T5-AXN-053

RISK MANAGEMENT AND CAPITAL ADEQUACY

RISK MANAGEMENT AND CAPITAL ADEQUACY

RETO R. GALLATI

McGraw-Hill

New York / Chicago / San Francisco / Lisbon

London / Madrid / Mexico City / Milan / New Delhi

San Juan / Singapore / Sydney / Toronto

The McGraw-Hill Companies

1 2 3 4 5 6 7 8 9 0 DOC/DOC 0 9 8 7 6 5 4 3

ISBN 0-07-140763-4

McGraw-Hill books are available at special discounts to use as premiums and sales promotions, or for use in corporate training programs. For more information, please write to the Director of Special Sales, Professional Publishing, McGraw-Hill, Two Penn Plaza, New York, NY 10121-2298. Or contact your local bookstore.

This book is printed on recycled, acid-free paper containing a minimum of 50% recycled de-inked paper.

When I was young, people called me a gambler. As the scale of my operations increased I became known as a speculator. Now I am called a banker. But I have been doing the same thing all the time.

—Sir Ernest Cassell
Banker to Edward VII

To my parents with love and gratitude

ACKNOWLEDGMENTS

The suggestion that I write a book about risk came from the late Fischer Black, while I was working at Goldman Sachs. The vastness of the project is daunting. The topic touches on the most profound depths of statistics, mathematics, psychology, and economics. I would like to thank the editors and reviewers and those who provided comments, especially M.R. Carey and Jean Eske, who carefully read the entire manuscript and provided valuable comments, corrections, and advice.

I end with a note of thanks to my family, my friends, and my faculty colleagues at Sloan, who inspired much of the enthusiasm that went into the creation of this book and endured me with patience.

RETO R. GALLATI
Cambridge, Massachusetts
February 2003

CONTENTS

Chapter 4
Operational Risk 283

Chapter 5
Building Blocks for Integration of Risk Categories 341

Chapter 6

Case Studies 441

INTRODUCTION

Over the past decades, investors, regulators, and industry self-regulatory bodies have forced banks, other financial institutions, and insurance companies to develop organizational structures and processes for the management of credit, market, and operational risk. Risk management became a hot topic for many institutions, as a means of increasing shareholder value and demonstrating the willingness and capability of top management to handle this issue. In most financial organizations, risk management is mainly understood as the job area of the chief risk officer and is limited, for the most part, to market risks. The credit risk officer usually takes care of credit risk issues. Both areas are supervised at the board level by separate competence and reporting lines and separate directives. More and more instruments, strategies, and structured services have combined the profile characteristics of credit and market risk, but most management concepts treat the different parts of risk management separately. Only a few institutions have started to develop an overall risk management approach, with the aim of quantifying the overall risk exposures of the company (Figure I-1).

This book presents an inventory of the different approaches to market, credit and, operational risk. The following chapters provide an in-depth analysis of how the different risk areas diverge regarding methodologies, assumptions, and conditions. The book also discusses how the different approaches can be identified and measured, and how their various parts contribute to the discipline of risk management as a whole. The closing chapter provides case studies showing the relevance of the different risk categories and discusses the "crash-testing" of regulatory rules through their application to various crises and accidents.

The objective of this book is to demonstrate the extent to which these risk areas can be combined from a management standpoint, and to which some of the methodologies and approaches are or are not reasonable for economic, regulatory, or other purposes.

PROBLEMS AND OBJECTIVES

Most institutions treat market, credit, operational, and systemic risk as separate management issues, which are therefore managed through separate competence directives and reporting lines. With the increased complexity and speed of events, regulators have implemented more and more regulations regarding how to measure, report, and disclose risk manage-

FIGURE I-1

Interaction and Integration of Risk Categories.

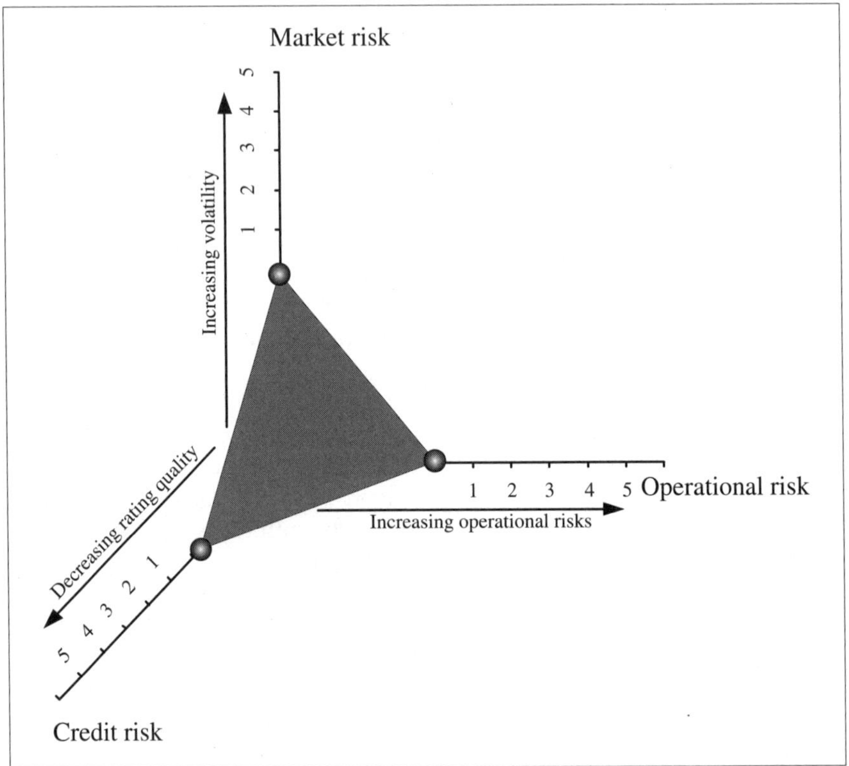

ment issues. As a result, one problem is to understand how the different risk categories are defined, and what characteristics, assumptions, and conditions are connected to the terms used to describe them. This allows us to understand the different natures of different types of risk. And because risk has to be measured, measurement tools, methodologies, and so forth must also be examined.

To this end, a scheme has been developed which allows a systematic screening of the different issues characterizing the natures of the different risk areas. It also helps determine the extent to which different risks can be combined. Many methodologies that claim to provide "total enterprise risk management," "enterprisewide risk management," and the like do not prove whether the underlying risks share enough similarities, or the risk areas share close enough assumptions, to justify considering them as a homogeneous whole.

This scheme is applied to case studies, to examine the extent to which some organizational structures, processes, models, assumptions, methodologies, and so forth have proved applicable, and the extent of the serious financial, reputational, and sometimes existential damages that have resulted when they have not.

APPROACH

This work focuses on the level above the financial instruments and is intended to add value at the organization, transaction, and process levels so as to increase the store of knowledge already accumulated. The pricing of instruments and the valuation of portfolios are not the primary objects of this book. Substantial knowledge has already been developed in this area and is in continuous development. Risk management at the instrument level is an essential basis for understanding how to make an institution's risk management structures, processes, and organizations efficient and effective.

This book aims to develop a scheme or structure to screen and compare the different risk areas. This scheme must be structured in such a way that it considers the appropriateness and usefulness of the different methodologies, assumptions, and conditions for economic and regulatory purposes.

The objectives of this book are as follows:

- Define the main terms used for the setup of the scheme, such as *systemic, market, credit,* and *operational risk.*
- Review the methodologies, assumptions, and conditions connected to these terms.
- Structure the characteristics of the different risk areas in such a way that the screening of these risk areas allows comparison of the different risk areas for economic and regulatory purposes.

In a subsequent step, this scheme is applied to a selection of case studies. These are mainly publicized banking failures from the past decade or so. The structured analysis of these relevant case studies should demonstrate the major causes and effects of each loss and the extent to which risk control measures were or were not appropriate and effective.

The objectives of the case study analyses are as follows:

- Highlight past loss experiences.
- Detail previous losses in terms of systemic, market, credit, and operational risks.
- Highlight the impact of the losses.
- Provide practical assistance in the development of improved risk management through knowledge transfer and management information.
- Generate future risk management indicators to mitigate the potential likelihood of such disasters.

CHAPTER 1

Risk Management: A Maturing Discipline

1.1 BACKGROUND

The entire history of human society is a chronology of exposure to risks of all kinds and human efforts to deal with those risks. From the first emergence of the species *Homo sapiens,* our ancestors practiced risk management in order to survive, not only as individuals but as a species. The survival instinct drove humans to avoid the risks that threatened extinction and strive for security. Our actual physical existence is proof of our ancestors' success in applying risk management strategies.

Originally, our ancestors faced the same risks as other animals: the hazardous environment, weather, starvation, and the threat of being hunted by predators that were stronger and faster than humans. The environment was one of continuous peril, with chronic hunger and danger, and we can only speculate how hard it must have been to achieve a semblance of security in such a threatening world.

In response to risk, our early ancestors learned to avoid dangerous areas and situations. However, their instinctive reactions to risk and their adaptive behavior do not adequately answer our questions about how they successfully managed the different risks they faced. Other hominids did not attain the ultimate goal of survival—including *H. sapiens neanderthalensis,* despite the fact that they were larger and stronger than modern humans. The modern humans, *H. sapiens sapiens,* not only survived all their relatives but proved more resilient and excelled in adaptation and risk management.

Figure 1-1 shows the threats that humans have been exposed to over the ages, and which probably will continue in the next century, as well. It is obvious that these threats have shifted from the individual to society

FIGURE 1-1

Development of the Threats to Individuals, Groups, Nations, and the World.

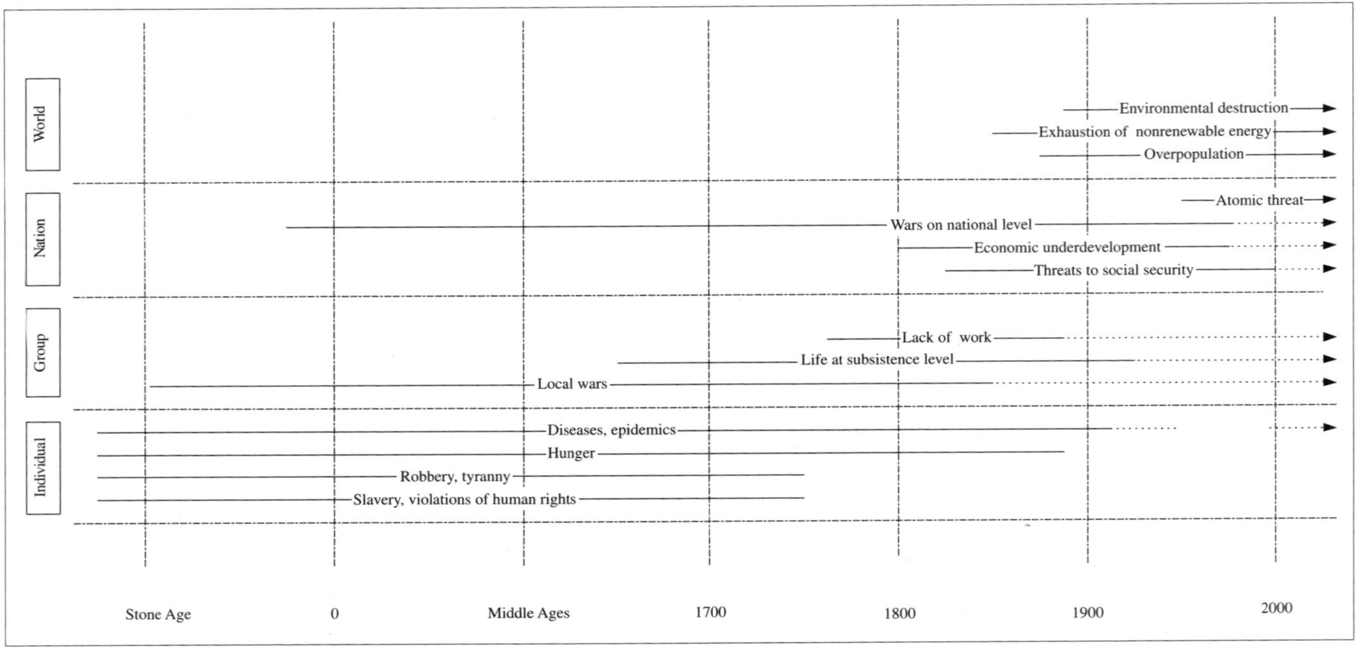

World
Environmental destruction
Exhaustion of nonrenewable energy
Overpopulation

Nation
Atomic threat
Wars on national level
Economic underdevelopment
Threats to social security

Group
Lack of work
Life at subsistence level
Local wars

Individual
Diseases, epidemics
Hunger
Robbery, tyranny
Slavery, violations of human rights

Stone Age
0
Middle Ages
1700
1800
1900
2000

and the global community. Thousands of years ago, humans first learned to cultivate the wild herbs, grasses, grains, and roots that they had traditionally gathered. Concurrently, humans were creating the first settlements and domesticating wild animals. Next, humans began to grow, harvest, and stockpile grain, which helped to form the concept of ownership. Over time, humans learned to defend their possessions and their interests, to accumulate foodstuffs and other goods for the future, and to live together in tribal and other communal settings. As wealth accumulated in modest increments, rules about how to live together were needed, and the first laws to govern human interaction were developed. Thus, the beginning of civilization was launched. Walled cities, fortifications, and other measures to protect property and communities demonstrate that with increases in wealth came increased risk in a new form. Old forms, which had threatened humans for generations, were replaced by new threats. Famine and pestilence were frequent crises, and the perils of nature destroyed what communities and individuals had built. Warfare and plundering increased the threats. As a result, our ancestors created technologies, war strategies, and social and legal rules to survive.

The evolution of business risks coincides with the start of trading and commerce. We do not know exactly when trading and commerce began, but their rise is clearly connected with the fact that society took advantage of specialization, which increased the capacity to produce and stockpile goods for future use. Stockpiling goods acts as a cushion against misfortune, the perils of nature, and the ravages of war. It is very probable that business, in the form of trading and commerce, was one of the first active efforts of society to deal with risk. Artifacts unearthed by archaeologists prove that those early businesspeople developed techniques for dealing with risk. Two major techniques are noteworthy and should be mentioned.

First, in 3000 B.C., the Babylonian civilization, with its extensive trade relations, exhibited a highly developed bureaucracy and trading sector with a monetary and legal system.

One consequence of the concept of private property was the evolution of a market economy, but until the innovation of money was introduced, commerce was on a barter basis. There is some debate regarding the exact moment when money was first used, but its use revolutionized commerce, private property, and the accumulation of wealth. It provided a new means of stockpiling resources, and thus had an important impact on risk management. With the introduction of money as a storage medium, wealth could be held in the form of tangible property or as an asset that could be exchanged for tangible properties. Physical assets could be acquired even by those who did not have financial assets, provided someone was willing to lend the money, which was the innovation of credit. This created risk for the lender, who was compensated by charging interest for loans.

The legal system was the second innovation that revolutionized society. Laws or rules originated as tribal conventions, which became more formalized over time. One of the first formal legal codes was established by Hammurabi between 1792 and 1750 B.C. There were no other major legal system innovations until the beginning of the Industrial Revolution, so we can fly over the periods of the Egyptian, Greek, and Roman empires, feudalism, the rise of the merchant class, and mercantilism. The beginning of the Industrial Revolution was characterized by two major events. Modern capitalism emerged after a transition period over several centuries, during which the conditions needed for a capitalistic market society were created. Among these conditions were formalized private ownership of the means of production, profit orientation, and the mechanisms of a market economy. With expanding industrial and economic activity, new organizational forms were needed to raise large amounts of capital and build production capacity. The *corporation* limited individual risk and leveraged production, distribution, and capital resources. The earliest form of shareholder organization, the *joint stock company,* appeared at the end of the seventeenth century. The investors pooled their funds, allowing multiple investors to share in both the profits and risks of the enterprise. This feature was equivalent to partnerships and other joint forms and was not an innovation. But the corporation addressed risk in a different way, by limiting the liability of the investors based on the amount invested. From a legal standpoint, a corporation is an artificial construct or artificial person, whose competencies and responsibilities are separate from those of the investor-owners (with exceptions).

The Industrial Revolution created new sources of risks. The application of steam power to the production process and transportation replaced old threats with the new risks that accompany advancing technologies. With the emergence of the age of information technology, inherent risks include business system problems, fraud, and privacy issues, which can all interrupt the day-to-day operations of a business.

Although the term *risk management* originated in the 1950s, Henry Fayol recognized its significance earlier.[1] Fayol, a leading management authority, was influenced by growing mass production in the United States, and the existence of giant corporations and their management challenges. In 1916, he structured industrial activities into six functions, including one called *security,* which sounds surprisingly like the concept of risk management:

> The purpose of this function is to safeguard property and persons against theft, fire and flood, to ward off strikes and felonies and broadly all social disturbances or natural disturbances liable to endanger the progress and even the life of the business. It is the master's eye, the watchdog of the one-man business, the police or the army in the case of the state. It is generally speaking all measures conferring security upon the undertaking and requisite peace of mind upon the personnel.[2]

Centuries ago, bandits and pirates threatened traders. Now hackers are engaged in vandalism and commit electronic larceny.

The media are full of news about the perils of human-made and natural hazards. The nuclear power plant accidents at the Three Mile Island facility in Pennsylvania in 1979 and at Chernobyl in Ukraine in 1987 show the new risks posed by human-made hazards and the seriousness of these threats. Destructive natural hazards exist as well. Hurricane Andrew caused damages of around $22 billion; and the floods in the midwestern United States in 1993 and the earthquakes in California in 1993 and in Kobe, Japan, in 1994 had devastating effects. In addition, terrorist activities have become more dangerous over the years, as demonstrated by the 1993 and 2001 bombings of the World Trade Center in New York, and the 1995 bombing of the Murrah Federal Building in Oklahoma City.

A review of the past along with an assessment of the growing array of risks shows that the impact of risks (in terms of financial losses) has increased. This is not only a consequence of the increased numbers of risks we are confronted with; the severity and frequency of disasters has increased as well. The financial losses from natural perils, such as floods, forest fires, and earthquakes, are not only a function of the number of events, as natural disasters occur with a certain average frequency as in the past. However, each catastrophe seems to be worse than the one that came before it. The ultimate reason is obvious: as more and more people live close together, business has become more capital intensive, and our infrastructure is more vulnerable and capital intensive as well. With the increased growth of capital investment in infrastructure, manufacturing capacity, and private ownership of real estate and other goods, the risk of financial losses increased substantially.

1.2 RISKS: A VIEW OF THE PAST DECADES

Recently, there have been a number of massive financial losses due to inadequate risk management procedures and processes (Figure 1-2). The failures of risk management in the world of finance were not primarily due to the incorrect pricing of derivative instruments. Rather, the necessary supervisory oversight was inadequate. The decision makers in control of organizations left them exposed to risks from derivative transactions and institutional money. Risk management does not primarily involve the correct pricing of derivative instruments—rather, it involves the supervision, management, and control of *organizational structures and processes* that deal with derivatives and other instruments.

Many cases in which managers focused on the correct pricing of financial instruments and neglected the other dimensions show the dramatic consequences of this one-dimensional understanding of risk management. In Switzerland, the pension fund scheme of Landis & Gyr

FIGURE 1-2

Overview of the Most Important and Obvious "Accidents" of the Past Decades.

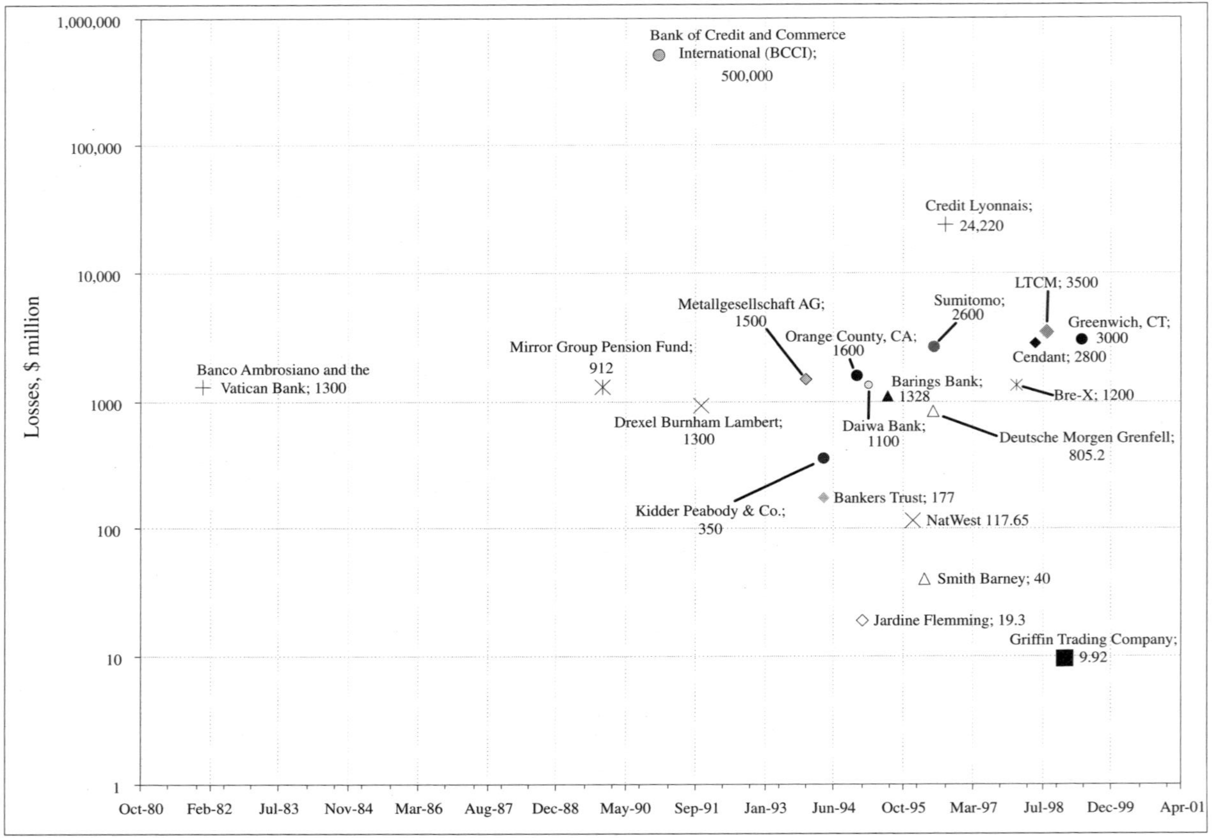

Losses, $ million
1,000,000
100,000
10,000
1000
100
10
1
Oct-80 Feb-82 Jul-83 Nov-84 Mar-86 Aug-87 Dec-88 May-90 Sep-91 Jan-93 Jun-94 Oct-95 Mar-97 Jul-98 Dec-99 Apr-01
Bank of Credit and Commerce International (BCCI); 500,000
Credit Lyonnais; 24,220
LTCM; 3500
Greenwich, CT; 3000
Cendant; 2800
Sumitomo; 2600
Metallgesellschaft AG; 1500
Orange County, CA; 1600
Mirror Group Pension Fund; 912
Banco Ambrosiano and the Vatican Bank; 1300
Barings Bank; 1328
Bre-X; 1200
Drexel Burnham Lambert; 1300
Daiwa Bank; 1100
Deutsche Morgen Grenfell; 805.2
Kidder Peabody & Co.; 350
Bankers Trust; 177
NatWest 117.65
Smith Barney; 40
Jardine Flemming; 19.3
Griffin Trading Company; 9.92

resulted in the loss of a substantial part of the fund's assets. Robert Maxwell swindled the Mirror Group's pension fund for £480 million. Daiwa lost more than $1 billion. Barings lost £850 million. Kidder Peabody lost more than $300 million. Orange County, California, lost more than $1 billion. This list of accidents, frauds, and willful swindles in the world of finance is never-ending. The reasons include behavioral risk, pricing risk, an incorrect understanding of products and services, and simple credit and market risks. Risk is not a one-dimensional, well-defined concept. Rather, it is a shifting concept whose meaning varies according to the environment in which it is used. Thus far, the term *risk* has been used in this discussion to mean "exposure to adversity." In this loose sense, the term *risk* has been adequate for the explanation of the history of risk. Now, *risk* and its associated terms have to be analyzed and defined more precisely, and the context in which these terms are used must be outlined. Each activity or area of knowledge has its own individual concept and terms. The terminology of risk, like many simple terms in everyday usage, takes on different meanings in specialized fields. The term *risk* shimmers with all the colors of the rainbow; it depends on how we define it. Risk is often linked with uncertainty and insecurity. Statisticians, economists, bankers, and academicians try and try again to develop a common understanding and definition of the term *risk.* But at present there is no agreed definition that can be applied to all areas; the concept of risk that is suitable for the economist can not be used by the social psychologist or the insurance mathematician. This book does not attempt to develop a concept for all areas of knowledge. The discussion is limited to economics and finance. However, there are some concepts that are shared with the fields of insurance, mathematics, and statistics, as many products and services in the economic and financial field are based on calculations that include risk. In the insurance industry, *risk* means either a peril insured against (e.g., flood damage) or a person or property protected by insurance (e.g., a driver and vehicle protected against financial damages from personal injury or collision by car insurance). For the moment, however, the term *risk* will be applied here in an abstract way, to indicate a situation in which a certain exposure exists. Therefore, risk is not strictly related to loss for present purposes, as this again would be one-dimensional and would unnecessarily restrict the discussion.

1.3 DEFINITION OF RISK

For the purposes of this discussion, *risk* is defined as "a condition in which there exists an exposure to adversity." In addition, there is an expectation of what the outcome should look like. Therefore, risk is defined here as follows:

risk A condition in which there exists a possibility of deviation from a desired outcome that is expected or hoped for.

Other definitions include the restriction that risk is based on real-world events, including a combination of circumstances in the external environment. We do not agree with this limitation. Potential risks that might occur in the future are excluded. In addition, we do not limit the range of risk to circumstances in the external environment. Many crises in the economy and the financial services industry happen because of problems within organizations. These often have to do with problems in the human resource area, which belong in the realm of the behavioral sciences.

The term *risk* is linked to the possibility of deviation. This means that the possibility of risk can be expressed as a probability, ranging from 0 to 100 percent. Therefore, the probability is neither impossible nor definite. This definition does not require that the probability be quantified, only that it must exist. The degree of risk may not be measurable, for whatever reason, but the probability of the adverse outcome must be between 0 and 100 percent.

Another key element of the definition is the "deviation from a desired outcome that is expected or hoped for." The definition does not say how such an undesirable deviation is defined. There are many ways of building expectations. By projecting historical data into the future, we build expectations. This pattern of behavior can be observed in our everyday lives. Another way of building expectations is to forecast by using information directed toward the future, not by looking back. The definition of *expectations* is absolutely key in the concept of risk, as it is used to define the benchmark. Any misconception of the expectations will distort the measurement of risk substantially. This issue is discussed in full in the auditing and consulting literature, which analyzes the problem of risk and control in great depth.[3]

Many definitions of risk include the term *adverse deviation* to express the negative dimension of the expected or hoped-for outcome. We do not agree with this limitation, which implies that risk exists only with adverse deviations, which must be negative and thus are linked to losses. Such a restriction would implicitly exclude any positive connotations from the concept of risk. We believe that risk has two sides, which both have to be included in the definition, and that risk itself has no dimension, negative or positive.

1.4 RELATED TERMS AND DIFFERENTIATION

Frequently, terms such as *peril, hazard, danger,* and *jeopardy* are used interchangeably with each other and with the term *risk.* But to be more precise about risk, it is useful to distinguish these terms:

- *Peril.* A peril creates the potential for loss. Perils include floods, fire, hail, and so forth. Peril is a common term to define a danger resulting from a natural phenomenon. Each of the events mentioned is a potential cause of loss.
- *Hazard.* A hazard is a condition that may create or increase the chance of a loss arising from a given peril. It is possible for something to be both a peril and a hazard at the same time. For instance, a damaged brake rotor on a car is a peril that causes an economic loss (the brake has to be repaired, causing financial loss). It is also a hazard that increases the likelihood of loss from the peril of a car accident that causes premature death.

Hazards can be classified into the following four main categories:

- *Physical hazard.* This type of hazard involves the physical properties that influence the chances of loss from various perils.
- *Moral hazard.* This type of hazard involves the character of persons involved in the situation, which might increase the likelihood of a loss. One example of a moral hazard is the dishonest behavior of a person who commits fraud by intentionally damaging property in order to collect an insurance payment. This dishonest behavior results in a loss to the insurance company.
- *Morale hazard.* This type of hazard involves a careless attitude toward the occurrence of losses. An insured person or organization, knowing that the insurance company will bear the brunt of any loss, may exercise less care than if forced to bear any loss alone, and may thereby cause a condition of morale hazard, resulting in a loss to the insurance company. This hazard should not be confused with *moral hazard,* as it requires neither intentional behavior nor criminal tendencies.
- *Legal hazard.* This type of hazard involves an increase in the severity and frequency of losses (legal costs, compensation payments, etc.) that arises from regulatory and legal requirements enacted by legislatures and self-regulating bodies and interpreted and enforced by the courts. Legal hazards flourish in jurisdictions in which legal doctrines favor a plaintiff, because this represents a hazard to persons or organizations that may be sued. The American and European systems of jurisprudence are quite different. In the American system, it is much easier to go to court, and producers of goods and services thus face an almost unlimited legal exposure to potential lawsuits. The European courts have placed higher hurdles in the path of those who might take legal action against another party. In addition, "commonsense" standards of what is actionable are different in Europe and the United States.

For a risk manager, the legal and criminal hazards are especially important. Legal and regulatory hazards arise out of statutes and court decisions. The hazard varies from one jurisdiction to another, which means global companies must watch legal and regulatory developments carefully.

1.5 DEGREE OF RISK

Risk itself does not say anything about the dimension of measurement. How can we express that a certain event or condition carries more or less risk than another? Most definitions link the degree of risk with the likelihood of occurrence. We intuitively consider events with a higher likelihood of occurrence to be riskier than those with a lower likelihood. This intuitive perception fits well with our definition of the term *risk*. Most definitions regard a higher likelihood of loss to be riskier than a lower likelihood. We do not agree, as this view is already affected by the insurance industry's definition of risk. If risk is defined as the possibility of a deviation from a desired outcome that is expected or hoped for, the degree of risk is expressed by the likelihood of deviation from the desired outcome.

Thus far we have not included the size of potential loss or profit in our analysis. We say that a situation carries more or less risk, and mean as well the value impact of the deviation. The expected value of a loss or profit in a given situation is the likelihood of the deviation multiplied by the amount of the potential loss or profit. If the money at risk is $100 and the likelihood of a loss is 10 percent, the expected value of the loss is $10. If the money at risk is $50 and the likelihood of a loss is 20 percent, the expected value of the loss is still $10. The same calculation applies to a profit situation. This separation of likelihood and value impact is very important, but we do not always consider this when we talk about more or less risk. Later we will see how the separation of likelihood and impact can help us analyze processes, structures, and instruments to create an overall view of organizational risk.

Frequently, persons who sit on supervisory committees (e.g., board members and trustees of endowment institutions and other organizations) have to make decisions with long-ranging financial impact but have inadequate backgrounds and training to do so. Organizational structures and processes are rarely set up to support risk management, as these structures are usually adopted from the operational areas. But with increased staff turnover, higher production volumes, expansion into new markets, and so forth, the control structures and processes are rarely adapted and developed to match the changing situation.

New problems challenge management, as the existing control processes and reporting lines no longer provide alerts and appropriate information to protect the firm from serious damage or bankruptcy, as was the case with Barings or Yamaichy.

Banks and other regulated financial institutions have been forced by government regulations and industry self-regulating bodies to develop the culture, infrastructure, and organizational processes and structures for adequate risk management. Risk management has become a nondelegable part of top management's function and thus a nondelegable responsibility and liability. Driven by law, the financial sector has developed over the past years strategies, culture, and considerable technical and management know-how relating to risk management, which represents a competitive advantage against the manufacturing and insurance sectors.

1.6 RISK MANAGEMENT: A MULTILAYERED TERM

1.6.1 Background

As previously discussed, risk management is a shifting concept that has had different definitions and interpretations. Risk management is basically a scientific approach to the problem of managing the pure risks faced by individuals and institutions. The concept of risk management evolved from corporate insurance management and has as its focal point the possibility of accidental losses to the assets and income of the organization. Those who carry the responsibility for risk management (among whom the insurance case is only one example) are called *risk managers*. The term *risk management* is a recent creation, but the actual practice of risk management is as old as civilization itself. The following is the definition of risk management as used used throughout this work:

risk management In a broad sense, the process of protecting one's person or organization intact in terms of assets and income. In the narrow sense, it is the managerial function of business, using a scientific approach to dealing with risk. As such, it is based on a distinct philosophy and follows a well-defined sequence of steps.

1.6.2 History of Modern Risk Management

Risk management is an evolving concept and has been used in the sense defined here since the dawn of human society. As previously mentioned, risk management has its roots in the corporate insurance industry. The earliest insurance managers were employed at the turn of the twentieth century by the first giant companies, the railroads and steel manufacturers. As capital investment in other industries grew, insurance contracts became an increasingly significant line item in the budgets of firms in those industries, as well.

It would be mistaken to say that risk management evolved naturally from the purchase of insurance by corporations. The emergence of risk management as an independent approach signaled a dramatic, revolutionary shift in philosophy and methodology, occurring when attitudes toward various insurance approaches shifted. One of the earliest references to the risk management concept in literature appeared in 1956 in the *Harvard Business Review.*[4] In this article, Russell Gallagher proposed a revolutionary idea, for the time, that someone within the organization should be responsible for managing the organization's pure risk:

> The aim of this article is to outline the most important principles of a workable program for "risk management"—so far so it must be conceived, even to the extent of putting it under one executive, who in a large company might be a full-time "risk manager."

Within the insurance industry, managers had always considered insurance to be the standard approach to dealing with risk. Though insurance management included approaches and techniques other than insurance (such as noninsurance, retention, and loss prevention and control), these approaches had been considered primarily as alternatives to insurance.

But in the current understanding, risk management began in the early 1950s. The change in attitude and philosophy and the shift to the risk management philosophy had to await management science, with its emphasis on cost-benefit analysis, expected value, and a scientific approach to decision making under uncertainty. The development from insurance management to risk management occurred over a period of time and paralleled the evolution of the academic discipline of risk management (Figure 1-3). Operations research seems to have originated during World War II, when scientists were engaged in solving logistical problems, developing methodologies for deciphering unknown codes, and assisting in other aspects of military operations. It appears that in the industry and in the academic discipline the development happened simultaneously, but without question the academic discipline produced valuable approaches, methodologies, and models that supported the further development of risk management in the industry. New courses such as operations research and management science emphasize the shift in focus from a descriptive to a normative decision theory.

Markowitz was the first financial theorist to explicitly include risk in the portfolio and diversification discussion.[5] He linked terms such as *return* and *utility* with the concept of risk. Combining approaches from operations research and mathematics with his new portfolio theory, he built the basis for later developments in finance. This approach became the *modern portfolio theory,* and was followed by other developments, such as Fischer Black's option-pricing theory, which is considered the foundation of the derivatives industry. In the early 1970s, Black and Scholes made a breakthrough by deriving a differential equation which must be satisfied by the price of any derivative instrument dependent on a nondividend stock.[6] This approach has been developed further and is one of the driving factors for the actual financial engineering of structured products.

FIGURE 1-3

Evolution of Insurance and Risk Management.

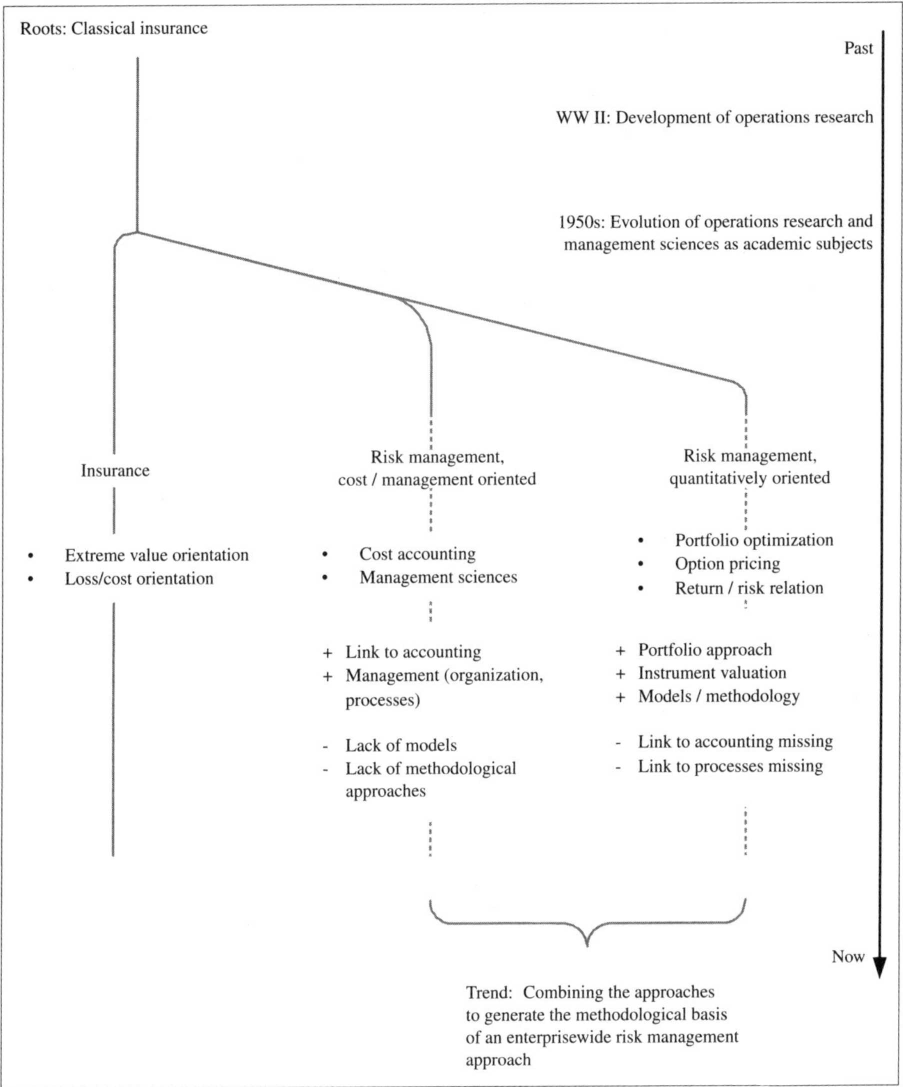

The current trend in risk management is a convergence of the differing approaches, as both trends have positive aspects (see Figure 1-4). Almost all leading consulting practices have developed value-at-risk concepts for enterprisewide risk management. Process pricing is the ultimate challenge for the pricing of operational risk.

FIGURE 1-4

Development Levels of Different Risk Categories.

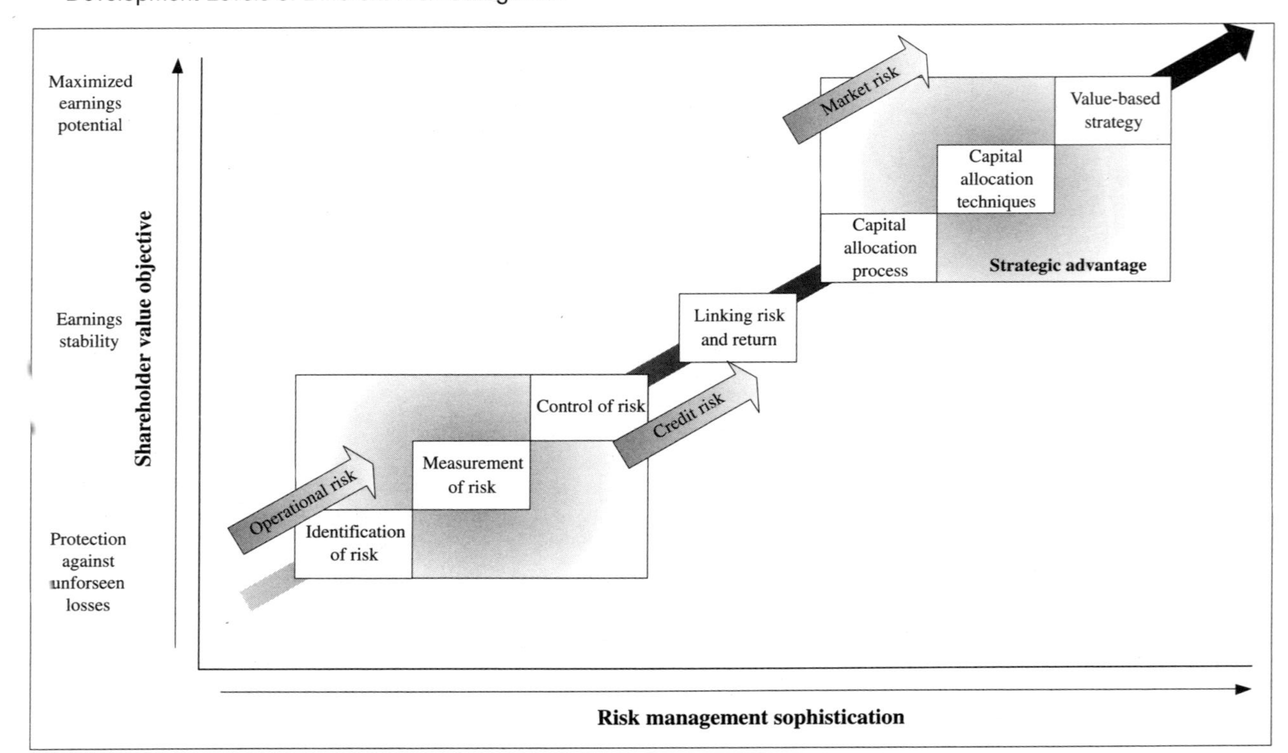

1.6.3 Related Approaches

1.6.3.1 Total Risk Management

Total risk management, enterprisewide risk management, integrated risk management, and other terms are used for approaches that implement firmwide concepts including measurement and aggregation techniques for market, credit, and operational risks. This book uses the following definition for total risk management, based on the understanding in the market regarding the concept:

total risk management The development and implementation of an enterprisewide risk management system that spans markets, products, and processes and requires the successful integration of analytics, management, and technology.

The following paragraphs highlight some concepts developed by consulting and auditing companies. *Enterprise risk management,* as developed by Ernst & Young, emphasizes *corporate governance* as a key element of a firmwide risk management solution. Boards that implement leading-edge corporate governance practices stimulate chief executives to sponsor implementation of risk management programs that align with their businesses. In fulfilling their risk oversight duties, board members request regular updates regarding the key risks across the organization and the processes in place to manage them. Given these new practices, boards are increasingly turning to the discipline of enterprise risk management as a means of meeting their fiduciary obligations. As a result, pioneering organizations and their boards are initiating enterprisewide risk management programs designed to provide collective risk knowledge for effective decision making and advocating the alignment of management processes with these risks. These organizations have recognized the advantages of:

- Achieving strategic objectives and improving financial performance by managing risks that have the largest potential impact
- Assessing risk in the aggregate to minimize surprises and reduce earnings fluctuations
- Fostering better decision making by establishing a common understanding of accepted risk levels and consistent monitoring of risks across business units
- Improving corporate governance with better risk management and reporting processes, thereby fulfilling stakeholder responsibilities and ensuring compliance with regulatory requirements

At present, many risk management programs attempt to provide a level of assurance that the most significant risks are identified and managed. However, they frequently fall short in aggregating and evaluating those risks across the enterprise from a strategic perspective. Effective enterprise risk management represents a sophisticated, full-fledged management discipline that links risk to shareholder value and correlates with the complexity of the organization and the dynamic environments in which it operates (Figure 1-5).

Once an organization has transformed its risk management capabilities, it will be in a position to promote its success through an effective, integrated risk management process. Ernst & Young's point of view is that effective enterprise risk management includes the following points (see Figure 1-6):[7]

- A culture that embraces a common understanding and vision of enterprise risk management
- A risk strategy that formalizes enterprise risk management and strategically embeds risk thinking within the enterprise

FIGURE 1-5

Evolving Trends and the Development of an Integrated Risk Framework to Support the Increasing Gap Between Business Opportunities and Risk Management Capabilities. (*Source: Ernst & Young,* Enterprise Risk Management, *Ernst & Young LLP, 2000. Copyright © 2000 by Ernst & Young LLP; reprinted with permission of Ernst & Young LLP.*)

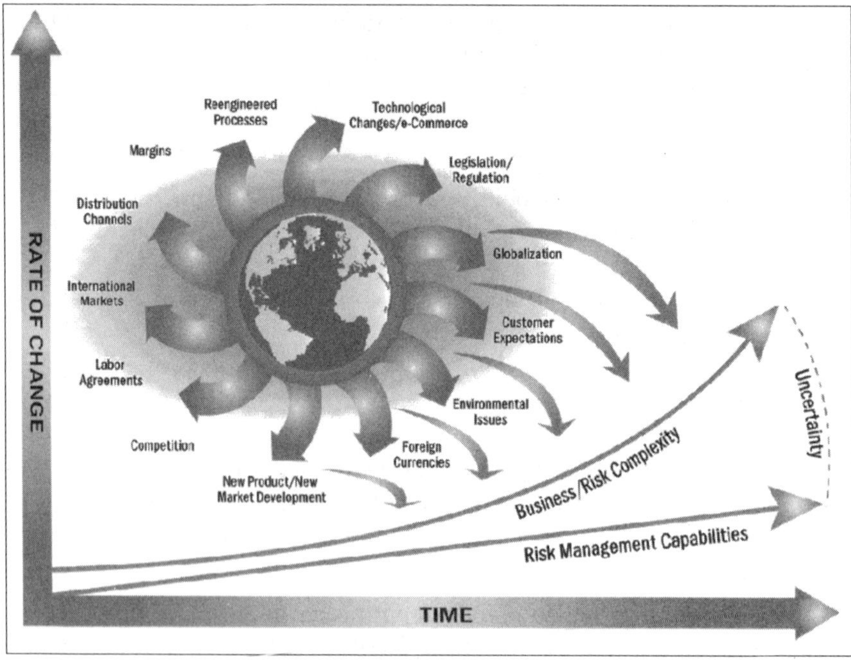

FIGURE 1-6

Enterprise Risk Management Point of View. *(Source: Ernst & Young LLP, a member of Ernst & Young Global. Copyright © 2002 by Ernst & Young LLP; reprinted with permission of Ernst & Young LLP.)*

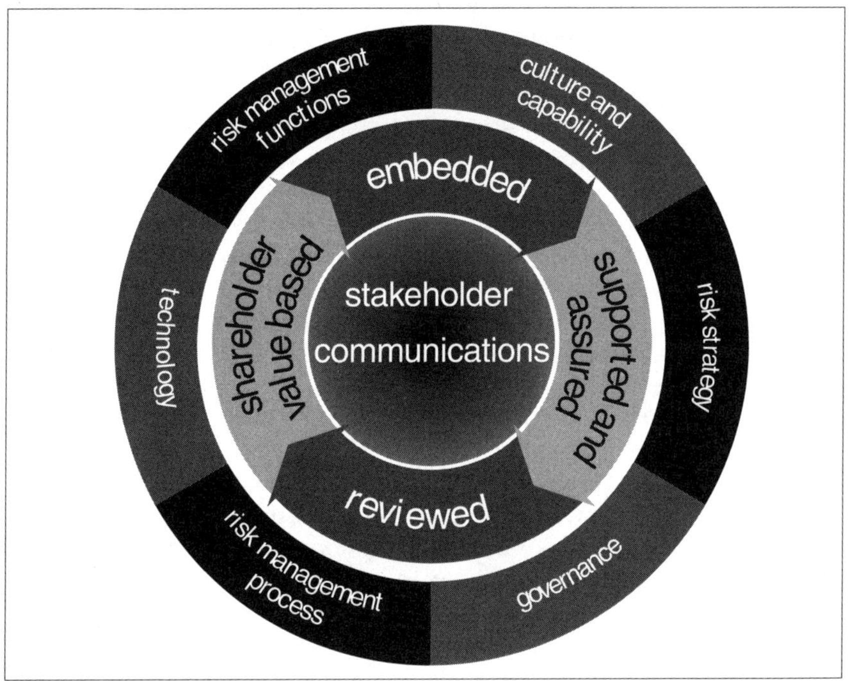

- An evolved governance practice that champions an effective enterprisewide risk management system
- Competent and integrated risk management capabilities for effective risk identification, assessment, and management

Coopers & Lybrand has developed its own version of an enterprisewide risk management solution in the form of *generally accepted risk principles* (GARP).[8] The GARP approach seeks to distil and codify major principles for managing and controlling risk from the guidance issued to date by practitioners, regulators, and other advisors. The framework uses the experience and expertise of all parties involved in its development to expand these principles so as to establish a comprehensive framework within which each firm can manage its risks and through which regulators can assess the adequacy of risk management in place. It presents a set of principles for the management of risk by firms, and for the maintenance of a proper internal control framework, going further than the mere assessment of the algorithms within risk management models. It covers such matters as the organization of the firm, the operation of its overall control framework, the means and principles of risk measurement and reporting, and the systems themselves. The approach is based around *principles,* each of which is supported by relevant details. The extent of the detail varies depending on the principle concerned. In all cases, the guidance provided is based on the assumption that the level of trading in a firm is likely to give rise to material risks. In certain cases an indication of alternative acceptable practices is given.

KPMG has developed a risk management approach based on the shareholder value concept, in which the value of an organization is not solely dependent on market risks, such as interest or exchange rate fluctuations. It is much more important to study all types of risks. This means that *macroeconomic* or *microeconomic* risks, on both the *strategic* and *operational* levels, have to be analyzed and considered in relation to every single decision. An organization can seize a chance for lasting and long-term success only if *all risks are defined and considered* in its overall decision-making process as well as in that of its individual business units. KPMG assumes (as do other leading companies) that the key factor for a total risk management approach is the phase of *risk identification,* which forms the basis for risk evaluation, risk management, and control. Figure 1-7 shows the Risk Reference Matrix, KPMG's systematic and integrated approach to the identification of risk across all areas of the business.[9] This is a high-level overview, which can be further broken down into details.

Many other approaches from leading consulting and auditing practices could be mentioned. They all assume that they have a framework that contains all the risks that must be identified and measured to get the overall risk management.

Figure 1-8 shows a risk map that covers many different risk areas, from a high-level to low-level view. From an analytical standpoint, it looks consistent and comprehensive, covering all risks in an extended framework. The allocation of individual risks may be arbitrary, depending on what concept is used. But the combination and complexity of all risks, their conditions and assumptions, might make it difficult to identify and measure the risk for an enterprisewide setup.

In practice, significant problems often occur at this stage. A systematic and consistent procedure to identify risk across all areas of the business, adhering to an integrated concept, is essential to this first sequence of the risk management process. But this integrated concept is, in certain regards, a matter of wishful thinking. The definition of certain individual risks—for example, development, distribution, and technology risks—is not overly problematic. The concepts span the complete range of risk terms. But in many cases the categorization and definition of some terms are ambiguous. One example is the term *liquidity.* Liquidity can be seen as

FIGURE 1-7

KPMG Risk Reference Matrix. *(Source: Cristoph Auckenthaler and Jürg Gabathuler,* Gedanken zum Konzept eines Total Enterprise Wide Risk Management (TERM), *Zurich: University of Zurich, 1997, 9, fig. 2.)*

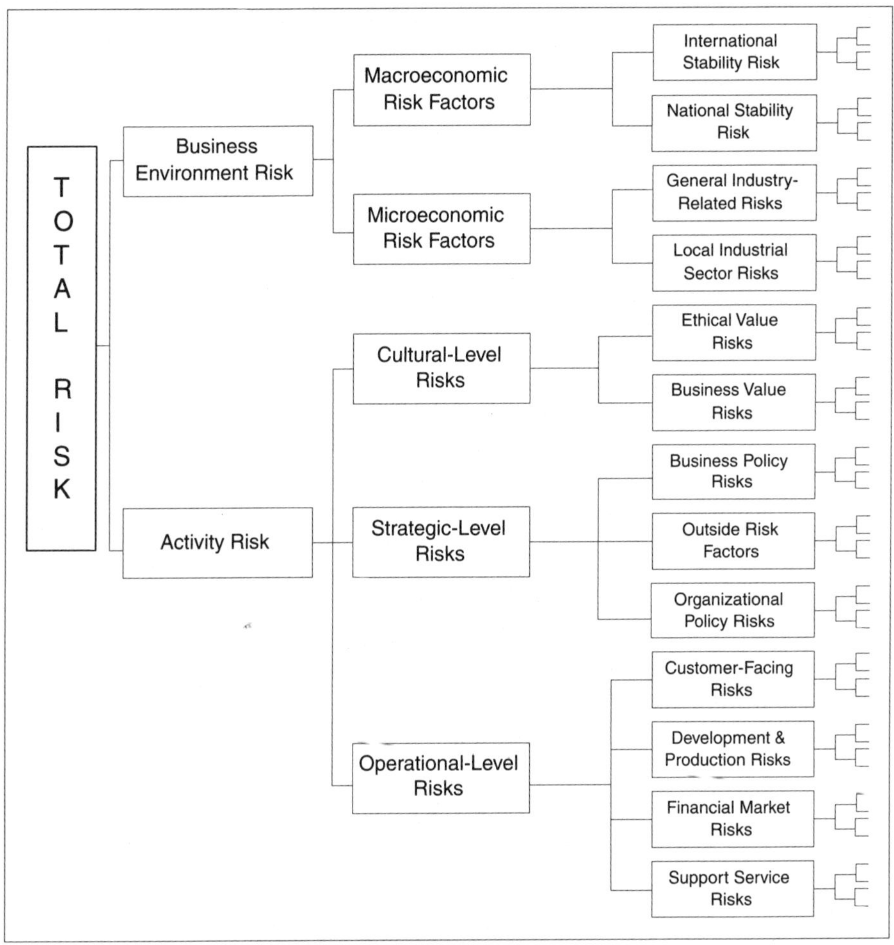

part of market and credit risks, but it also affects systemic risk. The total risk management concept appears to be complete, consistent, and adequate. But this interpretation is too optimistic, as some of the concepts still lack major elements and assumptions.

In an overall approach, the *interaction* between individual risks, as well as the definition of the weighting factors between the risk trees that must be attached to this correlation, creates serious difficulties. Portfolio theory tells us that correlation between the individual risk elements rep-

FIGURE 1-8

Risk Map of a Total Risk Management Approach. *(Source: Modified from KPMG.)*

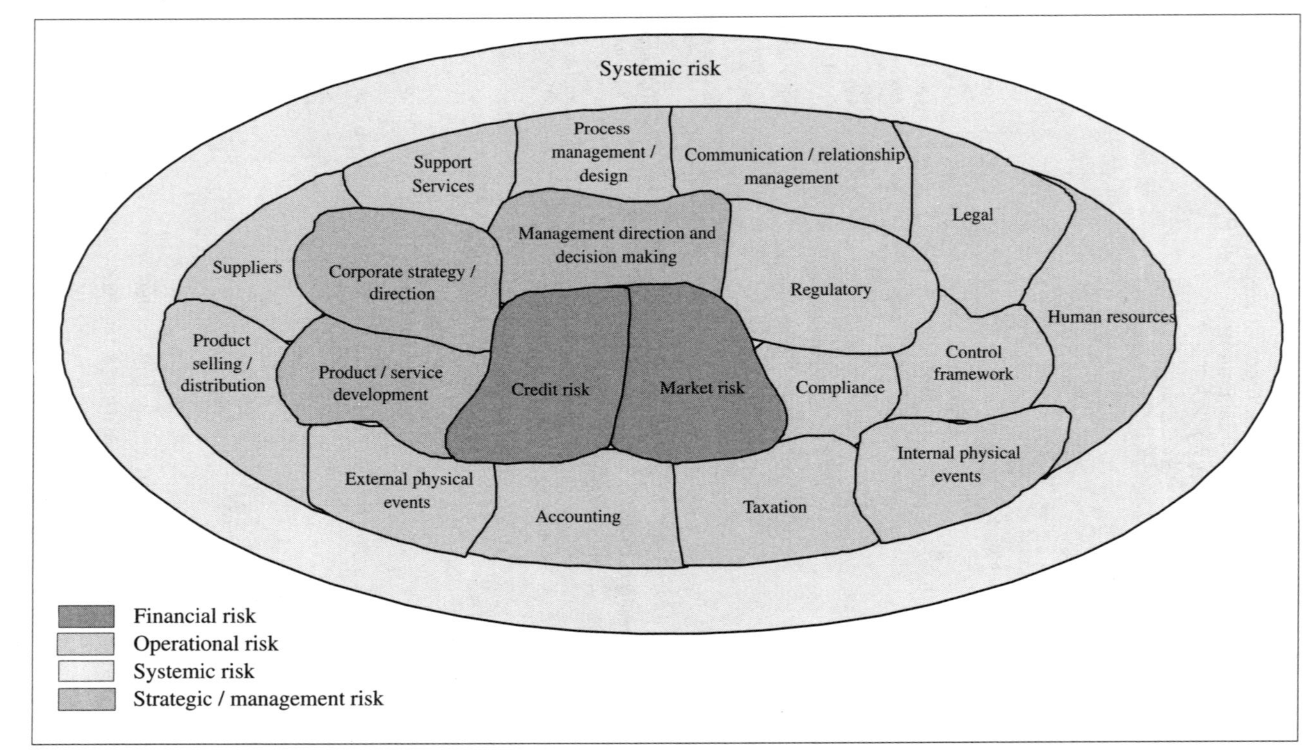

resents a central role in the establishment of risk definitions and strategies, and therefore in the risk management and hedging process (provided hedging is feasible). The same is also true for the risk management of a business (with elements such as new product risks, model risks, counterparty risks, etc.). From a practical standpoint, it is often not possible to get data and calculate risk coefficients if the overall scheme of a total risk management concept represents a widely branching system, because the number of interactions (correlations) and the required data increase substantially as the number of elements increases. Such approaches require the combined and well-orchestrated use of questionnaires, checklists, flowcharts, organization charts, analyses of yearly financial statements and transactions, and inspections of the individual business locations. This requires substantial expenditures and commitment from management.

As can be seen from the preceding descriptions of the different enterprise risk management solutions, the major consulting firms approach the same issues from different perspectives. Whereas KPMG and Ernst & Young have a more holistic approach, Coopers & Lybrand takes a more normative, trading-oriented, and regulatory approach. Regardless of the different approaches offered by the various auditing and consulting companies, a company has to adapt the approach it selects based on its own needs, its understanding of risk management, and the extent to which risk management is an integrated part of upper management's responsibilities or an independent control and oversight function.

1.6.3.2 Total Quality Management

Virtually every activity within an organization changes the organization's exposure to risk. It is part of a risk manager's responsibility to educate others on the risk-creating and risk-reducing aspects of their activities. The recognition that risk control is everyone's responsibility closely links risk control to principles of quality improvement, an approach to management that has been employed with considerable success in Japan and the United States. The movement toward quality improvement often is known by code names and acronyms such as *total quality management* (TQM) and *total quality improvement* (TQI). TQM was developed in Japan after World War II, with important contributions from American experts. Ultimately, Japanese companies recognized that production volume itself does not create competitive advantage, only quality and product differentiation can do so. In the context of TQM, quality is here defined as follows:[10]

quality The fulfillment of the agreed-upon requirements communicated by the customer regarding products, services, and delivery performance. Quality is measured by customer satisfaction.

TQM has five approaches, reflecting the different dimensions of quality:[11]

- *Transcendent approach.* Quality is universally recognizable and is a synonym for high standards for the functionality of a product. The problem is that quality cannot be measured precisely under this approach.
- *Product-oriented approach.* Differences in quality are observable characteristics linked to specific products. Thus, quality is precisely measurable.
- *User-oriented approach.* Quality is defined by the user, depending on the utility value.
- *Process-oriented approach.* The production process is the focus of quality efforts. Quality results when product specifications and standards are met through the use of the proper production process.
- *Value-oriented approach.* Quality is defined through the price-product-service relationship. A quality product or service is identified as one that provides the defined utility at an acceptable price.

The TQM approach has four characteristics:

- *Zero-error principle.* Only impeccable components and perfect processes may be used in the production process to ensure systematic error avoidance in the quality circle.
- *Method of "why."* This is a rule of thumb: the basis of a problem can be evaluated by asking why five times. This avoids taking the symptoms of a problem to be the problem itself.
- *Kaizen.* Kaizen is a continuous process of improvement through systematic learning. This means turning away from the traditional tayloristic division of labor and returning to an integrated organization of different tasks that includes continuous training to develop personnel's technical and human relations skills.
- *Simultaneous engineering.* Simultaneous engineering demands feedback loops between different organizational units and different processes. This requires overlapping teams and process orientation.[12]

Table 1-1 highlights the profiles of the total quality management and total risk management approaches.

Total quality management has its own very distinct terms and definitions, which make it a different approach from total risk management. It is a multidimensional client-oriented approach, in which management takes preventive measures to ensure that all processes, organizational en-

TABLE 1-1

Differences and Similarities Between Total Quality Management and Total Risk Management

Total Quality Management (TQM)	Total Risk Management (TRM)
Extended, multidimensional, client-oriented quality term.	Integrated, multidimensional enterprise-oriented term.
Extended client definition: clients are internal and external.	Internal client definition: clients are internal.
Preventive quality assurance policy.	Preventive and product-oriented risk management policy.
Quality assurance is the duty of all employees.	TRM assurance is the duty of specially assigned and responsible persons.
Enterprisewide quality assurance.	TRM assurance within the limits and for the risk factors to be measured according to the risk policy.
Systematic quality improvement with zero-error target.	Systematic risk control within the defined limits.
Quality assurance is a strategic job.	TRM is a strategic job.
Quality is a fundamental goal of the enterprise.	TRM is a fundamental goal of the enterprise.
Productivity through quality.	TRM to ensure ongoing production.

SOURCE: Hans-Jörg Bullinger, "Customer Focus: Neue Trends für eine zukunftsorientierte Unternehmungsführung," in Hans-Jörg Bullinger (ed.), "Neue Impulse für eine erfolgreiche Unternehmungsführung, 13. IAO-Arbeitstagung," *Forschung und Praxis,* Band 43, Heidelberg u.a., 1994.

tities, and employees focus on quality assurance and continuous improvement throughout the organization.

1.6.4 Approach and Risk Maps

Figures 1-9 and 1-10 present the approach and risk maps used in this book.

1.7 SYSTEMIC RISK

1.7.1 Definition

There is no uniform accepted definition of systemic risk. This book uses the definition contained in a 1992 report of the Bank for International Settlement (BIS):[13]

FIGURE 1-9

Risk Categorization Used as an Integrative Framework in This Book.

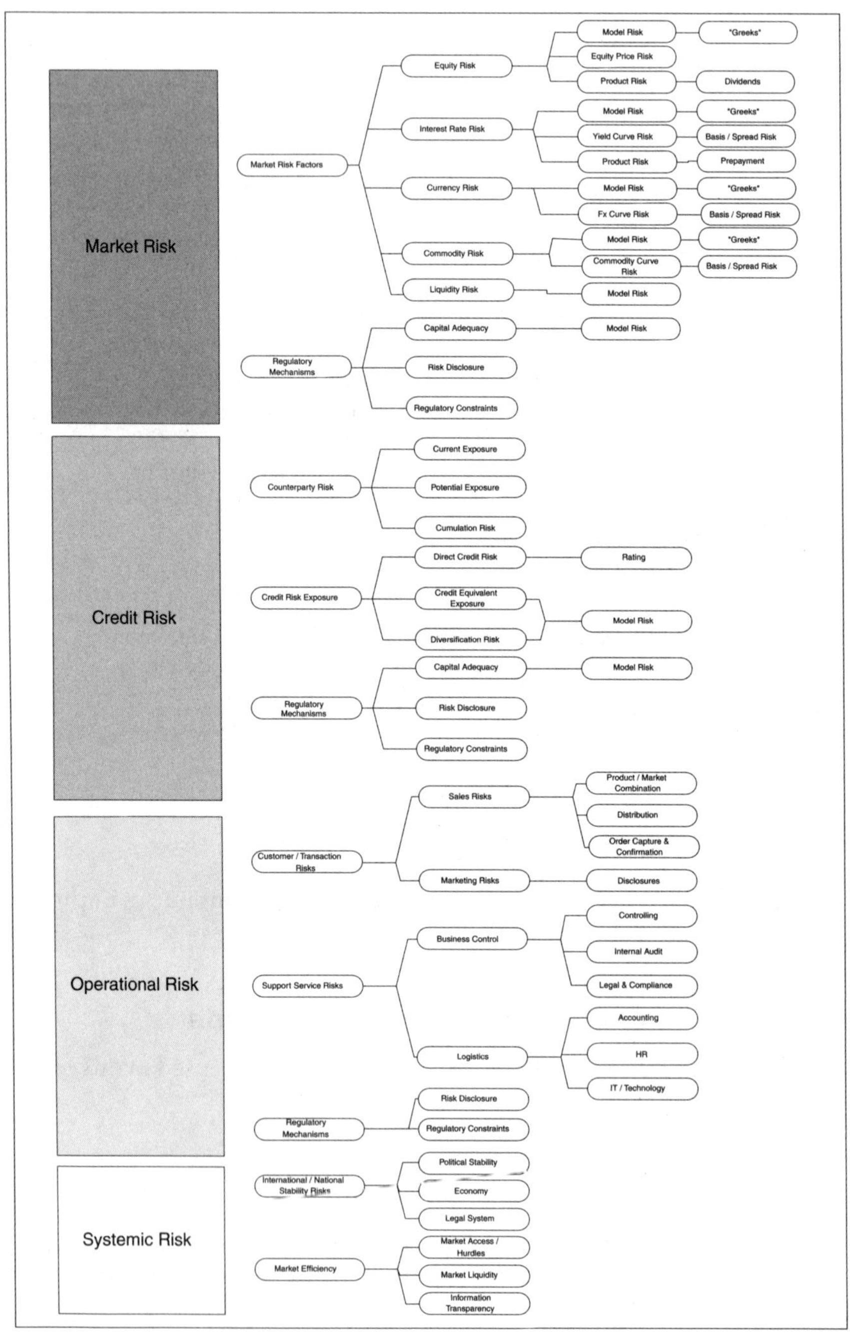

FIGURE 1-10

Example of Transaction Breakdown, Process-Oriented Flow of Different Risk Categories Involved.

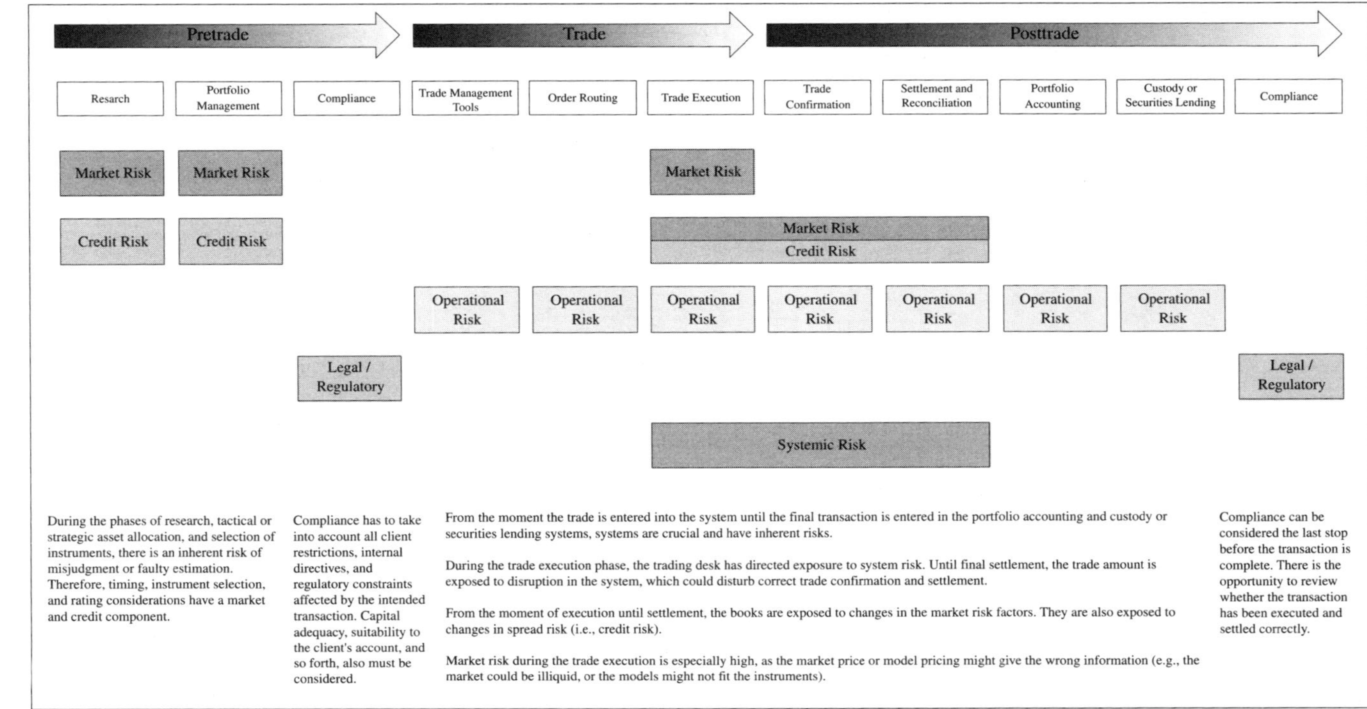

systemic risk The risk that a disruption (at a firm, in a market segment, to a settlement system, etc.) causes widespread difficulties at other firms, in other market segments, or in the financial system as a whole.

In this definition, systemic risk is based on a shock or disruption originating either within or outside the financial system that triggers disruptions to other market participants and mechanisms. Such a risk thereby substantially impairs credit allocation, payments, or the pricing of financial assets. While many would argue that no shock would be sufficient to cause a total breakdown of the financial system, there is little doubt that shocks of substantial magnitude could occur, and that their rapid propagation through the system could cause a serious system disruption, sufficient to threaten the continued operation of major financial institutions, exchanges, or settlement systems, or result in the need for supervisory agencies to step in rapidly.

1.7.2 Causes of Systemic Risk

Under the BIS definition, one should consider not only the steps taken within the institution to guard against a major internal breakdown. One should also consider those features of the global financial marketplace and current approaches to risk management and supervision that could adversely affect the institution's ability to react quickly and appropriately to a shock or disturbance elsewhere.

Recent developments in the financial market have produced a broad range of highly developed pricing models. Shareholder value, which is often mistakenly thought of as the generation of higher return on equity, leads financial institutions to reduce the proprietary capital used for activities that increase the profitability of equity capital. The financial institution reduces the equity capital to the bare regulatory minimum with the result that less and less capital supports the expanded trading activities, because the shareholder value concept has nothing to do with capital support. This trend is quite dangerous, as less and less capital serves as security capital in the return-generation process for more and more risk, without generating commensurate returns, and this trend alone promotes systemic risks. The development of an internationally linked settlement system has progressed significantly; nevertheless, there are still other factors that create systemic risk.

1.7.3 Factors That Support Systemic Risk

The following factors support systemic risk, based on empirical experience from previous crises or near-misses in the market:

- *Economic implications.* Our understanding of the relationship between the financial markets and the real state of the economy is questionable. The pricing of individual positions or positions for a portfolio can be done with any desired precision. The economic implications of the created models are often overlooked. It is not always a simple matter to understand the basic economic assumptions and parameters of complex mathematical models. This is one of the biggest systemic risks and a possible reason for the irritating, erratic movements of the markets. The participants—especially the "rocket scientists," highly intelligent but with a narrow horizon—do not understand the impact of coordination and feedback loops among the many individual decisions on the financial markets, especially concerning derivative constructs.

- *Liquidity.* Pricing models work under the ideal assumption that markets are liquid. Even worst-case scenarios and stress testing of market situations assume liquid markets. Valuation models are still hedge and arbitrage models, and are always based on the assumptions that positions can be liquidated and cash positions can be adjusted. With illiquid markets, strategy changes or position liquidation are difficult and sometimes impossible. Such a situation might cause a domino effect—an institution trying to liquidate positions in an illiquid market experiences cash problems, which causes the market to react negatively, sweeping away other institutions. The LTCM case is a typical example of this kind of systemic risk exposure (see case study in Chapter 6).

It is important to distinguish between liquidity risk as part of systemic risk and liquidity risk as part of market and credit risk. Market liquidity risk as part of systemic risk relates to the market itself, not to the pricing of individual positions.

The over-the-counter (OTC) market is a very attractive market for financial institutions, as the margins in this market are higher than on traded exchanges. The volume in the OTC market is enormous, but nontransparent. Transactions are not subject to the same clearing, settlement, and margin requirements as on traded exchanges. The risk of the OTC market, then, is that it is nontransparent, noninstitutionalized, and almost unregulated. Surprises may appear out of nowhere, and they may cause quick market reactions, disrupting the financial system with feedback loops and affecting financial institutions.

1.7.4 Regulatory Mechanisms for Risk Management

The regulatory bodies have recognized the need for adequate risk measurement and management techniques and approaches. The toolbox of the regulators is not limited to quantitative models, as many accidents and near-misses have highlighted the need for transparency and disclosure of market, credit, and operational risk information. A well-informed investor is well positioned to adjust the price based on available information, reflecting the expected risk premium for the entity being invested in.

Minimum disclosure requirements, risk management and control guidance through local supervisors, cross-border coordination of local regulators, and shared control of supranational organizations are some of the options regulators can select to keep systemic risk under control. The following topics highlight the focus of regulations recently published by BIS, and also indicate the mindset of the regulators, based on some recent accidents:

- *Enhancing Bank Transparency,* September 1998. Public disclosure and supervisory information that promote safety and soundness in banking systems.[14]
- *Supervisory Information Framework for Derivatives and Trading Activities,* September 1998. Joint Report by the Basel Committee on Banking Supervision and the Technical Committee of the International Organization of Securities Commissions (IOSCO).[15]
- *Framework for Internal Control Systems in Banking Organisations,* September 1998.[16]
- *Essential Elements of a Statement of Cooperation Between Banking Supervisors,* May, 2001. Framework for cross-border cooperation among different local regulators.[17]
- *Conducting a Supervisory Self-Assessment: Practical Application,* April 2001; *The Relationship Between Banking Supervisors and Banks' External Auditors,* February 2001. Guidelines for local regulators to assess their own supervisory abilities and the national supervisory frameworks.[18]
- *Best Practices for Credit Risk Disclosure,* September 2000; *Industry Views on Credit Risk Mitigation,* January 2000; *Range of Practice in Banks' Internal Ratings Systems,* January 2000. Reviews of current best practices for credit risk disclosures, which became part of the new capital adequacy framework to increase the quality level of disclosed information and generate peer pressure.[19]
- *Review of Issues Relating to Highly Leveraged Institutions,* March 2001; *Banks' Interactions with Highly Leveraged Institutions,* January 2000. Reviews and recommendations regarding banks' exposure and transactions with highly leveraged institutions, based on the LTCM crisis of September 1998.[20]

The approach of the BIS regulations is clearly a combination of the various measures available to the supervisory organizations, designed to avoid systemic risks and protect clients through increased disclosure and transparency and more precise calculation of the capital needed to support risks.

None of the previously mentioned approaches would achieve these objectives on their own. Thus, the new capital adequacy approach integrates the different risk categories and the different supervisory tools in the form of capital adequacy calculation, disclosure requirements, cross-border cooperation among supervisors, and the like.

1.8 SUMMARY

Risk management is not a new function or gadget in the financial industry. However, based on recent events, regulators and the media have increasingly scrutinized risk management practices and techniques. A closer look at some of the accidents makes it apparent that managers, regulators, and investors have partially lost control of risk management, overestimated their own capabilities and capacities, and brought companies and entire markets to the edge of the abyss.

For well over 100 years, farmers, for example, have engaged in risk management as they have sought to hedge their crops against price fluctuations in commodity markets. Their preferred strategy has been to sell short some or all of their anticipated crops before harvest time to another party on what are called *futures markets.* The Chicago Board of Trade (CBOT) was the first exchange to offer futures contracts. This strategy guarantees the farmer a known price for a crop, regardless of what the commodity's future price turns out to be when the crop is harvested. Risk management along these lines makes sense for farmers for at least two reasons. First, agricultural prices are exposed to volatility. Many of these farmers are not diversified and must also borrow in order to finance their crops. Therefore, setting the future sale price now migrates the risk of price fluctuations.

For another example that demonstrates the same approach, consider a large aluminum extraction company, owned by numerous shareholders, facing similar commodity price risk. For concreteness, consider a firm primarily engaged in the extraction and sale of raw aluminum on a global basis. Given that aluminum prices are relatively volatile and are exposed to global economic cycles, the first rationale for risk management might seem similar to the farmer's. However, unlike the farmer's circumstance, this firm is owned by a large number of shareholders, who can, if they wish, greatly reduce or eliminate their risk from low aluminum prices simply by holding a diversified portfolio that includes only a small fraction of assets invested in the aluminum extraction company. More generally, if investors can freely trade securities in many firms, they can choose their exposure to volatility in aluminum prices. Indeed, in two studies, Modigliani and Miller[21] showed that, in a world with no transactions costs or taxes and with equal information, managers could not benefit their shareholders by altering the risk profile of the firm's cash flow. Essentially, in this situation, shareholders can already do whatever they choose at no cost; actions by managers are redundant.

Although the Modigliani and Miller studies considered the options of changing the firm's risk profile only through the use of debt financing (1958),[22] or the distribution (or lack thereof) of dividends (1961),[23] and not through the use of financial derivative securities, the powerful implication here is the same as that outlined earlier.

However, the practical world is not without transaction costs and not as transparent as academic assumptions would have it. Several times over the past decades, investors and the market have been surprised by the announcement that a company has incurred substantial losses through speculation, fraud, or money laundering, leaving investors with dramatically devalued investments or even in bankruptcy. No risk management strategy as proposed by Miller and Modigliani could have prevented such a disaster, as shareholders were unable to take any action to offset or mitigate the risks.

Regulators have become more active over the past decades and have launched several initiatives regarding credit, market, and operational risks, forcing financial organizations to invest in their infrastructure, processes, and knowledge bases. The objective of both management and the regulators is to build and enforce an integrated risk management framework. However, although the objective might be the same, the strategy is completely different from the regulatory and management viewpoints, which is why risk management has become a hot issue. Management seeks to protect clients' assets at the lowest possible cost by avoiding losses and by increasing the value of the shareholders' investment through business decisions that optimize the risk premium. Regulators seek to protect the clients' assets without regard to cost, maintaining market stability and protecting the financial market by excluding systemic risk.

Risk management has to serve both purposes and thus has to be structured, built, and managed in such a way that it can answer these different needs simultaneously. The models and approaches used in the different risk categories must give statements about the risk exposures and allow aggregation of risk information across different risk categories. It is the purpose of this book to look into the different models and analyze the compatibility, assumptions, and conditions between the different models and risk categories.

1.9 NOTES

1. Henri Fayol, *General and Industrial Management*, New York: Pitman, 1949. English translation of book originally published in French in 1916.

2. Ibid.
3. KPMG Peat Marwick, *Understanding Risks and Controls: A Practical Guide*, Amsterdam: KPMG International Audit and Accounting Department, March 1995.
4. Russell B. Gallagher, "Risk Management: A New Phase of Cost Control," *Harvard Business Review* (September–October 1956).
5. Harry M. Markowitz, "Portfolio Selection (1)," *Journal of Finance* 7 (March 1952), 77–91. This is a path-breaking work in the field.
6. Fischer Black and Myron Scholes, "The Pricing of Options and Corporate Liabilities," *Journal of Political Economy* 81 (May–June 1973), 637–654.
7. Ernst & Young, *Enterprise Risk Management*, New York: Ernst & Young LLP, 2000; *Enterprise Risk Management—Implications for Boards of Directors*, New York: Ernst & Young LLP, 2000.
8. Coopers & Lybrand, *GARP—Generally Accepted Risk Principles*, London: Coopers & Lybrand, January 1996.
9. Christoph Auckenthaler and Jürg Gabathuler, *Gedanken zum Konzept eines Total Enterprise Wide Risk Management* (*TERM*), Zurich: University of Zurich, 1997.
10. Philip B. Crosby, *Qualität bringt Gewinn*, Hamburg: McGraw-Hill, 1986.
11. David A. Garvin, *Managing Quality*, New York: Free Press, 1988.
12. Hans-Jörg Bullinger, Joachim Warschaft, Stefan Bendes, and Alexander Stanke, "Simultaneous Engineering," in E. Zahn (ed.), *Handbuch Technologiemanagement*, Stuttgart: Schäffer-Pöschel Verlag, 1995.
13. Bank for International Settlement (BIS), Basel Committee on Banking Supervision, *Delivery Versus Payment in Security Settlement Systems*, Basel, Switzerland: Bank for International Settlement, September 1992.
14. Bank for International Settlement (BIS), Basel Committee on Banking Supervision, *Enhancing Bank Transparency*, Basel, Switzerland: Bank for International Settlement, September 1998.
15. Bank for International Settlement (BIS), Basel Committee on Banking Supervision, *Supervisory Information Framework for Derivatives and Trading Activities: Joint Report by the Basel Committee on Banking Supervision and the Technical Committee of the International Organisation of Securities Commissions*, Basel, Switzerland: Bank for International Settlement, September 1998; *Trading and Derivatives Disclosures of Banks and Securities Firms: Joint Report by the Basel Committee on Banking Supervision and the Technical Committee of the International Organisation of Securities Commissions*, Basel, Switzerland: Bank for International Settlement, December 1988; *Risk Concentrations Principles: Joint Report by the Basel Committee on Banking Supervision, the International Organisation of Securities Commissions, and the International Association of Insurance Supervisors*, Basel, Switzerland: Bank for International Settlement, December 1999.
16. Bank for International Settlement (BIS), Basel Committee on Banking Supervision, *Framework for Internal Control Systems in Banking Organisations*, Bank for International Settlement, Basel, Switzerland, September 1998.

17. Bank for International Settlement (BIS), Basel Committee on Banking Supervision, *Essential Elements of a Statement of Cooperation Between Banking Supervisors*, Basel, Switzerland: Bank for International Settlement, May 2001.
18. Bank for International Settlement (BIS), Basel Committee on Banking Supervision, *Conducting a Supervisory Self-Assessment: Practical Application*, Basel, Switzerland: Bank for International Settlement, April 2001; *The Relationship Between Banking Supervisors and Banks' External Auditors: Consultative Document, Issued for Comment by 12 June 2001*, Basel, Switzerland: Bank for International Settlement, February 2001.
19. Bank for International Settlement (BIS), Basel Committee on Banking Supervision, *Best Practices for Credit Risk Disclosure*, Basel, Switzerland: Bank for International Settlement, September 2000; *Industry Views on Credit Risk Mitigation*, Basel, Switzerland: Bank for International Settlement, January 2000; *Range of Practice in Banks' Internal Ratings Systems: Discussion Paper*, Basel, Switzerland: Bank for International Settlement, January 2000.
20. Bank for International Settlement (BIS), Basel Committee on Banking Supervision, *Review of Issues Relating to Highly Leveraged Institutions*, Basel, Switzerland: Bank for International Settlement, March 2001; *Banks' Interactions with Highly Leveraged Institutions: Implementation of the Basel Committee's Sound Practices Paper*, Basel, Switzerland: Bank for International Settlement, January 2000.
21. M. H. Miller and F. Modigliani, "Dividend Policy, Growth and the Valuation of Shares," *Journal of Business* 34 (1961), 411–433; F. Modigliani and M. H. Miller, "The Cost of Capital, Corporation Finance and the Theory of Investment," *American Economic Review* 48 (1958), 261–297.
22. Ibid.
23. Ibid.

CHAPTER 2

Market Risk

2.1 BACKGROUND

Many of the basic concepts used in risk management have evolved from models and methodologies that were originally developed decades ago. Nowadays, most financial organizations have established sophisticated risk management infrastructures, policies, and processes, which support senior management in the steering and fine-tuning of the risk appetite and risk capacity of institutions. However, crises and accidents have happened in the past and will happen again in the future. Regulators have established rules and methods to measure the risks of individual institutions and to force them to support these risks with capital. Many quantitative models and methodologies have evolved from modern portfolio theory, option pricing theories, and other investment-oriented methodologies. The models have been refined for different instruments and asset types, for short and long investment horizons, etc. But the mapping of regulatory-oriented policies onto academic models and practical everyday applications is not without problems.

This chapter analyzes the different models and approaches to market risk, including assumptions and conditions underlying these models and approaches. It also discusses the tolerance and compatibility of both the practical and regulatory approaches to market risk. We will focus on topics such as time horizon, calculation approaches for probability, volatility and correlation, stability of assumptions, and the impact of liquidity. Financial institutions, faced with the need to comply with far-reaching regulations, have a natural incentive to achieve an understanding of the details of risk models and approaches, and to reduce the regulatory required capital. The capital saved through understanding academic and regulatory frameworks allows organizations to invest the "exempt" capital in new and other business opportunities.

2.2 DEFINITION OF MARKET RISK

The Bank for International Settlement (BIS) defines *market risk* as "the risk of losses in on- and off-balance-sheet positions arising from movements in market prices."[1]

The main factors contributing to market risk are equity, interest rate, foreign exchange, and commodity risk. The total market risk is the aggregation of all risk factors. In addition to market risk, the price of financial instruments may be influenced by the following residual risks: spread risk, basis risk, specific risk, and volatility risk:

- *Spread risk* is the potential loss due to changes in spreads between two instruments. For example, there is a credit spread risk between corporate and government bonds.
- *Basis risk* is the potential loss due to pricing differences between equivalent instruments, such as futures, bonds, and swaps.
- *Specific risk* refers to issuer-specific risk—e.g., the risk of holding a corporate bond versus a Treasury futures contract. How to best manage specific risk has been extensively researched and is still a topic of debate. According to the capital asset pricing model (CAPM), specific risk is entirely diversifiable. (See Section 2.4.1 for a discussion of the CAPM.)
- *Volatility risk* is defined as the potential loss due to fluctuations in (implied) volatilities and is referred to as *vega risk.*

To determine the *total price risk* of financial instruments, market risk and residual risk have to be aggregated. Risk is not additive. Total risk is less than the sum of its parts, because the diversification between different assets and risk components has to be considered (i.e., the correlation would never be 1). This effect is described as *diversification effect.* High diversification effect between market and residual risk is expected due to the low correlation.

Table 2-1 lists the key risk dimensions that give rise to market and credit exposure.

Risk can be analyzed in many dimensions. Typically, risk dimensions are quantified as shown in Figure 2-1, which illustrates their interrelationship. Fluctuations in market rates can also give rise to counterparty credit exposure and credit risk, as an increasing interest-rate level makes it more difficult for the issuer to pay the accrued interest rate from the operative cash flow, and as the higher interest rates lower the profit margin.

TABLE 2-1

Key Risk Dimensions Giving Rise to Market and Credit Exposure

Dimension	Example
Risk taker	Position, portfolio, trading desk, business unit
Risk factor	Equity, interest rate, foreign-exchange currency, and commodity
Country or region	Europe, Americas, Asia Pacific
Maturity or duration	1 week, 1 month, 3 months . . . 30 years
Instrument or instrument type	Cash, options, forwards, futures
Counterparty	Crédit Suisse, UBS, Morgan Stanley

Counterparty trading limits should be in place to limit credit exposure due to market-driven instruments, such as *swaps* and *forwards*. The management of credit exposure for market-driven instruments is discussed further in Chapter 3.

Business risk is not included in the definition of risk used in this book (see Chapter 1). Business and market risk are two key sources of risk that can impact a company's ability to achieve earnings or cash-flow targets (see Figure 2-2). The relative magnitude of business risk to market risk varies from company to company and thus reflects the approach and pol-

FIGURE 2-1

Key Risk Dimensions Giving Rise to Market and Credit Exposure. (*Source: Modified from RiskMetrics Group,* Risk Management: A Practical Guide, *New York: RiskMetrics Group, 1999, p. 15. Copyright © 1999 by RiskMetrics Group, all rights reserved. RiskMetrics is a registered trademark of RiskMetrics Group, Inc., in the United States and in other countries. Reproduced with permission of RiskMetrics Group, LLC.*)

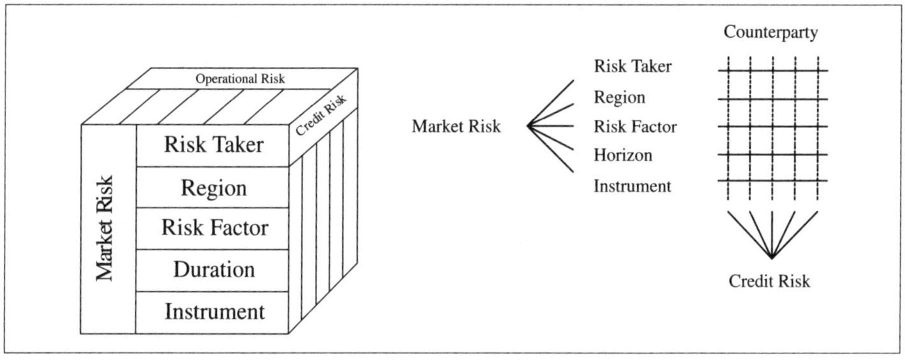

FIGURE 2-2

Differentiation Between Market Risk and Business Risk. (*Source: Modified from RiskMetrics Group,* CorporateMetrics–Technical Document, *New York: RiskMetrics Group, 1999, p. 5, chart 1. Copyright © 1999 by RiskMetrics Group, all rights reserved. CorporateMetrics is a registered trademark of RiskMetrics Group, Inc., in the United States and in other countries. Reproduced with permission of RiskMetrics Group, LLC.*)

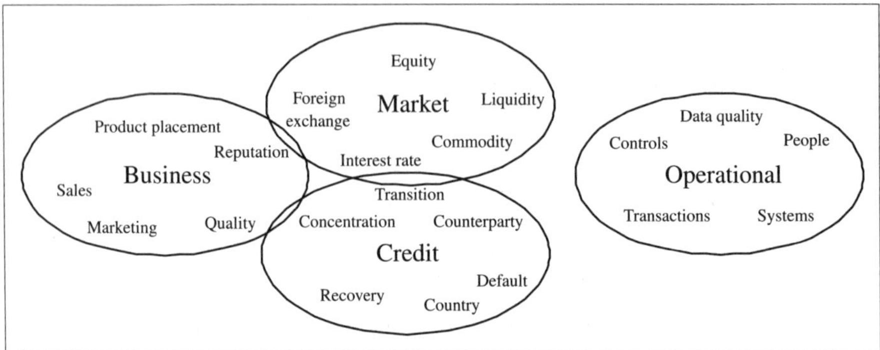

icy for managing both types of risks; it also helps set the tone for a company's risk management culture and awareness. When discussing *business risk,* we are referring to the uncertainty (positive and negative) related to the business decisions that companies make and to the business environment in which companies operate. For example, business risk can arise from investment decisions and strategy, product development choices, marketing approaches, product placement issues, and client behavior uncertainty. Broadly speaking, these are decisions with an inherent long-term horizon and involve structural risks that companies are "paid to take" in order to generate profits. Companies evaluate and take business risks in areas based on their expertise and, to varying degrees, with significant influence over potential returns. In contrast, *market risk* refers to the uncertainty of future financial results that arises from market-rate changes.

Market risk can impact on a company's business in many different ways. For example, operating margins can be eroded due to the rising prices of raw materials or depreciating currencies in countries in which a company has foreign sales (direct market risk impact). Changes in the market environment may eventually force companies to adjust the prices of their products or services, potentially altering sales volumes or competitiveness, depending on the positioning and market exposures of the company's competitors (the indirect impact of market risk on business results). Some organizations may be "paid" to take market risks (e.g., financial organizations), but most seek to manage the impact of market risk on financial results (this is especially true of most nonfinancial organizations).

Financial organizations have overlapping business and market risks. However, as their "raw materials" are currencies, interest rates, etc., financial organizations have to keep business and market risks separated to realize success from intended business strategies and decisions, and from the risk-return relationship of these decisions.

2.3 CONCEPTUAL APPROACHES FOR MODELING MARKET RISK

Investment diversification was a well-established practice long before Markowitz published his paper on portfolio selection in 1952.[2] The development of the modern portfolio theory and of option pricing theories had its roots some decades before Markowitz. These mostly quantitative approaches were not the first to provide diversification for their customers, because such approaches were modeled on the investment trusts of Scotland and England, which began in the middle of the nineteenth century, and diversification had occurred even earlier. In *The Merchant of Venice,* Shakespeare has the merchant Antonio say:

> My ventures are not in one bottom trusted,
> Nor to one place; Nor is my whole estate
> Upon the fortune of this present year;
> Therefore, my merchandise makes me not sad.[3]

Prior to Markowitz's 1952 article, there was no adequate quantitative theory of investment established that covered the effects of diversification when risks are correlated, distinguished between efficient and inefficient portfolios, and analyzed risk–return trade-offs on the portfolio as a whole. In order to understand the benefits and pitfalls of the theories and models currently used for regulatory and management purposes, it is necessary to understand the development of portfolio theory. In 1935, Hicks discussed the need for an improved theory of money and the desirability of building a theory of money along the same lines as the already existing theory of value.[4] Hicks introduced risk into his analysis. Specifically, he noted: "The risk-factor comes into our problem in two ways: First, as affecting the expected period of investment, and second, as affecting the expected net yield of investment."[5] Hicks represents the probabilities of risk dispersions by a mean value and by some appropriate measure of dispersion. Hicks was a forerunner of Tobin[6] in seeking to explain the demand for money as a consequence of the investor's desire for low risk as well as high return. Beyond that, there is little similarity between the two authors. Hicks, unlike Tobin or the appendix in Hicks[7] (1962), did not designate standard deviation or any other specific measure of dispersion as representing risk for the purposes of analysis. Hicks could not demonstrate a formula relating risk on the portfolio to risk on individual assets. Hicks did not distinguish between efficient and inefficient portfolios, lacked a coherent image of an efficient frontier, and gave no hint of any kind of theorem explaining that all efficient portfolios that include cash have the same allocation of distribution among risky assets.

Hicks's article on liquidity (1962) is more precise about the formulation of risk by mentioning the standard deviation as a measure of "certainty" and the mean.[8] The formalization was spelled out in a mathematical appendix to Hicks (1962) titled "The Pure Theory of Portfolio Investment" and in a footnote on page 796 of the work that presents a $\mu\sigma$-efficient set diagram. The appendix presents a mathematical model that is almost identical to Tobin's, but with no reference to Tobin's work. The difference between the Hicks and Tobin models is that Hicks assumed that all correlations are zero, whereas Tobin permitted any nonsingular covariance matrix. Specifically, Hicks presented the general formula for portfolio variance, written in terms of correlations rather than covariances. Hicks (1962) derived the Tobin conclusion that among portfolios which include cash, there is a linear relationship between portfolio mean and standard deviation, and that the proportions among risky assets remain constant along this linear portion of the efficient frontier. Hicks presented what later was called the *Tobin separation theorem.*

Marschak (1938) was clearer in formulating risk by constructing an ordinal theory of choice under uncertainty.[9] He assumed a preference ordering in the space of parameters of probability distributions—in the simplest form—expressed by the mean and the variance. From this formulation to the analysis of portfolio selection in general is the shortest of steps, but one not fully taken by Marschak,[10] though he made tentative moves in this direction, expressing preferences for investments by indifference curves in the mean-variance space. Marschak's 1938 work is a landmark on the road to a theory of markets whose participants act under risk and uncertainty, as later developed in Tobin[11] and the CAPMs.[12] It is the most significant advance of economic theory regarding risk and uncertainty prior to the publication of von Neumann and Morgenstern in 1944.[13] The asset allocation decision had not been adequately addressed by neoclassical economists at the time of Marschak. The methodology of deterministic calculus is adequate for the decision of maximizing a consumer's utility subject to a budget constraint (as part of the neoclassic approach), whereas portfolio selection involves making a decision amidst uncertainty. Under these circumstances, the probabilistic notions of expected return and risk become very important.

In 1938, Williams highlighted the importance of diversification.[14] He concluded that probabilities should be assigned to possible values of a security and the mean of these values used as the value of that security. He also concluded that by investing in many securities, risk could be virtually eliminated. This presumption, that the law of large numbers applies to a portfolio of securities, cannot be accepted. The returns from securities are too intercorrelated. Diversification cannot eliminate all variance. Williams suggested that the way to find the value of a risky security has always been to add a "premium for risk" to the pure interest rate, and then use the sum as the interest rate for discounting future receipts. Williams discussed the separation of specific and systematic risk, without giving a clear overall framework. It should be noted, however, that Williams's "dividend discount model" remains one of the standard ways to estimate the security means needed for a mean-variance analysis.[15]

Leavens' 1945 article on the diversification of investments concluded that each security is acted upon by independent causes.[16] Leavens made the assumptions behind the systemic/specific risk separation very clear, without directly tying his findings to a theoretical formulation.

2.4 MODERN PORTFOLIO THEORY

On the basis of his path-breaking 1952 article, Markowitz became the father of modern portfolio theory (MPT).[17] At the same time, Roy (1952) published an article on the same topic with similar conclusions and a clear theoretical framework.[18] The 1952 article on portfolio selection by Markowitz proposed expected (mean) return, and variance of return, of the portfolio as a whole as criteria for portfolio selection, both as a possible hypothesis about actual behavior and as a maxim for how investors ought to act. The article assumed that *beliefs* or projections about securities follow the same probability rules that random variables obey. From this assumption, Markowitz concluded that the expected return on the portfolio is a weighted average of the expected returns on individual securities and that the variance of return on the portfolio is a particular function of the variances of, and the covariances between, securities and their weights in the portfolio. Markowitz distinguished between efficient and inefficient portfolios. Subsequently, this frontier became the "efficient frontier" for what Markowitz referred to as the set of *mean-variance efficient combinations*. Markowitz proposed that means, variances, and covariances of securities be estimated by a combination of statistical analyses. From these estimates, the set of mean-variance efficient combinations can be derived and presented to the investor, who can choose the desired risk-return combination. Markowitz used geometrical analyses of various security examples to illustrate properties of efficient sets, assuming nonnegative investments subject to a budget constraint. He showed in his 1952 article that the set of efficient portfolios is piecewise linear (made up of connected straight lines) and the set of efficient mean-variance combinations is piecewise parabolic.

Roy (1952) similarly proposed making choices on the basis of mean and variance of the portfolio as a whole. Specifically, he proposed choosing the positions that maximize the portfolio's utility, based on the return, with σ as the standard deviation of return. Roy's formula for the variance of the portfolio included the covariances of returns among securities. The main differences between the Roy and Markowitz approaches were that Markowitz required nonnegative investments, whereas Roy allowed the amount invested in any security to be positive or negative. Furthermore, Markowitz proposed allowing the investor to choose a desired portfolio from the efficient frontier, whereas Roy recommended choosing a specific portfolio. Roy's 1952 article was his first and last article in finance. He made this one tremendous contribution and then disappeared from the field, whereas Markowitz wrote several books and many articles on the portfolio-selection problem and enhancements of his 1952 article.[19]

The conceptual approach to market risk is closely linked historically to the development of modern portfolio theory and the option pricing theory. Modern portfolio theory started with the path-breaking theory of Markowitz.[20] Markowitz was the first finance theorist who explicitly included risk in portfolio analysis. The Markowitz approach is based on the assumption of a relation between risk and return and considers the effect of diversification, using the standard deviation or variance as a measure for risk.

$$\sigma_p^2 = \sum_{i=1}^{N} X_i^2 \sigma_1^2 + \sum_{i=1}^{N} \sum_{\substack{j=1 \\ i \neq 1}}^{N} X_i X_j \rho_{ij} \sigma_i \sigma_j \tag{2.1}$$

The portfolio return is the weighted return of the individual positions, and the portfolio risk is the weighted risk of all individual assets and the covariance between those assets:

$$\bar{R}_p = \sum_{i=1}^{n} X_i r_i$$

$$\sigma = \sum_{i=1}^{N} X_i^2 \sigma_1^2 + \sum_{i=1}^{N} \sum_{\substack{j=1 \\ i \neq 1}}^{N} X_i X_j \sigma_{ij} \tag{2.2}$$

The covariance can be expressed as a correlation term as follows:

$$\sigma_{ij} = \rho_{ij} \sigma_i \sigma_j \tag{2.3}$$

The risk-adjusted portfolio return is:

$$\frac{r_p - r_f}{\sigma_p} \tag{2.4}$$

The efficient frontier is an outcome of Markowitz's theory, a borderline of all portfolios with optimal risk–return relations (Figure 2-3). His ap-

FIGURE 2-3

Efficient Frontier Curve and Capital Market Line.

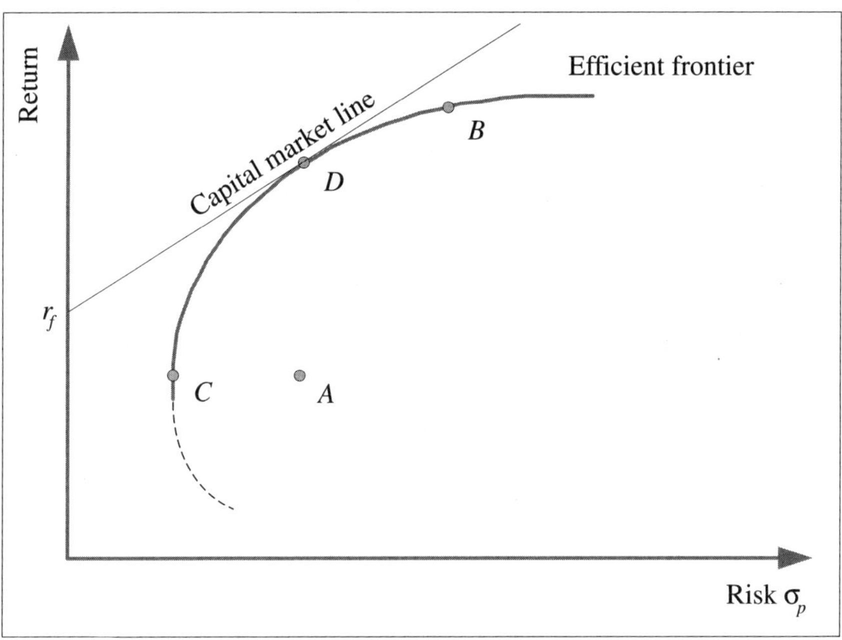

proach was developed further by Tobin.[21] Tobin improved the correlation between the assets and the risk aversion by including a risk-free position. Through combining the portfolios on the efficient frontier of Markowitz and a risk-free position, Sharpe further developed the conceptual modeling of market risks and introduced the capital market line as the tangent from the risk-free asset to the efficient frontier.

2.4.1 The Capital Asset Pricing Model

The complexity of Markowitz's portfolio model and some generalization of assumptions led to further developments. The capital asset pricing model (CAPM) was developed by Sharpe,[22] Lintner,[23] and Mossin,[24] and later was enhanced by Black. It is a logical extension of the ideas behind modern portfolio theory as first outlined by Markowitz. Because the Markowitz approach makes no statement about the pricing of equities, the CAPM offers a statement on the relevant investment risks and the risk–return relation under the condition that the markets are in equilibrium. The CAPM is an equilibrium model for the capital market.

The CAPM is based on the following nine assumptions:[25]

- *Utility maximization.* Investors try to maximize their own utilities; they are risk-averse.
- *Decision basis.* Investors make their decisions only on the basis of risk and return.
- *Expectations.* Investors have homogeneous expectations regarding return and risk (variance and covariance) of the assets.
- *One-period time horizon.* Investors have identical time horizons of one period.
- *Information efficiency.* Information is free and simultaneously available to all market participants.
- *Risk-free asset.* Investors can borrow or invest in an unlimited amount of risk-free assets.
- *Markets without friction.* No taxes, transaction fees, restrictions on short positions or other market restrictions exist.
- *Capital market equilibrium.* The sum of all instruments is given and in possession of the investors. All instruments are marketable, and the assets are divisible to any degree. Supply and demand are not influenced by anything other than price.
- *Distribution.* The CAPM, like the Markowitz approach, is based on the normal distribution of returns or a quadratic utility function.

All combinations are on the line between a risk-free investment and the uncertain investment of the efficient frontier. The part between r_f and D is called the capital market line (CML) and contains only one efficient portfolio, which is at the tangential point between the efficient frontier and the capital market line (see Figure 2-3).

It is not enough to know the return distribution (variance) of a position; the return must be viewed relative to the market and risk components. The CAPM assumes that a certain portion of the risk of a position is a reflection of the overall market risk, which is carried by all positions in the market and thus cannot be diversified. This part of the risk is defined as *systematic risk,* which cannot be eliminated through diversification. This risk premium is defined as the market risk premium. In contrast, the *specific risk* (or unsystematic risk) cannot be explained by market events and has its origins in position-specific factors (e.g., management errors and competitive disadvantages). This component can be diversified and is not rewarded by a premium.

The expected return of a specific stock is calculated as follows:

$$E(r_i) = r_f + \beta_i \cdot [E(r_m) - r_f] + \varepsilon_i \tag{2.5}$$

where r_i = return of security i
r_f = return of the risk-free asset
r_m = return of the market
β_i = sensitivity of security i relative to market movement m
ε_i = error term

2.4.2 The Security Market Line

One of the key elements of modern portfolio theory is that, despite diversification, some risk still exists. The sensitivity of a specific position relative to the market is expressed by β_i (see Figure 2-4). The CAPM defines β_i as the relation of the systematic risk of a security i to the overall risk of the market.

FIGURE 2-4

Security Market Line.

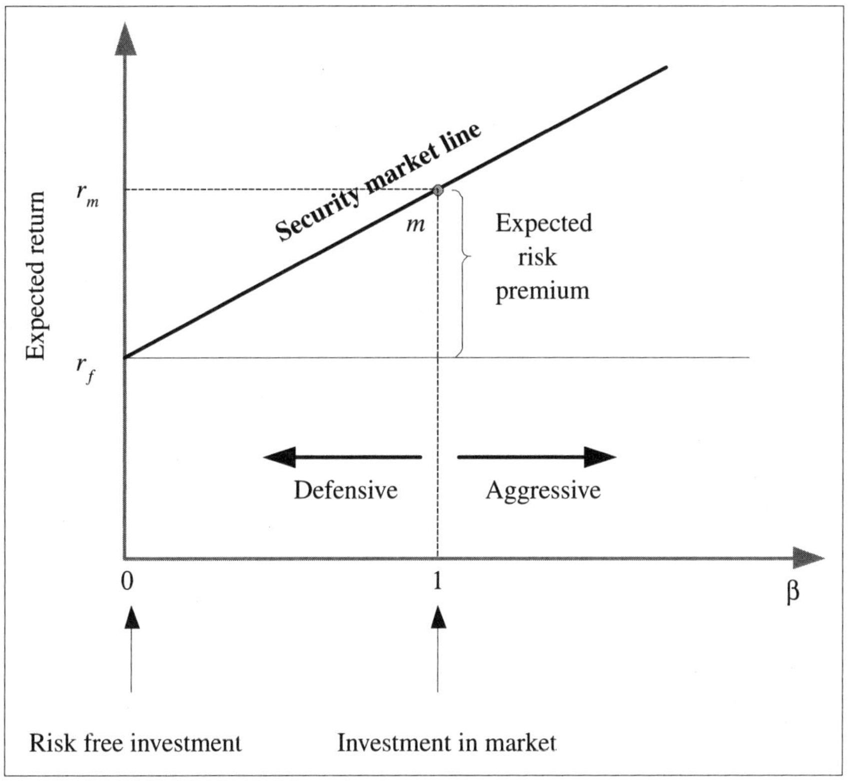

$$\beta_i = \frac{\text{covariance }(r_m, r_i)}{\text{variance }(r_m)} = \frac{\text{systematic risk of title } i}{\text{risk of market portfolios}}$$

$$\frac{\beta_i = \text{cov }(r_i, r_m)}{\sigma r_m} \tag{2.6}$$

where r_i = return of security i
r_f = return of the risk-free asset
r_m = return of the market
β_i = sensitivity of security i relative to market movement m
ε_i = error term

The one-factor model is a strong simplification of the Markowitz model, and the CAPM is a theory. The main criticisms of the CAPM are as follows:

- The market efficiency is not given in its strong form, as not all information is reflected in the market. This presents an opportunity for arbitrage profits, which can be generated as long as insider information is not available to the public.
- The *normal distribution* is a generalization, which distorts the results, especially for idiosyncratic risks.

The main message of market efficiency as it pertains to capital market models is that a market is considered efficient if all available data and information are reflected in the pricing and in the demand-and-supply relation.[26] Fama distinguishes three types of market efficiency: weak, semistrong, and strong.[27]

In a study on Swiss equities, Zimmermann and Vock[28] came to the conclusion that the test statistics (the standardized third and fourth moment as a measure for the skewness and kurtosis, the standardized span or *studentized range,* and the test from Kolmogorov-Smirnov) point to a leptokurtic return distribution (see Figure 2-5). The study concluded that the normal distribution has to be questioned from a statistical point of view. The deviations are empirically marginal. The leptokurtosis has been confirmed for U.S. equities in studies by Fama,[29] Kon,[30] Westerfield,[31] and Wasserfallen and Zimmermann[32] (see Figure 2-5). Zimmermann[33] concluded that over a longer time horizon (1927 to 1987), the normal distribution fits the return distribution of Swiss equities.

FIGURE 2-5

Normal and Leptokurtic Distribution of Equity Returns.

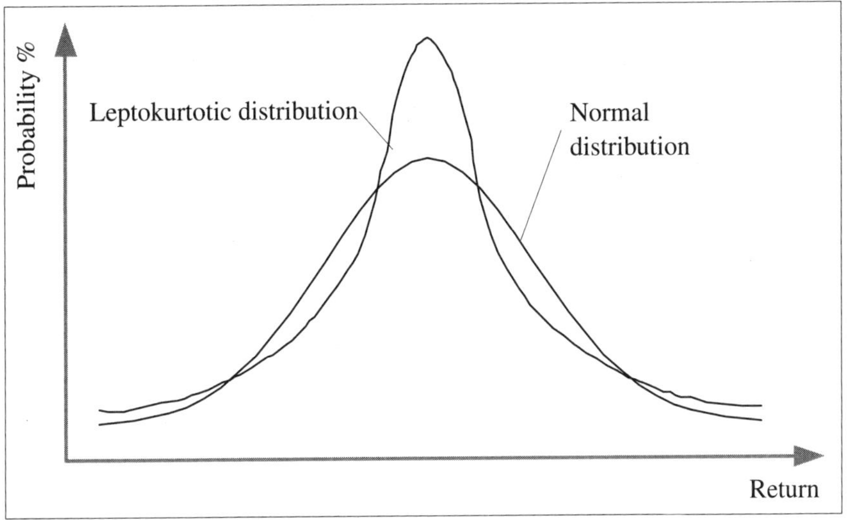

2.4.3 Modified Form of CAPM by Black, Jensen, and Scholes

Black, Jensen, and Scholes conducted an empirical examination of the CAPM in 1972. They used a model without a risk-free interest rate, because the existence of a risk-free interest rate was controversial.[34] In the model without a risk-free return, the security market line (SML) is no longer defined by the risk-free return and the market portfolio; instead, it is a multitude of combinations, as there is a multitude of zero-beta portfolios.[35]

The return that they were able to explain was significantly higher than the average risk-free return within the observation period. They concluded that the model is compatible with the standard form of the CAPM, but differentiates between borrowing and lending. The study supports the practical observation that borrowing is more expensive than lending money. Empirical studies support the development of the capital market line with two interest rates, one for borrowing and one for lending money. It is an important improvement, as it excludes the assumption that borrowing and lending are based on the same risk-free rate.[36] Figure 2-6 is based on the following equations:

$$E(r_i) = r_L + \beta_i \cdot [E(r_m) - r_L] + \varepsilon_i \tag{2.7}$$

$$E(r_i) = r_B + \beta_i \cdot [E(r_m) - r_B] + \varepsilon_i \tag{2.8}$$

FIGURE 2-6

Efficient Frontier with Different Interest Rates for Borrowing and Lending Capital.

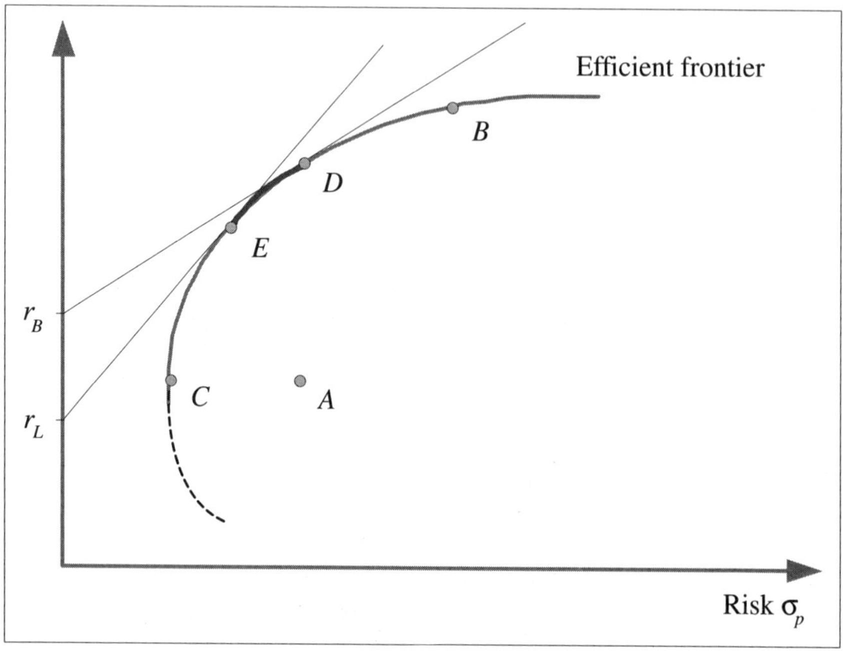

2.4.4 Arbitrage Pricing Theory

Empirical examinations of the CAPM showed significant deficiencies in its ability to forecast and alleviate risk. These studies led to the development of the arbitrage pricing theory (APT), first introduced by Ross[37] and further developed by other scientists.

APT is based on the empirical observation that different instruments have simultaneous and homogeneous development ranges. The theory implicitly assumes that the returns are linked to a certain number of factors which influence the instrument prices. The part explained by these factors is assigned to the systematic factors, whereas the nonexplainable part of the return (and thus the risk) is assigned to specific factors.

In theory, the factors are uncorrelated, as empirical examination supports correlated factors. Such correlated factors have to be transformed into an observation-equivalent model with uncorrelated factors. The factors cannot be observed and have to be examined empirically.

A critical difference between CAPM and APT is that APT is an equilibrium theory, based on the arbitrage condition. As long as it is possible with intensive research to find factors that systematically impact the return of a position, it is possible to do arbitrage based on this superior knowledge.

2.4.5 Approaches to Option Pricing

Modern portfolio theory is not based solely on return calculations. Risk and risk management become increasingly important. As the portfolio theory shows, despite diversification, an investor is still exposed to systematic risk. With the development of portfolio and position insurance, an approach has been created to hedge (insure) against unwanted moves of the underlying position. The theoretical framework introduced a range of applications, such as replication of indices, dynamic insurance, leveraging, immunization, structured products, etc. To understand the current state of option pricing, the different approaches, and the critics, it is necessary to summarize the development of, and approaches to, modern option-valuation theory.

Valuation and pricing of income streams is one of the central problems of finance. The issue seems straightforward conceptually, as it amounts to identifying the amount and the timing of the cash flows expected from holding the claims and then discounting them back to the present. Valuation of a European-style call option requires that the mean of the call option's payout distribution on the expiration date be estimated, and the discount rate be applied to the option's expected terminal payout.

The first documented attempt to value a call option occurred near the turn of the twentieth century. Bachelier wrote in his 1900 thesis that the call option can be valued under the assumption that the underlying claim follows an arithmetic Brownian motion.[38] Sprenkle and Samuelson used a geometric Brownian motion in their attempt to value options.[39] As the underlying asset prices have multiplicative, rather than additive (as with the arithmetic motion) fluctuations, the asset price distribution at the expiration date is lognormal, rather then normal. Sprenkle and Samuelson's research set the stage, but there was still a problem. Specifically, for implementation of their approach, the risk-adjusted rates of price appreciation for both the asset and the option are required. Precise estimation was the problem, which was made more difficult as the option's return depends on the asset's return, and the passage of time.

The breakthrough came in 1973 with Black, Scholes, and Merton.[40] They showed that as long as a risk-free hedge may be formed between the option and its underlying asset, the value of an option relative to the asset will be the same for all investors, regardless of their risk preferences. The argument of the risk-free hedge is convincing, because in equilibrium, no arbitrage opportunities can exist, and any arbitrage opportunity is obvious for all market participants and will be eliminated. If the observed price of the call is above (or below) its theoretical price, risk-free arbitrage profits are possible by selling the call and buying (or selling) a portfolio consisting of a long position in a half unit of the asset, and a short position in the other half in risk-free bonds. In equilibrium, no arbitrage opportunities can exist, and any arbitrage opportunity can exist.

2.4.5.1 Analytical Formulas

The option valuation theory goes beyond the mathematical part of the formula. The economic insight is that if a risk-free hedge between the option and its underlying asset my be formed, risk-neutral valuation may be applied. The Black-Scholes model follows the work of Sprenkle and Samuelson. In a risk-neutral market, all assets (and options) have an expected rate of return equal to the risk-free interest rate. Not all assets have the same expected rate of price appreciation. Some assets, such as bonds, have coupons, and equities have dividends. If the asset's income is modeled as a constant and continuous proportion of the asset price, the expected rate of price appreciation on the asset equals the interest rate less the cash disbursement rate. The Black-Scholes formula covers a wide range of underlying assets. The distinction between the valuation problems described as follows rests in the asset's risk-neutral price appreciation parameter:

- *Non-dividend-paying stock options.* The best-known option valuation problem is that of valuing options on non-dividend-paying stocks. This is, in fact, the valuation problem addressed by Black and Scholes in 1973.[41] With no dividends paid on the underlying stock, the expected price appreciation rate of the stock equals the risk-free rate of interest, and the call option valuation equation becomes the familiar Black-Scholes formula.
- *Constant-dividend-yield stock options.* Merton generalized stock option valuation in 1973 by assuming that stocks pay dividends at a constant, continuous dividend yield.[42]
- *Futures options.* Black valued options on futures in 1976.[43] In a risk-neutral world with constant interest rates, the expected rate of price appreciation on a futures contract is zero, because it involves no cash outlay.
- *Futures-style futures options.* Following the work of Black, Asay valued futures-style futures options.[44] Such options, traded on various exchanges, have the distinguishing feature that the option premium is not paid up front. Instead, the option position is marked to market in the same manner as the underlying futures contract.
- *Foreign currency options.* Garman and Kohlhagen valued options on foreign currency in 1983.[45] The expected rate of price appreciation of a foreign currency equals the domestic rate of interest less the foreign interest.
- *Dynamic portfolio insurance.* Dynamic replication is at the heart of one of the most popular financial products of the 1980s—dynamic portfolio insurance. Because long-term index put options were not traded at the time, stock portfolio managers had

to create their own insurance by dynamically rebalancing a portfolio consisting of stocks and risk-free bonds. The weights in the portfolio show that as stock prices rise, funds are transferred from bonds to stocks, and vice versa.

- *Compound options.* An important extension of the Black-Scholes model that falls in the single underlying asset category is the compound option valuation theory developed by Geske.[46] Compound options are options on options. A call on a call, for example, provides its holder with the right to buy a call on the underlying asset at some future date. Geske shows that if these options are European-style, valuation formulas can be derived.
- *American-style call options on dividend-paying stocks.* The Geske compound option model has been applied in other contexts. Roll, Geske, and Whaley developed a formula for valuing an American-style call option on a stock with known discrete dividends.[47] If a stock pays a cash dividend during the call's life, it may be optimal to exercise the call early, just prior to dividend payment. An American-style call on a dividend-paying stock, therefore, can be modeled as a compound option providing its holder with the right, on the ex-dividend date, either to exercise early and collect the dividend, or to leave the position open.
- *Chooser options.* Rubinstein used the compound option framework in 1991 to value the "chooser" or "as-you-like-it" options traded in the over-the-counter market.[48] The holder of a chooser option has the right to decide at some future date whether the option is a call or a put. The call and the put usually have the same exercise price and the same time remaining to expiration.
- *Bear market warrants with a periodic reset.* Gray and Whaley used the compound option framework to value yet another type of contingent claim, S&P 500 bear market warrants with a periodic reset traded on the Chicago Board Options Exchange and the New York Stock Exchange.[49] The warrants are originally issued as at-the-money put options but have the distinguishing feature that if the underlying index level is above the original exercise on some prespecified future date, the exercise price of the warrant is reset at the then-prevailing index level. These warrants offer an intriguing form of portfolio insurance whose floor value adjusts automatically as the index level rises. The structure of the valuation problem is again a compound option, and Gray and Whaley's 1997 paper provides the valuation formula.
- *Lookback options.* A lookback option is another exotic that has only one underlying source of price uncertainty. Such an option's

exercise price is determined at the end of its life. For a call, the exercise price is set equal to the lowest price that the asset reached during the life of the option; for a put, the exercise price equals the highest asset price. These buy-at-the-low and sell-at-the-high options can be valued analytically. Formulas are provided in Goldman, Sosin, and Gatto's 1979 paper.[50]

- *Barrier options.* Barrier options are options that either cease to exist or come into existence when some predefined asset price barrier is hit during the option's life. A down-and-out call, for example, is a call that gets knocked out when the asset price falls to some prespecified level prior to the option's expiration. Rubinstein and Reiner's 1991 paper provides valuation equations for a large family of barrier options.[51]

2.4.5.2 Approximation Methods

Many valuation problems do not have explicit closed-form solutions. Probably the best-known example of this is the valuation of American-style options. With American-style options, the option holder has an infinite number of exercise opportunities between the current date and the option's expiration date, making the problem challenging from a mathematical standpoint. Hundreds of different types of exotic options trade in the OTC market, and many, if not most, do not have analytical formulas. Nonetheless, they can all be valued accurately using the Black-Scholes model. If a risk-free hedge can be formed between the option and the underlying asset, the Black-Scholes model risk-neutral valuation theory can be applied, albeit using numerical methods. A number of numerical methods for valuing options are lattice based. These methods replace the Black-Scholes model assumption that asset price moves smoothly and continuously through time with an assumption that the asset price moves in discrete jumps over discrete intervals during the option's life:

- *Binomial method.* Perhaps the best-known lattice-based method is the binomial method, developed independently in 1979 by Cox, Ross, and Rubinstein and Rendleman and Bartter.[52] In the binomial method, the asset price jumps up or down, by a fixed proportion, at each of a number of discrete time steps during the option's life. The length of each time step is determined when the user specifies the number of time steps. The greater the number of time steps, the more precise the method. The cost of the increased precision, however, is computational speed. With n time steps, $2n$ asset price paths over the life of the option are considered. With 20 time steps, this means more than 1 million paths.

  The binomial method has wide applicability. Aside from the American-style option feature, which is easily incorporated within the framework, the binomial method can be used to value many types of exotic options. Knockout options, for example, can be valued using this technique. One simply imposes a different check on the calculated option values at the nodes of the intermediate time steps between 0 and n, i.e., if the underlying asset price falls below the option's barrier, the option value at that node is set equal to 0. The method can also be extended to handle multiple sources of asset price uncertainty. Boyle, Evnine, and Gibbs adapt the binomial procedure to handle exotics with multiple sources of uncertainty, including options on the minimum and maximum, spread options, and so on.[53]

- *Trinomial method.* The trinomial method is another popular lattice-based method. As outlined by Boyle, this method allows the asset to move up, move down, or stay the same at each time increment.[54] Again, the parameters of the discrete distribution are chosen in a manner consistent with the lognormal distribution, and the procedure begins at the end of the option's life and works backward. By having three branches instead of two, the trinomial method provides greater accuracy than the binomial method for a given number of time steps. The cost, of course, is that the greater the number of branches, the slower the computational speed.
- *Finite difference method.* The explicit finite difference method was the first lattice-based procedure to be applied to option valuation. Schwartz applied it to warrants, and Brennan and Schwartz applied it to American-style put options on common stocks.[55] The finite difference method is similar to the trinomial method in the sense that the asset price moves up, moves down, or stays the same at each time step during the option's life. The difference in the techniques arise only from how the price increments and the probabilities are set. In addition, finite difference methods calculate an entire rectangle of node values rather than simply a tree.
- *Monte Carlo simulation.* Boyle introduced Monte Carlo simulation to option valuation.[56] Like the lattice-based procedures, the technique involves simulating possible paths that the asset price may take over the life of the option. Again, the simulation is performed in a manner consistent with the lognormal asset price process. To value a European-style option, each sample run is used to produce a terminal asset price, which, in turn, is used to determine the terminal option value. With repeated sample runs, a distribution of terminal options values is obtained, and the expected terminal option value may be calculated. This expected value is then discounted to the present to obtain the option valuation. An advantage of the Monte Carlo method is that the

degree of valuation error can be assessed directly, using the standard error of the estimate. The standard error equals the standard deviation of the terminal option values divided by the square root of the number of trials. Another advantage of the Monte Carlo technique is its flexibility. Because the path of the asset price beginning at time 0 and continuing throughout the life of the option is observed, the technique is well suited for handling barrier-style options, Asian-style options, Bermuda-style options, and the like. Moreover, it can easily be adapted to handle multiple sources of price uncertainty. The technique's chief disadvantage is that it can be applied only when the option payout does not depend on its value at future points in time. This eliminates the possibility of applying the technique to American-style option valuation, in which the decision to exercise early depends on the value of the option that will be forfeit.

- *Compound option approximation.* The quasi-analytical methods for option valuation are quite different from the procedures that attempt to describe asset price paths. Geske and Johnson, for example, use a Geske compound option model to develop an approximate value for an American-style option.[57] The approach is intuitively appealing. An American-style option, after all, is a compound option with an infinite number of early exercise opportunities. While valuing an option in this way makes intuitive sense, the problem is intractable from a computational standpoint. The Geske-Johnson insight is that although we cannot value an option with an infinite number of early exercise opportunities, we can extrapolate its value by valuing a sequence of "pseudo-American" options with zero, one, two, and perhaps more early exercise opportunities at discrete, equally spaced intervals during the option's life. The advantage that this offers is that each of these options can be valued analytically. With each new option added to the sequence, however, the valuation of a higher-order multivariate normal integral is required. With no early exercise opportunities, only a univariate function is required. However, with one early exercise opportunity, a bivariate function is required; with two opportunities, a trivariate function is required, and so on. The more of these options used in the series, the greater the precision in approximating the limiting value of the sequence. The cost of increased precision is that higher-order multivariate integral valuations are time-consuming computationally.
- *Quadratic approximation.* Barone-Adesi and Whaley presented a quadratic approximation in 1987.[58] Their approach, based on the

work of MacMillan, separates the value of an American-style option into two components: the European-style option value and an early exercise premium.[59] Because the Black-Scholes model formula provides the value of the European-style option, they focus on approximating the value of the early exercise premium. By imposing a subtle change on the Black-Scholes model partial differential equation, they obtain an analytical expression for the early exercise premium, which they then add to the European-style option value, thereby providing an approximation of the American-style option value. The advantages of the quadratic approximation method are speed and accuracy.

2.4.5.3 Generalizations

The generalizations of the Black-Scholes option valuation theory focus on the assumed asset price dynamics. Some examine the valuation implications of modeling the local volatility rate as a deterministic function of the asset price or time or both. Others examine the valuation implications when volatility, like asset price, is stochastic.

Under the assumption that the local volatility rate is a deterministic function of time or the asset price or both, the Black-Scholes model risk-free hedge mechanisms are preserved, so risk-neutral valuation remains possible. The simplest in this class of models is the case in which the local volatility rate is a deterministic function of time. For this case, Merton showed that the valuation equation for a European-style call option is the Black-Scholes model formula, where the volatility parameter is the average local volatility rate over the life of the option.[60]

Other models focus on the relationship between asset price and volatility and attempt to account for the empirical fact that, in at least some markets, volatility varies inversely with the level of asset price. One such model is the constant elasticity of variance model proposed by Cox and Ross.[61] However, valuation can be handled straightforwardly using lattice-based or Monte Carlo simulation procedures.

Derman and Kani, Dupire, and Rubinstein and Reiner recently developed a valuation framework in which the local volatility rate is a deterministic (but unspecified) function of asset price and time.[62] If the specification of the volatility function is known, any of the lattice-based or simulation procedures can be applied to option valuation. Unfortunately, the structural form is not known. To circumvent this problem, these authors parameterize their model by searching for a binomial or trinomial lattice that achieves an exact cross-sectional fit of reported option prices. An exact cross-sectional fit is always possible, because there are as many degrees of freedom in defining the lattice (and, hence, the local volatility-rate function) as there are option prices. With the structure of the implied tree identified, it becomes possible to value other, more exotic, OTC options and to refine hedge ratio computations.

The effects of stochastic volatility on option valuation are modeled by either superimposing jumps on the asset price process or allowing volatility to have its own diffusion process or both. Unfortunately, the introduction of stochastic volatility negates the Black-Scholes model risk-free hedge argument, because volatility movements cannot be hedged. An exception to this rule is provided by Merton, who adds a jump term to the usual geometric Brownian motion governing asset price dynamics.[63] By assuming that the jump component of an asset's return is unsystematic, the Merton model can create a risk-free portfolio in the Black-Scholes model sense and apply risk-neutral valuation. Indeed, Merton finds analytical valuation formulas for European-style options. If the jump risk is systematic, however, the Black-Scholes model risk-free hedge cannot be formed, and option valuation will be utility-dependent.

A number of authors model asset price and asset price volatility as separate, but correlated, diffusion processes. Asset price is usually assumed to follow geometric Brownian motion. The assumptions governing volatility vary. Hull and White, for example, assume that volatility follows geometric Brownian motion.[64] Scott models volatility using a mean-reverting process, and Wiggins uses a general Wiener process.[65] Bates combines both jump and volatility diffusions in valuing foreign currency options. Except in the uninteresting case in which asset price and volatility movements are independent, these models require the estimation of risk premiums.[66] The problem when volatility is stochastic is that a risk-free hedge cannot be created, because volatility is not a traded asset. But perhaps this problem is only temporary. The critical issue for all options, of course, is correct contract design.

2.5 REGULATORY INITIATIVES FOR MARKET RISKS AND VALUE AT RISK

Alan Greenspan has made it very clear that the assumptions and conditions must be fully discussed and understood when applying quantitative models such as value at risk (VaR):

> Probability distributions estimated largely, or exclusively, over cycles that do not include periods of panic will underestimate the likelihood of extreme price movements because they fail to capture a secondary peak at the extreme negative tail that reflects the probability of occurrence of a panic. Furthermore, joint distributions estimated over periods that do not include panics will underestimate correlations between asset returns during panics. Under these circumstances, fear and disengagement on the part of investors holdings net long positions often lead to simultaneously declines in the values of private obligations, as investors no longer realistically differentiate

among degrees of risk and liquidity, and to increase in the values of riskless government securities. Consequently, the benefits of portfolio diversification will tend to be overestimated when the rare panic periods are not taken into account.[67]

The 1988 Basel accord provided the first step toward tighter risk management and enforceable international regulation with similar structural conditions for financial supervision.[68] The Basel accord set minimum capital requirements that must be met by banks to guard against credit risk. This agreement led to a still-evolving framework to impose capital adequacy requirements to guard against market risks.

The reasoning behind regulation is multilayered and complex. One could ask why regulations are necessary. In a free market, investors should be free to invest in firms that they believe to be profitable, and as owners of an institution, they should be free to define the risk profile within which the institution should be free to act and evolve. Essentially, this is what happened to Barings, where complacent shareholders failed to monitor the firm's management (see Section 6.6). Poor control over traders led to increasingly risky activities and, ultimately, bankruptcy. In freely functioning capital markets, badly managed institutions should be allowed to fail. Such failures also serve as powerful object lessons in risk management.

Nevertheless, supervision is generally viewed as necessary when free markets appear to be unable, themselves, to allocate resources efficiently. For financial institutions, this is the rationale behind regulations to protect against systemic risk (externalities) and to protect client assets (i.e., deposit insurance).

Systemic risk arises when an institution's failure affects other participants in the market. Here the fear is that a default by one institution will have a cascading effect on other institutions, thus threatening to destabilize the entire financial system. Systemic risk is rather difficult to evaluate, because it involves situations of extreme instability, which happen infrequently. In addition, regulators tend to take preventive measures to protect the system before real systemic damage is caused.[69]

Deposit insurance also provides a rationale for regulative measures. By nature, bank deposits have destabilizing potential. Depositors are promised that the full face value of their investments will be repaid on demand. If customers fear that a bank's assets have fallen behind its liabilities, they may then rationally trigger a run on the bank. Given that banks invest in illiquid assets, including securities and real estate, the demand for repayment will force liquidation at great cost.

One solution to this problem is government guarantees on bank deposits, which reduce the risk of bank runs. These guarantees are also viewed as necessary to protect small depositors who have limited financial experience and cannot efficiently monitor their banks.

There is an ongoing argument that deposit insurance could be provided by the private sector instead of the government. Realistically, however, private financial organizations may not be able to provide financial transfers to investors if large macroeconomic shocks or sector collapses occur, such as the U.S. savings and loan crisis of the 1980s. On the other hand, applying Darwinism to capital markets, it should be possible to eliminate failing institutions from the market and replace them with fitter organizations.[70]

This government guarantee is no "panacea, for it creates a host of other problems, generally described under the rubric of moral hazard (see Section 1.4). Given government guarantees, there is even less incentive for depositors to monitor their banks. As long as the cost of the deposit insurance is not related to the risk-profile of the activities, there will be perverse incentives to take additional risks. The moral hazard problem, due to deposit insurance, is a rationale behind regulatory attempts to supervise risk-taking activities. This is achieved by regulating the bank's minimum levels of capital, providing a reserve for failures of the institution or systemic risks. Capital adequacy requirements can also serve as a deterrent to unusual risk taking if the amount of capital set aside is tied to the amount of risk undertaken.

Alan Greenspan stated in 1999 that the current regulatory standards had been misused due to inconsistent and arbitrary treatment:

> The current international standards for bank capital had encouraged bank transactions that reduce regulatory requirements more than they reduce a bank's risk position. The fundamental credibility of regulatory capital standards as a tool for prudential oversight and prompt corrective action at the largest banking organizations has been seriously undermined.[71]

2.5.1 Development of an International Framework for Risk Regulation

The Basel Committee on Banking Supervision was founded in 1975; it is the driving force for harmonization of banking supervision regulation on an international level, and it substantially supports cross-border enforcement of cooperation among national regulators. The committee's recommendations have no internal binding power, but based on the material power of persuasion and the implementation of its recommendations at the local level by the members of the Committee, it has a worldwide impact.[72]

Capital adequacy is the primary focus of the committee, as capital calculation has a central role in all local regulations, and the standards of the BIS are broadly implemented. The standards are intended to strengthen the international finance system and reduce the distortion of normal trading conditions by arbitrary national requirements. The BIS recommendations apply only to international banks and consolidated banking groups. They are minimum standards, allowing local regulators to set or introduce higher requirements. The Basel Committee intends to develop and enhance an international regulatory network to increase the quality of banking supervision worldwide.

2.5.2 Framework of the 1988 BIS Capital Adequacy Calculation

Since its inception, the Basel Committee has been very active on the issue of capital adequacy. A landmark financial agreement was reached with the Basel accord, concluded on July 15, 1988, by the central bankers of the G-10 countries.[73] The regulators announced that the accord would result in international convergence of supervisory regulations governing the capital adequacy of international banks. Though minimal, these capital adequacy standards increase the quality and stability of the international banking system, and thus help to reduce distortion between international banks. The main purpose of the 1988 Basel accord was to provide general terms and conditions for commercial banks by means of a minimum standard of capital requirements to be applied in all member countries. The accord contained minimal capital standards for the support of credit risks in balance and off-balance positions, as well as a definition of the countable equity capital. The Basel capital accord was modified in 1994 and 1995 with regard to derivatives instruments and recognition of bilateral netting agreements.[74]

With the Cooke defined ratio, the 1988 accord created a common measure of solvency. However, it covers only credit risks and thus deals solely with the identity of banks' debtors. The new ratios became binding by regulation in 1993, covering all insured banks of the signatory countries.

2.5.2.1 The Cooke Ratio

The Basel accord requires that banks hold capital equal to at least 8 percent of their total risk-weighted assets. *Capital,* however, is interpreted more broadly than the usual definition of equity, because its goal is to protect deposits. It consists of two components:

- *Tier 1 capital.* Tier 1 capital, or *core capital,* includes stock issues and disclosed reserves. General loan loss reserves constitute capital that has been dedicated to funds to absorb potential future losses. Real losses in the future are funded from the reserve account rather than through limitation of earnings, smoothing out income over time.
- *Tier 2 capital.* Tier 2 capital, or *supplementary capital,* includes perpetual securities, undisclosed reserves, subordinated debt

with maturity longer than five years, and shares redeemable at the option of the issuer. Because long-term debt has a junior status relative to deposits, debt acts as a buffer to protect depositors (and the deposit insurer).

The Cooke ratio requires an 8 percent capital charge, at least 50 percent of which must be covered by Tier 1 capital. The general 8 percent capital charge is multiplied by risk capital weights according to predetermined asset classes. Government bonds, such as Treasuries, Bundesobligationen, Eidgenossen, and so forth are obligations allocated to the Organization for Economic Cooperation and Development (OECD) government papers, which have a risk weight of zero. In the same class fall cash and gold held by banks. As the perceived credit risk increases (nominally), so does the risk weight. Other asset classes, such as claims on corporations (including loans, bonds, and equities), receive a 100 percent weight, resulting in the required coverage of 8 percent of capital.

Signatories of the Basel accord are free to impose higher local capital requirements in their home countries.[75] For example, under the newly established bank capital requirements, U.S. regulators have added a capital restriction which requires that Tier 1 capital must comprise no less than 3 percent of total assets.

2.5.2.2 Activity Restrictions

In addition to the weights for the capital adequacy calculation, the Basel accord set limits on excessive risk taking. These restrictions relate to large risks, defined as positions exceeding 10 percent of the bank's capital. Large risks must be reported to regulatory authorities on a formal basis. Positions exceeding 25 percent of the bank's capital are not allowed (unless a bank has the approval of the local regulator). The sum of all large-risk exposures may not exceed 800 percent of the capital.

2.5.3 Criticisms of the 1988 Approach

The 1988 Basel accord had several drawbacks, which became obvious with implementation. The main criticisms were the lack of accommodation of the portfolio approach, the lack of netting possibilities, and the way in which market risks were incorporated.

- *The portfolio approach was not accommodated.* Thus, correlations between different positions of the bank's portfolio did not account for the portfolio risk of the bank's activities. The Basel accord increased the capital requirements resulting from hedging strategies, as offsetting hedging positions were not allowed.
- *Netting was not allowed.* If a bank nets corresponding lenders and borrowers, the total net exposure may be small. If a

counterparty fails to fulfill its obligations, the overall loss may be reduced, as the positions lent are matched by the positions borrowed. Netting was an important driving force behind the creation of swaps and time deposits. *Swaps* (of currencies and interest rates) are derivatives contracts involving a series of exchanges of payments and are contracted with explicit offset provisions. In the event of a counterparty default, the bank is exposed only to the net of the interest payments, not to the notional amount.[76]

- *Exposures to market risk were vaguely regulated.* According to the 1988 Basel accord, assets were recorded at book value. These positions could deviate substantially from their current market values. As a result, the accounting approach created a potential situation in which an apparently healthy balance sheet with acceptable capital (recorded at book value) hid losses in market value. This regulatory approach concerning accounting created problems for the trading portfolios of banks with substantial positions in derivatives. This specific drawback convinced the Basel Committee to move toward measuring market risk by the value-at-risk approach and mark-to-market position booking.

2.5.4 Evolution of the 1996 Amendment on Market Risks

In view of the increasing exposure to market risks in securities and derivatives trading, the Basel Committee created a substantial enhancement of the credit-risk-oriented capital adequacy regulations through new measurement rules and capital requirements to support market risks throughout an institution. The committee published the results of its work for discussion in January 1996.[77] The discussion paper proposed two alternative methods for risk measurement and capital requirements to support market risks. The standard model approach was to be used by small and midsized banks lacking the complex technological infrastructure and expertise needed to calculate daily market risk exposures. The internal model approach could be used if the local regulator explicitly allowed the bank to use its own technological infrastructure and expertise to calculate daily market risk exposures. Banks would have the opportunity to use both approaches simultaneously during a transition period. After a certain time, banks would be expected to use only one model across the institution.

Originally, the aim had been for a harmonized standard, which should have balanced the terms of competition between the securities dealers and the banks regarding capital requirements. The development of such a regulative framework would have been supported by a joint project between the Basel Committee and the stock exchange supervisory authorities, for whom market risks have always been in the foreground. The discussion with the Technical Committee of the International Organization of Securities Commission (IOSCO)—the international association of supervisory authorities of the securities houses of the Western industrialized nations—failed, because the IOSCO members could not agree on a common approach. Partly responsible for the failure was the fact that IOSCO had no concrete capital adequacy standard. This would have required a substantial reworking of IOSCO's regulations.

Based on this discussion, the Basel Committee published a first consultation paper in 1993, which included proposals for the regulatory treatment of market risks of debt and equity positions in the trading books. For trading positions, the related derivatives instruments, and foreign currency risks from the banking books, the committee proposed a binding standard approach for measurement and capital requirements to support market risks. In addition, a proposal for the measurement of interest rate risks based on the bank's complete activity has been developed to identify unexceptionally high interest rate risks (the so-called outlier concept). As an alternative to the proposed standard approach for the measurement and capital requirements to support market risks, the committee also considered the banks' own internal models for the measurement and capital requirements to support market risks. The modified recommendations of the Basel Committee were published in April 1995. Simultaneously, another globally coordinated consultation procedure was carried out with market participants and representatives from the local regulators. The final capital adequacy accord for measurement and capital requirements to support market risks was adopted by the committee in December 1995 and published in January 1996. The member countries had until the end of 1997 to include the modified capital adequacy regulation in their national supervisory regulations.

2.6 AMENDMENT TO THE CAPITAL ACCORD TO INCORPORATE MARKET RISKS

Starting at the end of 1997, or earlier, if their supervisory authority so prescribed, banks were required to measure and apply capital charges to their market risks in addition to their credit risks.[78] *Market risk* is defined as "the risk of losses in on- and off-balance-sheet positions arising from movements in market prices." The following risks are subject to this requirement:

- Risks pertaining to interest-rate-related instruments and equities in the trading book
- Foreign exchange risk and commodities risk throughout the bank

2.6.1 Scope and Coverage of Capital Charges

The final version of the amendment to the capital accord to incorporate market risks regulates capital charges for interest-rate-related instruments and equities and applies to the current market value of items in the bank's trading books. By *trading book* is meant the bank's proprietary positions in financial instruments (including positions in derivative products and off-balance-sheet instruments) which are intentionally held for short-term resale. The financial instruments may also be acquired by the bank with the intention of benefiting in the short term from actual or expected differences between their buying and selling prices, or from other price or interest-rate variations; positions in financial instruments arising from matched principal brokering and market making; or positions taken in order to hedge other elements of the trading book.[79]

Capital charges for foreign exchange risk and for commodities risk apply to the bank's total currency and commodity positions, subject to some discretion to exclude structural foreign exchange positions:

> For the time being, the Committee does not believe that it is necessary to allow any de minimis exemptions from the capital requirements for market risk, except for those for foreign exchange risk set out in paragraph 13 of A.3, because the Capital Accord applies only to internationally active banks, and then essentially on a consolidated basis; all of these are likely to be involved in trading to some extent.[80]

2.6.2 Countable Capital Components

The definition of capital is based on that of the BIS, from the *Amendment to the Capital Accord to Incorporate Market Risks:*

> The principal form of eligible capital to cover market risks consists of shareholders' equity and retained earnings (tier 1 capital) and supplementary capital (tier 2 capital) as defined in the 1988 Accord. But banks may also, at the discretion of their national authority, employ a third tier of capital ("tier 3"), consisting of short-term subordinated debt as defined in paragraph 2 below for the sole purpose of meeting a proportion of the capital requirements for market risks, subject to the following conditions. . . .[81]

The definition of eligible regulatory capital remains the same as outlined in the 1988 accord and clarified in the October 27, 1998, press release on instruments eligible for inclusion in Tier 1 capital. The ratio must be no lower than 8 percent for total capital. Tier 2 capital continues to be limited to 100 percent of Tier 1 capital.[82]

To clarify the impact of the amendment for market risk on the risk steering of the banks, the capital definitions are summarized as follows:

- Banks are entitled to use Tier 3 capital solely to support market risks as defined in Parts A and B of the amendment. This means that any capital requirement arising in respect of credit and counterparty risk in the terms of the 1988 accord, including the credit counterparty risk in respect of derivatives in both trading and banking books, needs to be met by the existing definition of capital in the 1988 accord (i.e., Tiers 1 and 2).
- Tier 3 capital is limited to 250 percent of a bank's Tier 1 capital that is required to support market risks. This means that a minimum of about 28.5 percent of market risks needs to be supported by Tier 1 capital that is not required to support risks in the remainder of the book.
- Tier 2 elements may be substituted for Tier 3 up to the same limit of 250 percent if the overall limits in the 1988 accord are not breached. That is, eligible Tier 2 capital may not exceed total Tier 1 capital, and long-term subordinated debt may not exceed 50 percent of Tier 1 capital.
- In addition, because the committee believes that Tier 3 capital is appropriate only to meet market risk, a significant number of member countries are in favor of retaining the principle in the present accord that Tier 1 capital should represent at least half of total eligible capital—that is, that the sum total of Tier 2 plus Tier 3 capital should not exceed total Tier 1. However, the committee has decided that any decision whether to apply such a rule should be a matter for national discretion. Some member countries may keep the constraint, except in cases in which banking activities are proportionately very small. In addition, national authorities will have discretion to refuse the use of short-term subordinated debt for individual banks or for their banking systems generally.

For short-term subordinated debt to be eligible as Tier 3 capital, it must, if circumstances demand, be capable of becoming part of a bank's permanent capital and thus be available to absorb losses in the event of insolvency. It must, therefore, at a minimum:

- Be unsecured, subordinated, and fully paid up
- Have an original maturity of at least two years
- Not be repayable before the agreed repayment date unless the supervisory authority agrees
- Be subject to a lock-in clause which stipulates that neither interest nor principal may be paid (even at maturity) if such payment means that the bank will fall below or remain below its minimum capital requirement

2.6.3 The de Minimis Rule

The Basel Committee has ruled out the use of simplifying approaches, allowing small institutions with negligible exposures to be excluded from the capital requirement for market risks:

> For the time being, the Committee does not believe that it is necessary to allow any de minimis exemptions from the capital requirements for market risk, except for those for foreign exchange risk set out in paragraph 13 of A.3, because the Capital Accord applies only to internationally active banks, and then essentially on a consolidated basis; all of these are likely to be involved in trading to some extent.[83]

However, several countries, such as Germany and Switzerland, have included de minimis rules in their national regulations, especially with regard to asset management–oriented institutions which have negligible market risk positions.[84] Assuming the approval of the national authorities (subject to compliance with the criteria for de minimis exception), local supervisors are free to monitor the relevant exposures in the non–de minimis institutions more carefully. The approach is reasonable for smaller asset management and private banking institutions, which do not take substantial amounts of risk on their own books, as they execute on behalf of their clients. The important distinction is between organizations subject to the standard model approach and those subject to the internal model approach, as this difference determines how risk has to be supported by capital. Thus it fixes capital that could be used for other business purposes.[85]

2.7 THE STANDARDIZED MEASUREMENT METHOD

With the standard approach, a standardized framework for a quantitative measurement of market risks and the capital calculation to support market risks is given for all banks. The capital adequacy requirements are preset, depending on the risk factor categories:

- Interest-rate and equity-price risks in the trading book
- Currency, precious metals, and commodity risks in the entire organization

The capital adequacy requirements are calculated for each individual position and then added to the total capital requirement for the institution; see Table 2-2.

For interest-rate risk, the regulations define a set of maturity bands, within which net positions are identified across all on- and off-balance-sheet items. A duration weight is then assigned to each of the 13 bands, varying from 0.20 percent for positions under 3 months to 12.50 percent

TABLE 2-2

Capital Adequacy Requirements with the Standardized Measurement Method

Instrument	Risk Decomposition
Interest-rate-sensitive position	General market risk: duration or maturity method
	Specific market risk: net position by issuer × weight factor, depending on the instrument class
Equity instruments	General market risk: 8% of the net position per national market
	Specific market risk: 8% of the net position per issuer
Precious metals	10% of the net position
Currencies	10% of all net long positions or all net short positions, whichever is greater
Commodities	20% of the net position per commodity group + 3% of the brutto position of all commodity groups

for positions over 20 years. The sum of all weighted net positions then yields an overall interest-rate-risk indicator. Note that the netting of positions within a band (horizontal) and aggregation across bands (vertical) essentially assumes perfect correlation across debt instruments.

For currency and equity risk, the market risk capital charge is essentially 8 percent of the net position; for commodities, the charge is 15 percent. All of these capital charges apply to the trading books of commercial banks, except for currency risks, which apply to both trading and banking books.

The framework for measurement of market risks and the capital calculation to support market risks has to ensure that banks and securities dealers have adequate capital to cover potential changes in value (losses) caused by changes in the market price. Not including derivatives, which usually exhibit nonlinear price behavior, the potential loss based on the linear relationship between the risk factors and the financial instruments corresponds to the product of position amount, sensitivity of the position value regarding the relevant risk factors, and potential changes in the relevant risk factors. Equation (2.9) provides a methodological basis for the measurement of market risks as well as the calculation of the capital requirements based on the standard approach.

$$\Delta_w = w \cdot s \cdot \Delta_f \tag{2.9}$$

where Δ_w = change in value of the position
w = value of the position
s = sensitivity
Δ_f = change in the price-relevant factor

For the quantification of market risks using Equation (2.9), the direction of the change of the relevant risk factors is less important than the change per se. This is based on the assumption that the long and short positions are influenced by the same risk factors, which causes a loss on the net position. The extent of the potential changes of the relevant risk factors has been defined by BIS such that the computed potential losses, which would have to be supported by capital, cover approximately 99 percent of the value changes that have been observable over the last 5 to 10 years with an investment horizon of 2 weeks.

The framework of the standard approach is based on the building-block concept, which calculates interest rate and equity risks in the trading book and currency, precious metals, and commodity risks in the entire institution separate from capital requirements, which are subsequently aggregated by simple addition. The building-block concept is also used within the risk categories. As with equity and interest-rate risks, separate requirements for general and specific market risk components are calculated and aggregated. From an economic viewpoint, this concept implies that correlations between the movements—the changes in the respective risk factors—are not included in the calculation and aggregation. With movements in the same direction, a correlation of +1 between the risk factors is assumed, and with movements in opposite directions, a correlation of –1 is assumed. The standard approach is thus a strong simplification of reality, as the diversification effect based on the correlations between the risk factors is completely neglected, which results in a conservative risk calculation. Related to this risk measurement approach is a higher capital requirement (relative to the internal model).

Contrary to the internal model, apart from the general requirements for risk management in trading and for derivatives, no further specific qualitative minimums are required. The implementation must be carefully examined by the external auditor, in compliance with the capital adequacy regulations, and the results confirmed to the national regulator.

2.7.1 General and Specific Risks for Equity- and Interest-Rate-Sensitive Instruments

In the standard approach, the general and specific components of market risk for the equity- and interest-rate-sensitive instruments in the trading book are calculated separately. The different types of market risks can be defined as follows:

- *Specific risk* includes the risk that an individual debt or equity security may move by more or less than the general market in day-to-day trading (including periods when the whole market is volatile) and event risk (when the price of an individual debt or equity security moves precipitously relative to the general market, e.g., on a takeover bid or some other shock event; such events would also include the risk of default).[86] The specific market risk corresponds to the fraction of market risk associated with the volatility of positions or a portfolio that can be explained by events related to the issuer of specific instruments and not in terms of general market factors. Price changes can thus be explained by changes in the rating (upgrade or downgrade) of the issuer or acquiring or merging partner.
- *General market risk* corresponds to the fraction of market risk associated with the volatility of positions or a portfolio that can be explained in terms of general market factors, such as changes in the term structure of interest rates, changes in equity index prices, currency fluctuation, etc.

The capital adequacy requirements of the revised regulation assume that splitting the individual risk components is possible. The credit risk components of market risk positions may not be neglected, as they as well are regulated and require capital support.

Forward transactions have a credit risk if a positive *replacement value* (claims against the counterparties) exists. Off-balance-sheet positions have to be converted into the credit equivalents and supported by capital.

A critical condition for the application of the current market risk measurement regulations is the correct mapping of the positions. In order to do so, all trading-book positions must be valued *mark-to-market* on a daily basis. In an additional step, all derivatives belonging to the trading book must be decomposed adequately to allocate the risk exposure to the corresponding risk factors. An aggregation between spot and forward rates requires the mapping of forwards, futures, and swaps as combinations of long and short positions, in which the forward position is mapped as either of the following:

- A long (or short) position in the underlying physical or fictive (e.g., derivatives) basis instruments
- An opposite short (or long) position in the underlying physical or fictive (e.g., derivatives) basis instruments

An interest-rate swap can be decomposed as shown in Figure 2-7.

FIGURE 2-7

Decomposition of an Interest-Rate Swap.

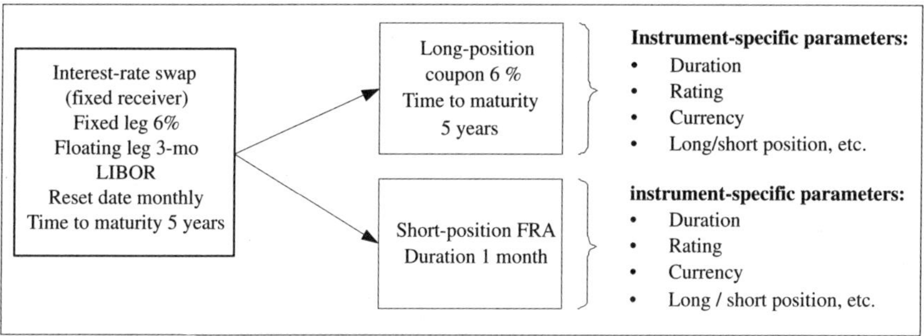

In this example, a fixed-rate-receiver swap is decomposed in a long position, in which the bank receives from the swap counterparty a fixed coupon of 5 percent and pays a variable 3-month London interbank offered rate (LIBOR) with monthly interest-rate resets.

2.7.2 Interest-Rate Risks

This subsection describes the standard framework for measuring the risk of holding or taking positions in debt securities and other interest-rate-related instruments in the trading book. The trading book itself is not discussed in detail here.[87]

The instruments covered include all fixed-rate and floating-rate debt securities and instruments that behave like them, including nonconvertible preference shares.[88] Convertible bonds—i.e., debt issues or preference shares that are convertible, at a stated price, into common shares—are treated as debt securities if they trade like debt securities and as equities if they trade like equities. The basis for dealing with derivative products is considered later under Treatment of Options (Section 2.7.6). The minimum capital requirement is expressed in terms of two separately calculated charges, one applying to the *specific risk* of each security, whether it is a short or a long position, and the other to the interest-rate risk in the portfolio (termed *general market risk*), where long and short positions in different securities or instruments can be offset. In computing the interest-rate risk in the trading book, all fixed-rate and floating-rate debt securities and instruments, including derivatives, are to be included, as well as all other positions that present risks induced by interest rates.

The capital requirements for interest-rate risks are composed of two elements, which are to be computed separately:

- *Requirements applying to specific risk.* All risks that relate to factors other than changes in the general interest-rate structure are to be captured and subjected to a capital charge.
- *Requirements applying to market risk.* All risks that relate to changes in the general interest-rate structure are to be captured and subjected to a capital charge.

The capital requirements applying to specific risks are to be computed separately for each issuer and those applying to general market risk, per currency. An exception exists for general market risk in foreign currencies with little business activity.

Should interest-rate instruments present other risks in addition to the interest-rate risks dealt with here, such as foreign-exchange risks, these other risks are to be captured in accordance with the related provisions as outlined in Part A.1-4 of the amendment.

2.7.2.1 Mapping of Positions

The systems of measurement shall include all derivatives and off-balance-sheet instruments in the trading book that are interest-rate sensitive. These are to be presented as positions that correspond to the net present value of the actual or notional underlying value (contract volume—i.e., market values of the underlying instruments) and subsequently are to be dealt with for general market and specific risk in accordance with the rules presented.

Positions in identical instruments fulfilling the regulatory requirements and which fully or almost fully offset each other are excluded from the computation of capital requirements for general market and specific risks. In computing the requirements for specific risks, those derivatives which are based on reference rates (e.g., interest-rate swaps, currency swaps, forward rate agreements, forward foreign-exchange contracts, interest-rate futures, and futures on an interest-rate index) are to be ignored.

Allowable Offsetting of Matching Positions

Offsetting is allowed for the following matching positions:

- Positions that match each other in terms of amount in a futures or forward contract and related underlying instrument (i.e., all deliverable securities). Both positions, however, must be denominated in the same currency. It should be kept in mind that futures and forwards are to be treated as a combination of a long and a short position (see Figure 2-7); therefore, one of the two futures or forward positions remains when offsetting it against a related spot position in the underlying instrument.
- Opposite positions in derivatives that relate to the same underlying instrument and are denominated in the same currency. In addition, the following conditions must be met:

Futures. Offsetting positions in the notional or underlying instruments to which the futures contract relates must be for identical products and must mature within seven days of each other.

Swaps and forward rate agreements. The reference rate (for floating-rate positions) must be identical, and the coupon must be closely matched (i.e., within 15 basis points).

Swaps, forward rate agreements, and forwards. The next interest-fixing date; or, for fixed coupon positions or forwards, the residual maturity must correspond within the following limits:

- Less than one month from cutoff date—same day
- One month to one year from cutoff date—within seven days
- Over one year from cutoff date—within 30 days

2.7.2.2 Futures, Forwards, and Forward Rate Agreements

Futures, forwards and forward rate agreements (FRAs) are treated as a combination of a long and a short position. The duration of a futures contract, a forward, or an FRA corresponds to the time until delivery or exercise of the contract plus (if applicable) the duration of the underlying value.

A long position in an interest-rate futures contract is, for example, to be treated as follows:

- A notional long position in the underlying interest-rate instrument with an interest-rate maturity as of its maturity
- A short position in a notional government security with the same amount and maturity on the settlement date of the futures contract

If different instruments can be delivered to fulfill the contract, the institution can choose which deliverable financial instruments are to be fitted into the maturity ladder. In doing so, however, the conversion factors set by the exchange are to be taken into consideration. In the case of a futures contract on an index of company debentures, the positions are to be mapped at the market value of the notional underlying portfolio.

2.7.2.3 Swaps

Swaps are treated as two notional positions in government securities with respective maturities. For instance, when an institution receives a floating interest rate and pays a fixed rate, the interest-rate swap is treated as follows:

- A long position in a floating-rate instrument with a duration that corresponds to the period until the next interest-rate repricing date
- A short position in a fixed-interest instrument with a duration that corresponds to the remaining duration of the swap

Should one leg of a swap be linked to another reference value, such as a stock index, the interest component is to be taken into consideration, with a remaining duration (interest maturity) that corresponds to the duration of the swap or the period until the next interest-rate repricing date, while the equity component is to be handled according to the rules pertaining to equities. In the case of interest-rate and currency swaps, the long and short positions are to be considered in the computations for the applicable currencies.

Institutes with significant swap books, and which do not avail themselves of the offsetting possibilities dealt with previously under Mapping of Positions (Section 2.7.2.1), may also compute the positions to be reported in the maturity or duration ladders with so-called sensitivity models or preprocessing models. The following possibilities exist:

- *Computation of the present value of the payment flows caused by each swap by discounting each individual payment with a corresponding zero-coupon equivalent.* The net present values aggregated over the individual swaps are slotted into the corresponding duration band for low-interest-bearing bonds (i.e., coupon <3 percent) and dealt with in accordance with the maturity method.
- *Computation of the sensitivity of net present values of the individual payment flows on the basis of the changes in yield arrived at under the duration method.* The sensitivities are then slotted into the corresponding time bands and dealt with in accordance with the duration method.

2.7.2.4 Specific Risk

The capital charge for specific risk is designed to protect against an adverse movement in the price of an individual security owing to factors related to the individual issuer. In measuring the risk, offsetting is restricted to matched positions in the identical issue (including positions in derivatives). Even if the issuer is the same, no offsetting is permitted between different issues, because differences in coupon rates, liquidity, call features, etc. mean that prices may diverge in the short run.

In computing the capital adequacy requirements for specific risk, the net position per issuer is determined. Within a category—government, qualified, other, or high-yield interest-rate instruments—all interest-rate instruments of the same issuer may be offset against each other, irrespective of their duration. In addition, the individual institution is free to allocate all interest-rate instruments of an issuer to that category corresponding to the highest capital charge for an interest-rate instrument of the issuer in question contained in the relevant portfolio. The institution shall opt for one method and apply this method consistently.

The capital requirements for specific risk are determined by multiplying the open position per issuer by the appropriate rate, as listed in Table 2-3.

TABLE 2-3

Capital Requirements for Specific Risks of Interest-Rate Instruments

Category	Capital Requirements
Interest-rate instruments	0%
Qualified interest-rate instruments	2.5
Other interest-rate instruments	8.0
High-yield interest-rate instruments	10.0

The *government* category includes all forms of G-10 paper, including bonds, Treasury bills, and other short-term instruments, but national authorities reserve the right to apply a specific risk weight to securities issued by certain foreign governments, especially securities denominated in a currency other than that of the issuing government.

Qualified interest-rate instruments are those that meet one of the following criteria:

- Investment-grade rating or higher from at least two credit-rating agencies recognized by the local supervisory authority
- Investment-grade rating or higher from one credit-rating agency recognized by the local supervisory authority in the absence of a lower rating from a rating agency recognized by the local supervisory authority
- Unrated, but with a yield to maturity and remaining duration comparable with those of investment-grade-rated instruments of the same issuer and trading on a recognized exchange or a representative market

Rating agencies deemed to be recognized by the local regulator would typically include those such as the following:

- Dominion Bond Rating Service (DBRS), Ltd., Toronto
- Fitch IBCA [International Bank Classification Agency], Duff & Phelps, London
- Mikuni & Company, Ltd., Tokyo
- Moody's Investors Service, Inc., New York
- Standard & Poor's (S&P) Ratings Services, New York
- Thomson Bank Watch (TBW), Inc., New York

Accordingly, instruments with investment-grade ratings are long-term interest-rate instruments with a rating of BBB (DBRS, IBCA, Mikuni, S&P, and TBW) or Baa (Moody's) and higher, and short-term interest-rate instruments with a rating such as Prime-3 (Moody's), A-3 (S&P and IBCA), M-4 (Mikuni), R-2 high (DBRS), or TBW-3 (TBW) and higher. Each supervisory authority is responsible for monitoring the application of these qualifying criteria, particularly in relation to the last criterion, where the initial classification is essentially left to the reporting banks.

The *other* category receives the same specific risk charge as a private-sector borrower under the credit risk requirements (i.e., 8 percent). However, because this may in certain cases considerably underestimate the specific risk for debt securities that have a high yield to redemption relative to government debt securities, each member country has the discretion to apply a specific risk charge higher than 8 percent to such securities and to disallow offsetting for the purposes of defining the extent of general market risk between such securities and any other debt securities.

High-yield interest-rate instruments are those which meet one of the following criteria:

- Rating such as CCC, Caa, or lower for long-term or an equivalent rating for short-term interest-rate instruments from a rating agency recognized by the local supervisory authority
- Unrated, but with a yield to maturity and remaining duration comparable to those with a rating such as CCC, Caa, or lower for long-term or an equivalent rating for short-term interest-rate instruments

This means that long-term interest-rate instruments with a rating such as CCC (DBRS, IBCA, Mikuni, S&P, and TBW), Caa (Moody's), or lower are deemed to be high-yield instruments. The high-yield rate is applicable to short-term interest-rate instruments if the rating is C (S&P), D (IBCA), M-D (Mikuni), R-3 (DBRS), TBW-4 (TBW), or lower.

2.7.2.5 General Market Risk

The capital requirements for general market risk are designed to capture the risk of loss arising from changes in market interest rates. A choice between two principal methods of measuring the risk is permitted, a *maturity* method and a *duration* method. In each method, the capital charge is the sum of four components:

- The net short or long position in the whole trading book
- A small proportion of the matched positions in each time band (the *vertical disallowance*)
- A larger proportion of the matched positions across different time bands (the *horizontal disallowance*)
- A net charge for positions in options, where appropriate

The capital requirements are computed for each currency separately by means of a maturity ladder. Currencies in which the institution has a small activity volume may be regrouped into one maturity ladder. In this case, no net position value is determined, but an absolute position value (i.e., all net long and short positions of all currencies in one time band) is determined by adding all the net positions together, irrespective of whether they are long or short positions, and no further offsetting is permitted.

Maturity Method

When applying the maturity method, the equity requirements for general market risk are computed as follows:

- *Slotting the positions valued at market into the maturity ladders.* All long and short positions are entered into the corresponding time bands of the maturity ladder. Fixed-interest instruments are classified according to their remaining duration until final maturity, and floating-rate instruments according to the remaining term until the next repricing date. The boundaries of the maturity bands are defined differently for instruments whose coupons are equal to or greater than 3 percent and those whose coupons are less than 3 percent (see Table 2-4). The maturity bands are allocated to three different zones.

TABLE 2-4

Maturity Method: Time Bands and Risk-Weighting Factors

	Coupon ≥ *3%*		*Coupon* < *3%*		
Zone	**Over**	**Up to**	**Over**	**Up to**	**Risk Weighting**
1		1 month		1 month	0.00%
	1 month	3 months	1 month	3 months	0.20
	3 months	6 months	3 months	6 months	0.40
	6 months	12 months	6 months	12 months	0.70
2	1 year	2 years	1.0 year	1.9 years	1.25
	2 years	3 years	1.9 years	2.8 years	1.75
	3 years	4 years	3.6 years	3.6 years	2.25
3	4 years	5 years	3.6 years	4.3 years	2.75
	5 years	7 years	4.3 years	5.7 years	3.25
	7 years	10 years	5.7 years	7.3 years	3.75
	10 years	15 years	7.3 years	9.3 years	4.50
	15 years	20 years	9.3 years	10.6 years	5.25
	20 years		10.6 years	12 years	6.00
			12 years	20 years	8.00
			20 years		12.50

- *Weighting by maturity band.* In order to take account of the price sensitivity in relation to interest-rate changes, the positions in the individual maturity bands are multiplied by the risk-weighting factors listed in Table 2-4.
- *Vertical offsetting.* The net position is determined for each maturity band from all weighted long and short positions. The risk-weighted net position is subject to a capital charge of 10 percent for each maturity band. This serves to account for the base and interest structure risk within each maturity band.
- *Horizontal offsetting.* To determine the total net interest positions, offsetting between opposed positions of differing maturities is possible, whereby the resulting closed net positions in turn receive a capital charge. This process is called *horizontal offsetting.* Horizontal offsetting takes place at two levels: within each of the three zones and between the zones.
- *Horizontal offsetting within the zones.* The risk-weighted open net positions of individual maturity bands are aggregated and offset against each other within their respective zones to obtain a net position for each zone. The closed positions arising from offsetting are subject to a capital charge. This charge amounts to 40 percent for Zone 1 and 30 percent each for Zones 2 and 3.
- *Horizontal offsetting between various zones.* Zone net positions of adjacent zones may be offset against each other, provided they bear opposing polarities (plus and minus signs). The resulting closed net positions are subject to a capital charge of 40 percent. An open position remaining after offsetting two adjacent zones remains in its respective zone and forms the basis for further offsetting, if applicable. Closed net positions arising from offsetting between nonadjacent zones (Zones 1 and 3), if applicable, are subject to a capital charge of 100 percent.

The result of the preceding calculations is to produce two sets of weighted positions, the net long or short positions in each time band and the vertical disallowances, which have no sign. In addition, however, banks are allowed to conduct two rounds of horizontal offsetting, first between the net positions in each of three zones (0 to 1 year, 1 year to 4 years, and 4 years and over), and subsequently between the net positions in the three different zones. The offsetting is subject to a scale of disallowances expressed as a fraction of the matched positions, as set out in Table 2-5. The weighted long and short positions in each of the three zones may be offset, subject to the matched portion, attracting a disallowance factor that is part of the capital charge. The residual net position in each zone may be carried over and offset against opposite positions in other zones, subject to a second set of disallowance factors.

TABLE 2-5

Components of Capital Requirements

Component	Weighting Factor
1. Net long or net short positions, total	100%
2. Vertical offsetting: weighted closed position in each maturity band	10
3. Horizontal offsetting	
Closed position in Zone 1	40
Closed position in Zone 2	30
Closed position in Zone 3	30
Closed position from offsetting between adjacent zones	40
Closed position from offsetting between nonadjacent zones	100
4. Add-on for option positions, if applicable (pursuant to Sections 5.3.1, 5.3.2b, 5.3.2c, and 5.3.3 of the amendment)	100

Using the maturity method, the capital requirements for interest-rate risk in a certain currency equal the sum of the components that require weighting, as listed in Table 2-5.

Offsetting is to be applied only if positions with opposing polarities (minus and plus signs) can be offset against each other within a maturity band, within a zone, or between the zones.

Duration Method

Under the alternative duration method, banks with the necessary capability may, with the consent of their regulatory supervisors, use a more accurate method of measuring all of their general market risk by calculating the price sensitivity of each position separately. Banks that elect to do so must use the method on a continuous basis (unless a change in method is approved by the national authority), and they are subject to supervisory monitoring of the systems used.

Institutions that possess the necessary organizational, personnel, and technical capacities may apply the duration method as an alternative to the maturity method. If they opt for the duration method, they may change back to the maturity method only in justified cases. The duration method is to be used, in principle, by all branches and for all products.

As already mentioned, the price sensitivity of each financial instrument is computed separately under this method. It is also possible to split the financial instrument into its payment flows and to take account of the duration for each individual payment flow. The capital requirements for general market risk are computed in the following manner:

- *Computation of price sensitivities.* Price sensitivity is computed separately for each instrument or its payment flows; the different changes in yield dependent on duration, as listed in Table 2-6, are subject to a capital charge. The price sensitivity is calculated by multiplying the market value of the instrument or of its payment flows by its modified duration and the assumed change in yield.
- *Entering price sensitivities into the time bands.* The resulting sensitivities are entered into one of the ladders. There are 15 time bands, based on the duration of the instrument or its payment flows, as shown in Table 2-6.

TABLE 2-6

Duration Method: Maturity Bands and Assumed Changes in Yield

	Duration		
Zone	**Over**	**Up to**	**Change in Yield**
1		1 month	1.00%
	1 month	3 months	1.00
	3 months	6 months	1.00
	6 months	12 months	1.00
2	1.0 years	1.9 months	0.90
	1.9 years	2.8 years	0.80
	2.9 years	3.6 years	0.75
3	3.6 years	4.3 years	0.75
	4.3 years	5.7 years	0.70
	5.7 years	7.3 years	0.65
	7.3 years	9.3 years	0.60
	9.3 years	10.6 years	0.60
	10.6 years	12 years	0.60
	12 years	20 years	0.60
	20 years		0.60

- *Vertical offsetting.* The vertical offsetting within the individual time bands is to be effected in a manner analogous to that used under the maturity method, whereby the risk-weighted closed position for each maturity band is subject to a capital charge of 5 percent.
- *Horizontal offsetting.* The horizontal offsetting between the time bands is to be effected in a manner analogous to that used under the maturity method.

Under the duration method, the required equity for general market risk per currency is thus calculated from the sum of the net position, the various offsets, and, where applicable, an add-on for option positions.

2.7.2.6 Interest-Rate Derivatives

The measurement system should include all interest-rate derivatives and off-balance-sheet instruments in the trading book that react to changes in interest rates, (e.g., forward rate agreements, other forward contracts, bond futures, interest-rate and cross-currency swaps, and forward foreign-exchange positions). Options can be treated in a variety of ways. A summary of the rules for dealing with interest rate derivatives is set out later under Treatment of Options (Section 2.7.6).

Calculation of Positions

Derivatives should be converted into positions in the relevant underlying instruments (see Table 2-7) and become subject to specific and general market risk charges as previously described. In order to calculate the standard formula as previously described, the amounts reported should be the market value of the principal amount of the underlying instrument or of the notional underlying instrument. When the apparent notional amount of the instrument differs from the effective notional amount, banks must use the effective notional amount.

- Futures and forward contracts, including forward rate agreements, are treated as a combination of a long and a short position in a notional government security. The maturity of a future or an FRA will be the period until delivery or exercise of the contract, plus (where applicable) the life of the underlying instrument. For example, a long position in a June three-month interest-rate future (taken in April) is to be reported as a long position in a government security with a maturity of five months and a short position in a government security with a maturity of two months. Where a range of deliverable instruments may be delivered to fulfill the contract, the bank has flexibility to elect which deliverable security goes into the maturity or duration ladder but should take account of any conversion factor defined

TABLE 2-7

Summary of Treatment of Interest-Rate Derivatives

Instrument	Specific Risk Charge*	General Market Risk Charge
Exchange-traded future		
Government debt security	No	Yes, as two positions
Corporate debt security	Yes	Yes, as two positions
Index on interest rates (e.g., LIBOR)	No	Yes, as two positions
OTC forward		
Government debt security	No	Yes, as two positions
Corporate debt security	Yes	Yes, as two positions
Index on interest rates (e.g., LIBOR)	No	Yes, as two positions
FRAs, swaps	No	Yes, as two positions
Forward foreign exchange	No	Yes, as one position in each currency
Options		
Government debt security	No	Either: Carve out together with the associated hedging positions: Simplified approach; Scenario analysis; Internal models
Corporate debt security	Yes	General market risk change according to the delta-plus method (gamma and vega should receive separate capital charges)
Index on interest rates	No	
FRAs, swaps	No	

*This is the specific risk charge relating to the issuer of the instrument. Under the existing credit risk rules, there remains a separate capital charge for the counterparty risk.

by the exchange. In the case of a future on a corporate bond index, positions are included at the market value of the notional underlying portfolio of securities.

- Swaps are treated as two notional positions in government securities with relevant maturities. For example, an interest-rate swap under which a bank receives floating-rate interest and pays fixed-rate interest is treated as a long position in a floating-rate instrument of maturity equivalent to the period until the next interest fixing and a short position in a fixed-rate instrument of maturity equivalent to the residual life of the swap. For swaps that pay or receive a fixed or floating interest rate against some other reference price (e.g., a stock index), the interest-rate component should be slotted into the appropriate repricing maturity category, with the equity component being included in the equity framework. The separate legs of cross-currency swaps are to be reported in the relevant maturity ladders for the currencies concerned.

Calculation of Capital Charges for Derivatives Under the Standardized Methodology

Matched positions may be offset if certain conditions are fulfilled. Banks may exclude from the interest-rate maturity framework altogether (for both specific and general market risk) long and short positions (both actual and notional) in identical instruments with exactly the same issuer, coupon, currency, and maturity. A matched position in a future or forward and its corresponding underlying instrument may also be fully offset, and thus excluded from the calculation; however, the leg representing the time to expiry of the future should be reported. When the future or the forward comprises a range of deliverable instruments, offsetting of positions in the future or forward contract and its underlying instrument is permissible only in cases in which there is a readily identifiable underlying security that is the most profitable for the short-position trader to deliver. The price of this security—sometimes called the *cheapest to deliver*—and the price of the future or forward contract should, in such cases, move in close alignment. No offsetting is allowed between positions in different currencies; the separate legs of cross-currency swaps or forward foreign-exchange deals are to be treated as notional positions in the relevant instruments and included in the appropriate calculation for each currency.

In addition, opposite positions in the same category of instruments can, in certain circumstances, be regarded as matched and allowed to offset fully. To qualify for this treatment, the positions must relate to the same underlying instruments,[89] be of the same nominal value, and be denominated in the same currency.[90]

In addition, the following conditions have to be considered for the calculation of the regulatory risk exposure:

- *Futures.* Offsetting positions in the notional or underlying instruments to which the futures contract relates must be for identical products and must mature within seven days of each other.
- *Swaps and FRAs.* The reference rate (for floating-rate positions) must be identical, and the coupon must be closely matched (i.e., within 15 basis points).

- *Swaps, FRAs, and forwards.* The next interest-fixing date or, for fixed coupon positions or forwards, the residual maturity must correspond within the following limits:
  Less than one month hence—same day
  One month to one year hence—within seven days
  Over one year hence—within 30 days

Banks with large swap books may use alternative formulas for these swaps to calculate the positions to be included in the maturity or duration ladder. One method would be to first convert the payments required by the swap into their present values. For this purpose, each payment should be discounted using zero-coupon yields, and a single net figure for the present value of the cash flows should be entered into the appropriate time band, using procedures that apply to zero- (or low-) coupon bonds; these figures should be slotted into the general market risk framework as set out earlier. An alternative method would be to calculate the sensitivity of the net present value implied by the change in yield used in the maturity or duration method and allocate these sensitivities into the time bands.

Other methods that produce similar results could also be used. Such alternative treatments will, however, be allowed only if:

- The supervisory authority is fully satisfied with the accuracy of the systems being used.
- The positions calculated fully reflect the sensitivity of the cash flows to interest-rate changes and are entered into the appropriate time bands.
- The positions are denominated in the same currency.

Interest-rate and currency swaps, FRAs, forward foreign-exchange contracts, and interest-rate futures are not subject to a specific risk charge. This exemption also applies to futures on an interest-rate index (e.g., LIBOR). However, in the case of futures contracts where the underlying instrument is a debt security, or an index representing a basket of debt securities, a specific risk charge will apply according to the credit risk of the issuer, as set out in the preceding paragraphs.

General market risk applies to positions in all derivative products in the same manner as for cash positions, subject only to an exemption for fully or very closely matched positions in identical instruments as defined. The various categories of instruments should be slotted into the maturity ladder and treated according to the rules identified earlier.

2.7.3 Equity Position Risk

To determine the capital requirements for equity price risks, all positions in equities and derivatives, as well as positions whose behavior is similar to equities (hereinafter these are referred to as *equities*) are to be included.

Shares in investment funds are also be dealt with like equities, unless they are split into their component parts and the capital charges are determined in accordance with the provisions relating to each risk category.

Capital requirements for equity price risks comprise the following two components, which are to be computed separately:

- *Specific risk requirements.* Those risks which are related to the issuer of the equities and cannot be explained by general market fluctuations are to be captured and subjected to a capital charge.
- *General market risk requirements.* Risks in the form of fluctuations of the national equity market or the equity market of a single monetary area are to be captured and subjected to a capital charge.

Should positions present risks other than the equity price risk dealt with here, such as foreign-exchange risks or interest-rate risks, these are to be captured in accordance with the corresponding sections of these guidelines.

2.7.3.1 Mapping of Positions

Initially, all positions are to be marked to market. Foreign currencies must be translated into the local currency at the current spot rate.

Index positions may be either treated as index instruments or split into the individual equity positions and dealt with as normal equity positions. The institution shall decide on one approach and then apply it on a consistent basis.

Derivatives based on equities and off-balance-sheet positions whose value is influenced by changes in equity prices are to be recorded in the measurement system at their market value of the actual or nominal underlying values (contract volume, such as market values of the underlying instruments).

Allowable Offsetting of Matched Positions

Opposite positions (differing positions in derivatives or in derivatives and related underlying instruments) in each identical equity or each identical stock index may be offset against each other. It is to be noted that futures and forwards are to be treated as a combination of a long and a short position, and therefore the interest-rate position remains in the case of the offsetting with a corresponding spot position in the underlying value.

Equity Derivatives

Except for options, which are dealt with under Futures and Forward Contracts, equity derivatives and off-balance-sheet positions that are affected by changes in equity prices should be included in the measurement system.[91] These include futures and swaps on both individual equities and stock indexes. The derivatives are to be converted into positions in the relevant underlying instrument. The treatment of equity derivatives is summarized in Table 2-8.

TABLE 2-8

Summary of Treatment of Equity Derivatives

Instrument	Specific Risk*	General Market Risk
Exchange-traded or OTC future		
Individual equity	Yes	Yes, as underlying
Index	2%	Yes, as underlying
Options		
Individual equity	Yes	Either: Carve out together with the associated hedging positions: Simplified approach Scenario approach Internal models
Index	2%	General market risk charge according to the delta-plus method (gamma and vega should receive separate capital charges)

*This is the specific risk charge relating to the issuer of the instrument. Under the existing credit risk rules, there remains a separate capital charge for the counterparty risk.

Futures and Forward Contracts

Futures and forward contracts are to be dealt with as a combination of a long and a short position in an equity, a basket of equities, or a stock index, on the one hand; and as a notional government bond, on the other. Equity positions are thereby captured at their current market price. Equity-basket or stock-index positions are captured at the current value of the notional underlying equity portfolio, valued at market prices.

Swaps

Equity swaps are also treated as a combination of a long and a short position. They may relate to a combination of two equity, equity-basket, or stock-index positions or a combination of a equity, equity-basket, or stock-index position and an interest-rate position.

2.7.3.2 Calculation of Positions

In order to calculate the standard formula for specific and general market risk, positions in derivatives should be converted into notional equity positions:

- Futures and forward contracts relating to individual equities should in principle be reported at current market prices.
- Futures relating to stock indexes should be reported as the marked-to-market value of the notional underlying equity portfolio.
- Equity swaps are to be treated as two notional positions.[92]
- Equity options and stock-index options should be either carved out together with the associated underlying instruments or be incorporated in the measure of general market risk described in this section according to the delta-plus method.

2.7.3.3 Calculation of Capital Charges

Several risk components have to be considered in the calculation of the capital charges:

- *Measurement of specific and general market risk.* Matched positions in each identical equity or stock index in each market may be fully offset, resulting in a single net short or long position to which the specific and general market risk charges will apply. For example, a future in a given equity may be offset against an opposite cash position in the same equity. However, the interest-rate risk arising from the future should be reported.
- *Risk in relation to an index.* Besides general market risk, a further capital charge of 2 percent is applied to the net long or short position in an index contract comprising a diversified portfolio of equities. This capital charge is intended to cover factors such as execution risk. National supervisory authorities will take care to ensure that this 2 percent risk weight applies only to well-diversified indexes and not, for example, to sectoral indexes.
- *Arbitrage.* In the case of the futures-related arbitrage strategies described later, the additional 2 percent capital charge previously described may be applied to only one index with the opposite position exempt from a capital charge. The strategies are:

  When the bank takes an opposite position in exactly the same index at different dates or in different market centers

  When the bank has an opposite position in contracts at the same date in different but similar indexes, subject to supervisory oversight that the two indexes contain sufficient common components to justify offsetting

When a bank engages in a deliberate arbitrage strategy, in which a futures contract on a broadly based index matches a basket of stocks, it is allowed to carve out both positions from the standardized methodology on condition that:

- The trade has been deliberately entered into and separately controlled.
- The composition of the basket of stocks represents at least 90 percent of the index when broken down into its notional components.

In such a case the minimum capital requirement is 4 percent (i.e., 2 percent of the gross value of the positions on each side) to reflect divergence and execution risks. This applies even if all of the stocks comprising the index are held in identical proportions. Any excess value of the stocks comprising the basket over the value of the futures contract or excess value of the futures contract over the value of the basket is to be treated as an open long or short position.

If a bank takes a position in depository receipts against an opposite position in the underlying equity or identical equities in different markets, it may offset the position (i.e., bear no capital charge), but only on condition that any costs on conversion are fully taken into account. Any foreign exchange risk arising out of these positions has to be reported.

2.7.3.4 Specific Risk

To determine the capital requirements for specific risk, the net position by issuer is determined; that is, positions with differing plus and minus signs for the same issuer may be offset.

The capital charge corresponds to 8 percent of the net position per issuer.

For diversified and liquid equity portfolios, the requirements to support specific risks are reduced to 4 percent of the net position per issuer. A diversified and liquid portfolio exists whenever the equities are quoted on an exchange and no individual issuer position exceeds 5 percent of the global equity portfolio or a subportfolio. The reference value to determine the 5 percent limit in this context means the sum of the absolute values of the net positions of all issuers. The global equity portfolio may be split into two subportfolios so that one of the two subportfolios falls into the diversified and liquid category, and the specific risks within this portfolio need only be subject to a 4 percent capital charge.

If stock-index contracts are not split into their components, a net long or net short position in a stock-index contract representing a widely diversified equity portfolio is subject to a capital charge of 2 percent of equity. The rate of 2 percent, however, shall not apply to sector indexes, for example.

2.7.3.5 General Market Risk

The capital requirements for general market risk amount to 8 percent of the net position per domestic equity market or per single currency zone. A separate computation is to be made for each domestic equity market, whereby long and short positions in instruments of differing issuers of the same domestic market may be offset.

2.7.4 Foreign-Exchange Risk

All positions in foreign currency and gold are to be included in the computation of capital requirements for foreign-exchange risk.

2.7.4.1 Determination of Net Position

The net position of an institution in a foreign currency is computed as the sum of the following positions:

- *Net spot position.* All assets less all liabilities and shareholders' equity.
- *Net forward positions.* All amounts outstanding less all amounts to be paid within the framework of forward transactions executed in this currency. The net present values are to be included; that is, positions discounted with the current foreign-currency interest rates. Because they relate to present values, forward positions (including guarantees and similar instruments that are certain to be called and are likely to be irrecoverable) are also translated into the local currency at the spot rate and not the forward rate.
- *Net amount of known, future income or expense that is fully hedged.* Future unhedged income and expense items can be taken into consideration at the institution's discretion, but thereafter on a uniform and consistent basis.
- Foreign-currency options.

In this manner, a net long or a net short position is arrived at. This is translated at the respective spot rate into the local currency.

Basket currencies can be dealt with as a separate currency or broken down into their currency components. The treatment, however, has to be consistent.

Positions in gold (cash and forward positions) are translated into a common standard unit of measurement (in general, ounces or kilograms). The net position is then valued at the respective spot price in the local currency. Any interest-rate or foreign-exchange risks arising from forward gold transactions are to be recorded. Institutions may, in addition and at their discretion, treat positions in gold as foreign-currency positions, but then only in a uniform and consistent manner.

2.7.4.2 Exclusions

The following positions can be excluded from the computation:

- Positions that were deducted from equity in the computation of the equity base
- Other participating interests that are disclosed at acquisition cost
- Positions that demonstrably serve on an ongoing basis as a hedge against foreign-currency fluctuations in order to secure the equity ratio

2.7.4.3 Determination of Capital Requirements

The capital requirements for foreign exchange and gold amount to 10 percent of the sum of net long or net short foreign-exchange positions, whichever is greater, translated into the local currency, plus the net gold position, ignoring plus or minus signs.

2.7.5 Commodities Risk

This section establishes a minimum capital standard to cover the risk of holding or taking positions in commodities, including precious metals, but excluding gold (which is treated as a foreign currency). A *commodity* is defined as a physical product which is or can be traded on a secondary market—e.g., agricultural products, minerals (including oil), and precious metals.

The standard approach for commodities risk is suitable only for institutions with insignificant commodities positions. Institutions with significant trading positions either in relative or absolute terms must apply the model-based approach. In computing the capital charges for risks arising from raw materials, in principle, the following risks must be taken account of.[93]

The price risk in commodities is often more complex and volatile than that associated with currencies and interest rates. Commodity markets may also be less liquid than those for interest rates and currencies and, as a result, changes in supply and demand can have a more dramatic effect on price and volatility. Banks also need to guard against the risk that arises when the short position falls due before the long position. Owing to a shortage of liquidity in some markets, it might be difficult to close the short position, and the bank might be squeezed by the market. These market characteristics can make price transparency and the effective hedging of commodities risk more difficult.

For spot or physical trading, the directional risk arising from a change in the spot price is the most important risk. However, banks using portfolio strategies involving forward and derivative contracts are exposed to a variety of additional risks, which may well be larger than the risk of a change in spot prices. These include:

- The risk of changes in spot prices
- The *forward gap risk*—that is, the risk of changes in the forward price which cannot be explained by changes in interest rates
- The base risk to capture the risk of changes in the price correlation between two similar, but not identical, raw materials

In addition, banks may face credit counterparty risk on over-the-counter derivatives, but this is captured by the 1988 capital accord. The funding of commodities positions may well open a bank to interest-rate or foreign-exchange exposure; if so, the relevant positions should be included in the measures of interest-rate and foreign-exchange risk. When a commodity is part of a forward contract (quantity of commodities to be received or delivered), any interest-rate or foreign-currency exposure from the other leg of the contract should be reported. Positions which are purely stock financing (i.e., a physical stock has been sold forward and the cost of funding has been locked in until the date of the forward sale) may be omitted from the commodities risk calculation, although they will be subject to interest-rate and counterparty risk requirements.

The interest-rate and foreign-exchange risks arising in connection with commodity transactions are to be dealt with in accordance with the related sections of these guidelines.

2.7.5.1 Determination of Net Positions

All commodity positions are to be allocated to a commodity group in accordance with Table 2-9. Within the group, the net position can be computed; that is, long and short positions may be offset. For markets that have daily delivery dates, any contracts maturing within 10 days of one another may be offset.

Banks may choose to adopt the models approach. It is essential that the methodology used encompasses the following risks:

- *Directional risk,* to capture the exposure from changes in spot prices arising from net open positions
- *Forward gap and interest rate risk,* to capture the exposure to changes in forward prices arising from maturity mismatches
- *Basis risk,* to capture the exposure to changes in the price relationship between two similar, but not identical, commodities

All commodity derivatives and off-balance-sheet positions that are affected by changes in commodity prices should be included in this measurement framework. These include commodity futures, commodity swaps, and options where the delta-plus method is used. (Banks using other approaches to measure options risk should exclude all options and the associated underlying instruments from both the maturity ladder approach and the simplified approach.) In order to calculate the risk, com-

TABLE 2-9

Commodity Groups

Category	Commodity Group
Crude oil	Allocation according to geographic criteria; e.g., Dubai (Persian Gulf), Brent (Europe and Africa), WTI (America), Tapis (Asia-Pacific), etc.
Refined products	Allocation according to quality; e.g., gasoline, naphtha, aircraft fuel, light heating oil (incl. diesel), heavy heating oil, etc.
Natural gas	Natural gas
Precious metals	Allocation according to chemical elements; e.g., silver, platinum, etc.
Nonferrous metals	Allocation according to chemical elements; e.g., aluminum, copper, zinc, etc.
Agricultural products	Allocation according to basic products, but without differentiating between quality; e.g., soya (incl. soybeans, oil, and flour), maize, sugar, coffee, cotton, etc.

modity derivatives should be converted into notional commodities positions and assigned to maturities as follows:

- Futures and forward contracts relating to individual commodities should be incorporated in the measurement system as notional amounts of barrels, kilos, etc. and should be assigned a maturity with reference to expiry date.
- Commodity swaps in which one leg is a fixed price and the other the current market price should be incorporated as a series of positions equal to the notional amount of the contract, with one position corresponding to each payment on the swap and slotted into the maturity ladder accordingly. The positions would be long positions if the bank is paying fixed and receiving floating, and short positions if the bank is receiving fixed and paying floating.
- Commodity swaps in which the legs are in different commodities are to be incorporated in the relevant maturity ladder. No offsetting is allowed in this regard except where the commodities belong to the same subcategory.

2.7.5.2 Commodity Derivatives

Futures and forward contracts are to be dealt with as a combination of a long and a short position in a commodity on the one hand, and as a notional government bond on the other.

Commodity swaps with a fixed price on the one hand and with the respective market price on the other are to be considered as a string of positions that correspond to the nominal value of the contract. In this context, each payment in the framework of the swap is to be regarded as a position. A long position arises when the bank pays a fixed price and receives a variable price (short position: vice versa). Commodity swaps concerning different commodities are to be captured separately in the corresponding groups.

Commodities futures and forwards are dealt with in a manner analogous to that of equity futures and forwards.

Banks may choose to adopt the models approach. It is essential that the methodology used encompasses the following risks:

- *Directional risk,* to capture the exposure from changes in spot prices arising from net open positions
- *Forward gap and interest-rate risk,* to capture the exposure to changes in forward prices arising from maturity mismatches
- *Basis risk,* to capture the exposure to changes in the price relationship between two similar, but not identical, commodities

All commodity derivatives and off-balance-sheet positions that are affected by changes in commodity prices should be included in this measurement framework. These include commodity futures, commodity swaps, and options where the delta-plus method is used. (Banks using other approaches to measure options risk should exclude all options and the associated underlying instruments from both the maturity ladder approach and the simplified approach.) In order to calculate the risk, commodity derivatives should be converted into notional commodities positions and assigned to maturities as follows:

- Futures and forward contracts relating to individual commodities should be incorporated in the measurement system as notional amounts of barrels, kilos, etc. and should be assigned a maturity with reference to expiry date.
- Commodity swaps in which one leg is a fixed price and the other the current market price should be incorporated as a series of positions equal to the notional amount of the contract, with one position corresponding to each payment on the swap and slotted into the maturity ladder covering interest-rate-related instruments accordingly. The positions would be long positions if the bank is paying fixed and receiving floating, and short positions if the bank is receiving fixed and paying floating.
- Commodity swaps in which the legs are in different commodities are to be incorporated in the relevant maturity ladder. No offsetting is allowed in this regard except where the commodities belong to the same subcategory, as previously defined.

2.7.5.3 Determination of Capital Requirements

The requirements to support commodities risk amount to 20 percent of the net position per commodities group. In order to take account of the base and time-structure risk, an additional capital charge of 3 percent of gross positions (sum of the absolute values of long and short positions) of all commodities groups is applied.

2.7.6 Treatment of Options

2.7.6.1 Segregation

In the case of financial instruments containing an option component that does not appear in a substantial and dominant manner, it is not compulsory to deal with the option component thereof as an option. Convertible bonds may be treated as bonds or as equities in accordance with the specific characteristics of each financial instrument. Bonds with a right of the issuer to early redemption can be dealt with as pure bonds and entered into the corresponding time band based on the most probable date of repayment.

2.7.6.2 Treatment of Financial Instruments with Option Characteristics

If the option component appears in a substantial and dominant manner, the financial instruments in question are to be dealt with by one of the following methods:

- Analytical breakdown into option and underlying instrument
- Approximation of the risk profiles by means of synthetic portfolios of options and basis instruments

2.7.6.3 Approach to Compute Capital Requirements

In recognition of the wide diversity of banks' activities in options and the difficulties of measuring price risk for options, several alternative approaches are permissible at the discretion of the national supervisory authority:

- Those banks which solely use purchased options are free to use the simplified approach, unless all their written option positions are hedged by perfectly matched long positions in exactly the same options, in which case no capital charge for market risk is required.
- Those banks which also write options are expected to use one of the intermediate approaches or a comprehensive risk management model approach. The more significant its trading, the more the bank will be expected to use a sophisticated approach.

In the simplified approach, the positions for the options and the associated underlying instrument, cash, or forward are not subject to the standardized methodology but rather are carved out and subject to separately calculated capital charges that incorporate both general market risk and specific risk. The risk numbers thus generated are then added to the capital charges for the relevant category—that is, interest-rate-related instruments, equities, foreign exchange, and commodities. The delta-plus method uses the sensitivity parameters or "Greek letters" associated with options to measure their market risk and capital requirements. Under this method, the delta-equivalent position of each option becomes part of the standardized methodology, with the delta-equivalent amount subject to the applicable general market risk charges. Separate capital charges are then applied to the gamma and vega risks of the option positions. The scenario approach uses simulation techniques to calculate changes in the value of an options portfolio for changes in the level and volatility of its associated underlying instruments. Under this approach, the general market risk charge is determined by the scenario grid (i.e., the specified combination of underlying and volatility changes) that produces the largest loss. For the delta-plus method and the scenario approach, the specific risk capital charges are determined separately by multiplying the delta equivalent of each option by the specific risk weights.

Three approaches are admissible for the computation of capital requirements on option positions: the simplified procedure for institutions that use only purchased options, the delta-plus method, and scenario analysis for all other institutions.

Simplified Approach

In the case of the simplified approach, options are not to be included under the standard approach in regard to specific risk and general market risk, but they are subject to capital requirements computed separately. The risk values so computed are then added to the capital requirements for the individual categories—that is, interest-rate instruments, equities, foreign exchange, gold, and commodities.

- *Purchased call and put options.* The capital requirements correspond to the smaller of:

  The market value of the option

  The market value of the underlying instrument (contract volume, i.e., market values of the underlying instruments) multiplied by the sum of the rates for general market risk and (if applicable) for specific market risk in relation to the underlying instrument.
- *Long cash position and purchased put option or short cash position and purchased call option.* The capital requirements correspond to the market value of the underlying instrument (contract volume, i.e.,

market values of the underlying instruments) multiplied by the sum of the rates for general market risk and (if applicable) for specific risk in relation to the underlying instrument less the intrinsic value of the option. The total requirement, however, cannot be a negative value. The corresponding underlying instruments are no longer to be included in the standard method. (See Table 2-10.)

Intermediate Approach: Delta-Plus Method

Banks that write options are allowed to include delta-weighted options positions within the standardized methodology. If options are dealt with in accordance with the delta-plus method, they are to be mapped as positions that correspond to the market value of the underlying instrument (contract volume, i.e., market values of the underlying instruments) multiplied by the delta (sensitivity of the option price in relation to changes in the price of the underlying instrument). Depending on the underlying instrument, they are included in the computation of capital requirements for specific and general market risk. As the risks of options are, however, inadequately captured by the delta, institutions must also measure the

TABLE 2-10

Simplified Approach: Capital Charges

Position	Treatment
Long cash and long put Short cash and long call	The capital charge is the market value of the underlying security* multiplied by the sum of specific and general market risk charges† for the underlying security less the amount the option is in the money (if any) bounded at zero.‡
Long call or long put	The capital charge is the lesser of: The market value of the underlying security multiplied by the sum of specific and general market risk charges for the underlying security The market value of the option

*In some cases, such as foreign exchange, it may be unclear which side is the underlying security; this should be taken to be the asset that would be received if the option were exercised. In addition, the nominal value should be used for items where the market value of the underlying instrument could be zero—caps and floors, swaptions, etc.

†Some options (e.g., where the underlying security is an interest rate, a currency, or a commodity) bear no specific risk but specific risk will be present in the case of options on certain interest-rate-related instruments (e.g., options on a corporate debt security or corporate bond index) and for options on equities and stock indexes. The charge under this measure for currency options will be 8 percent and for options on commodities 15 percent.

‡For options with a residual maturity of more than six months, the strike price should be compared with the forward, not current, price. A bank unable to do this must take the in-the-money amount to be zero.

¶Where the position does not fall within the trading book (i.e., options on certain foreign-exchange or commodities positions not belonging to the trading book), it may be acceptable to use the book value instead.

gamma risk (risk resulting from nonlinear relationships between option price changes and changes in the underlying instrument) and vega risk (risk resulting from the sensitivity of the option price to fluctuations of volatility of the underlying instrument).

- *Delta risk.* Capital requirements for delta risk on options with interest-rate instruments, equities, foreign exchange, and commodities are based on the delta-weighted positions.

In computing the general market risk, delta-weighted options on debentures or interest rates are allocated to the time bands for interest-rate instruments and (if applicable) also for computing specific risk. Options on derivatives are to be mapped twice, like the corresponding derivatives themselves. Thus, an April purchase of a June call option on a three-month interest-rate future—on the basis of its delta equivalent—will be considered as a long position with a maturity of five months and as a short position with a maturity of two months. The written option will similarly be entered as a long position with a maturity of two months and a short position with a maturity of five months.

Options on equities, foreign exchange, gold, and commodities will also be incorporated into the measurement values as delta-weighted positions.

- *Gamma risk.* For each individual option, a gamma effect, as defined here, is to be computed:

$$\text{Gamma effect} = 0.5 \cdot \gamma \cdot \delta^2 \qquad (2.10)$$

where γ designates gamma and δ the change in the underlying value of the option. δ is computed by multiplying the market value of the (notional) underlying value (contract volume, i.e., amount receivable of the underlying value or nominal value) by the following factors:

Interest-rate options: risk weight in accordance with Table 2-4 [dependent on the maturity of the (notional) underlying instrument]

Options on equities or stock indexes: 8 percent

Options on foreign exchange or gold: 10 percent

Options on commodities: 20 percent

A net gamma effect is to be computed from the gamma effects for the same categories of underlying instruments. The individual categories are defined as follows:

- Interest-rate instruments of the same currency and the same time band

- Equities and stock indexes of the same national market or the same currency zone
- Foreign currencies of each identical currency pair
- Gold
- Commodities

Only the negative net gamma effects are to be included in the computation of required equity and to be summed as absolute values to arrive at the total capital requirement.

The method of computing the gamma capital requirements presented here takes into account only general market risk. Banks that possess significant positions in options on specific equities or debt instruments must, however, take specific risks into consideration in computing gamma effects.

- *Vega risk.* For each individual option, a vega effect, as defined here, is to be computed:

$$\text{Vega effect} = 0.25 \cdot \nu \cdot \text{volatility} \tag{2.11}$$

where ν designates the value of vega.

For each category of underlying instruments, a net vega effect is to be computed by addition of all vega effects of long positions (purchased options) and subtraction of all vega effects of short positions (sold options). The total capital requirements for the vega risk subject to a capital charge result from the aggregation of the sum of absolute values of net vega effects computed for each category.

The computation of vega effects is to be made based on implicit volatilities. In the case of illiquid underlying instruments, other methods may be used on an exception basis to determine the volatility structure.

Intermediate Approach: Scenario Method

More sophisticated banks also have the right to base the market risk capital charge for options portfolios and associated hedging positions on scenario matrix analysis. This is accomplished by specifying a fixed range of changes in the option portfolio's risk factors and calculating changes in the value of the option portfolio at various points along this grid. For the purpose of calculating the capital charge, the bank revalues the option portfolio using matrices for simultaneous changes in the option's underlying rate or price and in the volatility of that rate or price. A different matrix is set up for each individual underlying instrument, as previously defined. As an alternative, at the discretion of each national authority, banks that are significant traders in options are permitted to base the calculation for interest-rate options on a minimum of six sets of time bands.

When using this method, no more than three time bands should be combined into any one set.

In computing the capital requirements for options and related hedging positions using scenario analysis, the potential change in value for all possible combinations of changes in the underlying instrument or rate (dimension 1) and volatility (dimension 2), within the framework of a separate standard matrix, is to be computed for each category of underlying instruments or rates.[94] In the case of interest-rate instruments, it is possible to carry out a separate analysis not for the instruments of each time band but to summarize the time bands into groups. However, a maximum of three time bands may grouped together, and at least six different groups must be formed. For foreign-exchange options in the scenario definition, the arbitrage relationship between the underlying instruments may be taken into consideration. In such cases, the scenarios can be defined uniformly against the U.S. dollar.

The dimensions of the matrices to be used are defined as follows:

- *Change in value of underlying instrument or rate (dimension 1).* The computations are to be made within the range for at least seven different changes in value (including a change of 0 percent), where the assumed changes in value are at equally spaced intervals. The ranges are to be defined as follows:

  Interest-rate options: Plus or minus the change in yield, in accordance with Table 2-6. Should several time bands be regrouped, the highest of the rates of the regrouped time bands shall apply for the group.

  Options on equities and stock indexes: ±8 percent.

  Options on foreign exchange and gold: ±10 percent.

  Options on commodities: ±20 percent.

  Computations on the basis of these value changes take into account only general market risk, not specific risk. The requirement for specific risk is thus to be computed separately, based on the delta-weighted positions (cf. secs. 1.2 and 1.3 of the 1996 amendment).
- *Change in volatility (dimension 2).* In regard to the variation in volatility, computations are to be conducted for at least three points: an unchanged volatility as well as relative changes in volatility of ±25 percent each.

After the computation of the matrix, each cell contains the net gain or loss of options and related hedging positions. The capital requirement computed for each category of underlying instrument corresponds in this case to the greatest of the losses contained in the matrix.

The scenario analysis is to be made based upon implicit volatilities. In the case of illiquid underlying instruments, other methods may be used on an exception basis to determine the volatility structure.

2.7.7 Criticisms of the Standard Approach

Although the standard approach aims to identify banks with unusual exposure, it is still beset by problems, such as duration, diversification, interdependencies of market risk and credit risk, and qualitative requirements.

- The duration of some instruments cannot be easily identified. Mortgages, for instance, contain prepayment options that allow the homeowner to refinance the loan if interest rates fall. Conversely, homeowners will make payments over a longer period if interest rates increase. The effective duration of mortgages thus changes with the level of interest rates and the history of prepayments for a mortgage pool. Assigning a duration band to one of these instruments becomes highly questionable. More generally, the risk classification is arbitrary. The capital charges of 8 percent are applied uniformly to equities and currencies (and gold) without regard for their actual return volatilities.
- The standard approach does not account for diversification across risks. Low correlations imply that the risk of a portfolio can be much less than the sum of individual component risks. This diversification effect applies across market risks or across different types of financial risks. Diversification across market risks is the easiest to measure. Historical data are available; they reveal that correlations across sources of risk generate diversification and lower the total risk. These diversification benefits are not recognized by simply aggregating across risk factors. Similarly, exchange movements are not perfectly correlated, nor are movements between interest rates and exchange rates. Assuming perfect correlations across various types of risks overestimates portfolio risk and leads to capital adequacy requirements that are too high.
- Correlations across different types of risks are more difficult to deal with. Most notably, default risk may be related to interest-rate risk. This is true for most floating-rate instruments (such as adjustable-rate mortgages, where borrowers may default should interest rates increase to insufferable amounts).
- At times, even credit rating agencies have overlooked the effect of market risk on the possibility of default. A prime example is the Orange County bankruptcy in December 1994. At that time, S&P's and Moody's long-term credit ratings for the county were close to the highest possible—AA and Aa1, respectively—in spite of more than $1 billion in unrealized losses in the investment pool. The agencies claimed to have

conducted a thorough examination of the county's finances, yet they remained unaware of the impending cash crisis. This occurred because the agencies focused only on credit risk—that is, the possibility that a borrower could fail to repay. The rating agencies failed to recognize that market risk can lead to credit risk.

2.8 THE INTERNAL MODEL APPROACH

In April 1995, the Basel Committee presented a major extension of the market risk models.[95] For the first time, it gave banks the option of using their own risk measurement models to determine their capital charge. This decision stemmed from a recognition that many banks have developed sophisticated risk management systems, in many cases far more complex than can be dictated by regulators. As for institutions lagging behind the times, this proposal provided a further impetus to create sound risk management systems.

To use this approach, banks have to satisfy various qualitative requirements, including regular review by various management levels within the bank and by regulators.

To summarize, the general market risk charge on any day t is:

$$MRC_t = \max\left(k - \frac{1}{60} \cdot \sum_{i=1}^{60} \text{VaR}_{t-i}, \text{VaR}_{t-1}\right) \tag{2.12}$$

where k is the multiplication factor determined by the supervisory authority, which can be set higher than its minimum of 3 if the supervisor is not satisfied with the bank's internal risk model.

To obtain total capital adequacy requirements, banks add their credit risk charges to their market risk charges applied to trading operations. Upon application, the local supervisory authority can authorize an institution to compute the capital requirements for market risks by means of risk aggregation models specific to each institution.

Risk aggregation models are statistical processes used to determine the potential changes in the value of portfolios on the basis of changes in the factors that determine such risks. In this connection, *value at risk* (VaR) is defined as that value which represents the maximum potential change in value of the total position, given a certain confidence level during a predetermined period of time.

The equity requirements for interest-rate and equity price risks in the trading book, and for foreign-exchange and commodity risks throughout an institution, result from the aggregation of VaR-based capital charges and any applicable additional requirements for specific risks on equity and interest-rate instruments.

2.8.1 Conditions for and Process of Granting Approval

Should an institution desire to apply the model-based approach, it should make application to the local supervisory authority and submit documentation demanded by that authority.

The local supervisory authority shall base its decision concerning its consent to use the model-based approach on the results of testing conducted under its aegis together with the banking law auditors. Furthermore, the local supervisory authority can base its decision on the review results of foreign supervisory authorities, other banking law auditors aside from those of the applicant, or other independent professional experts.

The approval to use the model-based approach is dependent on certain conditions.

The costs associated with testing the model during the preapproval phase, as well as any subsequent necessary testing, are to be borne by the institution.

The local supervisory authority shall grant approval for the use of the model-based approach only if the following conditions have been met on a continual basis:

- The institution possesses a sufficient number of staff who are familiar with complex models not only in the area of trading, but also in risk control, internal auditing, and back-office functions.
- The areas of trading, back office, and risk control possess an adequate electronic data processing (EDP) infrastructure.
- The risk aggregation model, in relation to the specific activities of the institution (composition of its trading book and its role within the individual markets—market maker, dealer, or end user), is constructed on a sound concept and is correctly implemented.
- The preciseness of measurement of the risk aggregation model is adequate.

The local supervisory authority can demand that the risk aggregation model first be monitored during a specific time frame and tested under real-time conditions before it is implemented for the computation of capital requirements for market risks to ensure that the following conditions are met:

- The risk factors set as minimum requirements are taken account of by the risk aggregation model.
- The risk aggregation model corresponds to the set minimum quantitative requirements.
- The set minimum qualitative requirements are complied with.

After granting approval for the use of the model-based approach, the local supervisory authority is to be notified whenever:

- Significant modifications are made to the risk aggregation model.
- The risk policy is changed.

The local supervisory authority shall decide whether and which further verification is necessary.

2.8.2 VaR-Based Components and Multiplication Factor

The *internal model* proposal is based on the following approach:

- The computation of VaR shall be based on a set of uniform quantitative inputs.
- A horizon of 10 trading days, or two calendar weeks, shall be used.
- A 99 percent confidence interval is required.
- An observation period based on at least a year of historical data and updated at least once a quarter shall be used.
- Correlations can be recognized in broad categories (such as fixed income) as well as across categories (e.g., between fixed income and currencies). As discussed before, this is an improvement over previous proposals.

The capital charge shall be set as the higher of the previous day's VaR or the average VaR over the last 60 business days, times a multiplication factor. The exact value of this factor is to be determined by the local regulators, subject to an absolute floor of 3. This factor is intended to provide additional protection against environments that are much less stable than historical data would lead one to believe.

A penalty component shall be added to the multiplication factor if backtesting reveals that the bank's internal model incorrectly forecasts risks. The purpose of this factor is to give incentives to banks to improve the predictive accuracy of the models and to avoid overly optimistic projections of profits and losses due to model fitting. As the penalty factor may depend on the quality of internal controls at the bank, this system is designed to reward internal monitoring, as well as to develop sound risk management systems.

The VaR-based equity requirement on a certain day corresponds to the greater of the following two amounts:

- The VaR computed within the framework of the model-based approach for the portfolio held on the preceding day

- The average of the daily VaR values computed using the model-based approach for the preceding 60 trading days multiplied by the multiplication factor for the specific institution as fixed by the local supervisory authority.

The multiplication factor for each specific institution shall be at least 3. Its precise size will depend on the following:

- The fulfillment of the qualitative minimum requirements
- The preciseness of forecasting by the risk aggregation model, which is to be tested using so-called backtesting

2.8.3 Requirement for Specific Risks

Institutions that model specific risks neither in the form of residual risks nor in the form of event and default risks shall determine capital requirements for specific risks in accordance with the standard approach.

Institutions that model specific risks in accordance with the prerequisites, but which in doing so limit themselves to capturing residual risks, and do not capture event and default risks at all or only partially, are subject to additional capital requirements for the specific risks of equity and interest-rate instruments. At the discretion of the institution, these may be determined using one of the following two approaches:

- Amount of VaR for equity and interest-rate portfolios
- Amount of VaR for the specific risks inherent in the equity and interest-rate portfolio

To determine the additional requirements, the amount of specific risk captured by the risk aggregation model for equity or interest-rate portfolio shall, in this case, correspond to one of the following:

- The increase in VaR for the related subportfolio caused by the inclusion of specific risks
- The difference between the VaR for the related portfolio and the VaR, which ensues when all positions are substituted by positions whose fluctuation in value is determined exclusively through fluctuations of share market index or the reference interest-rate curve
- The result of the analytical separation of general market risk from specific risk within the framework of a certain model

For the purposes of determining these additional capital requirements, the general market risk for equities is to be defined by means of a single risk factor: a representative market index or the first factor or a linear combination of factors for the purposes of an empirical factor model.

For interest-rate instruments, the general market risk shall correspond to the fluctuation of the reference curve per currency based upon an established liquid market.

The institution must opt for a method for determining the additional requirements for specific risks and apply this method on a continual basis.

Should an institution provide the local supervisory authority with evidence that not only residual risks but also event and default risks are fully modeled, it may be dispensed from additional capital requirements for specific risks.

2.8.4 Combination of Model-Based and Standard Approaches

Institutions wishing to use internal models must in principle possess a risk aggregation model which, at minimum, covers all risk factor categories (foreign exchange, interest rates, equity prices, and commodity prices) with respect to general market risks.

During the phase when an institution is migrating to the model-based approach, the local regulator can allow it to combine the model-based and standard approaches under the condition that the same approach is applied within the same risk factor category, i.e., either the model-based or standard approach.

If positions in a certain risk factor category (such as commodities risk) are absolute and insignificant when considered relatively, the local regulator may also allow an institution not to integrate these into the model-based approach, but to deal with them separately in accordance with the standard approach.

If the model-based and standard approaches are combined, the total capital requirement for market risks is arrived at through a simple addition of the capital requirements for each component.

2.8.5 Specification of Market Risk Factors to Be Captured

An important part of a bank's internal market risk measurement system is the specification of an appropriate set of market risk factors, i.e., the market rates and prices that affect the value of the bank's trading positions. The risk factors contained in a market risk measurement system should be sufficient to capture the risks inherent in the bank's portfolio of on- and off-balance-sheet trading positions. Although banks will have some discretion in specifying the risk factors for their internal models, the following guidelines should be fulfilled.

In principle, the risk aggregation model must take into consideration all risk factors that impact the relevant positions of the institution. An exception exists for the specific risks of equity and interest-rate instruments whose capital requirements may also be computed in accordance with the standard approach.

The following minimum requirements apply for the individual risk factor categories:

- *Interest-rate risks.* The interest-structure risks in each currency in which notable interest-rate-sensitive positions are held are to be captured. In this respect, the following shall apply:

  The modeling of the interest maturity structure is to be made in accordance with a recognized method.

  The number and distribution of the time bands must be appropriate to the size and structure of operations; there must be six at a minimum.

  The risk aggregation model must capture spread risks. These exist in that changes in value of cash flows with similar maturity and currency but issuers of different rating categories are not fully correlated.
- *Foreign-exchange risks.* Risk factors for the exchange rates between the domestic currency and each foreign currency in which the institution holds a significant exposure are to be taken into consideration.
- *Equity price risks.* The risk aggregation model must take into consideration a risk factor (e.g., a stock market index) at least for each national market or single currency zone in which significant positions are held. Risk factor definitions based on sector or branch indexes are also possible.
- *Commodities risks.* Risk factors are to be modeled for each group of commodities. In addition, the risk aggregation model must take into consideration risks in the form of so-called convenience yields—i.e., different developments in spot and forward prices not induced by interest rates.
- *Risks of option positions.* For options, the VaR measure, in addition to delta risks, must capture at least the following risks:

  Gamma risks. Risks arising from nonlinear relationships between option price changes and changes in the price of the underlying instrument.

  Vega risks. Risks arising from the sensitivity of option prices against changes in volatility of the underlying instrument. Institutions with large and complex option portfolios must take appropriate account of volatility risks of option positions according to different maturities.

- *Specific risks of equity and interest-rate instruments.* Specific risks equate those parts of aggregate volatility which relate to occurrences in connection with the issuer of the individual instruments and which cannot be explained by general market risks. To determine the capital requirements, the following further differentiation is to be made:

  Specific risks in the form of residual risks. A residual risk represents that part of the volatility of price fluctuations of equity and interest-rate instruments which cannot be explained empirically by general market factors within the context of a single- or multiple-factor model.

  Specific risks in the form of event and default risks. Specific event risks correspond to the risk that the price of a certain equity or interest-rate instrument changes abruptly as a result of occurrences in connection with the issuer and to an extent which cannot be explained as a general rule by the analysis of historic price fluctuations. In addition to default risk, any abrupt price fluctuations in connection with shocklike occurrences—such as, for instance, a takeover bid—constitute event risks.

An appropriate modeling of specific risks in the form of residual risks presupposes that the model satisfies all quantitative and qualitative minimum requirements, as well as that the following conditions are met:

- The historic change in the portfolio value is explained to a large degree.
- The model demonstrably captures concentrations; i.e., it is sensitive to fluctuations in the composition of the portfolio.
- The model has proven itself to be robust even in periods of strained market situations.

A complete capture of specific risks presupposes that residual risks as well as event and default risks are captured by the risk aggregation model.

2.8.6 Minimum Quantitative Requirements

No specific type of risk aggregation model is prescribed for the determination of capital requirements for market risks. Institutions may determine the VaR on the basis of variance-covariance models, historical simulations, Monte Carlo simulations, and the like. The risk aggregation model, however, must fulfill the following quantitative minimum requirements:

- *Periodicity of computation.* The VaR is to be computed daily on the basis of the prior day's positions.

- *Confidence level.* The computation of VaR should be effected using a one-tailed forecasting interval with a confidence level of 99 percent.
- *Holding period.* In computing VaR, a change in the risk factors corresponding to a change over a 10-day period is to be used. Also allowed are VaR numbers which are, for instance, determined on the basis of a holding period of 1 day and converted to a value corresponding to a holding period of 10 days by multiplication by 10. Institutions with significant option positions must, however, convert in due course to capturing in the risk aggregation model the nonlinear relationship between option price changes and changes in the price of the corresponding underlying instrument by means of 10-day changes in risk factors.
- *Historical observation period and updating of data sets.* The observation period for the forecasting of future changes and volatilities in risk factors, including the correlation between them which is at the basis of the VaR computation, must amount to one year at least. Should the individual daily observations be taken into consideration with individual weights in the computation of volatility and correlations (weighting), the weighted average observation period (weighted lag) must be at least six months (i.e., the individual values in the weighted average must be at least six months old). The data sets must be updated at least each quarter unless market conditions require immediate updating.
- *Correlations.* The VaR computation may be effected by recognizing empirical correlations both within the general risk factor categories (i.e., interest rates, exchange rates, equity prices, and commodity prices, including related volatilities) and between the risk factor categories in case the correlation system of the institution is based on sound concepts and correctly implemented. The correlations are to be continuously monitored with particular care. Above all, the impact on the VaR of abrupt changes in correlations between the risk factor categories are to be computed and evaluated regularly during stress testing. Should the computation of VaR be effected without considering empirical correlations between the general risk factor categories, the VaR for the individual risk factor categories is to be aggregated through addition.

Alan Greenspan was very explicit about stress testing, highlighting its importance in the context of liquidity and systemic risk:

> The use of internal models for risk analysis, and as the basis for regulatory capital charges has become common so far as market risk is concerned. While the limits of models, and the importance of the assumptions that must be made to put them to use, have been reasonably well understood, those issues have been brought into sharp focus by the Asian crisis. For example, firms now appreciate more fully the importance of the tails of the probability distribution of the shocks and of the assumptions about the covariance of prices charges. The use of stress tests, which address the implications of extreme scenarios, has properly increased.[96]

2.8.7 Minimum Qualitative Requirements

The supervisory authorities are able to assure themselves that banks using models have market risk management systems that are conceptually sound and that are implemented with integrity. Accordingly, the supervisory authorities have specified a number of qualitative criteria that banks have to meet before they are permitted to use a models-based approach. The extent to which banks meet the qualitative criteria may influence the level at which supervisory authorities set the multiplication factor. Only those banks whose models are in full compliance with the qualitative criteria are eligible for application of the minimum multiplication factor.

2.8.7.1 Integrity of Data

The institution shall demonstrate that it possesses sound, documented, internally tested, and approved procedures which ensure that all transactions are captured, valued, and prepared for risk measurement in a complete, accurate, and timely manner. Manual corrections to data are to be documented so that the reason and exact content of the correction may be reconstructed. In particular, the following principles shall apply:

- All transactions are to be confirmed daily with the counterparty. The confirmation of transactions as well as their reconciliation is to be effected by a unit independent of the trading department. Differences are to be investigated at once.
- A procedure must be in force which will ensure the appropriateness, uniformity, consistency, timeliness, and independence of the data used in the valuation models.
- All positions are to be processed in a manner which ensures complete recording in terms of risk.

2.8.7.2 Independent Risk Control Department

The institution must possess a risk control department which has qualified employees in sufficient number, is independent of the trading activities, and reports directly to a member of the management team responsible for risk control.

Risk control shall support the following functions in particular:

- Organization and implementation of risk monitoring systems (trading and control systems).
- Close control over daily operations (limits, profit and loss statement, etc.) including measurement criteria for market risk.
- Daily VaR computations, analyses, controls, and reporting:

  Preparation of daily reports on the results of the risk aggregation model, as well as analyses of the results, including the relationship between VaR and trading limits.

  Daily reporting to the responsible member of management.
- Completion of regular backtesting.[97]
- Completion of regular stress testing.
- Testing and authorization of risk aggregation models, valuation models for computing the daily profit and loss statement, and models to generate input factors (e.g., yield-curve models).
- Ongoing review and updating of the documentation for the risk monitoring system (trading and control systems).

2.8.7.3 Management

The following provisions shall apply to management for the purposes of using the model-based approach:

- The responsible member of management must be informed directly on a daily basis, and in an appropriate manner, of the results of the risk aggregation model, and he or she shall subject these to a critical review.
- The responsible member of management who evaluates the daily reports of the independent risk-monitoring department must possess the authority to reduce the positions of individual traders as well as to reduce the overall risk exposure of the bank.
- The responsible member of management must be informed periodically of the results of backtesting and stress testing by the risk control department, and he or she must subject these results to critical review.

2.8.7.4 Risk Aggregation Model, Daily Risk Management, and System of Limits

The following principles shall apply for the relationship between the risk aggregation model, daily risk control, and limits:

- The risk aggregation model must be closely integrated into daily risk control. In particular, its results must be an integral part of the planning, monitoring, and management of the market risk profile of the institution.
- There must exist a clear and permanent relationship between the internal trading limits and the VaR (as it is used to determine capital requirements for market risks). The relationship must be known by both dealers and management.
- The limits are to be reviewed regularly.
- The procedures to be followed in case the limits are exceeded, and any applicable sanctions, must be clearly defined and documented.

2.8.7.5 Backtesting

An institution using the model-based approach must possess regular, sound, documented, and internally tested procedures for backtesting. In principle, backtesting serves the purpose of obtaining feedback on the quality and precision of the risk measurement system.

The process of backtesting retrospectively compares the trading income during a defined period of time with the dispersion area of trading income predicted by the risk aggregation model for that period. The goal of the process is to be able to state, within certain probabilities of error, whether the VaR determined by the risk aggregation model actually covers 99 percent of the trading outcome. For reasons of statistical reliability of the assertions, the daily trading profits and the daily VaR are compared over a longer observation period.

For the purposes of the model-based approach, a standardized backtesting process is required to determine the multiplier specific to the institution. Regardless, institutions should also use backtesting on a lower level than that of the global risk aggregation model—for example, for individual risk factors or product categories—in order to investigate questions regarding risk measurement. In this manner, parameters other than those of the standardized backtesting process can be used in backtesting.

Institutions which determine not only requirements for general market risks but also those for specific risks by means of a risk aggregation model must also possess procedures for backtesting which indicate the adequacy of modeling specific risks. In particular, separate backtesting is to be conducted for subportfolios (equity and interest-bearing portfolios) containing specific risks, and the results are to be analyzed and reported upon demand to the local supervisory authority as well as to the banking law auditors.

Backtesting is to be conducted with consideration given to the following standards in order to determine the multiplication factor specific to the institution:

- The test must be based on the VaR computed for the daily market risk report. The only difference relates to the fact that a holding period of 1 day, not 10 days, is subject to a capital charge.
- The decision whether backtesting should be carried out on the basis of actual trading results (i.e., inclusive of results of intraday trading and inclusive of commissions), trading results from which these items have been eliminated, or hypothetical trading results determined by revaluation to market of the financial instruments in the institution's portfolio on the preceding day is left, in principle, to each individual institution. The condition is that the process may be declared to be sound, and the income figures used must not systemically distort the test outcome. In addition, a uniform process over the time period is to be applied; i.e., the institution is not free to change the backtesting methodology without consulting the local supervisory authority.
- The sampling method applied is to be based on 250 prior observations.

The daily VaR reported internally, as well as the trading result on the day of computation, are to be documented in a manner that is irreversible and that may be inspected at any time by the local supervisory authority and the banking law auditors.

The institution shall daily compare the trading result with the VaR computed for the day before. Cases in which a trading loss exceeds that of the corresponding VaR are designated as exceptions. The review and documentation of these exceptions (for observations for the 250 preceding trading days) is to be undertaken at least each quarter. The result of this quarterly review is to be reported to the local supervisory authority and the banking law auditors.

The increase in the multiplication factor specific to the institution corresponds to the number of exceptions noted during the observation period of the preceding 250 trading days (Table 2-11). In the case of the increase of the multiplication factor dependent on backtesting, the local supervisory authority can ignore individual exceptions if the institution demonstrates that the exception does not relate to an imprecise (forecasting quality) risk aggregation model.

If there are more than four exceptions for the relevant observation period before 250 observations are available, the local supervisory authority is to be notified immediately. From that day forward, the institution must compute VaR with an increased multiplier until the local supervisory authority has made a final decision.

If an institution-specific multiplication factor greater than 3 should be set as a result of backtesting, it is expected that the origin of the imprecise estimates of the risk aggregation model will be investigated and, if possible, eliminated. The setting of the multiplier to 4 requires a compul-

TABLE 2-11

Multiplication Factor Specific to the Institution

Number of Exceptions	Increase in Multiplication Factor
4 or fewer	0.00
5	0.40
6	0.50
7	0.65
8	0.75
9	0.85
10 or more	1.00

sory rapid and careful review of the model. The shortcomings are to be eliminated swiftly. Otherwise, the conditions for using the model-based approach will be deemed violated.

A reduction of the multiplication factor by the local supervisory authority will ensue only if the institution can demonstrate that the error has been remedied and that the revised model presents an appropriate forecasting quality.

2.8.7.6 Stress Testing

An institution using the model-based approach must apply regular, sound, consistent, documented, and internally tested stress-testing procedures. Important goals of stress testing are to ascertain whether the equity can absorb large potential losses and to derive possible corrective action.

The definition of meaningful stress scenarios is left, in principle, to the individual institution. The following guidelines, however, shall apply:

- Scenarios which lead to extraordinary losses or which render the control of risks difficult or impossible are to be considered.
- Scenarios with extreme changes in market risk factors and the correlation between these (arbitrarily set scenarios or historic scenarios corresponding to periods of significant market turbulence) are to be applied.
- Scenarios specific to the institution which must be considered particularly grave in regard to the specific risk positions are to be applied.
- The analyses must capture liquidity aspects of market disturbances in addition to extreme changes in market risk factors and their intercorrelation.

- The risks of all positions are to be included in stress testing, especially option positions.

In addition to actual quantitative stress tests and analyses thereof, lines of responsibility must exist to ensure that the outcome of stress testing will trigger the necessary measures:

- The results of stress testing must be periodically reviewed by the responsible member of management and be reflected in the policy and limits that are set by management and the internal authority for direction, supervision, and control.
- If certain weaknesses are uncovered through stress testing, steps must be taken immediately to deal with these risks appropriately (e.g., by hedging or by reduction of the risk exposure).

2.8.7.7 Criticisms of the Internal Model Approach

The internal model approach has been highly welcomed and criticized at the same time. This part of the accord has been severely criticized by the International Swaps and Derivatives Association (ISDA). In particular, the multiplication factor of 3 is viewed as too large. The ISDA showed that a factor of 1 would have provided enough capital to cover periods of global turmoil, such as the 1987 stock market crash, the 1990 Gulf War, and the 1992 European Monetary System (EMS) crisis. An even more serious criticism is that the method based on an internal VaR creates a capital requirement that is generally higher than the standard model prescribed by the Basel Committee. Hence, the current approach provides a negative incentive to the development of internal risk models.

2.9 THE PRECOMMITMENT MODEL

The debate on the appropriate risk measurement system took another turn when the U.S. Federal Reserve Board proposed a *precommitment* approach to bank regulation in 1995. Under this third alternative, the bank would precommit to a maximum trading loss over a designated horizon. This loss would become the capital charge for market risk. The supervisor would then observe, after, say, a quarterly reporting period, whether trading losses exceeded the limit. If so, the bank would be penalized, which might include a fine, regulatory discipline, or higher future capital charges. Violations of the limits would also bring public scrutiny to the bank, which provides a further feedback mechanism for good management.

The main advantage of this "incentive-compatible" approach is that the bank itself chooses its capital requirement. As Kupiec and O'Brien have shown, this choice is made optimally in response to regulatory penalties for violations.[98] Regulators can then choose the penalty that will induce appropriate behavior.

This proposal was welcomed by the ISDA, which argued that this approach explicitly recognizes the links between risk management practices and firm-selected deployment of capital. Critics, in contrast, pointed out that quarterly verification is very slow in comparison to the real-time daily capital requirements of the Basel proposals. Others worried that dynamic portfolio adjustments to avoid exceeding the maximum loss could exacerbate market movements, in the same way that portfolio insurance supposedly caused the crash of 1987.

2.10 COMPARISON OF APPROACHES

At this point, it is useful to compare the pros and cons of each method. The first, the standard model method, is generally viewed as least adequate because of the following factors:

- *Portfolio considerations.* The model ignores diversification effects across sources of risk.
- *Arbitrary capital charges.* The capital charges are only loosely related to the actual volatility of each asset category. This can distort portfolio choices, as banks move away from assets for which the capital charge is abnormally high.
- *Compliance costs.* Given that many banks already run sophisticated risk measurement systems, the standard model imposes a significant additional reporting burden.

The second method, the internal model, addresses all of these issues. It relies on the self-interest of banks to develop accurate risk management systems. Internal VaR systems measure the total portfolio risk of the bank, account for differences in asset volatilities, and impose only small additional costs. In addition, regulatory requirements will automatically evolve at the same speed as risk measurement techniques, as new developments will be automatically incorporated into internal VaRs.

Unfortunately, from the viewpoint of regulators, the internal model still has some drawbacks:

- *Performance verification.* Supervisors are supposed to monitor whether internal VaRs indeed provide good estimates of future profits and losses in trading portfolios. As capital charges are based on VaRs, there may be an incentive to artificially lower the VaR figure to lower capital requirements; thus, verification by regulators is important. The problem is that, even with a well-calibrated model, there will be instances when losses will exceed the VaR by chance (e.g., 5 percent of the time using a 95 percent confidence level). Unfortunately, long periods may be needed to distinguish between chance losses and model inaccuracies. This issue makes verification difficult.

- *Endogenity of positions.* The banks' internal VaRs typically measure risk over a short interval, such as a day. Extending these numbers to a 10-day trading period ignores the fact that positions will change, especially in response to losses or unexpectedly high volatility. Therefore, measures of long-horizon exposure ignore efficient risk management procedures and controls. Perhaps this is why the ISDA found that the current approach appeared too conservative.

Note that these problems do not detract from the usefulness of VaR models for corporate risk management. From the viewpoint of regulators, however, the precommitment approach has much to recommend, because it automatically accounts for changing positions. In addition, the risk coverage level is endogenously chosen by the bank, in response to the penalty for failure, which creates fewer distortions in capital markets.

Unfortunately, all models suffer from a performance verification problem. The regulator can compare only *ex post,* or realized, performance to *ex ante* estimates of risk or maximum loss. Unless the maximum loss is set extremely high, there always will be instances in which a loss will exceed the limit even with the correct model. The key then for regulators is to separate good intentions and bad luck from reckless behavior.

2.11 REVISION AND MODIFICATION OF THE BASEL ACCORD ON MARKET RISKS

2.11.1 The E.U. Capital Adequacy Directive

The history of capital adequacy requirements in Europe must be put in the perspective of plodding movements toward European economic and political integration. The Single European Act of 1985 committed member countries to achieving a free market in goods, services, capital, and labor. To this end, the European Union's Investment Services Directive (ISD), which came into effect on January 1, 1996, swept away restrictions against nonlocal financial services. Up until then, a securities firm that wanted to do business in another European Union country had to abide by local rules—for instance, having to establish separately capitalized subsidiaries (and expensive offices) in foreign countries. In effect, this raised the cost of doing business abroad and made Europe's internal market less efficient than it might otherwise have been.[99]

Under the new regulations, firms based in one E.U. country were authorized to carry out business in any other E.U. country. This was expected to lead to the general consolidation of office networks. For instance, Deutsche Bank announced that its global investment banking activities would be centralized in London. Also, the centralization of risk management would provide for better control of financial risks. In addition to efficiency gains, more competition was expected to drive down transaction costs and increase the liquidity of European financial markets.

To discourage firms from rushing to set up shop in the country with the lowest level of regulations, however, the European Union adopted Europe-wide capital requirements known as the Capital Adequacy Directive (CAD I). The CAD, published in March 1993, laid down minimum levels of capital to be adopted for E.U. banks and securities houses by January 1996.

In many ways, the CAD paralleled the Basel guidelines. It extended the 1989 Solvency Ratio and Own Funds Directives, which were similar to the 1988 Basel accord. The 1993 requirements were very similar and in some cases identical to those laid out in the 1993 Basel proposal. The amendment to incorporate market risks led to the updated version, CAD II (April 1997), which allowed all E.U. institutions to run their own VaR models for daily calculation.

There were some differences, however. First, the Basel guidelines were aimed only at banks, not securities houses. Regulation of securities houses is concerned mainly with orderly liquidation, while bank regulators aim to prevent outright failure. Second, the CAD II guidelines were put into effect in 1996, whereas the Basel rules became effective in 1998, which left a period during which European firms had to comply with a separate set of guidelines.

2.11.2 New Capital Adequacy Framework to Replace the 1988 Accord

The market risk approaches remained unchanged.[100] Refer back to the discussion earlier in this chapter of the 1996 Amendment to the Capital Accord to Incorporate Market Risks (Section 2.6), which outlines the quantitative approaches in detail.

2.12 REGULATION OF NONBANKS

In many ways, the regulation of nonbank financial intermediaries parallels that of banks. Each of these institutions must learn to deal effectively with similar sources of financial risk.

Also, there is a tendency for lines of business to become increasingly blurred. Commercial banks have moved into trading securities and provide some underwriting and insurance functions. The trading portfolios of banks contain assets, liabilities, and derivatives that are no different from those of securities houses. Therefore, trading portfolios are measured at market values, while traditional banking items are still reported at book value. With the trend toward securitization, however, more and more assets (such as bank loans) have become liquid and tradable.

2.12.1 Pension Funds

Although pension funds are not subject to capital adequacy requirements, a number of similar restrictions govern defined-benefit plans. The current U.S. regulatory framework was defined by the Employee Retirement Income Security Act (ERISA) promulgated in 1974. Under ERISA, companies are required to make contributions that are sufficient to provide coverage for pension payments. In effect, the minimum capital is the present value of future pension liabilities. The obligation to make up for unfunded liabilities parallels the obligation to maintain some minimal capital ratio. Also, asterisk weights are replaced by a looser provision of diversification and of not taking excessive risks, as defined under the "prudent man" rule.

As in the case of banking regulation, federal guarantees are provided to pensioners. In the United States, the Pension Benefit Guarantee Corporation (PBGC), like the Federal Deposit Insurance Corporation (FDIC), charges an insurance premium and promises to cover defaults by corporations. Other countries have similar systems, although most other countries rely much more heavily on public pay-as-you-go schemes, in which contributions from current employees directly fund current retirees. The United States, Britain, and the Netherlands are far more advanced in their reliance on private pension funds. Public systems in countries afflicted by large government deficits can ill afford generous benefits to an increasingly aging population. As a result, private pension funds are likely to take on increasing importance all over the world. With those will come the need for prudential regulation.

2.12.2 Insurance Companies

Regulation of insurance companies is globally less centralized than that of other financial institutions, whose insurance is regulated at the national level. In the United States, the insurance industry is regulated at the state level. As in the case of FDIC protection, insurance contracts are ultimately covered by a state guaranty association. State insurance regulators set nationwide standards through the National Association of Insurance Commissioners (NAIC).

In December 1992, the NAIC announced new capital adequacy requirements for insurers. As in the case of the early 1988 Basel accord, the new rules emphasized credit risk. For instance, no capital would be needed to cover holdings of government bonds and just 0.5 percent for mortgages, but 30 percent of the value of equities would have to be covered. This ratio was much higher than the 8 percent ratio required for banks, which some insurers claimed put them at a competitive disadvantage vis-à-vis other financial institutions that were increasingly branching out into insurance products.

In the European Union, insurance regulation parallels that of banks, with capital requirements, portfolio restrictions, and regulatory intervention in cases of violation. For life insurance companies, capital must exceed 4 percent of mathematical reserves, computed as the present values of future premiums minus future death liabilities. For non-life insurance companies, capital must exceed the highest of about 17 percent of premiums charged for the current year and about 24 percent of annual settlements over the past three years.

2.12.3 Securities Firms

The regulation of securities firms is still evolving. Securities firms hold securities on the asset and liability sides (usually called *long* and *short positions*) of their balance sheets. Regulators generally agree that some prudent reserve should be available to cover financial risks. There is no agreement, however, as to whether securities firms should hold capital to cover their net positions, consisting of assets minus liabilities, or their gross positions, consisting of the sum of all long plus short positions.

The United States and Japan use the gross position approach, the United Kingdom uses the net position, and the Basel Committee and the European Union consider a variant of both approaches. The European Union, for instance, required firms to have equity equal to 2 percent of their gross positions plus 8 percent of their net positions as of 1996.

Dimson and Marsh compare the effectiveness of these approaches for a sample of detailed holdings of British market makers.[101] Comparing the riskiness of the portfolio to various capital requirements, they show that the net position approach, as required by the United Kingdom, dominates the E.U. and U.S. approaches, as it best approximates the actual portfolio risk. The net position approach comes closest to what portfolio theory would suggest.

Although there are differences in the regulations of banks and securities firms, capital requirements are likely to converge as banks and securities firms increasingly compete in the same markets. Currently, the same accounting rules apply to the trading-book activities of banks and the trading activities of securities firms. In the United States, the 1933 Glass-Steagall Act, which separates the commercial and investment bank functions, is slowly being chipped away. The 1933 act is widely viewed as obsolete and overly restrictive, especially in comparison with the universal banking system prevalent in Europe. Cracks in the Glass-Steagall wall started to appear in 1989, when commercial banks were allowed to underwrite stocks and bonds on a limited basis (although no more than 10 percent of their revenues could come from underwriting). Banks have also been expanding into insurance products, such as annuities, although further expansion is being fiercely resisted by U.S. insurance companies.

More recently, VaR has been gaining prominence in the regulation of securities firms. The Securities and Exchange Commission, the Commodity Futures Trading Commission, and six major Wall Street securities houses have entered an agreement to base capital requirements on VaR methodology. An authoritative resource for counterparty risk management, published by the Counterparty Risk Management Policy Group (CRMPG) in June 1999, is improving counterparty risk management practices. CRMPG was formed by a group of 12 parties in the aftermath of the 1998 market turmoil to promote better industrywide counterparty market and credit risk practices. As for the commercial banking system, VaR is bound to become a universally accepted benchmark.[102]

2.12.4 The Trend Toward Risk-Based Disclosures

In addition to deriving strategic benefits from risk measurement and management, institutions can use their risk management systems to generate the kinds of reports that regulators are seeking. Disclosure guidelines released by the U.S. Securities and Exchange Commission (SEC) in 1997 allow companies to use VaR-type measures to communicate information about market risk. While many companies may be interested in measuring the aggregate market risk of their underlying exposures and hedge instruments for internal purposes, current regulations require only the disclosure of market risk–sensitive instruments (e.g., derivative contracts). Disclosure of underlying exposures and other positions is encouraged, but not required. Whether companies decide to report only the required disclosures or to also include the encouraged disclosures, the systems being used for internal risk measurement can be leveraged to meet regulatory disclosure requirements.

2.12.5 Disclosure Requirements

SEC market risk disclosure requirements affect all companies reporting their financial results in the United States.[103] These regulations apply to derivative commodity instruments, derivative financial instruments, and other financial instruments (investments, loans, structured notes, mortgage-backed securities, indexed debt instruments, interest-only and principal-only obligations, deposits, and other debt obligations) that are sensitive to market risk, all of which are collectively called *market risk–sensitive instruments.*

The SEC requires that companies provide both quantitative and qualitative information about the market risk–sensitive instruments they are using.[104] Currently, the allowed alternatives for the reporting of quantitative information include tabular summaries of contract fair values; measures of sensitivity to market rate changes; and VaR measures expressing potential loss of earnings, cash flows, or fair values.

The New Basel Capital Accord has integrated disclosure requirements as an integral part of the entire accord, across all risk factors:

> The third pillar, market discipline, will encourage high disclosure standards and enhance the role of market participants in encouraging banks to hold adequate capital. The Committee proposes to issue later this year [2001] guidance on public disclosure that will strengthen the capital framework.[105]

2.12.6 Encouraged Disclosures

Apart from setting requirements on market risk–sensitive instruments, the SEC encourages, but does not require, risk disclosures on instruments, positions, and transactions not covered by Item 305 of Regulation S-K and Item 9A of Form 20-F. Such instruments can include physically settled commodity derivatives, commodity positions, cash flows from anticipated transactions, and other financial instruments, such as insurance contracts. The BIS emphasizes disclosure practices and requires that regulations on the disclosure of specific, relevant information regarding market, credit, and operational risk be enforced; thus, the banks become more transparent.

In general, the reporting of the combined market risk of underlying business exposures and market risk–sensitive instruments should provide a more accurate portrayal of a firm's total risk profile than reporting for market risk–sensitive instruments alone.

2.13 MARKET INSTRUMENTS AND CREDIT RISKS

Credit exposure and market risk are interrelated, and the boundaries between credit and market risk increasingly overlap and merge; this is particularly obvious in the case of credit risk derivatives. It can be argued that credit risk is a component of market risk, as it reflects the company- or issuer-specific risk. A change in the quality of a company and its ability to fulfill its financial obligations is, in an efficient market, immediately reflected in the specific risk, either on the equity side through the idiosyncratic risk or on the fixed-income side through the spread on top of the risk-free term structure. This reflects the balance sheet, as all financing instruments ultimately lead back to the balance sheet of the original underlying company and should therefore reflect the same company-specific risk.

Credit exposures from market-driven transactions such as swaps, forwards, and purchased options are an issue for all participants in the

OTC derivatives markets. Credit or market risk can result from fluctuations in market rates. (More instrument types are analyzed and decomposed regarding market, credit, and operational risk in Chapter 3.)

In the case of a swap, the interrelationship of credit and market risk can be illustrated in a simple example. Party A engages in an interest-rate swap with Party B, paying a five-year fixed rate and receiving a three-month LIBOR. If the five-year rate goes down, A incurs a market loss because it agreed to pay B an above-market interest rate. On the other hand, if a 10-year rate falls, the swap is in the money for A. However, this mark-to-market (MTM) gain on the swap is now a credit exposure to B—if B defaults, A forsakes the MTM gain on the swap. Therefore, a company has credit exposure whenever rates fluctuate in its favor. A company has potential credit exposure from the time a contract is initiated up to final settlement.

For example, simulating a simple equity-index fall would do little to uncover the risk of a market-neutral risk arbitrage book. In a real-world example, Long Term Capital Management (LTCM) had leveraged credit-spread-tightening positions (i.e., long corporate bond positions were interest-rate hedged with short Treasuries) in August 1998. This portfolio was supposedly market neutral.[106]

A stress test for spread widening (i.e., flight-to-safety phenomenon) would have uncovered the potential for extreme losses. Stressed markets often give rise to counterparty credit risk issues that may be much more significant than pure market impacts. For example, a market-neutral swap portfolio could result in huge credit exposures if interest rates moved significantly and counterparties defaulted on their contractual obligations. While market rates and creditworthiness are unrelated for small market movements, large market movements could precipitate credit events, and vice versa. Note that it is much more straightforward to reduce market risk than credit risk. To reduce the market risk in our example, Party A can purchase a 10-year government bond or futures contract, or enter into an opposite swap transaction with another counterparty. Credit risk presents a more complex problem. For example, taking an offsetting swap with another counterparty to reduce market risk actually increases credit risk (one counterparty will always end up owing the party the net present value of the swap). Solutions to the credit problem are available, however. Party A could arrange a credit enhancement structure with Party B, such as structuring a collateral or MTM agreement (e.g., Party B agrees to post collateral or pay the MTM of a swap on a periodic basis, or if a certain threshold is reached). Furthermore, a credit derivative could be written by a third party to insure the swap contract.

Options have their own credit and market risk profile (Figure 2-8). Only purchasers of options have credit exposure to their counterparts. If the option is in the money and the counterparty defaults, the party is in trouble. For example, Party A has potential credit exposure when it buys a

FIGURE 2-8

Market, Credit, and Operational Risks from a Transaction Perspective.

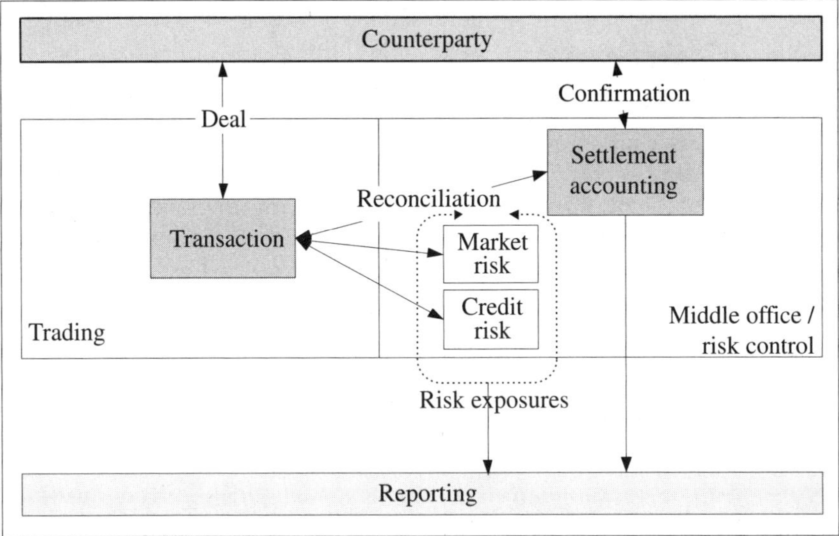

put option on the S&P 500 Stock Index to insure an equity portfolio. If the equity market falls and Party A's counterparty defaults on its obligation to honor the put option, A would incur a credit loss (for example, if the insurer of its equity portfolio does not fulfill its obligation). Sellers of options do not have credit exposure. After a party sells an option and collects the premium, it is not exposed to its counterparty (for example, the counterparty will not owe it anything, but it will potentially owe something to the counterparty). As a seller of options, a party incurs only market risk (i.e., the risk that market rates will move out of its favor). The projected credit exposure of options increases with time, with the peak exposure expected just before final settlement.

The credit risk of swaps and forwards is mostly counterparty risk. Counterparties engaging in swaps and forwards incur credit exposure to each other. Swaps and forwards are generally initiated at the money. That is, at the beginning of a contract, neither counterparty owes the other anything. However, as rates change, the MTM value of the contract changes, and one counterparty will always owe another counterparty money (the amount owed will be the MTM value).

Usually, the projected credit exposure of an interest-rate swap has a concave shape. Projected exposure of a currency swap, however, increases with time and peaks just before settlement. A currency swap has a larger, and continually upward sloping, exposure profile due to the foreign-exchange risk of the principal amount, which is exchanged only at final settlement. Projected credit exposure of a forward also slopes continually upward, as there is no exchange of payments before settlement.

2.14 SUMMARY

Market risk management has become a relatively mature discipline. Therefore, this chapter focuses on the evolution of the different models and approaches, and on the conditions and assumptions which are linked to those models and approaches. The groundbreaking works of Markowitz and Black and Scholes 50 years ago set the framework in the market risk area, subsequently enhanced and modified by others. These origins have shaped the profile of the discipline and provided a substantial set of specialized parameters and assumptions, typical for a discipline considered to have an integrated framework. The terms *time horizon, diversification,* and *volatility,* just to mention three parameters, have a different meaning within the market risk framework than in credit risk or operational risk. The international regulatory body has developed the supervisory framework for each risk category independently from the other categories, and tries to bring the individual components together in the new capital adequacy framework.

The discussion of different models and their application within the regulatory framework covering market risk–related issues is a central part of this chapter. The Basel Committee on Banking Supervision of the Bank for International Settlement has moved from a prescriptive approach on supporting risk with capital to a risk-sensitive framework, and the latest approach is intended to integrate the market, credit, and operational risk categories into an integrated risk framework. This chapter focuses on the conceptual approaches regarding the modeling of market risk and the regulatory initiatives on market risk and VaR.

2.15 NOTES

1. Bank for International Settlement (BIS), Basel Committee on Banking Supervision, *Amendment to the Capital Accord to Incorporate Market Risks,* Basel, Switzerland: Bank for International Settlement, January 1996, sec. I.1. p. 3.
2. Harry M. Markowitz, "Portfolio Selection (1)," *Journal of Finance* 7 (March 1952), 77–91.
3. William Shakespeare, *The Merchant of Venice,* ca. 1596–1598, Antonio in act 1, scene 1.
4. J. R. Hicks, "A Suggestion for Simplifying the Theory of Money," *Economica* (February 1935), 1–19.
5. Ibid., 7.

6. James Tobin, "Liquidity Preference as Behavior Towards Risk," *Review of Economic Studies* 26/1 (February 1958), 65–86.
7. J. R. Hicks, "Liquidity," *Economic Journal* 72 (December 1962), 787–802.
8. Ibid.
9. J. Marschak, "Money and the Theory of Assets," *Econometrica* 6 (1938), 311–325.
10. Ibid., 314.
11. James Tobin, "Liquidity Preference as Behavior Towards Risk," *Review of Economic Studies* 26/1 (February 1958), 65–86.
12. William F. Sharpe, "Capital Asset Prices: A Theory of Market Equilibrium Under Conditions of Risk," *Journal of Finance* 19/3 (September 1964), 425–442; John Lintner, "The Valuation of Risk Assets and the Selection of Risky Investments in Stock Portfolios and Capital Budgets," *Review of Economics and Statistics* 47/1 (February 1965), 13–37.
13. Johnann von Neumann and Oskar Morgenstern, "Theory of Games and Economic Behavior," 3d ed., Princeton, NJ: Princeton University Press, 1967 (1st ed., 1944).
14. J. B. Williams, *The Theory of Investment Value,* Cambridge, MA: Harvard University Press, 1938.
15. J. L. Farrell, "The Dividend Discount Model: A Primer," *Financial Analysts Journal* 41 (November–December 1985), 16–19, 22–25.
16. D. H. Leavens, "Diversification of Investments," *Trusts and Estates* 80 (May 1945), 469–473.
17. Harry M. Markowitz, "Portfolio Selection (1)," *Journal of Finance* 7 (March 1952), 77–91.
18. A. D. Roy, "Safety First and the Holding of Assets," *Econometrica* 20/3 (July 1952), 431–449.
19. Harry M. Markowitz, "The Optimization of a Quadratic Function Subject to Linear Constraints," *Naval Research Logistics Quarterly* 3 (1956), 111–133; *Portfolio Selection—Efficient Diversification of Investments,* New York: John Wiley & Sons, 1959; *Mean-Variance Analysis in Portfolio Choice and Capital Markets,* Oxford, U.K.: Basil Blackwell, 1987.
20. Harry M. Markowitz, *Portfolio Selection (2),* 2d ed., Oxford, U.K.: Basil Blackwell, 1992, p. 154ff.
21. James Tobin, "Liquidity Preference as Behavior Towards Risk," *Review of Economic Studies* 26/1 (February 1958), 65–86.
22. William F. Sharpe, "Capital Asset Prices, A Theory of Market Equilibrium Under Conditions of Risk," *Journal of Finance* 19/3 (September 1964), 425–442.
23. John Lintner, "The Valuation of Risk Assets and the Selection of Risky Investments in Stock Portfolios and Capital Budgets," *Review of Economics and Statistics* 47/1 (February 1965), 13–37; "Security Prices, Risk, and Maximal Gains from Diversification," *Journal of Finance* 20 (1965), 587–615.

24. Jan Mossin, "Equilibrium in a Capital Asset Market," *Econometrica* 35/4 (October 1966), 768–783.

25. Diana R. Harrington, *Modern Portfolio Theory, the Capital Asset Pricing Model and Arbitrage Pricing Theory: A User's Guide,* 2d ed., Englewood Cliffs, NJ: Prentice-Hall, 1987, p. 35.

26. For a detailed discussion, see Christoph Aukenthaler, "Trust Banking, Theorie und Praxis des Anlagegeschäftes," PhD thesis, University of Zurich, Haupt, Bern, 1991, 244ff., or Pirmin Hotz, "Das Capital Asset Pricing Model und die Markteffizienzhypothese unter besonderer Berücksichtigung der empirisch beobachteten 'Anomalien' in den amerikanischen und anderen internationalen Aktienmärkten," PhD thesis, University St. Gall, Victor Hotz AG, Baar, 1989, p. 43ff.

27. Eugene Fama, "Efficient Capital Market: A Review of Theory and Empirical Work," *Journal of Finance* 3 (1970), 383–417.

28. Thomas Vock and Heinz Zimmermann, "Risiken und Renditen schweizerischer Aktien," *Schweizerzische Zeitschrift für Volkwirtschaft und Statistik* 4 (1984), 547–576.

29. Eugene Fama, *Foundations of Finance,* New York: Basic Books, 1976, p. 25ff.

30. Stanley J. Kon, "Models of Stock Returns—A Comparison," *Journal of Finance* 39 (1984), 147–165.

31. Randolph Westerfield, "An Examination of Foreign Exchange Risk and Fixed and Floating Exchange Rate Regimes," *Journal of International Economics* 7 (1977), 181–200.

32. Walter Wasserfallen and Heinz Zimmermann, "The Behaviour of Interdaily Exchange Rates," *Journal of Banking and Finance* 9 (1985), 55–72.

33. Heinz Zimmermann, "Zeithorizont, Risiko und Performance, eine Übersicht," *Finanzmarkt und Portfolio Management* 2 (1991), 169.

34. Fischer Black, "Capital Market Equilibrium with Restricted Borrowing," *Journal of Business* 7, 444–454.

35. For a detailed analysis see Fischer Black, Michael C. Jensen, and Myron Scholes, "The Capital Asset Pricing Model: Some Empirical Tests," in Michael Jensen, *Studies in the Theory of Capital Markets,* New York: Praeger, 1972.

36. Eugene Fama, "Efficient Capital Market: A Review of Theory and Empirical Work," *Journal of Finance* 3 (1970), 383–417; Fischer Black, Michael C. Jensen, and Myron Scholes, "The Capital Asset Pricing Model: Some Empirical Tests," in Michael Jensen, *Studies in the Theory of Capital Markets,* New York: Praeger, 1972; Eugene Fama and James MacBeth, "Risk, Return and Equilibrium: Empirical Tests," *Journal of Political Economy* 9 (1973), 601–636.

37. Stephen A. Ross, "The Arbitrage Theory of Capital Asset Pricing," *Journal of Economic Theory* 13 (1976), 341–360.

38. Louis Bachelier, "Theorie de la Speculation," *Annales de l'Ecole Normale Superieure* 17 (1900), 21–86. English translation by A.J. Boness in Paul H. Cootner (ed.), *The Random Character of Stock Market Prices,* Cambridge, MA: MIT Press, 1967, pp. 17–78.

39. C. Sprenkle, "Warrant Prices as Indicators of Expectations and Preferences," *Yale Economic Essays* 1 (1961), 172–231; P. Samuelson, "Rational Theory of Warrant Pricing," *Industrial Management Review* 10 (1965), 15–31.

40. Fischer Black and Myron Scholes, "The Pricing of Options and Corporate Liabilities," *Journal of Political Economy* 81 (May–June 1973), 637–654; R. C. Merton, "Theory of Rational Option Pricing," *Bell Journal of Economics and Management Science* 4/1 (June 1974), 141–183.

41. Ibid., Black and Scholes.

42. Ibid., Merton.

43. Fischer Black, "The Pricing of Commodity Contracts," *Journal of Financial Economics* 3 (1976), 167–179.

44. M. Asay, "A Note on the Design of Commodity Option Contracts," *Journal of Finance* 2 (1982), 1–8.

45. M. Garman and S. Kohlhagen, "Foreign Currency Option Values," *Journal of International Money and Finance* 2 (1983), 231–238.

46. R. Geske, "The Valuation of Compound Options," *Journal of Financial Economics* 7 (1979), 63–81.

47. Richard Roll, "An Analytic Valuation Formula for Unprotected American Call Options on Stocks with Known Dividends," *Journal of Financial Economics* 5 (1977), 251–258; R. Geske, "A Note on an Analytical Formula for Unprotected American Call Options on Stocks with Known Dividends," *Journal of Financial Economics* 7 (1979), 375–380; R. Whaley, "On the Valuation of American Call Options on Stocks with Known Dividends," *Journal of Financial Economics* 9 (1981), 207–211.

48. M. Rubinstein, "Pay Now, Choose Later," *Risk* (February 1991), 13.

49. S. Gray and R. Whaley, "Valuing S&P 500 Bear Market Warrants with a Periodic Reset," *Journal of Derivatives* 5 (1997), 99–106.

50. B. Goldman, H. Sosin, and M. Gatto, "Path Dependent Options: Buy at the Low, Sell at the High," *Journal of Finance* 34 (1979), 1111–1127.

51. M. Rubinstein and E. Reiner, "Breaking Down the Barriers," *Risk* (September 1991), 31–35.

52. J. Cox, S. Ross, and M. Rubinstein, "Option Pricing: A Simplified Approach," *Journal of Financial Economics* 7 (1979), 229–264; R. Rendleman Jr. and B. Bartter, "Two-State Option Pricing," *Journal of Finance* 34 (1979), 1093–1110.

53. P. Boyle, J. Evnine, and S. Gibbs, "Numerical Evaluation of Multivariate Contingent Claims," *Review of Financial Studies* 2 (1989), 241–250.

54. P. Boyle, "A Lattice Framework for Option Pricing with Two State Variables," *Journal of Financial and Quantitative Analysis* 23 (1988), 1–12.

55. E. Schwartz, "The Valuation of Warrants: Implementing a New Approach," *Journal of Financial Economics* 4 (1977), 79–93; M. Brennen and E. Schwartz, "The Valuation of American Put Options," *Journal of Finance* 32 (1977), 449–462.

56. P. Boyle, "Options: A Monte Carlo Approach," *Journal of Financial Economics* 4 (1977), 323–338.

57. R. Geske and H. Johnson, "The American Put Valued Analytically," *Journal of Finance* 39 (1984), 1511–1524.

58. G. Barone-Adesi and R. Whaley, "Efficient Analytic Approximation of American Option Values," *Journal of Finance* 42 (1987), 301–320.

59. L. MacMillan, "Analytic Approximation for the American Put Option," *Advances in Futures and Options Research* 1 (1986), 119–139.

60. R. Merton, "Theory of Rational Option Pricing," *Bell Journal of Economics and Management Science* 4/1 (1973), 141–183.

61. J. Cox and S. Ross, "The Valuation of Options for Alternative Stochastic Processes," *Journal of Financial Economics* 3 (1976), 145–166.

62. E. Derman and I. Kani, "Riding on the Smile," *Risk* (July 1994), 32–39; D. Dupire, "Pricing with a Smile," *Risk* (July 1994), 18–20; M. Rubinstein and E. Reiner, "Implied Binomial Trees," *Journal of Finance* 49 (1994), 771–818.

63. R. C. Merton, "Option Pricing when Underlying Stock Returns are Discontinuous," *Journal of Financial Economics* 3 (1976), 125–143.

64. J. Hull and A. White, "The Pricing of Options and Assets with Stochastic Volatilities," *Journal of Finance* 42 (1987), 281–300.

65. L. Scott, "Option Pricing when the Variance Changes Randomly: Theory Estimation, and an Application," *Journal of Financial and Quantitative Analysis* 22 (1987), 419–438; J. Wiggins, "Option Values Under Stochastic Volatility: Theory and Empirical Estimates," *Journal of Financial Economics* 19 (1987), 351–372.

66. D. Bates, "Jumps and Stochastic Volatility: Exchange Rate Processes Implicit in PHLX Deutschemark Options," *Review of Financial Studies* 9 (1996), 69–108.

67. Alan Greenspan, "Measuring Financial Risk in the Twenty-First Century," remarks before a conference sponsored by the Office of the Comptroller of the Currency, Washington, D.C., October 14, 1999.

68. Bank for International Settlement (BIS), Basel Committee on Banking Supervision, *International Convergence of Capital Measurement and Capital Standards*, Basel, Switzerland: Bank for International Settlement, July 1988.

69. See U.S. General Accounting Office, *Long-Term Capital Management, Regulators Need to Focus Greater Attention on Systemic Risk*, Washington, DC: General Accounting Office, October 1999.

70. See the analysis and recommendations in Commodity Futures Trading Commission (CFTC), Hedge Funds, Leverage, and the Lessons of Long-Term Capital Management: Report of the President's Working Group on Financial Markets, Washington, DC: Commodity Futures Trading Commission, April 1999, www.cftc.gov/tm/hedgefundreport.html, accessed May 19, 2000.

71. *Financial Times*, "Greenspan Hits Out at Way Banks Treat Risk" (October 12, 1999), 10.

72. The Basel Committee's members are representatives of the central banks and local regulatory organizations of the Group of Ten (G-10) countries: Belgium, Canada, France, Germany, Italy, Japan, the Netherlands, Sweden, the United Kingdom, and the United States, plus Luxembourg and

Switzerland. The committee meets four times a year, usually in Basel, Switzerland, under the chairmanship of the Bank for International Settlement, where the permanent secretariat of the committee is located.

73. Bank for International Settlement (BIS), Basel Committee on Banking Supervision, *International Convergence of Capital Measurement and Capital Standards,* Basel, Switzerland: Bank for International Settlement, July 1988.

74. Bank for International Settlement (BIS), Basel Committee on Banking Supervision, *Prudential Supervision of Banks' Derivatives Activities,* Basel, Switzerland: Bank for International Settlement, December 1994; *Amendment to the Capital Accord of July 1988,* Basel, Switzerland: Bank for International Settlement, July 1994; *Basel Capital Accord: The Treatment of the Credit Risk Associated with Certain Off-Balance-Sheet Items,* Basel, Switzerland: Bank for International Settlement, July 1994.

75. The U.S. banking industry regulators consist of the Federal Reserve Board, the Office of the Comptroller of the Currency, and the Federal Deposit Insurance Corporation.

76. The Basel Committee has extended the add-ons on equities, precious metals, and commodities contracts and increased the add-ons in general for longer maturities. See Bank for International Settlement (BIS), Basel Committee on Banking Supervision, *Treatment of Potential Exposure for Off-Balance-Sheet Items,* Basel, Switzerland: Bank for International Settlement, April 1995. See as well the discussion of the Basel Committee's 1994 and 1995 modifications in Section 2.8. See also the regulations issued in Bank for International Settlement (BIS), Basel Committee on Banking Supervision, *Interpretation of the Capital Accord for the Multilateral Netting of Forward Value Foreign Exchange Transactions,* Basel, Switzerland: Bank for International Settlement, April 1996; and *Survey of Disclosures About Trading and Derivatives Activities of Banks and Securities Firms: Joint Report by the Basel Committee on Banking Supervision and the Technical Committee of the International Organisation of Securities Commission,* Basel, Switzerland: Bank for International Settlement, November 1996.

77. Bank for International Settlement (BIS), Basel Committee on Banking Supervision, *Amendment to the Capital Accord to Incorporate Market Risks,* Basel, Switzerland: Bank for International Settlement, January 1996, modified in September 1997.

78. Ibid.

79. Committee members who are also members of the European Union regard this definition as being consistent with (albeit less detailed than) the definition of the trading book in the EU's Capital Adequacy Directive.

80. Bank for International Settlement (BIS), Basel Committee on Banking Supervision, *Amendment to the Capital Accord to Incorporate Market Risks,* Basel, Switzerland: Bank for International Settlement, January 1996, modified September 1997.

81. Ibid., para. II.a.

82. Bank for International Settlement (BIS), Basel Committee on Banking Supervision, *The New Basel Capital Accord: Consultative Document, Issued for*

Comment by 31 May 2001, Basel, Switzerland: Bank for International Settlement, January 2001, part 2I, para. 20.

83. Bank for International Settlement (BIS), Basel Committee on Banking Supervision, *Amendment to the Capital Accord to Incorporate Market Risks,* Basel, Switzerland: Bank for International Settlement, January 1996, modified September 1997, para. 7.

84. Switzerland Federal Banking Commission, "Guidelines Governing Capital Adequacy Requirements to Support Market Risks," EG-FBC Circular No. 97/1, October 22, 1997.

85. See comments in Reto R. Gallati, "De-Minimis-Regel diskriminiert," *Schweizer Bank* (Zurich), 9 (1998), 41–43.

86. See definition of specific risk in Bank for International Settlement (BIS), Basel Committee on Banking Supervision, *Amendment to the Capital Accord to Incorporate Market Risks,* Basel, Switzerland: Bank for International Settlement, January 1996, modified September 1997, para. I.b, footnote 5.

87. See Bank for International Settlement (BIS), Basel Committee on Banking Supervision, *International Convergence of Capital Measurement and Capital Standards,* Basel, Switzerland: Bank for International Settlement, July 1988.

88. Traded mortgage securities and mortgage derivative products possess unique characteristics because of the risk of prepayment. Accordingly, for the time being, no common treatment applies to these securities, which are dealt with at national discretion. A security that is the subject of a repurchase or securities-lending agreement will be treated as if it were still owned by the lender of the security—i.e., it will be treated in the same manner as other securities positions.

89. This includes the delta-equivalent value of options. The delta equivalent of the legs arising out of the treatment of caps and floors can also be offset against each other under the rules laid down in this paragraph.

90. The separate legs of different swaps may also be matched, subject to the same conditions.

91. Where equities are part of a forward contract, a future, or an option (quantity of equities to be received or to be delivered), any interest rate or foreign currency exposure from the other leg of the contract should be reported.

92. For example, an equity swap, in which a bank receives an amount based on the change in value of one particular equity or stock index, and pays on a different index will be treated as a long position in the former and a short position in the latter. Where one of the legs involves receiving or paying a fixed or floating interest rate, that exposure should be slotted into the appropriate repricing time band for interest-rate-related instruments. The stock index should be covered by the equity treatment.

93. Bank for International Settlement (BIS), Basel Committee on Banking Supervision, *Amendment to the Capital Accord to Incorporate Market Risks,* Basel, Switzerland: Bank for International Settlement, January 1996, modified September 1997, sec. 5.3.1, para. 130.

94. Ibid., sec. 5.3.2.b, para. 96.

95. Bank for International Settlement (BIS), Basel Committee on Banking Supervision, *Proposal to Issue a Supplement to the Basel Capital Accord to Cover Market Risks,* Basel, Switzerland: Bank for International Settlement, April 1995; *An Internal Model–Based Approach to Market Risk Capital Requirements,* Basel, Switzerland: Bank for International Settlement, 1995.

96. Alan Greenspan, "Risk Management in the Global Financial System—Before the Annual Financial Markets Conference of the Federal Reserve Bank of Atlanta," Miami Beach, Florida, February 27, 1998.

97. Bank for International Settlement (BIS), Basel Committee on Banking Supervision, *Supervisory Framework for the Use of "Backtesting" in Conjunction with the Internal Models Approach to Market Risk Capital Requirements,* Basel, Switzerland: Bank for International Settlement, January 1996.

98. P. Kupiec and J. O'Brien, "A Pre-Commitment Approach to Capital Requirements for Market Risk," FEDS Working Paper no. 95-34, Washington, DC: Federal Reserve Board of Governors, 1995.

99. A typical management response is to cut positions as losses accumulate. This pattern of trading can be compared to portfolio insurance, which attempts to replicate a put option. Therefore, attempts by management to control losses will create a pattern of payoffs over long horizons that will be asymmetrical, similar to options. The problem is that traditional VaR measures are inadequate with highly nonlinear payoffs.

100. Bank for International Settlement (BIS), Basel Committee on Banking Supervision, *The New Basel Capital Accord: Consultative Document, Issued for Comment by 31 May 2001,* Basel, Switzerland: Bank for International Settlement, January 2001, 6ff.; *Amendment to the Capital Accord to Incorporate Market Risks,* Basel, Switzerland: Bank for International Settlement, January 1996, modified September 1997.

101. E. Dimson and R. Marsh, "Capital Requirements for Securities Firms," *Journal of Finance* 50 (1995), 821–851.

102. Misconceptions of models are that they are conceptually built for "normal conditions". See comments from Tim Shepheard-Walwyn and Robert Litterman, "Building a Coherent Risk Measurement and Capital Optimization Model for Financial Firms," paper presented at the Conference on Financial Services at the Crossroads: Capital Regulation in the 21st Century, New York, February 26–27, 1998, *FRBNY Economic Policy Review* (October 1998), 173ff. and Section 5.8 of this book, which discusses misconceptions of models.

103. See Securities and Exchange Commission Item 305 of Regulation S-K and Item 9A of Form 20-F.

104. For a description of the required qualitative market risk disclosures, see Securities and Exchange Commission Item 305(b) of Regulation S-K and Item 9A(b) of Form 20-F.

105. Bank for International Settlement (BIS), Basel Committee on Banking Supervision, *The New Basel Capital Accord: Consultative Document, Issued for*

Comment by 31 May 2001, Basel, Switzerland: Bank for International Settlement, January 2001, paras. 74, 655ff.

106. A market-neutral risk arbitrage book would consist of a series of long and short positions; this hedges out market risk but leaves exposure to firm-specific risk. A trading strategy that eliminates broad market risk (equity, interest rate, foreign exchange, or commodity) leaves only residual risk. For example, a hedge fund manager can hedge the market risk of a U.S. stock portfolio by shorting S&P 500 Stock Index futures, leaving only firm-specific residual risk.

CHAPTER 3

Credit Risk

3.1 BACKGROUND

Over the past decade, a number of the world's largest banks and research and academic institutions have developed sophisticated systems that model the credit risk arising from important aspects of their businesses. Such systems have been designed for identifying, quantifying, aggregating, and managing credit risk exposures. The output and analysis of these systems have become increasingly important in risk management, performance measurement (including performance-oriented compensation), and customer profitability analysis, as well as in forming the base for decisions in credit portfolio management and for equity-capital allocation by the institution.

These systems and models are used for internal purposes by those who manage credit risks, and they also have the potential to be used in the supervisory oversight of the entire organization. The authorization of the modeling approach to be used in the formal process of setting regulatory capital requirements for credit risks depends on several conditions. Regulators have to be confident that the models are used to actively manage risk, that the models are conceptually sound and empirically validated, and that the procedures for capital requirements are adequate and comparable across institutions. The major concerns are data integrity and availability and validation of the conceptual model.

The following paragraphs discuss the different approaches to credit risk management, including how economic and regulatory conditions and assumptions are congruent. The increase of structured products that have simultaneous credit risk and market risk components has to be taken into account when designing such models.

3.2 DEFINITION

This work uses the definition of *credit risk* contained in a 1996 report of the Bank for International Settlement (BIS):[1]

> Credit risk/exposure: the risk that a counterparty will not settle an obligation for full value, either when due or at any time thereafter. In exchange-for-value systems, the risk is generally defined to include replacement risk and principal risk.

This work also uses a consistent definition of *loan:*[2]

> A "loan" is a financial asset resulting from the delivery of cash or other assets by a lender to a borrower in return for an obligation to repay on a specified date or dates, or on demand, usually with interest.

Loans include the following:

- Consumer installments, overdrafts and credit card loans
- Residential mortgages
- Nonpersonal loans, such as commercial mortgages, project finance loans, and loans to businesses, financial institutions, governments, and their agencies
- Direct financing leases
- Other financing arrangements that are, in substance, loans

Loan *impairment* represents deterioration in the credit quality of one or more loans such that it is probable that the bank will be unable to collect, or there is no longer reasonable assurance that the bank will be able to collect, all amounts due according to the contractual terms of the loan agreements.[3]

3.3 CURRENT CREDIT RISK REGULATIONS

Current credit risk regulations are based on the 1988 BIS guidelines. These minimum requirements have been subsequently enforced and implemented by local regulators at the national level by more than 100 nations, and they include minimum standards for capital adequacy for credit risks and the definition of the countable equity capital. Since 1988 the regulations have been modified five times, primarily during the transitional period of 1988 to 1992.[4] In 1989 the regulations were materially modified by substantially differentiating capital requirements for balance and off-balance positions, and by extending the incorporation of subordinated loans to the equity calculation. Based on the BIS guidelines, the calculation approach was switched to the indirect capital requirement calculation method in 1994. Balance sheet positions are first weighted according to their relative counterparty risk and then multiplied by the standard capital requirement of 8 percent. The basic problem with this approach is that securitization and other forms of capital arbitrage allow banks to achieve effective capital requirements well below the nominal 8 percent Basel standard.

The regulatory risk weights do not reflect certain risks, such as interest-rate and operating risks. More important, they ignore critical differences in credit risk among financial instruments (for example, all commercial credits incur a 100 percent risk weight), as well as differences across banks in hedging, portfolio diversification, and the quality of risk management systems. These anomalies create opportunities for "regulatory capital arbitrage" that render the formal risk-based capital ratios increasingly less meaningful for the largest, most sophisticated banks. Through securitization and other financial innovations, many large banks have lowered their risk-based capital requirements substantially without reducing materially their overall credit risk exposures. More recently, the September 1997 Market Risk Amendment to the Basel Accord created additional arbitrage opportunities by affording certain credit risk positions much lower risk-based capital requirements when held in the trading account rather than in the banking book.

Despite several substantial modifications, the current framework for capital requirements does not reflect the fact that market and risk management have evolved over the past 10 years (see Figure 3-1). The BIS has published a consultative paper on reform of its 1998 capital accord.[5]

3.4 DEFICIENCIES OF THE CURRENT REGULATIONS

The fundamental concept of the capital accord is relatively simple—it assumes that for all banks, independent of their size, business activity, and level of development of risk management, only one standardized approach exists, which contains several defects. The original accord focused mainly on credit risk; it has since been amended to address market risk. Interest-rate risk in the banking book and other risks, such as operational, liquidity, legal, and reputational risks, are not explicitly addressed:

- The risk weightings for counterparties are not differentiated in detail and thus do not represent the risk in an adequate and sensitive form.
- Correlations between the positions in a credit portfolio are not considered. A risk reducing diversification from a portfolio management approach is not rewarded with lower capital requirements. An individual credit position of $50 million is treated in the same way as a portfolio of five different credits of $10 million each.
- The current regulations do not consider hedging of credit risk positions with credit derivatives. Offsetting positions that economically net out each have to be supported with capital.

FIGURE 3-1

Trend of Risk Management Sophistication and Capital Adequacy Regulation.

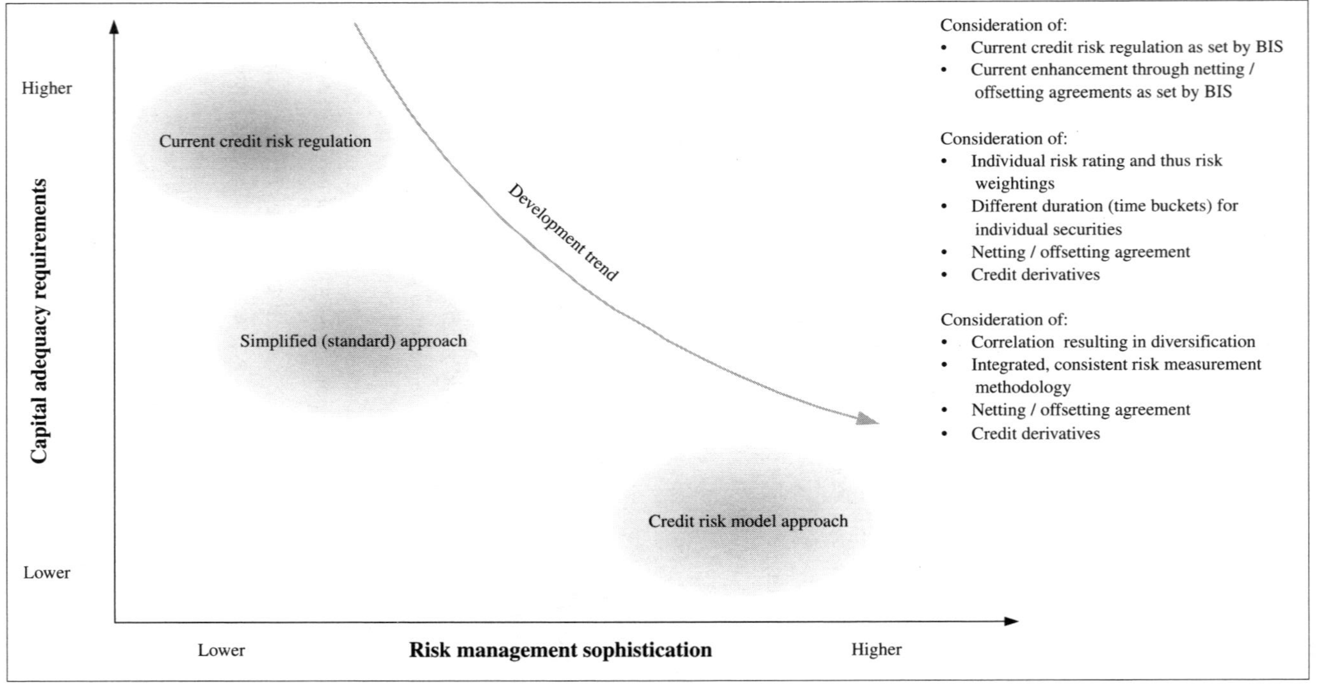

- Convergence from capital markets to commercial lending drive risk analytics, e.g., credit securitization, credit derivatives, and option-pricing models.

The following factors challenge credit risk management and must be included in the discussion to develop a useful credit risk methodology:

- The current practice does not distinguish between transaction and portfolio approaches. These approaches represent different levels in the credit process and must be integrated together.
- Commercial loans are often complex heterogeneous contracts with a number of complicated embedded options and other structural elements.
- Measuring risk-adjusted profitability is difficult due to a lack of good understanding of "true" operating and economic capital costs.
- Due to limited loan trading, a market view of loan value is hard to come by, making it cumbersome to compare value between loans and other traded asset classes.

3.5 DEFICIENCIES OF CURRENT CONCEPTUAL APPROACHES FOR MODELING CREDIT RISK

The existing credit risk models use a conceptual setup similar to that for the measurement of market risks. Most market risk models have evolved from a mean-variance approach and developed further, as the profit-and-loss (P&L) distribution did not fit the assumptions of the models. For market risks, a variety of different approaches are used to calculate P&L distributions: the RiskMetrics approach, historical simulation, and Monte Carlo simulation. Delta-gamma methods have been developed to identify and adjust distributions for the nonlinear component of risk.[6] The regulatory requirements can be better covered with an insurance or actuarial approach, which uses econometric methods such as autoregressive conditional heteroskedasticity (ARCH) and generalized ARCH (GARCH) and scenario analysis and historical databases reaching back a long time to analyze and calculate these extreme events.

The existing commercial credit risk models are based on the concept of covering losses with adequate pricing and provisions. This is basically a cost approach applied to a portfolio of credit positions, whereas the regulatory approach is more of a loss approach implemented to identify and measure individual extreme events and to calculate the loss from such events.

To calculate the default probability, the ratings for the borrowers' positions are needed. Data availability and data integrity generally dictate the methods used to estimate expected default frequency (EDF)/transition matrices. At most banks, internal credit ratings are a key variable—or in some cases the sole criterion—for assigning borrowers to risk segments. This is especially true with large corporate credit customers. Most banks have stored historical aggregate performance data by broad loan types or lines of business, but not by risk grade. Furthermore, such databases generally go back only a few years, at best.

Since banks typically have comparatively little useful internal default and migration data, they often attempt to estimate EDF/transition matrices using historical performance studies published by the rating agencies, such as Standard & Poor's, Moody's or Duff & Phelps. Such historical data often reports historical default, loss, and rating migration experience by rating category, covering time spans of 20 or more years. However, in some cases, the geographical and industry composition of this published data may not be appropriate to the characteristics of the loan portfolio being modeled. For example, published rating agency data is often dominated by U.S. experience and based on U.S. accounting practices. Using inappropriate transition matrices will result in misleading assessments of credit risk.[7] External rating information is sometimes adjusted based on judgment to incorporate internal information on the borrower's creditability. To use an experience database for credits, a bank must first develop or assume some economic and econometric relations between the internal rating categories and the grading systems applied by the rating agencies. Such correspondences are commonly developed using four basic approaches, either individually or in combination:

- The first approach involves matching historical default frequencies within each internal rating grade to the default frequencies by the agency's rating category.
- The second approach compares a bank's own internal grades with those of the rating agencies for borrowers that are rated by both. Such comparisons may not be possible for major segments of the portfolio (middle-market customers, non-U.S. business firms).
- The third method attempts to expand the population of firms for which such comparisons are possible by constructing pseudo–credit agency ratings for firms not formally rated by the agencies. This is accomplished by estimating the relationship between agency ratings and financial and other characteristics of firms using publicly available data for agency-rated firms.
- The fourth approach involves subjective comparison of the bank's rating criteria for assigning internal grades with the rating agencies' published rating criteria.

Unlike the market risk approach, backtesting is not yet seriously applicable. The methodology applied to backtesting market risk value-at-risk (VaR) models is not easily transferable to credit risk models due to the data constraints. The market risk amendment requires a minimum of 250 trading days of forecasts and realized losses. A similar standard for credit risk models would require an impractical number of years of data, given the models' longer time horizons. Given the limited availability of data for out-of-sample testing, backtesting estimates of unexpected credit loss is certain to be problematic in practice, as previously mentioned. Where analyses of ex-ante estimates and ex-post experience are made, banks typically compare the historical time series of estimated credit risk losses to historical series of current credit losses captured over some years. However, the comparison of expected and actual credit losses does not address the accuracy of the model's forecasting ability of unexpected losses, against which economic capital is allocated. While such independent work on backtesting is limited, some literature indicates the difficulty of ensuring that capital requirements generated using credit risk models will provide an adequately large capital buffer.[8]

However, the assumption underlying these approaches is that prevailing market perceptions of credit spreads (for rate-of-return analysis) are substantially accurate and economically well founded. If this is not so, reliance on such techniques raises questions as to the comparability and consistency of credit risk models, an issue which may be of particular importance to supervisors.[9]

3.6 CONCEPTUAL APPROACHES FOR MODELING CREDIT RISK

The design of the credit risk management structure and culture varies from bank to bank. While some banks have implemented systems and structures that measure and monitor credit risk exposures throughout the organization, other institutions have structures that monitor credit risk exposures within given business lines or legal entities. In addition, some banks have separate models for corporate and retail clients.

The internal applications of model output also span a wide range, from the simple to the complex. The trend is increasing, but a few organizations still use the output for active credit portfolio management. The current applications include setting concentration and limit exposures, risk-based pricing, evaluation of the risk-return profile of business lines or portfolio managers using risk-adjusted return on capital (RAROC), and calculation of economic capital calculation for the different business lines. Institutions also rely on model estimates for setting or validating loan loss reserves, either for direct calculations or for validation purposes.

These models have some factors, conditions, and assumptions in common which must be analyzed in more detailed. When possible, it is best to bring all these factors and parameters to their highest common denominator.

The most critical factors of the different *conceptual approaches* to credit risk modeling are the following:

- Probability density function of credit loss
- Expected and unexpected credit loss
- Time horizon
- Default mode
- Conditional versus unconditional models
- Approaches to credit risk aggregation
- Correlations between credit events.

There are five main factors contributing to the *level of credit risk losses* with credit risk models:

- Changes in loss rate given defaults
- Rating migrations
- Correlations among default and rating transitions
- Changes in credit spreads
- Changes in exposure levels

3.6.1 Transaction and Portfolio Management

Transaction and portfolio management serve complementary objectives:

- *Transaction management* pursues value creation.
- *Portfolio management* pursues value preservation.

Transaction management is based on individual transaction optimization and added value through the use of appropriate risk and pricing models, methods for structuring loan instruments, and the like for individual positions. Relationships to other segments and markets are not included in this view. The portfolio management approach considers all factors (such as correlations, volatilities, etc.) for a portfolio in order to optimize and preserve the existing risk-return level in a portfolio.

Depending on the credit risk management setup, different activities (such as securitization, credit derivatives, syndicated loans, etc.) are possible with the given infrastructure and management know-how. Figure 3-2 gives an overview of the impact of the loan structure on credit risk management decisions.

Depending on the credit risk management type, the focus is on different objectives. At the transaction level, the focus is on:

- Measuring credit risk using risk ratings and default and loss probability calculations

FIGURE 3-2

Impact of Loan Structure on Credit Risk Management Approach.

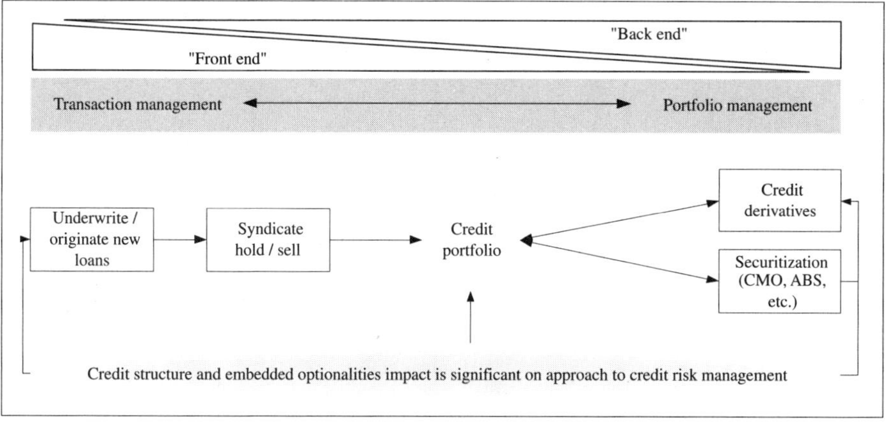

- Developing and using migration models
- Integrating risk ratings into the credit process.

The key input elements are *risk ratings*. Risk-rating methodology is developed with three objectives in mind:

- Measure credit risk (default and loss probability or potential) using good discrimination, separation, and accuracy across the full spectrum of credit risk.
- Provide management with accurate and meaningful information for decision making.
- Produce supportable and accurate information for regulatory and financial statement reporting purposes.

3.6.1.1 Primary Approaches to Risk Rating

Table 3-1 gives an overview of the primary approaches.

3.6.1.2 Migration Models

Migration models can help to calibrate the risk rating and the predicted losses by *default* frequency and amount of loss. The objectives are as follows:

- Adjust the internal rating process to external rating systems.
- Support provisioning requirements.
- Determine the risk cost by rating.
- Support risk-based pricing.

TABLE 3-1

Overview of Primary Approaches to Risk Rating

Technique	Description	Disadvantages	Advantages	Examples
Judgmental approach/ expert systems	Relationship managers and/or credit officers assign ratings based on financial ratios, opinions on management quality, and other data collected in due diligence review; expert system codifies rules of successful loan officers.	Subjective; ratings affected by fads or politics; vulnerable to relativity and anchoring; no numerical estimates of risk term structures except by reference to past experience.	In-place common, historical track record may be available; allows for nonquantitative factors; promotes identification of risk factors.	Most bank systems
Discriminant analysis	Classifies companies or facilities into several categories based on financial ratios measuring leverage, debt-service coverage, volatility; uses historical default data to calibrate model.	Oriented to the history; often calibrated over an arbitrary period; usually no term structure; prone to overfitting.	Simple to apply to all borrowers, allows testing of many variables and functional forms.	Altman's Z score
Contingent claims (options model)	Capital owners hold a default option, which they exercise when advantageous; associated with migration model; predicts cumulative default probabilities as a function of market leverage, term, and volatility.	Oriented to the future; parsimonious; determines default term structure; measures sensitivity to changing business conditions.	Hard to apply and probably less reliable for private firms; unbundling of volatility of structured and securitized products to identify risk factors.	KMV's CreditMonitor

FIGURE 3-3

Average Loss Rate Approach for Measuring Rating Transitions.

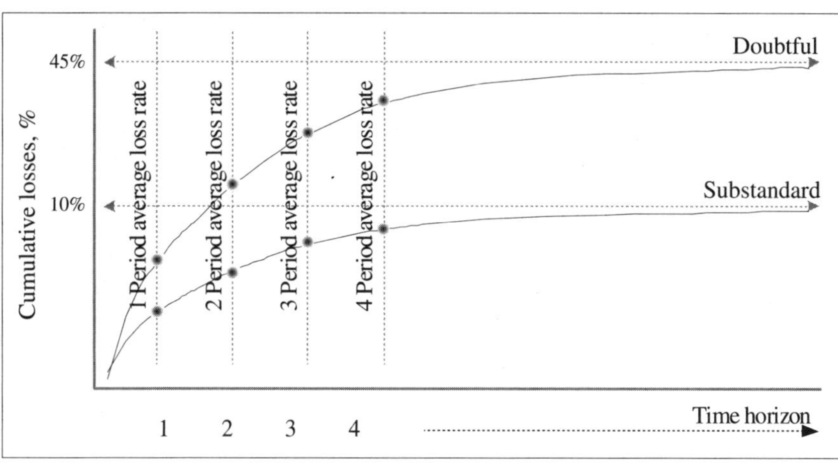

The *average loss rate model* measures *transactional losses* by risk rating. The cumulative loss over several periods is calculated on the basis of individual positions allocated to credit development curves, which are based on average loss rates based on historical experience. Figure 3-3 shows the development curves for two positions.

Applying a Markov approach, the model measures rating transitions through various *"credit" stages* (see Figure 3-4). The true Markov process probabilities are based on the following assumptions:

FIGURE 3-4

Markov Process for Measuring Rating Transitions.

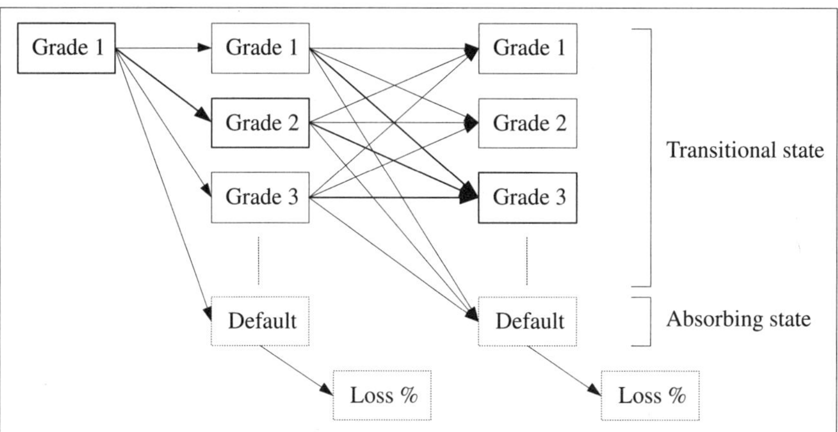

- The model is independent of its prior grade history.
- The model is constant over time.
- The probabilities are the same for all credits in a given category regardless of the specific credit characteristics.
- The probabilities are independent of the movements of other credits.

The results from the Markov process have to be mapped against standard ratings (e.g., from S&P) to review and calibrate the internal process to external rating information (see Figure 3-5).

The EDF is an essential input for many analytical methodologies and models, including risk-based pricing, RAROC, and quantitative models (e.g., CreditMetrics). EDFs also allow financial institutions to test the alignment of their own grading systems across different business units and against third-party data. (See comments on EDF in Section 3.7.3.2.)

3.6.2 Measuring Transaction Risk–Adjusted Profitability

The current performance measurement approaches use two different methodologies: RAROC and net present value (NPV). Performance measurement comes in many variations. The statements in Table 3-2

FIGURE 3-5

Mapping of the Markov Process to External Rating Information.

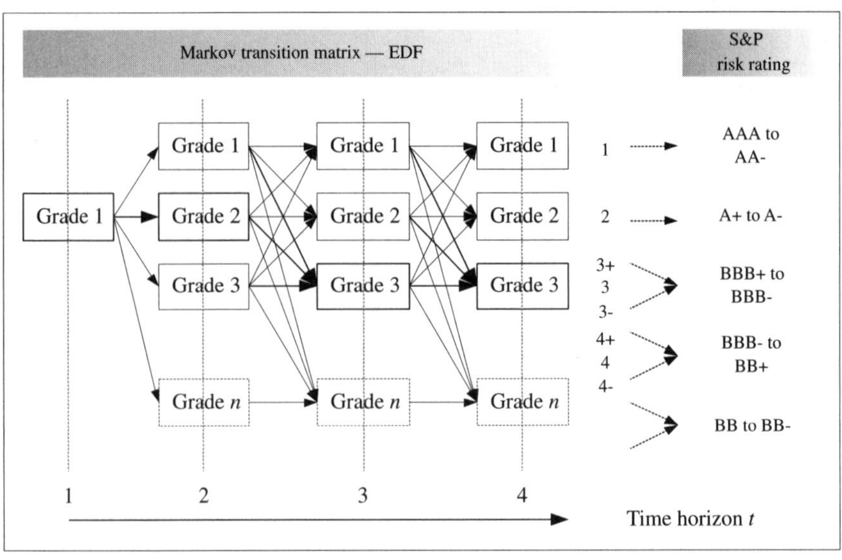

TABLE 3-2

Comparison of Current Performance Measurement Approaches

NPV	RAROC
Can treat credit risk as dynamic	Tends to take a static view of credit risk
Can value embedded optionalities and credit structure	Typically does not consider credit structure and optionalities
Can calibrate to the market or to an internal risk premium	Tends to be policy driven and accounting oriented
Can consider credit risk migrations in multistate framework	Tends to be two-state

refer to the way in which most transaction-level RAROC models are implemented.

3.7 MEASURING CREDIT RISK FOR CREDIT PORTFOLIOS

Credit portfolio management requires the following:

- Rich data and informational resources
- A structure that spans multiple organizations and functions
- A consistent organizational vision that promotes concerted action steps

To calculate a portfolio VaR, multiple input information is required:

- Ratings transition probabilities
- Correlations across borrowers
- Information on the pricing and structure of each loan position and contract:

  Loan type (revolving versus term)

  Amortization

  Collateral

  Spread and fees

  Tenor

  Options (e.g., prepayment,
  repricing or grid, and term-out)

In general, a portfolio model and a transaction model must be integrated in order to deliver useful output information.

3.7.1 Economic Capital Allocation

3.7.1.1 Probability Density Function of Credit Losses

Sophisticated financial organizations use an analytical setup that relates the overall required economic capital of the institute to its credit activities. The required economic capital is linked to the portfolio's credit risk with the *probability density function* (*PDF*) *of credit losses*, a key result from the credit risk model.[10] An important element is the probability that credit losses will exceed a given amount, which is represented by the area under the density function to the right of the given limit (the upper limit covering expected credit losses). A portfolio with a higher risk of credit loss is one whose density under the function has a relatively long and fat tail (see Figure 3-6).

The *expected credit loss* is defined as the total amount of credit losses the bank would expect from its credit portfolio over a specific time horizon (leftmost vertical line in Figure 3-6). The expected loss is one of the costs of transacting business that gives rise to credit risk. For marketing and other reasons, financial institutes prefer to express the risk of the credit portfolio by the *unexpected credit loss*, i.e., the amount by which the actual losses exceed the expected loss. The unexpected loss is a measure of the uncertainty or variability of actual losses versus expected losses. The estimated economic capital needed to support the institution's credit portfolio activities is generally referred to as its *required economic capital* for credit risk. A cushion of economic capital is required for loss absorption,

FIGURE 3-6

Probability Density Function (PDF) of Credit Losses.

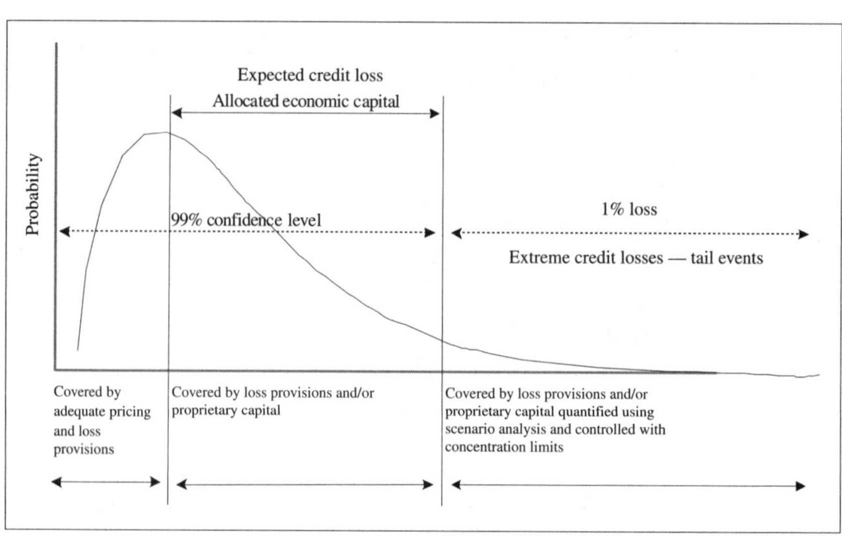

because the actual level of credit losses suffered in any one period could be significantly higher than the expected level. The procedure for calculating this amount is similar to the VaR methods used in allocating economic capital for market risks. The understanding is that economic capital for credit risk is determined in such a way that the estimated probability of unexpected credit loss exhausting economic capital is less than some target insolvency rate.

The capital allocation systems generally assume that it is the role of reserve funding to cover expected credit losses, while it is the role of economic capital to cover unexpected credit losses. The required economic capital represents the additional amount of capital necessary to achieve the target insolvency rate, over and above that needed for coverage of expected losses (the distance between the two lines in Figure 3-6).

3.7.1.2 Measuring Credit Loss

Loss in a credit portfolio is defined by three variables: the difference between the portfolio's *current value* and its *future value* at the end of a certain *time horizon*. Because many functions depend on the time dimension in one way or another, the time horizon is a key input variable for the definition of risk. There are basically two ways of selecting the time horizon over which credit risk is monitored:

- The first approach is the application of a *standardized time period* across all contracts (instruments). Most financial institutions adopt a one-year time horizon across all asset classes (not only credit instruments).
- The second is the *liquidation period* approach, in which each credit contract (instrument) is associated with a unique time period, coinciding with the instrument's maturity or with the time needed for liquidation. Some vendor systems allow specific time periods for asset classes or portfolios (for structured credit portfolios). The *hold-to-maturity* approach seems to be applicable if the exposures were intended to be held to maturity and/or liquid markets for trading these instruments are limited.

The factors influencing the fixing of the period are as follows:

- Availability or publication of default information
- Availability of borrower information
- Internal control rhythms and renewal processes
- Capital planning
- Account statement preparations; changes to the capital structure (capital increase or reduction).

3.7.1.3 Default-Mode Paradigm

The default-mode (DM) paradigm states that a credit loss occurs only if a borrower defaults on a repayment obligation within the planning horizon. As long as the default event does not become a fact, no credit loss would exist. In the event that the borrower defaults on obligations, the credit loss is calculated as the difference between the bank's credit exposure (the amount due to the bank at the moment of default) and the present value of future net recoveries (discounted cash flows from the borrower less workout expenses). The current and the future values of the credit are defined in the default-mode paradigm based on the underlying two-state (default versus nondefault) notion of the credit loss. The *current value* is typically calculated as the bank's credit exposure (e.g., book value). The *future value* of the loan is uncertain. It would depend on whether the borrower defaults during the defined time horizon. In the case of nondefault, the credit's future value is calculated as the bank's credit engagement at the end of the time horizon (adjusted so as to add back any principal payments made over the time horizon).

In the case of a default, the future value of the credit is calculated as the credit minus *loss rate given default* (LGD). The higher the recovery rate following default, the lower the LGD. Using a credit risk model, the current value of the credit instrument is assumed to be known, but the future value is uncertain. Applying a default-mode credit risk model for each individual credit contract (e.g., loan versus commitment versus counterparty risk), the financial institution must define or estimate the joint probability distribution between all credit contracts with respect to three types of random variables:

- The bank's associated credit exposure
- A binary zero/one indicator denoting whether the credit contract defaults during the defined time horizon
- In the event of default, the associated LGD

3.7.1.4 Mark-to-Market Paradigm

The mark-to-market (MTM) paradigm treats all credit contracts under the assumption that a credit loss can arise over time, deteriorating the asset's credit quality before the end of the planned time horizon. The mark-to-market paradigm treats all credit contracts as instruments of a portfolio being marked to market (or, more accurately, marked to model) at the beginning and end of the defined time horizon. The credit loss reflects the difference of the valuation at the beginning and at the end of the time horizon. This approach considers changes in the asset's creditworthiness, reflecting events that occur before the end of the time horizon. These models must incorporate the probabilities of credit rating migrations (through the rating transition matrix), reflecting the changes in creditworthiness.

For each credit position in the portfolio, migration paths have to be calculated, using the rating transition matrix and Monte Carlo simulation. For all positions, the simulated migration (including the risk premium associated with the contract's rating grade at the end of the rating period) is used to mark the position to market (or, more accurately, to model) as of the end of the time horizon. For the purpose of estimating the current and future values of the credit contracts, two approaches can be used:

- The discounted contractual cash flow (DCCF) approach
- The risk-neutral valuation (RNV) approach

3.7.1.5 Discounted Contractual Cash Flow Approach

The *discounted contractual cash flow* (DCCF) approach is commonly associated with J. P. Morgan's CreditMetrics methodology. The current value of a nondefaulted loan is calculated as the present discounted value of its future contractual cash flows. For a credit contract with an assigned risk rating (i.e., BBB), the credit spreads used for the calculation of the discounted cash flows of the credit contract equal the market-determined term structure of credit spreads corresponding to similar corporate bonds (maturity, coupon, sinking-fund provision, etc.) with that same rating. The current value is treated as known, because the future value of the credit depends on the (uncertain) end-of-period rating and the market-determined term structure of credit spreads associated with the specific rating. The future value of the credit is subject to changes in migration (creditworthiness) or in the credit spreads according to the market-determined term structure. In the event of default, the future value of a credit would be given by its recovery value, calculated as the credit minus loss rate given default (a similar approach to that used in the default-mode approach).

The DCCF approach is a practical approach, but it is not completely in line with modern finance theory. For all contracts with the same rating, the same discount rates are assigned. Thus, for all contracts not defaulted within the defined time horizon, the future value does not depend on the expected loss rate given default, as they are not defaulted. Modern finance theory holds that the value of an asset (borrower's asset) depends on the correlation of its return with that of the market. Borrowers in different market segments, exposed to different business cycles and other risk factors, will still be assigned to the same risk grade according to the DCCF approach.

3.7.1.6 Risk-Neutral Valuation Approach

To avoid the pitfalls of the discounted contractual cash flow approach, Robert Merton developed a structural approach imposing a model of firm value and bankruptcy.[11] A company defaults when the value of its underlying assets falls beneath the level required to serve its debt. The risk-neutral valuation (RNV) approach discounts contingent payments instead of discounting contractual payments. A credit can be considered as a set of derivative contracts on the underlying value of the borrower's assets. If a payment (interest rate, amortization, etc.) is contractually due at date *t*, the payment actually received by the lender will be the contractual amount only if the firm has not defaulted by date *t*. The lender receives a portion of the credit's face amount equal to the credit minus loss rate given default (an approach similar to that used in the default-mode method) if the borrower defaults at date *t*, and the lender receives nothing at date *t* if the borrower has defaulted prior to date *t*. The value of the credit equals the sum of the present values of these derivative contracts (each payment obligation at time *t* is regarded as an option). The difference from the discount rates used for the discounted contractual cash flow approach is that the discount rate applied to the contracts' contingent cash flows is determined using a risk-free term structure of interest rates and the risk-neutral pricing measure. Similar to the option-adjusted spread approach, the risk-neutral pricing measure can be regarded as an adjustment to the probabilities of borrower default at each horizon *t*, which incorporates the market risk premium associated with the borrower's default risk. The magnitude of the adjustment depends on the expected return and volatility of the borrower's asset value. Returns modeled consistently with the capital asset pricing model (CAPM) can be expressed in terms of the market expected return and the firm's correlation beta (β) with the market. This approach combines pricing of the credits with the respective credit losses:

- The expected default frequency and the loss rate given default by the borrower
- The correlation between the borrower's risk and the systematic (market) risk

This is consistent with modern finance theory.

The interpretation of default is key in understanding the risk-neutral valuation approach. A credit is considered to be in default once it migrates to a predefined limit. This worst-case scenario is not clearly defined; it varies according to the institution's risk appetite and risk capacity, thus affecting measures of default, migration, credit loss, and the probability density function.

3.7.2 Choice of Time Horizon

As mentioned earlier, most institutions use a one-year time horizon to measure their credit risk exposures. This has to do more with computational convenience and availability of information rather than with internal process and model optimization. The definition of default used in credit models is not congruent with that applied for legal purposes. The institution may consider a credit to be in default if the credit is classified as falling below an investment-grade rating, if cash flows are past due, if the credit is placed on a nonaccrual status, if recovery proceedings are initiated, and so forth.

The time horizon appears to be an important variable for the assessment of capacity of models to meet economic and regulatory needs.

The ability of a default-mode model to assess the effects of potentially unfavorable credit events due to the model's two-state nature (i.e., default/nondefault) may be particularly sensitive to the defined length of the time horizon.

3.7.3 Credit Loss Measurement Definition

3.7.3.1 DM Versus MTM Models

Both the default-mode (DM) and mark-to-market (MTM) approaches estimate the credit losses from adverse changes in credit quality. The quality of credit models is primarily influenced by the fit between the model output and the model application. The model choice should be made based on the circumstances of the use and application. An institution that uses a portfolio of liquid credits and exposure to credit spreads (i.e., the hedge transactions for credit portfolios using credit spreads between different term structures) may require a credit loss measurement definition that incorporates potential shifts in credit spreads and thus opt for the (more complicated) MTM model with the multistate nature.

3.7.3.2 DCCF Versus RNV Approaches

In practice, the difference between the approaches is smaller than in theory, because the credit value is priced as a discounted present value of its future cash flows in both approaches. The dichotomy is sharper in theory because the discount factors are calculated differently. The discounted contractual cash flow (DCCF) approach assumes a nonparametric approach to estimating these discount factors. The public debt issuers (issues) are grouped into rating categories, and the credit spreads on the issuers are then averaged within each rating "bucket." On the other hand, the risk-neutral valuation (RNV) approach is more complex. In a structural process, each credit is simultaneously modeled in an individual framework. This means that the modeling of the market risk premium for each credit in the RNV model is typically referenced to credit spreads from the debt market.

The empirical evidence of the econometric theory shows that highly structural estimators make efficient use of available data but are vulnerable to model misspecification. Nonparametric estimators make minimal use of modeling assumptions but underperform where data integrity is a problem. The two approaches will, in general, assign different credit losses to any given loan. Under normal market conditions (liquidity and information efficiency) and the stable assumptions of the RNV model, both approaches should deliver reasonable output for a well-diversified credit portfolio.

The probability that a particular credit contract will default during the time horizon is a critical input. The bank's credit staff has to assign internal credit risk ratings for all credit contracts. This is done for most corporate customers. The trend is that all customers, corporate or retail, are assigned risk ratings in order to obtain the overall risk profile of the credit portfolio, including the correlations between the different segments of the portfolio as they are exposed to different business cycles, macroeconomic factors, etc.

There are basically three approaches (which can be combined) for assigning a credit rating to a customer or the contract:

- The traditional approach, based on financial, accounting, and other characteristics of the customer. This approach is very subjective and is based on the reliability and availability of specific information.
- Credit-scoring models supplied by commercial vendors, which also deliver a database that reflects the best-practice standards in the market.
- Credit-scoring models developed internally, which reflect the structure and the processes of the credit department.

External ratings are frequently combined with internal rating categories, which allows combination of the internal credit authorization process and external rating data. The expected default frequency (EDF) can be interpreted as a credit's probability of migrating from its current internal rating grade to default within the credit model's time horizon. The likelihood of such a migration from its current risk rating category to another category is defined in the transition matrix, as illustrated in Table 3-3.

Given the contract's actual rating (defined by each row), the probability to migrate to another category (defined by the columns) is defined within the intersecting cell of the transition matrix. Thus, in Table 3-3, the likelihood of a credit contract rated A migrating to BBB within one year would be 7.4 percent. The likelihood of a credit contract rated CCC migrating to default within one year would be 18.6 percent.

3.7.3.3 Unconditional Versus Conditional Models

In a broad sense, all models are conditional, as they process input information on the credit quality of the borrower and the credit contracts. In a narrower sense, it is possible to distinguish between unconditional and conditional models. The unconditional models process information limited to the borrower and the credit contracts. The transition matrix and the correlations are modeled to capture the long-run values of these parameters. But such long-run averages may misrepresent the short-term condition, as correlations and default frequency tend to vary systematically

TABLE 3-3

Sample Credit Rating Transition Matrix: Probability of Migrating to Another Rating Within 1 Year

Initial Rating	Rating at Year End, %							
	AAA	AA	A	BBB	BB	B	CCC	Default
AAA	87.74	10.93	0.45	0.63	0.12	0.10	0.02	0.02
AA	0.84	88.23	7.47	2.16	1.11	0.13	0.05	0.02
A	0.27	1.59	89.05	7.40	1.48	0.13	0.06	0.03
BBB	1.84	1.89	5.00	84.21	6.51	0.32	0.16	0.07
BB	0.08	2.91	3.29	5.53	74.68	8.05	4.14	1.32
B	0.21	0.36	9.25	8.29	2.31	63.89	10.13	5.58
CCC	0.06	0.25	1.85	2.06	12.34	24.86	39.97	18.60

SOURCE: Greg M. Gupton, Christopher C. Finger, and Mickey Bhatia, *CreditMetrics Technical Document,* New York: Morgan Guaranty Trust Co., April 1997, 76.

with the course of the business cycle. The conditional models process information on the borrower and the credit contracts and, in addition, are linked to macroeconomic information such as gross domestic product, current levels and trends in domestic and international employment, inflation rates, indicators specific for particular sectors, etc.

CreditMetrics and CreditRisk are examples of unconditional risk models. They estimate the expected default frequency and correlations between historical default data and borrower- or contract-specific information, such as the rating. These models are based on data collected and estimated over many credit cycles to reflect the averages of these parameters. They should predict reasonable credit loss probabilities based on the transition matrix, if the credit portfolio is composed of similar credit contracts. This type of model has drawbacks; if the borrowers are upgraded or downgraded over time, their expected default rates will be revised downward or upward. Such a portfolio will not have a similar standard deviation over time and will be more complex to manage relative to given risk levels. The unconditional models are not able to incorporate macroeconomic parameters such as business cycle effects. The tendency for rating improvement or deterioration is positive during cyclical upturns or downturns, respectively.

The drawbacks of the unconditional models are avoided with the conditional models. Examples of conditional credit risk models include McKinsey and Company's CreditPortfolioView[12] and KMV's PortfolioManager.

Within its conceptual modeling, the transition matrices of CreditPortfolioView are related to the state of the economy, as the matrices of the covariance matrix are modified to give an increased likelihood of an upgrade (and decreased likelihood of a downgrade) during an upswing (or downswing) in a credit cycle. KMV's PortfolioManager links the process of estimating the asset values, rates of return, and volatility to current equity prices, which are information-efficient and incorporate all information available in the market. This approach is comparable to the arbitrage price theory (APT) and the multifactor models. Empirical research has generated empirical evidence. The drawbacks of these models are timing and parameterization. They might underestimate losses as the credit cycle enters a downturn and overestimate losses as the cycle bottoms out.

3.7.4 Risk Aggregation

Within most credit risk approaches, broadly similar conceptual approaches are implemented, modeling individual-level credit risk exposures for different type of positions. Most banks measure credit risk at the individual asset level for capital market and corporate instruments (*bottom-up approach*), while aggregate data is used for quantifying risk for different types of positions (*top-down approach*), including product lines such as consumer, credit card, or mortgage portfolios.

- *Bottom-up approaches* attempt to measure credit risk at the individual level of each facility based on an explicit evaluation of the creditworthiness of the portfolio's constituent debtors. Each specific position in the portfolio is linked with an individual risk rating, typically used as a proxy for the EDF or the probability of rating migration.[13] The data is then aggregated to the portfolio level, taking into account diversification effects based on the correlation matrix.
- *Top-down approaches* are used to cope with the sheer number of exposures. Typically, for retail positions, a top-down empirical approach is applied. The information for individual positions is allocated to specific factors and aggregated into buckets, such as credit scores, age, geographical location, collateralized exposures, and so forth. The credit risk is quantified at the level of these buckets. Facilities within each bucket are treated as statistically identical. In the process of estimating the distribution of credit losses, the model builder would attempt to model both the aggregate default rate and the LGD rate using historical time-series data for that risk segment (bucket) taken as a whole, rather than by arriving at this average through a joint consideration of default and migration risk factors for each specific facility in the pool.

The literature on credit risk models tends to make a distinction between these two approaches, whereas in practice the differences are less clear-cut. The differences in the implementation arise primarily in the ways the underlying parameters are estimated using the available data. The distinction between top-down and bottom-up approaches is not always precise. The key consideration is the degree to which a financial institution can distinguish meaningfully between borrower classes (buckets). Frequently, so-called bottom-up models rely on aggregate data to estimate individual borrower parameters. A practical example is the mapping of individual borrower ratings (a bottom-up approach) to a transition matrix calculated from pooled data, which is derived from published ratings by rating agencies or from internal statistics (an average of aggregate top-down data). The accuracy of aggregate data and the compatibility to the financial institution's actual credit portfolio influences the use of aggregate data and potentially distorts idiosyncratic loan-specific effects to which the financial institution is exposed.

3.8 DEVELOPMENT OF NEW APPROACHES TO CREDIT RISK MANAGEMENT

3.8.1 Background

Over the past few years, a revolution has been brewing in the way credit risk is both measured and managed. In contrast to the accounting-driven, relatively dull, and routine history of credit risk, new technologies and methodologies have emerged among a new generation of financial engineering professionals who are applying their engineering skills and analysis to this risk topic.

Why is this development happening now? The eight most obvious reasons for this sudden surge in interest are as follows:

- *Maturing market risk area.* Given the maturity of market risk models, the experience gained over the past decades, based on theoretical and academic research and practical experience which has relativized and improved the relevance of market risk modeling, the market risk area has evolved in a way that frees resources and welcomes new challenges, such as credit and operational risk.
- *Disintermediation of borrowers.* As capital markets have expanded and become accessible to small- and middle-market firms, borrowers left behind to raise funds from banks and other traditional financial institutions are increasingly likely to be smaller and have weaker credit ratings. Capital market growth has produced a "winner's curse" effect on the credit portfolio structure of traditional financial institutions.

- *Competitive margin structure.* Almost paradoxically, despite a decline in the average quality of loans (due to disintermediation), the respective margin spreads, especially in wholesale loan markets, have become very thin—that is, the risk–premium trade-off from lending has gotten worse. A number of reasons can be cited, but an important factor is the enhanced competition for lower-quality borrowers, such as from finance companies, much of whose lending activity is concentrated at the higher-risk, lower-quality end of the market.
- *Structural change in bankruptcies.* Although the most recent recessions hit at different times in different countries, most bankruptcy statistics showed a significant increase in bankruptcies, compared to the prior economic downsides. To the extent that there has been a permanent or structural increase in bankruptcies worldwide—possibly due to the increase in global competition and sectoral changes, such as the technology sector—accurate credit risk analysis becomes even more important today than in the past.
- *Diminishing and volatile values of collaterals.* Concurrent with the ongoing Asian crisis, banking crises in well-developed countries have shown that real estate values and precise asset values are very hard to predict and to realize through liquidation. The weaker the rating and the more uncertain collateral values are, the more risky lending is likely to be.
- *Exposures from off-balance-sheet derivatives.* The growth of credit exposure and counterparty risk, based on the phenomenal growth of the derivative markets, has extended the need for credit analysis beyond the loan book. In many of the largest banks, the notional (not market) value of the off-balance-sheet exposure to instruments such as over-the-counter (OTC) swaps and forwards exceeds more than 10 times the size of the loan portfolios. The growth in credit risk off the balance sheet was one of the reasons for the introduction of risk-based capital requirements in 1993.[14]
- *Capital requirements.* Under the BIS system, banks have to hold a capital requirement based on the marked-to-market current value of each OTC derivatives contract (so-called current exposure) plus an add-on for potential future exposure.
- *Technological advances.* Computer infrastructure developments and related advances in information technology—such as the development of historic information databases—have given banks and financial organizations the opportunity to test high-powered modeling techniques. In the case of credit risk

management, besides being able to analyze loan loss and value distribution functions and especially the tails distributions, the infrastructure enables the active management of loan portfolios, based on modern portfolio theory (MPT) models and techniques.[15]

3.8.2 BIS Risk-Based Capital Requirement Framework

Despite the importance of the reasons previously discussed, probably the greatest incentive and key impetus to the development of enhanced credit risk models has been dissatisfaction with the BIS and local regulators' imposition of capital requirements on loans. The current BIS regime has been described as a "one size fits all" policy; virtually all loans to private-sector counterparties are subjected to the same 8 percent capital ratio (or capital reserve requirement), not taking into account the different impacts of the size of the loan; the maturity of the loan; or, most important, the credit quality (rating) of the borrowing counterparty. Under current capital requirement terms, loans to a firm near bankruptcy are treated in the same fashion as loans to a AAA borrower or the government. Further, the current capital requirement is additive across all loans; there is no allowance for lower capital requirements because of a greater degree of diversification in the loan portfolio.

In 1997, the European Community was the first to give certain large banks the discretion to calculate capital requirements for their trading books—or market risk exposures—using *internal models* rather than the alternative regulatory (*standardized*) model. Internal models are subject to certain constraints imposed by regulators and are subjected to backtesting verification.[16] They potentially allow the following revisions:

- VaR of each tradable instrument to be more accurately measured (e.g., based on its price volatility, maturity, etc.)
- Correlations among assets (diversification effect) to be taken into account

In the context of market risk, VaR is defined as the predicted worst-case loss at a specific confidence level (e.g., 95 percent) over a certain period of time (e.g., 10 days). For example, under the BIS market risk regulations, when banks calculate their VaR-based capital requirements using their internal models, they are required to measure the worst-case day as the worst day that happens once every 100 business days. The current regulative framework is additive and does not consider diversification in the loan portfolio to allow lower capital requirements.

The critical questions for bankers and regulators developing a new framework are the following:

- Can an internal-model approach be used to measure the VaR or capital exposure of (nontradable) loans?
- Do internal models provide sufficient flexibility and accuracy to support the standardized 8 percent risk-based capital ratio that imposes the same capital requirement on virtually all private-sector loans?

Internal models require additional enhancements before they can replace the 8 percent rule, especially because of the nontradability of some types of loans compared to marketable instruments, and the lack of deep historic databases on loan defaults. However, the new internal models offer added value to financial organizations, regulators, and risk managers. Specifically, internal model approaches potentially offer better insight on how to value and manage outstanding loans and credit risk–exposed instruments such as bonds (corporate and emerging market), as well as better methods for estimating default risk probabilities regarding borrowers and derivative counterparties. Moreover, internal models have the following advantages:

- In many cases they allow a better estimation of the credit risk of portfolios of loans and credit risk–sensitive instruments.
- They enhance the pricing of new loans, in the context of a bank's RAROC, and of relatively new instruments in the credit derivatives markets (such as credit options, credit swaps, and credit forwards). The models provide an alternative opportunity to measure the optimal or economic amount of capital a bank should hold as part of its capital structure.

Before looking at some of these models and new approaches to credit risk measurement, a brief analysis of the more traditional approaches will heighten the contrast between the new and traditional approaches to credit risk measurement.

3.8.3 Traditional Credit Risk Measurement Approaches

3.8.3.1 Background

It is hard to draw a clear line between traditional and new approaches, as many of the superior concepts of the traditional models are used in the new models. For the purposes of this historical review, the traditional credit models are segregated into three types: expert systems, rating systems, and credit-scoring systems.[17]

3.8.3.2 Expert Systems

In an expert system, the credit decision is made by the local or branch credit officer. Implicitly, this person's expertise, skill set, subjective judgment, and weighting of certain key factors are the most important determinants in the decision to grant credit. The potential factors and expert systems a credit officer could look at are infinite. However, one of the most common expert systems, the "five Cs" of credit, will yield sufficient understanding. The expert analyzes these five key factors, subjectively weights them, and reaches a credit decision:

- *Capital structure.* The equity-to-debt ratio (leverage) is viewed as a good predictor of bankruptcy probability. High leverage suggests greater probability of bankruptcy than low leverage, as a low level of equity reduces the ability of the business to survive losses of income.
- *Capacity.* The ability to repay debts reflects the volatility of the borrower's earnings. If repayments on debt contracts proves to be a constant stream over time, but earnings are volatile (and thus have a high standard deviation), the probability is high that the firm's capacity to repay debt claims is at risk.
- *Collateral.* In the event of a default, a lender has a claim on the collateral pledged by the borrower. The greater the proportion of this claim and the greater the market value of the underlying collateral, the lower the remaining exposure risk of the loan in the case of a default.
- *Cycle/economic conditions.* An important factor in determining credit risk exposure is the state of the business cycle, especially for cycle-dependent industries. For example, the infrastructure sectors (such as the metal industries, construction, etc.) tend to be more cycle dependent than nondurable goods sectors, such as food, retail, and services. Similarly, industries that have exposure to international competitive conditions tend to be cycle sensitive. Taylor, in an analysis of Dun and Bradstreet bankruptcy data by industry (both means and standard deviations), found some quite dramatic differences in U.S. industry failure rates during the business cycle.[18]
- *Character.* This is a measure of the firm's reputation, its willingness to repay, and its credit history. In particular, it has been established empirically that the age factor of an organization is a good proxy for its repayment reputation.

Another factor, not covered by the five Cs, is the interest rate. It is well known from economic theory that the relationship between the interest-rate level and the expected return on a loan (loss probability) is highly nonlinear.[19] At low interest-rate levels, the expected return could increase if rates are raised. However, at high interest-rate levels, an increase in rates may lower the return on a loan, as the probability of loss increases.

This negative relationship between high loan rates and expected loan returns is due to two effects: (1) adverse selection and (2) risk shifting. When loan rates rise beyond some point, good borrowers drop out of the loan market, preferring to self-finance their investment projects or to seek equity capital funding (*adverse selection*). The remaining borrowers, who have limited liability and limited equity at stake—and thus lower ratings—have the incentive to shift into riskier projects (*risk shifting*). In upside economies and supporting conditions, they will be able to repay their debts to the bank. If economic conditions weaken, they will have limited downside loss from a borrower's perspective.

Although many financial institutions still use expert systems as part of their credit decision process, these systems face two main problems regarding the decision process:

- *Consistency.* What are the important common factors to analyze across different types of groups of borrowers?
- *Subjectivity.* What are the optimal weights to apply to the factors chosen?

In principle, the subjective weights applied to the five Cs derived by an expert can vary from borrower to borrower. This makes comparability of rankings and decisions across the loan portfolio very difficult for an individual attempting to monitor a personal decision and for other experts in general. As a result, quite different processes and standards can be applied within a financial organization to similar types of borrowers. It can be argued that the supervising committees or multilayered signature authorities are key mechanisms in avoiding consistency problems and subjectivity, but it is unclear how effectively they impose common standards in practice.[20]

3.8.3.3 Rating Systems

One of the oldest rating systems for loans was developed by the U.S. Office of the Comptroller of the Currency (OCC). The system has been used in the United States by regulators and bankers to assess the adequacy of their loan loss reserves. The OCC rating system allocates an existing loan into five rating buckets: four low-quality ratings and one high-quality rating. In Table 3-4, the required loss reserve appears next to each category.

Over the years, the financial institutions have extended and enhanced the OCC-based rating system by developing internal rating systems that more finely subdivide the pass/performing rating category.

The OCC pass grade is divided into six different categories (ratings 1 to 6). Ratings 7 to 10 correspond to the OCC's four low-quality loan ratings. These loan-rating systems do not exactly correspond with the bond-rating systems, especially at the lower-quality end of the spectrum (see Section 2.7.2.4 for a further discussion of bond-rating systems). One reason is the different focus of the approaches: loan-rating systems are sup-

TABLE 3-4

Example for Loss Reserves Based on Rating System

Rating Bucket	Loss Reserves, %
Low-quality ratings	
Other assets especially mentioned (OAEM)	0
Substandard assets	20
Doubtful assets	50
Loss assets	100
High-quality rating	
Pass/performing	0

NOTE: From a technical perspective, the 0 percent loss reserves for OAEM and pass loans are lower bounds. In practice, the reserve rates on these categories are determined by the bank in consultation with examiners and auditors, depending on some type of historical analysis of charge-off rates for the bank.

SOURCE: U.S. Office of the Comptroller of the Currency, EC-159 (rev.), December 10, 1979, www.occ.treas.gov/ftp/release.

posed to rate an individual loan (including its covenants and collateral backing). Bond-rating systems are more oriented toward rating the overall borrower. This gap of one-to-one mapping between bond and loan rating methodologies raises a flag as to the merits of those newer approaches that rely on bond data (spreads, transition matrices, etc.) to value and price loans individually and in a portfolio context.

Given this trend toward finer internal ratings of loans, compared to the OCC's regulatory model, the 1998 Federal Reserve System Task Force Report[21] and Mingo[22] give some tentative support for using an internal model ratings-based approach as an alternative to the OCC model, to calculate capital reserves against unexpected losses, and loan loss reserves against expected loan losses. For example, using the outstanding dollar value of loans in each internal rating class (1 to 10), a bank might calculate its capital requirement against unexpected loan losses as follows:

$$\text{Capital requirement} = \sum \begin{bmatrix} \text{total class 1 loans} \cdot 0.2\% \\ + \\ \vdots \\ + \\ \text{total class 10 loans} \cdot 100\% \end{bmatrix} \tag{3.1}$$

The 0.2 percent for rating class 1 is just suggestive of unexpected loss rates and should be based on historic loss probabilities of a loan in class 1 moving to class 10 (loss) over the next year.[23] However, an important problem remains, similar to the current 8 percent risk-based capital ratio of the BIS approach—the diversification in the loan portfolio is not considered. The credit risks of each rating class are simply added up to calculate a total capital requirement.

3.8.3.4 Credit-Scoring Systems

Credit-scoring approaches can be found in virtually all types of credit analysis. The basic concept is generally the same: certain key factors are preidentified. They determine the loss probability of default and the recovery rate (as opposed to repayment), and they are combined or weighted into a quantitative score schema. The score can be literally interpreted as a loss probability of default. In other scoring systems, the score can be regarded as a classification system: it allocates a potential or existing borrower into either a good group (higher rating) or a bad group (lower rating), based on a score and a cutoff point. Full reviews of the traditional approach to credit scoring, and the various methodologies, can be found in Caouette, Altman, and Narayanan[24] and in Saunders.[25] See Altman and Narayanan for a good review of the worldwide application of credit-scoring models.[26] One simple example of this new credit risk model type should cover the key issues supposedly addressed by many of these newer models. The Altman Z-score model is a classification model for corporate borrowers and can also be used to get a default probability prediction.[27] Based on a matched sample by year, size, and sectors of defaulted and solvent firms, and applying the linear discriminant analysis, the best-fitting scoring model for commercial loans results in the following equation:

$$Z = 1.2 \cdot X_1 + 1.4 \cdot X_2 + 3.3 \cdot X_3 + 0.6 \cdot X_4 + 1.0 \cdot X_5 \tag{3.2}$$

where X_1 = working capital/total assets ratio
X_2 = retained earnings/total assets ratio
X_3 = earnings before interest and taxes/total assets ratio
X_4 = market value of equity/book value of total liabilities ratio
X_5 = sales/total assets ratio

If a corporate borrower's accounting ratios X_i, weighted by the estimated coefficients in the Z function, result in a Z score below a critical value (in Altman's initial study, 1.81), the borrower would be classified as "insufficient" and the loan would be refused.

A number of issues need to be discussed here. First, the model is linear, whereas the path to bankruptcy can be assumed to be highly nonlinear, and the relationship between the X_i values itself is likely to be nonlinear. A second issue is that, with the exception of the market value of equity term in the leverage ratio, the model is essentially based on accounting ratios. In most countries, standards require accounting data only at discrete intervals (e.g., quarterly) and are generally based on historic- or book-value accounting principles. It is also questionable whether such models can capture the momentum of a firm whose condition is rapidly deteriorating (e.g., as in the Russia crisis of October 1998). As the world becomes more complex and competitive, and the decision flow becomes faster, the predictability of simple Z-score models may worsen. Brazil offers a good example. When fitted in the mid-1970s, the Z-score model did a quite good job of predicting default even two or three years prior to bankruptcy.[28] However, more recently, even with low inflation and greater economic stability, this type of model has performed less well as the Brazilian economy has become more open.[29]

The recent application of nonlinear methods (such as neural networks) to credit risk analysis shows potential to improve on the proven credit-scoring models. Rather than assuming there is only a linear and direct effect from the X_i variables on the Z credit score (or, in the language of neural networks, from the input layer to the output layer), neural networks allow for additional explanatory power via complex correlations or interactions among the X_i variables (many of which are nonlinear). For example, the five variables in the Altman Z-score model can be described by some nonlinearly transformed sum of X_1 and X_2 as a further explanatory variable.[30] In neural network terminology, the complex correlations among the X_i variables form a "hidden layer" which, when exploited (i.e., included in the model), can improve the fit and reduce type 1 and type 2 errors. (A type 1 error consists of misjudging a bad loan as good; a type 2 error consists of misjudging a good loan as bad.)

Yet, neural networks pose many problems for financial economists. How many additional hidden correlations should be included? In the language of neural networks, when should training stop? It is entirely possible that a large neural network, including large N nonlinear transformations of sums of the X_i variables, can reduce type 1 and type 2 errors of a historic loan database close to zero. However, as is well known, this creates the problem of *overfitting*—a model that well explains in-sample data may perform quite poorly in predicting out-of-sample data. More generally, the issue is when does one stop adding variables—when the remaining forecasting error is reduced to 10 percent, 5 percent, or less? Reality might prove that what is thought to be a global minimum forecast error may turn out to be just a local minimum. In general, the issue of economic meaning is probably the most troubling aspect of financial interpretation and use. For example, what is the economic meaning of an exponentially transformed sum of the GARCH-adjusted sales to total assets and the credit-spread-adjusted discount factor ratio? The ad hoc economic nature of these models and their tenuous links to existing financial theory separate them from some of the newer models that are discussed in the following chapters.

3.8.4 Option Theory, Credit Risk, and the KMV Model

3.8.4.1 Background

The idea of applying option pricing theory to the valuation of risky loans and bonds has been in the literature at least as far back as Merton.[31] In recent years, Merton's approach has been extended in many directions. KMV Corporation's CreditMonitor model, a default prediction model that produces (and updates) default predictions for all major companies and banks whose equity is publicly traded, is one well-known and widely applied option theory–based loan valuation model.[32] This section explains the link between loans and options, then investigates how this link can be used to derive a default prediction model. (Option theory is discussed in more detail in Section 2.4.5.)

3.8.4.2 Loans as Options

Figure 3-7 demonstrates the link between loans and optionality. Assume that this represents a one-year loan and the amount *OB* is borrowed on a discount basis. Technically, option formulas model loans as zero-coupon bonds with fixed maturities. Over the year, the borrowing firm will invest the funds in various investments or assets. Assuming that at the end of the year the market value of the borrowing firm's assets is OA_2, the borrower has an incentive to repay the loan (*OB*) and keep the residual as profit or return on investment ($OA_2 - OB$). Indeed, for any value of the firm's assets exceeding *OB*, the owners of the firm will have an incentive to repay the loan. However, if the market value of the firm's assets is less than *OB* (e.g., OA_1 in Figure 3-7), the owners have an incentive (or option) to default and to turn over the remaining assets of the firm to the lender (the bank).

FIGURE 3-7

Link Between Loans and Optionality.

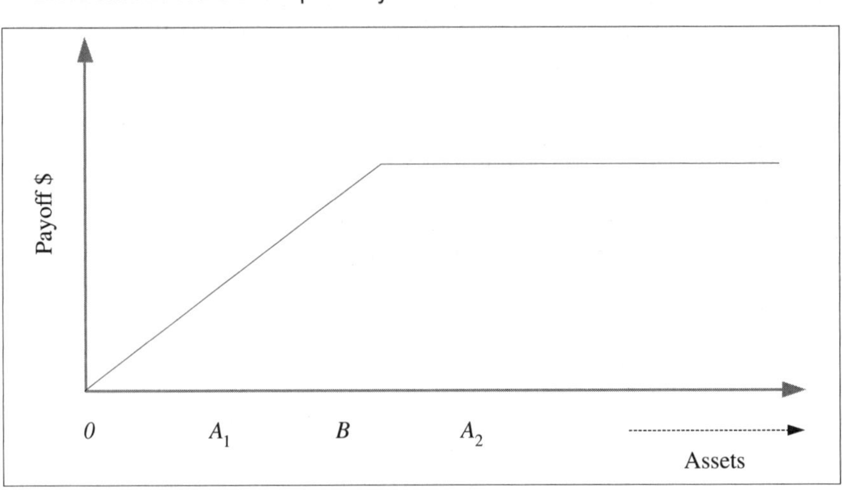

For market values of assets exceeding *OB*, the bank will earn a fixed upside return on the loan; essentially, interest and principal will be repaid in full. For asset values less than *OB*, the bank suffers increasingly large losses. In the extreme case, the bank's payoff is zero: principal and interest are a total loss.[33]

The loan payoff function shown in Figure 3-7—a fixed payoff on the upside and a long-tailed downside risk—looks familiar to an option theorist. Comparing this profile with the payoff profile of a short put option on a stock (shown in Figure 3-8) makes the correspondence more obvious. If the price of the stock *S* exceeds the strike price *K*, the writer of the option will keep the put premium received. If the price of the stock falls below *K*, the writer will lose successively larger amounts.

Merton noted this formal payoff equivalence; that is, if a bank grants a loan, its payoff is isomorphic to short a put option on the assets of the borrowing firm.[34] Moreover, just five variables enter the classic Black-Scholes-Merton model of a put option valuation for stocks (equity capital); the value of the default option (or, more generally, the value of a risky loan) will also depend on and reflect on the value of five similar variables.

In general form:

$$\text{Value of a put option on a stock} = f(S,K,r,T,\sigma_S) \tag{3.3}$$

$$\text{Value of a default option on a risky loan} = f(\overline{E},B,r,T,\overline{\sigma}_E) \tag{3.4}$$

where *S*, *K*, *E*, and *B* are as previously defined (a bar above a variable denotes that it is not directly observable); *r* is the short-term interest rate; *E* and σ_E are, respectively, the volatilities of the firm's equity value and the market value of its assets; and *r* is the maturity of the put option or, in the case of loans, the time horizon (default horizon) for the loan.

FIGURE 3-8

Payoff Profile of a Written Put Option on a Stock.

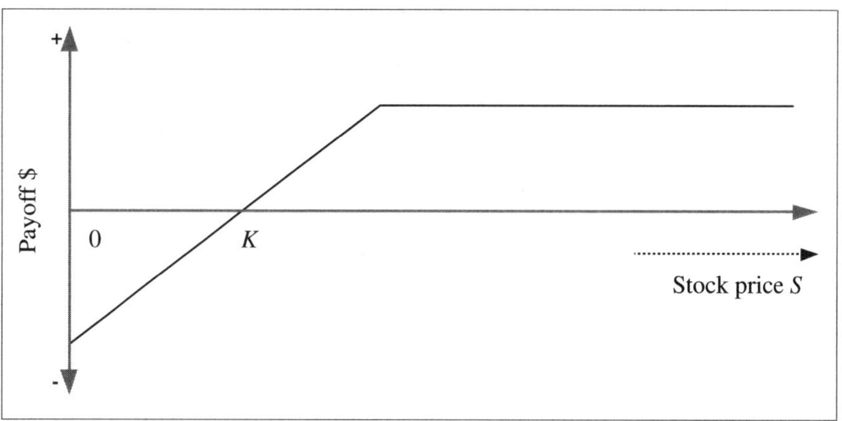

In general, for options on stocks, all five variables on the right-hand side of Equation (3.3) are directly observable; however, this is true for only three variables on the right-hand side of Equation (3.4). The market value of a firm's assets E and the volatility of the market value of a firm's assets σ_E are not directly observable. If E and σ_E could be directly measured, the value of a risky loan, the value of the default option, and the equilibrium spread on a risky loan over the risk-free rate could all be calculated.[35]

Some analysts have substituted the observed market value of risky debt on the left-hand side of Equation (3.4) (or, where appropriate, the observed interest spread between a firm's risky bonds and a matched risk-free Treasury rate) and have assumed that the book value of assets equals the market value of assets. This allows the implied volatility of assets σ_E to be backed out from Equation (3.4).[36] However, without additional assumptions, it is impossible to input two unobservable values (E and σ_E), based solely on one equation [Equation (3.4)]. Moreover, the market value of risky corporate debt is hard to get for all but a few firms.[37] Corporate bond price information is generally not easily available to the public, and quoted bond prices are often artificial matrix prices.[37]

3.8.4.3 KMV CreditMonitor Model

The innovation of the KMV CreditMonitor model is that it looks at the bank's lending problem from the viewpoint of the borrowing firm's equity holders and considers the loan repayment incentive problem (see bibliography). To solve the two unknown variables, E and σ_E, the system uses the following relationships:

- The structural relationship between the market value of a firm's equity and the market value of its assets.
- The relationship between the volatility of a firm's assets and the volatility of a firm's equity. After values of these variables are derived, an expected default frequency (EDF) measure for the borrower can be calculated.

Figure 3-9 shows the loan repayment issue from the side of the borrower (the equity owner of the borrowing firm). Suppose the firm borrows OB and the end-of-period market value of the firm's assets is OA_2 (where $OA_2 > OB$). The firm will then repay the loan, and the equity owners will keep the residual value of the firm's assets ($OA_2 - OB$). The larger the market value of the firm's assets at the end of the loan period, the greater the residual value of the firm's assets to the equity holders (borrowers). However, if the firm's assets fall below OB (e.g., are equal to OA_1), the borrowers of the firm will not be able to repay the loan.[39] They will be economically insolvent, will declare bankruptcy, and will turn the firm's assets over to the bank. Note that the downside risk to the equity owners is truncated no matter how low asset values are, compared to the amount borrowed. Specifi-

FIGURE 3-9

Call Option to Replicate the Equity of a Firm.

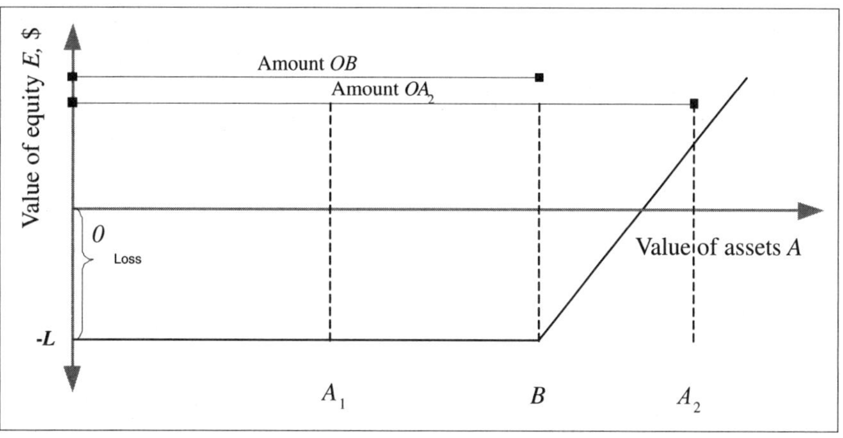

cally, "limited liability" protects the equity owners against losing more than *OL* (the owners' original stake in the firm). As shown in Figure 3-9, the payoff to the equity holder of a leveraged firm has a limited downside and a long-tailed upside. Being familiar with options, we recognize the similarity between the payoff function of an equity owner in a leveraged firm and buying a call option on a stock. Thus, we can view the market-value position of equity holders in a borrowing firm *E* as isomorphic to holding a call option on the assets of the firm *A*.

In general terms; equity can be valued as:

$$E = h(\overline{A}, \overline{\sigma}_A, r, B, T) \tag{3.5}$$

In Equation (3.5), the observed market value of a borrowing firm's equity (price of shares × number of shares) depends on the same five variables as in Equation (3.4), as per the Black-Scholes-Merton model for valuing a call option (on the assets of a firm). However, a problem still remains: how to solve two unknowns (A and σ_A) from one equation (where E, r, B, and T are all observable).

KMV and others in the literature have resolved this problem by noting that a second relationship can be exploited: the theoretical relationship between the observable volatility of a firm's equity value $\sigma_{\overline{E}}$ and the unobservable volatility of a firm's asset value σ_A. In general terms:

$$\overline{\sigma}_E = g(\sigma_A) \tag{3.6}$$

With two equations and two unknowns, Equations (3.5) and (3.6) can be used to derive a solution for A and σ_A by successive iteration. Explicit functional forms for the option-pricing model (OPM) in Equation (3.5) and for the stock price–asset volatility linkage in Equation (3.6) have to be specified.[40] KMV uses an option-pricing Black-Scholes-Merton-type model that allows for dividends. B, the default exercise point, is taken as the value of all short-term liabilities (one year and under), plus half the book value of outstanding long-term debt. While the KMV model uses a framework similar to that of Black-Scholes-Merton, the actual model implemented, which KMV calls the *Vasicek-Kealhofer model,* makes a number of changes in order to produce usable results. These modifications include defining five classes of liabilities, reflecting cash payouts such as dividends, handling convertible debt, assuming the default point is an absorbing barrier, and relying on an empirical distribution to convert distance to default into a default probability. The precise strike price or default boundary has varied under different generations of the model. There is a question as to whether net short-term liabilities should be used instead of total short-term liabilities.[41] The maturity variable t can also be altered according to the default horizon of the analyst; it is most commonly set equal to one year. A slightly different OPM was used by Ronn and Verma to solve a very similar problem, estimating the default risk of U.S. banks.[42]

After they have been calculated, the A and σ_A values can be employed, along with assumptions about the values of B and T, to generate a theoretically based EDF score for any given borrower.

The idea is shown in Figure 3-10. Suppose that the values backed out of Equations (3.5) and (3.6) for any given borrower are, respectively, A =

FIGURE 3-10

Theoretical EDF and Default Loss Region

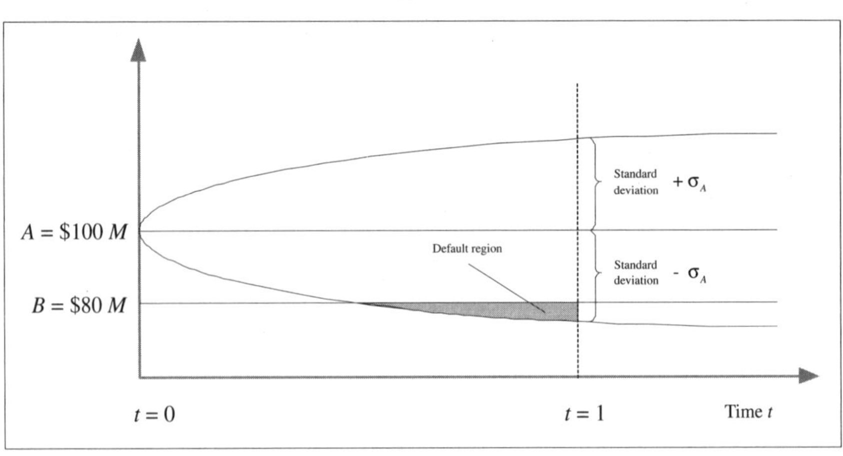

\$100 million and σ_A = \$10 million, where σ_A is the annual standard deviation of the asset value. The value of B is \$80 million. In practice, the user can set the default boundary or exercise price B equal to any proportion of total debt outstanding that is of interest. Suppose we want to calculate the EDF for a one-year horizon. Given the values of A, σ_A, B, and r, and with r equal to one year, what is the theoretical probability of a borrowing firm's failure at the one-year horizon? As can be seen in Figure 3-10, the EDF is the cross-hatched area of the distribution of asset values below B. This area represents the probability that the current value of the firm's assets, \$100 million, will drop below \$80 million at the one-year time horizon.

If it is assumed that future asset values are normally distributed around the firm's current asset value, we can measure the $t = 0$ (or today's) distance from default at the one-year horizon as follows:

$$\text{Distance from default} = \frac{A - B}{\sigma_A} = \frac{\$100\text{ M} - \$80\text{ M}}{\$10\text{ M}}$$
$$= 2 \text{ standard deviations} \qquad (3.7)$$

For the firm to enter the default region (the shaded area), asset values would have to drop by \$20 million, or 2 standard deviations, during the next year. If asset values are normally distributed, we know that there is a 95 percent probability that asset values will vary between plus and minus 2σ from their mean value. Thus, there is a 2.5 percent probability that asset values will increase by more than 2σ over the next year, and a 2.5 percent probability that they will fall by more than 2σ. In other words, there is an EDF of 2.5 percent. We have shown no growth in expected or mean asset values over the one-year period in Figure 3-10, but this can easily be incorporated. For example, if we project that the value of the firm's assets will grow 10 percent over the next year, then the relevant EDF would be lower because asset values would have to drop by 3σ, which is below the firm's expected asset growth path, for the firm to default at year-end. The distance from default is:[43]

$$\frac{A(1+g) - B}{\sigma_A} = \frac{\$110\text{ M} - \$80\text{ M}}{\$10\text{ M}} = 3 \text{ standard deviations} \qquad (3.8)$$

The normal distribution assumption of asset values around some mean level is critical in calculating joint default transition probabilities in J. P. Morgan's CreditMetrics (see Section 3.8.5.3), yet there is an important issue as to whether it is theoretically or empirically reasonable to make this assumption. With this in mind, rather than producing theoretical EDFs, the KMV approach generates an empirical EDF along the following lines. Suppose that we have a large historic database of firm defaults and no defaults (repayments), and we calculate that the firm we are analyzing has a theoretical distance from default of 2σ. We then ask the empirical questions:

- What percentage of the borrowers in the database actually defaulted within the one-year time horizon when their asset values placed them a distance of 2σ away from default at the beginning of the year?
- What is the percentage of the total population of borrowers that were 2σ away from default at the beginning of the year?

This produces an empirical EDF:

$$\text{Empirical EDF} = \frac{\begin{array}{l}\text{Number of borrowers that defaulted}\\ \text{within a year with asset values of } 2\sigma\\ \text{from } B \text{ at the beginning of the year}\end{array}}{\begin{array}{l}\text{Total population of borrowers with}\\ \text{asset values of } 2\sigma \text{ from } B \text{ at the}\\ \text{beginning of the year}\end{array}} \tag{3.9}$$

Assume that, based on a global database, it was estimated that 5 percent of all possible firms defaulted. As a result, this empirically based EDF can differ quite significantly from the theoretically based EDF. From a proprietary perspective, KMV's advantage comes from building up a large global database of firms (and firm defaults) that can produce such empirically based EDF scores.

The EDFs have a tendency to rise before the credit quality deterioration is reflected in the agency ratings. This greater sensitivity of EDF scores, compared to both accounting-based and rating-based systems, comes from the direct link between EDF scores and stock market prices. As new information about a borrower is generated, its stock price and stock price volatility will react, as will its implied asset value A and standard deviation of asset value σ_A.[44] Changes in A and σ_A generate changes in EDFs. For actively traded firms, it would be possible (in theory) to update an EDF every few minutes. In actuality, KMV can update EDF scores frequently for some 20,000 firms globally.

Because an EDF score reflects information signals transmitted from equity markets, it might be argued that the model is likely to work best in highly efficient equity market conditions and might not work well in many emerging markets. This argument ignores the fact that many thinly traded stocks are those of relatively closely held companies. Thus, major trades by insiders, such as sales of large blocks of shares (and thus major movements in a firm's stock price), may carry powerful signals about the future prospects of a borrowing firm.

Overall, the option-pricing approach to bankruptcy prediction has a number of strengths. It can be applied to any public company. Further, because it is based on stock market data rather than historic book value accounting data, it is forward-looking. In addition, it has a strong theoretical framework, because it is a structural model based on the modern theory of corporate finance and options, in which equity is viewed as a call option on the assets of a firm. However, the strengths can be offset by four weaknesses:

- Construction of theoretical EDFs is difficult without the assumption of normality of asset returns.
- It does not differentiate between different types of long-term bonds according to their seniority, collateral, covenants, or convertibility.
- The private firms' EDFs can be estimated only by using some comparability analysis based on accounting data and other observable characteristics of the borrower and thus are subject to the same criticisms regarding subjectivity and consistency as are the expert systems.
- It is static in that the Merton model assumes that once management puts a debt structure in place, it leaves this structure unchanged even if the value of a firm's assets has increased or decreased substantially. As a result, the Merton model cannot capture the financial behavior of those firms that seek to maintain a constant or target leverage ratio (debt to equity) across time.[45]

3.8.4.4 Structural and Intensity-Based Models

An additional potential problem with KMV-type models, and the Black-Scholes-Merton structural model approach on which they are based, is their implications for the calculation of the default probability and credit spreads as the time to default, or the maturity of debt, shrinks. Under normal Black-Scholes-Merton continuous time diffusion processes for asset values, the probability that a firm's asset value A will fall below its debt boundary B (Figure 3-10) declines substantially as the default horizon T approaches zero. Indeed, the implication of structural models is that the credit spread at the very short end of the risky debt market should be zero.[46]

In general, however, observable short-term credit spreads are nonzero. It could be argued that this is due to liquidity and transaction cost effects, but there is a conflicting opinion that the structural models of the Black-Scholes-Merton and KMV types—and especially the underlying assumptions of these models regarding the diffusion of asset values over time (see Figure 3-10)—underestimate the probability of default over short horizons.[47] Recent research efforts have focused on resolving this issue by modifying the basic assumptions of the Black-Scholes-Merton model. The work by Zhou[48] attempts to address underestimation of short-horizon risk by allowing for jumps in the asset value A of the firm. Related work on *intensity-based* models by Jarrow and Turnbull[49] and by Duffie and Singleton[50] presents an alternative approach to resolving the short-term horizon problem. Intensity-based models apply fixed or variable hazard functions to default risk. Essentially, rather than assuming a structural model of default (as in the Black-Scholes-Merton approach), in which a firm defaults when asset values fall below debt values, the intensity-based model is a *reduced-form* model; default follows a Poisson distribution, and default arises contingent on the arrival of some hazard.[51] Duffie and Lando[52] have sought to integrate the intensity based approach into the structural Black-Scholes-Merton approach. Assume that asset values in the context of the structural model are noisy in that they cannot be adequately observed by outsiders. In this context, accounting information releases may partially resolve this information gap and lead to jumps in asset values as investors revise their expectations based on partial information. Thus, imperfect information and noisiness in observed asset values may potentially be integrated into the OPM (structural) framework and resolve the underestimation of default risk at the short-term horizon. Work by Leland,[53] by Anderson, Sunderesan, and Tychon,[54] and by Mella-Barral and Perraudin[55] extends the classic Black-Scholes-Merton model by allowing for debt renegotiations (i.e., renegotiations of the debt boundary value), and thus a "dynamic" B.[56] Similarly, Leland[57] builds in agency costs as a friction to the traditional Black-Scholes-Merton model, and Acharya and Carpenter[58] model callable defaultable bonds under conditions of stochastic interest rates and endogenous bankruptcy.

3.8.5 J. P. Morgan's CreditMetrics and Other VaR Approaches

3.8.5.1 Background

Since 1993, when the Bank for International Settlement (BIS) announced its intention to introduce a capital requirement for market risk (see Section 2.5.4), great efforts have been made in developing and testing methodologies of value at risk (VaR). In 1995, the BIS amended its market risk proposal and agreed to allow certain banks to use their own internal models, rather than the standardized model approach, to calculate their market risk exposures. Since 1997, in the European Community and later in the United States, the largest banks (subject to local regulatory approval) have been allowed to use their internal models to calculate VaR exposures and the capital requirements for their trading books.[59]

The following sections review some general VaR concepts and subsequently discuss its potential extension to nontradable loans and its substitution or enhancement as a model for the 8 percent risk-based capital ratio currently applied when calculating the capital requirement for loans in the banking book. The focus is on CreditMetrics, developed by J. P. Morgan in conjunction with several other sponsors, including KMV.

3.8.5.2 Conceptual VaR Approach

Essentially, VaR models seek to measure the maximum loss of value on a given asset or liability over a given time period at a given confidence level (e.g., 95 percent, 97.5 percent, 99 percent, etc.).

This book defines VaR as the predicted worst-case loss at a specific confidence level over a certain period of time.

An example of a tradable instrument such as a corporate bond will suffice to describe the basic concept of VaR methodology (see Figure 3-11). Assume that the market price P of a corporate bond today is \$80, and the estimated daily standard deviation of the value σ is \$10. Because the trading book is managed over a relatively short horizon (usually with a one-day time horizon), a trader or risk manager may ask: "What is the potential loss tomorrow expressed in dollars at a 95 percent confidence level?" Assume that the trader is concerned with the potential loss on a bad day that occurs, on average, once in every 100 days, and that daily asset values (and thus returns) are normally distributed around the current bond value of \$80. Statistically speaking, the one bad day has a 1 percent probability of occurring tomorrow. The area under a normal distribution function carries information about probabilities. Roughly 68 percent of return observations must lie between +1 and –1 standard deviation from the mean; 95 percent of observations lie between +2 and –2 standard deviations from the mean; and 98 percent of observations lie between +2.33 and –2.33 standard deviations from the mean. With respect to the latter, and in terms of dollars, there is a 1 percent chance that the value of the bond will increase to a value of $\$80 + 2.33\sigma$ tomorrow, and a 1 percent chance that it will fall to a value of $\$80 - 2.33\sigma$. Because σ is assumed to be \$10, there is a 1 percent chance that the value of the bond will fall to \$56.70 or below; alternatively, there is a 99 percent probability that the bond holder will lose less than \$80 – \$56.70 = \$23.30 in value; that is, \$23.30 can be viewed as the VaR on the bond at the 99 percent confidence level. Note that, by implication, there is a 1 percent chance of losing \$23.30 or more tomorrow. As, by assumption, asset returns are normally distributed, the 1 bad day in every 100 can lead to the loss being placed anywhere in the shaded region below \$56.70 in Figure 3-11. In reality, losses on nonleveraged financial instruments are truncated at –100 percent of value, and the normal curve is at best an approximation to the log-normal.

The key input variables for the VaR calculation of a tradable instrument are its current market value P and the volatility or standard deviation of that market value σ. Given an assumed risk horizon (number of days, weeks, etc.) and a required confidence level (e.g., 99 percent), the VaR can be directly calculated.

FIGURE 3-11

VaR Exposure for a Traded Instrument for a Specific Time Horizon.

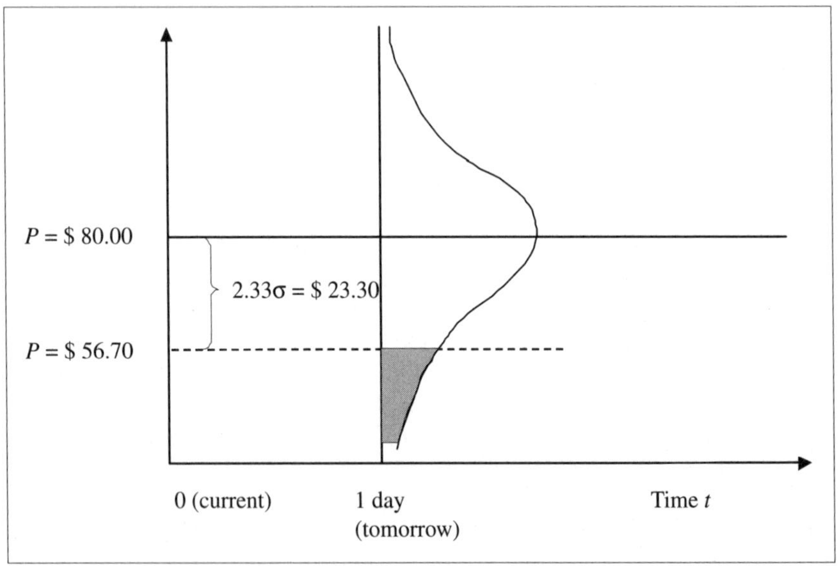

Application of this standardized methodology to nontradable loans creates direct problems:

- The current market value of a loan P is not directly observable, as most loans are not traded.
- As P is not observable, no time series is available to calculate σ, the volatility of P.

At best, the assumption of a normal distribution for returns on some tradable assets is a rough approximation, and the assumed approximation becomes critical when applied to the possible distribution of values for loans. Specifically, loans have both severely truncated upside returns and long downside risks (see Figure 3-12). As a result, even if we can and do measure P and σ, we still need to take into account the asymmetry of returns on making a loan.

3.8.5.3 CreditMetrics

CreditMetrics was introduced in 1997 by J. P. Morgan and its cosponsors (Bank of America, KMV, Union Bank of Switzerland, and others) as a VaR framework to apply to the valuation and risk of nontradable assets such as loans and privately placed bonds.[60] RiskMetrics seeks to answer the question: "If tomorrow is a bad day, how much will I lose on tradable assets

FIGURE 3-12

Nonnormal Distributed Returns and Impact on VaR Calculation. (*Source: J. P. Morgan,* CreditMetrics Technical Document, *New York: J. P. Morgan, April 2, 1997, 7, chart 1.1. Copyright © 1997 by J. P. Morgan & Co., Inc., all rights reserved. Reproduced with permission of RiskMetrics Group, Inc.*)

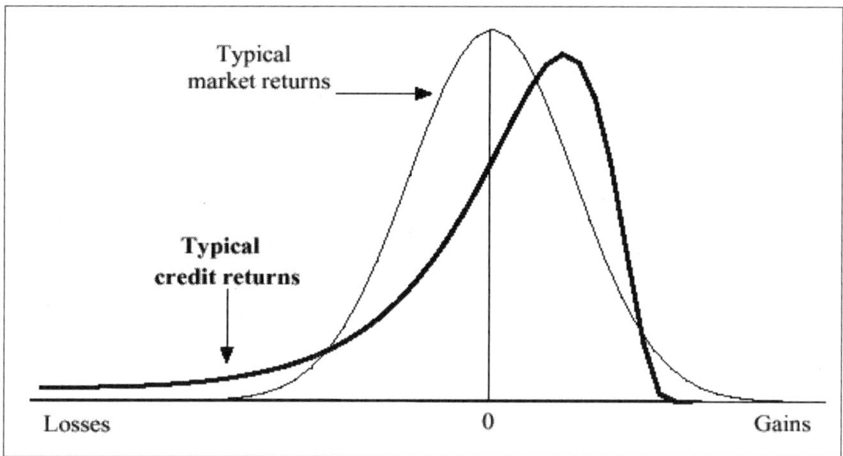

such as stocks, bonds, and equities?" CreditMetrics asks: "If next year is a bad year, how much will I lose on my loans and loan portfolio?"[61]

As mentioned earlier, loans are not publicly traded, thus neither P (the loan's market value) nor σ (the volatility of the loan value over the specified horizon) can be observed directly. However, using the following information, it is possible to calculate a hypothetical P and σ for any non-traded loan or bond, and, thus, a VaR figure for individual loans and the loan portfolio.[62]

- Available data on a borrower's credit rating
- The probability that the rating will change over the next year (the rating transition matrix)
- Recovery rates on defaulted loans (empirical data)
- Credit spreads and yields in the bond or loan market (market data)

The first step is the calculation of the VaR on a loan using a simple example; the second step is consideration of technical issues arising from the calculation. Consider, as the example, a five-year fixed-rate loan of $100 million at 6 percent annual interest.[63] The borrower is rated BBB.

Rating Migration

Based on historical data on publicly traded bonds and loans collected by Standard & Poor's, Moody's, KMV, or other bond or loan analysts, the probability that a BBB borrower will stay at BBB over the next year is estimated at 86.93 percent.[64] There is also some probability that the borrower will be upgraded (e.g., to A) or will be downgraded (e.g., to CCC or even to default, D). Indeed, eight transitions are possible for the borrower during the next year. Seven involve upgrades, downgrades, and no rating change, and one involves default.

Valuation

The effect of rating upgrades and downgrades is to reflect the required credit risk spreads or premiums (based on the changed ratings) on the loan's remaining cash flows and, thus, on the implied market (or present) value of the loan. If a loan is downgraded, the required credit spread premium should increase, so that the outstanding present value of the loan to the financial organization should decrease. The contractual loan rate in the example is assumed fixed at 6 percent. A credit rating upgrade has the opposite effect. Technically, because we are revaluing the five-year, $100 million, 6 percent loan at the end of the first year, after a credit event has occurred during that year, then (measured in millions of dollars):[65]

$$P = 6 + \frac{6}{1 + r_1 + s_1} + \frac{6}{(1 + r_2 + s_2)^2} + \frac{6}{(1 + r_3 + s_3)^3} + \frac{106}{(1 + r_4 + s_4)^4} \tag{3.10}$$

where r_i are the risk-free rates (so called forward zero rates) on zero-coupon T-bonds *expected* to exist one year into the future, and the one-year forward zero rates are calculated from the current treasury yield curve. Further, s is the annual credit spread on zero-coupon loans of the particular rating class of one-year, two-year, three-year, and four-year maturities (the latter are derived from observed spreads in the corporate bond market over treasuries). In the example, the first year's coupon or interest payment of $6 million is undiscounted and can be regarded as accrued interest earned on a bond or a loan.

Assume that during the first year, the borrower gets upgraded from BBB to A. The present or market value of the loan to the financial organization at the end of the one-year risk horizon (in millions) is then:[66]

$$P = 6 + \frac{6}{1.0372} + \frac{6}{(1.0432)^2} + \frac{6}{(1.0493)^3} + \frac{106}{(1.0532)^4} = \$108.66 \tag{3.11}$$

At the end of the first year, if the loan borrower is upgraded from BBB to A, the $100 million (book value) loan has a market value to the financial organization of $108.66 million. (This is the value the financial organization would theoretically be able to obtain at the year-1 horizon if it sold the loan to another financial organization at the fair market price.) Table 3-5 shows the value of the loan if other credit events occur. Note that

TABLE 3-5

Value of the Loan at the End of Year 1, Under Different Ratings (Including First-Year Coupon)

Year-End Rating	Value, Millions	Transition Probability, %
AAA	$109.37	0.02
AA	109.19	0.33
A	108.66	5.95
BBB	107.55	86.93
BB	102.02	5.30
B	98.10	1.17
CCC	83.64	0.12
Default	51.13	0.18

SOURCE: J. P. Morgan, *CreditMetrics Technical Document,* New York: J. P. Morgan, April 2, 1997, 11.

the loan has a maximum market value of $109.37 million (if the borrower is upgraded from BBB to AAA) and an estimated minimum value of $51.13 million if the borrower defaults. The latter is the estimated recovery value of the loan, or one minus the loss given default (LGD) if the borrower declares bankruptcy.[67]

The probability distribution of loan values is shown in Figure 3-13. The value of the loan has a relatively fixed upside and a long downside (i.e., a negative skew). The value of the loan is not symmetrically (or normally) distributed.

The maps are based on the rating transitions (nonnormal), whereas the returns of the underlying assets (loans) are assumed to be normally distributed. The VaR calculation in CreditMetrics has normally and nonnormally distributed components. In order to see how accurate the assumption of normal distribution is, we can now calculate two VaR measures, based on the *normal* and the *actual* distribution of loan values, respectively.

Calculation of VaR

Table 3-6 demonstrates the calculation of the VaR, based on two approaches, for both the 5 and 1 percent worst-case scenarios around the mean or expected (rather than original) loan value. Step 1 in determining VaR is to calculate the expected mean of the loan's value (or its expected value) at year 1. This is calculated as the sum of each possible loan value at the end of the year times its transition probability over this one-year pe-

FIGURE 3-13

Distribution of Loan Values on Five-Year BBB Loan at the End of Year 1. (*Source: J. P. Morgan*, CreditMetrics Technical Document, *New York: J. P. Morgan, April 2, 1997, 11, chart 1.2. Copyright © 1997 by J. P. Morgan & Co., Inc., all rights reserved. Reproduced with permission of RiskMetrics Group, Inc.*)

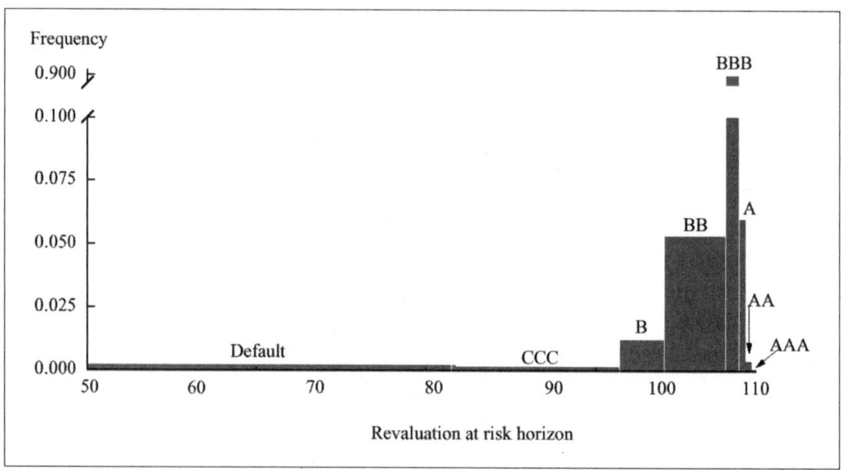

riod. The mean value of the loan is $107.09 (also see Figure 3-14). However, the financial organization is interested in knowing the unexpected losses or volatility in the loan's value. Specifically, if next year is a bad year, how much can the organization lose at a certain probability level? A bad year could be defined as occurring once every 20 years (the 5 percent confidence level) or once every 100 years (the 1 percent confidence level). This definition is similar to market risk VaR, except that for credit risk, the risk horizon is one year rather than one day.

Assuming that loan values are normally distributed, the variance of loan value (in millions) around its mean is $8.94 (squared), and its standard deviation, or volatility, is the square root of the variance, equal to $2.99. Thus, the VaR on a 5 percent confidence level for the loan is 1.65 × $2.99 = $4.93 million. The VaR on a 1 percent confidence level is 2.33 × $2.99 = $6.97 million. However, this likely underestimates the actual or true VaR of the loan, because, as shown in Figure 3-14, the distribution of the loan's value is clearly not normal. In particular, it demonstrates a negative skew or a long-tailed downside risk.

Applying the current distribution of loan values and probabilities in Table 3-6 results in a 6.77 percent probability that the loan value will fall below $102.02, implying an approximate VaR on a 5 percent confidence level of $5.07 million ($107.09 – $102.02 = $5.07 million), and a 1.47 percent probability that the loan value will fall below $98.10, implying an approxi-

TABLE 3-6

VaR Calculations for the BBB Loan (Benchmark Is Mean Value of Loan)

Year-End Rating	Probability	New Loan Value Plus Coupon, Millions	Probability Weighted Value, $	Difference of Value from Mean, $	Probability Weighted Difference Squared
AAA	0.02	$109.37	0.02	2.28	0.0010
AA	0.33	109.19	0.36	2.10	0.0146
A	5.95	108.66	6.47	1.57	0.1474
BBB	86.93	107.55	93.49	0.46	0.1853
BB	5.30	102.02	5.41	(5.06)	1.3592
B	1.17	98.10	1.15	(8.99)	0.9446
CCC	0.12	83.64	1.10	(23.45)	0.6598
Default	0.18	51.13	0.09	(55.96)	5.6358
			$107.09 = mean value	8.94 = variance of value	

σ = standard deviation = $2.99

Assuming normal distribution:

5 percent VaR = 1.65σ = $4.93

1 percent VaR = 2.33σ = $6.97

Assuming actual distribution:*

5 percent VaR 95 percent of actual distribution = $107.09 – $102.02 = $5.07

1 percent VaR 99 percent of actual distribution = $107.09 – $98.10 = $8.99

*5% VaR approximated by 6.77% VaR (i.e., 5.3% + 1.17% + 0.12% + 0.18%) and 1% VaR approximated by 1.47% VaR (i.e., 1.17% + 0.12% + 0.18%).

SOURCE: J. P. Morgan, *CreditMetrics Technical Document,* New York: J. P. Morgan, April 2, 1997, 28.

mate VaR on a 1 percent confidence level of $8.99 million ($107.09 – $98.10 = $8.99). These current VaR measures could be made less approximate by applying a linear interpolation to get at the 5 and 1 percent confidence levels. For example, because the 1.47 percentile equals $98.10 and the 0.3 percentile equals $83.64, using linear interpolation, the 1.00 percentile equals approximately $92.29. This suggests an actual 1 percent VaR of $107.09 – $92.29 = $14.80.[68]

3.8.5.4 Capital Adequacy Requirements

The critical test for a credit model is to compare these VaR figures with the 8 percent risk-based capital requirement against loans that is currently mandated by the BIS and the Federal Reserve. For a $100 million face

FIGURE 3-14

Actual Distribution of Loan Values on Five-Year BBB Loan at the End of Year 1.

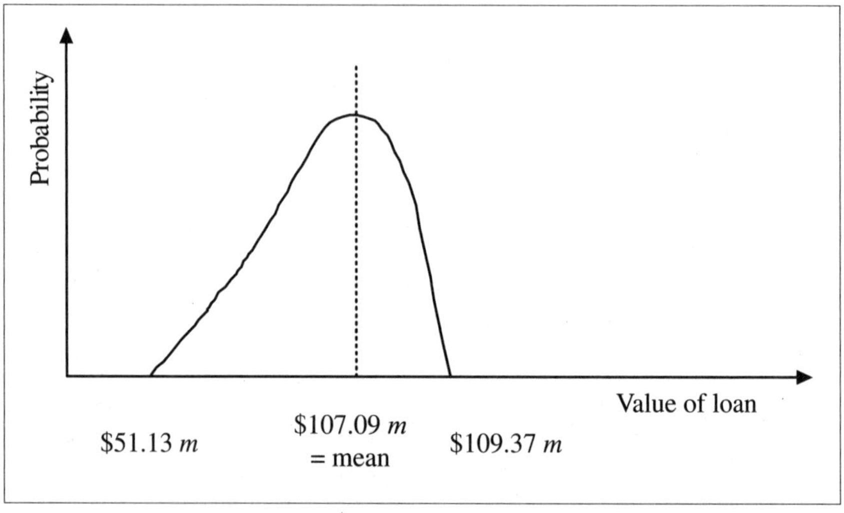

(book) value BBB loan to a private-sector borrower, the capital requirement would be $8 million. (Note the contrast to the two VaR measures developed previously.) Using the 1 percent VaR based on the normal distribution, the capital requirement against unexpected losses on the loan would be $6.97 million (i.e., less than the BIS requirement). Using the 1 percent VaR based on the interpolated value from the actual distribution, the capital requirement would be $14.80 million (an amount much greater than the BIS capital requirement).[69] Implementing the CreditMetrics approach, every loan is likely to have a different VaR and thus a different implied or economic capital requirement. This contrasts with the current BIS regulations, in which all loans of different ratings (AAA to CCC) and different maturities are subject to the same 8 percent capital requirement. Moreover, the question of a stress-test multiplier for an internally based capital requirement would also need to be addressed. In particular, estimated losses at the 99 percent confidence level have a distribution which might exceed the boundaries in extreme events. In extreme events (such as a catastrophic year), the loss will exceed the 99 percent measure calculated by a significant margin. Under the BIS approach to support market risk, this extreme loss (or stress-test issue) is addressed by requiring banks to multiply their estimated VaRs by a factor ranging between 3 and 4.[70]

Applying such a multiplication factor in the credit risk context to low-quality loans would raise capital requirements considerably. The process to derive the appropriate size of such a multiplication factor, given the problems of stress testing credit risk models, remains a critical issue for the success of credit risk models in the capital requirement context.

3.8.5.5 Technical Challenges and Solution Approaches

Rating Migration

A number of questions arise in applying the bond-rating transitions assumed in Table 3-6 to calculate the transition probabilities of ratings moving to different rating categories (or to default) over the one-year horizon:

- First, the way defaults and transitions occur and the transition probabilities are calculated is mapped in CreditMetrics with an average one-year transition period over past data (e.g., 20 years).[71] Specifically, the transition probabilities are assumed to follow a stable Markov process,[72] which assumes that the probability that a bond or loan will transition to any particular level during this period is independent of (not correlated with) any outcome in the past period. However, there is empirical evidence that rating transitions are autocorrelated over time. For example, a bond or loan that was downgraded in the previous period has a higher probability of being downgraded in the current period (compared to a borrower or a loan that was not downgraded).[73] This suggests that the ratings transitions can be described better with a second or higher Markov over time.
- Second, the transition matrix stability is assumed to be stable. The use of a single transition matrix assumes that transitions do not differ across borrower types (a detailed segregation of industrial firms versus banks, or Europe versus the United States) or across time (e.g., peaks versus troughs in the business cycle). There is considerable empirical evidence to assume that important industry factors, such as country factors or business cycle factors, impact rating transitions. For example, when analyzing a loan to a German industrial company, it is required to apply a rating transition matrix built around data for that specific country and industry. CreditPortfolioView, analyzed later in this chapter, can be regarded as a direct attempt to manage the issue of cyclical impact on the bond or loan transition matrix.[74]
- The third issue relates to the portfolio effect of bonds used in calculating the transition matrix. Altman and Kishore found a noticeable empirical impact of bond "aging" on the probabilities calculated in the transition matrix.[75] Indeed, a substantial impact has been found, depending on whether the bond sample used to calculate transitions is based on new bonds or on all bonds outstanding in a rating class during a specific time frame.

- The fourth issue relates to the methodology of applying bond transition matrices to value loans. As collateral, covenants, and other features make loans behave differently from bonds, applying bond transition matrices may result in an inherent valuation bias. This demands the internal development, by the banks, of loan-rating transitions based on historic loan databases, as a crucial step to improve the methodological accuracy of VaR measures of loan risk.[76]

Valuation

In the VaR calculation, as shown earlier, the amount recoverable on default (assumed to be $51.13 per $100 in this example), the forward zero interest rates r_i, and the credit spreads s_i are all assumed to be nonstochastic. Making any or all of them stochastic generally will increase any VaR measure and thus capital requirement. In particular, loan recovery rates have substantial variability, and the credit spread has empirically different sizes, where the credit spread variability is expected to vary over some rating class at a given moment in time (e.g., AAA and A+ bonds or loans are likely to have different credit spreads).[77] More generally, credit spreads and interest rates are likely to vary over time with the credit cycle and shifts, rotation, and convexity in the term structure, rather than being deterministic.

Another topic to mention is recovery rates. If the standard deviation of recovery rates is $25 to $45, around a mean value of $51.13 per $100 of loans, it can be shown that the VaR (assuming the 99 percent confidence level) will increase to 2.33 × $3.13 million = $7.38 million, or a VaR-based capital requirement of 7.38 percent of the face value of the BBB loan.[78] One reason for assuming that interest rates are nonstochastic or deterministic is to separate market risk from credit risk.[79] But this remains highly controversial, especially to those who feel that their measurement should be integrated rather than separated and that credit risk is positively correlated with the interest-rate cycle.[80]

Mark-to-Market Model versus Default Model

By allowing for the effects of credit-rating transitions (and hence, spread changes) on loan values, as well as default, CreditMetrics is viewed as a mark-to-market (MTM) model. Other models, such as CreditRisk$^+$, attribute spread risk as part of market risk and concentrate on calculation of expected and unexpected loss rather than on expected and unexpected changes in value as in CreditMetrics. This alternative approach is often called the default model or default mode (DM). (See Section 3.7.1.3.)

It is useful to compare the effects of the MTM model versus the DM model by calculating the expected and, more important, the unexpected losses for the same example.

The expected loss on the loan is:

$$\text{Expected loss} = p \times \text{LGD} \times \text{exposure} \tag{3.12}$$

To calculate the unexpected loss, some assumptions regarding the default probability distributions and recoveries have to be made. The simplest assumption is that recovery rates are fixed and are independent of the distribution of probabilities. As the borrower either defaults or does not default, the default probability can, most simply, be assumed to be binomially distributed with a standard deviation of:

$$\sigma = \sqrt{p \times (1 - p)} \tag{3.13}$$

The unexpected loss on the loan (given a fixed recovery rate and exposure amount) is:

$$\text{Unexpected loss} = \sqrt{p \times (1 - p)} \times \text{LGD} \times \text{exposure} \tag{3.14}$$

The difference between the MTM and the DM approaches occurs partly because the MTM approach allows an upside as well as a downside transition to the loan's value, whereas the DM approach fixes the maximum upside value of the loan to its book or face value of $100 million. Thus, economic capital under the DM approach is more closely related to book value accounting concepts than to the market value accounting concepts as applied in the MTM approach.

3.8.6 The McKinsey Model and Other Macrosimulation Models

3.8.6.1 Background

The current methodology underlying CreditMetrics VaR calculations assumes that transition probabilities are stable across borrower types and across the business cycle. The assumption of stability is critical to the CreditMetrics approach. A recent survey of the internal rating systems of 18 major bank holding companies suggested that as much as 60 percent of their collective loan portfolios may be below the equivalent of investment grade.[81] The study concludes further that the default rates on low-quality credits (including junk bonds) are highly sensitive to the state of the business cycle. Moreover, there is empirical evidence that rating transitions in general may be correlated to the state of the economy.[82] This empirical evidence suggests that the probability of downgrades and defaults may be significantly greater in a cyclical downturn than in an upturn, assuming that transitions do not follow a normal distributed probability function.

3.8.6.2 Incorporating Cyclical Factors

There are at least two approaches to how to incorporate cyclical factors:

- The past sample period is segregated into recession years and nonrecession years (a recession matrix and a nonrecession matrix) to yield two separate VaR calculations to calculate two separate historic transition matrices.
- The Relationship between transition probabilities and macrofactors is modeled directly, and in a secondary step, a model is fitted to simulate the evolution of transition probabilities over time by shocking the model with macroevents.

McKinsey's CreditPortfolioView is based on the second approach.

3.8.6.3 The Macrosimulation Multifactor Approach

One way to build in business cycle effects and to take a forward-looking view of VaR is to model macroeffects, both systematic and unsystematic, on the probability of default and associated rating transitions. The macrosimulation approach should be viewed as complementary to CreditMetrics, which overcomes some of the biases resulting from assuming static or stationary transition probabilities period to period.[83]

The essential concept is represented in the transition matrix for a given country, as shown in Figure 3-15. Note especially the cell of the matrix in the bottom right-hand corner, p_{CD}.

FIGURE 3-15

Historic (Unconditional) Transition Matrix.

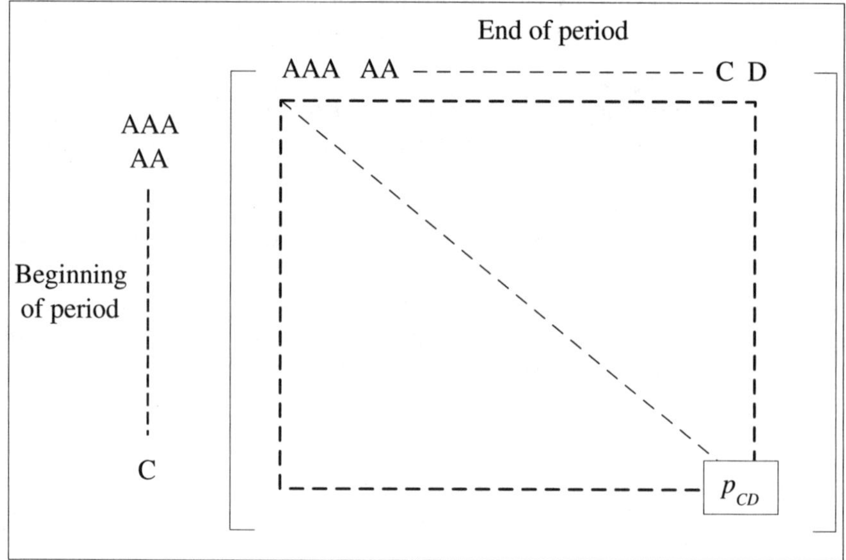

Each cell in the transition matrix shows the probability that a particular counterparty, rated at a given grade at the beginning of the period, will move to another rating by the end of the period. In Figure 3-15, p_{CD} shows the estimated probability that a C-rated borrower (in this example a speculative-grade borrower) will default over the next year—that is, it will transition from a C rating to a D rating.

In general, it can be expected that this probability moves significantly during the business cycle and is higher in recessions than in expansions. Because the probabilities in each row of the transition matrix must sum up to 1, an increase in p_{CD} must be compensated for by a decrease in other probabilities—for example, those involving upgrades of initially C-rated debt, where p_{CB} and p_{CA} represent the probabilities of the C-rated borrower's moving to, respectively, a B grade and an A grade during the next year. The probability density in the transition matrix moves increasingly in a southeast direction as a recession proceeds.[84]

With this in mind, let p_{CD} vary at time t along with a set of factors indexed by variable y. For convenience, the subscripts C and D will be dropped. However, there is an implicit probability that a C-rated borrower will default over the next one-year period. In general terms:[85]

$$p_t = f(y_t) \tag{3.15}$$

where $f < 0$

That is, there is an inverse correlation between the state of the economy and the default probability. The macroindicator, variable y, can be viewed as being driven by a set of i systematic macroeconomic variables at time t (X_{it}) as well as by unsystematic random shocks, structural changes to the economic system such as innovations, new industries and technology, and the like. In general:

$$Y_t = g(X_{it}, V_t) \tag{3.16}$$

where $i = 1, \ldots, n$
$V_t \sim N(0, \sigma)$

In turn, macroeconomic variables X_{it}, such as gross domestic product (GDP) growth, unemployment, and so on, can themselves be considered to be explained by their past histories (e.g., lagged GDP growth) as well as to be sensitive to shocks themselves, ε_{it}.[86] Thus:

$$X_{it} = h(X_{it-1}, X_{it-2}, \ldots, \varepsilon_{it}) \tag{3.17}$$

Different macromodel specifications can be applied in the context of Equations (3.16) and (3.17) to improve model fit, and different models can be used to explain transitions for different countries and industries.

Substituting Equation (3.17) into Equation (3.16), and Equation (3.16) into Equation (3.15), the probability that a speculative grade-C loan will transition to grade D during the next year will be determined by:

$$p_t = f(X_{it-j}; V_t, \varepsilon_{it}) \tag{3.18}$$

Equation (3.18) models the determinants of this transition probability as a function of lagged macrovariables, a general economic shock factor or innovation V_t, and shock factors or innovations for each of the *i* macrovariables ε_{it}. Because the X_{it-j} are predetermined, the key variables driving p_t will be the innovations or shocks V_t and ε_{it}. Using a structured Monte Carlo simulation approach (see Monte Carlo Simulation in Section 5.4.3.5), values for V_t and ε_{it} can be generated for periods in the future that occur with the same probability as that observed from history.[87] We can use the simulated *V* and ε values, along with the fitted macromodel, to simulate scenario values for p_{CD} in periods $t, t+1, t+2, \ldots, t+n$, and on into the future.

Suppose that, based on current macroconditions, the simulated value for p_{CD}, labeled p^*, is 0.35, and the number in the historic (unconditional) transition matrix is 0.30 (where the asterisk indicates the simulated value of the transition probability). Because the unconditional transition value of 0.30 is less than the value estimated conditional on the macroeconomic state (0.35), we are likely to underestimate the VaR of loans and a loan portfolio, especially at the low-quality end. Defining the ratio r_t:

$$r_t = \frac{p_t^*}{p_t} = \frac{0.35}{0.30} = 1.16 \tag{3.19}$$

Based on the simulated macromodel, the probability of a C-rated borrower's defaulting over the next year is 16 percent higher than the average unconditional historical transition relationship implies. We can also calculate this ratio for subsequent periods $t + 1$, $t + 2$, and so on. For example, suppose that, based on simulated innovations and macrofactor relationships, the simulation predicts $p_t^* + 1$ to be 0.38. The ratio relevant for the next year, r_{t+1}, is then:

$$r_{t+1} = \frac{p_{t+1}^*}{p_{t+1}} = \frac{0.38}{0.30} = 1.267 \tag{3.20}$$

The unconditional transition matrix will underestimate the predicted risk of default on low-grade loans in this period.

These calculated ratios can be used to adjust the elements in the projected $t, t+1, \ldots, t+n$ transition matrices. In McKinsey's CreditPortfolioView, the unconditional value of p_{CD} is adjusted by the ratio of the conditional value of p_{CD} to its unconditional value. Consider the transition

FIGURE 3-16

Conditional Transition Matrix M_t.

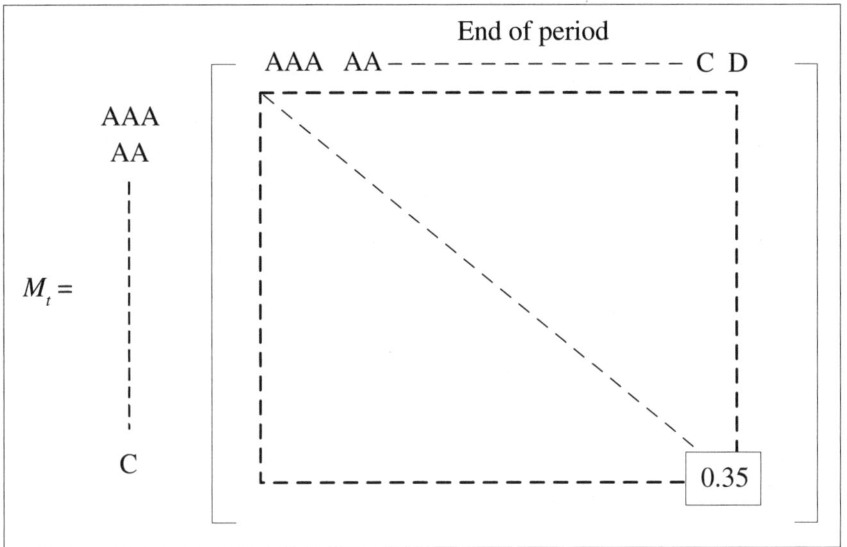

matrix for period t; then $r_t \times 0.30 = 0.35$ (which is the same as p_t^*), thus replacing 0.30 with 0.35 in the transition matrix p_{CD}, as shown in Figure 3-16. This also means that all the other elements in the transition matrix have to be adjusted (e.g., p_{CA}, p_{CB}, and so on). A number of procedures can be used to do this, including linear and nonlinear regressions of each element or cell in the transition matrix on the ratio r_t.[88] The rows of the transition matrix must sum up to 1.[89]

For the next period ($t + 1$), the transition matrix would have to be similarly adjusted by multiplying the unconditional value of p by r_{t+1}, or $0.30 \times 1.267 = 0.38$. This is shown in Figure 3-17.

Thus, there would be different transition matrices for each year into the future ($t, t + 1, \ldots, t + n$), reflecting the simulated effect of the macroeconomic shocks on transition probabilities. This type of approach, along with CreditMetrics, could be used to calculate a cyclically sensitive VaR for 1 year, 2 years, . . . , n years.[90]

Specifically, the simulated transition matrix M would replace the historically based unconditional (stable Markov) transition matrix, and, given any current rating for the loan (say C), the distribution of loan values based on the macroadjusted transition probabilities in the C row of the matrix M_t could be used to calculate VaR at the one-year horizon, in a fashion similar to that used by CreditMetrics in Section 3.8.5.3.

FIGURE 3-17

Conditional Transition Matrix M_{t+1}.

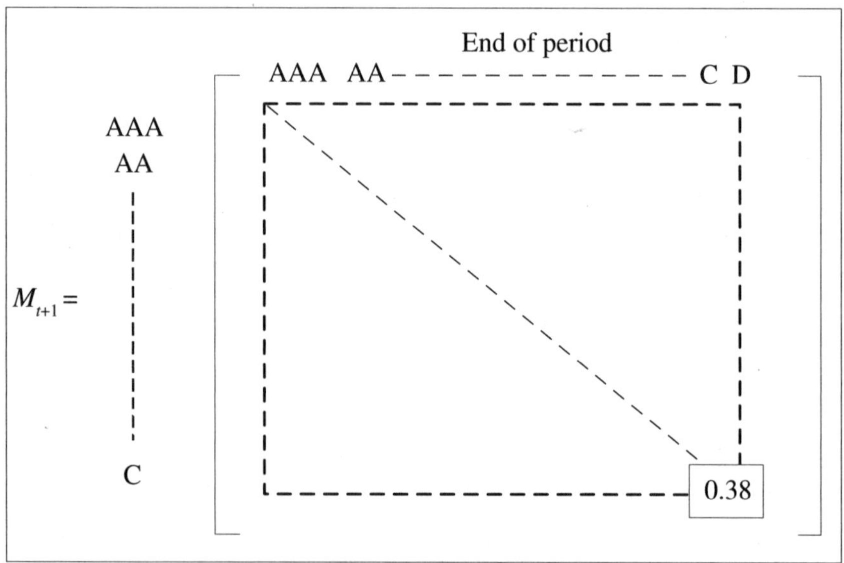

We could also calculate VaR estimates using longer horizons. Suppose we are interested in transitions over the next two years (t and $t + 1$). Multiplying the two matrices,

$$M_{t't+1} = M_t \cdot M_{t+1} \tag{3.21}$$

produces a new matrix, $M_{t't+1}$. The final column of this new matrix will give the simulated (cumulative) probabilities of default on differently rated loans over the next two years.

The macrosimulation approach described until now considered just one simulation of values for p^*, from one set of shocks V_t and ε_{it}. This process has to be repeated over and over again—for example, taking 10,000 random draws to generate 10,000 estimates of p_t^* and 10,000 possible transition matrices.

As shown in Figure 3-18, hypothetical simulated values can be plotted. The mean simulated value of p^* is 0.30, but the extreme value (99th percentile, or worst-case value) is 0.55. Calculating capital requirements when considering unexpected declines in loan values (the latter figure for p_t^*), and the transition matrix associated with this value, might be considered most relevant for the capital requirement calculation.

FIGURE 3-18

Probability Distribution of Simulated Values.

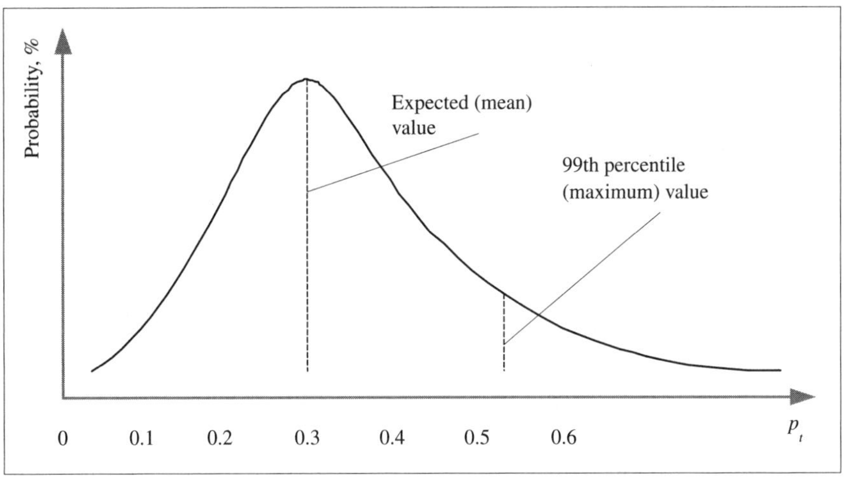

3.8.7 KPMG's Loan Analysis System and Other Risk-Neutral Valuation Approaches

3.8.7.1 Background

The application of risk-neutral probabilities to value risky assets has been in the finance literature at least as far back as Arrow (1953)[91] and has been subsequently enhanced by Harrison and Kreps (1979),[92] Harrison and Pliska (1981),[93] and Kreps (1982).[94] Traditionally, valuing risky assets by discounting cash flows is done on an asset by a risk-adjusted discount rate. To do this, the probability distribution for all cash flows and the risk-return preferences of investors have to be known or estimated. The latter are especially difficult to incorporate into the calculation. Suppose that all assets are assumed to trade in a market in which all investors are willing to accept, from any risky asset, the same expected return as that promised by the risk-free asset. Such a theoretical market can be described as behaving in a *risk-neutral* fashion. In a financial market in which investors behave in a risk-neutral manner, the prices of all assets can be determined by simply discounting the expected future cash flows on the asset by the risk-free rate.[95]

The equilibrium relationship, where the expected return on an asset equals the risk-free rate, can be applied to back out an implied risk-neutral probability of default, also called the *equivalent martingale measure.* This forward-looking estimate of the default risk of a security can be compared with historical estimated measures of transition probabilities. As long as an asset is risky, the forward-looking risk-neutral probability will not equal its historical measure (the realized value of the transition probability).[96]

3.8.7.2 Deriving Risk-Neutral Probabilities

The following paragraphs discuss two ways of deriving forward-looking default probability measures based on the risk-neutral valuation approach. After that is a discussion of the relationship between the risk-neutral measure of default and its historical measure. The last discussion focuses on the potential use of the risk-neutral concept in pricing loans and in calculating the market value of a loan and its VaR.

3.8.7.3 Deriving Risk-Neutral Measures from Spreads on Zero-Coupon Bonds

One methodology for deriving risk-neutral probabilities from spreads between risky bonds (ratings less than AAA; e.g., corporate bonds) and Treasuries has been used at Goldman Sachs and was described by Litterman and Iben.[97]

Consider the two zero-coupon bond yield curves shown in Figure 3-19. The annualized discount yield on one-year zero-coupon Treasuries is assumed to be 10 percent, and the annualized discount yield on one-year grade-B zero-coupon corporates is 15.8 percent. The methodology assumes that the zero-yield curves either exist or can be fitted. As noted

FIGURE 3-19

Comparison of the Zero-Coupon Treasury Bond Curve and the Zero-Coupon Grade-B Corporate Bond Curve.

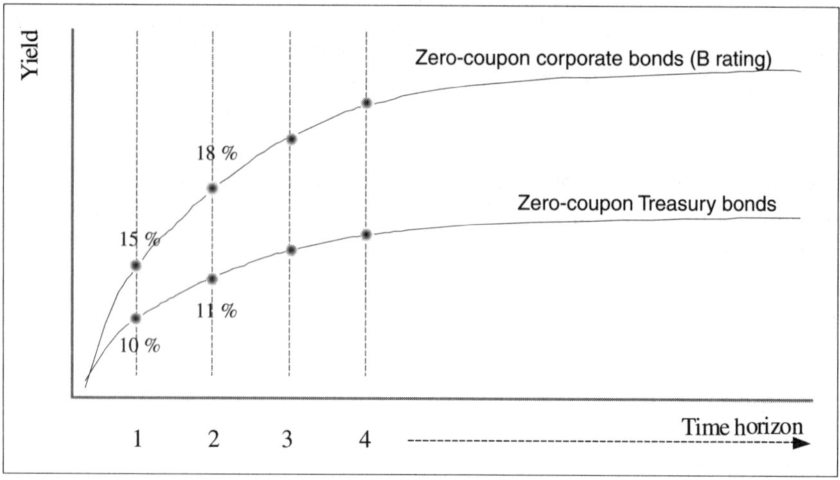

previously, in equilibrium, under risk-neutral valuation, the expected return on the risky bond must equal the risk-free return (the return on the risk-free Treasury bond), or:

$$p_1 \times (1 + k_1) = 1 + i_1 \tag{3.22}$$

where p_1 = implied risk-neutral probability of repayment in year 1
$1 + k_1$ = expected return on risky one-year corporate bond
$1 + i_1$ = risk-free return on one-year Treasury bond

We assume that if the risky bond defaults, the loss given default (LGD) equals 1, and the holder of the bond receives nothing (for simplicity).

From Equation (3.22), we can derive the implied risk-neutral probability of repayment p:

$$p_1 = \frac{1 + k_1}{1 + i_1} = \frac{1.1}{1.158} = 0.95 \tag{3.23}$$

Thus, the risk-neutral probability of default p_1^* is:

$$p_1^* = 1 - p_1 = 1 - 0.95 = 0.05 \tag{3.24}$$

We can also back out the risk-neutral probability of default in the year 2, . . . , year n by exploiting the forward rates embedded in the zero curves in Figure 3-19. For example, p_2^*, the risk-neutral probability of default in year 2 (essentially, the forward marginal probability that the B-rated corporate borrower will default between year 1 and year 2), can be derived in a two-step process. The first step is to derive the one-year expected forward rates on corporates and Treasuries from the existing zero curves. The second step is to back out the implied risk-neutral probability of default from the forward rates. By applying this approach, the entire term structure of forward-looking risk-neutral probabilities can be derived.

3.8.7.4 Deriving the Risk-Neutral Probability Measure from Stock Prices

Using bond prices and yield spreads, the preceding approach extracts the risk-neutral probability of default forecast for a particular borrower (e.g., rate B). This involves placing the borrower into a particular rating bucket. Thus, this implies a matched yield curve for that rating class and utilizes relationships between zero-coupon bond prices and yields for risky versus risk-free debt. An alternative approach is to exploit the type of option-pricing models discussed in Section 2.4.5, along with stock prices and the volatility of stock prices. A risk-neutral probability forecast for a particular borrower can also be backed out of an option-pricing model.[98] Indeed, from a Merton-type model, where equity is viewed as a call option on the value of the firm's assets, the probability that the value of a firm's assets at the time of debt maturity (e.g., $T = 1$) will be greater than the face value of the firm's debt is $N_1(k)$. The risk-neutral probability of default is then:

$$p_t^* = 1 - N_1(k) \tag{3.25}$$

$N_1(k)$ is the area under the normal distribution relating to a variable k, which, in turn, depends on the value of the firm's assets, the volatility of the firm's assets, leverage, time to maturity, and the risk-free rate. As with the KMV approach, neither the market value nor the volatility of the firm's assets is directly observable. These values have to be iterated from observable stock prices and the volatility of stock prices. Delianedis and Geske[99] have shown that using the risk-neutral probabilities derived from a standard Merton model[100] as a first step and the risk-neutral probabilities derived from an enhanced Merton-type model[101] as a second step allows for multiple classes of debt, demonstrating the ability of these measures to predict actual rating transitions and defaults. In other words, the risk-neutral measure has the potential to predict changes in the historical measure.[102]

3.8.7.5 The Relationship Between the Historical and the Risk-Neutral Measures

Following Ginzberg et al.[103] and Belkin et al.,[104] the relationship between the risk-neutral measure and the historical measure of default probability can be best viewed in terms of a risk premium.[105] That is, the spread Φ between the returns on a one-year risk-free asset (such as a corporate bond) will reflect the risk-neutral probability of default p_1^* and some loss given default (LGD):

$$\Phi_1 = p_1^* \times \text{LGD} \tag{3.26}$$

Alternatively, we can view the spread as compensating investors for both an expected loss ε_1 and an unexpected loss u_1 on the risky bond:

$$\Phi_1 = \varepsilon_1 + u_1 \tag{3.27}$$

The expected loss ε_1 can, in turn, be set equal to the average or historical probability of default of this type of borrower by multiplying the historic transition probability t_1 times the LGD:[106]

$$\varepsilon_1 = t_1 \times \text{LGD} \tag{3.28}$$

The unexpected loss component u_1 can be viewed as being equal to the unexpected default probability of default times the LGD.[107]

Substituting Equation (3.28) into Equation (3.27) and incorporating Equation (3.26) results in:

$$p_1^* \times \text{LGD} = (t_1 \times \text{LGD}) + u_1 \tag{3.29}$$

Given some fixed LGD, the difference between p^* (the risk-neutral probability of default) and t_1 (the historical probability of default) is a risk premium that reflects the unexpected default probability. For example, if $\Phi = 1$ percent, LGD = 40 percent, and $t_1 = 1$ percent, then:

$$\Phi_1 = p_1^* \times \text{LGD} = (t_1 \times \text{LGD}) + u_1 \tag{3.30}$$

$$\Phi_1 = p_1^* \times 0.40 = (0.01 \times 0.40) + u_1 = 0.01 \tag{3.31}$$

In the next step we solve for values of both p_1^* and u_1. From Equations (3.30) and (3.31), the risk-neutral probability of default $p_1^* = 2.5$ percent, which is higher than the historical default probability of $t_1 = 1$ percent, and the unexpected loss or risk premium $u_1 = 0.60$ percent.

Ginzberg et al.[108] offer an approach to how actual U.S. credit spreads can be segregated into an expected loss and a risk premium component. For example, an average (par) spread of 20.01 basis points on one-year AAA corporates over one-year Treasuries can be broken down into an expected loss component $t_1 \times$ LGD of 0.01 basis points and a risk premium u_1 of 20 basis points. An 1188.97 basis-point spread on one-year CCC bonds over Treasuries can be broken down into an expected loss component of 918.97 basis points and an unexpected loss component of 270 basis points.

3.8.7.6 Risk-Neutral Probabilities Applied to Credit Risk Valuation

Risk-neutral probabilities offer substantial potential value for a credit officer in pricing decisions and in making market valuations of loans. For example, risk-neutral probabilities can be used in setting the required spread or risk premium on a loan. Following Ginzberg et al.,[109] assume a credit officer wants to find the fixed spread W on a one-year loan that will yield \$1 of expected NPV from each \$1 lent. The loan would be a break-even project in an NPV sense. The credit officer knows that:

- r = one-year risk-free rate = 4 percent
- p_1^* = risk-neutral probability of default = 6.5 percent
- LGD = 33.434 percent

To solve for s:

$$E(\text{NPV}) = \frac{(1 - p_1^*)(1 + r + s) + p_1^*(1 - \text{LGD})}{1 + r}$$

$$= \frac{(0.935)(1.04 + s) + 0.65(0.66566)}{1.04} \tag{3.32}$$

The value of the loan spread s that solves Equation (3.32) is 2.602 percent. However, a major problem with this approach is seen in extending this type of analysis beyond the one-year horizon. The default or no-default scenario, under which risk-neutral probabilities are derived, fits the one-year loan case but not the multiyear loan case. For multiyear loans, a richer universe of possibilities exists. These include borrower migration upgrades and downgrades, which may trigger some loan repricing clauses, which may in turn affect the value of the loan and the borrower's option to prepay a loan early.

Ginzberg et al.[110] and KPMG's Loan Analysis System[111] have attempted to extend the valuation framework in Equation (3.32) to multiperiod loans with a variety of options. These options include loan spread repricing as nondefault transitions in credit quality occur and building in penalty fees for borrowers who prepay early.

Figure 3-20, from Aguis et al.,[112] describes, in a simplified fashion, the potential transitions of the credit rating of a B-rated borrower over a four-year loan period. Similarities with bond valuation models, especially lattice or "tree" diagrams for bond valuation (binominal model), are obvious. Given transition probabilities, the original grade-B borrower can migrate up or down over the loan's life to different ratings, and may even default and migrate to D (an absorbing state). Along with these migrations, a pricing grid that reflects the bank's current policy on spread repricing for borrowers of different quality can be built. This methodology has the potential to generate additional information regarding whether the credit model has a good or bad repricing grid in an expected NPV sense—basically, whether $E(\text{NPV}) \neq 1$.

When valuing a loan in this framework, valuation takes place recursively (from right to left in Figure 3-20), as it does when valuing bonds under binomial or multinomial models. For example, if the E(NPV) of the loan in its final year is too high (too rich), and given some prepayment fee, the model supports prepayment of the loan to take place at the end of period 3. Working backward through the tree from right to left, the total E(NPV) of the four-year loan can be calculated. Moreover, the credit officer can make different assumptions about spreads (the pricing grid) and prepayment fees to determine the loan's value. Other parameters of a

FIGURE 3-20

Multiperiod Loan Transitions Over Many Periods. [*Source: Scott D. Aguais and Anthony M. Santomero, "Incorporating New Fixed Income Approaches into Commercial Loan Valuation,"* Journal of Lending and Credit Risk Management *80/6 (February 1998), 58–65, fig. 2, http://fic.wharton.upenn.edu/fic/papers/98.html. Reproduced with permission of the authors.*]

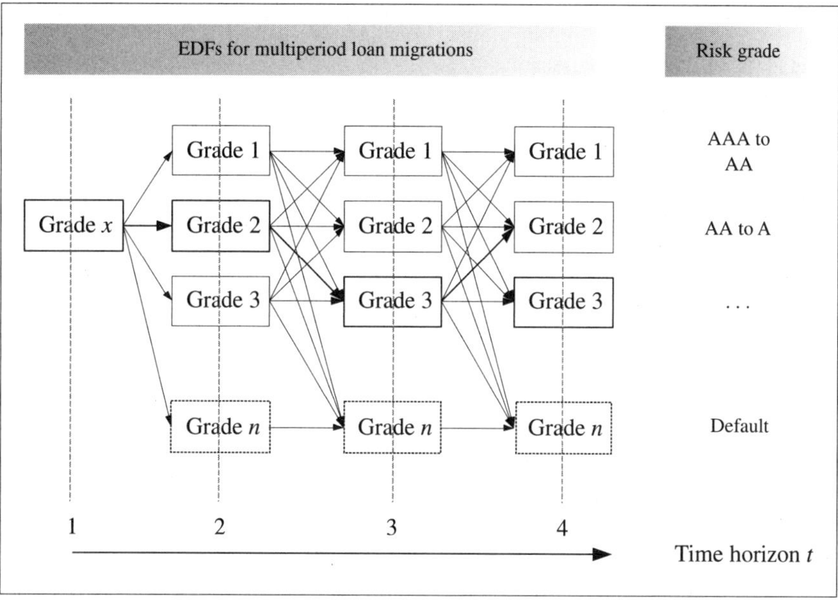

loan's structure, such as caps, and amortization schedules, can be built in, and a VaR can be calculated.[113]

The risk-neutral valuation framework supports the calculation for both default prediction and loan valuation. Compared to historic transition probabilities, the risk-neutral model gives the advantage of a forward-looking prediction of default. The risk-neutral prediction will generally exceed the history-based transition prediction over some horizon because, conceptually, it contains a risk premium reflecting the unexpected probability of default. Moreover, the risk-neutral framework considers only two credit states: default and nondefault; it does not recognize several rating buckets.

KPMG suggested a valuation approach that is potentially consistent with the risk-neutral model under no arbitrage.[114] Over its life, a loan can migrate to states other than default/nondefault. The valuation model is similar in spirit to a multinomial tree model for bond valuation, with the difference that transition probabilities replace interest-rate movement probabilities. This model has some flexibility, as credit spreads can vary, fees can be charged on prepayments, and other special provisions can be built into the valuation process. A question arises as to the link between the model and the existence of an underlying portfolio of replicating assets. In particular, the exact details of the construction of a replicating no-arbitrage portfolio for a multiperiod nontradable loan are still open.

3.8.8 The CSFB CreditRisk$^+$ Model

3.8.8.1 Background

Only quite recently have ideas and concepts from the insurance industry found their way into the new approaches for credit risk measurement and management. The following sections discuss two applications of insurance ideas, one from life insurance and one from property insurance. Altman[115] and others have developed mortality tables for loans and bonds using ideas (and models) similar to those that insurance actuaries use when they set premiums for life insurance policies. Credit Suisse Financial Products, a former subsidiary of Credit Suisse First Boston (CSFB), developed a model similar to the one used by household insurance vendors for assessing the risk of policy losses in setting premiums.

3.8.8.2 Migration of Mortality Approach for Credit Risk Measurement

The concept is quite simple: based on a portfolio of loans or bonds and their historic default experience, develop a table that can be applied in a predictive sense for one-year or marginal mortality rates (MMRs) and for multiyear or cumulative mortality rates (CMRs). Combining such calculations with LGDs allows us to create estimates of expected losses.[116]

To calculate the MMRs of a B-rated bond or loan defaulting in each year of its life, the analyst will pick a sample of years—say, 1971 through 1998—and, for *each individual year,* will analyze:

$$MMR_1 = \frac{\text{Total value of grade-B bonds defaulting in year 1 of issue}}{\text{Total value of a B-rated bond outstanding in year 1 of issue}}$$

$$MMR_2 = \frac{\text{Total value of B-rated bond defaulting in year 2 of issue}}{\begin{array}{l}\text{Total value of a B-rated bond outstanding in year 2 of}\\ \text{issue (adjusted for defaults, calls, sinking fund}\\ \text{redemptions, and maturities in the prior year)}\end{array}} \tag{3.33}$$

And so on for $MMR_3, \ldots, MMR_n$.

When the MMR for a specific individual year has been calculated, the credit officer calculates a weighted average of all MMRs, which becomes the figure entered into the mortality table. The weights used should reflect the relative issue sizes in different years, thus biasing the results toward the years with larger issues. The average MMR in year 1 for a particular rating bucket ($\overline{\text{MMR}}$) would be calculated as:

$$\overline{\text{MMR}}_1 = \sum_{i=1971}^{1998} \text{MMR}_{1i} \cdot w_i$$

$$\sum w_i = 1 \tag{3.34}$$

To calculate a CMR—the probability that a loan or bond will default over a period longer than a year (e.g., 2 years)—it is first necessary to specify the relationship between MMRs and survival rates (SRs):

$$\text{MMR}_i = 1 - \text{SR}_i$$

$$\text{SR}_i = 1 - \text{MMR}_i \tag{3.35}$$

Consequently,

$$\text{CMR}_N = 1 - \prod_{i=1}^{N} \text{SR}_i \tag{3.36}$$

where $\prod$ is the geometric sum or product $[\text{SR}_1 \times \text{SR}_2 \times \ldots \text{SR}_N]$ and N denotes the number of years over which the cumulative mortality rate is calculated.

3.8.8.3 Mortality Rates and Tables

Table 3-7 shows MMRs and CMRs for syndicated loans and bonds over a five-year horizon, as computed by Altman and Suggitt.[117] Looking at the table in more detail, we can see that for the higher-grade buckets the mortality rates are quite comparable, but this is not the case for the lowest-quality-rating buckets. For example, low-quality loans have substantially higher MMRs in the first three years of life than do similarly rated bonds. The critical question is whether high-yield loans and bonds have substantially different default profiles, or is this a statistical result due to a relatively small sample size? In particular, although not described, each of the MMR estimates has an implied standard error and confidence interval. It can be shown that with an increasing number of loans or bonds in the observation sample (i.e., as n gets bigger), the standard error on a mortality rate will fall (i.e., the degree of confidence level applied to calculate the MMR estimate of expected out-of-sample losses increases). As a loan or bond either dies or survives in any period, the standard error T of an MMR is:[118]

TABLE 3-7

Comparison of Syndicated Bank Loan Versus Corporate Bond Mortality Rates, Based on Original Issuance Principal Amounts (1991–1996)

Years after Issue	1		2		3		4		5	
Rating	**Bank**	**Bond**	**Bank**	**Bond**	**Bank**	**Bond**	**Bank**	**Bond**	**Bank**	**Bond**
AAA										
Marginal	0.00%	0.00%	0.00%	0.00%	0.00%	0.00%	0.00%	0.00%	0.00%	0.00%
Cumulative	0.00	0.00	0.00	0.00	0.00	0.00	0.00	0.00	0.00	0.00
Aa										
Marginal	0.00	0.00	0.00	0.00	0.00	0.00	0.00	0.00	0.00	0.00
Cumulative	0.00	0.00	0.00	0.00	0.00	0.00	0.00	0.00	0.00	0.00
A										
Marginal	0.00	0.00	0.12	0.00	0.00	0.00	0.00	0.00	0.00	0.05
Cumulative	0.00	0.00	0.12	0.00	0.12	0.00	0.12	0.00	0.12	0.05
Baa										
Marginal	0.04	0.00	0.00	0.00	0.00	0.00	0.00	0.54	0.00	0.00
Cumulative	0.04	0.00	0.04	0.00	0.04	0.00	0.04	0.54	0.04	0.54
Ba										
Marginal	0.17	0.00	0.60	0.38	0.60	2.30	0.97	1.80	4.89	0.00
Cumulative	0.17	0.00	0.77	0.38	1.36	2.67	2.32	4.42	7.10	4.42
B										
Marginal	2.30	0.81	1.86	1.97	2.59	4.99	1.79	1.76	1.86	0.00
Cumulative	2.30	0.81	4.11	2.76	6.60	7.61	8.27	9.24	9.97	9.24
Caa										
Marginal	15.24	2.65	7.44	3.09	13.03	4.55	0.00	21.72	0.00	0.00
Cumulative	15.24	2.65	21.55	5.66	31.77	9.95	31.77	29.51	31.77	29.51

SOURCE: E. I. Altman and H. J. Suggitt, "Default Rates in the Syndicated Loan Market: A Mortality Analysis," Working Paper S-97-39, New York University Salomon Center, New York, December 1997. Reproduced with permission of NYU Salomon Center.

$$\sigma = \frac{MMR_i \cdot (1 - MMR_i)}{N} \tag{3.37}$$

and rearranging:

$$N = \frac{MMR_i \cdot (1 - MMR_i)}{\sigma^2} \tag{3.38}$$

As can be derived from Equations (3.37) and (3.38), there is an inverse relationship between sample size N and the standard error σ of a mortality rate estimate.

Assume that $MMR_1 = 0.01$ is a mortality rate estimate, and extreme actuarial standards of confidence in the stability of the estimate for pricing and prediction out of sample have to be applied. Extreme actuarial standards might require σ to be one-tenth the size of the mortality rate estimate (or $\sigma = 0.001$). Plugging these values into Equation (3.38) results in:

$$N = \frac{(0.01) \cdot (0.99)}{(0.001)^2} = 9900 \tag{3.39}$$

This results in 10,000 loan observations per rating bucket required to obtain this type of confidence in the estimate. With, say, 10 rating classes, a portfolio of some 100,000 loans would have to be analyzed and calculated. Very few banks have the resources to build information systems of this type. To get to the requisite large size, a nationwide effort among the banks themselves may be required. The end result of such a cooperative effort might be a national loan mortality table per country that could be used for the calculation of the banks' loan loss reserves, based on expected losses, similar to the national life mortality tables applied in pricing life insurance.[119]

3.8.9 CSFB's CreditRisk$^+$ Approach

This section analyzes two insurance-based approaches to credit risk analysis. Mortality analysis offers an actuarial approach to predicting default rates, which is considered an alternative to some of the traditional accounting-based models for measuring expected losses and loan loss reserves. The added value of mortality rates very much depends on the size of the sample of loans or bonds from which they are calculated. CreditRisk$^+$, an alternative to CreditMetrics, calculates capital requirements based on actuarial approaches found in property insurance concepts. The major advantage is the rather minimal data input required (e.g., no data on credit spreads are required). Its major limitation is that it is not a full VaR model because it focuses on loss rates rather than loan value changes. It is a default-mode (DM) model rather than a mark-to-market (MTM) model.

The approach developed by CSFB stands in direct contrast to CreditMetrics in its objectives and its theoretical framework:

- CreditMetrics seeks to estimate the full VaR of a loan or loan portfolio by viewing rating upgrades and downgrades and the associated effects of spread changes in the discount rate as part of the credit's VaR exposure. In contrast, CreditRisk$^+$ considers spread risk as part of market risk rather than credit risk. As a result, in any period, only two states of the credit world are considered, default and nondefault. The focus is on measuring expected and unexpected losses rather than expected value and unexpected changes in value (or VaR) as under CreditMetrics. As mentioned, CreditMetrics is an MTM model, whereas CreditRisk$^+$ is a DM-based model.
- The second major conceptual difference is that in CreditMetrics, the default probability in any year is modeled based on a discrete assumption (as are the upgrade/downgrade probabilities). In CreditRisk$^+$, default is modeled as a continuous variable with a probability distribution. An analogy from home insurance is relevant. When a whole portfolio of home loans is insured, there is a small probability that all houses will burn down simultaneously. In general, the probability that each house will burn down can be considered as an independent event. Similarly, many types of loans, such as mortgages and small business loans, can be analyzed in a similar way, with respect to their default risk. In the CreditRisk$^+$ model, each individual loan is assumed to have a small default probability, and each loan's default probability is independent of the default on other loans.[120] This assumption of independent occurrence makes the default probability distribution of a loan portfolio resemble a Poisson distribution.

Figure 3-21 presents the difference in assumptions regarding default probability distribution in CreditRisk$^+$ and CreditMetrics.

The two degrees of uncertainty, the default frequency and the loss severity, produce a distribution of losses for each exposure band. Summing (or, more exactly, aggregating) these losses across exposure bands produces a distribution of losses for the loan portfolio (Figure 3-22). Although not labeled by CSFB as such, we shall call the model in Figure 3-23 Model 1. The computed loss function, assuming a Poisson distribution for individual default rates and the bucketing of losses, is displayed in Figure 3-23. The loss function is quite symmetric and is close to the normal distribution, which it increasingly approximates as the number of loans in the portfolio increases. However, as discussed by CSFB, default and loss rates tend to have fatter tails than is implied by Figure 3-23.[121] Specifically, the Poisson distribution implies that the mean default rate of a portfolio of loans should equal its variance, that is:

FIGURE 3-21

Comparison of the CreditRisk+ and CreditMetrics Models.

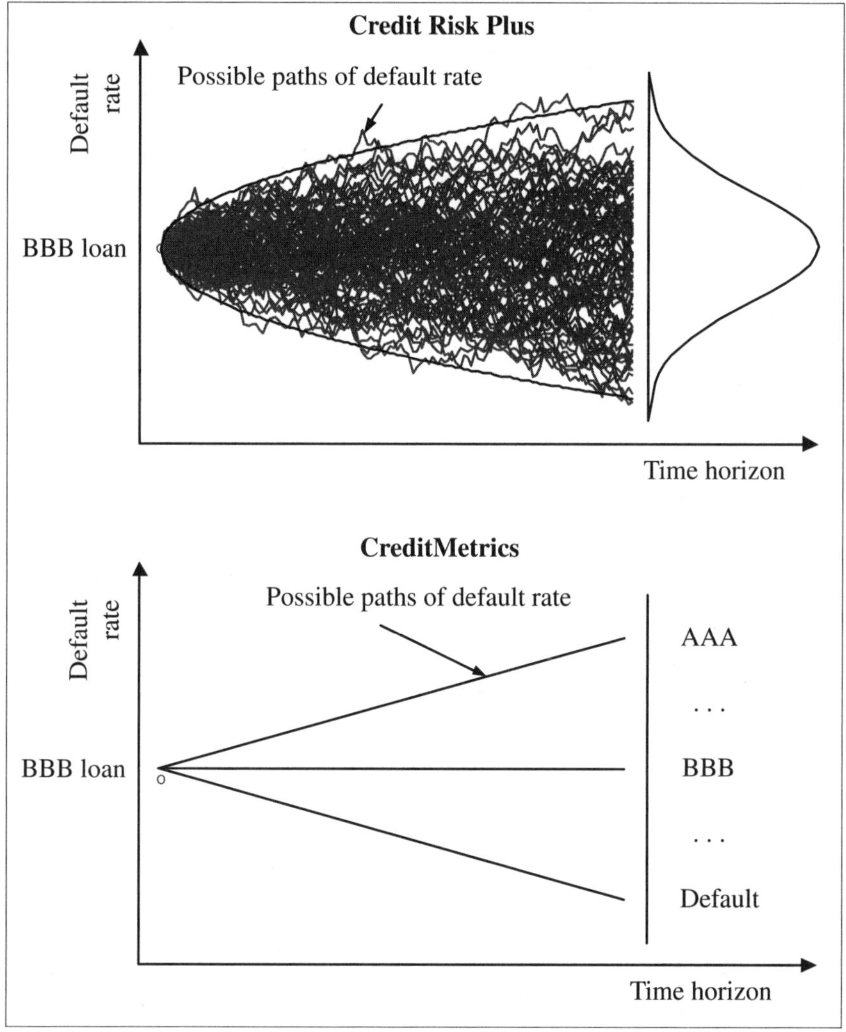

$$\sigma^2 = \text{mean} \tag{3.40}$$

$$\sigma = \sqrt{\text{mean}} \tag{3.41}$$

Using figures on default rates from Carty and Lieberman,[122] CSFB shows that, in general, Equation (3.41) does not hold, especially for lower-quality credit. For B-rated bonds, Carty and Lieberman found that the mean default rate was 7.27 percent, its square root was 2.69 percent, and its σ was

FIGURE 3-22

Influencing Factors on Distribution of Losses.

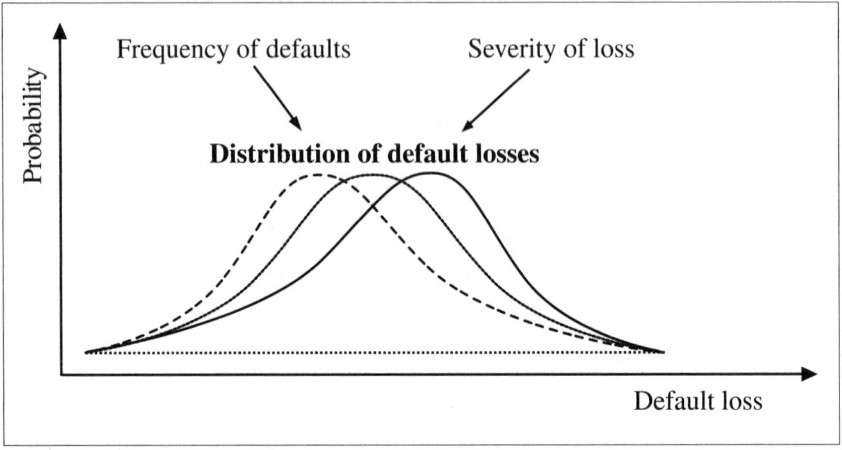

5.1 percent, or almost twice as large as the square root of the mean (see Figure 3-23). This answers the question of what extra degree of uncertainty might explain the higher variance (fatter tails) in observed loss distributions. The additional uncertainty modeled by CSFB is that the mean default rate itself can vary over time or over the business cycle. For example, in economic expansions, the mean default rate will be low; in eco-

FIGURE 3-23

Distribution of Credit Losses with Default Rate Uncertainty and Severity Uncertainty.

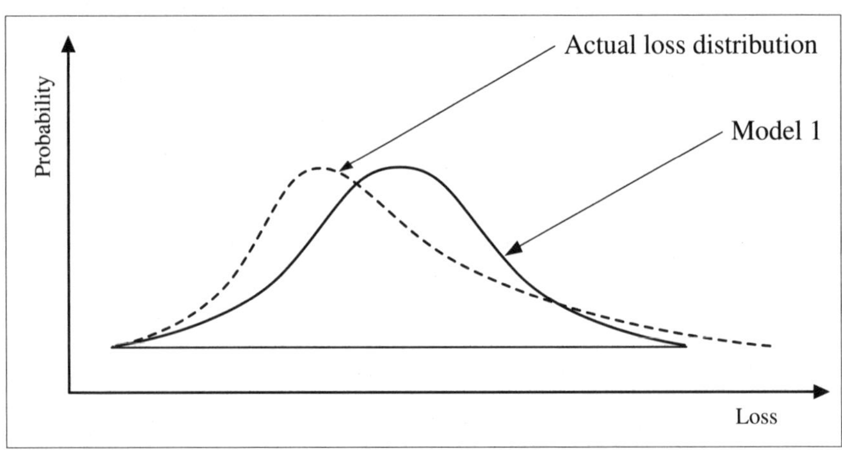

nomic contractions, it may rise substantially. In their extended model (henceforth called Model 2), there are three types of uncertainty:

- The uncertainty of the default rate around any given mean default rate
- The uncertainty about the loss severity
- The uncertainty about the mean default rate itself, modeled as a gamma distribution by CSFP[123]

Appropriately implemented, a loss distribution can be calculated along with expected losses and unexpected losses that exhibit observable fatter tails. The latter can then be used to calculate the capital requirement, as shown in Figure 3-24. Note that this economic capital measure is comparable with the VaR measured under CreditMetrics, because CreditMetrics allows for rating upgrades and downgrades that affect a loan's value. By contrast, there are no nondefault migrations in the CSFB model. Thus, the CSFB capital calculation is closer to a loss-of-earnings or book-value capital measure than a full market value of economic capital measure. Nevertheless, its great advantage lies in its parsimonious requirement of data. The key data inputs are mean loss rates and loss severities, for various loss buckets in the loan portfolio, both of which are potentially amenable to collection, either internally or externally. A simple discrete example of the CSFB Model 1 will illustrate the minimal data input that is required.

FIGURE 3-24

Capital Requirement Based on the CSFB CreditRisk+ Model.

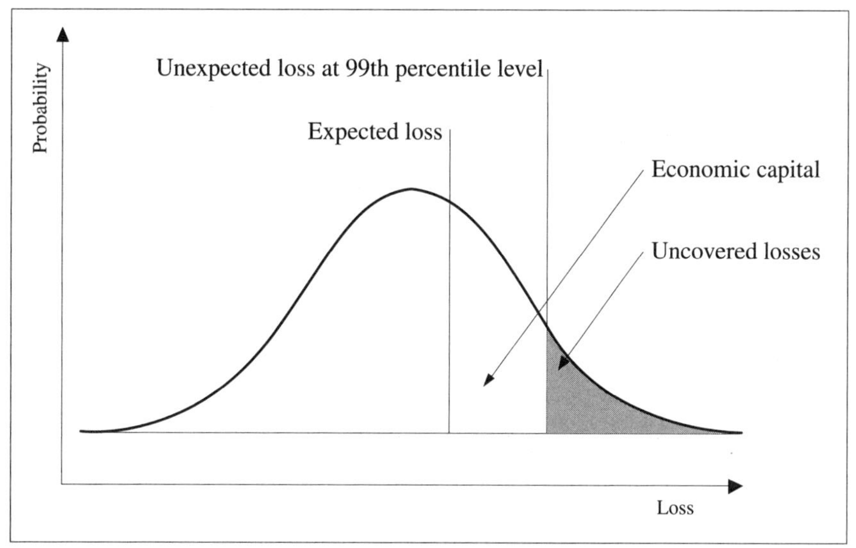

3.8.10 Summary and Comparison of New Internal Model Approaches

3.8.10.1 Background

The previous sections describe key features of some of the more prominent new quantitative models of credit risk measurement that are publicly available. At first glance, these approaches appear to be very different and likely to generate substantially different loan loss exposures and VaR measures. The following sections summarize and compare four of these new models and highlight key differences and similarities among them.

3.8.10.2 Model Comparison

Six key dimensions are used to compare the different approaches among the four models: (1) CreditMetrics, (2) CreditPortfolioView, (3) CreditRisk+, and (4) KMV. Analytically and empirically, these models are not as different as they may first appear. Indeed, similar arguments have been made by Gordy,[124] Koyluoglu and Hickman,[125] and Crouhy and Mark,[126] using different model anatomies. Table 3-8 displays the six key dimensions for comparing the models.

TABLE 3-8

Comparison of Different Approaches

Model				
Dimensions for Comparison	**CreditMetrics (J. P. Morgan)**	**CreditPortfolio-View (McKinsey)**	**CreditRisk+ (CSFP)**	**KMV**
Definition of risk	MTM	MTM or DM	DM	MTM or DM
Risk drivers	Asset values	Macrofactors	Expected default rates	Asset values
Volatility of credit events	Constant	Cyclical	Variable	Variable
Correlations of credit events	Multivariate normal asset returns	Factor loadings correlation of residual risk	Conditional independence assumption or correlation with expected default rate	Multivariate normal asset returns
Recovery rates	Random	Random	Constant with buckets	Constant or random
Numerical approach	Simulation or analytic (one-period VaR)	Simulation (one-period VaR)	Closed-form solution	Closed-form solution

3.8.10.3 Definition of Risk in the Different Models

As described in the previous sections, we distinguish between models that calculate VaR based on the change in the market value of loans using mark-to-market (MTM) models, and models that focus on predicting default losses using default-mode (DM) models.[127] The MTM models allow for credit upgrades and downgrades, and therefore spread changes, as well as defaults in calculating loan value losses and gains. Contrarily, the DM models consider only two states of the credit world: default and nondefault. The key difference between the MTM and DM approaches is the inclusion of spread risk in MTM models. Not surprisingly, if models incorporate different input, they are likely to produce different results. CreditMetrics is an MTM model, whereas CreditRisk+ and KMV are DM models. CreditPortfolioView can be implemented as an MTM or a DM model.

3.8.10.4 Risk Drivers

CreditMetrics and KMV have their analytic foundations in a Merton-type model; a firm's asset values and the volatility of asset values are the key drivers and input variables of default risk. In CreditPortfolioView, the risk drivers are macrofactors (such as inflation, credit spread, etc.); in CreditRisk+, the risk drivers are the mean level of default risk and its volatility. If expressed in terms of multifactor models, all four models can be viewed as having similar roots.[128] Specifically, the variability of a firm's asset returns in CreditMetrics (as well as in KMV) is modeled as being directly linked to the variability in a firm's stock returns. In calculating correlations among firms' asset returns, the stocks of individual firms are determined by a set of systematic risk factors (industry factors, country factors, etc.) and unsystematic risk factors. The systematic risk factors, along with correlations among systematic risk factors (and their weighted sensitivity, similar to the multifactor/arbitrage pricing theory of model portfolio theory), determine the asset returns of individual firms and the default correlations among firms.

The risk drivers in CreditPortfolioView have methodological foundations similar to those of CreditMetrics and KMV. In particular, a set of local systematic market macrofactors and unsystematic macroshocks drives default risk and the correlations of default risks among borrowers in the same local market. The key risk driver in CreditRisk+ is the variable *mean default rate* in the economy. This mean default rate can be linked systematically to the state of the macroeconomy—when the macroeconomy deteriorates, the mean default rate is likely to rise, as are default losses. Improvement in economic conditions has the opposite effect.

Risk drivers and correlations in all four models can be correlated to a certain extent to macrofactors describing the evolution of economywide conditions.

3.8.10.5 Volatility of Credit Events

A key difference in the methodology among the models is in the modeling of the one-year default probability or the probability of default distribution function. In CreditMetrics, the default probability (as well as upgrades and downgrades) is modeled as a fixed or discrete value based on historic data. In KMV, expected default frequencies (EDFs) are linked to the variability of the firm's stock returns, and will vary as new information is impounded in stock prices. Variations in stock prices and the volatility of stock prices determine the KMV's EDF scores. In CreditPortfolioView, the default probability is a logistic function of a set of macrofactors and normally distributed shocks. As the macroeconomy evolves, the default probability and the cells, or probabilities, in the rest of the transition matrix will evolve as well. In CreditRisk$^+$, the default probability of each loan is assumed to be variable, following a Poisson distribution around some mean default rate. The mean default rate is modeled as a variable with a gamma distribution. This produces a distribution of losses that may have fatter tails than those produced by either CreditMetrics or CreditPortfolioView.

3.8.10.6 Correlation of Credit Events

The similarity of the determinants of credit risk correlations has been discussed in the context of risk drivers. Specifically, the correlation structure in all four models can be attributed to systematic sensitivities of loans to key factors. The correlations among borrowers are discussed in Section 3.9.6, where the application of the new models and modern portfolio theory to support credit portfolio decisions is discussed.

3.8.10.7 Recovery Rates

The loss distribution and VaR calculations depend not only on the default probability but also on the loss severity or loss given default (LGD). Empirical evidence suggests that default severities and recovery rates are quite volatile over time. More precisely, building in a volatile recovery rate is likely to increase the VaR or unexpected loss rate.

CreditMetrics, in the context of its VaR calculations, allows for recoveries to be variable. In the current model version, which recognizes a skew in the tail of the loan value loss distribution function, recovery rates are assumed to follow a beta distribution, and the VaR of loans is calculated via a Monte Carlo simulation. In KMV's simplest model, recovery rates are considered constant over time. In more recent extended versions of the model, recovery rates are allowed to follow a beta distribution as well. In CreditPortfolioView, recovery rates are also estimated via a Monte Carlo simulation approach. By contrast, under CreditRisk$^+$, loss severities are clustered and allocated into subportfolios, and the loss severity in any subportfolio is considered constant over time.

3.8.10.8 Numerical Approach

The estimation approach of VaRs, or unexpected losses, differs across models. A VaR, at both the individual loan level and the loan portfolio level, can be calculated analytically under CreditMetrics. This approach becomes increasingly intractable as the number of loans in the portfolio increases. As a result, for large loan portfolios, Monte Carlo simulation techniques are applied to generate an approximate aggregate distribution of portfolio loan values, and thus a VaR. Similarly, CreditPortfolioView uses repeated Monte Carlo simulations to generate macroshocks and the distribution of losses (or loan values) of a loan portfolio. CreditRisk^{+}, based on its convenient distributional assumptions (the Poisson distribution for individual loans and the gamma distribution for the mean default rate, along with the fixed recovery assumption for loan losses in each subportfolio of loans), allows an analytic or closed-form solution to be generated for the probability density function of losses. KMV allows an analytic solution to the loss function.

The development of internal models for credit risk measurement and capital requirements is at an early stage. In some sense, its present level of development can be compared to that of market risk in 1994, when RiskMetrics first appeared and was followed by alternative methodologies such as historic simulation and Monte Carlo simulation. The credit risk models publicly available to date have exhibited quite different approaches across a number of important dimensions. Harmonizing these models across just a few key dimensions, however, can result in quite comparable unexpected loss calculations. This suggests that over time, with theoretical and model development, a consensus model or approach may eventually emerge. To some extent, this has already happened in the market risk modeling area, supported by regulatory incentives.

3.8.11 Comparison of Major Credit Risk Models

A variety of credit models exists, which are mainly portfolio approaches. The different conceptual approaches of the most current applications are summarized in the following list:

- KMV

  Conceptual model. Expected default frequency based on market value of assets. Borrower defaults when available resources have been depleted below a critical level. EDFs are linked to the variability of the firm's stock returns, which will vary as new information is impounded in stock prices. Variations in stock prices and the volatility of stock prices determine the KMV stock scores.

  Modeling of concentration. A multifactor stock return model is applied, from which correlations are calculated. The model reflects the correlation among the systemic risk factors affecting each firm's asset correlation, their individual default probabilities, and their appropriate weights. The approach to estimate correlations is similar to that used in CreditMetrics. However, KMV typically finds that correlations lie in the range of 0.002 to 0.15, which is relatively low.

- CreditMetrics

  Conceptual model. Simulation-based portfolio approach, in which changes in debt values are modeled based on changes in rating, and the market value of each position is a derived function of its rating. Simulations of credit migrations are time consuming.

  Modeling of concentration. Concentration risk is modeled by sector allocation, and borrower correlation is derived from sector correlations. Asset returns are simulated and mapped to simulated credit migrations. Recovery rates are random variables.

- CreditRisk$^+$

  Conceptual model. Insurance or actuarial type for modeling low-probability, high-impact events. Default probability of each loan is assumed to be a random, conditionally independent variable, following a Poisson distribution around some mean default rate. The mean default rate is modeled as a variable with a gamma distribution. The default probability on each sector is different.

  Modeling of concentration. Each position is allocated to sectors that represent countries and industries. Sectors are conditionally assumed to be independent, and one individual sector can be used for modeling the specific risk of positions.

- CreditPortfolioView

  Conceptual model. A conditioned transition matrix is calculated, simulating the evolution of transition probabilities over time by generating macroshocks to the model. The simulated transition matrix replaces the historically based unconditional (stable Markov) transition matrix. Given any current rating for the loan, the distribution of loan values, based on the macroadjusted transition probabilities in the row for a specific rating of the matrix, could be used to calculate VaR at the one-year horizon, in a fashion similar to that used in CreditMetrics. A cyclically sensitive VaR for 1, 2, . . . , n years can be calculated.

  Modeling of concentration. Directly models the relationship between transition probabilities and macrofactors; in a secondary step, a model is fitted to simulate the evolution of transition probabilities over time by shocking the model with macroevents. Each position is allocated to sectors that represent countries and industries. Sectors are not conditionally assumed to be independent.

Depending on the conceptual approach of the model, the input parameters are different, as is the way some of the key elements of credit risk are handled. Correlations that are inferred from equity indexes (such as the CreditMetrics model) require a three-step process for the computation of the credit correlation coefficient (Figure 3-25):

- CreditMetrics provides the correlation coefficients describing the comovements of various industry–country equity indexes.
- The user has to define (input) how much of the variance in an individual borrower's credit indicator is derived from the various country–industry indexes.
- The model then computes the borrower's credit correlation coefficients.

Volatility values are critical information for the portfolio approach, as they are the basis for the correlation calculation, a key component of the portfolio approach. To measure portfolio VaR, one starts with the loan-

FIGURE 3-25

Three-Step Process for Calculation of Credit Correlation Coefficients.

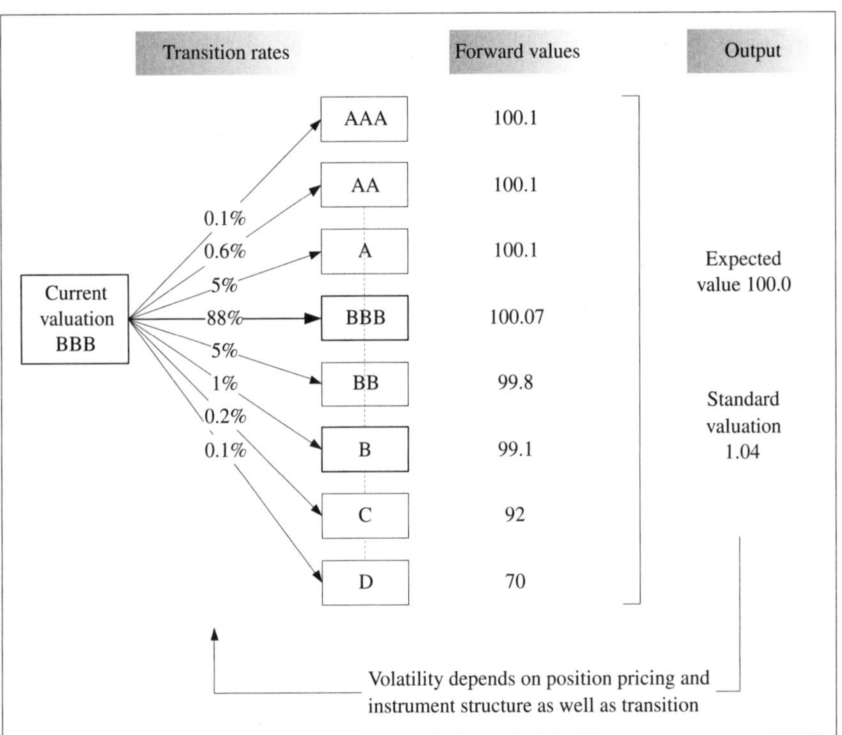

specific volatility, which reflects price (historical and future) and the structure of the loan. The volatility depends on the issue of price and structure as well as the transitions. The forward valuation depends on:

- Loan price and loan structure
- Collateral
- Spread and fees
- Amortization
- Tenor
- Options (e.g., prepayment, repricing or grid, term-out, and market conditions)

The portfolio distribution can be produced by simulation, using random draws of the loans' x_i values. In a second step, the end-of-period ratings are derived. In a third step, the loans are priced, based on the ratings and other input parameters. In a fourth step, the loans are summed up to get the portfolio value by using the values and the correlation from the random draws. This procedure is repeated many times to derive a stable distribution of the portfolio with the loans' x_i values (see Figure 3-26).

Instead of estimating the loans' x_i values, the distribution of common and specific factors can be estimated by using random draws of the factors. In a first step, random draws of the factors are taken. In a second step, the random draws of the factors are used to calculate the x_i values. In a third step, the loans are priced, based on the ratings and other input parameters. In a fourth step, the loans are summed up to get the portfolio value by using the values and the correlation from the random draws. This procedure is repeated many times to derive a stable distribution of the portfolio with the loans' x_i values (see Figure 3-27).

FIGURE 3-26

Computation of Portfolio Distribution Through Simulation Process.

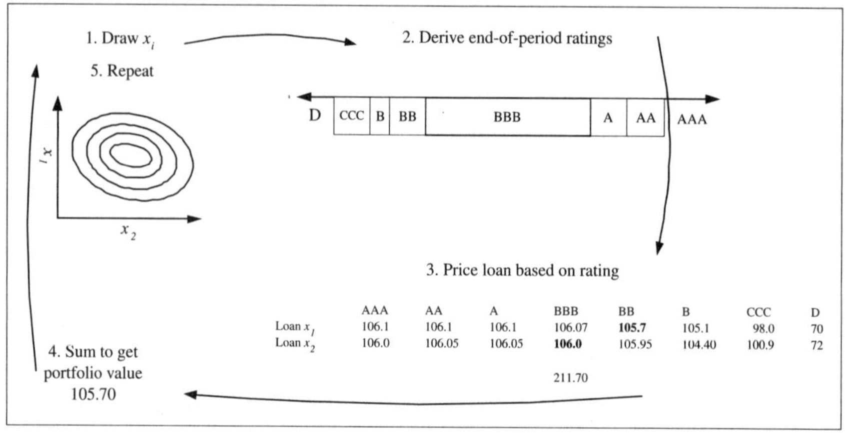

FIGURE 3-27

Distribution of Common and Specific Factors Through Random Drawing.

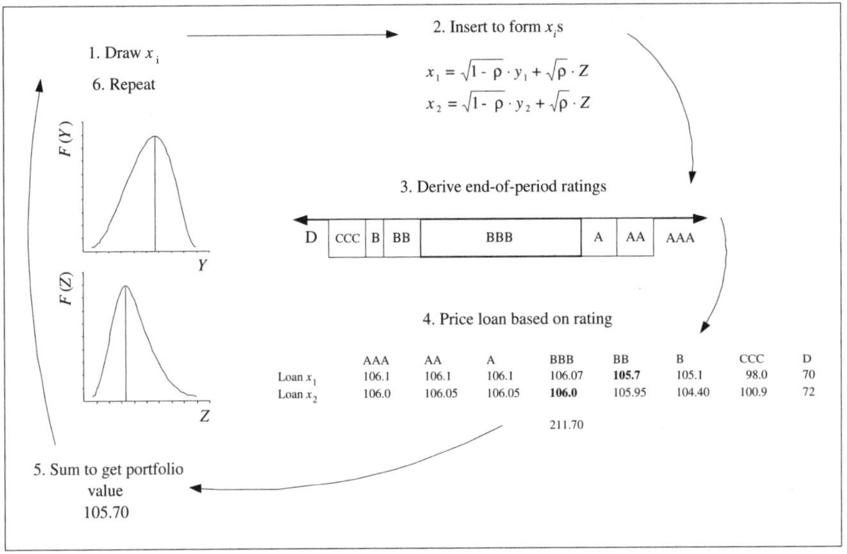

3.9 MODERN PORTFOLIO THEORY AND ITS APPLICATION TO LOAN PORTFOLIOS

3.9.1 Background

Default risk and credit risk exposure are commonly viewed on a single-borrower basis. Much of the banking theory literature views the personnel at banks and similar institutions as credit specialists who, over time, through monitoring and the development of long-term relationships with customers, gain a comparative advantage in lending to a specific borrower or group of borrowers. (The current BIS risk-based capital ratio is linearly additive across individual loans.) This advantage, developed by granting (and holding to maturity) loans to a select subset of long-term borrowers, can be viewed as inefficient from a risk–return perspective. Instead, loans publicly traded, or "swappable" with other financial organizations, could be considered as being similar to commodity-type assets such as equities, which are freely traded at low transaction costs and with high liquidity in public securities markets. By separating the credit-granting decision from the credit portfolio decision, a financial organization may be able to generate a better risk–return trade-off, and offset what KMV and others have called the *paradox of credit.*

Figure 3-28 illustrates the paradox of credit by applying the efficient frontier approach to loans. Portfolio A is a relatively concentrated loan

FIGURE 3-28

The Paradox of Credit.

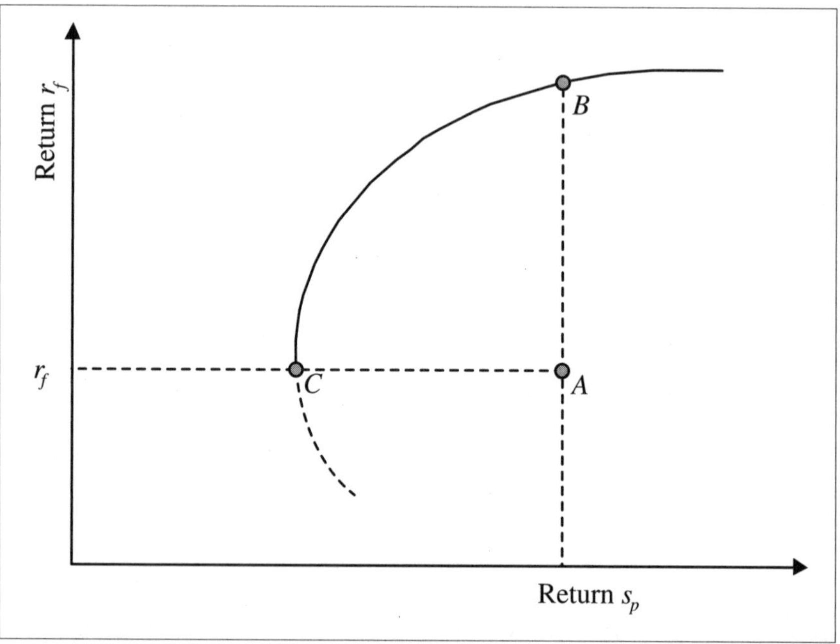

portfolio for a traditional bank that makes and monitors loans, and holds those loans to maturity. Portfolios B and C are on the *efficient frontier* of loan portfolios. They achieve either the maximum return for any level of risk *B* or the minimum risk for a given return C. To move from *A* to either *B* or *C*, the bank must actively manage its loan portfolio in a manner similar to the tenets of modern portfolio theory (MPT), where the key focus for improving the risk–return trade-off is on (1) the default correlations (diversification) among the assets held in the portfolio and (2) a willingness, as market conditions vary, to flexibly adjust the loan allocation rather than to make and hold loans to maturity, as is the traditional practice in banking.

Modern portfolio theory provides a useful framework for considering risk–return trade-offs in loan portfolio management. The MPT framework provides the analytical basis for the intuitive observation that the lower the correlation among loans in a portfolio, the greater the potential for a manager to reduce a bank's risk exposure through diversification. Assuming that a VaR-based capital requirement reflects the concentration risk and default correlations of the loan portfolio, such a diversified portfolio may have lower credit risk than a similar portfolio with loan exposures that are considered independently additive (as is the case with the current BIS 8 percent capital ratio).

There are a number of problems in directly applying MPT to loans and loan portfolios (and many bonds), including the following:

- The nonnormality of loan returns
- The unobservability of market-based loan returns (and, thus, correlations) as a result of the fact that most loans are nontraded

These issues and other related problems are discussed in Section 3.8.10.2, which analyzes approaches suggested by KMV, CreditMetrics, and other models. Specific attention is given to how these new approaches calculate returns, risk, and correlations of loans and loan portfolios.

3.9.2 Application to Nontraded Bonds and Credits

Modern portfolio theory has been around for almost 50 years and is now a common portfolio management tool, used by most money managers. It has also been applied with some success to publicly traded junk bonds when their returns have tended to be more equitylike (price driven) than bondlike (yield driven) and when historical returns have been available.[129] With respect to most loans and bonds, however, there are problems with nonnormal returns, unobservable returns, and unobservable correlations.

The following sections discuss various approaches to applying MPT techniques to loan portfolios. Most of the new credit models are not full-fledged MPT models (returns are often not modeled), but their importance is in the link they show between both default correlations and portfolio diversification and loan portfolio risk.

The consensus of the literature and the industry appears to be that default correlations are relatively low on average, and gains through loan portfolio diversification are potentially high. The current 8 percent BIS risk-based capital ratio ignores correlations among loans in setting capital requirements, and it may be an inadequate reflection of capital requirements. In particular, MPT-based models are more precise in suggesting that loan portfolios in which individual loan default risks are highly correlated should have higher capital requirements than loan portfolios of similar size in which default risk correlations are relatively low. In contrast, the current BIS regulations specify that the same capital requirement is to be imposed for equally sized portfolios of private-sector loans, independent of their country, industry, or borrower composition.

3.9.3 Nonnormal Returns

Loans and bonds tend to have relatively fixed upside returns and long-tailed downside risks. Thus, returns on these assets tend to show a strong negative skew and, in some cases, kurtosis (fat-tailedness) as well. MPT is built around a model in which only two moments—the mean and the variance—are required to describe the distribution of returns. To the extent that the third (skew) and fourth (kurtosis) moments of returns substantially describe the distribution of asset returns, the straightforward application of MPT models based on the simple two-moment approach becomes difficult to justify. It can be argued that as the number of loans in a portfolio gets bigger, the distribution of returns tends to become more normal.

3.9.4 Unobservable Returns

An additional issue relates to the fact that most loans and corporate bonds are nontraded or are traded as OTC products at irregular intervals with infrequent historical price or volume data. The estimation of mean returns $\bar{\mu}$ and the variance of returns σ_i^2 using historic time series thus becomes challenging.

3.9.5 Unobservable Correlations

Similarly, if price and return data are unavailable, or the estimates are unreliable given the previously mentioned issues, calculating the covariance σ_{ij} or correlation ρ_{ij} among asset returns also becomes difficult. The correlations are a key building block in MPT-type analysis.[130]

3.9.6 Modeling Risk–Return Trade-Off of Loans and Loan Portfolios

3.9.6.1 Background

The following discussion focuses on a number of ways to apply MPT-type techniques to a loan portfolio. It distinguishes between models that seek to calculate the full risk–return trade-off for a portfolio of loans (such as KMV's Portfolio Manager) and models that concentrate mostly on the risk dimension (such as CreditMetrics) and the VaR of the loan portfolio.

3.9.6.2 KMV's Portfolio Manager

KMV's Portfolio Manager can be considered a full-fledged modern portfolio theory optimization approach, because all three key variables—returns, risks, and correlations—are calculated. However, it can also be used to analyze risk effects alone, as discussed later. Next is a discussion of how the three key variables that enter into any MPT model can be calculated.

Loan Returns

In the absence of return histories on traded loans, the expected return on the ith loan R_{it} over any given time horizon can be expressed as:

$$R_{it} = [\text{spread}_i + \text{fees}_j] - [\text{expected loss}_i] \quad (3.42)$$

Or:

$$R_{it} = [\text{spread}_i + \text{fees}_j] - [\text{EDF}_i \cdot \text{LGD}_i] \quad (3.43)$$

The first component of returns is the spread of the loan rate over a benchmark rate (such as LIBOR), plus any fees directly allocated to the loan and expected over a given period (e.g., a year). Expected losses on the loan are subsequently deducted because they can be viewed as part of the normal cost of doing banking business. In the context of a KMV-type model, where the expected default frequency (EDF) is estimated from stock returns (the CreditMonitor model), then, for any given borrower, expected losses will equal $\text{EDF}_j \times \text{LGD}_j$, where LGD_i is the loss given default for the *i*th borrower (usually estimated from the bank's internal database).

Loan Risks

In the absence of historical return data on loans, a loan's risk σ_{LGD} can be approximated by the unexpected loss rate on the loan UL_i—essentially, the variability of the loss rate around its expected value $\text{EDF}_i \times \text{LGD}$. There are several approaches in which the unexpected loss can be calculated, depending on the assumptions made about the number of credit-rating transitions, the variability of LGD, and the correlation of LGDs with EDFs. For example, in the simplest case, we can assume a DM model in which the borrower either defaults or doesn't default, so that defaults are binomially distributed and LGD is fixed and constant across all borrowers. Then:

$$\sigma_i = \text{UL}_i = \sqrt{(\text{EDF}_i) \cdot (1 - \text{EDF}_i)} \cdot \text{LGD} \quad (3.44)$$

where $\sqrt{(\text{EDF}_i) \cdot (1 - \text{EDF}_i)}$ reflects the variability of a default-rate frequency that is binominally distributed. A slightly more sophisticated DM version would allow LGD to be variable, but factors affecting EDFs are assumed to be different from those affecting LGDs, and LGDs are assumed to be independent across borrowers. In this case:

$$\sigma_i = \sqrt{(\text{EDF}_i) \cdot (1 - \text{EDF}_i) \cdot \text{LGD}_i^2 + \text{EDF}_i \cdot \text{LGD}_i^2} \quad (3.45)$$

where σ_i is the standard deviation of borrower i's LGD.[131] If we want to develop σ_i measures, allowing for a full MTM model with credit upgrades and downgrades as well as default, then σ_i might be calculated similarly to CreditMetrics, as discussed later. Indeed, in recent versions of its model, KMV produces a rating transition matrix based on EDFs and allows a full MTM calculation of σ_i to be made.[132]

Loan Correlations

One important assumption in a KMV-type approach is that default correlations are likely to be low. To see why, consider the context of the two-state DM version of a KMV-type model. A default correlation would reflect the joint probability of two firms X and Y—say, Ericsson and Nokia—having their asset values fall simultaneously below their debt values over the same horizon (e.g., one year). In the context of Figure 3-29, the Ericsson asset value would have to fall below its debt value B_Y, and the Nokia asset value would have to fall below its debt value B_X. The joint area of default is shaded, and the joint probability distribution of asset values is represented by the isocircles. The isocircles are similar to those used in geography charts to describe hills. The inner circle is the top of the hill representing high probability, and the outer circles are the bottom of the hill (low probability). The joint probability that asset values will fall in the shaded region is comparably low and will depend, in part, on the asset

FIGURE 3-29

Joint Default Probabilities. [*Source: Harry M. Markowitz,* Portfolio Selection (2), *2d ed., Oxford, United Kingdom: Basil Blackwell, 1992, figure 4,* and *KMV,* Credit-Monitor Overview, *San Francisco: KMV Corporation,* 1993; Portfolio Management of Default Risk, *San Francisco: KMV Corporation, November 15, 1993, rev. May 31, 2001, 10. Reproduced with permission of Blackwell Publishing and KMV LLC.*]

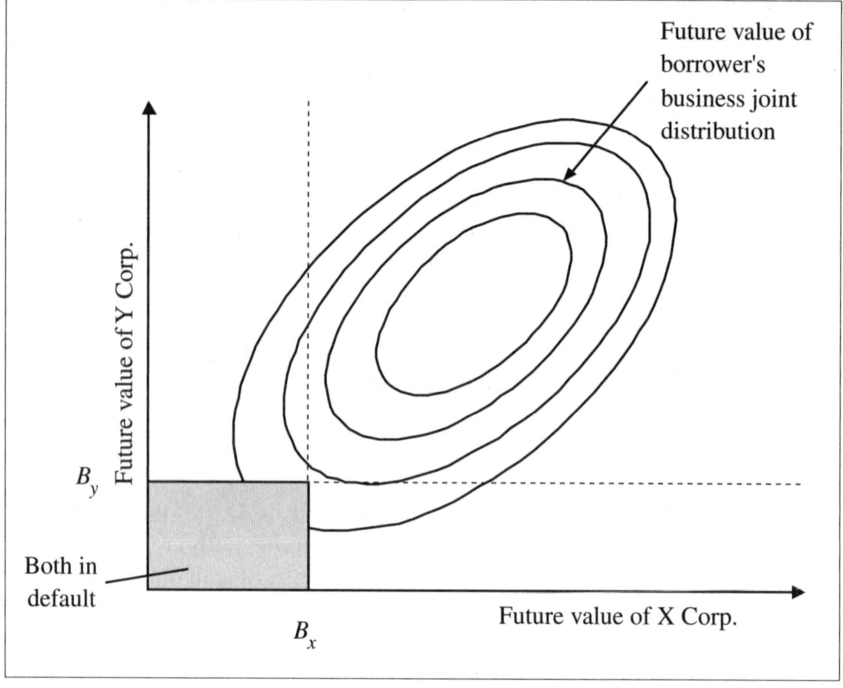

correlations between the two borrowers. In the context of the simple binomial model, for Nokia N and Ericsson E, respectively:

$$\rho_{NE} = \frac{\sigma_{NE}}{\sigma_N \cdot \sigma_E} \tag{3.46}$$

$$\rho_{NE} = \frac{\mathrm{JDF}_{NE} - (\mathrm{EDF}_N \cdot \mathrm{EDF}_E)}{\sqrt{(\mathrm{EDF}_N)(1 - \mathrm{EDF}_N)} \cdot \sqrt{(\mathrm{EDF}_E)(1 - \mathrm{EDF}_E)}} \tag{3.47}$$

The numerator of Equation (3.47), σ_{NE}, is the covariance between the asset values of the two firms, N and E. It reflects the difference between when the two asset values are jointly distributed (JDF_{NE}) and when they are independent ($\mathrm{EDF}_N \cdot \mathrm{EDF}_E$). The denominator, $\sigma_N \cdot \sigma_E$, reflects the standard deviation of default rates under the binomial distribution for each firm. Rather than seeking to directly estimate correlations using Equation (3.47), KMV uses a multifactor stock-return model from which correlations are calculated. The model reflects the correlation among the systematic risk factors affecting each firm and their appropriate weights. KMV's approach to estimate correlations is discussed under CreditMetrics. However, KMV typically finds that correlations lie in the range of 0.002 to 0.15, and are thus relatively low. After the estimation, the three inputs (returns, risks, and correlations) can be used in a number of ways. One potential use would be to calculate a risk–return efficient frontier for the loan portfolio, as discussed previously.

A second application is to measure the risk contribution of expanding lending to any given borrower. As discussed earlier, the risk (in a MPT portfolio sense) of any individual loan will depend on the risk of the individual loan on a stand-alone basis and its correlation with the risks of other loans. For example, a loan might be thought to be risky when viewed individually, but because its returns are negatively correlated with other loans, it may be quite valuable in a portfolio context by contributing to diversification and thus lowering portfolio risk.

The effects of granting additional loans to a particular borrower also depend crucially on assumptions made about the balance-sheet constraint of the financial organization. For example, if investable or loanable funds are viewed as fixed, then expanding the proportion of assets lent to any borrower i (i.e., increasing X) means reducing the proportion invested in all other loans (assets) as the overall amount of funds is constrained. However, if the funds constraint is viewed as nonbinding, then the amount lent to borrower i can be expanded without affecting the amount lent to other borrowers. In the KMV-type marginal risk contribution calculation, a funding constraint is assumed to be binding:

$$X_i + X_j + \cdots + X_n = 1 \tag{3.48}$$

By comparison, in CreditMetrics, the marginal risk contributions are calculated assuming no funding constraint. For example, a financial organization can make a loan to a tenth borrower without reducing the loans outstanding to the nine other borrowers.

Assuming a binding funding constraint, the marginal risk contribution (MRC) for the ith loan can be calculated as follows:

$$UL_p = \left[\sum_{i=1}^{N} X_i^2 \cdot UL_i^2 + \sum_{i=1}^{N}\sum_{\substack{i=1 \\ i \neq 1}}^{N} X_i X_j UL_i UL_j \rho_{ij}\right]^{1/2} \tag{3.49}$$

And

$$\sum_{i=1}^{N} X_i = 1 \tag{3.50}$$

The marginal risk contribution can also be viewed as a measure of the economic capital needed by the bank in order to grant a new loan to the ith borrower, because it reflects the sensitivity of portfolio risk (specifically, portfolio standard deviation) to a marginal percentage change in the weight of the asset. Note that the sum of MRCs is equal to UL_p; consequently, the required capital for each loan is just its MRC scaled by the capital multiple (the ratio of capital to UL_p).[133]

3.9.6.3 CreditMetrics

In contrast to KMV, CreditMetrics can be viewed more as a loan portfolio risk-minimizing model than a full-fledged MPT risk–return model. Returns on loans are not explicitly modeled. Thus, the discussion focuses on the measurement of the VaR for a loan portfolio. As with individual loans, two approaches to measuring VaR are considered:

- Loans are assumed to have normally distributed asset values.
- The actual distribution exhibits a long-tailed downside or negative skew.

The normal distribution approach is discussed; this approach produces a direct analytic solution to VaR calculations using conventional MPT techniques.

Portfolio VaR Under the Normal Distribution Model

In the normal distribution model, a two-loan case provides a useful benchmark. A two-loan case is readily generalizable to the N-loan case; that is, the risk of a portfolio of N loans can be shown to depend on the risk of each pair of loans in the portfolio.

To calculate the VaR of a portfolio of two loans, we need to estimate:

- The joint migration probabilities for each loan (assumed to be the \$100-million face value BBB loan discussed, and an A-rated loan of \$100 million face value)
- The joint payoffs or values of the loans for each possible one-year joint migration probability

Joint Migration Probabilities

Table 3-9 shows the one-year individual and joint migration probabilities for the BBB and A loans. Given the eight possible credit states for the BBB borrower and the eight possible credit states for the A borrower over the next year (the one-year horizon), there are 64 joint migration probabilities. The joint migration probabilities are not simply the additive product of the two individual migration probabilities. These can be recalculated by looking at the independent probabilities that the BBB loan will remain BBB (0.8693) and the A loan will remain A (0.9105) over the next year. The joint probability, assuming the correlation between the two migration probabilities is zero, would be $0.8693 \cdot 0.9105 = 0.7915$ or 79.15 percent. The joint probability in Table 3-9 is slightly higher, at 79.69 percent, because the assumed correlation between the rating classes of the two borrowers is 0.3.

Adjusting the migration table to reflect correlations is a two-step process. First, a model is required to explain migration transitions. Credit-Metrics applies a Merton-type model to link asset value or return volatil-

TABLE 3-9

Joint Migration Probabilities with 0.30 Asset Correlation

Obligor 1 (BBB)		*Obligor 2 (A)*							
		AAA	**AA**	**A**	**BBB**	**BB**	**B**	**CCC**	**Default**
		0.09	**2.27**	**91.05**	**5.52**	**0.74**	**0.26**	**0.01**	**0.06**
AAA	**0.02**	0.00	0.00	0.02	0.00	0.00	0.00	0.00	0.00
AA	**0.33**	0.00	0.04	0.29	0.00	0.00	0.00	0.00	0.00
A	**5.95**	0.02	0.39	5.44	0.08	0.01	0.00	0.00	0.00
BBB	**86.93**	0.07	1.81	79.69	4.55	0.57	0.19	0.01	0.04
BB	**5.30**	0.00	0.02	4.47	0.64	0.11	0.04	0.00	0.01
B	**1.17**	0.00	0.00	0.92	0.18	0.04	0.02	0.00	0.00
CCC	**0.12**	0.00	0.00	0.09	0.02	0.00	0.00	0.00	0.00
Default	**0.18**	0.00	0.00	0.13	0.04	0.01	0.00	0.00	0.00

SOURCE: J. P. Morgan, *CreditMetrics Technical Document,* New York: J. P. Morgan, April 2, 1997, 38.

ity to discrete rating migrations for individual borrowers. Second, a model is needed to calculate the correlations among the asset value volatilities of individual borrowers. Similar to KMV, asset values of borrowers are unobservable, as are correlations among those asset values. The correlations among the individual borrowers are therefore estimated from multifactor models driving borrowers' stock returns.

Linking Asset Volatilities and Rating Transitions

To see the link between asset volatilities and rating transitions, consider Figure 3-30, which links standardized normal asset return changes (measured in standard deviations) of a BB-rated borrower to rating transitions.[134]

If the unobservable (standardized) changes in asset values of the firm are assumed to be normally distributed, we can calculate how many standard deviations asset values would have to have to move the firm from BB into default. For example, the historic one-year default probability of this type of BB borrower is 1.06 percent. Using the standardized normal distribution tables, asset values would have to fall by 2.3 σ for the firm to default. Also, there is a 1 percent probability that the BB firm will move to a C rating over the year. Asset values would have to fall by at least 2.04σ to change the BB borrower's rating to C or below. There is a 2.06 percent probability (1.06% + 1.00%) that the BB-rated borrower will be downgraded to C or below (such as D). The full range of possibilities is graphed in Figure 3-30. Similar figures could be constructed for a BBB borrower, an

FIGURE 3-30

Link Between Asset Value Volatility σ and Rating Transitions for a BB-Rated Borrower. (*Source: Modified from J. P. Morgan,* CreditMetrics Technical Document, *New York: J. P. Morgan, April 2, 1997, 87, 88, tables 8.4 and 8.5, chart 8.2. Copyright © 1997 by J. P. Morgan & Co., Inc., all rights reserved. Reproduced with permission of RiskMetrics Group, Inc.)*

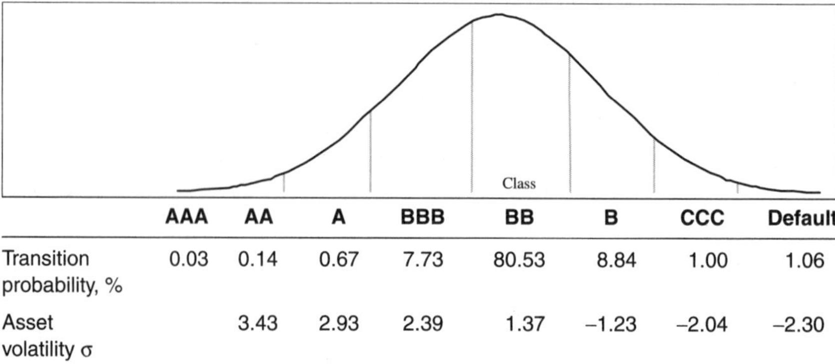

	AAA	AA	A	BBB	BB	B	CCC	Default
Transition probability, %	0.03	0.14	0.67	7.73	80.53	8.84	1.00	1.06
Asset volatility σ		3.43	2.93	2.39	1.37	−1.23	−2.04	−2.30

TABLE 3-10

Link Between Asset Value Volatility σ and Rating Transitions for an A-Rated Borrower

	Class							
	AAA	AA	A	BBB	BB	B	CCC	Default
Transition probability, %	0.09	2.27	91.05	5.52	0.74	0.26	0.01	0.06
Asset volatility σ		3.12	1.98	−1.51	−2.30	−2.72	−3.19	−3.24

SOURCE: J. P. Morgan, *CreditMetrics Technical Document,* New York: J. P. Morgan, April 2, 1997, 87, table 8.4.

A borrower, and so on. The links between asset volatility and rating changes for an A borrower are shown in Table 3-10.

From Figure 3-30, we can see that a BB-rated borrower will remain BB as long as the standardized normal asset returns of the borrowing firm fluctuate between −1.23 σ and +1.37 σ. The A borrower's rating will remain unchanged as long as the asset returns of the firm vary between −1.51 σ and +1.98 σ. Assume that the correlation p between those two firms' asset returns is 0.2 (to be calculated in more detail later).

The joint probability Pr that both borrowers will remain simultaneously in the same rating class during the next year can be found by integrating the bivariate normal density function as follows:

$$\Pr(-1.23 < BB < 1.37, -1.51 < 1.98) = \int_{-1.23}^{1.37} \int_{-1.51}^{1.98} f(\zeta_1 \zeta_2; \rho) \cdot \zeta_1 \zeta_2 = 0.7365 \quad (3.51)$$

where ζ_1 and ζ_2 are random, and $\rho = 0.20$.

In Equation (3.51), the correlation coefficient ρ_i is assumed to be equal to 0.2. As described next, these correlations, in general, are calculated in CreditMetrics based on multifactor models of stock returns for the individual borrower.[135]

Joint Loan Values

In addition to 64 joint migration probabilities (in this generic example), we can calculate 64 joint loan values in the two-loan case, as shown earlier (Table 3-9). The market value for each loan in each credit state is calculated and discussed under Joint Migration Probabilities. Individual loan values are then added to get a portfolio loan value, as shown in Table 3-11. Thus, if

TABLE 3-11

Loan Portfolio Value: All 64 Possible Year-End Values for a Two-Loan Portfolio

Obligor 1 (BBB)		*Obligor 2 (A)*							
		AAA	**AA**	**A**	**BBB**	**BB**	**B**	**CCC**	**Default**
		106.59	**106.49**	**106.30**	**105.64**	**103.15**	**101.39**	**88.71**	**51.13**
AAA	**109.37**	215.96	215.86	215.67	215.01	212.52	210.76	198.08	160.50
AA	**109.19**	215.78	215.68	215.49	214.83	212.34	210.58	197.90	160.32
A	**108.66**	215.25	215.15	214.96	214.30	211.81	210.05	197.37	159.79
BBB	**107.55**	214.14	214.04	213.85	213.19	210.70	208.94	196.26	158.68
BB	**102.02**	208.61	208.51	208.33	207.66	205.17	203.41	190.73	153.15
B	**98.10**	204.69	204.59	204.40	203.74	210.25	199.49	186.81	149.23
CCC	**83.64**	190.23	190.13	189.94	189.28	186.79	185.03	172.35	134.77
Default	**51.13**	157.72	157.62	157.43	156.77	154.28	152.52	139.84	102.26

SOURCE: J. P. Morgan, *CreditMetrics—Technical Document,* New York: J. P. Morgan, April 2, 1997, 12.

both loans get upgraded to AAA over the year, the market value of the loan portfolio at the one-year horizon becomes \$215.96 million. By comparison, if both loans default, the value of the loan portfolio becomes \$102.26 million.

With 64 possible joint probabilities and 64 possible loan values, the mean value of the portfolio and its variance are as computed in Equations (3.52) and (3.53):

$$\text{Mean} = p_1 \cdot V_1 + p_2 \cdot V_2 + \cdots + p_{64} \cdot V_{64} = \$213.63 \text{ million} \tag{3.52}$$

$$\begin{aligned}\text{Variance} &= p_1 \cdot (V_1 - \text{mean})^2 \\ &+ p_2 \cdot (V_2 - \text{mean})^2 + \cdots \\ &+ p_{64} \cdot (V_{64} - \text{mean})^2 \\ &= \$11.22 \text{ million}\end{aligned} \tag{3.53}$$

Taking the square root of the solution to Equation (3.53), the σ of the loan portfolio value is \$3.35 million and the VaR at the 99 percent confidence level under the normal distribution assumption is $2.33 \cdot \$3.35 = \$7.81$ million.

Comparing this result of \$7.81 million for a face-value credit portfolio of \$200 million with the 99 percent VaR-based capital requirement of \$6.97 million (for the single BBB loan of \$100 million face value as derived earlier, we can see that although the credit portfolio has doubled in face value, a VaR-based capital requirement (based on the 99th percentile of the loan portfolio's value distribution) has increased by only \$0.84 million (\$7.81 million – \$6.97 million). The reason for this low increase in VaR is portfolio diversification. A correlation of .3 between the default risks of the two loans is built into the joint transition probability matrix in Table 3-11.

Portfolio VaR Using the Actual Distribution

The capital requirement under the normal distribution is likely to underestimate the true VaR at the 99 percent level because of the skewness in the actual distribution of loan values. Using Table 3-9 in conjunction with Table 3-11, the 99 percent (worst-case scenario) loan value for the portfolio is \$204.40 million.[136] The unexpected change in value of the portfolio from its mean value is \$213.63 million – \$204.40 million = \$9.23 million. This is higher than the capital requirement under the normal distribution discussed previously (\$9.23 million versus \$7.81 million); however, the contribution of portfolio diversification is clear. In particular, the regulatory capital requirement of \$9.23 million for the combined \$200-million face-value portfolio can be favorably compared to the \$8.99 million for the individual BBB loan of \$100 million face value.

Parametric Approach with Many Large Loans

The normal distribution approach can be enhanced in two ways:

- The first way is to keep expanding the loan joint transition matrix, directly or analytically computing the mean and standard deviation of the portfolio. However, this rapidly becomes computationally difficult. For example, in a five-loan portfolio, there are 81 possible joint transition probabilities, or over 32,000 joint transitions.
- The second way is to manipulate the equation for the variance of a loan portfolio. It can be shown that the risk of a portfolio of *N* loans depends on the risk of each pairwise combination of loans in the portfolio as well as the risk of each individual loan. To consistently estimate the risk of a portfolio of *N* loans, only the risks of subportfolios containing two assets need to be calculated.

CreditMetrics uses Monte Carlo simulation to compute the distribution of loan values in the large sample case in which loan values are not normally distributed. Consider the portfolio of loans in Table 3-12 and the correlations among those loans (borrowers) in Table 3-13. For each loan, 20,000 (or more) different underlying borrower asset values are simulated, based on the original rating of the underlying loan, the joint transition probabilities, and the historical correlations among the loans.[137] The loan (or borrower) can either stay in its original rating class or migrate to another rating class. Each loan is then revalued after each simulation and rating transition. Adding across the simulated values for the 20 loans produces 20,000 different values for the loan portfolio as a whole. Based on the 99 percent worst-case scenario, a VaR for the loan portfolio can be calculated as the value of the loan portfolio that has the 200th worst value out of 20,000 possible loan portfolio values.

In conjunction with the mean loan portfolio value, a capital requirement can be derived. The CreditMetrics portfolio approach can also be applied to calculation of the marginal risk contribution for individual loans. Unlike the KMV approach, funds are considered as being flexibly adjustable to accommodate an expanded loan supply, and marginal-means loans are either granted or not granted to a borrower, rather than making an incremental amount of new loans to an existing borrower.

Table 3-14 demonstrates the stand-alone and marginal risk contributions of 20 loans in a hypothetical loan portfolio based on a standard deviation measure of risk σ. The stand-alone columns reflect the dollar and percentage risk of each loan, viewed individually. The stand-alone percentage risk for the CCC-rated asset (number 7) is 22.67 percent, and the B-rated asset (number 15) is 18.72 percent. The marginal risk contribution columns in Table 3-14 reflect the risk of adding each loan to a portfolio containing the remaining 19 loans (the standard deviation risk of a 20-loan

TABLE 3-12

Example Portfolio

Credit asset	Rating	Principal amount, $	Maturity, years	Market value, $
1	AAA	7,000,000	3	7,821,049
2	AA	1,000,000	4	1,177,268
3	A	1,000,000	3	1,120,831
4	BBB	1,000,000	4	1,189,432
5	BB	1,000,000	3	1,154,641
6	B	1,000,000	4	1,263,523
7	CCC	1,000,000	2	1,127,628
8	A	10,000,000	8	14,229,071
9	BB	5,000,000	2	5,386,603
10	A	3,000,000	2	3,181,246
11	A	1,000,000	4	1,181,246
12	A	2,000,000	5	2,483,322
13	B	600,000	3	705,409
14	B	1,000,000	2	1,087,841
15	B	3,000,000	2	3,263,523
16	B	2,000,000	4	2,527,046
17	BBB	1,000,000	6	1,315,720
18	BBB	8,000,000	5	10,020,611
19	BBB	1,000,000	3	1,118,178
20	AA	5,000,000	5	6,181,784

SOURCE: J. P. Morgan, *CreditMetrics—Technical Document,* New York: J. P. Morgan, April 2, 1997, 121.

portfolio minus the standard deviation risk of a 19-loan portfolio). Interestingly, Table 3-14, on a stand-alone basis, Asset 7 (CCC) is riskier than Asset 15 (B), but when risk is measured in a portfolio context (by its marginal risk contribution), Asset 15 is riskier. The reason can be seen from the correlation matrix in Table 3-13, where the B-rated loan (Asset 15) has a "high" correlation level of 0.45 with Assets 11, 12, 13, and 14. By comparison, the highest correlations of the CCC-rated loan (Asset 7) are with Assets 5, 6, 8, 9, and 10, at the 0.35 level.

One policy implication is immediate and is shown in Figure 3-31, where the total risk (in a portfolio context) of a loan is broken down into two

TABLE 3-13

Asset Correlations for Example Portfolio

	1	2	3	4	5	6	7	8	9	10	11	12	13	14	15	16	17	18	19	20
1	1	0.45	0.45	0.45	0.15	0.15	0.15	0.15	0.15	0.15	0.1	0.1	0.1	0.1	0.1	0.1	0.1	0.1	0.1	0.1
2	0.45	1	0.45	0.45	0.15	0.15	0.15	0.15	0.15	0.15	0.1	0.1	0.1	0.1	0.1	0.1	0.1	0.1	0.1	0.1
3	0.45	0.45	1	0.45	0.15	0.15	0.15	0.15	0.15	0.15	0.1	0.1	0.1	0.1	0.1	0.1	0.1	0.10	.1	0.1
4	0.45	0.45	0.45	1	0.15	0.15	0.15	0.15	0.15	0.15	0.1	0.1	0.1	0.1	0.1	0.1	0.1	0.1	0.1	0.1
5	0.15	0.15	0.15	0.15	1	0.35	0.35	0.35	0.35	0.35	0.2	0.2	0.2	0.2	0.2	0.15	0.15	0.15	0.1	0.1
6	0.15	0.15	0.15	0.15	0.35	1	0.35	0.35	0.35	0.35	0.2	0.2	0.2	0.2	0.2	0.15	0.15	0.15	0.1	0.1
7	0.15	0.15	0.15	0.15	0.35	0.35	1	0.35	0.35	0.35	0.2	0.2	0.2	0.2	0.2	0.15	0.15	0.15	0.1	0.1
8	0.15	0.15	0.15	0.15	0.35	0.35	0.35	1	0.35	0.35	0.2	0.2	0.2	0.2	0.2	0.15	0.15	0.15	0.1	0.1
9	0.15	0.15	0.15	0.15	0.35	0.35	0.35	0.35	1	0.35	0.2	0.2	0.2	0.2	0.2	0.15	0.15	0.15	0.1	0.1
10	0.15	0.15	0.15	0.15	0.35	0.35	0.35	0.35	0.35	1	0.2	0.2	0.2	0.2	0.2	0.15	0.15	0.15	0.1	0.1
11	0.1	0.1	0.1	0.1	0.2	0.2	0.2	0.2	0.2	0.2	1	0.45	0.45	0.45	0.45	0.2	0.2	0.2	0.1	0.1
12	0.1	0.1	0.1	0.1	0.2	0.2	0.2	0.2	0.2	0.2	0.45	1	0.45	0.45	0.45	0.2	0.2	0.2	0.1	0.1
13	0.1	0.1	0.1	0.1	0.2	0.2	0.2	0.2	0.2	0.2	0.45	0.45	1	0.45	0.45	0.2	0.2	0.2	0.1	0.1
14	0.1	0.1	0.1	0.1	0.2	0.2	0.2	0.2	0.2	0.2	0.45	0.45	0.45	1	0.45	0.2	0.2	0.2	0.1	0.1
15	0.1	0.1	0.1	0.1	0.2	0.2	0.2	0.2	0.2	0.2	0.45	0.45	0.45	0.45	1	0.2	0.2	0.2	0.1	0.1
16	0.1	0.1	0.1	0.1	0.15	0.15	0.15	0.15	0.15	0.15	0.2	0.2	0.2	0.2	0.2	1	0.55	0.55	0.25	0.2
17	0.1	0.1	0.1	0.1	0.15	0.15	0.15	0.15	0.15	0.15	0.2	0.2	0.2	0.2	0.2	0.55	1	0.55	0.25	0.2
18	0.1	0.1	0.1	0.1	0.15	0.15	0.15	0.15	0.15	0.15	0.2	0.2	0.2	0.2	0.2	0.55	0.55	1	0.25	0.2
19	0.1	0.1	0.1	0.1	0.1	0.1	0.1	0.1	0.1	0.1	0.1	0.1	0.1	0.1	0.1	0.25	0.25	0.25	1	0.6
20	0.1	0.1	0.1	0.1	0.1	0.1	0.1	0.1	0.1	0.1	0.1	0.1	0.1	0.1	0.1	0.25	0.25	0.25	0.65	1

SOURCE: J. P. Morgan, *CreditMetrics—Technical Document,* New York: J. P. Morgan, April 2, 1997, 122.

TABLE 3-14

Standard Deviation of Value Change

		Stand-alone		Marginal	
Asset	Credit rating	Absolute, $	Percent	Absolute, $	Percent
1	AAA	4,905	0.06	239	0.00
2	AA	2,007	0.17	114	0.01
3	A	17,523	1.56	693	0.06
4	BBB	40,043	3.37	2,934	0.25
5	BB	99,607	8.63	16,046	1.39
6	B	162,251	12.84	37,664	2.98
7	CCC	255,680	22.67	73,079	6.48
8	A	197,152	1.39	35,104	0.25
9	BB	380,141	7.06	105,949	1.97
10	A	63,207	1,99	5,068	0.16
11	A	15,360	1.30	1,232	0.10
12	A	43,085	1.73	4,531	0.18
13	B	107,314	15.21	25,684	3.64
14	B	167,511	15.40	44,827	4.12
15	B	610,900	18.72	270,000	8.27
16	B	322,720	12.77	89,190	3.53
17	BBB	28,051	2.13	2,775	0.21
18	BBB	306,892	3.06	69,624	0.69
19	BBB	1,837	0.16	120	0.01
20	AA	9,916	0.16	389	0.01

SOURCE: J. P. Morgan, *CreditMetrics—Technical Document,* New York: J. P. Morgan, April 2, 1997, 130.

components: (1) its percentage marginal standard deviation (vertical axis) and (2) the dollar amount of credit exposure (horizontal axis). We then have:

Total risk of a loan

$$= \text{marginal standard deviation, \%} \times \text{credit exposure, \$} \quad (3.54)$$

For the 13-rated loan the standard deviation results in a risk of:

$$\$270{,}000 = 8.27\% \times \$3{,}263{,}523$$

FIGURE 3-31

Credit Limits and Loan Selection in the CreditMetrics Framework. (*Source: Modified from J. P. Morgan,* CreditMetrics Technical Document, *New York: J. P. Morgan, April 2, 1997, 131. Copyright © 1997 by J. P. Morgan & Co., Inc., all rights reserved. Reproduced with permission of RiskMetrics Group, Inc.*)

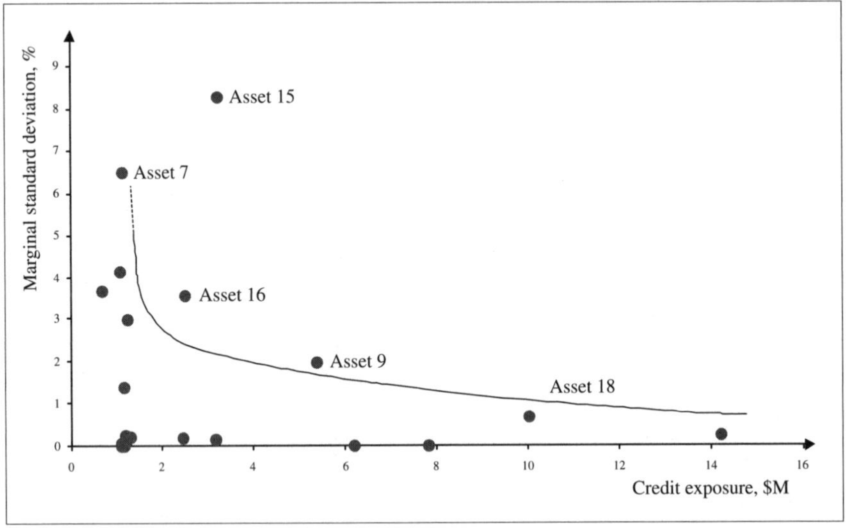

Also plotted in Figure 3-32 is an equal risk isoquant of $70,000. Suppose managers wish to impose a total credit risk exposure limit of $70,000 on each loan measured in a portfolio context. Then Asset 15 (the 13-rated loan) and Assets 16 and 9 are obvious outliers. One possible alternative would be for the financial institution to sell Asset 15 to another institution, or to swap it for another B-rated asset that has a lower correlation with the other loans (assets) in the institution's portfolio. In doing so, its expected returns may remain (approximately) unchanged, but its loan portfolio risk is likely to decrease due to an increased benefit from diversification.

3.9.6.4 Alternative Portfolio Approaches

CreditPortfolioView and CreditRisk+ can only be considered partial MPT models, similar to CreditMetrics, because the returns on loans and the loan portfolio are not explicitly modeled.

The role of diversification in CreditPortfolioView is obvious in the context of the macroshock factors (or unsystematic risk factors) U and V (see Section 3.8.6.3), which drive the probability of borrower default over time. As portfolio diversification increases (e.g., across countries in the CreditPortfolioView model), the relative importance of unsystematic risk to systematic risk will shrink, and the exposure of a loan portfolio to shocks will shrink. In the context of the Monte Carlo simulations of the model, the 99 percent worst-case loss for an internationally well diversified portfolio is likely to be less pronounced (other things being equal) than that for a concentrated one-country or industry-specialized loan portfolio.

In CreditRisk$^+$, two model cases have to be distinguished. In Model 1 (see Section 3.8.9), two sources of uncertainty can be identified: the frequency described by the Poisson distribution of the number of defaults (around a constant mean default rate), and the severity of losses (variable across loan exposure bands). Because the Poisson distribution implies that each loan has a small probability of default and that this probability is independent across loans, the correlation of default rates is, by definition, zero.

In Model 2, however, where the mean default rate itself is variable over time (described with a gamma distribution), correlations are induced among the loans in the portfolio because they show varying systematic linkages to the mean default rate movements. As discussed in Section 3.8.10, the movement in the mean default rate can be modeled in terms of factor sensitivities to different independent sectors (which could be countries or industries). For example, a company's default probability may be sensitive to both a U.S. factor and a UK factor. Given this trait, the default correlations in CreditRisk$^+$ are shown to be equal to:

$$\rho_{AB} = (m_A m_B)^{1/2} \sum_{k=1}^{N} \theta_{Ak}\theta_{Bk} \left(\frac{\sigma_k}{m_k}\right)^2 \tag{3.55}$$

where ρ_{AB} = default correlation between borrowers A and B
m_A = mean default rate for Type-A borrower
m_B = mean default rate for Type B borrower
θ_A = allocation of borrower A's default rate volatility across N sectors
θ_B = allocation of borrower B's default rate volatility across N sectors
$(\sigma_k/m_k)^2$ = proportional default rate volatility in sector k

Table 3-15 demonstrates an example of Equation (3.55) where each of the two borrowers is sensitive to one economywide sector only ($\theta_{Ak} = \theta_{Bk} = 1$), and $\sigma_k/m_k = 0.7$ is set at an empirically reasonable level. As can be seen from Table 3-15, as the credit quality of the borrowers declines (i.e., m_A and m_B get larger), correlations increase. Nevertheless, even in the case in which individual mean default rates are high (m_A = 10 percent and m_B = 7 percent), the correlation among the borrowers is still quite small (in this case, 4.1 percent).

Another issue to discuss is correlations derived from intensity-based models. The correlations among default rates reflect the effect of events in inducing *simultaneous* jumps in the default intensities of obligors. The causes of defaults themselves are not modeled explicitly. However, what

TABLE 3-15

Relationship Between Mean Default Rates and Default Correlations

m_A	0.5%	5%	10%
m_B	1%	2%	7%
θ_{Ak}	1	1	1
θ_{Bk}	1	1	1
σ_k/m_k	70%	70%	70%
ρ_{AB}	0.35%	1.55%	4.1%

SOURCE: Credit Suisse First Boston, *CreditRisk*+, technical document, London/New York, October 1997. Reproduced with permission of Credit Suisse First Boston (Europe) Ltd.

are modeled are various approaches to default-arrival intensity that focus on correlated times to default. This allows the model to answer questions such as the worst week, month, year, and so on, out of the past *N* years, in terms of loan portfolio risk. The worst period is derived when correlated default intensities were highest (defaults arrived at the same time). With joint credit events, some of the default intensity of each obligor is tied to such an event with some probability.[138]

3.9.7 Differences in Credit versus Market Risk Models

In analyzing the applicability of regulatory requirements to the credit risk issue, it appears that qualitative standards will play a similarly important role in the assessment of the accuracy of credit risk models and the credit process (such as management oversight). However, the application of quantitative standards to credit risk models is likely to be more difficult than for market risks for the following reasons:

- *Data limitation* and *data integrity* appear to be major hurdles in the design and implementation of credit risk models. Most credit instruments are not marked to market. The statistical evidence for credit risk models does not derive from a statistical analysis of prices; the comprehensive historical basis is not comparable to that for market risks. The scarcity of the data required for modeling credit risk also stems from the infrequent nature of default events and the longer-term time horizons used in measuring credit risk. The parameterization of credit risk models requires a more in-depth understanding of the model's sensitivity to structural assumptions and parameter estimates, requiring the use of simplifying assumptions, parameters, and proxy data.

- *Validation* and *verification* of credit risk models are also fundamentally more difficult than the backtesting procedure used for market risk models. Based on the frequency of the data available, market risk models typically employ a horizon of a few days, whereas credit risk models generally rely on a time frame of one year or more. Longer holding periods, combined with the higher target loss quantiles used in credit risk models, present design problems in assessing the accuracy of the models. A quantitative standard for the validation of the accuracy of models similar to that presented in the Market Risk Amendment would require an impractical number of years of data, spanning multiple credit cycles.
- The segment of an institution's banking book concerned with credit risk exposures and the length of the time horizon of such products are much greater than those of the trading books. Hence, errors in measuring credit risk are more likely to affect the assessment of the bank's overall soundness. It appears more likely that losses can accumulate over time unnoticed in the banking book, as it is not marked to market on a regular basis.

3.10 BACKTESTING AND STRESS TESTING CREDIT RISK MODELS

3.10.1 Background

A critical issue for financial organizations and regulators is the validation and predictive accuracy of internal models. In the context of market models, this issue has led to numerous efforts to backtest models to ascertain their predictive accuracy. Under the current BIS market risk–based capital requirements, a financial organization must validate the accuracy of its internal market models through backtesting over a minimum of 250 past days if they are used for capital requirement calculations. If the predicted VaR errors for those 250 days are outside a given confidence level (i.e., risk is underestimated on too many days), penalties are imposed by regulators to create incentives for bankers to improve the models.[139]

It can be argued, however, that backtesting over a 250-day time horizon is not enough, given the high standard-deviation errors that are likely to be involved if the period is not representative. To reduce errors of this type, suggestions have been made to increase the number of historical daily observations over which a backtest of a model is conducted. For example, a horizon of at least 1000 past daily observations is commonly believed to be adequate to ensure that the period chosen is representative in terms of testing the predictive accuracy of any given model. However, even for traded financial assets such as currencies, a period of 1000 past days requires going back in time more than four years and may involve covering a wide and unrepresentative range of foreign-exchange regimes, as such a horizon may include structural changes.

The key measure of the usefulness of internal credit risk models is their predictive ability. Tests of predictive ability, such as backtesting, are difficult for credit risk models because of the lack of the following requirements:

- *Sufficiently long time-series data.* Given a large and representative (in a default risk sense) loan portfolio, it is possible to stress-test credit risk models by using cross-sectional subportfolio sampling techniques that provide predictive information on average loss rates and unexpected loss rates.
- *Comparability of conditioning variables from model to model.* The predictive accuracy, in a cross-sectional sense, of different models can be used to select different models. In the future, wider-panel data sets, and time series of loan loss experience, are likely to be developed by financial institutions and consortiums of banks (e.g., the British Bankers' Association). The credit risk models are used at the beginning of such an exercise, and it is important to note that, to be really useful, these loan portfolio experience data sets should include not only loss experience but also the conditioning variables that the different models require (e.g., recoveries, loan size, ratings, and interest rates).

3.10.2 Credit Risk Models and Backtesting

To appropriately backtest or stress-test market risk models, 250 observations are required. But it is unlikely that a bank would be able to provide anywhere near that many past observations. With annual observations (which are the most likely to be available), a bank might be able to provide only a fraction of the required historical observations, severely limiting the institution to a capacity to perform only time-series backtesting similar to that which is currently available for market risk models.[140]

3.10.3 Stress Testing Based on Time-Series Versus Cross-Sectional Approaches

Recent studies from Granger and Huang[141] (at a theoretical level), and Carey[142] and Lopez and Saidenberg[143] (at a simulation and empirical level), provide evidence that stress tests similar to those conducted across time for market risk models can be conducted using cross-sectional or panel data for credit risk models. In particular, suppose that in any given year a bank has a sample of N loans in its portfolio, where N is sufficiently large. By repeated subsampling of the total loan portfolio, it is possible to generate a cross-sectional distribution of expected losses, unexpected losses, and the full probability density function of losses. By comparing cross-sectional subportfolio loss distributions with the actual full-portfolio loss distribution, it is possible to estimate the predictive accuracy of a credit risk model. If the model is a good predictor—and thus the backtesting results should support this statement—the mean average loss rate and the mean 99th percentile loss rate from a high number of randomly drawn subportfolios of the total loan portfolio (e.g., 10,000) should be statistically close to the actual average and 99th percentile loss rates of the full loan portfolio experienced in that year.[144]

A number of statistical problems arise with cross-sectional stress testing, but these are similar to those that arise with time-series stress testing (or backtesting):

- The first problem, and perhaps the most critical, is ensuring the representative nature of any given year or subperiod selected to determine statistical moments such as the mean (expected) loss rate and the 99 percent unexpected loss rate. Structural changes in the market can make past data invalid for the prediction of future losses. The emergence of new credit instruments, changes in the fiscal behavior of the government, and legal or regulatory changes regarding debt and equity treatment, tax law, and so forth can impact the way a model reflects systematic versus unsystematic risk factors. This suggests that some type of screening test needs to be conducted on various recession years before a given year's loss experience is chosen as a benchmark for testing predictive accuracy among credit risk models and for calculating capital requirements.[145]
- The second problem is the effect of outliers on simulated loss distributions. A few extreme outliers can seriously affect the mean, variance, skew, and kurtosis of an estimated distribution, as well as the correlations among the loans implied in the portfolio. In a market risk model context, it can be shown that only 5 outliers out of 1000 observations, in terms of foreign currency exchange rates, can have a major impact on estimated correlations among key currencies.[146] When applying this issue to credit risk, the danger is that a few major defaults in any given year could seriously bias the predictive power of any cross-sectional test of a given model.
- The third problem is that the number of loans in the portfolio has to be large; therefore, the data sample has to be very large. It will be big enough only in the case of a nationwide database.

For example, Carey's sample is based on 30,000 privately placed bonds held by a dozen life insurance companies from 1986 to 1992, a period during which more than 300 credit-related events (defaults, debt restructurings, and so on) occurred for the issuers of the bonds.[147] The subsamples chosen varied in size; for example, portfolios of $0.5 to $15 billion, containing no more than 3 percent of the bonds of any one issuer. Table 3-16 shows simulated loss rates from 50,000 subsample portfolios drawn from the 30,000-bond population. Subportfolios were limited to $1 billion in size.

Table 3-16 compares Monte Carlo estimates of portfolio loss rates at the mean and at various percentiles of the credit loss rate distribution, when Monte Carlo draws are limited to the good years, 1986 to 1989; the bad years, 1990 to 1992; and the worst year, 1991. All drawn portfolios are $1 billion in size. The two panels, each with three rows, report results when all simulated portfolio assets are investment grade and below investment grade (rated <BBB), respectively. An exposure-to-one-borrower limit of 3 percent of the portfolio size was enforced in building simulated portfolios. The results in each row are based on 50,000 simulated portfolios.

TABLE 3-16

Loss Rate Distribution When Monte Carlo Draws Are from Good Versus Bad Years

Portfolio Assets Rated < BBB, %	Years Used	*Simulated Portfolio Loss Rate, %*						
			Loss Distribution Percentile					
		Mean	95	97.5	99	99.5	99.9	99.95
0	Good: 1986–1989	0.09	0.53	0.74	1.40	1.46	1.98	2.14
0	Bad: 1990–1992	0.15	0.87	1.26	1.45	1.59	2.22	2.28
0	Very bad:	0.16	0.91	1.40	1.54	1.67	2.28	2.36
100	Good: 1.73 1986–1989	4.18	4.63	5.11	5.43	5.91	6.05	
100	Bad: 1990–1992	2.53	5.59	6.31	7.19	7.82	8.95	9.33
100	Very bad: 1991	3.76	6.68	7.30	8.04	8.55	9.72	10.19

SOURCE: Mark Carey, "Credit Risk in Private Debt Portfolios," *Journal of Finance* (August 1998), 1363–1387. Reproduced with permission of Blackwell Publishing.

The loss rates vary by year. In 1991, which was the trough of the last U.S. recession, 50,000 simulated portfolios containing <BBB bonds produced a mean 99 percent loss rate of 8.04 percent, which is quite close to the BIS 8 percent risk-based capital requirement. However, note that in relatively good years (e.g., 1986 to 1989), the 99 percent loss rate was much lower: 5.11 percent.

3.11 PRODUCTS WITH INHERENT CREDIT RISKS

3.11.1 Credit Lines

3.11.1.1 Description

Credit lines originate when a bank extends credit to a borrower with a specified maximum amount and a stated maturity. The borrower then draws and repays funds through the facility in accordance with its requirements. Lines of credit are useful for short-term financing of working capital or seasonal borrowings. A commitment fee is usually charged on the unused portion. These loans are often unsecured but may be collateralized by accounts receivable, securities, or inventory. The contractual profile depends on the risks involved and the experience of the bank with the specific client. Firms engaged in manufacturing, distribution, retailing, and the service sector often use lines of credit to finance short-term working-capital needs.

3.11.1.2 Inherent Risk Types

As with all credit, the primary risk is that the borrower will default and be unable to repay the principal amount amortization and interest outstanding at any point in time. Lines-of-credit facilities are exposed to an element of contingent principal risk in that the bank generally has a contractual commitment to lend additional funds on demand. Depending on the contractual profile, market risk through interest-rate fluctuations might affect the profitability of a credit line. Variable-interest payments from the borrower to the bank will change over time, depending on actual interest rates and the reset dates.

3.11.1.3 Quantification of Credit Risks

The bank's exposure on a line-of-credit facility consists of the following components:

- Outstanding principal amount (less amortization paid)
- Accrued interest outstanding
- Credit equivalent exposure from the remaining commitment to lend additional funds on demand (which can be quantified as the remaining amount of the maximal credit level multiplied by the probability of drawdown by the borrower)

The next step is to assess the borrower's total exposure. The bank has to determine the likelihood that the borrower will default. To collateralize the borrower's credit, the bank has to value the net realizable assets. All these factors are used to quantify the overall credit exposure and serve as a basis to calculate the provisioning.

3.11.1.4 Exposure to Market Risks

The bank has a market risk if the interest payments from the borrower to the bank are based on variable rates. The bank is thus exposed to changes in the level and the term structure of interest rates.

3.11.2 Secured Loans

3.11.2.1 Description

The less creditworthy a potential borrower is, the more likely it becomes that a bank will request some form of collateral in order to minimize its loss exposure. Securititization is regarded as characteristic of any type of credit, rather than a credit category of its own. Banks analyze their loan portfolios by reviewing the proportion of secured (collateralized) credits to the entire portfolio balance.

Loan security is usually not an activity performed expressly to generate business activity and profit. Maintenance, administration, and liquidation of collaterals are in fact often expensive, time consuming, and therefore unprofitable for the foreclosing institute. In many cases, the bank lacks the expertise to seize assets which have to be liquidated. It is more useful to sell the security. Considerations such as insurance, legal liability, and the cost of maintenance can be critical when deciding whether to repossess collateral.

Most credit security is formulated in some kind of fixed or floating claim over specified assets or a mortgage interest in property. Table 3-17 describes some common forms of credit security.

3.11.2.2 Inherent Risk Types

As with all loans, the lender is exposed to borrower default. It is the primary risk associated with loans—the risk that the borrower will be unable to meet the obligation to repay the principal and interest outstanding at any point in time. Banks collateralize loans to reduce their exposure to loss due to borrower default.

Liquidation of collaterals is usually not a profitable business for a bank. Rising interest rates increase the risk of default, as the outstanding interest might be higher than the financing power of the borrower. Decreasing market values of property increase the collateralized part of the loans and increase the risk that the bank will have higher loss exposures in case of borrower default.

TABLE 3-17

Common Forms of Credit Security

Loan Security	Comments
Lien	A lien is a right to retain someone's property until a debt due from the borrower has been repaid (the borrower and owner need not be identical). Banks require that liens used as security be in writing and refer specifically to the property under lien. Depending on local regulations and location of the property, the lien has to be officially approved by a notary and recorded in public records in order to be enforceable.
Mortgage	A mortgage is a lien on real property. The mortgage does not affect the rights of ownership, as they do not pass to the bank.
Assignment	An assignment is a transfer by a borrower of the right to receive a benefit from a third-party debtor. Usually the transfer is money or securities to be assigned as receivables to the bank as security for the loan.
Hypothecation	Hypothecation is a form of direct security involving only indirect legal title. This approach is chosen when it is not practical for the bank to take actual physical possession of either the goods or related title documents. The bank has a claim over items which it neither controls nor owns.
Guarantee	A guarantee is a common form of indirect security involving the acceptance by a third party of responsibility for the debts or defaults of the borrower.
Pledge	A pledge is a direct security based on an express agreement that gives a bank possession but not ownership of specific goods or title documents.

3.11.2.3 Quantification of Credit Risks

The quantification of credit risks can be considered the outcome of the process of assessing the risk exposure to a bank's secured lending. The first step is to classify the loans within the bank's credit analysis system. The bank will establish a limit up to which a secured loan can be granted. If the risk of default is determined to be substantial because of deterioration in the borrower's financial condition, poor payment history, decreased asset values, and the like, the bank must take action and prepare for liquidation of the collateral as the ultimate step.

Often the term *net realizable value* is used for the liquidation value. The net realizable value consists of the following components:

- The current market value of the collateral
- A provision for all costs of administration and maintenance from the time the bank takes possession of the collateral until the time of sale

- A reserve provision for potential decline in market value from the time the bank takes possession of the collateral until the time of sale
- A provision for insurance premiums
- A provision for selling costs
- Claims by other creditors (lenders) whose security interest in the collateral are ranked higher than the bank's ranking
- Revenues to be generated prior to disposing of the collateral

The realization of the net realizable value is generally a subjective and complex process—particularly the liquidation of collaterals where no liquid market exists (real estate in specific geographic areas, used manufacturing equipment, etc.).

The calculation of capital adequacy for credit risks uses different risk weightings. Specifically, loans that are fully collateralized by government securities or guaranteed by the government have a 0 percent weighting. Loans to private persons for purchase of a residence fully secured by a mortgage will have a weighting of 50 percent or more.

3.11.2.4 Exposure to Market Risks

Rising interest rates increase the risk of default, as the outstanding interest might be higher than the financing power of the borrower. Specifically, for loan contracts with a floating interest rate, increasing interest rates will be rolled over to the borrower at the reset dates. Contracts with a fixed interest rate might be foreclosed, which exposes the borrower to a reinvestment risk at a higher interest-rate level. Decreasing market values of property increase the collateralized part of the loans and increase the risk that the bank will have higher loss exposures in case of borrower default.

3.11.3 Money Market Instruments

3.11.3.1 Description

The traditional classification of securities separates the money market instruments and the capital market instruments. The money market includes short-term, marketable, liquid, low-risk debt securities. Money market instruments are sometimes called *cash equivalents* because of their safety and liquidity. They are usually highly marketable and trade in large denominations; therefore, they are beyond the reach of individual investors. Table 3-18 lists instruments commonly used as money market instruments. They have different profiles (legal structure, secured/unsecured, etc.) and the degree of their activity in the market differs, but there are also considerable similarities in their applications.

A bank using money market instruments for both borrowing and lending would pursue some or all of the following objectives:

TABLE 3-18

Common Forms of Money Market Securities

Money Market Instrument	Comments
Interbank placement	The interbank placement market is extremely liquid and active. It enables banks and other financial institutions to raise short-term funding or to place excess funds. Placements on a call basis are possible, from one day (overnight) to up to five years. The interbank placement market developed from the eurocurrency market. This market originally developed following the placement of U.S. dollars outside the United States; it first became the eurobond market, based on these eurodollars. Subsequently, it moved into shorter maturities in the eurocurrency market, including currencies such as sterling, euros, and Swiss francs. It now represents an international money market outside clear national boundaries, covering all financial centers worldwide, 24 hours a day. The interbank placement market is a global market not linked to a specific time zone. For international banks and institutions, it is possible to raise and place funds whenever required and to globally manage money market portfolios on a location-by-location basis. The portfolio can be transferred to the next location for ongoing management of the positions currently in the portfolio. Eurocurrency in the London market is usually linked to the LIBOR; the participants quote the rate at which they are willing to accept (borrow) or place (lend) funds. The spread between the bid and the ask reflects the liquidity of the market and the credit quality of the counterparty. Major banks have also begun to develop instruments with similar characteristics for foreign issuers, in different currencies. Large multinational firms offer these instruments to finance their short debts.[148]
Banker's acceptance	Similar to letters of credit, banker's acceptances are securities that are written when a bank places itself between the borrower and the investor and accepts responsibility for paying the loan. This shields the investor from the risk of default. A banker's acceptance is often preceded by a written promise from the lending bank that it will make the loan. The lending bank does not actually accept the banker's acceptance until the borrower takes down the loan. Later, if the lending bank wants to withdraw the money it has invested in the loan before the loan expires, the bank can sell the banker's acceptance to another investor. Banker's acceptances may be resold to any number of other investors before the loan is repaid. There is an active secondary market in these debts. Any investor who buys a banker's acceptance can collect the loan on the date it is scheduled to be repaid. Banker's acceptances are among the oldest money market securities. They are typically used to expedite foreign trade by financing accounts receivable between buyers and sellers from different countries. Large international banks create banker's acceptances for the interest rates on loans, with a provision depending on the creditworthiness.

TABLE 3-18

Common Forms of Money Market Securities (*Continued*)

Money Market Instrument	Comments
Certificates of deposits	Certificates of deposit (CDs) are an important source of medium-term funds. They are negotiable instruments issued by banks for deposits placed with them for a fixed period of time. CDs can be traded in an active secondary market. This liquidity gives CDs an advantage through a rate of interest which is slightly lower than that of an equivalent-time deposit in the interbank market. CDs can have fixed interest rates or floating and variable rates. Rates are normally priced as a spread over LIBOR.
Repo agreements	Sale and repurchase agreements are short-term loans secured by collateral in the form of securities. A repo agreement consists of the sale of the underlying securities for immediate cash settlement with a simultaneous agreement to repurchase the underlying securities at a higher price at a later date. The price difference between the spot and future price represents an interest charge for the use of cash received or lent during the time horizon of the contract. The counterparty to a repo transaction engages in a reserve repo, which is the purchase of the securities against cash settlement and simultaneous agreement to sell them at a higher price in the future. This is a particularly common interbank mechanism for transferring short-term funds from banks with excess funds to those with short-term requirements. For lenders of funds, it is important to reduce risk by ensuring that the securities purchased are received and held throughout the life of the transaction (usually through a depository). The borrower cannot use the same securities for another transaction. In addition, the borrower and lender have to agree on the initial price and must monitor subsequent price movements. In the event of falling market prices, the lender will require additional collateral to cover the initial transaction amount. In the event of increased market prices, the borrower will recall excess collateral. The collateral deposited is kept in balance with the initial transaction amount, as any unbalance hurts profitability and increases risk for either the borrower or the lender.
Commercial paper	Commercial paper consists of unsecured promissory notes with a fixed maturity. These notes are backed only by the credit rating of the issuing corporation and are therefore normally issued only by banks and other businesses with high credit ratings. Commercial paper is usually issued in bearer form and on a discounted basis. Commercial paper issuers typically maintain open lines of bank credit sufficient to pay back all of their outstanding commercial paper at maturity. They issue commercial paper only because that type of credit is quicker and easier to obtain than bank loans. The credit ratings of most commercial paper issuers are so high that the so-called prime (that is, highest-quality credit rating) commercial paper interest rate is essentially a riskless rate of interest, matching the yields on negotiable CDs and banker's acceptances.

- Generating arbitrage profits between the money markets and other related business activities (e.g., futures, swaps, and foreign exchange)
- Generating profits from dealing in money market instruments and from taking positions in interest-rate positions
- Generating profits from market making (dealing) from the bid–ask spread of interest-rate positions
- Optimizing the use of capital by gearing the balance sheet to the required level

Money market activities fund other business activities, manage liquidity, and define interest rates on leading transactions. These activities are centrally undertaken in the treasury department. Many banks generate more profit from nonoperative treasury activities by utilizing the money markets to generate profits from arbitrage between the markets and other products, by taking a view on future developments (speculation), or by dealing as a market maker in specific positions. Each of these means of participation in the money market generates risk exposure for the bank.

3.11.3.2 Inherent Risk Types

The money markets are highly liquid, and the credit risk of the counterparties is considered low. Apart from credit and market risk, settlement risk can be substantial and critical, as the volume of money market activities is high. The settlement of these transactions is therefore critical. But as the range of participants in the money market business is known, and supervision of the counterparties is required by regulation, the remaining counterparty exposures are reduced to a shorter time horizon than in the capital market.

3.11.3.3 Quantification of Credit Risks

The primary risk is the risk of borrower default. As most of the players in the money markets are banks, the effect of such a default would be a significant change in the bank's liquidity management as a result of the withdrawal of a large portion of the bank's deposit base or funding sources. A substantial default would affect the banking system through a ripple effect of defaults because of the substantial interbank deposit activity.

Listing authorized institutions with which the funds may be placed and limiting the amount of deposits or bank assets which may be placed with specific institutions reduces the counterparty risk. Approval for a counterparty to become an authorized institution is usually regulated. One key consideration is the institution's credit rating, as determined internally or externally.

3.11.3.4 Exposure to Market Risks

Money markets are highly liquid, as they serve to transfer funds from institutions that have excess funds to institutions that need additional funds. As this market acts globally, 24 hours a day, money market interest rates reflect all information in the market. Changes in expectations regarding inflation have an immediate impact, and interest rates change almost simultaneously with the revelation of new information. The steady flow of information continuously changes the shape and level of interest rates, and therefore the pricing and valuation of money market positions, hedges, and arbitrage strategies as well.

3.11.4 Futures Contracts

3.11.4.1 Description

The futures contract calls for delivery of an asset or its cash value at a specified delivery or maturity date for an agreed-upon price, called the *futures price,* to be paid at contract maturity. The *long position* is held by the investor who commits to purchasing the commodity on the delivery date. The counterparty who takes the *short position* commits to delivering the commodity at contract maturity. The terms and conditions of a futures contract are standardized depending on the future's exchange. Quantity, grade, or type of commodity, currency, or financial instrument at a specified future date and a specified price are set and regulated by the terms of the futures exchange where the future's instrument is traded. The terms include the details of the contract type, settlement, and margin requirement. Most of the basic principles are valid for the different futures exchanges and contract types.

Financial futures include stock indexes, currencies, interest-rate instruments, commodity indexes, and so forth. Futures contracts are based on specific financial instruments—for example, the futures contract on U.S. Treasury obligations is based on the standard contract amount of $100,000 used by the Chicago Board of Trade (CBOT). An investor who sells such a contract to hedge a portfolio has an obligation to sell the Treasury obligation (i.e., deliver cash) at a future date at a price agreed on at the time of the contract trade. Other futures contracts, such as currency futures, are based on a specific amount of one currency valued against another currency at a predetermined date in the future at a price agreed on at the time of the contract. For example, London International Financial Futures Exchange (LIFFE) is based on standardized contracts in sterling against dollars in increments of £25,000 each. Like currency futures contracts, forward contracts are made in advance of delivery, but they differ from futures in several respects:

- A forward contract is a private agreement between two parties; it is not created and traded on a standardized exchange.

- A futures contract can be closed out without delivery, while the forward contract requires delivery and can not be resold, since there is no secondary market.
- Futures have margins, requiring daily realization of profits and losses. Forward contracts realize profits and losses at delivery only.

A futures contract requires a deposit of an *initial margin* at the clearinghouse that handles the two sides of the transaction. For any transaction, two contracts are written: one between the buyer and the clearinghouse, and one between the seller and the clearinghouse. At the end of each trading day, the positions are compared to the market value, and as prices change, the proceeds accrue to the trader's margin account immediately. This daily settling is called *marking to market*. If an investor accrues sustained losses from daily marking to market, the margin account may fall below a critical value, called the *maintenance* or *variation* margin. Once the value of the margin account falls below this value, the investor receives a margin call to transfer new funds into the account, or the broker will close out enough of the position to meet the required margin for that position. This procedure safeguards the position of the clearinghouse. Marking to market is the major means of limiting risk. Initial margins may be less than 1 percent of the face value of the contract and may have no significant impact on the accounting. But the daily marking to market ensures that the profits and losses from futures are calculated and booked daily. Through this procedure, all contracts are standardized in terms of the other party, as well as in terms of size and delivery date. To cancel a position, the investor simply has to reverse the trades by selling contracts previously bought. This creates a highly liquid market in standardized instruments.

A futures contract obliges the long position to purchase the asset at the futures price. In contrast, the call option conveys the right to purchase the asset at the exercise rate. The purchase will be made only if it yields at profit.

Futures can be used for different purposes:

- *Hedging.* Buying or selling a future can be used to hedge the underlying position. Within a very short time a hedge can be built up to lengthen or shorten the duration of a portfolio, so the downside of an equity portfolio can be protected by selling a corresponding equity futures index, and so forth.
- *Position generation.* Exposures to markets, segments, and so forth can be built up with a fraction of the face value of the futures contract. Instead of buying the underlying instruments, only the initial margin is required to generate the equivalent exposure. It is an efficient way to generate exposure if direct exposure through buying the underlying instrument is not desired for any reason.

- *Arbitrage trading.* Options can be traded by buying and selling futures that appear to be over- or underpriced compared to similar products or markets issued by different counterparties, using different valuation models to generate an arbitrage position.
- *Asset–option and option–option trading.* Options can be traded by buying and selling options to combine these options with each other or in combination with underlying instruments to produce structured products with risk–reward profiles different from those of the underlying instrument or the individual option.
- *Speculation.* Speculation can be regarded as a special case of trading with open futures positions. The speculator expects that the actual future movements of the underlying instrument or the individual option will differ from the expected movements (expected parameters) inherent in the current futures price. The difference between the cash and futures prices is known as the *basis.* Speculators take direct open positions (i.e., selling futures without the underlying instrument and expecting the instrument price to decrease).

3.11.4.2 Inherent Risk Types

Credit risk is limited to margin amounts, or marking to market. Payments due to or from the broker, or to the clearinghouse, do not include the overall amount of the underlying instruments. The futures contract has a symmetrical risk–reward profile for both counterparties.

Market risks have an important influence on the overall risk exposure of futures, as most of the input variables (currencies, interest rates, equity prices, etc.) are market risk factors.

3.11.4.3 Quantification of Credit Risks

The credit risk of futures contracts can be categorized as follows:

- Credit risk arising from managing margin accounts.
- Credit risk when a counterparty is unable to deliver the contract (or its cash equivalent) or to meet the required margin call. In such cases, the futures contract can not be covered at current market rates, and a loss is incurred, which should not normally exceed the margin amount.

The risk involved with exchange-traded futures lies with the clearinghouse after all transactions have been registered and the credit risk is not with the original counterparties of the futures transaction. The greatest source of counterparty risk is brokers that are not members of a clearinghouse. Some financial institutions impose limits on the volume of futures business that can be undertaken with brokers that are not members of a clearinghouse. These limits reduce the risk by number and value of outstanding transactions with any particular broker. But the overall exposure for a futures broker is not as great as for the client, as the broker can call for margin from the customer in order to mitigate the credit risk.

Before the counterparties enter into contracts with one another, they usually agree on standard terms and conditions, to which both parties agree. They also agree to rules on how disputes are to be settled.

3.11.4.4 Exposure to Market Risks

Market risks have a substantial influence on valuation and on risk exposure. Input variables such as the volatility of the underlying instrument, interest rates, and equity price are required for the valuation of options. Any change in these variables directly influences the valuation and thus exposes these products to market risks with a higher leverage than the underlying instrument, as the option represents the right to sell or buy the principal amount of the underlying instrument for the price of the option, which is substantially less. The clearinghouse is not directly affected by market risk factors, as it passes the proceeds from the daily marking to market as an intermediary directly from one margin account to another, and thus carries no market risk. The customer carries the market risk in the form of the margin account. The customer can close out a contract by entering into a reverse transaction, thus limiting losses to the amount in the margin account.

3.11.5 Options

In general, an option gives to the buyer the right, but not the obligation, to buy or sell a good at a specific quantity at a specific price (*strike price*) on or before a specific date in the future (*maturity date*). Many different types of option contracts exist in the financial world. The two major types of contracts traded on organized options exchanges are *calls* and *puts.* The contracts are available for a wide variety of underlying instruments:

- Equities
- Interest-rate-sensitive products
- Currencies
- Commodities
- Other derivatives, such as futures, and so forth

Some options trade on over-the-counter (OTC) markets. The OTC market offers an advantage in that that the terms of the option contract (exercise price, maturity date, committed underlying instrument) can be tailored to the needs of the traders or clients. Option contracts traded on an exchange are for defined underlying instruments with standardized parameters.

3.11.5.1 Description

The option-pricing approach is a valuation technique that relies on estimating the value of the embedded option. Option premiums fluctuate so rapidly, as a function of price movements in the underlying instruments, that computerized models are necessary to properly value them. The most famous valuation model was developed by Black and Scholes; it is currently the foundation of models developed and used worldwide. Although the models are complex, their logic can be understood intuitively. The intrinsic value is the value of an option that is immediately exercised. A rational investor would never exercise a call when the underlying asset price is below the exercise price. When the option is not worth exercising, it is *out of the money* or *at the money*. The *intrinsic value* cannot be negative, as the buyer of a call has the right but not the obligation to exercise. The option has a *time value*, even if the intrinsic value is zero. The time value reflects the probability that the option will move into the money and therefore acquire an intrinsic value. The time value is an increasing function of the time to expiration. The likelihood of this happening decreases as the option's remaining time to maturity decreases. The influence of each of the input variables on a call option can be described as follows:

- *Exercise price.* The higher the exercise price, the lower the premium for the option on the same asset that has an identical expiration date.
- *Interest rate.* Options reduce the opportunity or financing cost for claiming an asset. Thus, as interest rates rise, this characteristic becomes more valuable, thereby raising the price of the option—or, in a sense, the present value of the asset to be purchased at expiration is reduced.
- *Volatility.* The more volatile the asset, the larger the expected gain on the option; hence, the larger its premium.
- *Time to expiration.* The value of an option is an increasing function of the time to expiration. The leveraging advantage mentioned earlier increases with time. The opportunity for the underlying instrument price to exceed the exercise price increases over time. Time compounds both the interest rate and volatility effects.

All determinants of the option premium, except the underlying asset volatility, can be measured precisely. The underlying asset volatility is usually estimated with the implicit volatility.

Options can be used for different purposes:

- *Hedging.* Buying an option can be used to hedge the underlying position. Options are potentially attractive, as they serve as hedges to equalize adverse movement in prices. Written options can also be used for hedging, particularly when the writer has the underlying position (covered call).

- *Arbitrage trading.* Options can be traded by buying and selling options that appear to be over- or underpriced compared to similar products issued by different counterparties, using different valuation models, to generate an arbitrage position.
- *Asset–option and option–option trading.* Options can be traded by buying and selling options to combine these options with each other or in combination with underlying instruments to produce structured products with risk–reward profiles different from those of the underlying instrument or the individual option.
- *Speculation.* Speculation can be regarded as a special case of trading with open option positions. The speculator expects that the actual future movements of the underlying instrument or the individual option will differ from the expected movements (expected parameters) inherent in the current option price. The speculators take direct open positions (i.e., selling a call without the underlying instrument and expecting the instrument price to decrease) or with structured combinations of options (i.e., selling a strangle).

3.11.5.2 Inherent Risk Types

Credit risk is limited to the valuation of an option and does not include the overall amount of the underlying instruments. A traded option purchased at the exchange has a credit risk limited to the price paid to the broker or the exchange. A written option (short selling) has a credit risk limited to the option premium to be received. But as written options are settled long before the option is exercised, the credit risk from the settlement of the premium rarely arises. The credit risk exposure from exchange-traded options is considered to be less than the exposure from OTC options, because settlement procedures and standardized parameters support efficiency in settlement.

Market risks have an important influence on the overall risk exposure of options, as most of the input variables (currencies, interest rates, equity prices, volatility coefficient, etc.) are market risk factors.

3.11.5.3 Quantification of Credit Risks

The quantification of credit risks from options can be treated similarly to that from other off-balance-sheet exposures. The bank's credit risk on a purchased exchange-traded option is limited to the price of the option and not to the overall value of the contract (principal value of the underlying instruments). The credit exposure can be measured by the margin deposits placed with brokers or exchanges. The credit exposure of short calls is limited to the price due from the counterparty. The credit risk exposure from exchange-traded options is considered to be less (almost risk free) than the exposure from OTC options purchased directly from counterparties, because settlement procedures and standardized parameters support efficiency in settlement.

Credit risk exposure is generally captured on a counterparty basis.

Banks usually apply two methods for the quantification of credit risks:

- Some banks apply a percentage on the principal amount of the underlying instruments to estimate a credit equivalent for these exposures. This method does not take into account the current market exposure of the option reflecting the changes in the input variables; and
- Most banks calculate the credit risk equivalent using the actual market value of the option plus a safety margin for likely future changes over the remaining time to expiration of the option. The two most important input variables for the option valuation market price and volatility are modified by adding a safety margin. The quantification of credit risk would be the revaluated option price based on the modified input parameters. This approach corresponds to scenario-analysis as required by different regulations (or regulators).

3.11.5.4 Exposure to Market Risks

Market risks have a substantial influence on valuation and on risk exposure. Input variables such as the volatility of the underlying instrument, interest rates, and equity price are required for the valuation of options. Any change in these variables directly influences the valuation and thus exposes these products to market risks with a higher leverage than the underlying instrument, as the option represents the right to sell or buy the principal amount of the underlying instrument for the price of the option, which is substantially less.

3.11.6 Forward Rate Agreements

3.11.6.1 Description

Forward rate agreements (FRAs) are private contracts between two parties (usually written by banks), which guarantee a client the borrowing or lending interest rate at a future time. On the expiration date of the FRA, the bank pays or receives the difference between the agreed interest rate and the interest rate prevailing in the marketplace at the time. An FRA is a contract for difference—the amount settled is the difference between the market interest rate at the settlement date and the interest rate fixed in the FRA contract. The FRA is disconnected from the actual lending or borrowing. The bank simply pays or receives the interest-rate difference at maturity but does not lend to or borrow from the client.

The effect of an FRA is to lock a fixed interest rate as an expense to one counterparty and as income to the other. No payment is required if market rates on the settlement date equal the forward rates as fixed on the contract date. To the extent that market rates diverge from the forward rate, one party has to compensate the other for the difference. The notional amount (principal) does not change hands. Forwards are like tailor-made futures to suit an investor's exact requirements, but they are mainly OTC products rather than exchange traded.

Forward rate agreements can be used for different purposes:

- As FRAs can be tailored to the client's needs, they can be used as *hedges.* An investor who expects a large amount at a specific date in the future, and a significant reduction in interest rates in the near future, may enter into a forward rate agreement to receive a fixed rate of interest in the future, which will become increasingly profitable to the extent that the interest rate decreases as expected. The investor is compensated by the profit from the FRA for the lower interest rate at which the expected amount can be invested in the future.
- FRAs can be used as *trading* instruments. A financial institution which expects a significant decrease in interest rates may engage in a FRA by receiving a fixed rate of interest, which will increase in value to the extent that the expected reduction in the market rate actually occurs.

3.11.6.2 Inherent Risk Types

The FRA is exposed to market and credit risks.

3.11.6.3 Quantification of Credit Risks

The term *credit risk* means an investor's exposure to a counterparty unable to fulfill obligations. The credit risk on an FRA is limited to the amount of the settlement payment and not the notional amount plus interest. The credit risk is calculated as the replacement value of the FRA (i.e., the current market value of the FRA). The *replacement value* is defined as the movement in interest rates since the contract date. Depending on the direction (up or down) of market interest rates relative to the contractual interest rates, an actual loss or profit can be generated. Credit risk must therefore be calculated in relation to future interest-rate volatility (i.e., implicit volatility), which can only be estimated. Using historical interest-rate fluctuations and option-pricing models (incorporating parameters such as time to maturity and the particular interest rate subject to the FRA contract), it is possible to calculate a range for the implicit volatility, within which interest-rate movements are expected to remain.

3.11.6.4 Exposure to Market Risks

As FRAs are based on interest rates, market risks have a substantial influence on the valuation and the risk exposure. For the time period between the settlement date and maturity, interest rates are locked in. After this time period, the amount is again exposed to movements in interest rates.

3.11.7 Asset-Backed Securities

3.11.7.1 Description

Asset-backed securities (ABSs) are a relatively new category of marketable securities that are collateralized by financial assets like accounts receivable (most commonly), mortgages, leases, or installment loan contracts. Asset-backed financing involves a process called *securitization*. Securitization is a disintermediation process in which the credit from commercial or investment banks and other lenders is replaced by marketable debt securities that can be issued at a lower cost. Securitization involves the formation of a pool of financial assets so that debt securities can be sold to external investors to finance the pool.

Securitization generates structured and complex instruments, which are not easy to price. But investors continue to demand all kinds of exotic forms of securities. Creative security design often calls for bundling basic and derivatives securities into one composite security. A *convertible* is a bundled security of preferred stock with options. Quite often, the creation of an attractive security requires the unbundling of an asset for pricing on the investor side. For example, a mortgage pass-through security is unbundled into two classes. Class 1 receives only principal payments from the mortgage pool, whereas Class 2 receives only interest payments. Other financial instruments have to be unbundled in a similar manner to assess an appropriate price.

Asset-backed securities can take the following forms:

- *Repurchase agreements (repos).* These are money market securities that date back to the 1950s. Repos are the oldest asset-backed security. (See the discussion of repo instruments in Section 3.11.3.)
- *Mortgage-backed securities.* A security is either an ownership claim in a pool of mortgages or an obligation that is secured by such a pool. These claims represent the securitization of mortgage loans. Mortgage lenders originate loans and then sell packages of these loans in the secondary market. The claims are sold for the cash inflows from the mortgages as those loans are paid off. The mortgage originator continues to service the loan, collecting principal and interest payments, and passes the payments along to the purchaser of the mortgage. *Mortgage pass-through securities (MPTSs)* are certificates backed by a pool of insured mortgages.

They were first sold in 1970 by the Government National Mortgage Association (GNMA), called *Ginnie Mae.* MPTs are popular in spite of their prepayment uncertainty because MPTS issuers get to remove the mortgage assets and all associated liabilities from their balance sheets. *Mortgage-backed bonds* (*MBBs*) are debt securities that have their credit enhanced by being overcollateralized and by the purchase of credit insurance. In overcollateralization, the MBB issuer takes a residual risk position in the pool.

- *Collateralized mortgage obligations (CMOs).* Issued by the Federal Home Loan Mortgage Corporation (FHLMC), called *Freddie Mac,* these are multiclass debt securities used to finance a pool of insured mortgages. CMO investors own bonds that are collateralized by a pool of mortgages or by a portfolio of mortgage-backed securities. The bonds are serviced with the cash flows from these mortgages; however, rather than using the straight pass-through arrangement, the CMO substitutes a sequential distribution process that creates a series of bonds with varying maturities to appeal to a wider range of investors.[149] The disadvantages of CMOs are that the issuer must retain the lowest class of CMO until the entire pool is liquidated, and the issuer must show the pool's assets and liabilities on its balance sheet.
- *Student loans.* First pooled and sold in 1973 by the Student Loan Marketing Association (SLMA), called *Sallie Mae.* The SLMA sponsors pass-throughs backed by loans originated under the Guaranteed Student Loan Program and by other loans granted under various U.S. federal programs for higher education.

These securities were supported by U.S. federal government agencies that insure the pools of financial assets against default. The profitability and liquidity of these government-subsidized financing plans set the stage for the private securitization programs, such as the following:

- *Trade-credit-receivable-backed bonds.* These are pools of trade-credit receivables, first issued by American Express in 1982.
- *Certificates amortizing revolving debts (CARDs).* These are pools of credit card receivables, first issued by Salomon Brothers in 1986.

Securitization usually involves the creation of new debt securities. As a result, the default risk, traditionally borne by equity investors, must be assumed by some other method. Credit enhancement is typically accomplished via the following procedures:

- The assets to be financed are placed in a trust as collateral with a third party, usually a depository bank.

- The next step is to provide for AAA- or at least AA-grade rating for the collateral from major credit-rating agencies such as Moody's or Standard & Poor's. If the proper credit enhancement arrangements can not be made, investors' risk aversion will keep them from buying the new debtlike securities. Several methods of obtaining a high credit rating for securitized assets exist, such as guarantees, overcollateralization, purchase of insurance from an insurance company, and diversification by geography or industry.

Typical benefits obtained from securitization are as follows:

- Funds flow more efficiently from investors to borrowers as the bundled financial assets gain liquidity. Assets may be illiquid individually (such as mortgages), but when repackaged and securitized they become liquid financial securities. Liquidity is one of the primary goals of securitization.
- Prepayment risks borne by the seller of the financial assets are transferred to the investor.
- Diversification opportunities are increased for the seller and the investor.
- The seller of the financial assets can avoid the interest rate risk and default risk associated with carrying assets in the books.
- Lower-cost financing for inventories of financial assets may be available.

3.11.7.2 Inherent Risk Types

As with all credit, the primary risk is that the borrowers will default and be unable to repay the principal and the interest outstanding. Thus, the rating and the corresponding term structure of interest rates (quality spread) reflect the credit risk.

As ABSs are based on interest rates, market risks have a substantial influence on the valuation and the risk exposure.

3.11.7.3 Quantification of Credit Risks

Credit risk exposure can be measured by the rating difference of the collateralized assets before and after the credit enhancement, which results in a quality spread in favor of the new debt securities. This risk is carried by the trust, which involves the collateralized assets on one side of the balance sheet and the equity capital, in the form of the securities, on the other side. The bank usually carries only the counterparty risk for the transaction if ABSs are bought from or sold to investors.

3.11.7.4 Exposure to Market Risks

As ABSs are based on interest rates, market risks have a substantial influence on the valuation and the risk exposure.

Most asset-backed securities are liquid, because the investment banking firm that securitizes the assets agrees to maintain a liquid secondary market in the securities.

3.11.8 Interest-Rate Swaps

3.11.8.1 Description

While there are numerous types of interest-rate swaps (IRSs), the most common is the plain-vanilla or generic swap that involves two parties (called *counterparties*) swapping fixed payments for floating-rate payments. For example, assume that one party has issued a floating-rate security that makes payments determined by a floating index. Floating-rate liabilities are risky because the borrower bears the risk of rising interest rates, which could prove unfortunate. It is possible that the firm or government that has issued a floating-rate security might prefer to make fixed-rate payments, while other parties in the market might have the opposite position, wherein they are required to make fixed payments but would prefer floating-rate payments. This might be the case if the party held assets that had floating-rate coupons. If it had floating-rate liabilities and floating-rate assets, the interest rate payments it makes would tend to move up and down with the interest-rate payments it receives. Changes in the level or structure of the term structure of interest rates would not affect the overall difference of interest rates to be paid and received.

The interest-rate benchmarks that are commonly used for the floating rate in an interest rate swap are those on various money market instruments: Treasury bills, the London interbank offered rate (LIBOR), commercial paper, banker's acceptances, certificates of deposit, and the prime rate.

Market participants can use an interest-rate swap to alter the cash-flow character of assets or liabilities from a fixed-rate basis to a floating-rate basis, or vice versa. The only cash flows that are exchanged between the parties are the interest payments, not the notional principal amount.

In most cases, an intermediary is needed, which is the function of the swap dealer, a firm that arranges swaps between other firms. In order to understand the swap activity, it is important to determine the various roles of the bank in this process. The different roles determine the risk exposures and the required control procedures as well as the accounting treatment. The bank can enter into a swap transaction for three reasons:

- For trading purposes
- As an intermediary
- For hedging purposes

A bank may act as trader and use swap transactions for trading or speculative purposes. Having a view on the future development of interest rates (or currency), the bank would not seek to enter an offsetting swap but would be exposed by a one-sided deal, depending on its view. For example, a bank expecting interest rates to decrease might enter into a swap paying a floating rate and receiving a fixed rate. This strategy is similar to lending in the money market for a contractual term at a fixed rate and borrowing the proceeds for shorter periods at variables rates.

Acting as an intermediary, the bank will arrange and administer the swap transaction. A counterparty seeking a swap will approach the bank, which will identify another counterparty with opposite interest-rate requirements. In most cases, the counterparties are unaware of each other, and the bank will exchange the interest payments and take a spread on the interest rate as compensation for its role as intermediary. The bank can act as principal or as an agent. If the bank acts as principal, the counterparties enter into a contract with the bank, and both parties rely on the bank, rather than on each other, for performance under the deal. Should one party default, the bank as principal is still obligated to the other party. The bank as intermediary substitutes its credit for the credit of the two counterparties, and in doing so, accepts the credit risks from both counterparties. The bank's exposure is not the full (notional) amount but is limited to the interest-rate cash flow to be paid by the defaulting party.

Using swap transactions to hedge existing or future transactions (with a forward swap) of assets and liabilities, the bank is exposed, for example, to the offset of variable-rate assets and fixed-rate liabilities. A decrease in interest rates would have a significant impact on hedged positions and profitability. In this example, the bank has two alternatives: it might enter a swap and convert the variable-rate assets into fixed-rate assets, or convert the fixed-rate liabilities into variable-rate obligations. In both cases the bank has the assurance that the overall earnings situation remains stable regardless of the direction in which interest rates move.

Smaller banks and individual portfolio managers tend to manage their portfolios on a deal-by-deal basis. Larger banks use portfolio hedging, in which all cash flows from all swap deals are aggregated. Because not all deals can be perfectly matched (in terms of principal, reset dates, etc.), the remaining exposure has to be hedged or not, based on known future cash flows or by reducing exposures that have different swap reset dates or maturity dates.

3.11.8.2 Inherent Risk Types

A swap is exposed to market, credit, and operational risks. The operational risk is primarily a settlement risk. Counterparty risk is part of the credit risk and is the main credit exposure. Like other off-balance-sheet instruments, the amount at risk is the cash flows (interest rates) to be exchanged and not the notional amount. Therefore, exposure is measured after determining an appropriate credit equivalent amount.

The amount at risk is exposed and is a function of the following factors:

- *Counterparty risk.* This presents the biggest part of the risk exposure.
- *Operational risk.* In particular, settlement risks.
- *Type of swap contract.* Swaps are generally riskier for a fixed maturity due to the added risk of exchange- or interest-rate movements.
- *Term to maturity of swap contract.* The longer the term to maturity, the more cash flows are outstanding and are exposed to interest-rate and currency movements over longer time horizons.
- *Payment mismatch.* Especially in a swap portfolio, swaps result in one party making payments prior to receiving payments—for example, one party makes semiannual payments (fixed rate) but receives quarterly payments (floating rate).

3.11.8.3 Quantification of Credit Risks

The quantification of credit risk is a function of the net present value of the swap and the counterparty ratings. Bank accountants and swap dealers use the net present value approach to determine the value of the swap. The replacement costs in terms of interest and currency rates for the fixed and variable cash flows are used to measure the present value. A swap, under which the bank receives 6 percent and pays LIBOR, where the replacement cost of the fixed leg is currently 4.5 percent, results in a profit upon valuation equal to the monetary effect of the 1.5 percent fixed-interest-rate differential over the term of the swap (with future cash flows discounted). If the bank paid 5.5 percent on the fixed leg (instead of the current market rate of 4.5 percent) this would result in a loss upon valuation of 1 percent discounted over the term of the swap. The matched transactions leave the bank a profit of 0.5 percent per annum on the national amount of the swap (the bank is receiving 6 percent and paying 5.5 percent on the offsetting legs of the two swaps). The NPV for a matched-swap deal will therefore generally be equal to the current value of the bank's spread on the cash flows being exchanged over the life of the deal.

This amount at risk can be used for the determination of the counterparty risk.

3.11.8.4 Exposure to Market Risks

The amount of interest-rate payments exchanged is based on the predetermined principal, which is called the *notional principal amount.* But as the counterparties agree to exchange periodic interest payments, the notional amount is not transferred. The swap position can be regarded as a series of forward or futures contracts, or a series of cash flows resulting from buying and selling cash market instruments. In both cases, the cash flows are exposed to interest- and currency-rate movements over the time horizon. Table 3-19 shows the risk–return profile in the case of interest-rate movements.

TABLE 3-19

Risk–Return Profile for Counterparties to an Interest-Rate Swap

	Interest-rate movement	
Counterparty	**Decrease**	**Increase**
Floating-rate payer	Gain	Loss
Fixed-rate payer	Loss	Gain

The long futures positions gain if interest rates decline and lose if interest rates rise. This is similar to the risk–return profile for a floating-rate payer. The risk–return profile for a fixed-rate payer is similar to that of the short futures position: a gain if interest rates increase and a loss if interest rates decrease.

3.12 PROPOSAL FOR A MODERN CAPITAL ACCORD FOR CREDIT RISK

A portfolio approach to credit risk management is the most important alternative approach to the current standardized capital rules. Portfolio credit risk modeling shares the advantages of portfolio market risk modeling, which have already been recognized by the leading regulatory bodies. These include:

- *Ability to take an* integrated view *of credit risk across a financial institution.* This makes possible the comparison of the relative risk of a 1-year $10-million loan, a 10-year $1-million bond, and a 10-year partly collateralized swap with a $10-million positive mark-to-market value.
- *Ability to assess* concentration *and* diversification. By taking a portfolio approach, a credit risk model recognizes the risks of concentrated exposures (to a single counterparty or to a group of highly correlated counterparties) and the benefits of diversification.
- *Ability to take a* dynamic view *of credit risk.* In contrast to the fixed standard capital rules, the model approach is based on actual default and recovery rates.

There has been dynamic development in the markets in recent years, which must be reflected in the regulations in order to support management dynamically in a business sense, instead of relying on the fixed standard capital rules:

- Lenders should focus on risk-adjusted performance measurement.
- Risk-adjusted capital allocation across different business activities is needed.
- Risk transfer by means of securitization is needed.

3.12.1 Institute of International Finance

In a 1998 discussion paper, the Institute of International Finance (IIF) proposed abandoning the rigid and inflexible system of 100 percent capital requirements for the private sector and introducing a more differentiated system for risk assessment, based on the credit quality of the borrower.[150]

The IIF also suggested introducing complex credit models, which could be developed and enhanced depending on the complexity of the instruments and the quality of the models used for modeling the risks. Similar to the model-based approach, the incentive for the implementation of complex credit risk management systems is risk-adequate valuation resulting in lower capital requirements for those risks.

The IIF uses the following premises, whereas the BIS, as the regulatory body, has to define the terms and assumptions in detail:

- Capital adequacy requirements based on the probability distribution of credit loss of the credit portfolio
- Consistent methodology for all counterparty ratings for all credit exposures
- Estimates of probability distribution regarding potential losses of the credit portfolios
- Estimates of correlations between the probability distributions of credit positions within a credit portfolio
- Estimates of the expected credit losses based on the ratings and the related statistical loss distributions as well as the loss severity in the case of credit defaults
- Estimates of the unexpected credit losses for the entire portfolio (e.g., with the VaR approach)
- Description of the data sources and documentation of the model approach assumptions
- Stress-testing procedures to quantify extreme credit losses over the statistical confidence levels

3.12.2 International Swaps and Derivatives Association

The International Swaps and Derivatives Association (ISDA) proposed a three-stage approach, which, like the IIF approach, is based on the incentive that a risk-adequate approach is directly related to lower capital requirements.[151]

The *first stage* is the current practice, with the possibility of offsetting risks by hedging positions in credit derivatives. The *second stage* is similar to the standard approach for supporting market risk; it is a simplified model that considers the counterparty rating and the term to maturity of the credit risk positions, and it includes several offsetting and netting possibilities. The *third stage* considers credit portfolio risk models. These models consider the correlations between credit positions and thus allow the use of the diversification effect of a risk-adequate, but complex and expensive, approach to the capital adequacy calculation for credit risks. This approach requires an enormous amount of input data, such as loss probability distributions, recovery rates, and credit spreads.

The discussion papers of the IIF and the ISDA are valuable contributions to the discussion of the next generation of credit risk regulations. The proposal of the ISDA to maintain the existing regulations in a slightly extended version could be misunderstood in view of the existing problems and weaknesses of the current regulations. A standardized approach that could be used by all institutions and would reflect the credit risk in a more accurate way would lead to more adequate capital requirements. This would be the basis for a concept similar to the capital accord supporting market risks, which requires that the lead regulators be able to approve internally used models (partially in use already). As in the market risk regulations, stringent quantitative and qualitative assumptions would have to be fulfilled before regulators could grant approval. Stress tests would be critical in reviewing the model quality, as backtesting is difficult with credit models.

3.12.3 Basel Committee on Banking Supervision and the New Capital Accord

The original accord focused mainly on credit risk. It has since been amended to address market risk. Interest-rate risk in the banking book and other risks, such as operational, liquidity, legal, and reputational risks, are not explicitly addressed. Implicitly, however, the present regulations take such risks into account by setting a minimum ratio that has an acknowledged buffer to cover unquantified risks.

The current risk weighting of assets results, at best, in a crude measure of economic risk, primarily because degrees of credit risk exposure are not sufficiently calibrated as to adequately differentiate between borrowers' differing default risks.

Another related and increasing problem with the existing accord is the ability of banks to arbitrage their regulatory capital requirement and exploit divergences between true economic risk and risk measured under the accord. Regulatory capital arbitrage can occur in several ways—for example, through some forms of securitization—and this can lead to a shift in banks' portfolio concentrations to lower-quality assets.

In 1999, the Basel Committee on Banking Supervision decided to introduce a new capital adequacy framework[152] to replace the initial accord from 1988.[153] The new accord is designed to improve the way regulatory capital requirements reflect underlying risks. This new capital framework consists of three pillars:

- Minimum capital requirements
- A supervisory review process
- Effective use of market discipline

With regard to minimum regulatory capital requirements, the BIS is building on the foundation of the current regulations, which will serve as a standardized approach for capital requirements at the majority of banks. In doing so, the paper proposes to clarify and broaden the scope of application of the current accord. With regard to risk weights to be applied to exposures to sovereigns, the BIS proposes replacing the existing rigid approach with a system that allows using external credit assessments for determining risk weights. It is intended that such an approach will also apply (either directly or indirectly and to varying degrees) to the risk weighting of exposures to banks, securities firms, and corporations. The result will be to reduce risk weights for high-quality corporate credits, and to introduce a risk weight higher than 100 percent for certain low-quality exposures. A new risk-weighting scheme to address asset securitization and the application of a 20 percent credit conversion factor for certain types of short-term commitments are also proposed.

For some sophisticated banks, the BIS believes that an internal ratings-based approach could form the basis for setting capital charges, subject to supervisory approval and adherence to quantitative and qualitative guidelines. The BIS believes that this will be an important step in the effort to align capital charges and underlying risk more closely.

The BIS wants to incorporate the model approach (similar to the capital adequacy regulation supporting market risks) in the credit portfolio risk modeling to be used for regulatory capital calculation.

At some of the more sophisticated banks that make use of internal ratings, credit risk models based on these ratings (and other factors) have also been developed. Such models are designed to capture the risk from the portfolio as a whole—an important element not found in approaches based solely on external credit assessments or internal ratings. The BIS supports the fact that these models are already in use in some banks' risk management systems, and it recognizes their use by some supervisors in their appraisals. However, the paper recognizes that due to a number of difficulties, including data availability and model validation, credit risk models are not yet at the stage where they can play an explicit part in setting regulatory capital requirements. The BIS will verify how this could become possible after further development and testing, and it intends to monitor progress on these issues closely.[154]

The recent development of credit risk mitigation techniques such as credit derivatives has also enabled banks to substantially improve their risk management systems. The current accord does not incorporate the development of specific forms of credit risk mitigation by placing restrictions on both the types of hedges acceptable for achieving capital reduction and the amount of capital relief. The current solution leaves open the treatment of imperfect credit risk protection (such as maturity mismatches, asset mismatches, or potential future exposure on hedges), resulting in the development of different national policies. The new accord committee proposes a more consistent and economic approach to credit risk mitigation techniques, covering credit derivatives, collateral, guarantees, and on-balance-sheet netting (see Annex 2 of the new capital accord).

The BIS recognizes that maturity of a claim is a factor in determining the overall credit risk it presents to the bank. The paper is somewhat unclear on this point, as it clearly says that the paper at present is not proposing to take maturity of claims into account for capital adequacy purposes, except in a very limited case. Nonetheless, it claims as well to distinguish more precisely among the credit quality of exposures, and it also will consider ways to factor maturity more explicitly into the assessment of credit risk.[155]

The BIS will also consider what changes may be needed to the market risk component of the regulations to enhance consistency of treatment between the banking and the trading books and to ensure adequate capital coverage for trading-book items, and it will consider ways to follow up on recommendations contained in earlier documents. For credit risk, the paper states that the objective of a more comprehensive treatment of risk, with capital charges that are more sensitive to risk, can be met in varying ways depending on the time frame under consideration (time to maturity) and on the technical abilities of banks and supervisors (models). The paper proposes three approaches for setting minimum capital requirements:

- A modified version of the existing approach
- The use of banks' internal ratings
- The use of portfolio credit risk models

The existing regulations specify explicit capital charges only for credit and market risks in the trading book (Figure 3-32). Other risks, including interest-rate risk in the banking book and operational risk, are also an important feature of banking. The committee therefore proposes to develop a capital charge for interest-rate risk in the banking book for banks whose interest-rate risk is significantly above average. The committee also proposes to develop capital charges for other risks, principally operational risk.[156]

The new operational risk regulations include the results of an informal survey that highlight the growing realization of the significance of risks other than credit and market risks, such as operational risk, which have been at the heart of some important banking problems in recent years. A capital charge based on a measure of business activities (such as revenues, costs, total assets, or, at a later stage, internal measurement systems) or a differentiated charge for businesses with high operational risk, based on measures commonly used to value those business lines, is calculated to support operational risks. Particular regard will need to be paid to the potential for capital arbitrage, to any disincentives to better risk control that might thereby be created, and to the capital impact for particular

FIGURE 3-32

New Structure of Capital Requirements, Broken Down by Risk Categories.

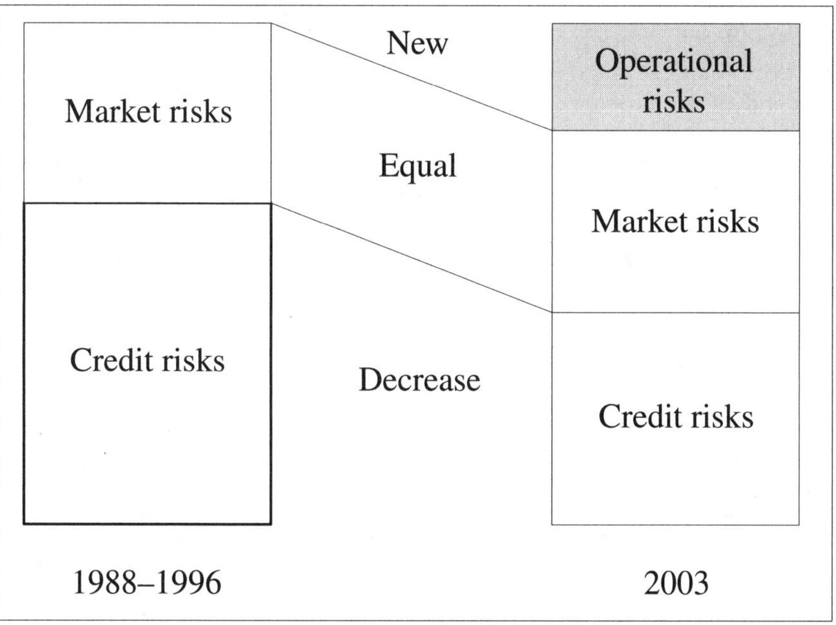

types of banks. Qualitative factors such as the integrity of the controls process and internal measures of operational risk should be considered.

The BIS has recognized the significance of interest-rate risk within some banking books, depending on a bank's risk profile and market conditions. Accordingly, the BIS proposes to develop a capital charge for interest-rate risk in the banking book for banks whose interest-rate risks are significantly above average (outliers). The BIS recognizes that some national discretion would be necessary regarding the definition of outliers and the methodology used to calculate interest-rate risk in the banking book. At the same time, the BIS intends to examine developments in methodologies as set out in its 1993 paper on the measurement of exposure to interest-rate risk to identify those banks which are outliers.[157] The BIS will consider alternative methodologies for capital charges, including allowing for national discretion and basing such charges on internal measurement systems that are subject to supervisory review, and it will seek comments from the industry.

For the measurement of credit risk, two principal options are being proposed in the new accord. The first is the standardized approach; the second is the internal ratings-based (IRB) approach. There are two variants of the IRB approach, foundation and advanced. Use of the IRB approach will be subject to approval by the supervisory body, based on the standards established by the committee.

3.12.3.1 Standardized Approach for Measuring Credit Risk

The standardized approach is conceptually the same as the present accord, but is more risk sensitive.[158] The bank allocates a risk weight to each of its assets and off-balance-sheet positions and produces a sum of risk-weighted asset values. A risk weight of 100 percent means that an exposure is included in the calculation of risk-weighted assets at its full value, which translates into a capital charge equal to 8 percent of that value. Similarly, a risk weight of 20 percent results in a capital charge of 1.6 percent (i.e., one-fifth of 8 percent).

Individual risk weights currently depend on the broad category of borrower (i.e., sovereign, bank, or corporate). Under the new accord, the risk weights are to be refined by reference to a rating provided by an external credit assessment institution (such as a rating agency) that meets strict standards. For example, for corporate lending, the existing accord provides only one risk-weight category of 100 percent, but the new accord will provide four categories (20, 50, 100, and 150 percent).

3.12.3.2 IRB Approach for Measuring Credit Risk

Under the internal ratings-based (IRB) approach, banks will be allowed to use their internal estimates of borrower creditworthiness to assess credit risk in their portfolios, subject to strict methodological and disclosure standards.[159] Distinct analytical frameworks will be provided for different types of loan exposures, such as corporate and retail lending, whose loss characteristics are different. Under the IRB approach, a bank estimates each borrower's creditworthiness, and the results are translated into estimates of potential future losses, which form the basis of minimum capital requirements. The framework allows for both a foundation method and more advanced methodologies for corporate, sovereign, and bank exposures. In the foundation methodology, banks estimate the probability of default associated with each borrower, and the supervisory authority supplies the other inputs. In the advanced approach, a bank with a sufficiently developed internal capital allocation process will be allowed to supply other necessary inputs as well. Under both the foundation and advanced IRB approaches, the range of risk weights will be far more diverse than those in the standardized approach, resulting in greater risk sensitivity.

Banks will be required to categorize banking-book exposures into six broad classes of assets, as shown in Figure 3-33. The internal rating systems must meet the following criteria:

- Must have been in use at least three years (except equity and project finance categories)
- Must be two-dimensional systems
- Must incorporate minimum annual ratings reviewed by an independent credit risk control unit
- Must incorporate an effect process for updating and reflecting changes in a borrower's financial condition within 90 days; 30 days for borrowers with weak credit

FIGURE 3-33

Banking Book Categories for Internal Ratings-Based Approach.

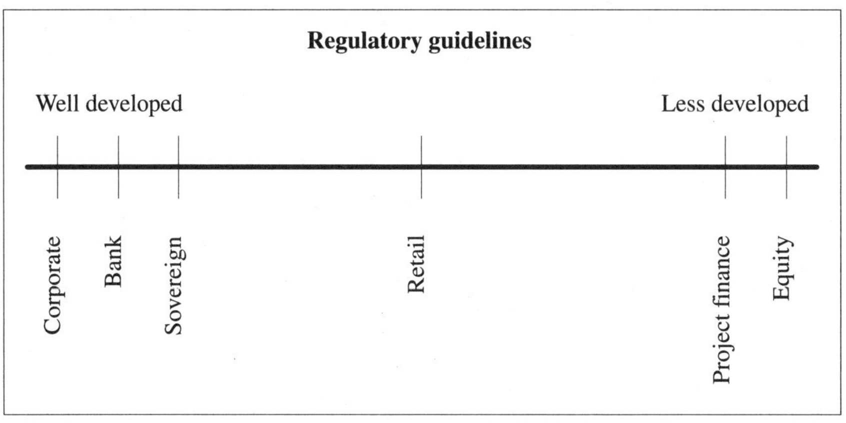

Probability of Default

Under the foundation and advanced IRB approaches, the probability of default (PD) defined by bank must comply with the following regulatory restrictions:[160]

- Must be consistent with the regulatory definition of default
- Must use a one-year time horizon
- Must be forward looking
- Must have a minimum default probability of 3 basis points
- Must be based on at least five years of data
- Must collect internal data and consider mapping to external data and statistical default models
- May use pooled data, but must demonstrate that the internal rating systems and criteria of other banks are comparable to own

Retail Exposures

The calculation of retail exposures is similar in most respects to that for corporate exposures, with some important exceptions. The bank is expected to segment its retail exposures on the basis of the following four techniques:

- Product type
- Borrower risk (e.g., credit score)
- Delinquency status (minimum of two categories for borrowers in arrears)
- Vintage (maximum one-year buckets).

Additional segmentation techniques may be employed (e.g., borrower type and demographics, loan size, maturity, loan to value).

There are two options for assessing the risk components:

- Separately assess PD and loss given default (LGD)
- Assess a single expected loss (PD × LGD).

The retail-exposure approach has no equivalent in the foundation approach.

3.12.3.3 Advanced IRB Approach

Only a small number of banks are expected to qualify due to rigorous eligibility requirements. The banks must agree to an aggressive rollout plan. Once a financial organization opts for the advanced IRB approach for one risk element, it must adopt its own estimates for other risk factors in a reasonably short period of time for all significant business units and exposure classes. During this period there will be no capital relief granted for intragroup transactions between the IRB bank and a business unit that uses the standardized approach for business lines and exposure classes (this restriction is intended to minimize "cherry picking"). For the first two years after implementation of the advanced IRB approach, the financial organization must calculate foundation and advanced approaches in parallel.

During the first two years following the date of implementation, the benefit of the advanced IRB approach is limited by a floor set equal to 90 percent of the capital requirements resulting from the foundation IRB approach.

The advanced IRB approach requires full compliance with all foundation requirements (internal ratings system and PDs).[161] In addition, the following requirements have to be met:

- Loss given default (LGD) grades must provide meaningful differentiation of loss rates.
- LGD and exposure at default (EAD) must be supported by at least seven years of historical data and preferably a full business cycle.
- The financial organization must provide evidence that it has a robust system for validating LGDs.
- Analysis of realized versus projected LGDs must be conducted at least annually.
- An independent unit must conduct stress testing of processes for evaluating estimates of PD, LGD, and EAD on at least a six-month basis.
- The Basel Committee is considering maturity as an explicit risk driver, particularly with regard to the treatment of maturity mismatches resulting from the use of certain credit risk mitigation techniques and instruments.
- All material aspects of the rating, PD, EAD, and LGD estimation process should be approved by the board of directors, management committee, and senior management.
- Internal audits must include an annual review of the internal ratings system.
- Internal ratings should be incorporated into the internal management reporting process.
- Management must ensure that the rating process, criteria, and outcome are comprehensively documented.
- Documentation of risk factor methodologies must:

  Provide a detailed outline of the theory, assumptions, and mathematical and empirical basis of the assignment of PD estimates to grades or individual obligors, and list the data sources used to estimate the model.

Establish a rigorous statistical process for validating the selection of explanatory variables.

Indicate the circumstances under which the model does not work effectively.

3.12.3.4 Validation and Stress Testing

The Basel Committee emphasizes validation and stress testing through regulatory requirements.[162] Banks must have in place a robust system to validate the accuracy and consistency of rating systems, processes, and internal estimates of risk factors. Historical data time frames used for assessing the degree of respective data correlation should be as long as possible, and should ideally cover a complete business cycle. Banks must have in place sound stress-testing processes for use in the assessment of capital adequacy. Testing must include identification of future changes in economic conditions, or possible events that could unfavorably impact a bank's default estimations and therefore its overall level of capital adequacy. Stress testing must be performed on at least a six-month basis. The output of testing should be periodically reported to senior management.

3.12.3.5 Collateral

The new accord contains many new components and definitions regarding collateral:

- The new accord provides for a broader definition of collateral.
- The new accord allows for recognition of cash, a defined range of debt securities, certain equity securities, units in mutual funds, and gold.
- Simple and comprehensive approaches to creating collateral transactions are proposed:

  The simple approach generally uses the current substitution approach.

  The comprehensive approach focuses on the cash value of collateral (conservative estimate).
- Banks are required to account for changes in the value of their exposures and in the value of collateral received.
- Accounting is to be accomplished through the use of "haircuts" to reflect exposure volatility, the volatility of the collateral received, and any currency volatility.
- Banks may choose to use either standard supervisory haircuts or those based on their own estimates of collateral volatility, subject to minimum requirements.
- The floor is set at 0 for very low risk transactions and 0.15 for all other collateralized transactions.

3.12.3.6 Credit Risk Mitigation and Securitization

The new framework introduces more risk-sensitive approaches to the treatment of collateral, guarantees, credit derivatives, netting, and securitization, under both the standardized approach and the IRB approach:[163]

- The mitigation must be direct, explicit, irrevocable, and unconditional.
- The proposed "substitution ceiling" approach for guarantees and credit derivatives is included under the advanced IRB methodology;[164]
- "Notching" is not permitted to extend beyond the higher of the borrower or guarantor grades, thereby preventing any treatment that is more favorable than full substitution.[165]
- Guarantees and credit derivatives recognized as giving protection receive a risk weight w of 0.15. Where the guarantor is a sovereign, a central bank, or a bank, w will be 0.[166]
- Guarantees that contain embedded options under which the guarantor may or may not be obligated to perform will be excluded from consideration.

3.12.3.7 Asset Securitization

The committee is increasingly concerned by the employment of securitization structures by some banks with the intention of avoiding maintenance of capital commensurate with their risk exposures.[167] Specifically, an institution must comply with the definition of a "clean break," and provide disclosure when the issuing bank removes securitized assets from its balance sheet. The new accord contains severe penalties for implicit recourse:

- Loss of favorable capital treatment for all assets associated with the structure
- Potential loss of favorable capital treatment for all securitized assets

The disclosure requirement of the new accord requires that banks disclose qualitiative items and quantitative data in order to obtain capital relief through the securitization process, as described in paragraphs 659 and 660 of the Pillar III section. These disclosures are required from banks in their statutory accounts, whether they act as originators or sponsors or third parties, and from issuers [special-purpose vehicles (SPVs)] in their offering circulars.[168]

3.12.3.8 Granularity Adjustment to Capital

The granularity adjustment is an addition or subtraction to the baseline level of risk-weighted assets described earlier in this document. IRB baseline risk weights are calibrated assuming a bank with exposures of "typical" granularity. The purpose of the granularity adjustment is to recognize that a bank with exposures characterized by coarse granularity, implying a large residual of undiversified idiosyncratic risk (i.e., single-borrower risk concentrations), should require additional capital. Similarly, a bank with exposures characterized by finer-than-average granularity should demand a smaller-than-average capital requirement. Adjustments are incorporated into the IRB approach in the form of an addition or subtraction to the baseline level of risk-weighted assets, and are applied across all nonretail exposures under the IRB approach.[169]

To be incorporated by means of a standard supervisory capital adjustment, the bank has to take into account industry, geographic, or other forms of credit risk concentration. There should be a meaningful distribution of exposure across grades, with no excessive concentrations in any particular grade. Specifically, the committee is proposing that no more than 30 percent of the gross exposure should fall in any single borrower grade.

Based on the distribution of its exposures and LGD estimates within (and across) its internal grades, a bank would calculate an adjustment to risk-weighted assets to reflect the degree of granularity relative to a standard reference portfolio. Should a bank's portfolio reflect a greater degree of granularity than the reference portfolio, a reduction of risk-weighted assets will be realized by the bank.

Conversely, upward adjustments to risk-weighted assets would be required for bank portfolios reflecting lesser degrees of granularity than the reference portfolio.

3.12.3.9 Credit Derivatives

The treatment of credit risk mitigation techniques, and in particular credit derivatives, is a contentious and highly technical area of the Basel Committee's proposals. Banks involved in trading these instruments have expressed concern that, unless the proposals are amended, Basel's plans could stunt the growth of the young credit derivatives market. If banks get preferential treatment for credit guarantees as opposed to credit derivatives, they may well be tempted to recharacterize derivatives as guarantees. This, too, could lead to market fragmentation and a rise in the cost of credit to the market.

The committee believes that the most effective way forward would be to treat this residual risk under the proposed framework's second pillar (the supervisory review process), rather than by using the w factor under the first pillar (minimum capital requirements) as proposed in the original approach. The committee believes that this approach will allow for a fairly simple, practical, and risk-sensitive framework for credit risk management techniques.[170]

Another justification from Basel for the treatment of credit derivatives is the legal risk of these instruments. The market has adopted the 1999

ISDA credit derivatives standard documentation. This has not proven foolproof, but it nonetheless represents a standardized agreement, as opposed to the generally bilateral nature of traditional bank guarantees. Another factor that may be worrying the regulators with regard to credit derivatives is the *double-default factor.* This refers to the fact that in credit derivative negotiations, the trader intuitively considers the correlation between the seller of protection and the underlying company it is selling protection against (the reference entity). The Basel Committee has not justified this omission by arguing that there is no correlation model that can explain it—in other words, it does not have a reliable way of explaining and measuring the correlation. Some financial institutions suggest that a good intermediate approach would be to divide the double-default issue into transactions where there is a very high risk and those where the risk is low, and set appropriate regulatory rules. Future developments, including an empirical correlation based on models with adequate historical default correlation data, should not be excluded by Basel.

The treatment of credit derivatives on the trading book is another important issue. If a bank sells protection on an entity in its trading book, and at the same time it buys protection against the same entity for itself, it would only obtain an 80 percent offset on regulatory capital. Some credit derivatives traders fear that this could lead to distortions in pricing to absorb this extra capital charge, which in turn might distort credit risk models that are based on market spreads.

3.13 SUMMARY

Credit risk has a long history; it evolved from an accounting foundation into a discipline of its own. The perception of balance-sheet-based debts, issued in many different forms (bonds, notes, subordinated, guaranteed, etc.) has changed substantially over the past decades, through major structural changes in the financial markets, such as the Brady bond crisis and the Russian default of September 1998, causing major impacts in the market and raising questions about the way credit risks are measured and managed. Credit derivatives are one example of how credit risk has evolved from a perceived loss area into a business line which generates both profits and credit instruments that can be traded on a daily basis.

Over the past decade, a number of the world's largest banks have developed sophisticated systems in an attempt to model the credit risk arising from important aspects of their business lines. Such models are intended to aid financial institutions in quantifying, aggregating, and managing risk across geographical and product lines. The outputs of these models also play increasingly important roles in banks' risk management and performance measurement processes, including performance-based compensation, customer profitability analysis, risk-based pricing and, to a lesser (but growing) degree, active portfolio management and capital structure decisions. Credit risk modeling has resulted in better internal risk management, and will be used in the supervisory oversight of banking organizations. However, before a portfolio modeling approach is approved for use in the formal process of setting regulatory capital requirements for credit risk, regulators want to be confident not only that models are being used to actively manage risk, but also that they are conceptually sound, are empirically validated, and produce capital requirements that are comparable across institutions. At this time, significant hurdles, principally concerning data availability and model validation, have to be cleared before an organization is entitled to use a credit model for calculating the capital requirements for credit risk. The new capital accord contains a new approach for looking at credit risk from a risk-sensitive standpoint, moving away from a formal and normative approach. It allows the banks to choose from alternative approaches, depending on the complexity of the credit portfolios, the credit instruments, and the capacity and complexity of credit risk management.

Models have already been incorporated into the determination of capital requirements for market risk. However, credit risk models are not a simple extension of their market risk counterparts for two key reasons:

- *Data limitations.* Banks and researchers alike report that data limitations are a key impediment to the design and implementation of credit risk models. Most credit instruments are not marked to market, and the predictive nature of a credit risk model does not derive from a statistical projection of future prices based on a comprehensive record of historical prices. The scarcity of the data required to estimate credit risk models also stems from the infrequent nature of default events and the longer time horizons used in measuring credit risk. Hence, in specifying model parameters, credit risk models require the use of simplifying assumptions and proxy data. The relative size of the banking book—and the potential repercussions on bank solvency if modeled credit risk estimates are inaccurate—underscore the need for a better understanding of a model's sensitivity to structural assumptions and parameter estimates.
- *Model validation.* The validation of credit risk models is fundamentally more difficult than the backtesting of market risk models. Whereas market risk models typically employ a horizon of a few days, credit risk models generally rely on a time frame of one year or more. The longer holding period, coupled with the higher confidence intervals used in credit risk models, presents problems to model builders in assessing the accuracy of their models. By the same token, a quantitative validation standard

similar to that in the Market Risk Amendment would require an impractical number of years of data, spanning multiple credit cycles.

This chapter analyzes the evolution of the credit risk models; the different approaches; the parameters, assumptions, and conditions which characterize them; and their similarities to market risk models. Core sections of this chapter link the credit risk models and the new capital framework. Modern portfolio theory is well established in market risk and is in the process of finding its way into credit risk. This chapter analyzes the compatibility of market risk–driven parameters and assumptions in the credit risk environment. A detailed section about the market risk component of credit risk instruments highlights the increasing overlap of the market and credit risk areas.

3.14 NOTES

1. Bank for International Settlement (BIS), Basel Committee on Banking Supervision, *Settlement Risk in Foreign Exchange Transactions: Report Prepared by the Committee on Payment and Settlement Systems of the Central Banks of the Group of Ten Countries,* Basel, Switzerland: Bank for International Settlement, March 1996.
2. Bank for International Settlement (BIS), Basel Committee on Banking Supervision, *Sound Practices for Loan Accounting and Disclosure,* Basel, Switzerland: Bank for International Settlement, July 1999.
3. It is recognized that accounting guidance sometimes indicates that one or the other of these two impairment tests ("it is probable that the bank will be unable to collect" and "there is no longer reasonable assurance that the bank will collect") should be used. For instance, the probability test is prescribed by IAS 39 and by the U.S. Financial Accounting Standards Board (FASB) Statements of Financial Accounting Standards 5 and 114, while a test of reasonable assurance is used in the Canadian Institute of Chartered Accountants (CICA) Handbook Section 3025.03, and in guidance issued by the British Bankers' Association. An insignificant delay or insignificant shortfall in amounts of payments does not necessarily constitute impairment if, during such a period of delay, the lender can reasonably expect to collect all amounts due.
4. The fifth amendment from the Basel Committee on Banking Supervision was Bank for International Settlement (BIS), Basel Committee on Banking Supervision, *Amendment to the Capital Accord to Incorporate Market Risks,* Basel, Switzerland: Bank for International Settlement, January 1996, modified September 1997.
5. Bank for International Settlement (BIS), Basel Committee on Banking Supervision, *A New Capital Adequacy Framework: Consultative Paper by the Basel Committee on Banking Supervision, Issued for Comment by 31 March 2000,* Basel, Switzerland: Bank for International Settlement, June 1999.

6. Christoph Rouvinez, "Mastering Delta Gamma," *Risk,* (February 1997); *Mastering Delta Gamma,* Zurich: Credit Suisse, 1999. For a detailed discussion, see Gerold Studer, "Maximum Loss for Measurement of Market Risk," Ph.D. thesis, Swiss Federal Institute of Technology, Zurich, 1997.
7. For a detailed discussion, see P. Nickell, W. Perraudin, and S. Varotto, "Stability of Rating Transitions," paper presented at the Bank of England Conference on Credit Risk Modeling and Regulatory Implications, London, September 21–22, 1998. This study examines Moody's ratings history over a 27-year period, indicating the influence of shifts in geographical and industrial composition of the data set on published average transition matrices, and it develops an ordered probit technique for deriving transition matrices that are appropriate to the characteristics of the credit exposures in the portfolio (e.g., industry and domicile of obligor, and stage of business cycle).
8. Pamela Nickell, William Perraudin, and Simone Varotto, "Ratings versus Equity-Based Credit Risk Modelling: An Empirical Analysis," Working Paper Series (132), Bank of England, London, 2001. This empirical study implemented and evaluated representative examples of two of the main types of credit risk models (ratings based and equity price based) and assessed their performance on an out-of-sample basis using large portfolios of eurobonds. Both models failed to provide an adequately large capital buffer across the 10-year sample period; the portfolios experienced "exceptions" at several times the rate predicted by VaR calculations based on the models' output.
9. For example, see J. A. Lopez and M. R. Saidenberg, "Evaluating Credit Risk Models," paper presented at the Bank of England Conference on Credit Risk Modeling and Regulatory Implications, September 21–22 1998. It is reported that a few survey participants relied on such alternative methods for backtesting. These included: (1) comparing loan pricing implied by the model with market pricing; (2) attempting to check the consistency of the main drivers of modeling output (internal ratings and recovery rates) through comparison with external benchmarks such as Moody's and S&P; and (3) backtesting on virtual portfolios, given the scarcity of data on credit events.
10. Bank for International Settlement (BIS), Basel Committee on Banking Supervision, *Credit Risk Modelling: Current Practices and Applications,* Basel, Switzerland: Bank for International Settlement, April 1999, 13.
11. R. C. Merton, "On the Pricing of Corporate Debt: The Risk Structure of Interest Rates," *Journal of Finance* 29 (June 1974), 449–470.
12. Thomas C. Wilson, "Credit Portfolio Risk (I)," *Risk* (October 1997); "Credit Portfolio Risk (II)," *Risk* (November 1997). McKinsey and Company, *CreditPortfolio View Approach Documentation and User's Documentation,* Zurich: McKinsey and Company, 1998.
13. In practice each facility of a debtor is analyzed, to consider additional features such as guarantees, options, etc. in the rating process. For simplification, the assumption that ratings are associated with borrowers is usually made.

14. Bank for International Settlement (BIS), Basel Committee on Banking Supervision, *Prudential Supervision of Banks' Derivatives Activities,* December 1994; *Risk Management Guidelines for Derivatives,* July 1994; *Amendment to the Capital Accord of July 1988,* July 1994; *Basel Capital Accord: The Treatment of the Credit Risk Associated with Certain Off-Balance-Sheet Items,* July 1994, Basel, Switzerland: Bank for International Settlement.
15. Technology and the increased liquidity in the secondary market for loans (along with the development of credit derivatives, though most are OTC) have helped to move the lending paradigm away from a buy-and-hold strategy to one in which credit risks are actively managed in a portfolio framework. See A. Kuritzkes, "Transforming Portfolio Management," *Banking Strategies* (July/August 1998).
16. For a discussion, see J. A. Lopez and M. R. Saidenberg, "Evaluating Credit Risk Models," paper presented at the Bank of England Conference on Credit Risk Modeling and Regulatory Implications, September 21–22, 1998; or Reto R. Gallati, "De-Minimis-Regel diskriminiert," *Schweizer Bank* 9 (Zurich, 1998), 41–43.
17. For a more complete discussion of these models, see J. B. Caouette, E. J. Altman, and P. Narayanan, *Managing Credit Risk: The Next Great Financial Challenge,* New York: John Wiley & Sons, 1998.
18. J. D. Taylor, "Cross-Industry Differences in Business Failure Rates: Implications for Portfolio Management," *Commercial Lending Review* (January 1998), 36–46.
19. J. Stiglitz and A. Weiss, "Credit Rationing in Markets with Imperfect Information," *American Economic Review* (June 1981), 393–410.
20. W. Treacy and M. Carey, "Internal Credit Risk Rating Systems at Large U.S. Banks," *Federal Reserve Bulletin* (November 1998). They argue that credit review organizations and processes are further enhanced mechanisms through which common standards can be enforced across credit officers.
21. Federal Reserve Systems Task Force on Internal Credit Risk Models, *Credit Models at Major U.S. Banking Institutions: Current State of the Art and Implications for Assessments of Capital Adequacy,* Washington, DC: U.S. Government Printing Office, May 1998.
22. J. J. Mingo, "Policy Implications of the Federal Reserve Study of Credit Risk Models at Major Banking Institutions," paper presented at the Bank of England Conference on Credit Risk Modeling and Regulatory Implications, London, September 21–22, 1998.
23. To calculate the estimated loan loss reserve against expected losses, a similar approach would be used, except that expected loss rates would replace unexpected loss rates.
24. J. B. Caouette, E. J. Altman, and P. Narayanan, *Managing Credit Risk: The Next Great Financial Challenge,* New York: John Wiley & Sons, 1998.
25. A. Saunders, *Financial Institutions Management: A Modern Perspective,* 2d ed., Burr Ridge, IL: Irwin/McGraw-Hill, 1997.

26. E. I. Altman and P. Narayanan, "An International Survey of Business Failure Classification Models," *Financial Markets, Instruments and Institutions* 6/2 (1997).
27. E. I. Altman, "Financial Ratios, Discriminant Analysis and the Prediction of Corporate Bankruptcy," *Journal of Finance* (September 1968), 589–609.
28. E. I. Altman, T. K. N. Baidya, and L. M. R. Dias, "Assessing Potential Financial Problems for Firms in Brazil," Working Paper 125, New York University Salomon Center, September 1977.
29. A. S. Sanvicente and F. L. C. Bader, "Filing for Financial Reorganization in Brazil: Event Prediction with Accounting and Financial variables and the Information Content of the Filing Announcement," working paper, São Paulo University, Brazil, March 1996.
30. P. K. Coates and L. F. Fant, "Recognizing Financial Distress Patterns Using a Neural Network Tool," *Financial Management* (Summer 1993), 142–155.
31. R. Merton, "On the Pricing of Corporate Debt: The Risk Structure of Interest Rates," *Journal of Finance* 29 (June 1974), 449–470.
32. EDF™ and CreditMonitor® are trademarks of KMV LLC.
33. In fact, if there are direct and indirect costs of bankruptcy (e.g., legal costs, inventory, maintenance costs, etc.), the lender's loss on a loan may exceed principal and interest. This makes the payoff profile in Figure 3-7 even more similar to that shown in Figure 3-8, where the loan may have a negative dollar payoff.
34. R. Merton, "On the Pricing of Corporate Debt: The Risk Structure of Interest Rates," *Journal of Finance* 29 (June 1974), 449–470.
35. Ibid.
36. For a detailed analysis, see G. Gorton and A. Santomero, "Market Discipline and Bank Subordinated Debt," *Journal of Money, Credit and Banking* (February 1990), 117–128 and M. J. Flannery and S. Sorescu, "Evidence of Bank Market Discipline in Subordinated Debenture Yields: 1983–1991," *Journal of Finance* (September 1996), 1347–1377.
37. Most corporate bonds are traded over the counter, not publicly. Price information is extremely difficult to get because most trades are interdealer (bank to bank).
38. See R. A. Jarrow and D. R. van Deventer, "Practical Usage of Credit Risk Models in Loan Portfolio and Counterparty Exposure Management," The Kamakura Corporation, March 15, 1999, for testing a Merton-type model using bond quotes (spreads) for one company. They find considerable instability in implied default probabilities. This may, in part, be due to the use of bond quotes rather than transaction prices. See also A. Saunders, A. Srinivasan, and I. Walter, "Price Formation in the OTC Corporate Bond Markets: A Field Study of the Inter-Dealer Market," Working Paper No. 98-89, New York University, Department of Finance, 1998 for a discussion of price formation in OTC corporate bond markets.

39. For example, if the company's assets are liquidated at current market values and the resulting funds are used to meet borrowing obligations.

40. R. A. Jarrow and S. M. Turnbull, "The Intersection of Market and Credit Risk," paper presented at the Bank of England Conference on Credit Risk Modeling and Regulatory Implications, London, September 21–22, 1998; G. Delianedis and R. Geske, "Credit Risk and Risk-Neutral Default Probabilities: Information About Rating Migrations and Defaults," paper presented at the Bank of England Conference on Credit Risk Modeling and Regulatory Implications, London, September 21–22, 1998.

41. KMV does not make distinctions in the liability structure with regard to seniority, collateral, covenants, or other parameters which distinguish the loans. Convertible debt and preferred stock are also as long-term liabilities, not breaking out the loan and equity components. However, users can input whatever value of B they feel is appropriate under a specific scenario.

42. E. Ronn and A. Verma, "Pricing Risk-Adjusted Deposit Insurance: An Option-Based Model," *Journal of Finance* (September 1986), 871–896.

43. The distance from default is 3 standard deviations. KMV Credit Monitor assumes a constant asset growth rate for all borrowers in the same market segment, which is the expected growth rate of the market as a whole. The rationale for this assumption is that in an efficient market, differences in growth rates between the market and individual firms are fully discounted (i.e., arbitraged away) and incorporated in the stock prices of the borrower. Thus, in equilibrium there should be no difference between asset growth of individual firms and the market. The only other adjustment to this constant across-the-board rate is for firm-specific payouts such as dividends or interest payments (keep in mind that the KMV Credit Monitor applies a Black-Scholes-Merton option model with dividends). The adjusted number is then applied to the implied current asset value in the distance-to-default formula.

44. Another reason for the better predictability of KMV scores over the short horizon is the approach to calibrating the model over time. Standard & Poor's and Moody's calibrate their rating to default experience over the past 20-plus years. Their probabilities therefore reflect a *cycle average* view. By comparison, KMV's EDFs reflect strong cyclicality over the business cycle. Some studies have shown that EDFs do not offer any advantage for time horizons over two years; see R. Miller, "Refining Ratings," *Risk* (August 1998).

45. R. A. Jarrow and D. R. van Deventer, "Practical Usage of Credit Risk Models in Loan Portfolio and Counterparty Exposure Management," The Kamakura Corporation, March 15, 1999.

46. H. Leland, "Corporate Debt Value, Bond Covenants and Optimal Capital Structure," *Journal of Finance* (September 1994), 1213–1252.

47. E. P. Jones, S. P. Mason, and E. Rosenfeld, "Contingent Claims Analysis of Corporate Capital Structures: An Empirical Investigation," *Journal of Finance* (July 1984), 611–625.

48. C. Zhou, "A Jump Diffusion Approach to Modeling Credit Risk and Valuing Defaultable Securities," working paper, Washington, DC: Federal Reserve Board of Governors, 1997.

49. R. A. Jarrow and S. M. Turnbull, "The Intersection of Market and Credit Risk," paper presented at the Bank of England Conference on Credit Risk Modeling and Regulatory Implications, London, September 21–22, 1998.

50. D. Duffie and K. Singleton, "Simulating Correlated Defaults," paper presented at the Bank of England Conference on Credit Risk Modeling and Regulatory Implications, London, September 21–22, 1998.

51. For a review of intensity-based models, see G. Duffee, "Estimating the Price of Default Risk," *Review of Financial Studies* (Spring 1999), 197–226.

52. D. Duffie and D. Lando, "Term Structures of Credit Spreads with Incomplete Accounting Information," working paper, Stanford University Graduate School of Business, 1997.

53. H. Leland, "Corporate Debt Value, Bond Covenants and Optimal Capital Structure," *Journal of Finance* (September 1994), 1213–1252.

54. R. Anderson, S. Sunderesan, and P. Tychon, "Strategic Analysis of Contingent Claims," *European Economic Review* (1996), 871–881.

55. P. Mella-Barral and W. Perraudin, "Strategic Debt Service," *Journal of Finance* (June 1997), 531–556.

56. For example, the boundary will become stochastic if there is liquidation cost to asset values. This gives borrowers power to renegotiate. In Merton's (1974) original model, there are no costs to liquidation; i.e., assets are liquidated and paid out costlessly. See also Francis A. Longstaff and E. Schwartz, "A Simple Approach to Valuing Risky Fixed and Floating Rate Debt," *Journal of Finance* (July 1995), 789–819.

57. H. Leland, "Agency Costs, Risk Management and Capital Structure," *Journal of Finance* (July 1998), 1213–1242.

58. V. V. Acharya and J. N. Carpenter, "Callable Defaultable Bonds: Valuation, Hedging and Optimal Exercise Boundaries," working paper, New York University Department of Finance, New York, March 15, 1999.

59. The current capital requirements for supporting market risk contain a general market risk component and a specific risk component. For example, with respect to corporate bonds that are held in the trading book, an internal model calculation of specific risk would include methodologies such as spread risk, downgrade risk, and concentration risk. Each of these is related to credit risk. The 1998 BIS market risk capital requirement contains a credit risk component.

60. J. P. Morgan, *CreditMetrics—Technical Document*, New York: J. P. Morgan, April 2, 1997. In 1998, the group that developed the RiskMetrics and CreditMetrics products was split off into a separate company called RiskMetrics Group.

61. For a discussion of the one-year time horizon, see the report from the Federal Reserve System Task Force on Internal Credit Risk Models, *Credit*

Models at Major U.S. Banking Institutions: Current State of the Art and Implications for Assessments of Capital Adequacy, Washington, DC: U.S. Government Printing Office, May 1998. For example, if the existence of autocorrelation or trend over the time toward default is suspected, a longer observation period (such as two years or more) might be appropriate.

62. As is discussed later, to calculate the VaR of a loan portfolio, default correlations among counterparties have to be estimated.
63. This example is based on the example used in J. P. Morgan, *CreditMetrics—Technical Document,* New York: J. P. Morgan, April 2, 1997, 9.
64. As is shown later, the choice of transition matrix has a substantial impact on the VaR calculations. Moreover, the choice to apply bond transitions to value loans raises the empirical question of how closely related bonds and loans are.
65. Technically, from a valuation perspective, the credit event is assumed to occur at the very end of the first year. The current version of CreditMetrics is being expanded to allow the credit event window to be as short as three months or as long as five years.
66. In this example, the discount rates reflect the appropriate zero-coupon rates plus credit spreads s_i on A-rated loans (bonds). If the borrower's rating were unchanged at BBB, the discount rates would be higher, because the credit spreads would reflect the default risk of a BBB borrower.
67. Recent empirical studies have shown that this LGD may be too high for bank loans. A Citibank study of 831 defaulted corporate loans and 89 asset-based loans for 1970 to 1993 found recovery rates of 79 percent (or, equivalently, LGD equal to 21 percent). Similarly, high recovery rates were found in a Fitch Investor Service report in October 1997 (82 percent) and a Moody's Investor Service Report in June 1998 (87 percent). For a detailed analysis of this issue, see E. Asarnow, "Managing Bank Loan Portfolios for Total Return," paper presented at the Conference on a New Market Equilibrium for the Credit Business, Frankfurt, Germany, March 11, 1999.
68. The calculation in Table 3-6 shows the risks of a loan that have been calculated from the perspective of its mean or expected forward value ($107.09). Using an alternative perspective, by looking at the distribution of changes in value around the value of the loan if the ratings continued to be BBB over the whole loan period, the forward value is $107.55. Applying this BBB benchmark value, the mean and the variance of the value changes are, respectively, –$0.46 and $3.13. The VaR at the 1 percent confidence level under the normal distribution assumption is then (2.33) × ($3.13) + (–$0.46) = –$7.75.
69. In 99 years out of 100, the capital requirements based on a VaR at a 1 percent confidence level would allow the bank to survive unexpected credit losses on loans. Note that under the specific risk component for market risk (which measures spread risk, downgrade risk, and concentration risk for tradable instruments such as corporate bonds), the VaR at a 1 percent confidence level has to be multiplied by a multiplication factor between 3 and 4 (subject to approval by the local regulator), and the sensitivity period is 10 days instead of one year.

70. Boudoukh and Whitelaw have demonstrated in simulation exercises that, for some financial assets, the multiplication factor can cover extreme losses such as the mean in the tail beyond the 99th percentile. However, they also found that the 3-to-4 multiplication factor badly underestimated extreme losses if there are runs of bad periods, as might be expected in a major long-term economic contraction. For the detailed analysis, see J. Boudoukh, M. Richardson, and R. Whitelaw, "Expect the Worst," *Risk* (September 1995), 101–105.

71. Using the simple approach to calculating a transition matrix, based on data for 1997 and 1998. In 1997, 5.0 percent of bonds rated BBB were downgraded to B. In 1998, 5.6 percent of bonds rated BBB were downgraded to B. The average transition probability of being downgraded from BBB to B is therefore 5.3 percent. See the transition matrix in Table 3-6. See the empirical results in P. Nickell, W. Perraudin, and S. Varotto, "Stability of Rating Transitions," paper presented at the Bank of England Conference on Credit Risk Modeling and Regulatory Implications, London, September 21–22, 1998, for an analysis of the assumption of one-year transition matrices.

72. E. I. Altman and D. L. Kao, "The Implications of Corporate Bond Ratings Drift," *Financial Analysts Journal* (May–June 1992), 64–75.

73. P. Nickell, W. Perraudin, and S. Varotto, "Stability of Rating Transitions," paper presented at the Bank of England Conference on Credit Risk Modeling and Regulatory Implications, London, September 21–22, 1998.

74. RiskMetrics is developing modifications to its CreditMetrics software to allow cyclicality to be incorporated in the transition matrix.

75. E. I. Altman and V. M. Kishore, "Defaults and Returns on High-Yield Bonds: Analysis Through 1997," working paper, New York University Salomon Center, January 1998.

76. An alternative approach would be to apply KMV's rating transition matrix, which is calculated around KMV's EDF scores. The correlation between KMV's transitions and the transitions of the ratings agencies is low.

77. L. V. Carty and D. Lieberman, *Corporate Bond Defaults and Default Rates 1938–1995,* New York: Global Credit Research, Moody's Investors Service, January 1996.

78. J. P. Morgan, *CreditMetrics—Technical Document,* New York: J. P. Morgan, April 2, 1997, 30, note 2.

79. The assumption of nonstochastic interest rates is also consistent with R. C. Merton, "On the Pricing of Corporate Debt: The Risk Structure of Interest Rates," *Journal of Finance* 29 (June 1974), 449–470. Shimko, Tejima, and van Deventer have extended the Merton model to include stochastic interest rates; see D. Shimko, N. Tejima, and D. R. van Deventer, "The Pricing of Risky Debt When Interest Rates Are Stochastic," *Journal of Fixed Income* (September 1993), 58–66.

80. See also M. Crouhy and R. Mark, "A Comparative Analysis of Current Credit Risk Models," paper presented at the Bank of England Conference on

Credit Risk Modeling and Regulatory Implications, London, September 21–22, 1998.

81. W. Treacy and M. Carey, "Internal Credit Risk Rating Systems at Large U.S. Banks," *Federal Reserve Bulletin* (November 1998).

82. P. Nickell, W. Perraudin, and S. Varotto, "Stability of Rating Transitions," paper presented at the Bank of England Conference on Credit Risk Modeling and Regulatory Implications, London, September 21–22, 1998, and Thomas C. Wilson, *Credit Risk Modeling: A New Approach,* New York: McKinsey Inc., 1997; "Credit Portfolio Risk (I)," *Risk* (October 1997); "Credit Portfolio Risk (II)," *Risk* (November 1997).

83. The unexpected loss rate could also be simulated using this type of binominal model for a two-state world of default versus no default, rather than a full VaR model.

84. In fact, all the probabilities in the final column of the transition matrix in Figure 3-15 will move cyclically and can be modeled in a way similar to p_{CD}.

85. In Thomas C. Wilson, *Credit Risk Modeling: A New Approach,* New York: McKinsey Inc., 1997, and "Portfolio Credit Risk (Parts I and II)," *Risk* (September and October, 1997), Equation (3.15) is modeled as a logistic function of the form $p_t = 1/(1 + e^{-yt})$. This constrains p to lie between 0 and 1.

86. In Thomas C. Wilson, *Credit Risk Modeling: A New Approach,* New York: McKinsey Inc., 1997, the macrovariables are modeled as levels of variables (rather than changes in levels), and the X variables are related to their lagged values by a second-order autoregressive process.

87. The variances and covariances of V and ε_{it} are technically calculated from the fitted model (the I matrix). The I matrix is then decomposed using the Cholesky decomposition $I = AA'$, where A and A' are symmetric matrices and A' is the transpose of A. Shocks can be simulated by multiplying the matrix A' by a random number generator: $Z \sim N(0,1)$.

88. Thomas C. Wilson, *Credit Risk Modeling: A New Approach,* New York: McKinsey Inc., 1997; "Credit Portfolio Risk (I)," *Risk* (October 1997); "Credit Portfolio Risk (II)," *Risk* (November 1997).

89. The precise procedure for the calculation is described in McKinsey and Company, *CreditPortfolio View Approach Documentation and User's Documentation,* Zurich: McKinsey and Company, 1998, 80–94. Basically, it involves the use of a shift operator (defined as the systematic risk sensitivity parameter) along with the imposition of the constraint that the shifted values in each row of the migration matrix sum to 1.

90. Alternatively, using a default model, and a default p/no-default $1 - p$ setup, unexpected loss rates can be derived for different stages of the business cycle.

91. K. Arrow, "Le Role des valeurs boursieres pour la repartition de la meilleure des risques," *Econometrie Colloque Internationaux du CNRS* 11 (1953), 41–47.

92. J. M. Harrison and D. Kreps, "Martingales and Arbitrage in Multi-Period Security Markets," *Journal of Economic Theory* (1979), 381–408.

93. J. M. Harrison and S. R. Pliska, "Martingales and Stochastic Integrals," *Stochastic Processes and Their Applications* (August 1981), 215–260.

94. D. Kreps, "Multiperiod Securities and the Efficient Allocation of Risk: A Comment on the Black-Scholes Option Pricing Model," in J.J. McCall, ed., *The Economics of Uncertainty and Information*, Chicago: University of Chicago Press, 1982.

95. For pricing of derivative assets, when the underlying asset is actively traded, the risk-neutral price is the correct one, irrespective of investor preferences. This is because, with an existing underlying asset, the derivative can be perfectly hedged to create a riskless portfolio. Assuming a portfolio is riskless, the portfolio's expected return equals to the risk-free rate.

96. R. K. Sundaram, "Equivalent Martingale Measures and Risk-Neutral Pricing: An Expository Note," *Journal of Derivatives* (Fall 1997), 85–98.

97. R. Litterman and Thomas Iben, "Corporate Bond Valuation and the Term Structure of Credit Spreads," *Journal of Portfolio Management* (Spring 1991), 52–64.

98. For a detailed discussion, see G. Delianedis and R. Geske, "Credit Risk and Risk-Neutral Default Probabilities: Information About Rating Migrations and Defaults," paper presented at the Bank of England Conference on Credit Risk Modeling and Regulatory Implications, London, September 21–22, 1998.

99. Ibid.

100. R. C. Merton, "On the Pricing of Corporate Debt: The Risk Structure of Interest Rates," *Journal of Finance* 29 (June 1974), 449–470.

101. R. Geske, "The Valuation of Corporation Liabilities as Compound Options," *Journal of Financial and Quantitative Analysis* (November 1977), 541–552.

102. The Merton (1974) model assumes that all long-term debt is of equal seniority and is unsecured.

103. A. Ginzberg, K. Maloney, and R. Wilner, "Risk Rating Migration and Valuation of Floating Rate Debt," working paper, Citicorp, March 1994.

104. B. Belkin, L. R. Forest, S. D. Aguais, and S. J. Suchower, *Credit Risk Premiums in Commercial Lending* (1) and *Credit Risk Premiums in Commercial Lending* (2), New York: KPMG, August 1998; B. Belkin, S. J. Suchower, and L. R. Forest, "The Effect of Systematic Credit Risk on Loan Portfolio Value at Risk and Loan Pricing," *CreditMetrics Monitor* (1998), 17–88; B. Belkin, S. J. Suchower, D. H. Wagner, and L. R. Forest, "Measures of Credit Risk and Loan Value in LAS," KPMG, *Risk Strategy Practice*, New York: KPMG, 1998.

105. This relationship has been described by A. Ginzberg, K. Maloney, and R. Wilner, "Risk Rating Migration and Valuation of Floating Rate Debt," Working Paper, Citicorp, March 1994, and by M. Crouhy and R. Mark, "A Comparative Analysis of Current Credit Risk Models," paper presented at the Bank of England Conference on Credit Risk Modeling and Regulatory Implications, London, September 21–22, 1998.

106. For example, the historic probability of a B-rated borrower transitioning into default during the next year and thus moving from B to D in a single year.

107. Unlike CreditMetrics, in which the VaR measure (or unexpected loss in value) is loan specific, these unexpected losses are specific to a rating bucket. CreditMetrics allows for upgrade and downgrade effects on loan value, whereas the simple risk-neutral approach assumes either default or no default (binary decision).

108. A. Ginzberg, K. Maloney, and R. Wilner, "Risk Rating Migration and Valuation of Floating Rate Debt," working paper, Citicorp, March 1994.

109. Ibid.

110. Ibid.

111. KPMG Peat Marwick, *Loan Analysis System*, New York: KPMG Financial Consulting Services, 1998.

112. See S.D. Aguais, L. Forest, S. Krishnamoorthy, and T. Mueller, "Creating Value from Both Loan Structure and Price," *Commercial Lending Review* (Winter 1997), 1–10.

113. As discussed in B. Belkin, S. J. Suchower, and L. R. Forest, "The Effect of Systematic Credit Risk on Loan Portfolio Value at Risk and Loan Pricing," *CreditMetrics Monitor* (1998), 17–88, the LAS model can also be used to calculate VaR measures. For example, a simple VaR figure can be calculated by using the LAS model to value the loan at the one-year (credit-event) horizon. Alternatively, model spread volatility can be introduced by allowing the transitions themselves to be variable (KPMG calls this Z risk).

114. KPMG Peat Marwick, *Loan Analysis System*, New York: KPMG Financial Consulting Services, 1998.

115. E. I. Altman, "Measuring Corporate Bond Mortality and Performance," *Journal of Finance* (September 1989), 909–922.

116. The combination of the volatility of annual MMRs with LGDs allows one to produce unexpected loss calculations as well. See E. I. Altman and A. Saunders, "Credit Risk Measurement: Developments over the Last Twenty Years," *Journal of Banking and Finance* (December 1997), 1721–1742 for details.

117. For details, see E. I. Altman and H. J. Suggitt, "Default Rates in the Syndicated Loan Market: A Mortality Analysis," Working Paper S-97-39, New York University Salomon Center, New York, December 1997.

118. A mortality rate is binomially distributed. For further discussion, see P. M. McAllister and J. J. Mingo, "Commercial Loan Risk Management, Credit Scoring and Pricing: The Need for a New Shared Database," *Journal of Commercial Lending* (May 1994), 6–20.

119. Most of the studies published show mortality tables that have been calculated on total samples of around 4000 bonds and loans; see E. I. Altman, "Measuring Corporate Bond Mortality and Performance," *Journal of Finance* (September 1989), 909–922, and E. I. Altman and H. J. Suggitt,

"Default Rates in the Syndicated Loan Market: A Mortality Analysis," Working Paper S-97-39, New York University Salomon Center, New York, December 1997. However, the Central Bank of Argentina has recently built transition matrices and mortality tables based on over 5 million loan observations. This loan data is available on the Central Bank's Web site (www.bcra.gov.ar/english/e_inferior.htm).

120. This is strictly true for only the simplest of the models in CreditRisk. A more sophisticated version ties loan default probabilities to the systematically varying mean default rate of the economy or sector of interest.

121. Credit Suisse First Boston, *Credit Risk*$^+$, technical document, London/New York, October 1997.

122. L. V. Carty and D. Lieberman, *Corporate Bond Defaults and Default Rates 1938–1995,* New York: Global Credit Research, Moody's Investors Service, January 1996.

123. Credit Suisse First Boston, *CreditRisk*$^+$, technical document, London/New York, October 1997.

124. Michael B. Gordy, "A Comparative Anatomy of Credit Risk Models," paper presented at the Bank of England Conference on Credit Risk Modeling and Regulatory Implications, London, September 21–22, 1998.

125. H. U. Koyluoglu and A. Hickman, *A Generalized Framework for Credit Risk Portfolio Models,* New York: Oliver, Wyman and Co., September 14, 1998.

126. M. Crouhy and R. Mark, "A Comparative Analysis of Current Credit Risk Models," paper presented at the Bank of England Conference on Credit Risk Modeling and Regulatory Implications, London, September 21–22, 1998.

127. For a detailed discussion of the MTM and DM approaches, see Bank for International Settlement (BIS), Basel Committee on Banking Supervision, *Credit Risk Modelling: Current Practices and Applications,* Basel, Switzerland: Bank for International Settlement, April 1999, 17, 22.

128. For a discussion of multifactor models, see Reto R. Gallati, "Empirical Application of APT Multifactor-Models to the Swiss Equity Market," Basic Report, Zurich: Credit Suisse Investment Research, September 1993, and M. J. Gruber, *Modern Portfolio Theory and Investment Analysis,* 5th ed., New York: John Wiley & Sons, 1998.

129. For a discussion, see E. I. Altman and A. Saunders, "Credit Risk Measurement: Developments over the Last Twenty Years," *Journal of Banking and Finance* (December 1997), 1721–1742.

130. Reto R. Gallati, "Empirical Application of APT Multifactor-Models to the Swiss Equity Market," basic report, Zurich: Credit Suisse Investment Research, September 1993

131. S. Kealhofer, "Managing Default Risk in Derivative Portfolios," in *Derivative Credit Risk: Advances in Measurement and Management,* London: Renaissance Risk Publications, 1995.

132. The EDFs of the KMV model vary from 0 to 20%. By allocating EDFs into score ranges or categories, a transition matrix can be generated based on EDF scores.

133. In recent documentation, KMV has applied a multiple of 10; thus, capital = $UL_p \cdot 10$.

134. A standardized return is a current return divided by its estimated standard deviation after subtracting the mean return. A standardized normal distribution has a mean of zero and a standard deviation of unity, $(x - \mu_i)/\sigma_i \rightarrow N(0,1)$

135. It can be argued that correlations should be measured between loans, not borrowers. For example, a low-quality borrower with a highly secured loan (e.g., collateralized, guarantees, etc.) would find the loan rated more highly than the borrower as a whole.

136. The calculation has been done by backward calculation of the probabilities of the worst outcome: the worst loan outcome, then the second-worst, and so forth.

137. Technically, the correlation matrix Σ among the loans is decomposed using the Cholesky factorization process, which finds two matrices A and A' (its transpose) such that $I = AA'$. Asset return scenarios y are generated by multiplying the matrix A' (which contains memory relating to historical correlation relationships) by a random number vector z; i.e., $y = A'z$.

138. D. Duffie and K. Singleton, "Simulating Correlated Defaults," paper presented at the Bank of England Conference on Credit Risk Modeling and Regulatory Implications, London, September 21–22, 1998 provides a discussion of various algorithms to estimate default correlation intensities and an extensive review of the intensity-modeling-based research.

139. The current regulations for the BIS internal model for market risk require that the bank's internal VaR be multiplied by a factor of 3 to 4, subject to approval of the local regulator. Intuitively, this multiplier can be regarded as a stress-test multiplier accommodating outliers in the 99 percent tail of the distribution. If, in backtesting a model, regulators or auditors find that the model underestimated VaR on fewer than 4 out of the past 250 days, the VaR multiplier remains at its minimum value of 3. If 4 to 9 days of underestimated risk are found, the multiplier is increased to a range of 3.4 to 3.85. If more than 10 daily errors are found, the multiplication factor for the internal VaR is set at 4. The multiplier is subject to other qualitative restrictions, which influence the multiplier granted by the regulator.

140. This assumption is still optimistic. Not even the rating agencies have current default histories going back that far. Most financial organizations can provide perhaps two or three years' usable data for the loans they grant.

141. C. W. J. Granger and L. L. Huang, "Evaluation of Panel Data Models: Some Suggestions from Time-Series," Discussion Paper 97-10, University of California, Department of Economics, San Diego, 1997.

142. Mark Carey, "Credit Risk in Private Debt Portfolios," *Journal of Finance* (August 1998), 1363–1387.

143. J. A. Lopez and M. R. Saidenberg, "Evaluating Credit Risk Models," paper presented at the Bank of England Conference on Credit Risk Modeling and Regulatory Implications, London, September 21–22, 1998.

144. For details, see ibid.

145. The analogy with backtesting market risk models using time-series data is linked to how representative the past period is (i.e., the last 250 days under the BIS rules).

146. G. Stahl, "Confidence Intervals for Different Capital Definitions in a Credit Risk Model," paper presented at Center for Economic Policy Research (CEPR) Conference, London, September 20, 1998.

147. Mark Carey, "Credit Risk in Private Debt Portfolios," *Journal of Finance* (August 1998), 1363–1387.

148. Reto R. Gallati, "Switzerland Money Markets," in Nick Battley, ed., *The European Bond Markets: An Overview and Analysis for Issuers and Investors,* 6th ed., Cambridge, MA: McGraw-Hill, 1997, 1373.

149. Paul Vienna, *An Investor's Guide to CMOs,* New York: Salomon Brothers, 1986 and Gregory J. Parseghian, "Collateralized Mortgage Obligations," in Frank Fabozzi, ed., *The Handbook of Fixed-Income Securities,* 3d ed., Homewood, IL: McGraw-Hill, 1991.

150. Institute of International Finance (IIF), *Recommendations for Revising the Regulatory Capital Rules for Credit Risk: Report of the Working Group on Capital Adequacy,* Washington, DC: Institute of International Finance, 1998.

151. International Swaps and Derivatives Association (ISDA), *Credit Risk and Regulatory Capital,* New York/London: International Swaps and Derivatives Association, March 1998.

152. Bank for International Settlement (BIS), Basel Committee on Banking Supervision, *A New Capital Adequacy Framework: Consultative Paper Issued by the Basel Committee on Banking Supervision for Comment by 31 March 2000,* Basel, Switzerland: Bank for International Settlement, June 1999.

153. See Bank for International Settlement (BIS), Basel Committee on Banking Supervision, *International Convergence of Capital Measurement and Capital Standards,* Basel, Switzerland: Bank for International Settlement, July 1988.

154. Bank for International Settlement (BIS), Basel Committee on Banking Supervision, *Credit Risk Modelling: Current Practices and Applications,* Basel, Switzerland: Bank for International Settlement, April 1999.

155. Bank for International Settlement (BIS), Basel Committee on Banking Supervision, *A New Capital Adequacy Framework: Consultative Paper Issued by the Basel Committee on Banking Supervision for Comment by 31 March 2000,* Basel, Switzerland: Bank for International Settlement, June 1999, 14, para. 28ff.

156. Bank for International Settlement (BIS), Basel Committee on Banking Supervision, *Operational Risk, Consultative Document: Supporting Document to the New Basel Capital Accord, Issued for Comment by 31 May 2001,* Basel, Switzerland: Bank for International Settlement, January 2001.

157. Bank for International Settlement (BIS), Basel Committee on Banking Supervision, *Measurement of Banks' Exposure to Interest Rate Risk,* Basel, Switzerland: Bank for International Settlement, April 1993.

158. Bank for International Settlement (BIS), Basel Committee on Banking Supervision, *A New Capital Adequacy Framework: Consultative Paper Issued by the Basel Committee on Banking Supervision for Comment by 31 March 2000*, Basel, Switzerland: Bank for International Settlement, June 1999, para. 21ff; *The Standardized Approach to Credit Risk, Consultative Document: Supporting Document to the New Basel Capital Accord, Issued for Comment by 31 May 2001*, Basel, Switzerland: Bank for International Settlement, January 2001.

159. Bank for International Settlement (BIS), Basel Committee on Banking Supervision, *A New Capital Adequacy Framework: Consultative Paper Issued by the Basel Committee on Banking Supervision for Comment by 31 March 2000*, Basle, Switzerland: Bank for International Settlement, June 1999, para. 150ff.; *The Internal Ratings-Based Approach, Consultative Document: Supporting Document to the New Basel Capital Accord, Issued for Comment by 31 May 2001*, Basel, Switzerland: Bank for International Settlement, January 2001.

160. Bank for International Settlement (BIS), Basel Committee on Banking Supervision, *The Internal Ratings-Based Approach, Consultative Document: Supporting Document to the New Basel Capital Accord, Issued for Comment by 31 May 2001*, Basel, Switzerland: Bank for International Settlement, January 2001, para. 24ff.

161. Ibid., para. 33ff.

162. Ibid., paras. 52ff and 392ff.

163. Bank for International Settlement (BIS), Basel Committee on Banking Supervision, *A New Capital Adequacy Framework: Consultative Paper Issued by the Basel Committee on Banking Supervision for Comment by 31 March 2000*, Basel, Switzerland: Bank for International Settlement, June 1999, paras. 61ff., 181, and 653ff.

164. Ibid., para. 404.

165. Ibid.

166. Ibid., para. 80ff.

167. Ibid., para. 516ff.

168. Ibid., para. 546ff.

169. Ibid., para. 503ff.

170. Bank for International Settlement (BIS), Basel Committee on Banking Supervision, "Update on Work on the New Basel Capital Accord," *Basel Committee Newsletter* 2 (September 2001).

CHAPTER 4

Operational Risk

4.1 BACKGROUND

Operational risk is not a new risk. In fact, it is the first risk a bank must manage, even before it makes its first loan or executes its first trade. However, the idea that operational risk management is a discipline with its own management structure, tools, and processes, much like credit or market risk, is new and has evolved over the last five years.

In 1998, the Basel Committee on Banking Supervision published a consultative paper related to operational risk.[1] Operational risk is an accepted part of sound risk management practice in modern financial markets. According to the BIS paper, the most important types of operational risk involve breakdowns in internal controls and corporate governance. Such breakdowns can lead to substantial financial losses through error, fraud, or failure to perform obligations in a timely manner, or can cause the interests and existence of the bank to be compromised in some other way. This may include dealers, lending officers, or other staff members exceeding their authority or conducting business in an unethical or risky manner. Other aspects of operational risk include the major failure of information technology systems, or events such as fires or other disasters.

Most financial institutions assign primary responsibility for managing operational risk to the business line head. Those banks that are developing measurement systems for operational risk are also often attempting to build incentive structures and processes for sound operational risk management practice by business managers. These incentive structures can take the form of allocating capital for operational risk, including operational risk measurement in the performance evaluation process, or requiring business line management to present operational loss details and resultant corrective action directly to the bank's highest levels of management.

Such a framework for managing operational risk is only in its early stages of development. Awareness of operational risk as a separate risk category is present and enforced by most auditors, as they include operational risk statements in their annual audit reports. Only a few sophisticated banks currently measure and report this risk on a regular basis, although many track operational performance indicators, analyze loss experiences, and monitor audit and supervisory ratings.

Significant conceptual issues and data needs have been identified that should be addressed to develop general measures of operational risk. Unlike market and perhaps credit risk, operational risk factors are largely internal to the bank, and a clear mathematical or statistical link between individual risk factors and the likelihood and size of operational loss (earnings volatility) does not yet exist. Experience with large losses is infrequent, and many banks lack a time series of historical data on their own operational losses and the causes of these losses. While the industry is far from converging on a set of standard models, such as are increasingly available for market and credit risk measurement, the banks that have developed or are developing models rely on a surprisingly similar set of risk factors. Those factors include internal audit ratings or control self-assessments; operational indicators such as volume, turnover, or rate of errors; loss experience; and income volatility.

One potential benefit of a formal approach to operational risk is that it becomes possible to develop incentives for business managers to adopt sound risk management practices through capital allocation charges, performance reviews, or other mechanisms. Many banks are also working toward some form of capital allocation as a business cost in order to create a risk pricing methodology.

Financial institutions are convinced that operational risk management programs protect and enhance shareholder value. Operational risk management as a distinct internal function with its own process, structure, tools, and measures is emerging, consisting of a set of integrated processes, tools, and mitigation strategies. This new trend is bringing a formal process and increased transparency to one of the oldest forms of risk. The key considerations are as follows:

- The creation of operational risk management programs has been driven by a combination of management commitment, need for an understanding of enterprisewide risks, a perceived increase in exposure to operational risk and risk events, and regulatory interest.

- There is consensus on the core definition of operational risk: the risk of direct or indirect loss resulting from inadequate or failed internal processes, people, and systems or from external events.
- Methodologies are evolving to quantify operational risk capital. While progress is being made, there is no consensus on approach, and methodologies are not yet used as a basis for decision making.

Lacking any guidance from the regulatory side, each firm may have developed its own understanding of operational risk management. Still, five stages of development of an operational risk management framework can be differentiated, which may help companies starting a program prioritize their efforts:

1. *Senior management commitment.* Senior management is committed to the vision that a new approach has merit.
2. *Perceived increase in operational risk.* Due to growing service businesses and diffusion of market and credit risks, operational risk receives increased attention from different interested groups, such as investors, regulators, clients, etc.
3. *Reaction to major loss events.* Losses have occurred internally or to others and forced senior managers to take action.
4. *Focus on enterprisewide risk management.* After the development of processes for market and credit risk management, operational risk is the next logical step.
5. *Regulatory attention.* The industry responds and moves ahead of expectations.

4.2 INCREASING FOCUS ON OPERATIONAL RISK

The operational form of risk is one of the most significant dimensions confronted by all businesses, financial and nonfinancial institutions alike. Historically, at least within the financial services industry, the more widely understood financial risks, such as market and credit risk, have taken precedence at both senior management and board levels. Investment decisions have focused on enhancing management's ability to identify, measure, monitor, and control traditional financial risks, with increasing emphasis on capabilities to deliver information on a real-time basis. More recently, however, operational risk has become increasingly prominent on the agenda of regulators, investors, and management.

4.2.1 Drivers of Operational Risk Management

Highly publicized organizational failures that have caught much media attention have increased the realization by management and regulators that many of the most severe operational losses could happen again almost anywhere. This prominence is fueled by a number of linked and equally important factors:

- Continuing changes in the regulation of the financial services sector have increased the focus on the prudential aspects of operational risk, including capital sufficiency and operational, control, and management effectiveness. Of particular interest is the introduction of personal accountability by management and boards of directors in more and more jurisdictions.
- Competitive pressures resulting from the smaller profit margins in traditional financial risk management products have increased the drive to innovate with ever more complex, nonstandard products or delivery mechanisms in less time. Each innovation, in its unique way, stretches to the limit the boundaries of existing business processes, which have largely been designed for high volume and relatively straightforward products and services. This continually changing product development and delivery process continues to undermine the capability of an organization to design and build a stable management infrastructure. What must be guarded against is a purely reactive, piecemeal evolution of not only the technology and supporting processes but, perhaps more important, the skill base of those charged with the responsibility of managing the new business model.
- Consolidation among financial service providers has created larger and more closely aligned institutions. These institutions are more complex as well as interconnected through internal and external organizations and substantial transactions. Accordingly, the frequency and complexity of operational problems will likely increase within institutions and on a concurrent basis with external organizations.
- Increasing use of technology in both the distribution and processing of transactions has increased the speed with which operational problems manifest themselves. To the extent that organizations use manual processes and "workarounds" that are neither efficient nor scalable, the probability of operational risks is further increased. Improved technology may mitigate this risk to some extent but, where mismanaged, can only serve to emphasize the impact of inadequacies. Technology, though on the whole an aid to greater efficiency and effectiveness, has also increased the capacity of operations, thus magnifying the effect of operational breakdown.

Shareholders increasingly expect compensation for investments and the risks associated with investment decisions. Management is now being asked to justify the nature and extent of capital invested in the business and to make appropriate disclosures of risk management and capital allocation processes in annual financial statements. The pressure to measure and disclose risk in capital terms will continue to increase as shareholder sophistication increases.

In a marketplace as ever changing and unpredictable as global financial services, the real challenge is to generate a management momentum equal in its dynamics to that of the environment so that processes and technology infrastructure can be consistently designed and redesigned to meet the needs of existing business. Figure 4-1 highlights the drivers of operational risk.

There are numerous examples of the complexity and risks associated with doing business in the 1990s, not least of which is the Barings collapse.

FIGURE 4-1

Drivers of Operational Risk.

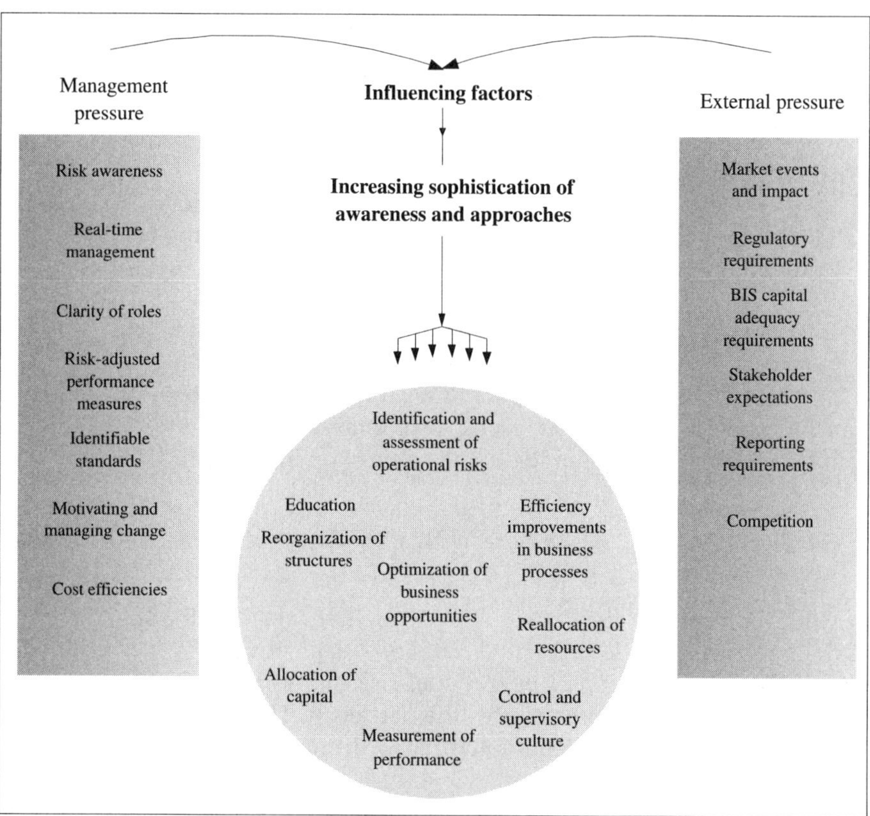

(See the case study on Barings in Chapter 6.) This, and a few others, are classic examples of operational failures where the ultimate price was paid by the shareholders and the institutions. Although many control failures and procedural breakdowns contribute to a collapse on this scale, it highlights the role that management can play in limiting the impact of operational failure. In the case of Barings, it is acknowledged in the final analysis that management, with limited resources available, had not selected the appropriate business segment on which to focus attention. Accumulations of competencies, supernormal profits, and unexpected losses are indicators of potential operating abnormalities. Management must simultaneously encourage good performance and continually question the validity of that performance.

4.2.2 Operational Risk and Shareholder Value

Operational risk management initiatives protect and enhance shareholder value. The evidence is qualitative rather than quantitative. The primary benefit received from an operational risk management program is the protection of shareholder value, encompassing internal awareness of operational risk, protection of reputation, and decreased levels of operational losses.

An effective operational risk management framework can add value by improving competitive advantage and reducing the level of losses from large events that can imperil financial condition and from smaller, more frequent incidents.

Risk-adjusted measures such as economic value added (EVA) and shareholder value added (SVA) are one way to measure the benefit from improved operational risk management.

$$\text{EVA} = \text{net result} - (\text{risk capital} \times \text{required interest rates}) \tag{4.1}$$

EVA is the numerator of RAROC. It measures the absolute value of an investment generated in excess of the target profitability. A business unit with a positive EVA adds to the value of an institution.

$$\text{SVA} = \sum_{t=1}^{T} \text{NPV}\,(\text{EVA}_t) \tag{4.2}$$

SVA measures the added value of an investment to the shareholder. An investment should be carried out if SVA is positive.

The quantification of operational risk allows us to express the loss (or potential loss), which reduces the net result. Thus, it is easy to figure out the added value of operational risk prevention in the context of EVA and SVA measures.

4.3 DEFINITION OF OPERATIONAL RISK

A common definition for operational risk is emerging. The debate on how to define operational risk has at times overshadowed the debate on how to manage it. How can institutions be expected to manage operational risk if they cannot define it? Many banks have their own internal definition of operational risk, and the great majority of them are satisfied with that definition.

In reviewing those definitions, analyzing common classifications, and eliminating linguistic, cultural, and organizational differences, it becomes obvious that there is a common core operational risk definition, specifically:

> Operational risk is the risk of direct or indirect loss resulting from inadequate or failed internal processes, people, and systems or from external events.[2]

This definition is a comprehensive, positive, and forward-looking statement that can be adapted by firms to reflect their own circumstances. An important distinction of the BIS definition is that it focuses on the sources of losses. But at an industry level this does express the core operational risk factors of most firms (and can facilitate exchange of information). It should also be understood that this definition is not intended to include defaults or changes to financial markets that are otherwise covered in the scope of market and credit risks.

The key distinction of the BIS definition is that it focuses on the impact of operational losses. This is a fundamental difference in the conceptual approach to creating a definition.

According to the BIS consultative paper, there is at present no agreed-upon universal definition of operational risk. A common definition of operational risk is any risk not categorized as market or credit risk. Other institutions have defined it as the risk of loss arising from various types of human or technical error. Still others associate operational risk with settlement or payment risk and business interruption, administrative, and legal risks. Several types of events (settlement, collateral, and netting risks) are seen by some institutions as not necessarily classifiable as operational risk and may contain elements of more than one type of risk. The institutions participating in the study all see some form of link between credit, market, and operational risk. In particular, an operational problem with a business transaction (for example, a settlement failure) could create market or credit risk. While most banks view technology risk as a type of operational risk, some view it as a separate risk category with its own discrete risk factors.

The majority of banks associate operational risk with all business lines, including infrastructure, although the mix of risks and their relative magnitude may vary considerably across businesses. Operational risk is tracked in business lines with high volume, high turnover (transactions/time), a high degree of structural change, and/or complex support systems. Operational risk is viewed as having a high potential impact on business lines with those characteristics, especially if the businesses also have low margins, as occurs in certain transaction-processing and payment system activities.

Operational risk for any institution arises from the influence and interaction of internal and external events on the people, processes, and technology applied to the business processes within that institution. Given that institutions are generally unique in the way they combine people, processes, and technology, it is difficult if not impossible to create a single generic definition for what constitutes operational risk.

Traditional definitions of operational risk are skewed and focused primarily on the negative aspects of risk, including the potential that, for one reason or another, business processes will be disrupted, resulting in a direct or indirect financial loss. Loss-incurring events may be driven by factors such as inadequate or failed information systems, inadequate or failed processes or controls, human error or fraud, or even unforeseeable natural catastrophes. *Direct loss* refers to losses on current earnings. *Indirect loss* refers to loss of potential earnings—for example, due to operational impediments to expanding the business or customer attrition resulting from reputation problems. This type of definition is backward looking, and historic information is of limited use to prevent future losses or to foretell threats to the existence of the organization.

Less traditional and potentially more strategic definitions of operational risk incorporate the positive view of risk (see Figure 4-2). Rather than viewing risk only as financial loss from market/credit risk exposures, operational risk includes consideration of the failure of operational processes or strategic investment decisions to optimize returns or financial gains. This definition introduces the concept of opportunity cost.

From a theoretical and academic standpoint, it is desirable to clarify discussions about operational risk and to identify and differentiate operational risk from all of the themes and categories discussed in previous chapters. This enables us to allocate and differentiate all risk definitions within a holistic framework and avoid the overlapping of well-defined risks. However, it is too big an undertaking for the purpose of this book, and we will restrict the identification and differentiation of operational risks to market and credit risks. Other risks, such as settlement, liquidity, and strategic risks, are summarized under "others" (see Table 4-1).

Analyzing recent losses, we are tempted to allocate negative developments to causes and impacts. Causes could be the undesirable deviation from an expected outcome, and impacts would be the risk, as it usually results in a loss that can be expressed in a value term. Many definitions do not explore this differentiation. Other definitions do not make a

FIGURE 4-2

Definition of Operational Risk as an Opportunity Instead of a Threat.

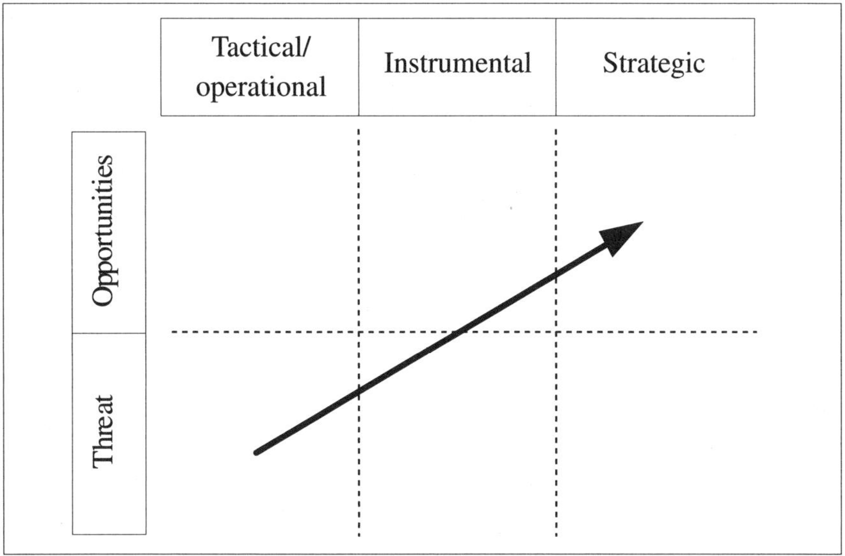

distinction and mix both dimensions, which makes identification and differentiation difficult. This is especially true for operational risk, as the process of building up loss databases requires a formal structure to categorize the losses. Quantitative analyses based on mixed definitions make less sense.

The analyses of losses, e.g., in the cases of Barings, Sumitomo, or Metallgesellschaft, tend to define losses as market risks. In the context of the cause-impact relationship, the definition of operational risk becomes meaningful, as the fundamental principles of internal control, segregation of dues, due diligence, etc. had been severely neglected in these cases.

For the purpose of this book, we will use the approach highlighted in Table 4-1. The definition of operational risk distinguishes between direct and indirect impacts from operational risk causes. The impact might be manifested in a market risk, resulting in a loss or profit. The matrix is based on the assumption that it is possible to identify the causes of operational risks, such as unexpected losses from internal errors; false assessment of situations, strategies, and external events; and so on. Sloppy oversight of counterparty risks can result in credit risk losses that could have been prevented by an appropriate internal control system and management culture. The direct impacts will immediately hit the P&L statement and the balance sheet at the moment of their occurrence, and the

TABLE 4-1

Definition Matrix for Identifying and Measuring Risk Based on Impact and Cause

Cause	*Impact*					
	Direct Appearance of Operational Risk					*Indirect Appearance of Operational Risk in Form of Loss of Market Value (Including Reputational Risk)*
				Operational Losses in Form of		
	Loss from Change in Credit-worthiness	**Loss from Change in Market Value**	**Other Losses**	**Extra Costs**	**Loss of Revenues**	
Unsafe or erroneous counterparty information	⇡	⇡		⇡	⇡	⇡
Unsafe or erroneous information regarding market development	⋮	⋮		⋮	⋮	⋮
Errors in areas such as: • Human resources • Processes • Systems • External events	⤴	⤴		⤴	⤴	⤴
Others, such as false assessment regarding: • Liquidity • Staging` • Strategy	⤴	⤴		⤴	⤴	⤴

SOURCE: Modified from Hans Geiger and Jean-Marc Piaz, "Identifikation und Bewertung von operationellen Risiken," in Henner Schierenbeck (ed.), *Handbuch Bank-Controlling,* 3d ed., Wiesbaden, Germany: Gabler Verlag, 2000.

indirect losses will result indirectly in discounted values of future expected cash flows. One example is the higher refinancing rates paid through the treasury department because the bank's counterparty risk is considered high. This decreases the bank's profit through higher costs, and, because of the low rating, the bank's market valuation is lower than it would be with a higher credit rating (higher discount rate including higher credit spread).

How does the matrix impact the definitions? It helps to distinguish between the causes and impacts and among the relationships between the different risk categories, creating an allocation of risk. The following examples will clarify the matrix:

- A constrained definition of credit risk in the form of a negative change in creditworthiness resulting in potential credit loss—and thus requiring a higher risk premium—which is based on unsafe or erroneous information on counterparties (first entry in first row of matrix). According to the preceding definition, this type of operationally caused unexpected credit loss would not be a credit risk subject to capital support.
- A day trader taking market risks by holding outdated positions due to failing processes and infrastructure. An outdated system that is reporting T+2 information through a batch process is inadequate.

The definition of operational risk by the Bank of International Settlement is subject to controversy. (See the preceding discussions.) The BIS defines operational risk as "the risk of direct or indirect loss resulting from inadequate or failed internal processes, people, and systems or from external events." While this definition includes legal risk, strategic and reputational risk are explicitly not included for the purpose of minimum regulation. We consider reputational risk as an integral part of the operational risk definition to be consistent with the BIS definition as an integrating framework. For the purpose of an international and regulatory binding definition, in this book we use the BIS definition of operational risk. We assume that the BIS (given all the feedback from the industry) will modify the definition and add reputational risk as a component of the definition.

4.4 REGULATORY UNDERSTANDING OF OPERATIONAL RISK DEFINITION

A first step in understanding the regulatory approach to operational risk is to read the relevant supplement of the consultation document for the revised Capital Accord issued by the Basel Committee of the Bank for International Settlement in January 2001.[3] Most remarkable is how much guidance the Committee is asking for from industry practitioners. Several times during the course of the document, the BIS requests feedback on a variety of topics. Some issues involved are very basic. For example, the discipline of operational risk management is so new that the BIS has only recently settled on a "final" definition of operational risk[4] (see Figure 4-3). This definition includes legal risk but not strategic or reputational risks. However, while the BIS may have heroically settled on a definition, the industry is still arguing over exactly what it means and how it relates to their attempts to put operational risk management on firm ground. While this definition has eliminated some sources of uncertainty (for example, it does not include the risks arising from botched business or strategic decisions, which were implied in earlier discussions), others remain. For example, the BIS specifically excludes reputational risk. Reputational risk is one of the key hazards for financial services companies, for which a good name is often a key intellectual property asset. Damage to that good name

FIGURE 4-3

Definition of Operational Risk Based on the BIS Approach.

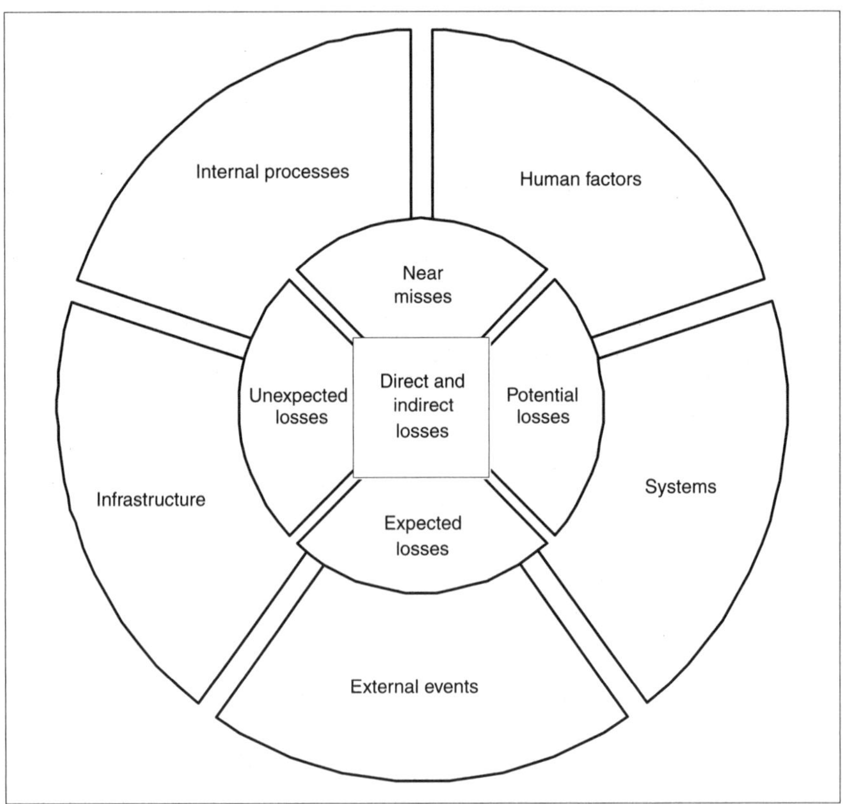

is one of the most difficult risks to overcome: you usually can't pay a fine or take a charge (no matter how painful) that will quickly reduce the risk to your firm's reputation. So quantifying and capitalizing reputational risk is no easy matter—and does not sit easily with attempts to quantify and capitalize many other forms of operational risk, such as systems failures or payment errors. That in turn has led to suggestions that reputational risk should not in fact be considered operational risk. While the BIS has settled on a definition of operational risk, the industry is still arguing over exactly what it means.

Part of the answer is that operational risk *measurement* is not the same thing as operational risk *management.* Quantifying those operational risks that lend themselves to quantification and neglecting the rest does not constitute best practice in operational risk management. As we will later discuss, and as the BIS consultation document acknowledges, there is a pronounced need for greater discussion (and management) of the qualitative aspects of operational risk.

So far, however, the banking industry has largely focused its efforts on coming up with measurement techniques that will allow it to take advantage of the "evolutionary" capital regime proposed by the Basel Committee on banking risks. But the best measurement techniques and capital models in the world will not reduce operational risks unless they are used in coordination with inherently solid management processes. While these techniques may assist firms in reducing their capital charges, allowing them to deploy their hard currency elsewhere, they remain exposed to risks that can harm (if not destroy) their reputations, or severely impair their liquidity and ability to meet financial commitments.

Most risks to financial firms can be divided into expected losses (covered by reserve provisions), unexpected losses (covered by regulatory and economic capital), and catastrophic losses that must simply be prevented by internal controls or transferred using insurance or alternative risk transfer (ART) instruments. The problem in devising rules for the capitalization of operational risk is that as yet it is quite unclear what proportion and type of operational risks fall into each category—and the boundaries keep moving as the industry changes.

To take a classic example, the management of Barings Bank was reportedly warned of the dangers of putting Nick Leeson in charge of both trading and settlement at a remote outpost with little additional oversight. They clearly felt that the operational risk involved was minor—but were proved dramatically wrong when it came to light in 1995 that Leeson had built up, and systematically concealed, a huge loss-making position. The operational risk was catastrophic. The most effective control over that risk would have been a change in organizational structure, not capitalization. Today, a number of firms offer "rogue trader" insurance, which could be viewed as a form of capitalization against operational risk. However, it is unlikely that they would agree to provide cover to companies with internal controls as botched as those of Barings. So operational risk management, in this case, is about internal controls, not about quantification and capitalization. (For details, see the analysis of Barings in Chapter 6.)

More generally, it is important to consider quantification and capitalization of operational risk as just two of many tools in the establishment of a viable program. The reality is that all financial organizations need to consider at least rudimentary approaches to operational risk capital, even where these do not lead to regulatory benefits; while operational risks are perhaps less tangible than market or credit risks, they have been responsible for some of the biggest losses in history. (See the discussion of case studies in Chapter 6.)

4.5 ENFORCEMENT OF OPERATIONAL RISK MANAGEMENT

The operational risk function is responsible for the development of firmwide operational risk policies, frameworks, and methodologies created to advise the business units. In this emerging model, the most common responsibilities for this new function are:

- Determining operational risk policies and definition
- Developing and deploying common tools
- Establishing indicators
- Assessing benefits of programs
- Analyzing linkages to credit and market risk
- Consolidating cross-enterprise information

In addition, operational risk managers focus on cross-enterprise operational risk management initiatives such as developing economic capital methodologies and building loss databases. They can also be charged with the management of the firm's portfolio of operational risks. Depending on the relationship with the business units, they may consult or participate in operational risk management projects with business units. There are a variety of stand-alone tools that companies are using to manage operational risk.

Operational risk management is developing a comprehensive set of tools for the identification and assessment of operational risk. Individual firms use a wide variety of techniques grouped around five topics: risk and self-assessment, risk mapping, risk indicators, escalation triggers, and loss event databases. The tool currently most valued and used is self-assessment (or risk assessment). However, the tool that most financial institutions are investigating, and that is next in line for development, is the internal loss database.

Methodologies to quantify operational risk capital are improving, but firms are not satisfied with the results so far. The majority of the financial institutions are in the process of developing a measure of economic capital for operational risk. However, the gap between what most firms want to achieve and what they are able to achieve remains large. The focus of current research and development efforts is the structural approach and the behavioral incentives that are created. As a consequence, operational risk capital measures are not yet used to drive economic decision making.

A healthy range of approaches are being applied along a continuum between top-down and more risk-based bottom-up approaches. These methodologies often rely on actual data, can quantify the level of exposure to each type of risk at the business line level, and react to changes in the control environment and actual operational risk results. Since no single approach is satisfactory, most firms currently use multiple methodologies to obtain a result. Overall, there is little movement toward risk-based and bottom-up methodologies (see Figure 4-4). To move forward, the industry will need to overcome three major obstacles: data, measurement, and management acceptance.

A framework for operational risk is emerging that consists of a set of integrated processes, tools, and mitigation strategies. Some key components contribute the most to the operational risk framework and reflect the company's culture, including the style of decision making, the level of formal processes, and the attributes of the core business:

FIGURE 4-4

Credit Risk: Bottom-Up Versus Top-Down Approaches.

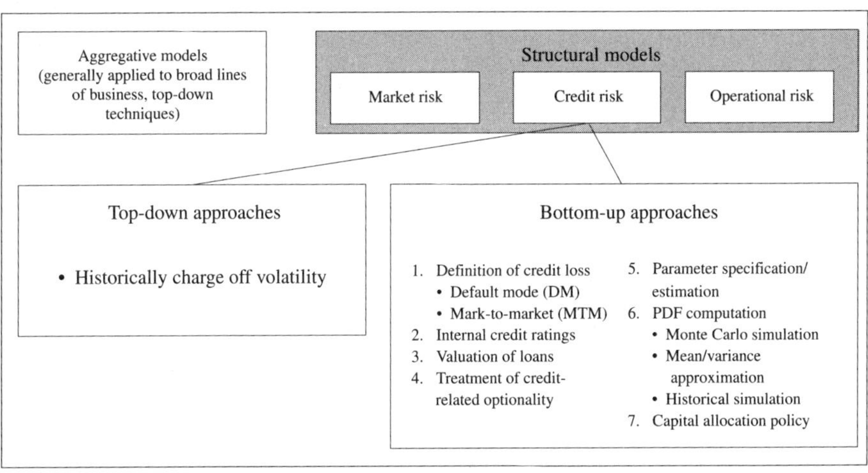

- *Strategy.* Risk management starts with the overall strategies and objectives of the institution and the subsequent goals for individual business units, products, or managers. This is followed by identification of associated inherent risks in strategies and objectives. Both negative events (e.g., a major loss that would have a significant impact on earnings) and opportunities (e.g., new products that depend on taking operational risk) are considered. As a result, a firm can set its risk tolerance—specifically, what risks the company understands, will take, and will manage versus those that should be transferred to others or eliminated. It is the basis for decision making and a reference point for the organization.
- *Risk policies.* Risk strategy is complemented by operational risk management policies, which are a formal communication to the organization as a whole on the approach to, and importance of, operational risk management. Policies typically include a definition of operational risk, the organization approach and related roles and responsibilities, key principles for management, and a high-level discussion of information and related technology.
- *Risk management process.* This sets out the overall procedures for operational risk management:

  Controls. Definition of internal controls, or selection of alternate mitigation strategy, such as insurance, for identified risks.

  Assessment. Programs to ensure that controls and policies are being followed and to determine the level of risk severity. These may include process flows, self-assessment programs, and audit programs.

  Measurement. A combination of financial and nonfinancial measures, risk indicators, escalation triggers, and economic capital to determine current risk levels and progress toward goals.

  Reporting. Information for management to increase awareness and prioritize resources.
- *Risk mitigation.* These are specific controls or programs designed to reduce the exposure, frequency, severity, or impact of an event or to eliminate (or transfer) an element of operational risk. Examples include business continuity planning, IT security, compliance reviews, project management, and merger integration and insurance. A variety of techniques are used to control or mitigate operational risk. As discussed later, internal controls and the internal audit process are seen as the primary means of controlling operational risk. Financial institutions have a variety of other possibilities. A few banks have established some form of

operational risk limits, usually based on their measures of operational risk, or other exception-reporting mechanisms to highlight potential problems. Some banks surveyed cited insurance as an important mitigator for some forms of operational risk. It is a standard accounting procedure to establish a provision for operational losses similar to traditional loan loss reserves now routinely maintained. Several banks are also exploring the use of reinsurance, in some cases from captive subsidiaries, to cover operational losses.

- *Operations management.* This refers to the day-to-day processes, such as front- and back-office functions, technology, performance improvement, management reporting, and people management. Every process has a component of operational risk management embedded in it.
- *Culture.* There is always a balance between formal policies and culture or the values of the people in the organization. In operational risk, cultural aspects such as communication, the tone at the top, clear ownership of each objective, training, performance measurement, and knowledge sharing all help set the expectations for sound decision making.

In addition, the integration with market and credit risk in an enterprisewide risk management framework is noted, as well as alignment with the needs of the stakeholders, e.g., customers, employees, suppliers, regulators, and shareholders.

4.6 EVOLUTION OF OPERATIONAL RISK INITIATIVES

The evolution of operational risk management practices varies in a number of ways depending on the company culture and operational risk event history. Although the surveyed companies had different experiences, after synthesizing the results we can see that there are five stages in the evolution of operational risk management (see Table 4-2). This should be helpful to companies developing operational risk initiatives.

Stage 1: traditional approach. Operational risks have always existed and are traditionally managed by focusing primarily on self-control and internal controls. This is the responsibility of individual managers and specialist functions, with periodic objective review by internal auditors. Usually, there is not a formal operational risk management framework such as is discussed in this book.

Stage 2: awareness. The second stage in the evolution begins with the commitment of senior management to make the organization

TABLE 4-2

Stages of Operational Risk

Trend of Development Stages

Traditional approach	Awareness	Monitoring	Quantification	Integration
Stage 1	**Stage 2**	**Stage 3**	**Stage 4**	**Stage 5**
Internal control Reliance on internal audit Individual mitigation programs—self-control Reliance on quality of people and culture	Operational risk manager Governance structure Definition policy Process maps/ self-assessment Early indicators Begin collection of event data and establishment of value proposition Top-down economic capital models	Clear vision and goals for operational risk management Comprehensive indicators Escalation triggers Early indicators Begin collection of event data and establishment of value proposition Top-down economic capital models	Comprehensive loss database Set quantitative goals for improvement Predict analysis and leading indicators Risk-based economic models Active operational committee	Full, linked set of tools Cross-functional risk analysis Correlation between indicators and losses Insurance linked with risk analysis and capital Risk-adjusted returns linked to compensation

more proactive in its understanding of operational risk and the appointment of someone to be responsible for operational risk. To gain awareness, there must be a common understanding and assessment of operational risk. This assessment begins with the formulation of an operational risk policy based on the business strategy, a definition of operational risk, and development of common tools. The tools in this stage usually include self-assessment and risk process mapping. In addition, early indicators of operational risk levels and collection of loss events are beginning to be developed. These provide a common framework for risk identification, definition of controls, and prioritization of issues and mitigation programs. However, the most important factor in this development stage is gaining senior management commitment and ownership buy-in of operational risk at the business unit level.

Stage 3: monitoring. Once all of the operational risks are identified, the need to understand the implications of these risks to the business becomes pronounced. The focus becomes tracking the current level of operational risk and the effectiveness of the management functions. Risk indicators (both quantitative and qualitative) and escalation criteria (which are goals or limits) are established to monitor and report performance. Measures are consolidated into an operational risk scorecard along with other relevant issues for senior management. More banks have some form of monitoring system for operational risk than have formal operational risk measures. Most financial institutions monitor operational performance measures such as volume, turnover, settlement failures, delays, and errors. Some banks monitor operational losses directly, with an analysis of each occurrence and a description of the nature and causes of the loss provided to senior managers or the board of directors. A consistent approach to monitoring the operational performance measures and analyzing them has not yet been agreed on because the various business models are too different. Only a few banks have yet reached this stage with their current information systems for capturing and reporting operational risks.

Stage 4: quantification. With a better understanding of the current situation, the need changes to focus on quantifying the relative risks and predicting what will happen. More analytic tools, based on actual data, are required to determine the financial impact of operational risk on the organization and provide data to conduct empirical analysis on causes and mitigants. The loss event database, initiated in stage 2, now contains sufficient information across businesses and risk types to provide insight into causes and more predictive models. There may be a significant investment in developing earnings and capital models, and establishment of a new committee to evaluate the results.

Stage 5: integration. Recognizing the value of lessons learned by each business unit (earnings volatility) and the complementary nature of the individual tools, management focuses on integrating and implementing processes and solutions. Balancing business and corporate values, qualitative versus quantitative analysis, and different levels of management needs, risk quantification is now fully integrated into the economic capital processes and linked to compensation. Quantification is also applied to make better cost/earnings decisions on investments and insurance programs. However, this integration goes beyond processes and tools. In most leading companies, operational risk management is being linked to the strategic planning process and quality initiative. When this linkage is established, the relationship between operational risk management and shareholder value is more directly understood.

4.7 MEASUREMENT OF OPERATIONAL RISK

Most banks considering measuring operational risk are at a very early stage, with only a few having formal measurement systems and several others actively considering how to measure operational risk. The existing methodologies are relatively simple and experimental, although a few banks seem to have made considerable progress in developing more advanced techniques for allocating capital with regard to operational risk. The experimental quality of existing operational risk measures reflects several issues. The risk factors usually identified by banks are typically measures of internal performance, such as internal audit ratings, volume, turnover, error rates, and income volatility, rather than external factors such as market price movements or a change in a borrower's condition. Uncertainty about which factors are important is due to the absence of a direct relationship between the risk factors usually identified and the size and frequency of losses. This contrasts with market risk, where changes in prices have an easily computed impact on the value of the bank's trading portfolio, and perhaps with credit risk, where changes in the borrower's credit quality are often associated with changes in the interest rate spread of the borrower's obligations over a risk-free rate. To date, there is little research correlating those operational risk factors with operational losses.

Capturing operational loss experience also raises measurement questions. A few banks noted that the costs of investigating and correcting the problems underlying a loss event were significant, and in many cases exceeded the direct costs of the operational losses. Several banks suggested creating two broad categories of operational losses. Frequent, smaller operational losses such as those caused by occasional human errors are viewed as common in many businesses. Major operational risk losses were seen to have low probabilities but a large impact perhaps exceeding those of market or credit risks. Banks varied widely in their willingness to discuss their operational loss experience, with only a handful acknowledging the larger losses.

Measuring operational risk requires estimating both the probability of an operational loss event and the potential size of the loss. Most approaches described in the interviews rely to some extent on risk factors that provide some indication of the likelihood of an operational loss event occurring. The risk factors are generally quantitative but may be qualitative and subjective assessments translated into scores (such as an audit assessment). The set of risk factors often used includes variables that measure risk in each business unit, such as grades from qualitative assessments including internal audit ratings; generic operational data such as volume, turnover, and complexity; and data on quality of operations such as error rate or measures of business riskiness such as revenue volatility. Banks incorporating risk factors into their measurement approach can use them to identify businesses with higher operational risk.

Ideally, the risk factors could be related to historical loss experience to create a comprehensive measurement methodology. Some institutions have started collecting data on their historical loss experience. Since few firms experience many large operational losses in any case, estimating a historical loss distribution requires data from many firms, especially if the low-probability, large-cost events are to be captured. Another issue that arises is whether data from several banks or firms comes from the same distribution. Some institutions have started building up proprietary databases of external loss experiences. Banks may choose different analytical or judgmental techniques to arrive at an overall operational risk level for the firm. Banks appear to be taking an interest in how some insurance risks are measured as possible models for operational risk measures.

4.8 CORE ELEMENTS OF AN OPERATIONAL RISK MANAGEMENT PROCESS

As with market risk and credit risk, institutions are continually designing, constructing, and improving operational risk management processes. Many approaches currently exist, and every consulting company claims to own the best practice standards. However, consulting organizations consistently assign operational risk responsibility to the management of the operational business units of a financial institution. In general, business units have been left to their own devices to build the appropriate infrastructure to manage their operations and the resultant risk. The challenge is the extent to which an organization builds centralized operational risk management processes to support this.

In order to create a consensus, it is most useful to consider the essential components of any effective risk management framework. A process has to be established and maintained to enable management and the board of directors to systematically:

- Identify operational risks
- Measure the extent of the identified operational risks
- Monitor the nature and extent of operational risk
- Control, within acceptable parameters, the operational risk exposure of the organization

The essential elements of that framework should include:

- The establishment of consistent standards for the identification of operational risk, including the development of definitions and terminology, from which the consolidated operational risk exposure can be generated.
- The establishment of reporting infrastructure to support the independent monitoring and control of operational risk. Effective organizational risk management requires independence between the management of operational risk, resident within the operational units, and oversight over the control of operational risk.
- The development of consistent measurement methodology to allow for consolidated analysis of the extent of operational risk. Furthermore, from this measurement base, decisions can be formulated on alternative risk transfer solutions, capital management and control, and the implementation of risk-adjusted performance measures.

4.9 ALTERNATIVE OPERATIONAL RISK MANAGEMENT APPROACHES

There seem to be two distinct operational risk management approaches being adopted across the financial services sector—a top-down and a bottom-up framework. However, even within these commonly used terms there is a range of interpretations. Some organizations understand bottom-up and top-down as the process through which the risks of the organization are identified, while others use the terms to describe the nature of the measurement process that supports the operational risk management framework.

The conceptual differences between the approaches can best be characterized by the way risk is identified, measured, and aggregated within the organization:

- Top-down approaches focus primarily on the view of risk within the organization generated from the top of the organization. Risk is identified, measured, and aggregated according to a preexisting structure decided on and agreed on by top management. As a result, a top-down approach tends to focus on known or identifiable operational risk loss events. The impact and likelihood of operational risks are generally determined by reference to a combination of known external events and internal views on relative exposures.
- Bottom-up approaches focus primarily on the origins of risk within the organization. Rather than focusing on views of risk after the fact, bottom-up approaches focus on originating factors (either internally or externally generated) to determine the likelihood and impact of operational risk. Organizations are generally managed through a combination of people, processes, and technologies that either implicitly or explicitly manage risk. Bottom-up approaches focus on the interaction between internal and external events and the people, processes, and technologies deployed throughout the organization. These points of interaction provide the basis for identifying and determining the likelihood and impact of operational risk.

The BIS approaches to operational risk can be compared with the bottom-up and top-down approaches: the basic approach is a top-down approach, and the internal approach is a bottom-up approach, whereas the standardized approach is a top-down framework with bottom-up constituents.[5]

4.9.1 Top-Down Approaches

The unique aspects of a top-down approach to operational risk are generally found in the identification, measurement, and monitoring of operational risk (see Figure 4-5).

4.9.1.1 Risk Identification

Risk identification in a top-down approach is driven by management belief that the organization is exposed to either direct or indirect loss. These loss events are normally aggregated into risk categories that are consistent with the organization's definition of risk (see Figure 4-5). For example, losses associated with the failure of technology would ordinarily be aggregated as technology risk.

The process of risk identification is ordinarily undertaken on either a centralized or decentralized basis through a combination of a prepopulated database of loss events, fed from either internal or external sources,

FIGURE 4-5

Top-Down Risk Identification and Aggregation.

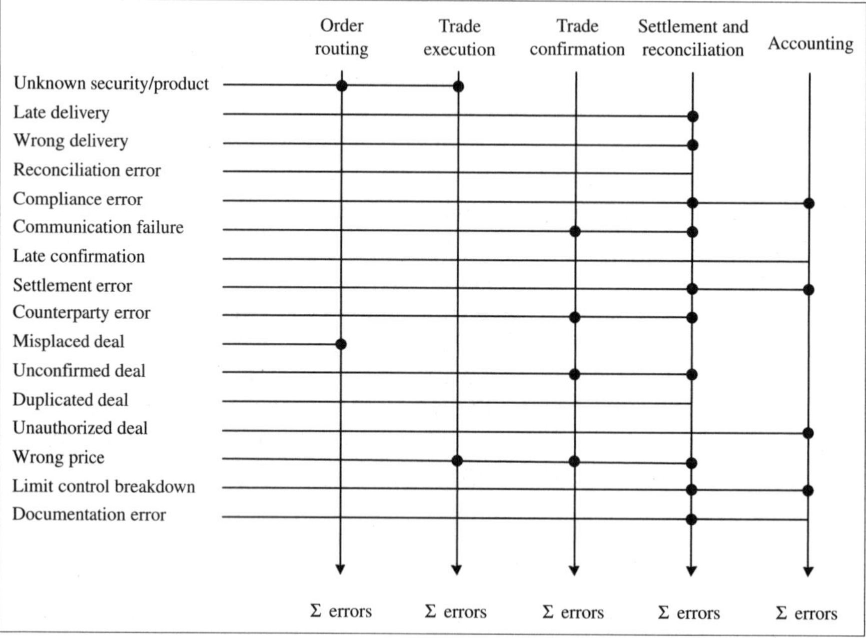

and traditional risk discovery techniques such as risk workshops and control and risk self-assessment in the form of checklist, questionnaire, or prepopulated automated tools.[6] Quite often organizations claim to have implemented a bottom-up approach because the identification and measurement of risk are undertaken on a decentralized basis, i.e., within the operational units. However, although the risks are identified from the bottom up, that identification and the resultant estimates of the likelihood of occurrence and impact are based on separation and aggregation of risk rather than origins of risk. In essence this would make these top-down approaches.

One key feature of top-down approaches is that they are most frequently established at a central point within the organization, such as the risk management team. As a result, risks can be readily aggregated to facilitate central analysis. This aggregation can then be used to support the measurement, management, monitoring, and control of operational risk.

4.9.1.2 Quantitative Risk Measurement

A variety of approaches are used to support the top-down measurement of operational risk. These approaches generally fall within two broad categories: quantitative measurement using mathematical approaches to quantify the level of risk, and qualitative measurement using more subjective assessment of risk (see Figure 4-6).

Operational risk in the context of quantitative risk measurement is the volatility of earnings that can be measured in the course of carrying on business, excluding the financial risks from market and credit risk.

Business risk in the context of quantitative risk measurement is the risk of operational earnings volatility due to changes in the earnings mix, margin, and volume volatility, and the level of variable and fixed costs.

Event risk in the context of quantitative risk measurement is the risk of financial loss due to operational processes and activities. Event risks such as earthquakes and terror attacks require special precautions. These include the costs of contingency plans for postdisaster recovery, system security, safeguarding of assets, and adherence to regulatory and legal requirements to maintain a minimum level of protection against event risks.

Business risk and market risk are two key types of risk that can affect a company's ability to achieve earnings or cash flow targets. While the relative magnitude of business risk and market risk varies across different organizations, the concept is the same for all with different exposures to different risks.

Business risk is defined as "the uncertainty of future financial results related to business decisions that organizations make and to the business environment in which organizations operate." For example, business risk can arise from strategy and investment decisions, marketing strategies,

FIGURE 4-6

Relationship of Frequency Versus Impact and Business Versus Event Risk.

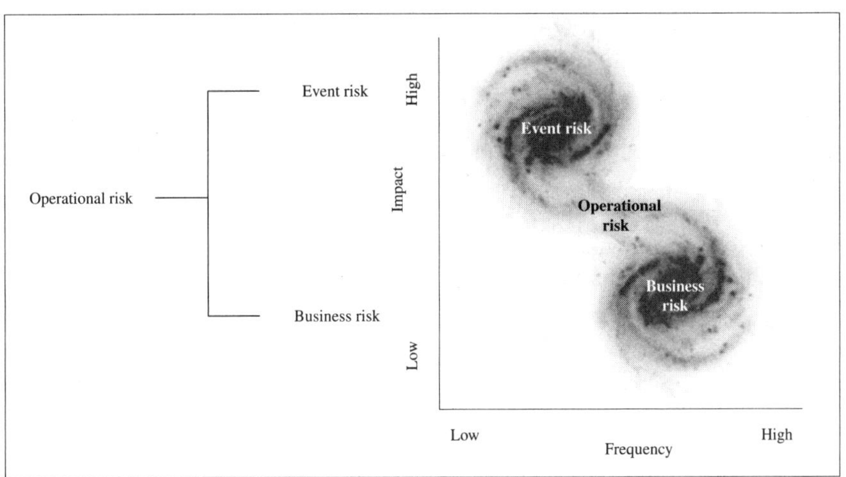

product development choices, competitive differentiation strategies, pricing decisions, and sales volume uncertainty. These are the decisions that contain inherent long-term conceptual risks that the management and shareholders of organizations are expected to take in order to generate profits and to be compensated for the risks taken. However, market risk refers to the uncertainty of future financial results arising from market rate changes (equities, fixed income, foreign exchange rates, etc.). Market risk can affect and expose an organization's business in a variety of ways. For example, operating margins can be eroded because of rising commodity prices or because of depreciating currencies for countries in which a company has foreign sales and thus cash flows in foreign currencies (direct market risk impact). Also, changes in market rates due to price competitiveness can potentially force an organization to adjust the prices of its products or services. In turn, this can affect sales volumes or competitive position depending on the positioning, market share, and market exposures of the company and its competitors (indirect impact of market risk on business profits).

Three of the more common top-down quantitative approaches focus on earnings volatility, the capital asset pricing model, and parametric methods for quantifying risk. Each of these methods is outlined in more detail in the following sections.

4.9.1.3 Earnings Volatility Approaches

Earnings volatility approaches are based on the assumption that volatility in earnings, business cash flows, asset values, interest, or commercial margins reflects the risk of the firm. Accordingly, if the volatility can be attributed to operational events rather than financial risks (market and credit risk), then this can be used to represent the operational risk of the firm. Institutions applying the earnings volatility approach will generally consider earnings volatility from a strategic and an event-driven basis.

When applying the earnings volatility approach, an institution needs to consider the source of information to support the estimate of earnings volatility and any other events to which the institution is exposed. In addition, earnings volatility may arise from nonoperational sources, and therefore these sources need to be excluded to ensure that only volatility from operational risk is being modeled. Before quantifying the operational risk, the data required to model the loss events and the volatility of income has to be run through a series of steps, as explained in the following sections.

Obtain Earnings Series

One possible source of earnings volatility can be discovered through the analysis of historical earnings. If the institution is prepared to accept the assumption that the historical earnings stream is an appropriate proxy for future earnings, this can form the input basis of the measurement process.

Accounting earnings are generally an easy source for historical earnings. This approach may be enhanced through budget data or other earning forecasts to extend the loss prediction into the future. The length of time over which the time series should be collected will vary from institution to institution, but should be long enough to support statistical evidence. A key element in collecting data is to ensure general consistency in the nature of the raw data. In some instances it will be impossible to generate consistently formed earnings streams, e.g., as a result of restructuring, takeover or merger, or significant changes in activities or divestments, etc. Additional attention is required to determine whether volatility in earnings streams is a result of changes in accounting policies.

Eliminate Volatility from Market and Credit Risk

A certain portion of the historical earnings volatility can be contributed to market and credit risk. An organization with an effective funds transfer pricing mechanism to account for earnings will be able to provide a reasonable proxy to separately identify volatility in earnings associated with nontraded market risk, whether related to interest or exchange rates.

The degree to which volatility in earnings contributes to credit risk can be difficult to assess, although there are generally clearly identifiable elements of earnings associated with the credit loss and provisioning process under existing accounting and regulative rules such as U.S. generally accepted accounting principles (GAAP) or international accounting standards (IAS). However, the impact from changes in the credit spread will not be identified separately from other impacts, such as market risks. Most accounting earnings series are set up on the basis of historical cost, and therefore any volatility associated with credit margin changes will be absorbed (and thus averaged) in the overall earnings volatility.

Careful analysis of the earnings series is required to avoid double-counting volatility arising from credit and market risk when combining market value at risk, credit value at risk, and net interest earnings at risk.

Eliminate Funding of Shareholder Equity

The cost of shareholder equity should be excluded from the accounting earnings series so that the mean of the series is appropriately calculated based on the underlying business and not the financing structure of the underlying organization.

Calculate Mean and Standard Deviation

The mean and standard deviation of the earnings series can be used as a starting point for the calculation of capital required to withstand the volatility of earnings as a result of operational risks. The critical assumption to be defined at this point is what is the appropriate confidence level on which to base the understanding of volatility from mean earnings. The first approach may be to select a confidence level consistent with the current credit rating of the organization.

Identify and Model Fat Tail Events

In the analysis of the earnings series, it is highly probable that the structural changes in earnings will impact the series generated from changes in market-related factors or from one-off events such as major operational failure changes in accounting rules, tax regulations, etc. Careful consideration needs to be given to whether these impacts should be separately identified or modeled.

Historical earning time series will generally involve losses associated with operational and process problems, but will not necessarily reflect all events that the organization may be potentially exposed to. As a result, separate consideration will need to be given to nonrelated one-off events that could occur. This can be taken into account through the estimation of the likelihood of impact and frequency determined during the risk identification and measurement process using filtering techniques (see Figure 4-7). Alternatively, external loss databases can be used to support the estimation of potential impacts and frequencies.

FIGURE 4-7

Distribution and Modeling of Fat Tails.

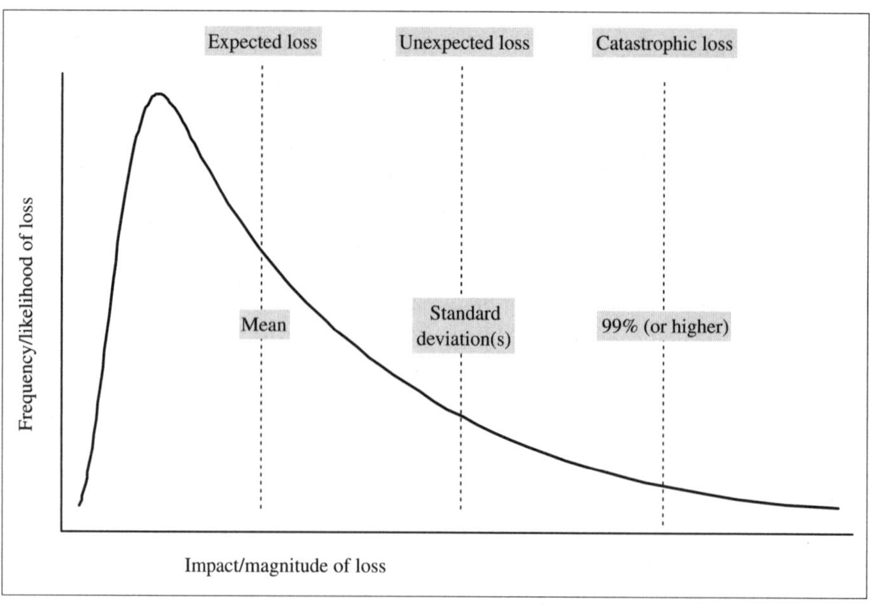

Combine the Impact of Separately Identifiable Loss Events and Volatility of Income

The outcomes of the two approaches need to be integrated to provide an estimate of the total measure of operational risk. There are a number of ways this integration can be undertaken, ranging from simple additive statistical techniques to the use of historical or Monte Carlo simulation.

4.9.1.4 Capital Asset Pricing Model Approaches

Several approaches based on financial market theories can be applied to the measurement of operational risk, such as the capital asset pricing model (CAPM). The CAPM claims that an investor should receive excess returns in compensation for any risk that is correlated to the risk in the return from the market as a whole. However, the investor should not receive excess returns for other risks. Risks that are correlated with return from the market are referred to as *systematic.* The remaining risks are referred to as *nonsystematic* or *endogenous.* The structure underlying the CAPM for an organization can be expressed as follows:

$$r_{\text{firm}} = r_{\text{risk free}} + \beta_{\text{firm}} \cdot [r_{\text{market}} - r_{\text{risk free}}] \tag{4.3}$$

The CAPM assumes that the risk of an individual position is well represented by its beta (β) coefficient. In statistical terms, the beta coefficient is defined as the covariance of the return of an individual position against the market portfolio return (or another benchmark) divided by the variance of the market's return. Companies with a beta of 1 tend to behave in direct proportion to the market; companies with a beta of less than 1 move in relative terms less than the market and, conversely, those with a beta of more than 1 move faster than the market.

The capital required by an organization is a function of the required return of the organization:

$$\text{equity at risk} = \frac{\text{required earnings}}{r_{\text{firm}}} \tag{4.4}$$

Equity is the equivalent amount of capital that is required to generate the required earnings given the risk-adjusted rate as determined under the CAPM. In order to convert the required rate of return into a numeric figure, the CAPM concept is applied to the market value of the firm, which drives the calculation of beta.

There are limitations in using the CAPM to measure equity requirements for operational risk:

- The beta concept is assumed to be fully leveraged in that is it is derived from market observations of returns from firms that use a combination of debt and equity to fund their financial needs. Leverage can be defined as being composed of financial leverage (the extent to which the institution relies on debt to generate revenue) and operating leverage (the extent to which the institution relies on fixed costs in the generation of revenue). In order to obtain a true measure of the capital requirements for operational risk, the effects of financial and operational leverage need to be separately identified.

- The beta concept is based on historical time series, and any change, such as in organizational structure, market structure, tax laws, etc., will only be adequately reflected in the beta measure after a certain amount of time has passed.

Applying the Approach in Practice

Measurement of the stock market beta is relatively transparent for listed companies, but becomes less transparent for unlisted companies. In practice this is overcome through a proxy process that assumes there are listed companies that can be considered peers for unlisted companies with similar country exposures, industry position, size, and organizational processes.

CAPM-based approaches can be difficult to apply without detailed knowledge of profit/loss accounting practices, tax considerations, etc. The calculation of operating leverage is difficult, as the organization has to maintain a consistent split between fixed and variable costs over time. There is no unique industry standard for the treatment of costs across industries and between the different national accounting structures.

4.9.1.5 Parametric Measurement

Parametric measurement has gained ready acceptance in the quantification of financial risk. Not surprisingly, concepts such as parametric value at risk (VaR) and similar simulation-based techniques are being frequently implemented to support the measurement of operational risk. Generally, these methods are similar to those being used for the modeling of one-off events in both the earnings volatility and CAPM measurement approaches.

Parametric approaches primarily focus on the ex post facto analysis of historical loss data to support the calculation of a loss distribution. The loss probability distribution can be either broken down into specific loss events or categories of risk or figured for the firm as a whole given the aggregation of all potential loss events. The loss probability distribution can be applied to the measurement of expected losses (forecasting), using the mean of the distribution, or of unexpected losses, using the standard deviation of the distribution.

Applying the Approach in Practice

Applying the parametric approach in practice has proven difficult due to the lack of historical loss data within most organizations. Collecting data has proven to be quite imperfect, requiring the application of extensive data collection techniques. In some instances, the absence of internal data has been addressed through the application of external loss databases. These loss databases provide proxy loss probability distributions that can be applied to support internal information sources.

While the parametric approach is a valid measurement alternative for most operational losses that have well-defined distributional characteristics, there are some loss events that create a statistical challenge. These losses, characterized by low frequency and high impact, require the introduction of alternative statistical methodologies, such as extreme value theory, to complete the full measurement framework. Based on historical experience, it is generally these events that are the most difficult to capture statistically and that lead to large numerical operational loss.

4.9.1.6 Qualitative Risk Measurement

As a result of the difficulties experienced in the quantitative measurement of operational risk, and given the fact that there has always been operational risk across and within organizations, there are a multitude of qualitative risk measurement approaches that have been employed. These approaches, while fundamental to support the management of operational risk, generally provide judgmental or relative rather than absolute measures of operational risk.

When applied in a top-down approach, qualitative measures tend to focus on the assessment of risk within the organization. Using techniques outlined in the preceding risk identification sections, organizations generally define a series of indicators that provide the basis for assessing whether the impressions of risk change over time. These indicators are often characterized according to what they indicate.

4.9.1.7 Key Performance Indicators (KPIs)

KPIs are simply tracked events that raise red flags if they go outside an established range. As the name suggests, KPIs are ordinarily associated with the monitoring of operational efficiency. Examples of KPIs include failed trades, customer complaints, staff turnover, transaction turnover, systems downtime, and transaction throughput.[7]

4.9.1.8 Key Control Indicators (KCIs)

KCIs are indicators that demonstrate the effectiveness of controls: for example, the number of items outstanding on a nostro reconciliation, the number of outstanding confirmations or unconfirmed trades, the number of fraudulent checks, etc.[8]

4.9.1.9 Key Risk Indicators (KRIs)

KRIs build on the concepts of KPIs and KCIs to construct leading indicators. By combining performance indicators and control indicators, such as staff turnover and transaction volume, an indicator can be created that allows insight about the stress that core processes will be facing. Rather than being considered new indicators, KRIs are a different means to combine traditional measures.[9]

Qualitative risk measures are generally built into the risk monitoring and control process in a manner consistent with the identification of risk.

4.9.2 Bottom-Up Approaches

Bottom-up approaches are characterized by the identification, measurement, and management of the causes of operational risk within the organization, rather than focusing on losses that are symptoms (outcomes) of operational failure.

4.9.2.1 Risk Identification

Bottom-up approaches focus primarily on the identification of the potential sources or causes of loss within the organization. These are generally driven by the interaction and reaction of the employees, processes, and technology of the institution combining both internal and external events. The sources of operational risk are generally not the result of a simple linear cause-and-effect relationship. Operational risks are viewed, rather, as a result of an entangled web of both internal and external influencing factors.

The process perspective is critical in the identification of risk because of the tendency for risks and losses to be transferred from one part of a process downstream. For example, if a reconciliation/after-trade compliance check is not performed in a timely manner, an investment decision might be based on unreconciled and thus (potentially) misleading information.

It follows that the basis for identifying operational risk in a bottom-up environment is to break the organization down into its core processes—those that are aligned with the achievement of the organization's strategic objectives and responsibilities (see Figure 4-8). Each core process can generally be broken down into a series of subprocesses. While this may appear to be a sisyphean task for a large and complex organization, it would probably not be necessary to extract all of the processes of the organization. It is likely that the majority of the organization's operational risks will result from a few critical processes and a relatively small number of possible loss events.

For each of the critical processes and subprocesses, an analysis is performed to determine the risk exposures, or potential risk exposures,

FIGURE 4-8

Bottom-Up Risk Identification and Aggregation.

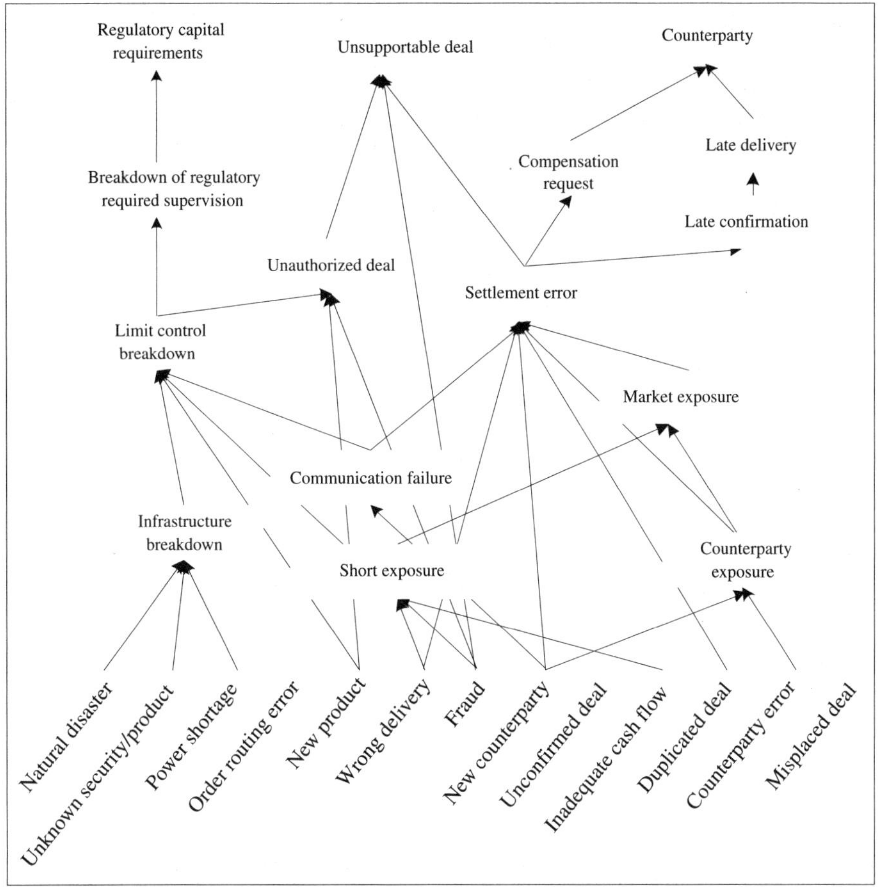

and the potential downside events that could result in the inability of the organization to meet its strategic objectives (and thus in losses). These risk exposures or potential weak processes have an inherent causal structure that needs to be identified and monitored to provide the appropriate inputs for the measurement and reporting of potential operational risk exposures.

For most loss-generating events there is usually a chain and a hierarchy of events that influence either the size or occurrence of a given event. These combinations/sequences are normally described as "and/or" events. Through the analysis of the hierarchies of events, a tree of causes can be constructed.

4.9.2.2 Quantitative Risk Measurement

There is a range of flexibility in the methodologies for modeling operational risk from the bottom up. These methodologies differ significantly. Therefore, the following sections cover the two main alternatives.

Agent-Based Simulation

One alternative is to measure the impact of operational risk through the application of complexity and simulation theory. The analysis of complexity is an interdisciplinary science that attempts to uncover the underlying principles governing complex systems and the emergent properties they exhibit. Such systems are composed of numerous simultaneous and varied interacting components.

In complex systems, sophisticated and unpredictable properties arise from an interacting group of agents. Examples of such emergent properties include how the system organizes itself, how it finds a balance between order and disorder, and how agents evolve new behaviors in response to change. Examples of emergent properties in business applications include the volatility of security prices, the speed with which supply chains can reconfigure themselves in response to changing market requirements, and the dominance of one technological alternative over another, such as a technological advantage.

Using the simulation capabilities afforded by computers, visionary biologists, mathematicians, physicists, and computer scientists have observed the emergent properties of complex adaptive systems in action. Models of artificial systems can be developed that run many different scenarios, and the resulting emergent properties can be analyzed without any risk to the system.

Agent-based modeling techniques can be used to study complex adaptive systems such as manufacturing plants, corporations, industries, markets, and sectors of the economy. In agent-based modeling, systems are modeled as clusters of autonomous decision-making entities called *agents.* These agents individually assess their situation and make decisions based on a set of rules. At the simplest level, an agent-based model consists of a cluster of agents and connections between these agents. Agents may execute various behaviors such as selling, buying, storing, reporting, etc. Compared to traditional modeling techniques, this distributed decision-making process does not result in a system of fixed equations that can be solved mathematically. However, by including repetitive, competitive interactions between agents using simulation techniques, it allows for a much more realistic estimation and presentation of a system because it emulates the manner in which the real world operates.

Applying an agent-based simulation approach requires the combination of a comprehensive understanding of the processes and operational characteristics of an organization and a detailed understanding of modeling techniques using complexity theory. The first step in applying an agent-based simulation to support the measurement of operational risk is the construction of a model of the business processes. This model is similar in principle to a traditional process decomposition of the organization. Each process within a business entity covers the interaction of people, technology, and generally observable events. The observed business process can be described by schematic figures or equations, and individual behaviors can be mapped by sets of if-then rules. The business model is translated into a computational description for the simulation environment.

A simulation environment is used to run multiple simulations of both the qualitative and quantitative dimensions of the model to determine loss probability distributions. Running the simulation enables calibration of the model with existing data and operational knowledge by comparing backtesting data with the realized data. Once it becomes apparent that the model is operating on a basis consistent with reality, it can be applied to support traditional techniques such as value at risk and stress testing to obtain robust risk measures.

Causal Modeling

Models that can be used in a bottom-up approach build from the causal tree as discussed earlier. These models range in practice from true internal causal models to hybrid models that combine external and internal data and simulation techniques to determine loss probability distributions. The loss probability distributions from either modeling approach can be used to generate estimates of expected and unexpected losses, which are traditional measures of risk.

Causal modeling uses the concept of conditional independence to generate joint probability distributions for all loss events. These distributions are used as a basis for calculating ranges of potential loss. Actual data is used to drive the generation of probability distributions. The absence of accurate and relevant historical data is one of the potential problems with the implementation of causal modeling. However, this can be overcome by combining internal data with external loss databases.

The events in a loss probability distribution have two attributes: frequency and impact. A bottom-up approach allows for the generation of separate distributions of both frequency and impact. From a risk management point of view, this allows for the separate analysis of the applications of controls and alternative risk transfer, and provides a financial incentive to assign personnel to reduce either the frequency or impact of loss (see Figures 4-9 and 4-10).

Data for frequency distributions can come from a variety of sources, including insurance data, external databases, management information systems, loss event analysis reports from expert groups, etc. The most obvious approach in developing a frequency distribution is to maintain a

FIGURE 4-9

Distribution of Operational Risk Events Under Equal Probability Assumption.

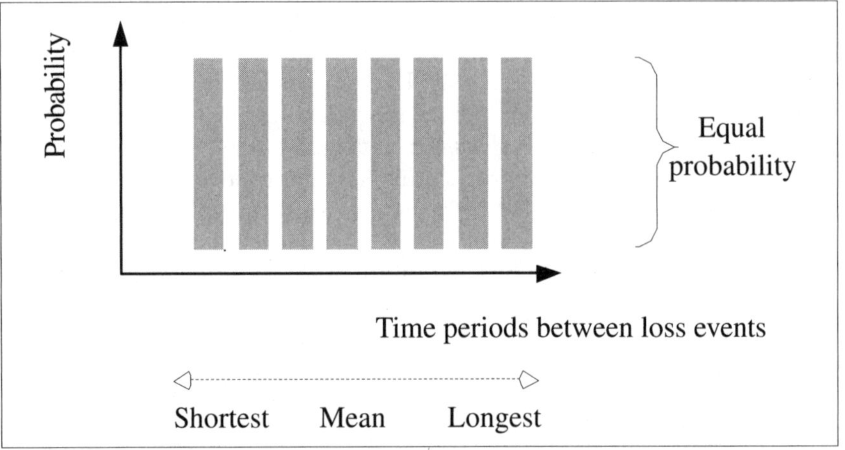

register of time-stamped loss events. A distribution can be fitted to this raw data and can serve as the basis for modeling probability. In the absence of actual data, a simulation tool could be used in combination with a subjective estimation of the parameters of that distribution, such as time horizon, standard deviation, confidence interval, distribution profile, etc.

The empirical data for generating and fitting impact distributions can come from a variety of sources depending on the nature of the events

FIGURE 4-10

Distribution of Operational Risk Events Under Unequal Probability Assumption.

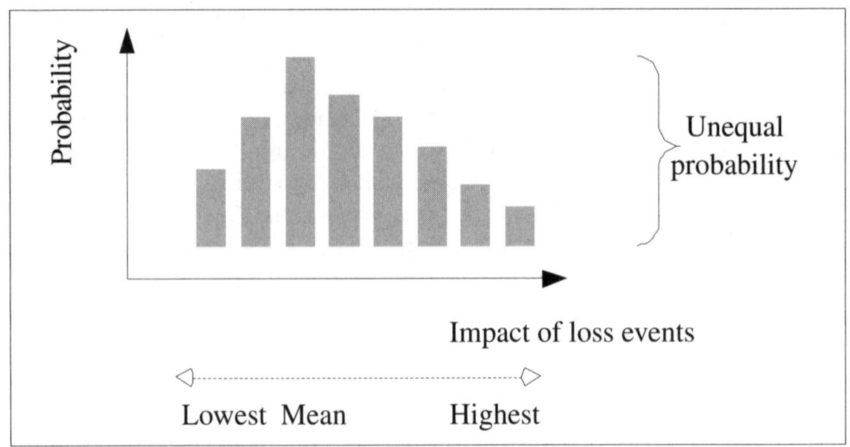

identified in the causal analysis. However, if there is insufficient historical data or statistical evidence from the existing historical data to support the generation of an appropriate probability distribution, simulation models can again be used to drive the generation of a distribution.

Combining the outcome of the separate estimation of frequency and impact in another simulation will provide a distribution of loss events. From the loss distribution, the expected loss (mean of the loss distribution) and the unexpected loss (the standard deviation of the loss distribution) can be calculated. The core limitation of using simulation in this way is the use of fixed conditional probabilities to create the causal tree. In a causal model, the conditional probabilities are not stationary, and application of a bayesian approach can be updated continuously.

4.9.2.3 Qualitative Risk Measurement

Bottom-up qualitative measures generally incorporate indicators that are found in the top-down approach. The critical difference is the extent of linkage with the causes of loss rather than the overall impressions of the indicators of the loss itself. This important difference is given from the basis of risk identification undertaken.

In a bottom-up approach, it is possible to focus on indicators that are meaningful for effective risk management and control, because the approach is driven from within the organization through the interaction of people, processes, and technologies with internal and external events. In general, these indicators will be largely consistent with those used on a daily basis by operational line management.

Organizations have realized that tracking too many KPIs can become overwhelming and confusing and, thus, ineffective. An efficient organization will need to decide and focus on which indicators are tracked continuously and which are sufficiently static to be tracked on a less dynamic basis.

4.9.3 Top-Down Versus Bottom-Up Approaches

Whether one approach or the other is more appropriate depends on the circumstances of each organization and that organization's view on the balance between the drivers for establishing operational risk management frameworks. There is no right answer to whether a top-down or bottom-up approach to operational risk is best. The discussion is ongoing as to the feasibility, accuracy, and value of quantifying operational risk. The soft and variable nature of many operational risk elements supports the skeptics' argument that it is just not possible to accurately quantify operational risk and that therefore there is little value to be derived from even attempting to do so. And, it is true that the range of factors underlying and influencing operational losses is so diverse that it makes finding a common basis on which to provide a measurement framework challenging. The fact remains that the ultimate organizational goal of measuring performance of the entire organization, on the basis of a fully risk-adjusted return on capital, will never be achieved without including a reasonable value for operational risk.

It may never be possible to model, and thereby quantify, all possible events of operational risk. The only data that will ever be available to use in modeling will be based on the frequencies and impacts of failure scenarios that occurred at some time in the past. Similarly, all VaR-based simulation is inherently flawed owing to the fact that what happens in the future is not necessarily related to the past. However, all simulation-based risk quantification models, including the assumed and proven market and credit risk modeling approaches, will be limited by these general assumptions. Despite these inherent limitations, there will always be value and benefit in risk management if there is a consistent basis for measurement such that management, the board of directors, and the shareholders have a clear understanding of their risk position and a reporting process that enables them to rank risks.

It should be clearly recognized that there are certain categories of operational risk events at the extreme ends of the risk spectrum for which it can be argued that modeling is irrelevant. For example, why try to model the likes of a major reputational failure scenario for the purpose of capital allocation, or a major loss such as in the Barings case, when it is more probable that should such an extreme event actually occur, it would wipe out the organization's capital base anyway? What is certain is that it will never be possible to get to the quantification end game without first developing the framework.

It is becoming increasingly obvious in the financial services sector that one or the other approach is not necessarily sufficient and that, although a specific method of capital allocation is useful, existing methods may not only be inaccurate but may be counterproductive and misleading for comprehensive operational risk management. Taking a purely top-down approach can limit an organization's ability to understand the practical risk drivers and may therefore restrict the management and mitigation function. Taking a purely bottom-up approach may result in a granular, low-level focus that might not contribute to achieving strategic objectives. More than likely the answer is to combine the two approaches.

4.9.4 The Emerging Operational Risk Discussion

Over the past months and years, the banking industry has entered into intensive discussion over capital requirements for operational risk. It seems that some institutions have come to initial conclusions in their strategic thinking about operational risk; what it means to their organization; and how they could go about quantifying it in a way that suits their strategic objectives, culture, and processes. Diverse approaches have evolved over a short period of time and/or have been adopted from other disciplines. Some approaches have resulted in top-down orientations and the attendant risk of overemphasis on capital management as opposed to risk management. Other organizations have done the reverse by starting with a nuclear look at business processes at the lowest operational level to discover where their operational risks might lie, then subsequently integrating and aggregating these risks into a quantification process.

To a certain extent, the pace of this evolution has been supported by an insatiable industry desire to understand and develop risk management concepts, terminology, and tools. In today's margin squeezing environments, where any potential marketing angle or competitive advantage is zealously guarded, operational risk management is perceived as another way to better allocate and use economic capital. The need for information and the problematic process associated with setting up an operational risk framework requires industry responses. Formal and informal discussions in academia and the financial services have increased and intensified and, to a certain degree, there is a need to intellectually stress-test them. These developments, together with structured research, have been responsible for some of the standard terminology that evolves in tandem with distinct methodology approaches to risk management.

4.10 CAPITAL ISSUES FROM THE REGULATORY PERSPECTIVE

Operational risk and regulatory capital have existed in separate spheres for some time. However, most formal papers that have been issued by regulatory bodies have merely committed to the intent to a capital adequacy structure for operational risk as a separate risk class. The Basel Committee, although not a supervisory body, has been providing the industry with regulatory best-practice guidelines and standards since 1975. It has been paving the way for an additional risk class to be implemented into the supervisory framework. For example, Principle 13 of the 1997 Basel core principles for effective banking supervision says:

> Banking supervisors must be satisfied that banks have in place a comprehensive risk management process (including appropriate board and senior management oversight) to identify, measure, monitor and control all other material risks and, where appropriate, to hold capital against these risks.[10]

Local regulators will be the ones to adopt and implement the Basel Committee's outline and be responsible for the day-to-day monitoring and enforcement of any regulatory capital charge. There is currently a tremendous amount of attention from local authorities on the industry discussion papers. Some local regulators will undoubtedly be more active than others. For example:

- In the United States, representatives of the Federal Reserve are cochairing the risk management subgroup of the Basel Committee. The topic of operational risk management is raised in virtually all U.S. bank examinations today, but the Fed and the Office of the Comptroller of the Currency (OCC) view operational risk from different sets of risk classes.
- In the United Kingdom, the Financial Services Authority (FSA) is a relatively new body and is undergoing incremental change in terms of its scope and powers. The FSA has been keen to immerse itself in the undercurrent of activity regarding operational risk evolution and has tried to draw from all spheres of expertise on the topic.[11]
- In Germany, the national regulator is following developments closely, but some representatives have expressed concerns over enforcement powers and the fact that there has not been adequate time for best practices to emerge.
- In Japan, regulators have already begun to implement a box-scoring approach to bank risk profiling. Meanwhile a 25 percent assessment of expense is already made on securities firms. From a risk management incentive standpoint, such an approach is less than optimal.[12]
- In Australia, the Australian Prudential Regulatory Authority (APRA) expects to follow the lead provided by overseas regulators, after careful local analysis, with discussion papers and policy statements in relation to operational risk capital.
- In Switzerland, the national regulator actively participates in the working committee of the Basel Committee and will adopt and enforce the recommendations rigorously, given the involvement of the Union Bank of Switzerland (UBS) in the LTCM debacle.[13]

Meanwhile, regulators in most countries agree that progress by banks is required. Some regulators already require an operational risk management function for domestic banks, e.g., the Saudi Arabian Monetary Authority (SAMA).

Following is a summary of comments reflecting the current regulatory discussions:

- There is a consensus that, because of its unique characteristics, a separate treatment of operational risk is appropriate.
- No common view exists regarding additional capital for operational risk. Critics of this approach suggest that a bank

demonstrating sound risk controls and systems might succeed in making a case for no additional capital. This would be enforced by local regulators and monitored and reported by auditors.

- Regarding additional capital requirements (beyond 8 percent), apparently few if any institutions are willing to commit to the notion that the industry is currently undercapitalized. Some institutions have noted that it may not be possible to resolve the "8 percent debate" until a common approach to credit risk capital is settled on.
- Practitioners express that the market risk guidelines have actually freed up capital for some institutions, and thus it should be possible to let overall capital percentages float above or below 8 percent.
- Recently, opinions were voiced favoring integration of the market and credit risk multiplier in one measure, given the difficulties of segregating market and credit risks in some cases and the potential to arbitrarily switch between regulatory regimes depending on what is deemed better for the bank.
- Any approach should support Pillar II regarding supervisory objectives. The value of risk assessments, the use of risk indicators, and control process assessments have all been discussed. However, one consistent concern is that many self-assessment approaches are too granular to use in support of modeling, especially given the fact the uniformity of such a granular approach applied across various organizations with different technologies, strategic objectives, etc. is not enforceable.
- There are thousands of registered banks worldwide, each with its own organizational structures, core competencies, and specializations. And there is a wide variety of influences on any particular institution. Regulators, consultants, vendors, and the banks themselves have to operate in markets around the world where there is a huge range of sophistication relating to the idiosyncracies just listed.

There has not yet been a worldwide operational risk initiatives survey that adequately captures and reflects the relative progress of a wide spectrum of banks relating to operational risk management efforts. Only approximately 3 to 5 percent of the worldwide banking population is actively investing time and money in developing an operational risk framework. If we were to look at the aggregate asset or balance sheet size represented by these groups, the percentage would definitely be much higher. But if we examine the size and activity of the banks that have failed or have sustained embarrassment or reputational damage, we see that operational risks at smaller institutions—e.g., the Banco Ambrosiano fiasco—cannot be ignored.[14]

4.11 CAPITAL ADEQUACY ISSUES FROM AN INDUSTRY PERSPECTIVE

The British Bankers' Association (BBA) set up an operational risk advisory panel in 1998, comprising a diverse group of banks believed to have an active interest in operational risk management. One of the panel's primary objectives was to assist the BBA in lobbying regulators about the type of frameworks that might work best for the industry as a whole, rather than having a methodology imposed on the industry that contradicted industry practice.

Later in 1998, the BBA panel, the International Swap and Derivatives Association (ISDA), and Robert Morris Associates (a U.S.-based industry body with a membership of over 3000 financial institutions) surveyed the financial services industry. The results of the survey, which were unveiled in early November 1999, have helped to crystallize the industry consensus on operational risk capital.[15]

The BBA lists several factors that it believes underlie the Basel proposals. These include:

- A recommendation to provide incentives for sound operational risk management.
- A recommendation to capture within the capital framework businesses that are, in regulatory capital terms, almost entirely risk free, e.g., custody and fund management.
- A perceived need for a balancing charge to redress an anticipated drop in regulatory capital held for credit risk. This line of thinking is also expressed in the argument that operational risk is implicit in current regulatory capital levels.

There are probably at least five perspectives emerging in the financial services community today about what an individual organization can accomplish with operational risk management, and how to accomplish these goals by applying objectives related to capital risk management and operational risk. These range in focus from risk management analytics and risk measurement, to control group focus, to business line management teams, to firmwide multidisciplinary operational risk management functions.

- *Risk measurement.* This dimension is perceived as a key objective driven by the recent urgings of banking regulators. Owing to the breathless pursuit of analytical precision, the first perspective has focused entirely on risk measurement, including finding a number or a series of numbers to represent the range of possible outcomes and demonstrating how this can be used to reduce potential losses or exploit opportunities in the market. This primary focus on modeling is based on the belief that a number is critical for emphasis, attention, and focus of purpose. The greatest challenge for these people will be in proving not only that they have achieved analytic precision, but also that these measures may be used to improve behavior and lower the downside or increase profits.

- *Internal controls.* The second perspective represents the opposite end of the spectrum—those who have practiced operational risk management in the form of one or more control disciplines (e.g., internal auditing, control, compliance, etc.), whose focus has been on maintaining tight controls or corporate risk management structures. It is tempting, and in some cases conceivable, that a move to the emerging discipline of operational risk management is a small leap from their current role(s).
- *Business management.* Business managers have managed their businesses based on several measures, such as KPIs, management accounting information, etc. They allocated the investable capital based on all this information. For this group, the move to track and analyze operational risk indicators is certainly not foreign, and may only require a slight refocusing supported by additional firmwide information available to them.
- *Insurance risk management.* This dimension is becoming more visible in the operational risk management discussion, as evidenced by the desire among firms for more effective operational risk hedges versus less relevant traditional insurance coverage.
- *Multidisciplinary operational risk management.* This emerging function is perceived as the most effective operational risk management program, which will incorporate the most effective features of all four previously mentioned schools of thought: (1) using quantitative and qualitative risk measurement tools for estimating the dimensions of the operational risk exposures; (2) applying the most effective risk management and risk control tools; (3) monitoring risk drivers and indicators, similar to the early warning indicators, through the use of management information systems (MIS) tools with the objective of creating a comprehensive operational risk management program; (4) applying well-known risk finance and insurance tools as operational risk hedges. Taken together, information from all of these efforts contributes to what we have begun to refer to as a firm's operational risk profile.

These practical risk management perspectives contrast with the regulatory objectives, known as the three pillars, which include minimum capital requirements, supervisory review, and effective use of market discipline. Regulators are seeking a strong but competitive banking system. The defining issues are when and how risk capital will be viewed alongside these objectives. A significant amount of banks note attempts to allocate economic capital to operational risk, but reportedly nearly all are dissatisfied with both their own methodology and the behavioral incentives created. Few if any use measures of operational risk capital to drive business decision making or behavior. There is widespread concern that any regulatory initiative in this area may retard or misdirect what have been very positive initial industry efforts to date.

Overall, the industry response to the proposal has been negative and a constant series of concerns has been articulated:

- *Definition.* It is difficult to conceive of how to develop a risk measure without a clearly defined risk boundary. No positive industry standard currently exists.
- *No additional capital.* The banking industry does not believe that regulatory capital to support operational risks in excess of current levels is justifiable. In the context of the opening Basel proposals, it is difficult to see how there would not be an additional charge for the majority of banks.
- *Duplication.* How will overlap between the various risk assessment processes (market risk, credit risk, operational risk, and supervisory review) be managed, and will the level at which current variable factors are set (market risk multiplier, target/trigger) be adjusted as a result? This would require modifying the existing credit and market risk regulations, meaning another lengthy process.
- *Level playing field.* This issue is a substantial concern for all banks. At an international level, there is concern that any regulatory capital charge for operational risk identified may well not be applied consistently—or at all—in some other jurisdictions. At a national level, this is more an issue of ensuring consistency of assessment and a positive bias toward better operational risk management.
- *Behavioral incentives.* The issue of developing positive behavioral incentives is based on the development of a risk-sensitive assessment methodology. All the available options have considerable flaws. There is a real concern that perverse behavior will be encouraged if the regulatory hurdles are blunt and high. Banks are much more likely to concentrate on arbitrage or avoidance.

- *Changing business environment.* In parallel with the development of risk management practice, the business of banking is itself undergoing a period of considerable change because of new businesses, products/services, organizational models, competitors, e-commerce, etc. This again supports the argument for a flexible methodological approach.
- *Developing efforts.* There is concern that the enforced implementation of a prescriptive methodology will retard or misdirect industry development efforts. There is also concern that the short-term regulatory need to develop an assessment methodology might obscure the pace of development. As a consequence, any methodological solution should, from the outset, be characterized as interim and open to replacement or change as industry practice progresses. Equally, there is a common opinion among many industry practitioners that a misaligned interim standard may do just as much damage even though it may be temporary.

4.11.1 Measurement Techniques and Progress in the Industry Today

The term *measurement* in the operational risk context can encompass a huge variety of concepts, tools, and information bases. It is virtually certain that the approaches might differ wildly. This could be one of the problems that regulators face even if they do stipulate a particular method, as the interpretation and application may give rise to many variations on the same theme. Perhaps the supervisors and the local regulators should actually rely on this happening.

The following sections summarize some of the more mainstream methodologies and provide an overview of what supervisors have been considering most recently.

4.11.1.1 Practitioner Measurement Methodologies

Risk indicator or factor-based models are methodologies that originate from risk indicator or loss information. These tend to give rise to bottom-up approaches due to the granularity and nature of the source of information.

Advantages

- Usually, information is readily available.
- If constructed properly, it is transparent to the management of the business line.
- Business line management tends to accept the outcomes.

Disadvantages

- Collection, filtering, and aggregation of consistent data across the firm is challenging.
- Capturing interdependencies or overlaps between areas is difficult (and sometimes impossible).
- Internal experience is required.
- Forecasting general trends is possible, but not particular predictive forecasts on a detailed level.

4.11.1.2 Economic Pricing Models

These models incorporate forecasting based on financial data and application of modeling. Probably the best known in operational risk circles is the capital asset pricing model (CAPM), which is based on the assumption that operational risk is responsible for an institution's stock price beta. It assumes that operational risk is the differential between credit and market risk and the security's market value.

Advantages

- Usually, information is readily available.
- If constructed properly, it is transparent to the management of the business line.
- Business line management tends to accept the outcomes.

Disadvantages

- Collection, filtering, and aggregation of consistent data across the firm is challenging.
- Capturing interdependencies or overlaps between areas is difficult (and sometimes impossible).
- Internal experience is required.
- Forecasting general trends is possible, but not particular predictive forecasts on a detailed level.

4.11.1.3 Risk or Loss Scenario–Based Models

These models attempt to summarize possible operational risk/loss outcomes for a variety of scenarios that are often mapped into a matrix of probabilities such as frequency and severity of outcome. Scenario models are reliant on the vision, breadth of knowledge, and experience of the person(s) conducting the modeling.

Advantages

- Experience and expectation of business line management is included in the process, and is well accepted.
- Conceptual, intuitive, and easy to understand and implement.

- Can help to accentuate areas for improvement in business strategy.
- Supports identifying and building a robust firmwide disaster recovery plan.
- Supports management in the development of a structured crisis management approach.

Disadvantages

- Often based on personal experience or expertise and thus subjective. (Individual perception has a high influence on scenario development.)
- It is difficult to implement an entire portfolio of scenarios that are really a representation of the institution's operational risk exposure.

4.11.1.4 Statistical/Actuarial Models

These are one of the more common modeling bases in banks today, although approaches differ. Commonly, the source information will be an operational risk event and loss data, which can also be a mix of data internal and external to the institution. Frequency and severity distributions are assembled based on the data and then simulated via a technique such as Monte Carlo to arrive at a range of possible loss outcomes. Figures are produced for a stipulated time horizon and range of confidence levels.

Advantages

- Forward-looking; ensures that users are aware of its predictive limitations.
- By definition, based on empirical data and thus more defensible than subjective scenarios. (See remarks regarding risk- or loss-based scenarios in Sec. 4.11.1.3.)

Disadvantages

- It is difficult and time intensive to ensure accurate and timely data collection and filtering processes given the depth of information required to calculate a firm's operational risk capital.
- In purely quantitative approaches, there is no qualitative assessment.
- Without a motivational incentive element built into the methodology, it is difficult to get buy-in from the business line.

4.11.1.5 Hybrid Models

In the end, an optimal modeling approach has not yet been identified. Each has its advantages and disadvantages. At Bankers Trust, the operational

RAROC framework and modeling process developed from 1992 to 1998 has been a combination, or hybrid, of several of the approaches outlined in the preceding sections, attempting to represent the best features of each.

Some important lessons were learned about operational risk modeling and capital adequacy in the process. For instance, from design through implementation we found ourselves having to battle the tendency of business line representatives to reduce their capital allocations as a prime objective, in contrast to, and at the expense of, more primary risk mitigation objectives. But through a combination of model approaches, including a statistical/actuarial and scenario-based measurement approach blended with risk factor and issues-based methods, we were able to make far greater headway toward satisfying the risk measurement objective and the objective of providing incentives for productive risk management behavior.

4.11.2 Regulatory Framework for Operational Risk Overview Under the New Capital Accord

In the 1998 accord, the Basel Committee made an implicit assumption that "all other risks" were included under the capital buffer related to credit risk.[16]

In its new recommendations, the committee proposes rather more accurate and complicated methods for calculating capital charges for credit risks, and has for the first time attempted to deal with operational risk as an entity in its own right.[17]

It is important to note that it is presently unclear whether all of the national bank supervisors who implemented the original 1988 capital accord will require all of their regulated institutions to meet the proposed BIS standards.

The mission for the banks that do eventually fall under the purview of the Basel guidelines is to quantify operational risk in order to set aside capital to cover future losses. The expectation is that around 20 percent of all bank capital will be allocated to operational risk, but individual banks may hold more or less than this proportion based on the sophistication of their operational risk management. In the spirit of the preceding discussion, the discretionary element of regulation means that capital discounts will only be given to banks that can demonstrate their ability to measure, control, and manage operational risks.

The Basel Committee is recommending an "evolutionary approach" to the quantification of operational risk capital. In essence, it specifies three approaches, based on the supposition that the appropriate capital charge for a typical bank will diminish as the bank takes progressive steps to address operational risk. This essentially allows banks to make increasingly large discounts to their regulatory capital as they make demonstrable progress toward a well-managed and properly controlled operating environment. Given that banks today vary widely in their preparedness, different banks will start at different points on the scale.

Work on operational risk is in a developmental stage, but three different approaches have been identified (in order of increasing sophistication: basic indicator, standardized, and internal measurement; see Figure 4-11).

1. The basic indicator approach utilizes one indicator of operational risk for a bank's total activity.
2. The standardized approach specifies different indicators for different business lines.
3. The internal measurement approach requires banks to utilize their internal loss data when estimating required capital.

Based on work to date, the committee expects operational risk to constitute on average approximately 20 percent of the overall capital requirements under the new framework. It will be important to collect sufficient loss data in the coming months to establish the accurate calibration of the operational risk charge as a basis for allowing the more advanced approaches.

FIGURE 4-11

Operational Risk Approaches and Industry Trend.

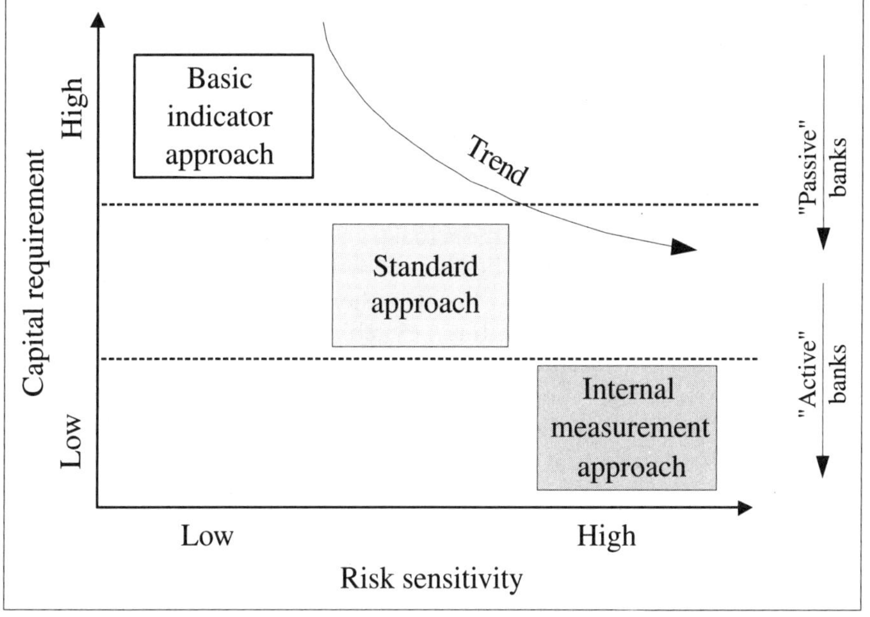

4.11.2.1 Basic Indicator Approach

The basic indicator approach (BIA),[18] also known as the single indicator approach, is designed for less sophisticated (and usually smaller) banks. This method allocates risk capital based on a single indicator of operational risk, the default being gross revenue. It is unclear whether gross revenue is a relevant indicator for operational risk. The single indicator approach is considered the easiest to implement, because it specifies a single number across the organization based on a well-known quantity. In order to satisfy this approach, banks will not have to do anything! However, all other things being equal, the BIA will likely result in higher capital charges than the other two approaches, and the hope is that banks will try to reduce these by moving up the evolutionary ladder—that is, by demonstrably improving their management of operational risk.

- Within each business line/risk type combination, a supervisor provides the exposure indicator (EI), which is the proxy for the size (or amount of risk) of each business line's operational risk exposure to each risk type.
- A single risk indicator (e.g., gross income) is used as a proxy for the institution's overall operational risk exposure.

$$C = \alpha \cdot \text{gross income} \tag{4.5}$$

where α is fixed at 30 percent of gross income.

4.11.2.2 Standardized Approach

The standardized approach[19] is the one the Basel Committee recommends that larger and more global banks use for the time being. It is also the approach that middle-tier banks should target in order to reduce their capital charges. While the single indicator approach is a crude, across-the-board measure, the standardized approach is based on information gathered from individual business units. It is suggested in the consultative paper that this approach best reflects the actual level of risk within a complicated organization with a variety of business activities, but does not require invoking complex and still controversial mathematical models.

The standardized approach is inevitably more complicated than the single indicator approach. The basic principle is that banks will have to map their own business units into a standard set of business units defined by the regulator. Each of these standard units is associated with a particular financial indicator—for example, the amount of assets under management for an asset management business—and the associated capital charge is defined by the level of these indicators:

- Bank activities are divided into standardized business units and business lines.

- A supervisor specifies an exposure indicator (EI) for each respective business line/risk type combination.
- Banks provide indicator data (e.g., gross revenue).
- There is an opportunity to migrate (on a business line basis) toward increasingly more sophisticated approaches.

$$C = \sum \beta_i \cdot \mathrm{EI}_i \tag{4.6}$$

and

$$\beta_i = \frac{[20\% \text{ current total MRC, \$}] \cdot [\text{business line weighting, \%}]}{\sum \text{financial indicator for the business line from bank sample, \$}} \tag{4.7}$$

where i = business line
β = capital factor (see Table 4-3)
EI = exposure indicator
MRC = minimum regulatory capital

This approach makes progress toward reflecting the makeup of an individual institution's business, making it a better measure than the one-size-fits-all approach based on gross revenue. Banks considering this approach will have good reason to start thinking about their business lines'

TABLE 4-3

Capital Factors for Individual Business Lines

Business Unit	Business Line(s)	Indicator	Capital Factor
Investment banking	Corporate finance	Gross income	β_1
	Trading and sales	Gross income (or VaR)	β_2
Banking	Retail banking	Annual average assets	β_3
	Commercial banking	Annual average assets	β_4
	Payment and settlement	Annual settlement throughput	β_5
Other	Retail brokerage	Gross income	β_6
	Asset management	Total funds under management	β_7

SOURCE: Bank for International Settlement (BIS), Basel Committee on Banking Supervision, *The New Basel Capital Accord, Consultative Document, Issued for Comment by 31 May 2001*, Basel, Switzerland: Bank for International Settlement, January 2001, para. 26.

operational risks and how they might be best managed, but will not have to go through the laborious and complicated exercise of collecting and evaluating internal loss data required under the third and most sophisticated approach.

The problem with the first and second methods is that they assume operational risk is linear and directly related to the size of the institution or business line. The concern about the third method is that it posits a fixed relationship between expected and unexpected losses that most experts in the field simply do not believe exists.

For the purposes of consistent and structured measurement of loss events, Basel breaks down operational risk loss experiences into the following loss types:[20]

- *Write-downs.* Direct reduction in value of assets due to theft, fraud, unauthorized activity, or market and credit losses resulting from operational events
- *Loss of recourse.* Payments or disbursements made to incorrect parties and not recovered
- *Restitution.* Restitution paid to clients in the form of principal and/or interest, or the cost of any other form of compensation paid to clients
- *Legal liability.* Judgments, settlements, and other legal costs
- *Regulatory and compliance.* Fines, or the direct cost of any other penalties, such as license revocations
- *Loss of or damage to assets.* Direct reduction in the value of physical assets, including certificates, due to some kind of accident (e.g., neglect, fire, earthquake)

The standard approach has not yet demonstrated how existing business fields (e.g., private banking) can be mapped into the preexisting business unit schema from the BIS. Business fields such as agency business, custody, etc. do not fit into the existing schema. The BIS wants to create additional business units.

4.11.2.3 Internal Measurement Approach

The internal measurement approach (IMA)[21] is reserved for banks with the most sophisticated risk management controls and programs in place. This approach breaks down the idea of indicators still further by introducing the concept of risk types. A bank needs to provide an exposure indicator for each risk type (tied to individual business units) based on internal loss data and the probability of a loss event occurring. This allows banks to align the capital charge for operational risk more closely with the actual economic risks of their business, in a way that reflects both their track record and their current operating environment.

No more than a handful of banks would qualify for this approach today, largely because of the lack of appropriate data. The Basel Committee recognizes that banks will move toward this approach as they start collecting internal loss data, and that this will be a step-by-step process. Among the tasks that need to be undertaken are the establishment of industry standards for loss data and the collection of a critical mass of loss data by pooling internal loss information from a number of institutions:

- The same business lines as in the standardized approach
- Based on internal data, banks' measurements of parameters and calculation of expected capital requirement:

$$C = \sum_i \sum_j [\gamma_{i,j} \cdot EI_{i,j} \cdot PE_{i,j} \cdot LGE_{i,j}] \tag{4.8}$$

where γ = conversion (translation) factor for the calculation of the capital requirements based on the expected loss
EI = exposure indicator (risk indicator), which is an estimate for the risk exposure per business line
PE = probability of loss event, an estimate for the frequency of a loss
LGE = loss given event, an estimate for the effective loss impact
i = index for the corresponding business line
j = index for the corresponding risk factor

4.11.3 Operational Risk Standards

The accord is quite demanding in regard to the operational risk standards that have to be applied. These qualifying criteria cover such areas as effective risk measurement and control, measurement, and validation.[22]

Regarding operational risk standards, the standardized approach requires:[23]

- Independent risk control and audit functions
- Effective use of risk reporting systems
- Appropriate documentation of risk management systems
- Independent operational risk management and control processes covering design, implementation, and review of operational risk measurement methodology
- Periodic reviews by internal auditors
- Development of specific, documented criteria for mapping current business lines and activities into the standardized framework

The internal measurement approach (IMA) requires regarding operational risk standards,[24] accuracy of loss data, and confidence in the results of calculations using that data (including PE and LGE), which must be established through "user tests":

- Banks not fully integrating IMA methodology into their day-to-day activities and major business decisions will not qualify for this approach.
- Appropriate historical loss experiences must be identified that are representative of current and future business activities.
- Periodic verification processes for estimating parameter inputs to regulatory capital charge must be performed and validated.
- Supervisory review and validation must be performed.

It can be assumed that the vast majority of regulated financial organizations will be most interested in the standardized approach—either aspiring to it, in the case of smaller organizations, or ensuring compliance with it, in the case of medium-sized and larger institutions. The standardized approach is in any case a natural precursor to the internal measurement approach, so even banks with more aggressive goals will find it useful to initially work through the requirements of the standardized approach.

Assuming that an acceptable form of the standardized approach is eventually implemented, where does that leave the banks? It is likely that many will fall into the first tier in the beginning and will be hit with the highest capital charges. It is also possible that many moderately sophisticated banks will be able to move quite quickly into the second tier once they have demonstrated they have the proper controls in place. In order to qualify for this stage, the banks will have to demonstrate the establishment of an operational risk management and control process, and a strategy for mapping an individual bank's business lines into the standardized formula. The BIS suggests the adoption of numerous qualitative items in a bank's quest to manage its operational risks. These items include:

- The establishment of a risk reporting system
- The establishment of an independent operational risk management and control process (which usually involves either a risk management, internal audit, or financial operations function)
- The identification of those historical loss events that are appropriate for an individual institution and its business units (which involves the use of an external loss database)

The business line controversy is not covered in this book. For details, refer to the committee's publications covering this issue.

4.11.4 Possible Role of Bank Supervisors

The discussion about the possible role of bank supervisors reflects the relatively early stage of the development of operational risk measurement and monitoring. Most banks agree that the process is not sufficiently developed to enable bank supervisors to mandate guidelines specifying particular measurement methodologies or quantitative limits on risk. Preference was expressed at this stage for supervisors to focus on qualitative improvement in operational risk management. At this stage, bank supervisors should become increasingly aware of the existence and importance of operational risk. As standards do not yet exist, financial institutions are skeptical about best-practices standards, given the perceived institution-specific nature of operational risk.

4.12 SUMMARY AND CONCLUSION

While the debate over operational risk has only just begun, the prospect of specific capital charges for operational risk looks inevitable. The scale and complexity of the underlying industry risks, and the systemic effect of losses incurred to date, are too large for regulators to ignore. Moreover, market and credit risk capital guidelines would be incomplete in the absence of an operational risk element.

However, no single approach to operational risk capital allocation has yet been adopted and implemented by a critical mass of institutions. This makes the supervisory task of devising such a method challenging, to say the least. And the challenges (in academia and in practice) are not limited to determining the formulae that underlie capital models; they also involve the quality and consistency of operational risk data in individual institutions and across the industry.

A key consideration will be whether the methodologies selected by regulators encourage operational risk mitigation on both institutional and industrywide levels. A badly designed set of capital regulations would spawn operational risk measurement functions within financial institutions, but would not promote effective risk mitigation and management functions.

Managing operational risk is becoming an important feature of sound risk management practice in modern financial markets. The most important types of operational risk involve breakdowns in internal controls and corporate governance. As recent cases in the market show, such breakdowns can lead to financial losses through error, fraud, or failure to perform in a timely manner or can cause the interests of the bank to be compromised in some other way (for example, dealers, lending officers, or other staff exceeding their authority or conducting business in an unethical or risky manner). Other aspects of operational risk include major failure of information technology systems or inability to report in a timely manner to investors, regulators, and clients.

The regulatory incentive takes the form of capital allocation for operational risk. In contrast, the management incentive consists of incorporating operational risk measurement into the performance evaluation process or requiring business line managers to present operational loss details and resultant corrective action directly to the bank's highest levels of management. While most banks have some framework for managing operational risk, many banks indicate that they are only in the early stages of developing an operational risk measurement and monitoring framework. Few banks currently measure and report this risk on a regular basis, although many track operational performance indicators, analyze loss experiences, and monitor audit and supervisory ratings. While the industry is far from converging on a set of standard models, such as are increasingly available for market and credit risk measurement, many banks have developed or are developing models relying on a surprisingly similar set of risk factors. Those factors include internal audit ratings or internal control self-assessments; operational indicators such as volume, turnover, or rate of errors; loss experience; and income volatility.

This chapter focuses on the origins of operational risk, the potential development path for operational risk models and approaches, and the regulatory framework from the Bank for International Settlement, as outlined in the latest version of the New Basel Capital Accord, which will force banks to measure operational risk with one of three alternative measurement approaches and to support operational risk with capital.

Core elements discussed in this chapter are the alternative methodologies for measuring operational risk and the framework for measuring and supporting operational risk from a regulatory standpoint.

4.13 NOTES

1. Bank for International Settlement (BIS), Basel Committee on Banking Supervision, *Operational Risk Management,* Basel, Switzerland: Bank for International Settlement, September 1998.
2. British Bankers' Association, "Operational Risk Management Study," London: British Bankers' Association, December 1999.
3. Bank for International Settlement (BIS), Basel Committee on Banking Supervision, *Operational Risk, Consultative Document: Supporting Document to the New Basel Capital Accord, Issued for Comment by 31 May 2001,* Basel, Switzerland: Bank for International Settlement, January 2001.
4. See also British Bankers' Association, *Operational Risk: The Next Frontier,* London: British Bankers' Association, December 1999. This study is based on a series of interviews with 55 global financial institutions located in North America, Europe, and Asia, and includes a discussion of operational risk, management structures, senior management reporting, operational

risk capital, insurance strategies, and tools. An executive summary and table of contents are available at the British Bankers' Association Web site (www.bba.org.uk/html/1154.html). The report concludes with an observation of seven major trends, including an industrywide acceptance of operational risk management as a core competency.

5. Bank for International Settlement (BIS), Basel Committee on Banking Supervision, *Operational Risk, Consultative Document: Supporting Document to the New Basel Capital Accord, Issued for Comment by 31 May 2001,* Basel, Switzerland: Bank for International Settlement, January 2001, para. 21ff.
6. Reto R. Gallati, *Methodology for Operational Risk,* Zurich: KPMG, July 1998.
7. Andrew Smith, *Operational Risk Management—Further Analytical Tools,* London: KPMG, January 1997.
8. KPMG Peat Marwick, "Operational Risk, Control Benchmarking Questionnaire," KPMG, March 1997.
9. Ibid.
10. Bank for International Settlement (BIS), Basel Committee on Banking Supervision, *Core Principles for Effective Banking Supervision,* Basel, Switzerland: Bank for International Settlement, September 1997, para. 13.
11. See the FSA Web site (www.fsa.gov.uk) for additional information.
12. See the Bank of Japan Web site (http://www.boj.or.jp/en/ronbun/fwp0003.html), "Challenges and Possible Solutions in Enhancing Operational Risk Measurement."
13. For a statement regarding the future revision of the Capital Adequacy Directive framework and operational risk, see the Swiss Federal Banking Commission Web site (www.ebk.admin.ch/d/aktuell/neu1-01.pdf).
14. For further details on Banco Ambrosiano and the Vatican Bank, see www.ex.ac.uk/~Rdavies/arian/scandal.classic.html.
15. For further details, see the BBA Web site (www.bba.org.uk), "BBA Operational Risk Database Association" and "BBA/ISDA/RMA Operational Risk Research."
16. Bank for International Settlement (BIS), Basel Committee on Banking Supervision, *Amendment to the Basel Capital Accord of July 1988,* Basel, Switzerland: Bank for International Settlement, April 1998.
17. Bank for International Settlement (BIS), Basel Committee on Banking Supervision, *Operational Risk, Consultative Document: Supporting Document to the New Basel Capital Accord, Issued for Comment by 31 May 2001,* Basel, Switzerland: Bank for International Settlement, January 2001, para. 15ff.
18. Ibid., para. 22f.
19. Ibid., para. 24ff.
20. Ibid., annex 4.
21. Ibid., para. 31ff.
22. Ibid., para. 51ff.
23. Ibid., para. 43f.
24. Ibid., para. 44ff.

CHAPTER 5

Building Blocks for Integration of Risk Categories

5.1 BACKGROUND

The integration of market, credit, and operational risk into a holistic risk management framework depends on the compatibility of the assumptions, conditions, and parameters of the individual risk categories. As all individual risk categories have, to a large extent, evolved naturally, the assumptions, conditions, and parameters linked with the risk categories are different. Any attempt to integrate the individual risk categories must involve verifying the compatibility of the different assumptions, models, and approaches. Currently, the biggest supporters of an integrated approach are the regulators.

The New Basel Capital Accord[1] attempts to unify the three risk categories with the purpose of supporting the risk of a financial organization with capital, based on models for market, credit, and operational risk. It is not an attempt to unify the models. Nevertheless, we will use the regulatory framework as a benchmark for comparing the different risks. The development of an integrated approach has not yet emerged, but, as with any complex development, it is just a question of time until the different risk dimensions are linked in a more coherent manner.

The discussion in this chapter deals with the basics of risk category integration; in Chapter 6 we will explore more integrated methodologies. Figure 5-1 highlights the typical development of a risk management practice. The future development will definitely depend largely on the agreed-upon and standardized definition and assumptions underlying the individual risk models. Today's "integrated risk management solutions" are really individual risk dimensions (such as market risk) deployed

FIGURE 5-1

Development Stages of Risk Management.

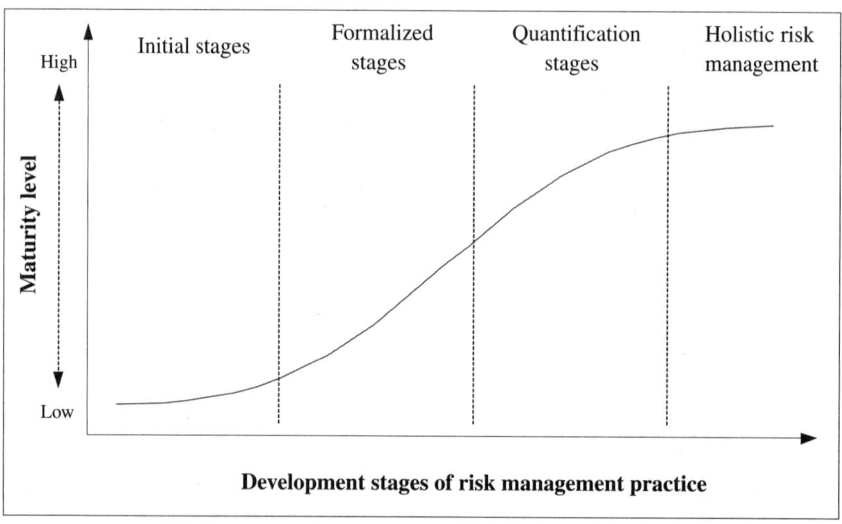

across a company rather than a holistic risk framework. To better understand the possibilities of integrated risk management, and the conflicts between different approaches from different risk dimensions, this chapter presents different assumptions, models, and approaches and examines how, if, and to what extent the three risk dimensions can be integrated.

The New Basel Capital Accord is used as a benchmarking framework in this chapter, while the individual approaches to calculating and supporting risk with capital (such as VaR for market risk) are analyzed in other chapters (e.g., Chapter 2 on market risk).

5.2 THE NEW BASEL CAPITAL ACCORD

5.2.1 Background

The New Basel Capital Accord[2] contains for the first time an integrated approach, attempting to bring together market, credit, and operational risk in order to calculate the overall risk exposure of a bank and to derive the required (regulatory) capital to support the bank's specific risk profile. Therefore, the Accord is explained in some detail in this chapter as well as in Chapters 2, 3, and 4.

More than a decade has passed since the Basel Committee on Banking Supervision introduced its 1988 capital accord. The New Basel Capital Accord has emerged over the past years, evolving from the 1988 Capital Accord:

• July 1988	Current accord published
• End of 1992	Deadline for implementation
• June 1999	First consultative package on the new accord
• January 2001	Second consultative package
• Late May 2002	Deadline for comments
• End of 2002	Publication of the new accord[3]
• 2005	Implementation of the New Basel Capital Accord

The new framework intends to provide approaches that are more comprehensive and more sensitive to risks than the 1988 accord, while maintaining the overall level of regulatory capital (see Table 5-1). Capital requirements reflect the underlying risks banks will allow in order to manage their businesses more efficiently.

The new framework's focus is primarily on internationally active banks. However, its underlying principles are intended to be suitable for application to banks of varying levels of complexity, sophistication, and size.

The new framework is less prescriptive than the original accord. At its simplest level, the new framework is somewhat more complex than the old one, but it offers a range of approaches to enable banks to use more risk-sensitive analytical methodologies (see Table 5-2). These inevitably require more detail in their application and thus a thicker rule book.

5.2.2 Existing Framework

The 1988 Accord focused on the total amount of bank capital, which is vital for reducing the risk of bank insolvency and the potential cost to depositors of a bank's failure. Building on this, the intent of the new framework is to improve the safety and soundness of the financial system by

TABLE 5-1

Rationale for a New Accord: Need for More Flexibility and Risk Sensitivity

Existing Accord	Proposed New Accord
Focus on a single risk measure	More emphasis on banks' own internal methodologies, supervisory review, and market discipline
One size fits all	Flexibility, menu of approaches, incentives for better risk management
Broad structure	More risk sensitivity

TABLE 5-2

Key Issues for Banks and Supervisors

Key Issues and Challenges for Supervisors	Key Issues and Challenges for Banks
Reliability of banks' internal ratings systems Validation of risk factors through the business cycle Historical data and changes in products/risk exposures Assessment of business practices and examiner resources Treatment of small business loans and project finance and equity exposures Calibration capital across the 6 exposure types Diversification benefits and proposed granularity adjustment Rewarding use of internal rating–based (IRB) approach while leaving capital in the banking system unchanged	Data collection and consistency • Establishing consistent ratings across business lines • Linking ratings and default probabilities • Collecting sufficient data over the business cycle Risk factor validation and adjustments for point in business cycle Disclosure requirements • Collection for dissemination in a timely manner • Comparability across institutions Requirement for rapid rollout of advanced IRB once started 90% floor on advanced IRB provides adequate incentive? Assessment of economic capital and capital allocation

placing more emphasis on a bank's own internal control and management, the supervisory review process, and market discipline.

The 1988 Accord essentially provided only one option for measuring the appropriate capital. However, the best way to measure, manage, and mitigate risks differs from bank to bank. An amendment was introduced in 1996 that focused on trading risks and allowed some banks for the first time to use their own systems to measure their market risks.[4]

The new framework provides a spectrum of approaches with different levels of complexity, from simple to advanced methodologies, for the measurement of both credit risk and operational risk in determining capital levels. It provides a flexible framework in which financial organizations, subject to supervisory review, will adopt approaches that best fit their business strategies, level of sophistication, and risk profile. The framework also deliberately provides embedded rewards for stronger and more sophisticated risk measurement.

The 1988 accord requires internationally active banks in the G-10 countries to hold capital equal to at least 8 percent of a group of assets measured in different ways according to their level of risk. The definition of capital is set (broadly) in two tiers. Tier 1 is shareholders' equity and retained earnings, and Tier 2 is additional internal and external resources available to the bank. The bank also has to hold at least half of its measured capital in Tier 1 form.

A portfolio approach is applied to the measurement of risk, with assets classified into four categories or "buckets" (0 percent, 20 percent, 50 percent, and 100 percent) according to the debtor category. This means that some assets (essentially bank holdings of government assets such as Treasury bills and bonds) have no capital requirement, while claims on banks have a 20 percent weight, which translates into a capital charge of 1.6 percent of the value of the claim. However, virtually all claims on the nonbank private sector receive the standard 8 percent capital requirement.

There is also a scale of charges for off-balance-sheet exposures through guarantees, commitments, forward claims, etc. This is the only complex section of the 1988 accord and requires a two-step approach whereby banks convert their off-balance-sheet positions into a credit equivalent amount through a scale of conversion factors, which are then weighted according to the counterparty's risk weighting.

The 1988 accord has been supplemented a number of times, with most changes relating to the treatment of off-balance-sheet activities. A significant amendment was enacted in 1996, when the Committee introduced a measure whereby trading positions in bonds, equities, foreign exchanges, and commodities were removed from the credit risk framework and given explicit capital charges related to the bank's open position in each instrument.

5.2.3 Impact of the 1988 Accord

The two principal purposes of the accord were to ensure an adequate level of capital in the international banking system and to create a "more level playing field" in competitive terms so that banks could no longer build business volume without adequate capital backing. These two objectives have been achieved. The merits of the accord were widely recognized, and during the 1990s the accord became an accepted world standard, with well over 100 countries applying the Basel framework to their banking systems. However, there also have been some less positive features. The regulatory capital requirement has been in conflict with increasingly sophisticated internal measures of economic capital. The simple bucket approach with a flat 8 percent charge for claims on the private sector has given banks an incentive to move high-quality assets off the balance sheet, thus reducing the average quality of bank loan portfolios. In addition, the 1988 Accord does not sufficiently recognize credit risk mitigation techniques, such as collateral and guarantees. These are the principal reasons why the Basel Committee decided to propose a more risk-sensitive framework in June 1999.

5.2.4 The June 1999 Proposal

The initial consultative proposal had a strong conceptual content and was deliberately rather vague on some details in order to solicit comment at a relatively early stage of the Basel Committee's thought process.[5] It contained three fundamental innovations, each designed to introduce greater risk sensitivity into the accord. One was to supplement the current quantitative standard with two additional pillars dealing with supervisory review and market discipline. These were intended to reduce the stress on the quantitative Pillar I by providing a more balanced approach to the capital assessment process. The second innovation was that banks with advanced risk management capabilities would be permitted to use their own internal systems for evaluating credit risk, known as *internal ratings,* instead of standardized risk weights for each class of assets. The third principal innovation was to allow banks to use the gradings provided by approved external credit assessment institutions (in most cases private rating agencies) to classify their sovereign claims into five risk buckets and their claims on corporations and banks into three risk buckets. In addition, there were a number of other proposals to refine the risk weightings and introduce a capital charge for other risks. The basic definition of capital stayed the same.

The comments on the June 1999 paper were numerous and reflected the important impact the 1988 accord has had. Nearly all those who commented welcomed the intention to refine the Accord and supported the three-pillar approach, but there were many comments on the details of the proposal. In particular, a widely expressed comment from banks was that the threshold for the use of the IRB approach should not be set so high as to prevent well-managed banks from using their internal ratings. Intensive work has taken place in the 18 months since June 1999. Much of this has been leveraged off work undertaken in parallel with industry representatives, whose cooperation has been greatly appreciated by the Basel Committee and its Secretariat.

As the U.S. energy markets discovered recently, the law of unintended consequences is the only certainty in any big regulatory upheaval. But some things seem pretty certain (see Table 5-3).

The New Basel Capital Accord tries to achieve the following objectives:

- Use three mutually reinforcing pillars to more closely align regulatory capital with economic capital
- Encourage integration of risk assessment into the management process

TABLE 5-3

Meaning of the New Accord

Basel II will mean:	A much greater variance in capital requirements between banks with different kinds of businesses, from retail to corporate
	A more complex regulatory regime, with banks and national jurisdictions likely to vary much more in the regulatory capital rules they follow and the quality of their enforcement
	A convergence (if incomplete) between economic capital (true cost of risk) and regulatory capital, and the introduction into bank regulations of many sophisticated risk concepts that will be the building blocks of future regulatory changes
Because Basel II will:	Allow qualifying banks to use internal ratings and economic capital concepts to measure regulatory capital for credit risk
	Set a specific charge for operational risk and allow qualifying banks to choose between more or less sophisticated ways of measuring this
	Oblige banks to release risk information to analysts that might affect bank share prices and credit ratings
Basel II will not:	Alter the way banks set aside capital for market risk, or change the kinds of capital that count as regulatory capital
	Allow banks to use internal portfolio models for either credit or operational risk—yet
	Alter the total amount of capital that the banking industry sets aside, providing the regulators get their sums right

- Achieve greater credit risk sensitivity
- Create flexibility in selecting approaches to setting regulatory capital
- Establish dynamic risk measurement methods for setting regulatory capital
- Reward institutions that adopt more sophisticated risk assessment techniques in order to assess the risks more adequately
- Apply an explicit capital charge for operational and all other risks, and thus reduce the need for a capital "cushion" (reserves)
- Maintain competitive equity between banks and nonbanks and across instrument types and national jurisdictions

The New Basel Capital Accord has still failed to address the following issues:

- The great degree to which the final figure for regulatory capital will diverge from that implied by economic capital calculations
- Definition and mechanics of the proposed charge for operational risk
- Treatment of retail portfolios
- Treatment of credit derivatives
- Proposed maturity factors for loan portfolios
- Lack of incentives to progress from basic to sophisticated risk estimation

Basel has indicated that it expects aggregate levels of regulatory capital to remain broadly steady; however, individual banks may well find themselves holding more or less regulatory capital than under the 1988 accord.

5.2.5 Potential Modifications to the Committee's Proposals

The Basel Committee has set as a standard that its next consultative paper must reflect the best possible effort to construct a revised accord that meets its objectives. Accordingly, the committee now plans to undertake an additional review aimed at assessing the overall impact of a new accord on banks and the banking system before releasing the next consultative paper. The committee's work during this quality assurance phase will focus on three issues:[6]

1. Balancing the need for a risk-sensitive accord with the need to make it sufficiently clear and flexible so that banks can apply it effectively
2. Ensuring that the accord leads to appropriate treatment of credit to small- and medium-sized enterprises, which are important for economic growth and job creation
3. Finalizing calibration of the minimum capital requirements to bring about a level of capital that, on average, is approximately equal to the requirements of the present Basel Accord, while providing some incentive to those banks using the more risk-sensitive internal ratings–based system

The Committee is undertaking a comprehensive quantitative impact study simultaneously during the next consultation period and believes that performing the impact assessment will help make the consultation period more constructive. On October 1, 2002, the Basel Committee on Banking Supervision launched a comprehensive field test for banks of its proposals for revising the 1988 capital accord. The field test, referred to as the third Quantitative Impact Survey or QIS3, is focused on the proposed minimum capital requirements under Pillar I of the New Basel Capital Accord. Banking organizations participating in the QIS3 were to submit completed questionnaires to their national supervisors by December 20, 2002.[7] Undertaking this additional review means that the committee's next consultative paper will not be issued in early 2002, as previously indicated. Instead, the committee will first seek to specify a complete version of its proposals in draft form, including those areas subject to modifications, such as asset securitization and specialized lending. Once a draft version of a fully specified proposal has been completed, the committee will undertake a comprehensive impact assessment of the draft proposal.

After incorporating the results of its comprehensive impact assessment, the committee will release these proposals to be reviewed during a formal consultation period. All interested parties will be invited to provide comment on this consultative paper. The committee intends to finalize the New accord following the completion of the formal consultation period. The Basel Committee has previously announced its intention to finalize the New accord in 2002 and for member countries to implement the New accord in 2005. The committee does not believe that its additional review process will be a lengthy one, and therefore is not at this time announcing a revised schedule for completion or implementation of the New accord.

In terms of potential modifications to the committee's proposals, it is important to note several of the potential changes that have already been described in working papers, press releases, and the results of the quantitative impact studies issued over the last few months.[8] These include the following:

- Modifications related to the coverage of expected losses, including the use of excess general provisions, specific provisions, and margin income (under certain circumstances) to offset IRB capital requirements
- Modifications to the proposed treatment of operational risk, including the introduction of the advanced measurement approach (AMA) and the reduction in the proposed target of operational risk capital as a percentage of current minimum capital requirements from 20 percent to 12 percent (with a further reduction potentially available under the AMA approach)
- Modifications to the credit risk mitigation framework such that residual risks will be assessed through Pillar II and the *w* factor will be eliminated from Pillar I of the framework
- Further specification of proposals relating to equity positions held outside the trading book, specialized lending exposures, and securitizations

In addition to these developments, the quantitative impact exercise seeks to assess the impact of other possible modifications to the committee's proposals, including:

- A modified risk weight curve for all corporate, sovereign, and interbank portfolios. The effects of this modified risk weight curve would also flow through to other portfolio treatments that are defined relative to the corporate IRB risk weights, including aspects of the securitization, equity, and specialized lending proposals.
- Greater recognition of physical collateral and receivables.
- Modified risk weight curves for both residential mortgage exposures and other retail exposures.

In April 2001, the Basel Committee on Banking Supervision initiated a Quantitative Impact Study (QIS2) involving a range of banks across the G-10 and beyond.[9] The objective of the study was to gather the data necessary to allow the committee to gauge the impact of the proposals for capital requirements set out in the January 2001 second consultative paper (CP2). An earlier, more limited study (QIS1) had been carried out in 2000 to inform the CP2 calibration.[10]

On average, the QIS2 results indicate that the CP2 proposals for credit risk would create an increase in capital requirements for all groups under both the standardized and IRB foundation approaches. Indeed, the foundation approach would generate higher capital requirements than the standardized approach, counter to the committee's desired incentives. Across the G-10, Group 1 banks' minimum capital requirements under the standardized approach would be 6 percent higher on average. Under the IRB foundation approach, minimum requirements would be 14 percent higher. Requirements seem likely to be lower under the IRB advanced approach, with an average change of –5 percent. For G-10 Group 2 banks, which would be more likely to use the standardized approach, the average increase in capital would be 1 percent. Results for Group 1 EU banks are similar, with increases of 6 percent and 10 percent under the standardized and IRB foundation approaches, respectively, but with a smaller change of –1 percent under the IRB advanced approach. For banks outside the G-10 and EU, the increase under the standardized approach was 5 percent on average.

These results do not include any charge for operational risk. As reported in a June 25, 2001 press release (available at www.bis.org/press/p010625.htm), the committee has concluded that its original target proportion of regulatory capital related to operational risk (i.e., 20 percent) will be reduced because this reflects too large an allocation of regulatory capital to this risk. For purposes of this exercise, and to illustrate the potential impact of the operational risk capital charge, Table 5-4 reflects an operational risk charge of 12 percent of current minimum regulatory capital for the standardized approach and 10 percent for the IRB approaches.

TABLE 5-4

Percentage Change in Capital Requirements Under the Second Consultative Proposal

	Standardized		*IRB Foundation*		*IRB Advanced*	
	Credit	**Overall**	**Credit**	**Overall**	**Credit**	**Overall**
G-10 Group 1	6%	18%	14%	24%	–5%	5%
G-10 Group 2	1%	13%				
EU Group 1	6%	18%	10%	20%	–1%	9%
EU Group 2	–1%	11%				
Other (non-G-10, non-EU)	5%	17%				

The committee has assumed that for the standardized approach on credit risk the standardized charge for operational risk will apply (i.e., 12 percent). For the IRB approaches, the figure of 10 percent has been used only as a working assumption for the purpose of this exercise. For further information, see also the Basel Committee's working paper on the regulatory treatment of operational risk at www.bis.org/publ/bcbs_wp8.htm.

The quantitative impact study for operational risk has delivered no clear direction regarding capital support for operational risk.[11] The study demonstrates the effort needed regarding data quality, standardization of units, formats (currencies, units, etc.), consistency checks, and so on.

Based on the results of the QIS2 exercise for operational risk, a new impact study regarding operational risks is required. The focus of the committee is on how any future QIS exercises might be improved to make them less burdensome both for the participating banks and in working with the submitted data and to enhance the value of the information received through the exercise. In this regard, the Committee is still open for feedback from the banking industry and other interested parties on the process of collecting this data and on the actual data collected, with the hope of identifying improvements that could be made in structuring any future rounds of QIS data requests on operational risk.

In considering the issues raised dealing with data and process problems regarding operational risk, it is important to note that the focus of any future QIS exercises for operational risk has not yet been determined. Nor has the scope of data to be requested—which might, for instance, include internal capital allocation information, exposure indicators, and/or loss event information—been decided on.

5.3 STRUCTURE OF THE NEW ACCORD AND IMPACT ON RISK MANAGEMENT

The three pillars of the new accord are:

- *Pillar I.* Minimum capital requirement (capital adequacy for market, credit, operational risk) due to increasing risk sensitivity and flexibility through updated standardized and new IRB approaches.
- *Pillar II.* Supervisory review process consisting of encouraging banks to develop and use better risk management techniques to monitor and manage risks; to review risk assessment and the level of integration into management reporting, decision making and processes; and to create a mechanism for regulators to require greater capital.
- *Pillar III.* Market discipline created by reinforcing capital regulation and other supervisory efforts to ensure safety and soundness.

These three mutually reinforcing pillars together should contribute to the safety and soundness of the financial system. The Committee stresses the need for rigorous application of all three pillars.

5.3.1 Pillar I: Minimum Capital Requirement

The Pillar I[12] establishes minimum capital requirements. The new framework maintains both the current definition of capital and the minimum requirement of 8 percent of capital to risk-weighted assets. To ensure that risks within the entire banking group are considered, the revised accord will be extended on a consolidated basis to holding companies of banking groups. (The Accord contains a discussion of the treatment of holdings and related issues.)

The committee's goal remains the same as detailed in the June 1999 paper: namely, to neither raise nor lower the aggregate regulatory capital, inclusive of operational risk, for internationally active banks using the standardized approach. With regard to the IRB approach, the committee's ultimate goal is to ensure that the regulatory capital requirement is sufficient to address underlying risks and contains incentives for banks to migrate from the standardized approach to the IRB approach. The committee invites the industry's cooperation in conducting the extensive testing and dialogue needed to attain these goals.

The capital adequacy is measured as follows:

$$\frac{\text{Total capital (unchanged)}}{\text{Market + credit + operational risk}} = \text{capital ratio (minimum 8\%)} \qquad (5.1)$$

TABLE 5-5

Menu of Alternative Approaches for the Different Risk Categories

Market Risk	Credit Risk	Operational Risk
Choice of approaches to measure market risk (unchanged): • Standardized approach • Internal models approach	Choice of approaches to measure credit risk: • Standardized approach (a modified version of the existing approach) • Foundation IRB approach • Advanced IRB approach	Choice of approaches to measure operational risk: • Basic indicator approach • Standardized approach • Internal measurement approach

Table 5-5 shows the menu to chose from regarding the different approaches within the different risk categories.

The enhancement within the new accord focuses on improvements in the measurement of risks, i.e., the calculation of the denominator of the capital ratio. The credit risk measurement methods are more elaborate than those in the current accord. The new framework proposes for the first time a measure for operational risk, while the market risk measure remains unchanged.

5.3.2 Pillar II: Supervisory Review Process

Pillar II[13] focuses on the supervisory process to be implemented on a national level. The supervisory review process requires supervisors to ensure that each bank has sound internal processes in place to assess the adequacy of its capital based on a thorough evaluation of its risks. Banks must have a process for assessing overall capital adequacy based on:

- Board and senior management oversight
- Sound capital assessment
- Comprehensive assessment of risks
- Monitoring and reporting
- Internal control review

The New Accord demands that local regulators (supervisors) review and evaluate a bank's assessments and strategies, that the bank operate above minimum regulatory capital ratios, and that supervisors intervene at an early stage.

The new framework stresses the importance of bank management developing an internal capital assessment process and setting targets for capital that are commensurate with the bank's particular risk profile and control environment. Supervisors would be responsible for evaluating how well banks are assessing their capital adequacy needs relative to their risks. This internal process would then be subject to supervisory review and intervention where appropriate. The implementation of these proposals will in many cases require a much more detailed dialogue between supervisors and banks. This in turn has implications for the training and expertise of bank supervisors, an area in which the committee and the BIS's Financial Stability Institute will be providing assistance.

This pillar is not a focus area of this book. For further information on Pillar II, refer to the BIS literature and literature from the industry.

5.3.3 Pillar III: Market Discipline and General Disclosure Requirements

Pillar III of the new framework[14] aims to bolster market discipline through enhanced disclosure by banks. Effective disclosure is essential to ensure that market participants can better understand banks' risk profiles and the adequacy of their capital positions. The new framework sets out disclosure requirements and recommendations in several areas, including the ways a bank calculates its capital adequacy and assesses its risks. The core set of disclosure recommendations applies to all banks, with more detailed requirements for supervisory recognition of internal methodologies for credit risk, credit risk mitigation techniques, and asset securitization:

- Banks should have a formal disclosure policy, approved by the board of directors, that describes the bank's objective and strategy for disclosure of public information about its financial condition and performance.
- Increasingly detailed disclosure requirements will apply for supervisory recognition of internal methodologies for credit risk, credit risk mitigation techniques, and asset securitization.
- Disclosures will include both core (qualitative and quantitative) and supplemental components. Additionally, banks will be required to implement a process for assessing the appropriateness of disclosure, including frequency. The verification process has to be performed at least annually.
- Disclosure should take place on a semiannual basis at a minimum. Quarterly disclosure will be expected for internationally active banks with certain exposures subject to rapid time decay.

The acceptance of IRB approaches is dependent on minimum disclosure requirements (see Table 5-6).

TABLE 5-6

Core Quantitative and Qualitative Disclosures for IRB Approaches

Core Quantitative Disclosures	Core Qualitative Disclosures
Overall risk breakdown of portfolio	Structure, management, and organizational credit risk management function
Geographic breakdown/concentration of credit exposures	Strategies, objectives, and practices in managing/controlling credit risk
Broad on/off-balance sheet breakdown	Information on techniques and methods for managing past due and impaired assets
Sector breakdown of credit exposures (e.g., by industry)	
Maturity profile of book	
Information on problem loans and provisioning	

Recommended supplementary disclosures include further detail regarding the form of credit risk exposures (e.g., loans, commitments, guarantees, tradable securities, counterparty risk in derivatives) and information about the mitigation of credit risk (securitization, credit derivatives, etc.) (see Table 5-7).

Market discipline is one of the focus areas at the heart of Basel II. It's new, it's trendy, and it should even be cheap. Banks accept that they will be expected to disclose more about their credit and operational risks and how they manage them, but they are not satisfied with the level of detail and the disclosure templates put forward in the regulators' proposals. The rationale behind the disclosure proposals is that, since banks are almost invariably ahead of the regulators when it comes to innovation, the best way to regulate a bank's capital adequacy is to leave it to the market itself. This does not mean taking an entirely laissez-faire approach to regulation, but allowing competitors, customers, and counterparties to make informed decisions about whether or not to trade with a particular bank based on its known exposures and the level of capital it holds to cover them. The regulator's function becomes one of making sure that the information is relevant, sufficient, and comparable. The actual content and extent of the information to be disclosed is hotly debated between players in the industry, regulators, credit agencies, accounting policy-setting bodies, etc. Disclosing information according to the New Accord guidelines is viewed as disclosing proprietary and confidential information to the public, overloading the shareholders with information, etc. The industry expects that the regulators will modify the concept substantially without removing the innovative third pillar of the proposal.

TABLE 5-7

Supplementary Disclosures in the New Accord

Subject	Type	Location in Supporting Document
Scope of application	Strong recommendations	Pillar III
Capital	Strong recommendations	Pillar III
Credit risk (general)	Strong recommendations	Pillar III
Credit risk (standardized approach)	Requirements and strong recommendations	Pillar III
Credit risk mitigation techniques	Requirements and strong recommendations	Pillar III
Credit risk (IRB approaches)	Requirements	Pillar III
Market risk	Strong recommendations	Pillar III
Operational risk	Strong recommendations and (in future) requirements	Pillar III
Interest rate risk in the banking book	Strong recommendations	Pillar III
Capital adequacy	Strong recommendations	Pillar III
Asset securitization	Requirements	Asset securitization
ECAI recognition	Requirements	Standardized approach
Supervisory transparency	Strong recommendations	Standardized approach and Pillar II

SOURCE: Bank for International Settlement (BIS), Basel Committee on Banking Supervision, *The New Basel Capital Accord, Consultative Document, Issued for Comment by 31 May 2001,* Basel, Switzerland: Bank for International Settlement, January 2001, para. 633 ff.

This pillar is not a focus area of this book. For further information, refer to the BIS literature and literature from the industry.

5.4 VALUE AT RISK AND REGULATORY CAPITAL REQUIREMENT

5.4.1 Background

The following discussion of VaR will help readers understand the benefits and pitfalls of VaR, which is used as a universal measurement in an integrated framework. Identifying and measuring the risks associated with instruments and participants in the financial markets has become the primary focus of intense study by academics, regulators, and financial institutions. Certain risks (such as default or counterparty risks) have figured at the top of most banks' concerns for a long time, and associated processes and infrastructures have been reviewed by auditors for a long time as well. Other risks, such as market risk, have been brought into the foreground by academic studies on portfolio optimization, derivatives pricing, and financial scandals, as well as by recent regulatory requirements to support market risks with capital. The reason for the shift in attention lies in the significant changes that the financial markets have undergone over the last two decades. Historically, risk was viewed from a nominal perspective, excluding the nature of risk and reduced risk information on pure financial numbers based on net present valuation.

5.4.2 Historical Development of VaR

Financial institutions developed VaR as a general measure of economic loss that could equate risk across product positions and aggregate risk on a portfolio basis. An important stimulus and condition for the development of VaR was the move toward marking to market, both for underlying instruments and derivatives. Prior to that, the focus was on net interest income including net present values, where the common risk measure was the repricing gap. Along with technological breakthroughs in data processing, the developments in risk management have gone hand in hand with changes in management practices, including a movement away from risk management based on accrual accounting and toward risk management based on the marking to market of positions. Increased liquidity and pricing availability, along with a new focus on trading, required and led to the frequent revaluation of positions and the concept of marking to market. As investments became more liquid, the need of management to frequently and accurately report investment gains and losses has led more and more firms to manage daily earnings from a mark-to-market perspective. The switch from accrual accounting to marking to market often results in higher swings in reported gains and losses, thereby increasing the need for managers to emphasize the volatility of the underlying markets. The markets have not become more volatile, but the focus on risks through marking to market has highlighted the volatility of earnings. Given the move to frequently revalue positions, managers and clients have become more concerned with estimating the potential impact of changes in market conditions on the value of their positions.

- *Instrument complexity.* As trading has increased and structured fixed-income products have evolved from pure coupon-carrying instrument, duration analysis has taken over. But duration's inadequacies led to the adoption of VaR.
- *Securitization and securities lending and borrowing.* Across markets, traded securities have replaced many illiquid

instruments. Foreign stocks (using American Depository Receipts, or ADRs) and loans and mortgages (using CMOs) have been securitized to permit disintermediation and trading. Global securities markets have expanded, and both exchange-traded and over-the-counter (OTC) derivatives have become major components of the markets, including securities lending and borrowing.

- *Performance.* Significant efforts have been made to develop methods and systems to measure financial performance. Indices for equities, fixed-income securities, commodities, and foreign exchanges have become commonplace and are used extensively to monitor returns within and/or across asset classes as well as to allocate funds. The somewhat one-sided focus on returns, however, has led to incomplete performance analysis. Return measurement gives no indication of the cost in terms of risk (volatility of returns). Studies by Markowitz and others on the efficient frontier clarify the relation of risk and return, and demonstrate that higher returns can only be obtained at the expense of higher risks. While this trade-off is well known, the risk component of the performance analysis has not yet received broad attention. Investors and trading managers are searching for common standards to measure market risks and to better estimate the risk–return profiles of individual assets or asset classes. Notwithstanding external constraints from regulatory agencies, the managers of financial firms have also been searching for ways to measure market risks, given the potentially damaging effect of miscalculated risks on company earnings. The Association for Investment Management and Research (AIMR) and Global Investment Performance Standard (GIPS) have established standard criteria for how to measure performance, including the risk component as input factor for risk-adjusted performance presentation.[15] As a result, banks, investment firms, and corporations are now in the process of incorporating measures of market risk into their management approaches.

Over the last few years, there have been significant developments in conceptualizing a common framework for measuring market risk. A wide variety of approaches to measure return have been developed, but little has been done to standardize the measurement of risk. Over the last two decades, many market participants, academics, and regulatory bodies have developed concepts for measuring risks, mainly market risks, using a nominal view of risk. Over the last years, two approaches have evolved as a means to measure market risk: VaR and scenario analysis.

5.4.3 VaR and Modern Financial Management

There are two steps to VaR measurement. First, all positions must be marked to market (valuation). Second, the future variability of the market value (volatility) must be estimated. Figure 5-2 illustrates this point.

5.4.3.1 Valuation

Frequently traded positions are valued at their current prices or rates as quoted in liquid secondary markets. To value transactions for which, in the absence of a liquid secondary market, no market value exists, the position is mapped into equivalent positions or decomposed into parts for which secondary market prices exist. The most basic such component is a

FIGURE 5-2

Steps for VaR Measurement, from Account (Records of Positions) Overvaluation to Risk Measurement.

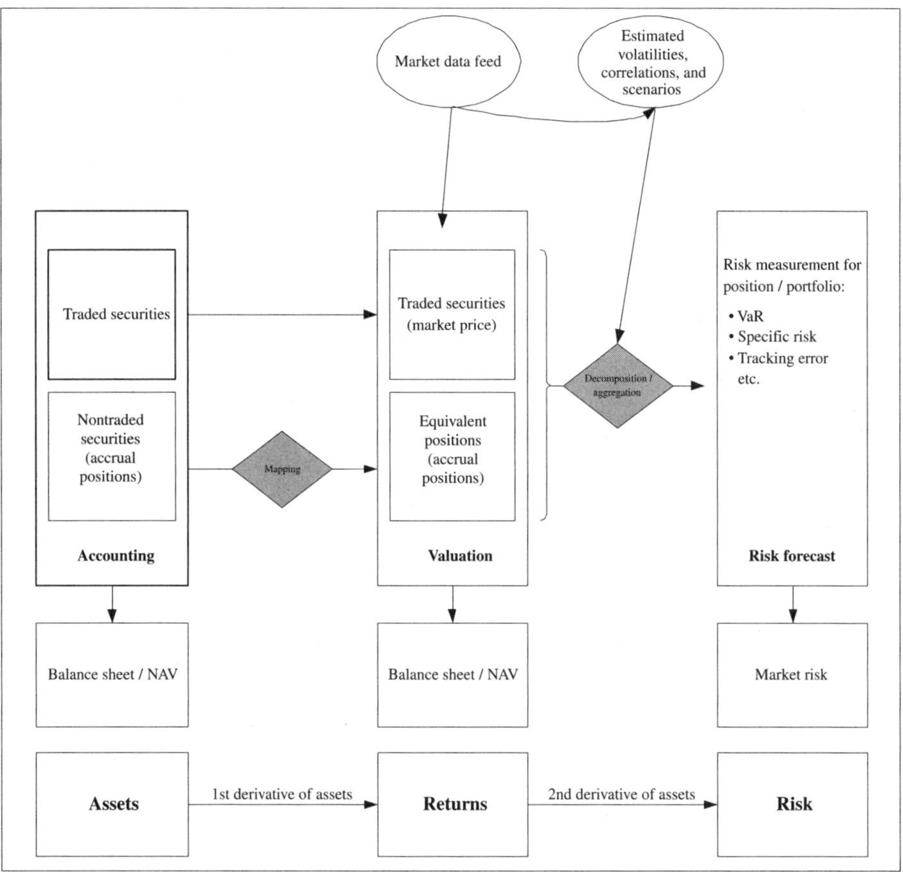

single cash flow with a given maturity and currency of the payor. Most transactions can be described as a combination of such cash flows and thus can be valued approximately as the sum of the market values of their component cash flows. Nonmarketable items, however, have embedded options that cannot be valued in this simple manner. To value them, expected volatilities and correlations of the prices and rates that affect their value are required, and an appropriate options pricing model is also required. For some valuations, volatilities and correlations are required.

5.4.3.2 Risk Estimation

Risk estimation is based on the change in values as a consequence of expected changes in prices and rates. The potential changes in prices are defined by either specific scenarios or a set of volatility and correlation estimates. If the value of a position depends on a single rate factor, then the potential change in value is a function of the factors in the scenarios or volatility of that rate. If the value of a position depends on multiple factors, then the potential change in its value is a function of the combination of factors in each scenario, or of each volatility, and of each correlation between all pairs of factors. Generating equivalent positions on an aggregate basis facilitates the simulation. As will be shown later, the simulation can be done algebraically using statistics and matrix algebra or exhaustively by computing estimated value changes for many combinations of factor changes. Forecasts of volatilities and correlations play a central role in the VaR approach.

5.4.3.3 Additional Approaches to Risk Estimation

Different approaches to the VaR calculation are currently being used, and most practitioners have selected an approach based on their specific needs, the types of positions they hold, their willingness to trade accuracy for speed (or vice versa), and other considerations. The models used today differ on two fronts:

1. How changes in the values of financial instruments are estimated as a result of market movements
2. How potential market movements are estimated

What creates the variety of models currently employed is the fact that the choices made on the basis of these two parameters can be mixed and matched in different ways.

5.4.3.4 Estimating Changes in Value

There are basically two approaches to estimating how the value of a portfolio changes as a result of market movements: analytical methods and simulation methods.

Analytical Methods

The analytical sensitivity approach is based on the following equation:

$$\text{Estimated value change} = f\,(\text{position sensitivity, estimated rate/price change}) \tag{5.2}$$

where the position sensitivity factor determines the relationship between the value of the instrument and the underlying rate or price (factor), and the accuracy of the risk approximation with the parameter of the estimation, such as probability. In its simplest form, the analytical sensitivity approach looks like this:

$$\text{Estimated value change} = \text{position sensitivity} \cdot \text{estimated rate change} \tag{5.3}$$

The value change of a fixed-income instrument can be estimated by using the instrument's duration. This linear approximation simplifies the convex price-yield relationship of a bond, and it is extensively used because the duration often accounts for the most significant part of the risk profile of a fixed-income instrument. Similar simplifications can be made for options using the option's delta for the estimated change in value. The analytical approach to account for nonlinear relationships between market value and rate changes (e.g., options) can be extended with the delta-gamma approach. The more refined version of the analytical approach looks like this:

$$\begin{aligned}\text{Estimated value change} = {} & (\text{position sensitivity}_1 \cdot \text{estimated rate change}) \\ & + \tfrac{1}{2}\,(\text{position sensitivity}_2) \cdot (\text{estimated rate change})^2 \\ & + \ldots\end{aligned} \tag{5.4}$$

In the case of an option, the first-order position sensitivity is the delta, while the second-order term is the gamma. The analytical approach requires that positions be summarized in some fashion so that the estimated rate changes can be applied. This process of aggregating positions is called *mapping*.

The advantages of analytical models are that they are computationally efficient and they enable users to estimate risk in a timely fashion.

Simulation Methods

The second type of approaches, typically referred to as *full valuation models*, rely on revaluing a position or a portfolio of instruments under different scenarios. How these scenarios are generated depends on the application of the models, from basic historical simulation to distributions of returns generated from a set of volatility and correlation estimates. Some models include user-defined scenarios that are based on major market events and aimed at estimating risk in crisis conditions. This process is often referred to as *stress testing*. Full valuation models enable the user to focus on the entire distribution of returns instead of a single VaR because they typically provide a richer set of risk measures. Their main drawback is the fact that the full valuation of large portfolios under a significant number of scenarios is computationally intensive and time consuming.

5.4.3.5 Estimating Market Movements

The second discriminant between VaR approaches is how market movements are estimated. There is much more variety here, and the following is not an exhaustive discussion of current practice.

Parametric Method

The parametric method uses historical time series analysis to derive estimates of volatilities and correlations on a large set of financial instruments. The parametric method, also called the *variance-covariance method,* assumes that the probability distribution of past returns can be modeled to provide reasonable forecasts of future returns over different time horizons. While the parametric approach assumes conditional normality of returns, the estimation process for the "normal" variance-covariance approach has to be refined to incorporate the empirically proven fact that most return distributions show kurtosis and leptokurtosis. These volatility and correlation estimates can be used as inputs in analytical VaR models and full valuation models.

Historical Simulation

The historical simulation approach, which is generally used for the full valuation model, makes no explicit assumptions about the probability distribution of asset returns. In historical simulation, portfolios are valued under a number of different historical time windows that are user defined. These lookback periods typically range from six months to two years.

Monte Carlo Simulation

While historical simulation approaches quantify risk by replicating one specific historical path of market evolution, stochastic simulation approaches attempt to generate many more paths of market returns. These stochastic returns are generated using a defined stochastic process (for example, they assume that the equity markets follow a random walk) and statistical parameters that drive the process (for example, the mean μ and standard deviation σ of the random variable).

The following parameters and assumptions add refinements to the VaR results generated by the approaches just listed:

- *Implied volatilities.* Looking forward, market returns are examined to give an indication of future potential return distributions. Implied volatility is extracted from a specific option pricing model to generate the market's forecast of future volatility. Implied volatilities are often used for the review and examination of historical volatility to refine the risk analysis. Implied volatilities are not only used to drive global VaR models as if all observable options prices on all instruments that compose a portfolio are analytically available. Unfortunately, the universe of consistently priced and available options prices is not large enough. Generally, only exchange-traded options are reliable sources of prices.
- *User-defined scenarios.* Most risk management models add user-defined rate and price movements to the standard VaR calculation. Some scenarios are subjectively chosen, while others are based on parameters derived from past crisis events. The latter is referred to as *stress testing* and is an integral part of a well-designed risk management process and required by regulation. Selecting the appropriate VaR methodology is not straightforward. Weighing the advantages and disadvantages of various methodologies will always be important. Cost-benefit trade-offs are different for each user, depending on his or her strategy and position in the markets, the number and types of instruments traded, and the technology available. Different choices can be made even at different levels of an organization, depending on the objectives. While trading desks of an institution may require precise risk estimation involving simulation on specific trading positions or portfolios, senior management may opt for an analytical approach that is cost efficient and timely and that gives an overview with adequate precision. It is important for senior management to know whether the risk-adjusted institution is risking $10 million or $50 million, but it is irrelevant for them to make the distinction between $10 million and $11 million. This degree of accuracy at the senior management level is not only irrelevant, but also may be unachievable operationally or may require a cost that is not consistent with shareholder value.

5.4.4 Definition of VaR

VaR is defined as the predicted worst-case loss at a specific confidence level (e.g., 95 percent) over a certain period of time (e.g., 10 days). The elegance of the VaR solution is that it works on multiple levels, from the position-specific micro level to the portfolio-based macro level using instruments or organizational entities as portfolio positions. VaR has become a common language for communication about aggregate risk taking, both within and outside of an organization (e.g., with analysts, regulators, rating agencies, and shareholders).

The application of VaR analysis and reporting has extended from position/portfolio VaR, to nonfinancial organizations, to expanded application of the VaR methodology, such as earnings at risk (EaR), earnings per share at risk (EPSaR), and cash flow at risk (CFaR). Statistical models of risk measurement, such as VaR, allow an objective, independent assessment of how much risk is actually being taken in a specific situation. Results are reported in various levels of detail by business unit and in the aggregate. These measures take into account the corporate environment of an institution, such as accrual vs. mark-to-market accounting or hedge accounting for qualifying transactions. Furthermore, the focus is now on the longer-term impact of risk on cash flows and earnings (quarterly or even annually) in the budgeting and planning process.

There are three major methodologies for calculating VaR, each with unique characteristics. Parametric VaR is simple and quick to calculate, but is inaccurate for nonlinear positions. The two simulation methodologies, historical and Monte Carlo, capture nonlinear risks and give a full distribution of potential outcomes, but require more computational power. Before calculating VaR, three parameters must be specified: (1) confidence level, (2) forecast horizon, and (3) base currency. The square root of time scaling of VaR may be applied to roughly extrapolate VaR to horizons longer than 1 day, such as 10 days or 1 month. Square root of time scaling assumes a random diffusion process with no autocorrelation, trending, or mean reversion.

5.4.4.1 VaR, Relative VaR, Marginal VaR, and Incremental VaR

Assuming 95 percent confidence and a 1-day horizon, a VaR of $1 million means that, on average, only on 1 day in 20 would an institution expect to lose more than $1 million due to market movements. This definition of VaR uses a 5 percent risk level (95 percent confidence). On average, losses exceeding the VaR amount would occur 5 percent of the time, or losses less than the VaR amount of $1 million would occur 95 percent of the time. Within a company, uncertainty in future earnings and cash flow is caused not only by uncertainty in an institution's underlying activity (e.g., sales volumes), but also by a number of other risks, including market risk. Market risk can arise from a number of factors, including foreign exchange exposures, interest rate exposures, commodity price–sensitive revenues or expenses, pension liabilities, and stock option plans. To address the institution's need to quantify the impact of market risk factors on earnings and cash flow, additional coefficients for volatility have been defined:

- *Earnings at risk (EaR).* The maximum shortfall of earnings, relative to a specified target, that could be expected based on the impact of market risk factors on a specified set of exposures for a prespecified time horizon and confidence level. Generally, earnings are reported on a per share of equity basis. Therefore, many companies prefer to use an earnings per share at risk (EPSaR) measure.
- *Cash flow at risk (CFaR).* The maximum shortfall of net cash generated, relative to a specified target, that could be expected based on the impact of market risk factors on a specified set of exposures for a specified time horizon and confidence level.

To better understand and interpret VaR, it is important to keep in mind that VaR is a flexible risk measurement in different dimensions:

- VaR can be defined for various horizons and confidence levels.
- VaR can be expressed as a percentage of market value or in absolute currency terms.

Apart from the normal VaR, there are three related VaR measures:

1. *Relative VaR.* The relative VaR coefficient expresses the risk of underperformance relative to a predefined benchmark, such as an index, a portfolio, or another position. Relative VaR is also commonly expressed as a percentage of present value.
2. *Marginal VaR.* The marginal VaR coefficient expresses how the removal of an entire specific position changes the risk of a portfolio. Marginal VaR can be computed for both absolute VaR and relative VaR. Marginal VaR is useful for identifying which position or risk category factor is the largest contributor to portfolio risk.
3. *Incremental VaR.* Marginal VaR measures the difference in portfolio risk caused by removing an entire position, whereas incremental VaR measures the impact of gradual small changes in position weighting. The overall sum of all incremental VaR adds up to the total diversified portfolio VaR. Therefore, incremental VaR may be used to calculate percentage contribution to risk. One of the most useful applications of incremental VaR is in reporting the rank contribution to risk-hedging opportunities. Incremental VaR is also useful for identifying positions for gradual risk reduction using partial hedges.

5.5 CONCEPTUAL OVERVIEW OF RISK METHODOLOGIES

Market risk models are designed to measure potential losses due to adverse changes in the value of financial instruments. There are several approaches to forecasting market risk, and no single method is best for every situation. Over the last years, VaR models have been developed and implemented throughout the financial sector and by nonfinancial institutions as well. Having roots in modern portfolio theory, VaR models forecast risk by analyzing historical patterns of market variables. Over time, three main methods have evolved and become established: parametric analysis, historical simulation, and Monte Carlo simulation. To understand the strengths and weaknesses of the different methods, it is important to discuss the nature and impact of linear and nonlinear instruments. A financial instrument is regarded as nonlinear if its price (and thus its value) changes disproportionately relative to the price changes in the underlying asset. The risk of nonlinear instruments (e.g., options and structured products) is more complex to estimate than the risk of linear instruments (e.g., traditional stocks, bonds, swaps, forwards, and futures). To account for the discontinuous payoff of nonlinear instruments such as options, risk simulations should use full valuation formulas (e.g., Black-Scholes) rather than derived first-order sensitivities (e.g., delta). Table 5-8 describes the three main methodologies for calculating VaR.

Monte Carlo and historical simulations are mechanically somewhat similar, as they both revalue instruments given changes in market rates (scenarios). The difference lies in how the scenarios are defined. Monte Carlo simulation generates random hypothetical scenarios using a random generator, while historical simulation estimates parameters from actual past market movements as scenarios. From a practical perspective, the important impact of the methodology choice is that a portfolio/position with significant nonlinear exposures, and a simulation approach (Monte Carlo or historical) with full position revaluation, will estimate the loss distribution conceptually with more accuracy than a parametric approximation for estimating VaR. Table 5-8 summarizes the advantages and disadvantages of each methodology. All three approaches for estimating VaR have something to offer and can be used together to provide a more robust estimate of VaR.

5.6 LIMITATIONS OF VAR

The choice of a methodology has some far-reaching impacts. The model's user should not view models as black boxes that produce magic numbers. It's important to realize that all three methodologies for measuring VaR are limited by a fundamental assumption that future risk can be predicted from the historical distribution of returns. The parametric approach assumes normally distributed returns, which implies that parametric VaR is only meant to describe losses on a "normal" day. Other types of days, such as crises (fat-tail events), which happen rarely but have a serious impact, do not exist within the "normal" view. While Monte Carlo simulation of-

Summary of Advantages and Disadvantages of Alternative Methodologies of Calculating VaR

Methodology	Advantages	Disadvantages
Parametric/variance-covariance approach	Fast and simple calculation. No need for extensive historical data (only volatility and correlation matrix are required). Estimates VaR with an equation that specifies parameters such as volatility, correlation, delta, and gamma.	Less accurate for nonlinear portfolios, or for skewed distributions. Accurate for traditional assets and linear derivatives; less accurate for nonlinear derivatives. Historical correlation and volatilities can be misleading under specific market conditions. Cash flow mapping required.
Monte Carlo simulation	Accurate* for all instruments. Provides a full distribution of potential portfolio values (not just a specific percentile). Permits use of various distributional assumptions (normal, T-distribution, normal mixture, etc.), and therefore has potential to address the issue of fat tails (formally known as leptokurtosis). No need for extensive historical data. No assumption on linearity, distribution, correlation, and volatilities required.	Computationally intensive and time consuming (involves revaluing the portfolio under each scenario). Quantifies fat-tailed risk only if market scenarios are generated from the appropriate distributions. Appropriate for all types of instruments, linear and nonlinear.
Historical simulation	Accurate* for all instruments. Provides a full distribution of potential portfolio values (not just a specific percentile). No need to make distributional assumptions (although parameter fitting may be performed on the resulting distribution). Faster than Monte Carlo simulation because fewer scenarios are used. Estimates VaR by regenerating history; requires actual historical rates and revalues positions for each change in the market.	Requires a significant amount of daily rate history (note, however, that sampling far back may be a problem when data is irrelevant to current conditions, e.g., currencies that have already devalued). Difficult to scale far into the future (long horizons). Coarse at high confidence levels (e.g., 99% and beyond) Somewhat computationally intensive and time consuming (involves re-valuing the portfolio under each scenario, although far fewer scenarios are required than for Monte Carlo) Incorporates tail risk only if historical data set includes tail events. Pricing models required, increasing complexity.

*If used with complete pricing algorithm.

fers a way to address the fat-tail problem by allowing a variety of distributional assumptions, volatility and correlation forecasts are still based on statistical fitting of historical returns. While historical simulation performs no statistical fitting, it implicitly assumes that the exact distribution of past returns forecasts future returns distributions. This means that all three approaches are vulnerable to structural changes or sudden changes in market behavior. Stress testing is required to explore potential regime shifts to best complement VaR and to review the accuracy of the VaR assumptions.

5.6.1 Parameters for VaR Analysis

Before calculating VaR, we need to specify three parameters: confidence level, forecast horizon, and base currency.

5.6.1.1 Confidence Level

The first step is to determine a confidence level or probability of loss associated with VaR measurement. Confidence levels generally range between 90 and 99 percent. Generally, a 95 percent confidence level as a baseline is common in the market. Instead of fixing only a single parameter, some institutions use several confidence levels (e.g., 95 percent and 99 percent) and forecast periods (e.g., one day, one week, and one year). It can be argued that using implied volatilities links risk prediction to market expectations as opposed to past market movements, and thus is forward looking. For a portfolio view of risk, however, historical correlations of market returns must still be applied, as it is generally impossible to get such information from option prices, especially for OTC-traded instruments.

Determining Confidence Levels

In choosing confidence levels for market risk, the institution should consider worst-case loss amounts that are large enough to be substantial, but that occur frequently enough to be observable. For example, with a 95 percent confidence level, potential losses should exceed VaR about once a month on average (or once in 20 trading days), giving this risk statistic a visceral meaning. Using a higher level of confidence, such as 99.9 percent, is generally regarded as more conservative. But one might also reason that a higher confidence level might mistakenly lead to a false sense of security. A 99.9 percent VaR will not be understood as thoroughly or taken as seriously by risk takers and managers because losses will rarely exceed that level, as a loss of that magnitude is expected to occur about once in four years. Due to fat-tailed market return distributions, a high confidence level VaR is difficult to model and verify statistically. VaR models tend to lose accuracy beyond the 95 percent mark and even more beyond 99 percent. When using VaR for measuring credit risk and capital, however, a 99 percent or higher confidence level VaR should be applied because of the likelihood of low-probability, event-driven risks (i.e., tail risk). Beyond a certain confidence level, rigorous stress testing becomes more important than statistical analysis.

5.6.1.2 Forecast Horizon

Generally, active financial institutions (e.g., investment banks, hedge funds) consistently use a one-day forecast horizon for their VaR analysis of all market risk–driven positions. For banks, it simply doesn't make sense to project market risks much further because trading positions can change dynamically from one day to the next. On the other hand, investment managers often use a one-month forecast horizon, while corporations may apply quarterly or even annual projections of risk for their financial positions.

Applying Longer Horizon for Illiquid Assets

Instead of applying a single horizon, some institutions apply different forecast horizons across asset classes to account for liquidity risk. It can be argued that the unwind period for an illiquid emerging market asset is much longer than for a government bond, and therefore a longer horizon (e.g., one week) for emerging markets should be used. However, a better solution is to treat market risk and liquidity risk as separate issues. Liquidity risk is currently a hot research topic, and new quantitative methodologies are being developed.[15]

Simply using a longer time horizon for illiquid assets is not adequate, and confuses liquidity risk with market risk in an overly simply manner that is not appropriate in relation to the complexity of this topic. A standard horizon for VaR across asset classes facilitates the risk communication process and allows comparison for market risk across asset classes.

5.6.1.3 Confidence Level Scaling Factors

Using a parametric approach, standard deviations can be used to estimate lower-tail probabilities of loss. *Lower-tail probability of loss* refers to the chance of loss exceeding a prespecified amount. Because returns tend to cluster around the mean, larger standard deviation movements have a lower probability of occurring. To arrive at the tail probability of loss levels and implied VaR confidence levels, standard deviations (confidence level scaling factors) are used. Figure 5-3 shows three confidence level scaling factors and their associated levels of tail probability of loss.

Assuming normality, one confidence level can be easily converted to a two-standard confidence level. For example, a 95 percent confidence level VaR is translated to the BIS standard of 99 percent confidence level through a simple multiplication, as shown in Table 5-9.

The confidence level transformation is based on the critical assumption of a normal distribution. As will be discussed later, the assumption of

FIGURE 5-3

Confidence Level Scaling Factors.

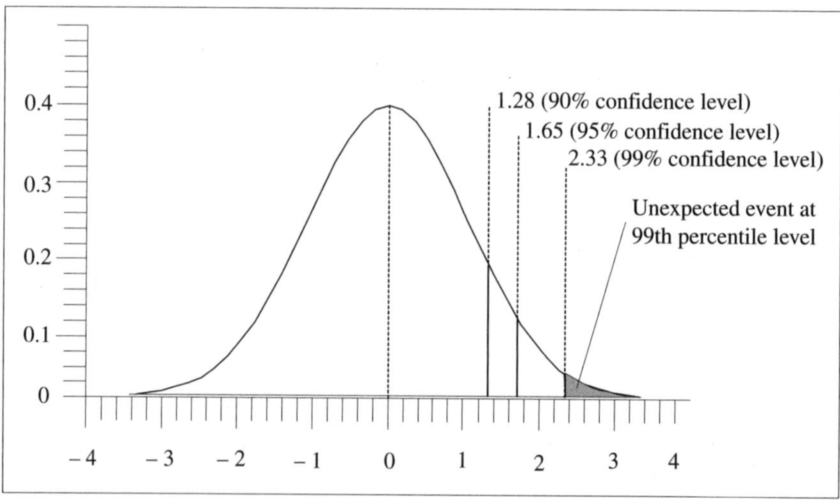

normal distribution is not supported by empirical evidence over time and depends as well on the asset class the distribution is calculated for. Regulators are increasingly discouraging this simple conversion, as the assumption of normally distributed P&Ls is often an oversimplification, especially when portfolios contain nonlinear positions.

5.6.1.4 Base Currency

The base currency for calculating VaR is typically the currency of the equity capital and reporting currency of a company. For example, Goldman, Sachs & Co. would use U.S. dollars to calculate and report its worldwide risks, while the Credit Suisse Group would use Swiss francs.

TABLE 5-9

Confidence Level Transformation from RiskMetrics Approach to BIS Standard

VaR Methodology	Confidence Level	Confidence Level Scaling Factor
BIS VaR	99%	2.33
RiskMetrics VaR	95%	1.65
Converting RiskMetrics to BIS	95% to 99%	RiskMetrics VaR × 2.33/1.65

5.6.1.5 Time Scaling of Volatility

Risk increases with time: the longer a position is held, the greater the potential for loss. But, unlike expected returns, volatility does not increase linearly with time. Long-horizon forecasting is complicated due to mean reversion of market returns, autocorrelation, trending, and the interrelationship of many macroeconomic factors. Autocorrelation refers to correlation between successive days' returns; mean reversion is the tendency for time series to revert to a long-term average (this is observed especially for interest rates). VaR estimates have to be time scaled (for example, when converting a daily VaR to a 10-day-horizon regulatory VaR standard). A commonly applied method is square root of time scaling, which (approximately) extrapolates one-day volatilities as well as one-day VaR to longer horizons. This method assumes that daily price changes are independent of each other and that there is no mean reversion, trending, or auto-correlation in the markets. To scale volatility, time the number of trading days as opposed to actual days (5 trading days per week, 21 days per month). For example:

$$\begin{aligned} \text{Weekly volatility} &= \text{1-day VaR} \cdot \sqrt{5} \\ &= \text{1-day VaR} \cdot 2.24 \\ \text{Monthly VaR} &= \text{1-day VaR} \cdot \sqrt{21} \\ &= \text{1-day VaR} \cdot 4.58 \end{aligned} \tag{5.5}$$

The simplified time-scaling approach can be useful for converting one-day management VaR figures to 10-day figures, for example for BIS regulatory VaR standards. However, regulators are not supportive of this approach, which has prompted some institutions to adopt more accurate methodologies.

5.6.1.6 Time Horizon and Credit Risk

Much of the academic analysis and industry rating data is expressed on an annual basis. This is a convention rather than an empirically supported fact. It is important to note that there is nothing about the credit risk methodology that supports a one-year horizon per se. Indeed, it is difficult to support the argument than any one particular risk horizon is best. Illiquidity, credit relationships, credit deterioration, and common lack of credit hedging instruments can all lead to prolonged risk-mitigating actions. The choice of risk horizon raises two practical questions:

1. Should credit risk be calculated for only one risk horizon or for longer or shorter periods?
2. Is there any empirical evidence that any one particular horizon is best?

Should there be one horizon or many? The choice of time horizon for risk measurement and risk management is not clear because there is no explicit theory to guide us. Many different security types bear credit risk. One of the common arguments in favor of multiple credit risk horizons is that they allow us to calculate risk at horizons tailored to each credit security type. For instance, it may be that interest rate swaps are more liquid than loans. The managers for each security type (e.g., loans versus swaps) may wish to see their security type calculated at their own risk horizon. However, the risk estimates for these different subportfolios cannot be aggregated if there is a mismatch in time horizons. Additionally, the periodic disclosure statements required for all listed companies (generally quarterly) and annual fiscal and business reporting disclose credit information on a quarterly/annual basis, unlike market prices for listed companies, which are listed daily.

What is a good risk horizon? Almost any risk measurement system is better at stating relative risk than absolute risk. Since relative risk measurements will likely drive investment decisions, the choice of risk horizon is not likely to make an appreciable difference. The key element of any risk measurement system is the resulting risk-mitigating actions of the underlying positions, as any given risk horizon is likely to lead to the same qualitative decisions. Although these actions may differ among institutions, the risk horizon is not likely to be significantly less than one quarter for a bank with loans, commitments, financial letters of credit, etc. On the other hand, the natural turnover due to ongoing maturity and reinvestment of positions provides appreciable room for risk-mitigating action even for highly illiquid instruments. Thus, using as a convention a one-year risk horizon—not unlike the convention for annualized interest rates—is common, at least for reporting purposes. Even if risk-mitigating actions are performed daily, recalculating risk at a longer horizon can still provide guidance on changes in relative risk.

Two credit risk modeling parameters must reflect the different risk horizons:

1. The transition from one risk horizon to another must be reflected in the formulas used to reevaluate all parameters influenced by or linked to alternating risk horizons.
2. The likelihood of credit quality migration, as shown in the transition matrix, must incorporate the new risk horizon in order to reevaluate the transition matrix for the new risk horizon, including all linked parameters.

One way of doing the latter is simply to multiply the short-horizon transition matrices to obtain the transition matrix for a longer horizon. For example, a two-year transition matrix could be obtained by multiplying the one-year transition matrix by itself. However, this methodology unfortunately ignores the impact of autocorrelation on the credit quality changes over multiple time horizons. A nonzero autocorrelation would indicate that successive credit quality movements from one rating bucket to another are not statistically independent between adjoining periods. The impact of autocorrelation is relevant for market risk calculations as well. For instance, some markets tend to exhibit mean reversion (that is, a tendency for prices to return to some stable long-term level). Autocorrelation prevents us from directly translating daily volatilities to monthly or yearly volatilities in a simple way. Regrettably, the issue of time period interdependencies can also arise for credit quality migrations.[17] The issues surrounding transition matrices are discussed in more detail in Sections 3.5 to 3.8.

5.6.2 Different Approaches to Measuring VaR

5.6.2.1 Delta-Normal Method

Calculating VaR for a single position is relatively simple. However, questions arise as VaR must be measured for large portfolios with complex positions that evolve over time. The portfolio return can be written as:

$$R_{p,t+1} = \sum_{i=1}^{N} w_{i,t} \cdot R_{i,t+1} \tag{5.6}$$

where the weights $w_{i,t}$ are indexed by time to emphasize the dynamic nature of trading positions.

The delta-normal approach assumes that all asset returns are normally distributed. As the portfolio is a combination of the assumed normal distributed positions, the portfolio return is a linear combination of normal variables and thus also normally distributed. Using matrix notations, the variance of a portfolio can be written as:

$$V(R_{p,t+1}) = w_t^1 \cdot \sum_{i=1}^{N} w_{i,t} \cdot R_{i,t+1} \tag{5.7}$$

Written in this form, risk is generated by a combination of linear exposures to the factors that are assumed to be normally distributed and by the forecast of the covariance matrix $\sum_{t+1}$. This approach supposes a local approximation to price movements. The covariance can be generated by two methods. First, it can be measured solely based on historical data. The alternative approach is to apply risk measures from options to the measurement of the covariance matrix, or a combination of both methods.

The advantages of the delta-normal method are that:

- It can be applied to a large number of assets and is simple to implement.

- The assumption of normal distributed asset returns is true for a large number of frequently traded positions in a liquid market.

The criticisms of the delta-normal method are that:

- The option-implied measures of risk are superior to historical data, but are not available for every asset position.
- This approach accounts inadequately for event risk. The normal distribution based on historical data does not represent infrequent and extreme events by the structure of the probability distribution per se. This is a general and structural shortcoming of all methods relying on historical data.
- Fat tail distribution is a common problem in the measurement of the distribution of returns on most financial assets. As VaR attempts to measure the behavior of the portfolio return on the left tail, fat tails are particularly worrisome. In a model based on normal distributed returns but with fat tails in the position or portfolio return distribution, the normal approximation underestimates the proportion of outliers and thus the true value of risk.

The delta-normal approach reflects nonlinear exposures inadequately. Option positions are represented by their deltas to the underlying asset. With an at-the-money call, $\Delta = 0.5$ and a long position in the option is replaced by a 50 percent position in the underlying asset. Unfortunately, however, changes in the values of option positions depend on changes in underlying spot rates but also on the level of the spot rates. At-the-money options display high convexity, which generates unstable deltas. The linear approximation to nonlinear positions is valid for only a very narrow range of underlying spot prices.

5.6.2.2 Delta Versus Full Valuation

The assumption of normal distribution is particularly convenient because of the invariance property of normal distributed variables; thus portfolios of normal distributed variables are themselves normally distributed. As mentioned earlier, because portfolios are linear combinations of specific positions, the delta-normal approach is fundamentally linear.

Because utilizing the Black-Scholes formula can be computationally intensive, particularly when there is a large number of scenarios and securities, it is often desirable to use a simple approximation of the formula. The simplest such approximation is to estimate changes in the option value via a linear mode, which is commonly known as the *delta approximation.* In this case, the initial value V_0 and a price change from P_0 to P_1 results in:

$$V_1 = V_0 + \delta(P_1 - P_0) \tag{5.8}$$

where

$$\delta = \frac{\partial}{\partial R} V(P,S,\tau) \mid_{P_0} \tag{5.9}$$

The potential loss in value V is thus defined as:

$$\Delta V = \beta_0 \cdot \Delta S \tag{5.10}$$

where β_0 is the portfolio sensitivity to change in prices
V_0 is the current position
ΔS is the potential change in prices

The normality assumption allows the calculation of the portfolio beta as the (weighted) average of the individual betas. A fundamental advantage of this approach is that it requires the measurement of the portfolio only once at the current position V_0, which is directly linked to the current prices S_0. The delta-normal approach applies to portfolios that are exposed to many different risk factors, such as equity, interest and fx factors, as the computation is simple and straightforward. However, the delta-normal approach does not fit well with a portfolio with options because:

- The portfolio delta can change very fast (given high gamma parameters).
- The portfolio delta may be asymmetric for up and down moves.
- The worst loss may not be reflected for two extreme realizations of the spot rate of the underlying asset.

The latter problem is clarified by this example: a portfolio consists of a call and a put on the same underlying asset. The worst payoff possible (the sum of the premiums) will be realized if the underlying spot rate does not move. It is not enough to measure the portfolio at the two extremes. All intermediate values must be verified and measured as well.

The full valuation approach, in contrast to the delta-normal valuation, requires the computation of the values of the portfolio for different levels of prices:

$$\Delta V = V(S_1) - V(S_0) \tag{5.11}$$

Although this approach is theoretically more correct, it has the drawback of being quite computationally demanding. It requires marking to market the complete portfolio over a large number of realizations (prices) of underlying random variables (equity prices, interest rates, etc.). Full valuation must be performed to measure the risk option trading books exposed to a limited and well-known number of risk factors.

The difference between the results of linear and nonlinear exposures is illustrated in Figures 5-4 and 5-5. In both cases, the underlying market factor is assumed to follow a normal distribution. In Figure 5-4, the payoff is a linear function of the underlying price and is displayed in the upper left graph. The price of the underlying asset is normally distributed as shown in the upper right graph. As a result of the linear function, the profit itself is normally distributed, as shown at the bottom of the figure. The VaR of the P&L can be found from the exposure and the VaR for the underlying price. There is one-to-one mapping between the two VaR measures.

Figure 5-5 displays the profit function for an option, which is nonlinear. (See the case study of Barings in Section 6.5, where Nick Leeson used straddles and failed, and his market assumptions and the complexity of the instrument worked against him.) The resulting profit distribution is skewed to the left. The VaR of the portfolio and the underlying asset cannot be directly linked, as there is a nonlinear relation.

FIGURE 5-4

Distribution with Linear Exposures.

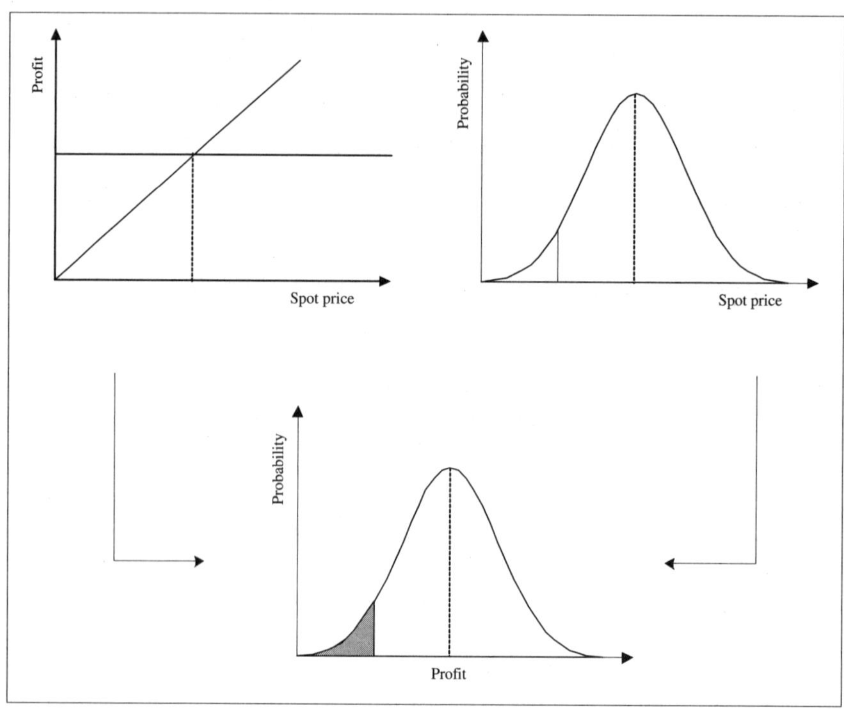

FIGURE 5-5

Distribution with Nonlinear Exposures.

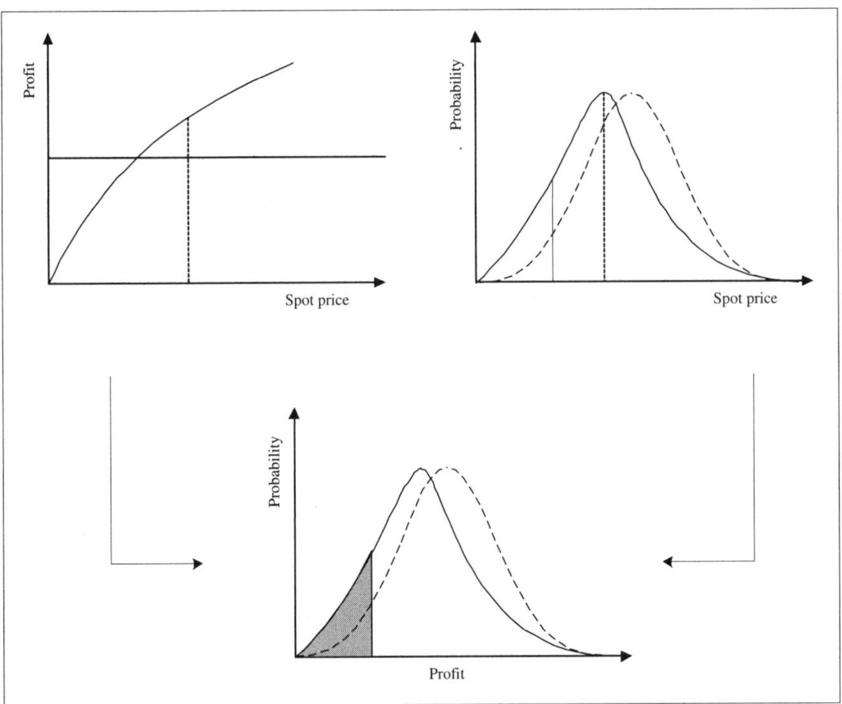

5.6.2.3 Delta-Gamma Method

The main drawback of the delta-normal method is that all risk parameters except the delta coefficient are lost. The elegance of the standardized application on different risk factors and among large portfolios is that it is given a simplification that strips away all nonlinear components. The Taylor expansion contains gamma and theta risks, which can be added to capture the nonlinear risk components (the expansion can also include vega risk to reflect exposures in volatility changes; however, this has been dropped in this example for simplicity).

$$V_1 = V_0 + \delta(P_1 - P_0) + \frac{1}{2}\Gamma(P_1 - P_0)^2 \tag{5.12}$$

and

$$V_1 = V_0 + \delta(P_1 - P_0) + \frac{1}{2}\Gamma(P_1 - P_0)^2 - \theta t \tag{5.13}$$

where t is the length of the forecast horizon and δ, Γ, and θ are net values for the total portfolio including options, which are all written on the same underlying instrument[18] and are defined by:

$$\Gamma = \frac{\partial^2}{\partial R^2} V(P,S,\tau) \mid_{P_0} \tag{5.14}$$

$$\theta = \frac{\partial}{\partial \tau} V(P,S,\tau) \mid_{\tau_0} \tag{5.15}$$

Figure 5-6 shows the delta, delta and gamma, and full valuation for an option. As can be seen, the delta-gamma-theta approximation almost perfectly duplicates the full valuation case.

Using a delta-normal approach, VaR is written as:

$$\text{VaR}_1 = \mid \delta \mid (\alpha \sigma S) \tag{5.16}$$

where α is a function of the selected confidence level.

FIGURE 5-6

Delta-Gamma-Theta Approximation versus Full and Delta Approximation.

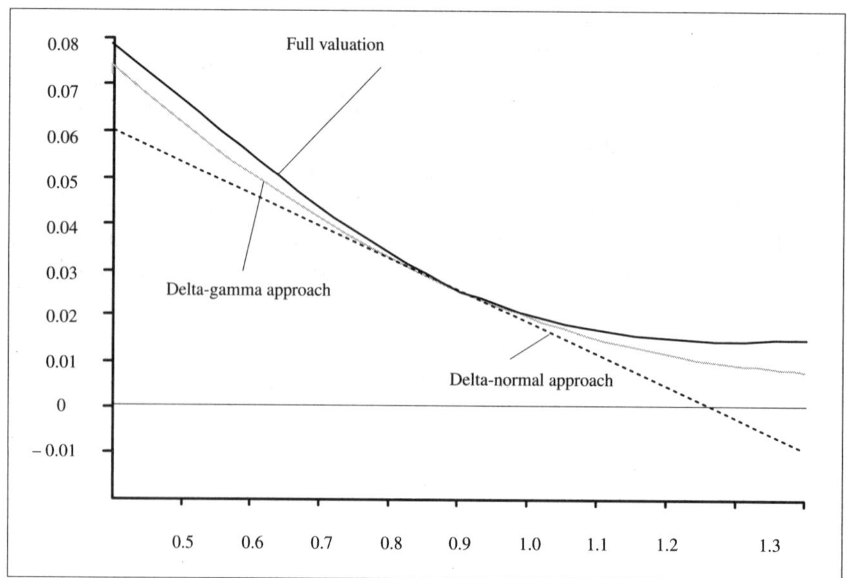

Using higher-order terms, VaR can be written as:

$$\text{VaR}_1 = |\delta|(\alpha\sigma S) - \frac{1}{2}\Gamma(\alpha\sigma S)^2 - |\theta|\ |Sd\sigma| \tag{5.17}$$

A negative Γ represents a net short position in options, which results in an add-on for the second term; otherwise the second term will decrease the total VaR. The third term θ represents an add-on to VaR due to exposures in changes in the time to maturity. Given a net long position with a negative θ, $d\sigma$ leads to a positive change (increase) in time at the α confidence level; otherwise, for a net short position with a positive θ, $d\sigma$ leads to a decreasing volatility at the α confidence level.

Moving away from linearity, the calculation of the distribution of changes in the portfolio value V becomes complex and cannot be directly linked to the VaR of the underlying position or portfolio.

The delta-gamma approach can be applied to many sources of risk. One approach to finding the portfolio VaR is the simulation of the movements in the market prices dS. Using a simulation technique, a large realization can be derived from the distribution

$$dS \approx N(0,\Sigma) \tag{5.18}$$

where Σ represents the covariance matrix of changes in prices.

The delta-gamma approach is unfortunately not very practical because, as it requires many sources of risk, the required amount of data increases geometrically. For example, for a portfolio with N = 100, 100 estimates are required of δ, 5050 estimates for the covariance matrix Σ, and an additional 5050 estimates for the matrix Γ, including the second derivatives of each position within the portfolio with respect to each source of risk. Thus, for such a portfolio, a full Monte Carlo simulation approach provides a more efficient and effective VaR measurement.

5.6.2.4 Comparison of Delta Versus Full Valuation

Each of the discussed methods is best adapted to a different application:

- The delta-normal approach fits best with large portfolios where optionality is not a dominant component.
- The delta-gamma approach fits best with portfolios with limited exposures to risk factors and with a dominant optionality component, as it provides superior precision with reasonable computational requirements.
- The full valuation or Monte Carlo simulation approaches fit best with portfolios with substantial components of optionality and exposures to several risk factors.

The discussion of the linear/nonlinear component has direct implications for the selection of the time horizon. With linear approaches, VaR can be easily adjusted to other periods by simply scaling a square root of time factor. These time horizon adjustments are based on the assumption that the position is constant and that all (daily) returns are independent and identically distributed. These time horizon adjustments are not applicable for positions with substantial components of optionality. As derivative instruments can be replicated by dynamically changing positions in the underlying assets, the risk of the derivative instruments can be dramatically different from the scaled measure of daily risk. Thus, time horizon adjustments of daily volatility to longer time horizons using the square root of the time scaling factor are valid only when positions are constant and when optionality in the portfolio is negligible. The full valuation or Monte Carlo simulation approach must be applied for portfolios or positions with substantial optionality components over the required time horizon, instead of scaling a daily VaR measure.

5.6.3 Historical Simulation Method

The historical simulation method can be viewed as a straightforward implementation of the full valuation method. By going back in time—say, for 250 days—and applying current weights to a time series of historical asset returns, the history of a hypothetical portfolio using the current position is generated.

$$R_{p,\tau} = \sum_{i=1}^{N} w_{i,t} \cdot R_{i,\tau} \qquad \tau = 1, \ldots, t \tag{5.19}$$

The weights w_t are kept at their current values, not the historical values. The full valuation requires a set of complete prices, such as yield curves. Hypothetical future prices for scenario τ are derived from applying historical price movements to the current level of prices:

$$P^*_{i,\tau} = P^*_{i,0} + \Delta P_{i,\tau} \qquad i = 1, \ldots, N \tag{5.20}$$

A new portfolio value $P^*_{p,\tau}$ is calculated from the full set of hypothetical prices, including nonlinear optionality components. In order to capture vega risks, the set of prices used can incorporate implied volatility measures to accommodate the option's price change relative to changes in volatility. This generates the hypothetical return corresponding to observation τ:

$$R_{p,\tau} = \frac{P^*_{p,\tau} - P_{p,0}}{P_{p,0}} \tag{5.21}$$

VaR is then calculated from the entire distribution of hypothetical returns. This method is relatively straightforward to implement if historical data has been collected over a certain time period. The choice of the length of the sample period reflects the trade-off between longer and shorter sample sizes. Longer time periods increase the accuracy of the estimates; in contrast, the estimate based on a shorter time frame might be irrelevant due to missing important changes in the underlying data caused by short-term structural changes.

This method considers the selection of time horizon for measuring VaR as the returns are calculated simply over intervals that correspond to the length of the VaR time horizon. For example, to calculate a monthly VaR, historical monthly portfolio returns are calculated over the last five years.

Being based on actual prices, this method is independent regarding nonlinearities and nonnormal distribution and thus captures gamma, vega risk, and correlations. The full valuation is based in its simplest form on historical data. The approach does not depend on assumptions and conditions about valuation models or the underlying stochastic structure of the instruments. It considers fat tails and is not prone to model risk.

However, the historical simulation method is subject to a number of criticisms. The most critical assumption of the historical simulation method is that the past foretells the future. Another issue is that risk contains significant and predictable time variation. The historical simulation approach tends to overestimate the meaningfulness of historical data for the future and to miss situations with temporarily elevated volatilities or structural changes.

The quality of VaR measures calculated with the historical simulation method is linked to the length of the historical period, with the same advantages and disadvantages discussed earlier. Another debated issue is the moving average estimation of variances. The historical simulation method allocates the same weight to all observations over the length of the time horizon. As the observation period can include data from structural changes, and short-term elevated volatilities, the measure of risk can change significantly after an old observation is excluded from the time window.

The last critical issue relates to large portfolios with complex instruments, which require extensive databases and computational power. A simplification used in practice is the bucketing approach, where cash flows are allocated into time bands, such as interest rate payoffs, dividends, etc. This increases the speed of computation and is accepted and adopted by the regulators. If the bucketing approach is used with too many simplifications, the benefits of full valuation can be lost due to lowered accuracy and precision of the VaR information received.

5.6.4 Stress Testing

Stress testing is completely different from historical or Monte Carlo simulation. Stress tests, sometimes called *scenario analyses,* are designed to estimate potential economic losses in abnormal markets to examine the effect on key financial variables on the portfolio. Historical analysis of markets shows that returns have fat tails, where extreme market moves (i.e., beyond 99 percent confidence) occur far more frequently than a normal distribution would suggest. Although risk management as a practice has improved considerably, events such as natural disasters, wars, and political coups still lie beyond statistical forecasting. For instance, a scenario where the yield curve moves up by 100 basis points over a month, or where a currency is suddently devalued by 20 percent, can be specified.

Regular stress testing is increasingly viewed as indispensable by risk managers and regulators. Stress tests should enhance transparency by exploring a range of potential low-probability events when VaR bands are dramatically exceeded. Stress testing combined with VaR gives a more comprehensive picture of risk. Such scenarios are well known within the traditional asset liability management (ALM) approach.

The usefulness of such an approach depends on whether such scenarios adequately represent typical market moves. Stress testing should answer two central questions:

1. How much is the loss if a stress scenario occurs, e.g., if the U.S. equity market crashes by 20 percent?
2. What event or risk factor could cause an institution to lose more than a predefined threshold amount, e.g., $1 million?

The first issue is commonly covered by a top-down approach for stress testing. Senior management or regulators want to be informed about how much the firm may lose in a major equity market crash. The second issue is usually raised in a bottom-up environment, such as at the book or business level. After scenarios are collected from individual risk takers, their potential losses can be measured and aggregated over the different exposures of the risk takers. For example, a stress scenario of depreciation of Euros vs. U.S. dollars might be ruled unimportant due to generally offsetting sensitivities (or nonmaterial reported sensitivities), while a scenario of widening credit spreads (e.g., lower ratings) could be identified as relevant. This approach could therefore be viewed as a bottom-up search for relevant stress scenarios.

5.6.4.1 How to Use Stress Tests

The key issue with stress tests is how to create and use them. To be meaningful, stress tests should tie back into the decision-making process. Corporate-level stress test results should be discussed in a regular forum by risk monitors, senior management, and risk takers. Just as for VaR limits, companies should have a set of stress loss limits categorized by risk type and risk-taking unit.

Stress testing should be performed at multiple levels of the micro, macro, and strategic risk pyramid at different frequencies. At a senior management level, stress results should guide the firm's appetite for aggregate risk taking and influence the internal capital allocation process. At the book level, stress tests may trigger discussions on how best to unwind or hedge a position.

5.6.4.2 Development of Stress Test Parameters

The goal of stress testing is to uncover potential concentration risks and make them more transparent. Good stress tests should therefore:

- *Be relevant to current exposures.* A concentrated portfolio with large risks may incur substantial losses from relatively small movements in certain risk factors.
- *Consider changes in all relevant risk factors.* Stress scenarios should consider all potential changes in a complete set of risk factors. A stress scenario in isolation does not reflect reality, as risk factors don't move in isolation (especially when they are extreme).
- *Examine potential structural changes.* A key question in developing a stress scenario is whether current risk parameters will hold or break down under extreme conditions. It is key to know if observed correlations hold or increase, or to what extent a structural change (i.e., decoupling of risk factors) could occur. For example, during large equity shocks (e.g., the 1987 crash and the 1997 and 1998 sell-offs), a flight to safety often results in a reversal of the normally highly positive correlation between stocks and government bonds: as stocks plummet, bonds rise because investors move into safer and more liquid assets. In the market turmoil of September 1998, LTCM experienced this problem when credit spreads widened and interest rates fell due to a flight to safety.
- *Consider market illiquidity.* Stressed markets are often characterized by material loss of liquidity. Liquidity can be viewed from two perspectives: the ability to trade positions without moving the prices and the ability to fund positions. For example, Brazilian bond traders reported that bid-ask spreads were so wide during the October 1997 liquidity crisis that it was unclear whether the local yield curve was upward or downward sloping. As prices in the marketplace cease to exist, it becomes impossible to mark positions to market. The threat of liquidity risk motivated the recapitalization of LTCM by a consortium of

14 commercial and investment banks in September 1998. In a statement to the U.S. House of Representatives, Federal Reserve Chairman Alan Greenspan stated that "the consequences of a fire sale triggered by cross-default clauses, should LTCM fail on some of its obligations, risked a severe drying up of market liquidity.[19]

- *Consider the interplay of market and credit risk.* Stressed markets often give rise to counterparty exposures that may be much more significant than pure market impacts. While market rates and creditworthiness are unrelated for small market moves, large market movements could precipitate credit events, and vice versa. A market-neutral risk arbitrage book would consist of a series of long and short positions, which hedges out market risk but is exposed to firm-specific risk. A trading strategy that eliminates broad market risk (equity, interest rates, foreign exchanges, or commodities) leaves only residual risk. For example, a hedge fund manager can hedge the market risk of a U.S. stock portfolio by shorting S&P 500 Index futures, leaving only firm-specific residual risk.

5.6.4.3 Forecasting Time Frame

The forecast time horizon for the stress scenario should reflect the institution's typical holding period. Banks, brokers, and hedge funds tend to look at one-day to one-week worst-case forecasts, while longer-term investors, such as mutual and pension funds, may view a one-month to three-month time frame as adequate. Corporations may use up to an annual horizon for strategic scenario analysis.

Steps for Stress Testing

There are three basic steps for stress testing:

1. *Generate scenarios.* The most challenging aspect of stress testing is generating credible worst-case forecasts that are relevant to portfolio positions. Scenarios should address both the magnitude of movement of individual market variables and the interrelationship of variables (i.e., correlation or causality).
2. *Revaluate the portfolio/positions.* Revaluing a portfolio or position involves marking to market all financial instruments under new worst-case market rates. Stress test results are generally changes in present value, not VaR.
3. *Aggregate results.* The results have to be aggregated to show expected levels of mark-to-market losses or gains for each stress scenario and in which entity the losses or gains are concentrated.

Creating Stress Scenarios

There are a variety of approaches to generating stress tests, such as:

- The predictive scenario generation, in which a subset of stressed risk factors is used with historical volatilities or correlations to predict the moves of all other market variables.
- A natural approach, in which scenarios are based on historical periods with extreme market conditions (see Table 5-10). Some infamous events include the 1987 U.S. stock market crash, the Exchange Rate Mechanism (ERM) crisis, the Fed rate hike in 1994, the 1995 Tequila crisis, the 1997 Asian crisis, the volatile markets in 1998, and the 1999 Brazil devaluation. In this approach, data is captured from relevant historical stress periods and a portfolio is valued with historical simulation to measure potential losses. RiskMetrics research has assembled a representative global model portfolio consisting of 60 percent equities and 40 percent fixed-income instruments to identify pertinent time periods for historical stress tests. Both one-day and five-day portfolio returns were used to identify extreme loss periods.

How does the severity of loss depend on global volatility? Figure 5-7 shows the volatility of the Nasdaq index for a period that includes three of the historical scenario dates. Obvious patterns can be seen during the time of the Gulf War, the Asian crisis, and the TMT crisis in March/April 2000.

TABLE 5-10

Major Loss Events of the Past 20 Years

	Date	One-Day Return (%)	Date	Five-Day Return (%)
Black Monday	10/19/87	–2.20	10/20/87	–5.9
Gulf War	8/3/90	–0.90	8/27/98	–3.8
Mexican peso fallout*	1/23/95	–1.00	1/23/95	–2.7
Asian crisis	10/27/97	–1.90	8/7/90	–3.6
Russian currency devaluations	8/27/98	–3.80	10/27/97	–2.6

SOURCE: RiskMetrics Group, *Risk Management: A Practical Guide,* New York: RiskMetrics Group, 1999, p. 28, reproduction with permission of RiskMetrics Group, Inc.

*The Mexican peso was actually devalued at the end of 1994. On January 23, 1995, the peso lost 6 percent and several Eastern European markets incurred losses of around 5 to 10 percent.

FIGURE 5-7

Nasdaq Index Returns from July 1989 to July 2001. *Data source:* Bloomberg Professional.

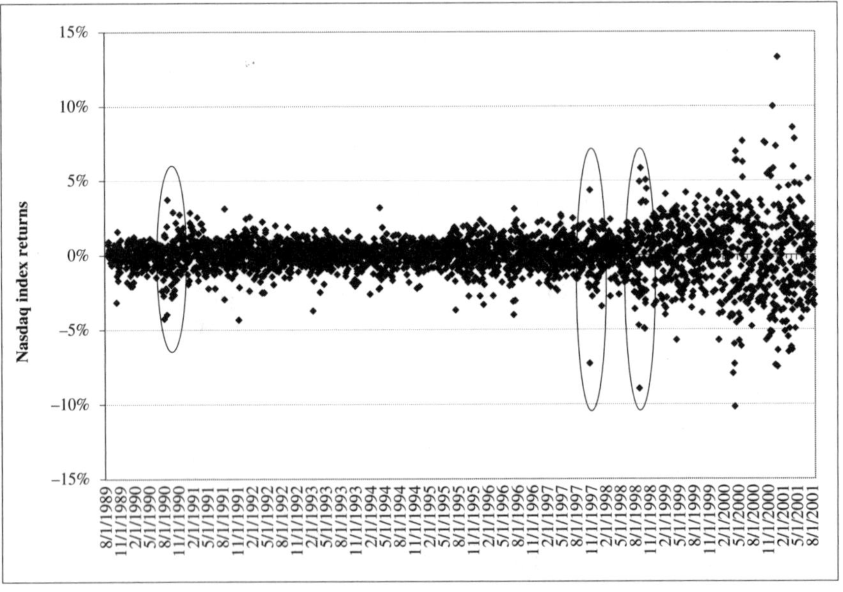

5.6.4.4 Evolution of Shocks from Volatility

The severity of portfolio losses appears to be related to the level of volatility in the world. For example, the Mexican peso fallout, which occurred during a period of relative market calm when the RiskMetrics Volatility Index (RMVI) was at an average level of approximately 100, only resulted in a one-day return of –1 percent, while the Asian crisis and Russian devaluation, which occurred while the RMVI was significantly above 100, resulted in more severe portfolio losses of 1.9 percent and 3.8 percent (see Figure 5-8). This suggests that it make no sense to run the same static stress tests in all market regimes—more volatile markets require more severe stress tests. To make stress scenarios more responsive to market conditions, the RMVI can be used as a dynamic scaling factor for stress scenarios. The RMVI is a benchmark portfolio that measures global volatility and is composed of equity, fixed income, and foreign exchange markets in 28 countries, as well as three major commodity markets. Observing the daily returns of these 87 markets, RiskMetrics calculates a total volatility across all countries and asset classes and compares it to a historical average. For more information, see Christopher Finger, *RMG Volatility Index: Technical Document*, New York: RiskMetrics Group, 1998.

FIGURE 5-8

Riskmetrics RMVI Methodology Applied to the Mexican Peso and U.S. Dollar from December 1995 to March 1999. (*Source: RiskMetrics Group,* Risk Management: A Practical Guide, *New York: RiskMetrics Group, 1999, 28. Copyright © 1999 by RiskMetrics Group, all rights reserved. Reproduction with permission of RiskMetrics Group, LLC.*)

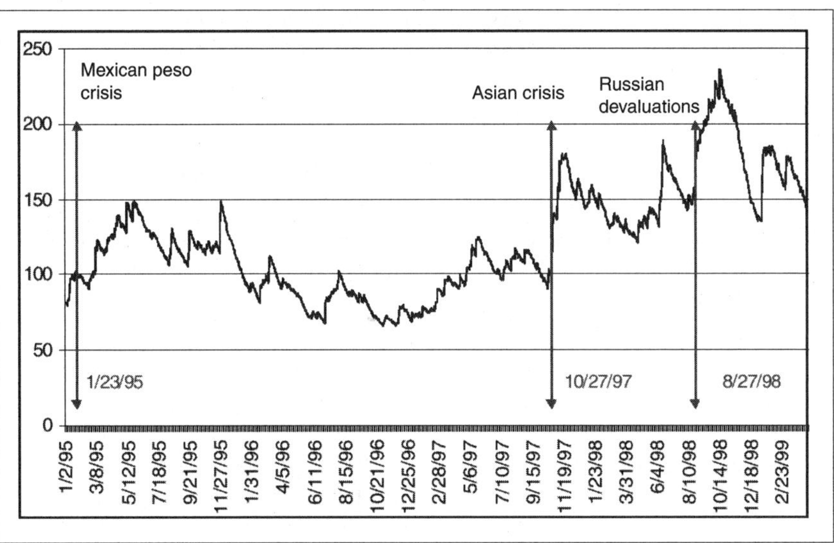

5.6.4.5 Applying Shocks to Market Factors or Correlations

A second approach to generating stress tests is to apply large shocks to either market factors or volatilities and correlations. This method can provide a good measure of the sensitivity to risk factors and can therefore be useful in identifying trouble spots in a portfolio.

It is straightforward to alter a market rate (e.g., to lower the S&P 500 by 10 percent) or many market rates (e.g., to lower all points on the U.S. government yield curve by 50 basis points), but the real challenge is to determine which market rates to shock and by how much. In general, these decisions will be based on historical moves, intuition, and the characteristics of the portfolio itself.

5.6.4.6 Applying Shocks to Volatilities and Correlations

VaR estimates can be stressed by applying shocks to volatilities or correlations. While volatilities can be adjusted up and down like market rates, special care must be taken with correlation matrices because nonsensical correlation structures can often be created from the interrelationship between factors. These correlation structures can, in turn, result in nonsensical (imaginary) VaRs.

For example, consider a three-party government. If party A and party B always vote on opposite sides of every issue (correlation of –1), it is impossible for party C to be positively correlated with both A and B. RiskMetrics has published a methodology to adjust correlations in a mathematically consistent fashion. The general idea is to mix an average correlation term into a prespecified group of assets and then to adjust all diagonal terms. This methodology is implemented in CreditManager, where it can be used to change the average correlation among industries and countries.

5.6.4.7 Anticipatory Scenarios

In generating an anticipatory scenario, a risk manager must determine the event of interest (e.g., flight to quality within Asian markets, stock market crash), the severity of the event (e.g., from once a year to once a decade), and the effects of such an event on the global market. For the third determination, it is essential to move all market rates in a consistent fashion. For example, in a flight to quality, not only will government-corporate spreads widen, but equity prices will fall.

The next step in the stress test is to revalue the portfolio under this scenario and to analyze sensitivities and summarize the results.

5.6.4.8 Applying Portfolio-Specific Stress Tests

Another stress testing approach searches for stress scenarios by analyzing the vulnerabilities of the specific portfolio in question. One way to discern the vulnerabilities is by conducting a historical or Monte Carlo simulation on a portfolio and searching for all scenarios that could cause a loss exceeding a defined threshold amount. Instead of specifying the scenario and calculating potential losses, as in the three approaches described previously, we specify what constitutes a severe loss and search for scenarios.

5.6.5 Summary of Stress Tests

Most models make assumptions that don't hold up in abnormal markets. Stress tests are therefore essential for a comprehensive risk picture and should be an integral component of risk analysis and communication.

As with VaR analysis, stress testing must be done at different levels of the organization. The organizational hierarchy for stress testing is even more important than for VaR reporting. At the desk level, traders are interested in stressing individual positions and specific risk factors. On a corporate level, senior management is concerned about macro stress scenarios that could pose a threat to firmwide operations. The process of generating and discussing stress scenarios is a collective exercise in risk analysis. Stress tests are an opportunity to consider scenarios that most view as unlikely, but that are possible. Make stress tests workable, realistic, and timely. Rather than stress-testing everything, focus on relevant position-specific stresses. It is important for stress tests to tie into the decision-making process: stress test results should guide corporate risk appetite decisions, impact limits, and be a judgmental factor in capital allocation.

Stress testing can be viewed from two perspectives: what would be the potential losses if certain events occurred, or what stress events could lead to losses of a certain magnitude? There are four major approaches for generating stress scenarios. The first uses historical scenarios and the second shocks market rates to examine portfolio sensitivities and concentrations. The third approach considers hypothetical future scenarios based on current market conditions. The fourth approach searches for stress scenarios by analyzing portfolio vulnerabilities.

5.7 PORTFOLIO RISK

As discussed earlier, portfolio risk is not new to the investment industry. Traders and merchants realized early that diversification reduces the risk of loss. In 1959, Harry Markowitz developed an analytical framework for portfolio analysis and looking at return and risk. The concept of portfolio risk is not new. In order to gain better insight, the following sections focus on the concept of VaR in the portfolio context. VaR is applied systematically to many sources of risk in the investment industry. We will mainly apply a delta-normal approach, as this approach is a direct extension of traditional portfolio risk analysis and is based on variances and covariances, well known from Markowitz and others.

VaR measures portfolio risk and, through decomposition in incremental VaR components, enables identification of the asset contributing the most to the overall portfolio risk. A drawback of the linear VaR models (based on the delta-normal approach) is that the size of the covariance matrix increases geometrically with the number of assets. Alternative approaches to reduce the size of the covariance matrix involve using diagonal and factor models.

5.7.1 Portfolio VaR

A portfolio p can be characterized by positions on a certain number of risk factors. Once the structure of the decomposition is defined, the portfolio return is a linear combination of the returns on underlying assets, where the weights w_i are given by the relative dollar amounts invested at the beginning of the period. Therefore, the VaR of a portfolio can be reconstructed from a combination of the risks of underlying securities.

The portfolio's return from t to $t + 1$ is defined as:

$$r_{p,t+1} = \sum_{i=1}^{N} w_{i,t} \cdot r_{i,t+1} \tag{5.22}$$

where the weights $w_{i,t}$ are measured at the beginning of the observation period and sum to unity of 1 (100 percent). In matrix notation, the same portfolio return can be defined as:

$$r_p = [w_1, w_2, \ldots, w_N] \begin{bmatrix} r_1 \\ r_2 \\ \vdots \\ r_N \end{bmatrix} = w'r \tag{5.23}$$

where w' represents the transposed vector (i.e., horizontal) of weights and r is the vertical vector containing individual asset returns $(r_1, r_2, \ldots, r_N)$.

The expected value $E(X)$ or the mean can be estimated as the weighted sum of all possible values, each weighted by its probability of occurence:

$$E(X) = \sum_{i-1}^{N} p_i \cdot x_i \tag{5.24}$$

By extension of Equation (5.24), the portfolio's expected return is defined as:

$$E(r_p) = \mu_p = \sum_{i-1}^{N} w_i \cdot \mu_i$$

and the portfolio's variance is:

$$\begin{aligned} \sigma_p^2 &= \sum_{i=1}^{N} w_1{}^2\sigma_1{}^2 + \sum_{i=1}^{N}\sum_{j=1}^{N} w_i w_j \sigma_{ij} \\ &= \sum_{i=1}^{N} w_1{}^2\sigma_1{}^2 + 2\sum_{i=1}^{N}\sum_{j<1}^{N} w_i w_j \sigma_{ij} \end{aligned} \tag{5.25}$$

The variance includes the risk of the individual positions and all the cross-products, reflected in $N(N-1)/2$ different covariances.

With an increasing number of assets, it becomes difficult to generate and manage all the different covariances on an equation basis. In matrix notation, the variance is written as:

$$\sigma_p^2 = [w_1, w_2, \ldots, w_N] \begin{bmatrix} \sigma_{1,1} & \sigma_{1,2} & \sigma_{1,3} & \cdots & \sigma_{1,N} \\ \vdots & & & & \vdots \\ \sigma_{N,1} & \sigma_{N,1} & \sigma_{N,1} & \cdots & \sigma_{N,N} \end{bmatrix} \begin{bmatrix} w_1 \\ w_2 \\ \\ w_N \end{bmatrix} \tag{5.26}$$

Defining cov as the covariance matrix, the portfolio variance can be written more compactly as:

$$\sigma_p^2 = w' \text{ cov } w \tag{5.27}$$

Using a normal distribution, the VaR measure is then $\alpha\sigma_p$ times the initial investment. Lower portfolio risk can be achieved through low correlations or a large number of assets. To see the effect of N, assume that all assets have the same risk, that all correlations are the same, and that equal weight is put on each asset. Figure 5-9 shows how portfolio risk decreases with the number of assets.

Start with the risk of one security, which is assumed to be 12 percent. When p is equal to 0, the risk of a 10-asset portfolio drops to 3.8 percent; increasing N to 100 drops the risk even further to 1.2 percent. Risk tends asymptotically to 0. More generally, portfolio risk is:

$$\sigma_p = \sqrt{\sigma \frac{1}{N} + \left(1 - \frac{1}{N}\right)\rho} \tag{5.28}$$

So, when $p = 0.5$, risk decreases rapidly from 12 percent to 8.9 percent as N goes to 10, but then converges much more slowly toward its minimum value of 8.5 percent. Correlations are essential in lowering portfolio risk.

FIGURE 5-9

Number of Securities in Portfolio and Impact on Correlation (Diversification).

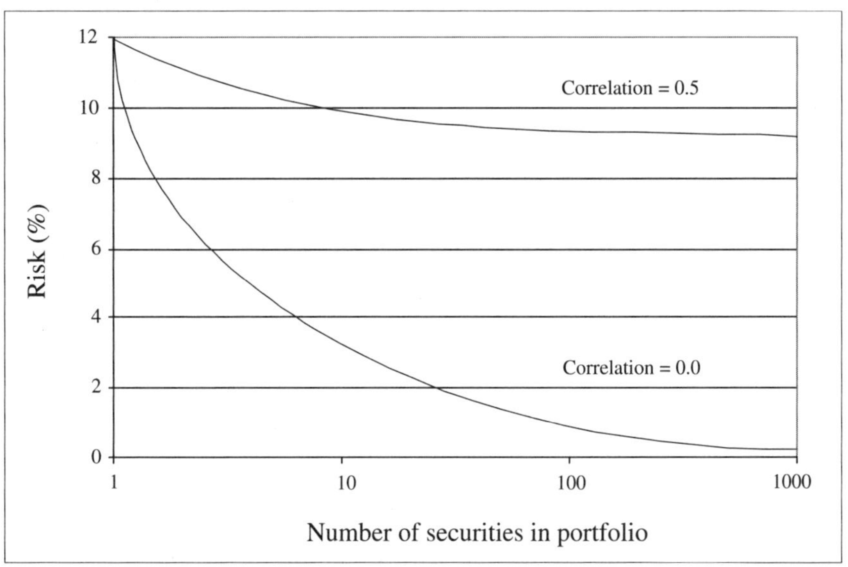

Covariances can be estimated from sample data as:

$$\hat{\sigma}_{ij} = \frac{1}{T-1}\sum_{t=1}^{T}(x_{t,i} - \hat{\mu}_i)(x_{t,j} - \hat{\mu}_i) \tag{5.29}$$

The covariance is a measure of the extent to which two variables move linearly together. If two variables are independent, their covariance is equal to 0. A positive covariance means that the two variables tend to move in the same direction; a negative covariance means that they tend to move in opposite directions.

The magnitude of covariance, however, depends on the variances of the individual components and is not easily interpreted. The correlation coefficient is a more convenient, scale-free measure of linear dependence:

$$\rho_{12} = \frac{\sigma_{1,2}}{\sigma_1\sigma_2} \tag{5.30}$$

The correlation coefficient ρ always lies between −1 and +1. When ρ is equal to unity, the two variables are said to be perfectly correlated. When ρ is 0, the variables are uncorrelated.

Correlations help to diversify portfolio risk. With two assets, the diversified portfolio variance is:

$$\sigma_p^2 = w_1{}^2\sigma_1^2 + w_2^2\sigma_2^2 + 2w_1w_2\sigma_1\rho_{1,2}\sigma_2 \tag{5.31}$$

The portfolio risk must be lower than individual risk. When the correlation is exactly unity, Equation (5.31) reduces the variance of the portfolio to the weighted variance of the underlying positions, since the portfolio weights sum to unity. Generally, the undiversified VaR is the sum of individual VaR measures. Diversification into perfectly correlated assets does not pay.

So far, nothing has been said about the distribution of the portfolio return. Ultimately, we would like to translate the portfolio variance into a VaR measure. To do so, we need to know the distribution of the portfolio return. In the delta-normal model, all individual security returns are assumed to be normally distributed. This is particularly convenient since the portfolio, a linear combination of normal random variables, is then also normally distributed. At a given confidence level, the portfolio VaR is value at risk = $\alpha\sigma_p$.

5.7.2 Incremental VaR

An important aspect of calculating VaR is to understand which asset, or combination of assets, contributes most to risk. Armed with this information, users can alter positions to modify their VaR most efficiently.

For this purpose, individual VaRs are not sufficient. Volatility measures the uncertainty in the return of an asset taken in isolation. When this asset belongs to a portfolio, however, what matters is the contribution to portfolio risk.

Suppose now that an existing portfolio is made up of N-1 securities, numbered as $j = 1, \ldots, N-1$. A new portfolio is obtained by adding one security, called i. The marginal contribution to risk from security i is measured by differentiating Equation (5.25) with respect to w_i.

$$\frac{\partial \sigma_p^2}{\partial w_i} = 2w_i\sigma_i^2 + 2\sum_{j=1, j\neq i}^{N} w_j\sigma_{i,j}$$

$$= 2\,\mathrm{cov}\left(r_i, w_i r_i + \sum_{j\neq i}^{N} w_j r_j\right) = 2\,\mathrm{cov}\,(r_i, r_j) \qquad (5.32)$$

We note that $\partial\sigma_p^2/\partial w_i = 2\sigma_p \partial\sigma_p/\partial w_i$. The sensitivity of the relative change in portfolio volatility to a change in the weight is then:

$$\frac{\partial \sigma_p}{\sigma_p \partial w_i} = \frac{\mathrm{cov}\,(r_i, r_j)}{\sigma_p^2} = \beta_i \qquad (5.33)$$

Therefore, β measures the contribution of one security to total portfolio risk. This is also called the systematic risk of security i vis-à-vis portfolio p. Using matrix notation, β is:

$$\beta = \frac{\mathrm{cov}\ w}{w'\ \mathrm{cov}\ w} \qquad (5.34)$$

Beta risk is the basis for the capital asset pricing model (CAPM), developed by Sharpe (1964). According to the CAPM, well-diversified investors want to be compensated for the systematic risk of securities only. In other words, the risk premium on all assets should depend on beta only. Whether this is an appropriate description of capital markets has been the subject of much of finance research over the last 20 years. Even though this proposition is much debated, the fact remains that systematic risk is a useful statistical measure of portfolio risk.

The measure of β is particularly useful for decomposing a portfolio's VaR into sources of risk. We can expand the portfolio variance into:

$$\sigma_p^2 = w_1\left(w_1{\sigma_1}^2 + \sum_{j=1, j\neq 1}^{N} w_i\sigma_{1,j}\right)$$

$$+ w_2\left(w_2{\sigma_2}^2 + \sum_{j=1, j\neq 2}^{N} w_i\sigma_{2,j}\right)$$

$$+ \cdots \qquad (5.35)$$

This is also:

$$\sigma_p^2 = w_1 \operatorname{cov}(r_1, r_p) + w_2 \operatorname{cov}(r_2, r_p) + \cdots$$
$$= w_1(\beta_1\sigma_p^2) + w_2(\beta_2\sigma_p^2) + \cdots$$
$$= \sigma_p^2\left(\sum_{i=1}^{N} w_i\beta_i\right) \tag{5.36}$$

which shows that the portfolio variance can be decomposed into a sum of components each due to asset *i*. Using a similar decomposition, VaR is then:

$$\text{VaR} = \text{VaR}\left(\sum_{i=1}^{N} w_i\beta_i\right) = \text{VaR}_1 + \text{VaR}_2 + \cdots \tag{5.37}$$

Here we have decomposed the total VaR into incremental measures. This provides vital information, as risk should be viewed in relation to the total portfolio and not in isolation.

5.7.3 Alternative Covariance Matrix Approaches

So far, we have shown that correlations are essential driving forces behind portfolio risk. When the number of assets is large, however, the measurement of the covariance matrix becomes increasingly difficult. With 10 assets, for instance, we need to estimate $10 \times 11/2 = 55$ different variance and covariance terms. With 100 assets, this number climbs to 5500. The number of correlations increases geometrically with the number of assets. For large portfolios, this causes real problems: the portfolio VaR may not be positive, and correlations may be imprecisely estimated.

The following sections discuss the extent to which such problems can affect VaR measures and propose some solutions. For many users, however, such problems may not be relevant because they have no control over the measurement of inputs. Until such users encounter zero VaR measures, these sections can be safely skipped.

5.7.3.1 Zero VaR Measures

The VaR measure derives from the portfolio variance, expressed as:

$$\sigma_p^2 = w' \operatorname{cov} w \tag{5.38}$$

In order to generate statistically useful measures, the cov has to be positive definite. This is not always the case. The status of the cov can be verified under two conditions:

1. The number of historical observations T must be greater than the number of assets N.
2. The return time series cannot be linearly correlated.

The first condition states that if a portfolio consists of 100 assets, there must be at least 100 historical observations to ensure that whatever portfolio is selected, the portfolio variance will be positive. The second condition rules out cases where an asset can be replicated exactly through a linear combination of other assets.

An example of a non-positive-definite matrix is obtained when two assets are identical (thus $\rho = 1$). In this situation, a portfolio consisting of \$1 on the first asset and –\$1 on the second will have exactly zero risk.

In practice, this problem is more likely to occur with a large number of assets that are highly correlated (such as currencies fixed to each other, zero coupon bonds, or ADRs and the original foreign stock). In addition, positions must be precisely matched with assets to yield zero risk. This is most likely to occur if the weights have been optimized on the basis of the covariance matrix itself. Such optimization is particularly dangerous because it can create positions that are very large, yet that apparently offset each other with little total risk.

If users notice that VaR measures appear abnormally low in relation to positions, they should check whether small changes in correlations lead to large changes in their VaRs.

5.7.3.2 Diagonal Model

A related problem is that as the number of assets increases, it is more likely that some correlations will be erroneously measured. Some models can help to simplify this process by providing a simpler structure for the covariance matrix. One such model is the diagonal model, originally proposed by Sharpe in the context of stock portfolios. This model is often referred to as the CAPM, which is not correct. The diagonal (one-factor) model is only a simplification of the covariance matrix and says nothing about the nature of expected returns, whose description through the relationship to the market factor is the essence of the CAPM.

The assumption is that the common movement in all assets is due to one common factor only, the market. Formally, the model is:

$$\begin{gathered} r_i = \alpha_i + \beta_i r_m + \varepsilon_i \qquad E(\varepsilon_i) = 0 \qquad E(\varepsilon_i r_m) = 0 \\ E(\varepsilon_i, \varepsilon_j) = 0 \quad E(\varepsilon_i^2) = \sigma_{\varepsilon,i}^2 \end{gathered} \tag{5.39}$$

The return on asset i is driven by the market return R and an idiosyncratic term ε_i, which is not correlated with the market or across assets. As a result, the variance can be broken down as:

$$\sigma_i^2 = \beta_i^2 \sigma_m^2 + \sigma_{\varepsilon,i}^2 \tag{5.40}$$

The covariance between two assets is:

$$\sigma_i^2 = \beta_i \beta_j \sigma_m^2 \tag{5.41}$$

which is solely due to the common factor. The full covariance matrix is:

$$\text{Cov} = \begin{bmatrix} \beta_1 \\ \vdots \\ \beta_N \end{bmatrix} [\beta_1 \ \dots \ \beta_N] \sigma_m^2 \begin{bmatrix} \sigma_{\varepsilon,i}^2 & \dots & 0 \\ \vdots & & \vdots \\ 0 & \dots & \sigma_{\varepsilon,N}^2 \end{bmatrix} \tag{5.42}$$

Written in matrix notation, the covariance matrix is:

$$\text{Cov} = \beta\beta'\sigma_m^2 + D_\varepsilon \tag{5.43}$$

As the matrix D is diagonal, the number of parameters is reduced from $N \times (N + 1)/2$ to $2N + 1(N$ for the betas, N in D and one for $0 - m)$. With 100 assets, for instance, the number is reduced from 5500 to 201, a considerable improvement regarding equation complexity and calculation time. Furthermore, the variance of large, well-diversified portfolios is simplified even further, reflecting only exposure to the common factor. The variance of the portfolio is:

$$\text{VaR}(r_p) = \text{VaR}(w'r) = w' \text{ cov } w = (w'\beta\beta'w)\sigma_m^2 + w'D_\varepsilon w \tag{5.44}$$

The second term consists of

$$\sum_{i=1}^{N} w_i^2 \sigma_{\varepsilon,i}^2$$

But this term becomes very small as the number of securities in the portfolio increases. For instance, if all the residual variances are identical and have equal weights, this second term is

$$\left[\sum_{i=1}^{N} (1/N)^2\right] \sigma_{\varepsilon,i}^2$$

which converges to 0 as N increases. Therefore, the variance of the portfolio converges to:

$$\text{VaR}(r_p) \rightarrow (w'\beta\beta'w)\sigma_m^2 \tag{5.45}$$

which depends on one factor only. This approximation is particularly useful when assessing the VaR of a portfolio consisting of many stocks. It has been adopted by the Basel Committee to reflect the market risk of well-diversified portfolios.

The actual correlations are all positive, as are those under the diagonal model. Although the diagonal model matrix resembles the original covariance matrix, the approximation is not perfect. The diagonal model measures risk in relation to the market, and thus the correlation is driven by exposure to the market and is different (usually lower) than the true correlation. This is because the market is the only source of common variation. Whether this model produces acceptable approximations depends on the purpose at hand. Despite the drawback of limitation in the explanatory power of the model given only one source of common variation, there is no question that the diagonal model provides a considerable simplification.

5.7.3.3 Factor Models

If a one-factor model is not sufficient, better precision and more statistical stability can be obtained with multiple-factor models. Equation (5.46) can be generalized to K factors:

$$r_i = \alpha_i + \beta_{i,1} r_i + \ldots + \beta_{i,k} r_k + \varepsilon_i \tag{5.46}$$

where $r_1, \ldots, r_k$ are factors independent of each other. In the previous three-stock example, the covariance matrix model can be improved with a second factor, such as the performance of the transportation industry, that would pick up the higher correlation between two stocks. With multiple factors, the covariance matrix acquires a richer structure:

$$\text{Cov} = \beta_1 \beta_1' \sigma_1^2 + \ldots + \beta_k \beta_k' \sigma_k^2 + D_\varepsilon \tag{5.47}$$

The total number of parameters is $(K + N \times K + N)$, which may still be considerably less than for the full model. With 100 assets and five factors, for instance, the number is reduced from 5500 to 605, which is no minor decrease.

Factor models are also important because they can help us decide on the number of VaR building blocks for each market. Consider, for instance, a government bond market that displays a continuum of maturities ranging from one day to 30 years. The question is, how many VaR building blocks do we need to represent this market adequately?

To illustrate, consider an equity market—say, the Swiss equity market—and calculate the principal components for the returns of the securities of the Swiss Mark Index (SMI). The next step is to regress in an orthogonal space the principal components against the factors, which can best explain the principal components (variation of returns). The principal components are by construction orthogonal. The factors contain multicolinearity, and, through an additional condition during the Lagrange optimization—introduction of unit vectors with components summing to 1—a series of vectors can be estimated that provide the best explanation of diagonal terms (the common factors, e.g., the market) and are orthogonal to each other. The results are presented in Table 5-11. Principal component 1 can be best explained by the Euro Currency Swiss Franc 1 Month factor, explaining 42.28 percent of the principal component. With an R^2 of 15.03, the second principle component was acceptably explained by the EFFAS Switzerland Government Bond Index, but the result was already considerably weaker, as reflected in the corresponding statistics. The following factors do not fully help us understand the return variation. However, the overall impact of such a multifactor model is to help us understand more than we would using solely a diagonal model, as it breaks down the common factor into several multiple factors.

Table 5-12 illustrates the relationship between the principal components and the factors. The factor loadings of the factors to the principal com-

TABLE 5-11

Principal Component and Factor Combination

Principal component	Factor	Name	R_2	$C(p)$	F Value
1	ECSWF1M	Euro Currency Swiss Franc 1 Month	0.4228	1117.36	104.73
2	DEFSWAL	EFFAS Switzerland Government	0.1503	47.383	26.69
3	ECWGM7D	Euro Currency German Mark 7 Days	0.0353	–23.544	5.23
4	SAPCOMP	Standard & Poor's 500 Composite	0.0443	–10.774	6.63
5	ECWGM3M	Euro Currency German Mark 3 Months	0.06	3.5143	9.13
6	BDBRYLD	EFFAS Germany Benchmark Bond	0.0382	–37.938	5.67
7	DEFJPG5	EFFAS Japan Government over 5 Years	0.0598	–14.104	9.1
8	FTSE100	FTSE100 Index	0.0479	48.0762	7.19
9	DEFUSG5	EFFAS U.S. Government over 5 Years	0.0362	–27.495	5.73
10	DEFBDAL	EFFAS Germany Government	0.0758	4.0806	11.72

SOURCE: Reto R. Gallati, "Empirical Application of APT Multifactor-Models to the Swiss Equity Market," Basic Report, Zurich: Credit Suisse Investment Research, September 1993.

TABLE 5-12

Correlation of Principal Components to Factors from 08/08/1988 to 03/31/1993

	PRIN1	PRIN2	PRIN3	PRIN4	PRIN5	PRIN6	PRIN7	PRIN8	PRIN9	PRIN10
ECSWF1M	**–0.60**	0.11	0.09	0.06	0.01	–0.12	0.03	0.01	0.08	0.07
DEFSWAL	0.02	**0.35**	–0.16	0.02	–0.12	–0.05	–0.04	–0.09	0.24	0.09
ECWGM7D	–0.01	0.01	**–0.13**	0.08	0.07	–0.08	0.12	–0.02	0.01	0.03
SAPCOMP	0.02	–0.01	0.06	**–0.21**	0.07	–0.07	–0.03	–0.10	–0.02	–0.09
ECWGM3M	–0.02	–0.06	0.14	0.07	**–0.14**	0.05	0.02	0.08	–0.04	0.05
BDBRYLD	0.00	–0.04	0.01	0.10	–0.05	**–0.12**	–0.03	0.05	–0.10	–0.01
DEFJPG5	–0.01	0.04	0.02	0.09	0.01	–0.09	**0.21**	0.04	–0.03	–0.01
FTSE100	0.04	0.15	0.03	0.12	0.02	0.12	0.06	**–0.19**	0.05	–0.04
DEFUSG5	–0.02	–0.01	0.04	0.05	–0.08	0.08	0.14	–0.09	**–0.18**	–0.05
DEFBDAL	0.00	–0.01	–0.03	0.02	0.06	–0.05	0.06	–0.01	0.05	**–0.24**

SOURCE: Reto R. Gallati, "Empirical Application of APT Multifactor-Models to the Swiss Equity Market," Basic Report, Zurich: Credit Suisse Investment Research, September 1993.

TABLE 5-13

Risk Premiums for Multifactor Models after Burmeister/McElroy

Factors	Code	λ_j	σ_j	Skewness	*t* Distribution	Curtosis
Euro Currency Swiss Franc 1 Month	ECSWF1M	–0.00626	0.2082	–8.9527	2.3533	98.9352
EFFAS Switzerland Government	DEFSWAL	–0.00025	0.0035	–0.5999	–1.8494	23.9291
Euro Currency German Mark 7 Days	ECWGM7D	–0.00416	0.1436	–4.0971	–0.3405	64.578
Standard & Poor's 500 Composite	SAPCOMP	–0.0011	0.0075	–5.6272	–1.72	42.3718
Euro Currency German Mark 3 Months	ECWGM3M	–0.004559	0.0072	–10.0413	2.2423	112.749
EFFAS Germany Benchmark Bond	BDBRYLD	0.000719	0.0274	5.4124	0.308	56.2529
EFFAS Japan Government over 5 Years	DEFJPG5	–0.0002	0.0036	–5.1681	–0.6504	45.158
FTSE100 Index	FTSE100	0.00061	0.0225	0.3397	–2.1186	10.5209
EFFAS U.S. Government over 5 Years	DEFUSG5	0.000125	0.0034	0.004	0.4298	22.3211
EFFAS Germany Government	DEFBDAL	–0.00053	0.0063	–2.409	–0.9945	12.4523

SOURCE: Reto R. Gallati, "Empirical Application of APT Multifactor-Models to the Swiss Equity Market," Basic Report, Zurich: Credit Suisse Investment Research, September 1993.

TABLE 5-14

Correlations of SMI Securities on Excess Returns

	CSH	UBS	RUKP	WI	ZUR	ALU	CIG	CIGN	ROG	NES	NESN	SR	HOL
CSH	1.00												
UBS	0.72	1.00											
RUKP	0.56	0.59	1.00										
WI	0.55	0.59	0.72	1.00									
ZUR	0.55	0.63	0.74	0.82	1.00								
ALU	0.52	0.53	0.48	0.53	0.49	1.00							
CIG	0.45	0.52	0.59	0.62	0.64	0.63	1.00						
CIGN	0.43	0.46	0.40	0.40	0.41	0.61	0.69	1.00					
ROG	0.54	0.59	0.56	0.57	0.58	0.58	0.70	0.67	1.00				
NES	0.43	0.45	0.55	0.55	0.57	0.47	0.62	0.35	0.57	1.00			
NESN	0.31	0.34	0.06	0.14	0.12	0.31	0.12	0.48	0.36	0.05	1.00		
SR	0.36	0.50	0.37	0.44	0.41	0.40	0.50	0.43	0.51	0.38	0.30	1.00	
HOL	0.45	0.47	0.44	0.42	0.43	0.53	0.51	0.49	0.52	0.38	0.28	0.45	1.00

SOURCE: Reto R. Gallati, "Empirical Application of APT Multifactor-Models to the Swiss Equity Market," Basic Report, Zurich: Credit Suisse Investment Research, September 1993.

TABLE 5-15

Factor Loadings According to Multifactor Calculations for SMI, Compiled 02/14/1992

SMI TS	SMI Security	ECSWF1M	DEFSWAL	ECWGM3M	FTSE100	R^2	R^2 Adjusted
ALU	Alusuisse-Lonza BS	–1.85	0.63	–0.70	0.98	28.4%	26.9%
CIG	Ciba-Geigy BS	–1.97	0.46	–0.67	1.40	31.6%	30.2%
CIGN	Ciba-Geigy RS	–1.86	0.39	–0.83	1.01	29.0%	27.4%
CSH	CSHolding BS	–1.92	0.54	–0.58	0.73	34.4%	33.0%
HOL	Holderbank BS	–1.97	0.27	0.12	0.58	35.3%	33.9%
NES	Nestlé BS	–2.04	0.12	–0.31	0.72	36.9%	38.6%
NESN	Nestlé RS	–1.67	–0.0099	–0.68	0.71	26.8%	25.2%
ROG	Roche DRC	–1.97	0.42	–0.49	0.57	35.6%	34.2%
RUKP	Schweizer Rück PC	–2.00	0.54	–0.09	0.26	32.5%	31.1%
UBS	UBS BS	–1.96	0.48	–0.78	0.80	37.4%	36.1%
SR	Swissair BS	–1.82	0.42	0.68	1.48	28.7%	27.1%
WI	Winterthur BS	–1.96	0.74	0.12	0.45	33.2%	31.8%
ZUR	Zurich BS	–1.94	0.73	–0.36	0.31	33.5%	32.1%

SOURCE: Reto R. Gallati, "Empirical Application of APT Multifactor-Models to the Swiss Equity Market," Basic Report, Zurich: Credit Suisse Investment Research, September 1993.

ponents are highlighted with bold numbers. In this context, the sign is not relevant, but the absolute correlation is important. The factor sensitivity reflects the sign with a positive or a negative factor sensitivity (factor-beta β_i).

Table 5-13 shows the risk premiums associated with this specific multifactor model. The available test lambdas confirm the selection of five indices according to the risk premium from the two-stage least-squares procedure. On a basis of the results, the selected risk factors represent so-called priced factors, that is, factors that are rewarded with a risk premium because they significantly influence the return on Swiss equities at the corresponding level. From the test statistics of the principal component analysis, the risk premium, and other analysis, we can conclude that the following four factors are of sufficient significance for use in a multifactor APT model:

1. Euro Currency Swiss Franc 1 Month
2. EFFAS Switzerland Government
3. Euro Currency German Mark 3 Months
4. FTSE100 Index

Table 5-14 displays the correlations between the securities, highlighting the fact that for a small market like the Swiss equity market, the correlations between the securities can be small, offering good diversification but requiring different approaches in the return and risk evaluation, as the companies in the different sectors are exposed to different industry factors and different company-specific factors.

Table 5-15 provides a summary of the results and contains the betas of the securities to the defined factors as analyzed and evaluated in the previous statistical procedures.

This decomposition shows that the risk of an equity portfolio can be usefully summarized by its exposures to a limited number of factors. Different types of models exist, such as models that keep the factors constant and allow tracking the same factors over time. Other models estimate the factors on a regular basis and provide insight into the different factors as they change over time and keep the overall explanatory power high.

5.8 PITFALLS IN THE APPLICATION AND INTERPRETATION OF VAR

Although VaR provides a line of defense against financial risks, it is no panacea. Users must understand the limitations of VaR measures.

5.8.1 Event and Stability Risks

The main drawback of models based on historical data is that they assume that the recent past is a good projection of future randomness. Even if the data has been perfectly fitted, there is no guarantee that the future will not hide nasty surprises that did not occur in the past.

Surprises can take two forms: either one-time events (such as a devaluation or default) or structural changes (such as going from fixed to floating exchange rates). Situations where historical patterns change abruptly cause havoc with models based on historical data.

Stability risk can be addressed by stress testing (discussed in Section 5.6.4), which aims at addressing the effect of drastic changes on portfolio risk. To some extent, structural changes can also be captured by models that allow risk to change through time or by volatility forecasts contained in options. An example of structural change is the 1994 devaluation of the Mexican peso, which is further detailed in the following text.

In December 1994, the emerging market turned sour as Mexico devalued the peso by 40 percent. The devaluation was widely viewed as having been bungled by the government, and led to a collapsing Mexican stock market. Investors who had poured money into the developing economies of Latin America and Asia faced large losses as the Mexican devaluation led to a widespread decrease in emerging markets all over the world.

Figure 5-10 plots the peso-dollar exchange rate, which was fixed around 3.45 pesos for most of 1994 and then jumped to 5.64 by mid-December. Figure 5-11 shows the distribution of the peso-dollar exchange rates for the same time frame. Apparently, the devaluation was widely unanticipated, even with a ballooning current account deficit running at 10 percent of Mexico's GDP and a currency widely overvalued according to purchasing power parity.

This episode indicates that, especially when price controls are left in place for long periods, VaR models based on historical data cannot capture potential losses. These models must be augmented by an analysis of economic fundamentals and stress testing. Interestingly, shortly after the

FIGURE 5-10

Mexican Peso–U.S. Dollar Exchange Rate from 1993 to 1996. (*Data source:* Bloomberg Professional.)

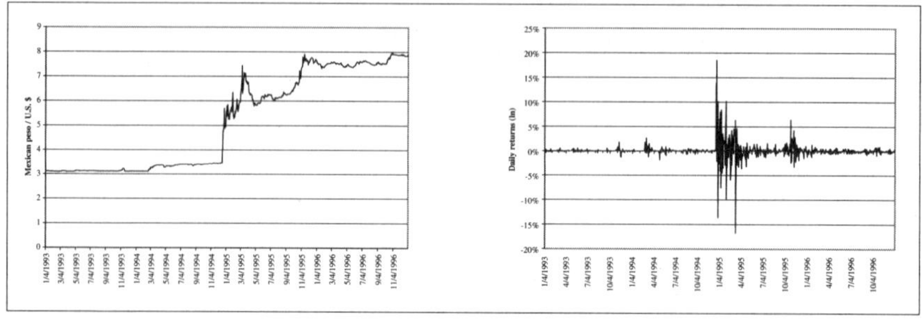

FIGURE 5-11

Distribution of Mexican Peso–U.S. Dollar Exchange Rates from 1993 to 1996, Including (left) and Excluding (right) the Week Before and After the Devaluation. (*Data source:* Bloomberg Professional.)

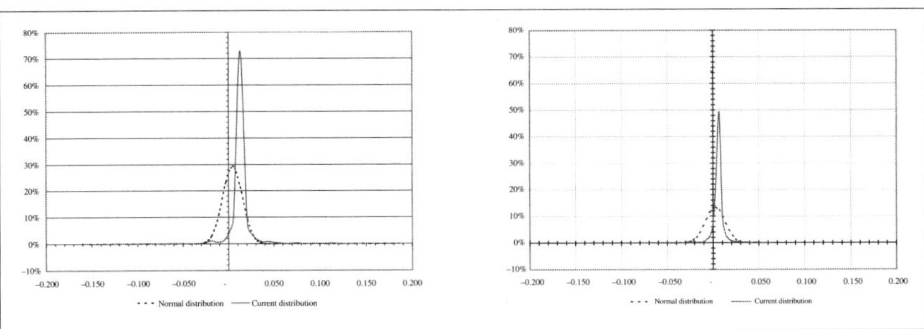

devaluation, the Mexican government authorized the creation of currency futures on the peso. It was argued that the existence of forward-looking prices for the peso would have provided market participants, as well as the central bank, with an indication of market pressures. In any event, this disaster was not blamed on derivatives.

5.8.2 Transition Risk

Whenever there is a major change, a potential exists for errors. This applies, for instance, to organizational changes, expansion into new markets or products, implementation of a new system, or new regulations. Since existing controls deal with existing risks, they may be less effective during a transition.

Transition risk is difficult to deal with because it cannot be explicitly modeled. The only safeguard is increased vigilance in times of transition.

5.8.3 Changing Holdings

A similar problem of instability occurs when trying to extrapolate daily risk to a longer horizon, which is of special concern to bank regulators. As we have seen in Secs. 3.6.2 and 3.7.5.2, the typical adjustment is by a square root of time factor, assuming constant positions. However, the adjustment ignores the fact that the trading position might very well change over time in response to changing market conditions. There is no simple way to assess the impact on the portfolio VaR, but it is likely that prudent risk management systems will decrease risk relative to conventional VaR measures. For instance, the enforcement of loss limits will gradually decrease exposure as losses accumulate. This dynamic trading pattern is similar to purchasing an option that has limited downside potential. It is also possible, however, as Barings has demonstrated, that traders who lose money increase their bets in the hope of recouping their losses.

5.8.4 Problem Positions

Problem positions are in a category similar to transition. All the analytical methods underlying VaR assume that some data is available to measure risks. However, for some securities, such as infrequently traded emerging market stocks, private placements, or exotic currencies, meaningful market-clearing prices may not exist.

Without adequate price information, risk cannot be assessed from historical data (not to mention implied data). Yet, a position in these assets will create the potential for losses that is difficult to quantify. In the absence of good data, educated stress testing appears to be the only method to assess risks.

5.8.5 Model Risks

Most risk management systems use past history as a guide to future risks. However, extrapolating from past data can be hazardous. This is why it is essential to beware of the pitfalls of model risks.

5.8.5.1 Functional Form Risk

This is the purest form of model risk. Valuation errors can arise if the specific functional form selected for valuing a security is incorrect. The Black-Scholes model, for instance, relies on a rather restrictive set of assumptions (geometric Brownian motion, constant interest rates, and volatility). For conventional stock options, departures from these assumptions generally have few consequences. However, there are situations where the model is inappropriate, such as for short-term interest rate options.

Model risk also becomes more dangerous as the instrument becomes more complicated. Pricing CMOs requires heavy investments in the development of models, which may prove inaccurate under some market conditions.

5.8.5.2 Parametric Risk

Also known as estimation risk, parameter risk stems from imprecision in the measurement of parameters. Even in a perfectly stable environment, we do not observe the true expected returns and volatilities. Thus, some random errors are bound to happen just because of sampling variation.

As shown in the previous chapters, the effect of estimating risk could be formally assessed by replacing the sample estimates with values that are statistically equivalent. An alternative method consists of sampling over different intervals. If the risk measures appear to be sensitive to a particular sample period, then estimation risk may be considerable.

Estimation risk increases with the number of estimated parameters. The more parameters that are estimated, the greater the chance that errors will interact with each other and create a misleading picture of risk. Errors in correlations are particularly dangerous when they are associated with large arbitrage positions. Parsimony breeds robustness.

The problem of estimation risk is often ignored in VaR analyses. Users should realize the fundamental trade-off between using more data, which leads to more precise estimates, and focusing on more recent data, which may be safer if risk changes over time.

Unfortunately, data may not be available for very long periods. For instance, only very limited histories are available for emerging markets or exotic currencies. This is all the more reason to remember that VaR numbers are just estimates.

5.8.5.3 Data Mining Risk

This is among the most insidious forms of risk. It occurs when searching various models and reporting only the one that gives positive results. This is particularly a problem with nonlinear models (such as neural network or chaos models), which involve searching not only over parameter values but also over different functional forms.

Data mining also consists of analyzing the data until some significant relationship is found. For instance, consider an investment manager who tries to find calendar anomalies in stock returns. The manager tries to see whether stock returns systematically differ across months, weeks, days, and so on. So many different comparisons can be tried that, in 1 case out of 20, we would expect to find significant results at the usual 5 percent level. Of course, the results are significant only because of the search process, which discards nonsignificant models. Data mining risk manifests itself in overly optimistic simulation results based on historical data. Often, results break down outside the sample period because they are fallacious.

Data mining risks can be best addressed by running paper portfolios, where an objective observer records the decisions and checks how the investment process performs using actual data.

5.8.5.4 Survivorship Risk

Survivorship is an issue when an investment process only considers series, markets, stocks, bonds, or contracts that are still in existence. The problem is that assets that have fared badly are not observed. Analyses based on current data, therefore, tend to project an overly optimistic image or display certain characteristics.

Survivorship effects are related to the "peso problem" in the foreign exchange market. Before the devaluation of 1982, the Mexican peso was selling at a large discount in the forward market (the forward price of the peso was well below the price for current delivery). This discount rationally anticipated a possible devaluation of the peso. An observer analyzing the discount before 1982 would have concluded that the market was inefficient. The failure, however, was not that of the market, but rather of the observer, who chose a sample period in which the data did not reflect any probability of a devaluation.

More generally, unusual events that have a low probability of occurrence but that may have severe effects on prices, such as wars or nationalizations, are not likely to be well represented in samples, and may be totally omitted from survivorship series. Unfortunately, these unusual events are very difficult to capture with conventional risk models.

5.8.6 Strategic Risks

As explained in Chapter 1, VaR can help to measure and control financial risk. However, it is impotent in the face of strategic risks that pose a challenge to corporations. Strategic risks are those resulting from fundamental shifts in the economy or political environment. One such example is the story of Bankers Trust, which before 1994 was widely admired as a leader in risk management, but became a victim of the backlash against derivatives. (See analysis of case studies in Section 6.1.) The derivatives market has been subject to political and regulatory risks, which are part of the menagerie of strategic risks affecting corporations either at the firm or the industry level.

Political risks arise from actions taken by policy makers that significantly affect the way an organization runs its business. These policies may impose limitations on the use of derivatives, thus negatively affecting the profitability of many firms involved in that market. It is perhaps in response to these threats that the private sector has come up with initiatives to address the issue of measuring market risks.

Regulatory risks are the result of changes in regulations or interpretation of existing regulations that can negatively affect a firm. For instance, as a result of the Bankers Trust case, the Commodities and Futures Trading Commission (CFTC) and the Securities and Exchange Commission (SEC) have extended their jurisdiction over market participants by declaring swaps to be "futures contracts" and "securities," respectively. This has allowed the CFTC to classify Bankers Trust as a commodity trading advisor subject to specific statutes. Another example is recent guidelines by federal bank regulators prohibiting the sale of certain types of structured notes to money market mutual funds, small savings institutions, and community banks.

5.8.7 Time Aggregation

If return is seen as the first derivative (momentum) of an asset, risk can be considered as a derivative of return and thus the second derivative (momentum) of the asset. It is important to understand what role time plays in this calculation.

Computing VaR first requires defining the period of time during which unfavorable outcomes can be measured. This period may be hours, days, or weeks. The time horizon is different depending on the purpose of the information. For an investment manager, it may correspond to the regular monthly or quarterly reporting period. For a trader, the horizon should be sufficiently long to catch traders taking positions in excess of their limits. Regulators are now leaning toward enforcing a horizon of two weeks, which is viewed as the period necessary to force bank compliance.

To compare risk across horizons, we need a translation method, a problem known in econometrics as *time aggregation*. Suppose we observe daily data, from which we obtain a VaR measure. Using higher-frequency data is generally more efficient because it uses more information. The investment horizon, however, may still be three months. The distribution for daily data must now be transformed into a distribution over a quarterly horizon. If returns are uncorrelated over time (or behave like a random walk), this transformation is straightforward.

$$\begin{aligned} R_{t,2} &= \ln\left(\frac{P_t}{P_{t-2}}\right) \\ &= \ln\left(\frac{P_t}{P_{t-1}}\right) + \ln\left(\frac{P_{t-1}}{P_{t-2}}\right) \\ &= R_{t-1} + R_t \end{aligned} \tag{5.48}$$

The problem of time aggregation can be traced to the problem of finding the expected return and variance of a sum of random variables. From Equation (5.48), the two-period return (from $t-2$ to t) $R_{t,2}$ is equal to $R_{t-1} + R_t$, where the subscript 2 indicates that the time interval is two periods. Following a Brownian motion, we know that:

$$E(X_1 + X_2) = E(X_2) \tag{5.49}$$

and

$$\sigma_{x_1 + x_2} = \sigma_{x_1} + \sigma_{x_2} + 2\sigma_{x_1, x_2} \tag{5.50}$$

Expressed formally, a variable z $(X_1 - X_n)$ follows a Wiener process if it has the following two properties. First, the change Δz during a small period of time Δt is:

$$\Delta z = \varepsilon\sqrt{\Delta t} \tag{5.51}$$

where ε is a random drawing from a standardized normal distribution $N(0,1)$. Second, the values of Δz for any two different short intervals of time Δt are independent.

It follows from the first property that Δz itself has a normal distribution with:

$$\begin{aligned} \text{Mean of } \Delta z &= 0 \\ \text{Standard deviation of } \Delta z &= \sqrt{\Delta t} \\ \text{Variance of } \Delta z &= \Delta t \end{aligned} \tag{5.52}$$

The second property implies that z follows a Markow process. Consider the increase in the value of z (distance between two observations) during a relatively long period of time T. This can be denoted by $z(T) - z(0)$ and can be regarded as the sum of the increases in z in N small time intervals of length Δt, where:

$$N = \frac{T}{\Delta t} \tag{5.53}$$

It follows that:

$$z(T) - z(0) = \sum_{i=1}^{N} \varepsilon_i \sqrt{\Delta t} \tag{5.54}$$

where ε_i ($i = 1,2, \ldots ,N$) are random drawing from $N(0,1)$. From the second property of the Wiener processes, the ε_i values are independent of each other. It follows from Equation (5.54) that $z(T) - z(0)$ is normally distributed with:

$$\begin{aligned} \text{Mean of } [z(T) - z(0)] &= 0 \\ \text{Standard deviation of } [z(T) - z(0)] &= N\Delta t = T \\ \text{Variance of } [z(T) - z(0)] &= \sqrt{T} \end{aligned} \tag{5.55}$$

This is consistent with the discussion earlier in this section in regard to time aggregation of the expected return and variance of a sum of random variables.

The key assumption has to be verified to allow a straightforward application of time aggregation: to aggregate over time, we assume that returns are uncorrelated over any successive time intervals, following a Brownian motion. This assumption is consistent with efficient markets, where the current price includes all relevant information about a particular asset at any time. If so, all price changes must be due to news that, by definition, cannot be anticipated and therefore must be uncorrelated over time: prices follow a random walk. The cross-product term σ_{x_1,x_2} must then be 0. In addition, we could reasonably assume that returns are identically distributed over time, which means that $E(R_{t-1}) = E(R_t) = E(R)$ and that $\sigma(R_{t-1}) = \sigma(R_t) = \sigma(R)$.

Based on these two assumptions, the expected return over a two-period horizon is $E(R_{t,2}) = E(R_{t-1}) + E(R_t) = 2E(R)$. The variance is $\sigma(R_{1,2}) = \sigma(R_{t-1}) + \sigma(R_t) = 2\sigma(R)$. The expected return over two days is twice the expected return over one day; likewise for the variance. Both the expected return and the variance increase linearly with time. However, volatility, in contrast, grows with the square root of time. In summary, to go from daily, monthly, or quarterly data to annual data, we can write:

$$\mu = \mu_{\text{annual}} T \tag{5.56}$$

$$\sigma = \sigma_{\text{annual}} \sqrt{T} \tag{5.57}$$

where T is the number of periods over the time horizon, usually in fractions relative to one year (e.g., 1/12 for monthly data or 1/252 for daily data if the number of trading days in a year is 252). Therefore, adjustments of volatility for different horizons can be based on a square root of time factor when positions are constant over time.

As an example, let us go back to the German mark–U.S. dollar rate data that we wish to convert to annual parameters. The mean of changes is −0.21% per month × 12 = −2.6% per annum. The risk is 3.51% per month × √12 = 12.2% per annum.

Table 5-16 compares the risk and average return for a number of financial series measured in percent per annum over the period from 1973 to 1994. Stocks are typically the most volatile of the lot (15 percent). Next come exchange rates against the dollar (12 percent) and U.S. bonds (9 per-

TABLE 5-16

Risk and Return, 1973 to 1994 (Percent per Annum)

Volatility	German Mark–U.S. Dollar	French Franc–German Mark	Canadian Dollar–U.S. Dollar	Yen–U.S. Dollar	U.S. Stocks	U.S. Bonds
Volatility	12.2	4.9	4.5	11.1	15.4	8.7
Average	−2.6	3.6	17	−4.4	11.1	8.6

cent). Some currencies, however, are relatively more stable. Such is the case for the French franc versus the German mark, which have been fixed to each other since March 1979.

Keep in mind that since the volatility grows with the square root of time and the mean with time, the mean will dominate the volatility over long horizons. Over short horizons, such as a day, volatility dominates. This provides a rationale for focusing on measures of VaR based on volatility only and ignoring expected returns. It also provides a rationale for analyzing the appropriateness of time horizon assumptions between different risk models. Whereas market risk information is readily available in different frequencies and formats, credit risk information is difficult to receive on a broad basis. This means that any data quality issue or low data frequency will lead to return information that contains errors. Errors will be maximized by any transformation through multiplication with the square root of time to adjust volatility from short to long time horizons.

To illustrate this point, consider an investment in U.S. stocks that, according to Table 5-16, returns an average of 11.1 percent per annum with a risk of 15.4 percent. Table 5-17 compares the risks and average returns of holding a position over successively shorter intervals, using Equations (5.56) and (5.57). Going from annual to daily and even hourly data, the mean shrinks much faster than the volatility. Based on a 252-trading-day year, the daily expected return is 0.04 percent—very small compared to the volatility of 0.97 percent.

Table 5-17 can be used to infer the probability of a loss over a given measurement interval. For annual data, this is the probability that the re-

TABLE 5-17

Risk and Return over Various Horizons Based on Average Volatility for S&P 500 Index from July 1989 to July 2001

Horizon	Years T	Mean μ	Risk σ	Ratio μ/σ	Probability of Loss (%)	Scales
Annual	1.0000	11.1000	15.8481	0.7004	24.18	1
Quarterly	0.2500	2.7750	7.920	0.3502	36.31	4
Monthly	0.0833	0.9250	4.5750	0.2022	41.99	12
Weekly	0.0019	0.2135	2.1977	0.0971	46.13	52
Daily	0.0040	0.0440	0.9083	0.0441	48.24	252
Hourly	0.0005	0.0052	0.3424	0.0151	49.40	8.5

DATA SOURCE: Bloomberg Professional.

turn, distributed $N(\mu = 11.1\%, \sigma^2 = 15.4\%^2)$, falls below 0. Transforming to a standard normal variable, this is the probability that $\varepsilon = (R - 0.111)/0.154$ falls below 0, which is the area to the left of the standard normal variable $-0.111/0.154 = -0.7208$. From normal tables, we find that the area to the left of 0.7208 is 23.6 percent. Thus, the probability of losing money over a year is 23.6 percent, as shown in the last column of Table 5-17. In contrast, the probability of losing money over one day is 48.2 percent, which is much higher!

This observation is sometimes interpreted as support for the conventional wisdom that stocks are less risky in the long run than over a short horizon. Unfortunately, this is not necessarily correct, since the dollar amount of the loss also increases with time.[20] The statistical tools necessary to compute VaR are discussed in the next section.

5.8.8 Predicting Volatility and Correlations

The volatility of financial markets and instruments can be observed and is to a certain extent predictable, which has substantial impact on risk management. Increasing volatility will lead to higher VaR. However, the observation and estimation of volatility do not follow a linear projection from the past into the future. Reviewing some historical time series regarding the stability of risk, it becomes obvious that the risk profile changes over time. For exchange rates this is intuitively obvious, as regime changes impact the risk profile. For example, return patterns changed dramatically after President Richard Nixon ended the 1944 Bretton-Woods agreement on August 15, 1971, declaring that the U.S. government no longer supported the gold-dollar exchange rate at $35 per fine ounce. On March 16, 1973, the exchange rates of the industrialized countries became free-floating. Bond yields were also more volatile and had a different risk profile in the early 1980s, as the creation of Brady bonds was a driving factor to eliminate systemic and counterparty risk. These examples demonstrate structural changes to risk. As a consequence, investors have to review their portfolios to reduce their exposures to those assets whose volatility is predicted to increase. Also, forecasted volatility means that assets directly dependent on volatility, such as derivatives, will change in value in a predictable fashion. Additionally, in a rational market, equilibrium prices will be affected by changes in volatility. A better understanding of the risk profiles, and thus the volatilities, enables participants in the market to better predict changes in volatility, diversification, exposures, and hedges, and thus to better control financial market risks.

Figure 5-12 shows return and volatility data over several years and different time series. Several periods are of particular interest: the Asian crisis, starting in July 1997; the Russian crisis in September/October 1998; and the technology, media, and telecommunications (TMT) sectors crisis in April 2000. 1998 was particularly tumultuous—the Russian crisis was

FIGURE 5-12

S&P 500 Index Returns from July 1989 to July 2001. (*Data source:* Bloomberg Professional.)

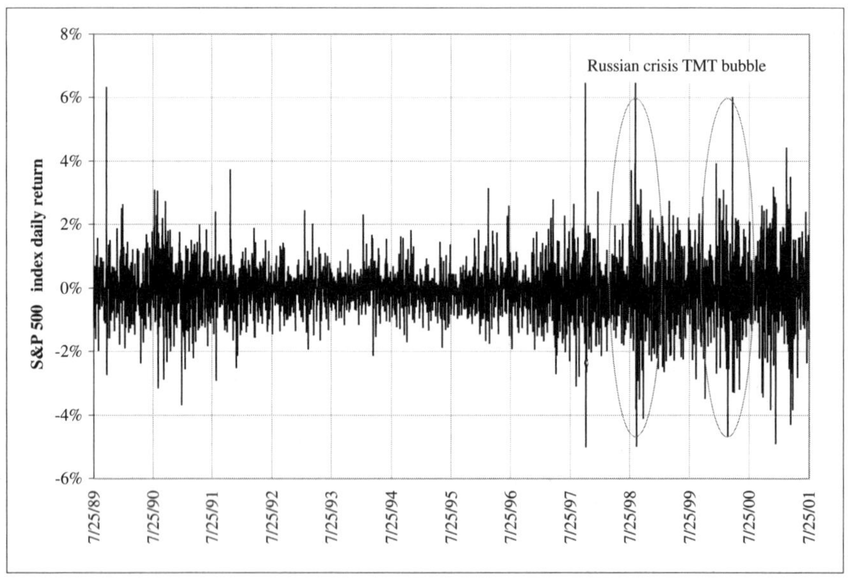

linked to LTCM hedge fund speculation on the narrowing of bond spreads in Russia, which increased volatility dramatically. April 2000 was another interesting period, as the TMT sectors abruptly downturned after almost 10 years of uninterrupted growth. The following sections discuss techniques of estimating and forecasting variation in risk and correlations.

5.8.9 Modeling Time-Varying Risk

5.8.9.1 Risk Around Mean and Fat Tail Events

To illustrate our point, we will use the S&P 500, the FTSE, and the Nasdaq to analyze the risk profiles and changes over time. In Figure 5-12 the S&P 500 index returns are displayed from July 1989 to July 2001. The period from 1990 to 1996 was fairly typical, with mostly narrow trading ranges and some wide swings. The years 1994 to 1996 were characterized by a steady upside in the equity markets with narrow volatilities, following the unexpected increase in lending rates by the Federal Reserve in February 1994. The result was increased volatilities and a bad year for the fixed income market with steady inflows to the equity market. The average volatility from 1994 to 1996 was 9.5 percent (using a 252-trading day adjustment). Volatility was not constant over time. More important is that the time variation in risk could explain the fact that the empirical distribution of return does not fit a normal distribution. The empirical distribution is better explained by a leptokurtotic distribution than a normal distribution, as we will see later.

The fat tails are of particular interest because the deviation of the empirical profile from the normal distribution profile causes issues with risk modeling, hedging, etc. (see Figure 5-13). Two obvious alternative hypotheses can explain fat tails:

1. The first explanation is that the true distribution is stationary and the empirical return distribution contains fat tails. In this case a normal distribution approximation is inappropriate.
2. The alternative view is that the distribution does change over time. Consequently, in times of increased volatilities in the markets, a stationary model could measure large observations as outliers, whereas they are really drawn from a distribution with temporarily greater dispersion.

In reality, both explanations carry some truth. This is why forecasting volatility is particularly critical for risk management. In the following section, we will focus on traditional approaches based on parametric time series modeling.[21]

5.8.9.2 Moving Averages

A very simple but widely employed method is to use a moving window of fixed length to estimate volatility. For instance, a typical length is 20 trading days (about a calendar month) or 60 trading days (about a calendar quarter).

FIGURE 5-13

Distribution of the Nasdaq Index Returns for 2000, 1999, and 1998 (left to right). (*Data source:* Bloomberg Professional.)

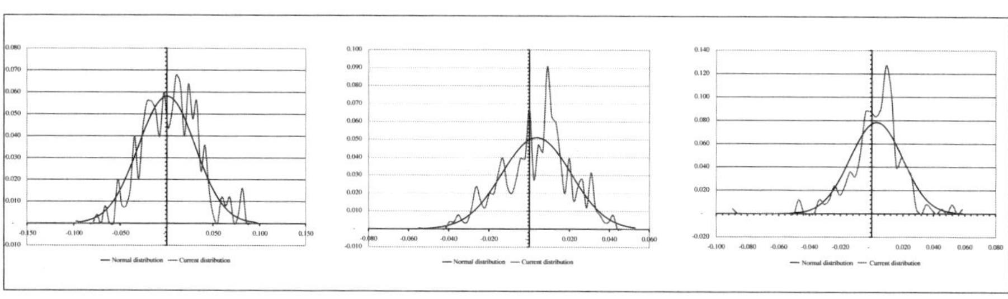

Assuming that we observe returns r over n days, this volatility estimate is constructed from a moving average (MA):

$$\sigma = \sqrt{\left(\frac{1}{n}\right)\sum_{i=1}^{n} r_{t-1}^2} \tag{5.58}$$

$$\sigma = \sqrt{\left(\frac{1}{n}\right)\sum_{i=1}^{N} (r_n - \bar{r})^2} \tag{5.59}$$

In Equation (5.58), we focus on absolute returns instead of returns around the mean. The second approach (Equation 5.59) includes the expected returns for the volatility estimation. We will use the second approach for the following calculations.

Each day, the volatility forecast is updated by adding information from the preceding day and dropping information from $(n + 1)$ days ago. All weights on past returns are equal and set to $(1/n)$. While simple to implement, this model has serious drawbacks. Most important, it ignores the dynamic ordering of observations. Recent information receives the same weight (importance) as older information, but recent data should intuitively be more relevant. For example, if there was a large return n days ago, dropping this return as the window moves one day forward will substantially affect the volatility estimate. As a result, moving average measures of volatility tend to look like levels of width n when plotted against time.

Figure 5-14 displays 20-day and 60-day moving averages for the S&P 500 index changes. Movements in the 60-day average are much more stable than those in the 20-day average. This is understandable, because longer periods decrease the weight of any single day. But is the longer time horizon adding value? Longer periods increase the precision of the estimate but could miss underlying variation in volatility. The answer to this question is left open to the investor, depending on his or her time horizon and other parameters.

5.8.9.3 GARCH Estimation

As mentioned earlier, longer periods increase the precision of the estimate but could miss underlying variation in volatility. This is why volatility estimation has moved toward models that put more weight on recent information. One of the first approaches to modeling volatility with a time-dependent component was the generalized autoregressive heteroskedastic (GARCH) model proposed by Engle and Bollerslev.[22]

The GARCH approach assumes that the variance of returns follows a predictable process. The forecasted conditional variance depends on the latest observation but also on the previous conditional variance. Define h as the conditional variance, using information up to time $t - 1$, and r_{t-1} as the previous day's return. The simplest such model is the GARCH (1,1) process:

$$h_t = \alpha_0 + \alpha_1 r_{t-1}^2 + \beta h_{t-1} \tag{5.60}$$

FIGURE 5-14

Moving Average (MA) Volatility Forecasts for Mexican Peso–U.S. Dollar Foreign Exchange. (*Data source:* Bloomberg Professional.)

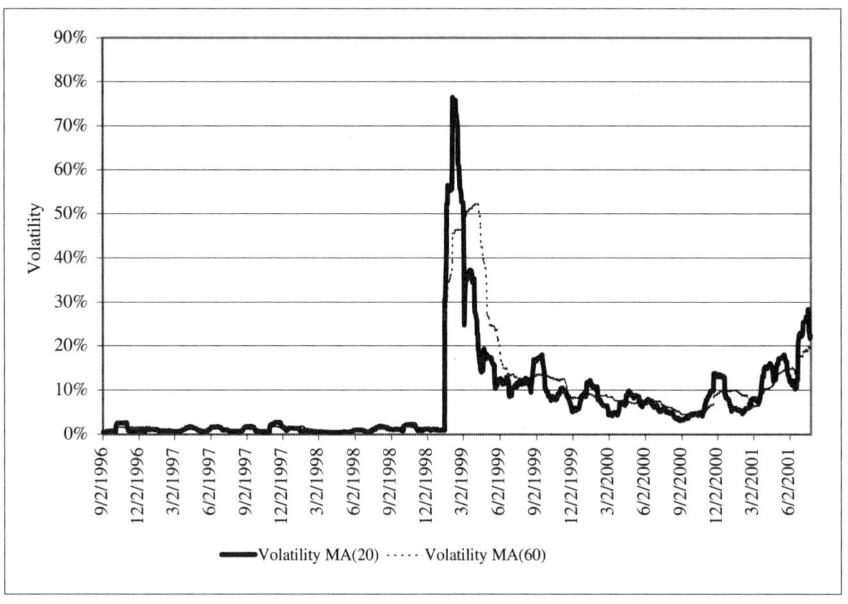

The average unconditional variance is found by setting

$$E[r_{t-1}^2] = h_t = h_{t-1} = h \tag{5.61}$$

Solving for h, we find:

$$h = \frac{\alpha_0}{1 - \alpha_1 - \beta} \tag{5.62}$$

For this model to be stationary, the sum of parameters $\alpha_1 + \beta$ must be less than unity. This sum is also called the *persistence,* for reasons that will become clear later on. This specification provides a parsimonious model, with few parameters, that seems to fit the data quite well.[23]

GARCH models have become a mainstay of time series analyses of financial markets, which systematically display volatility clustering. Literally hundreds of papers have applied GARCH models to stock return data,[24] to interest rate data,[25] and to foreign exchange data.[26] Econometricians have also created many variants of the GARCH model, most of which provide marginal improvement on the original GARCH model. A comprehensive review of the GARCH literature has been generated by

Bollerslev, Chou, and Kroner.[27] The drawback of GARCH models is their nonlinearity. The parameters mentioned earlier must be estimated regularly by maximization of the likelihood function, which involves a numerical optimization. Typically, researchers assume that the scaled residual

$$\varepsilon_t = \frac{r_t}{\sqrt{h_t}}$$

has a normal distribution.

The GARCH approach provides other interesting features. The returns r can be serially uncorrelated but are not independent as they are nonlinearly related through second moments. This class of models is also related to chaos theory. Recent work has revealed that many financial prices display chaotic properties. Often, the nonlinearities behind chaos theory can be traced to the time variation in variances. The GARCH models can explain some of the reported chaotic behavior of financial markets.

Figure 5-15 shows the GARCH forecast of volatility for the S&P 500 index changes. It shows increased volatility from fall 1996 on. Afterward, volatility spikes upward during the Asian crisis in summer 1997, the Rus-

FIGURE 5-15

GARCH Volatility Forecast for the S&P 500 Index. (*Data source:* Bloomberg Professional.)

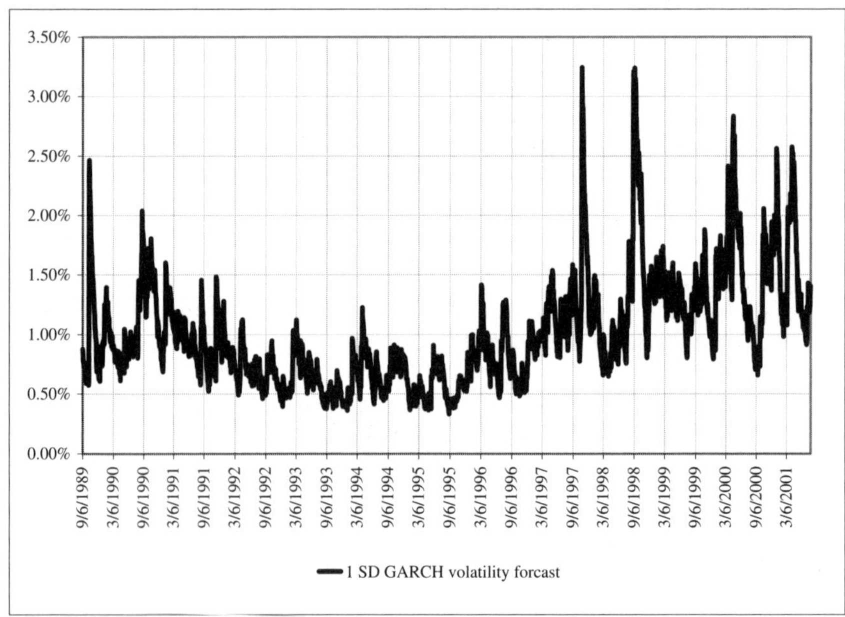

sian crisis in September/October 1998, and the TMT meltdown in April 2000 and the months following. A simple Autoregressive Integrated Moving Average (ARIMA) test run on the S&P index (Figure 5-16) shows that the assumption of stable volatility is closer to an acceptable level (p value ≥ 0.05) in the years until 1996. After 1996, the p values show clearly unacceptable low levels.

The practical application of this information is illustrated in Figure 5-17, which shows daily returns along with conditional 95 percent confidence bands. This model appears to adequately capture variation in risk. Most of the returns fall within the 95 percent band. The few outside the bands correspond to the remaining 5 percent of occurrences.

5.8.9.4 Long-Horizon Forecasts

The GARCH approach can also be used to compute volatility over various time horizons. We assume that the volatility is estimated based on daily information. To compute a monthly volatility, we first decompose the multiperiod (geometric) return into daily returns as in Equation (5.63):

FIGURE 5-16

ARIMA Test for S&P 500 Index. (*Data source:* Bloomberg Professional.)

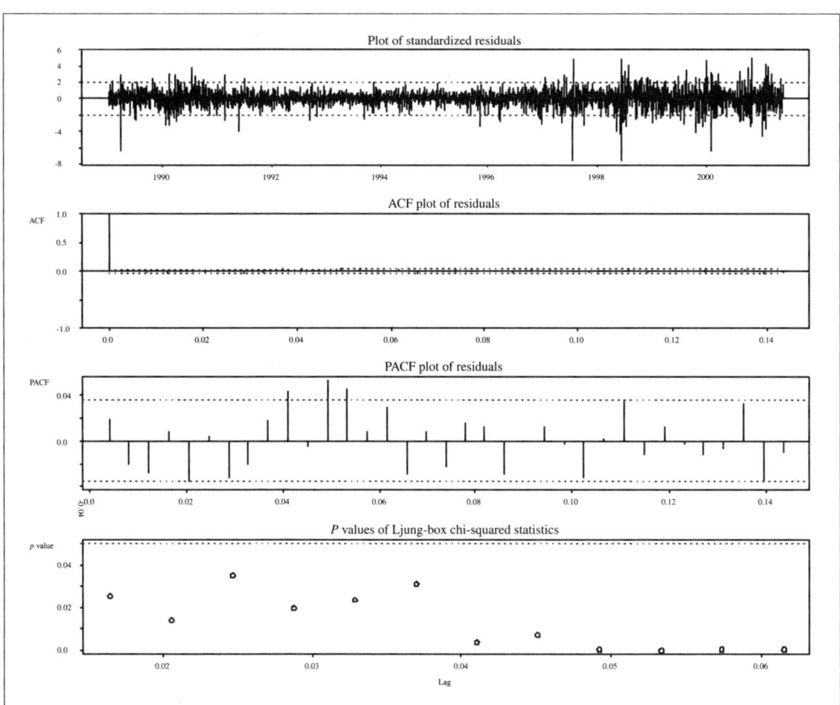

FIGURE 5-17

Returns and GARCH Confidence Bands for S&P 500 Index. (*Data source:* Bloomberg Professional.)

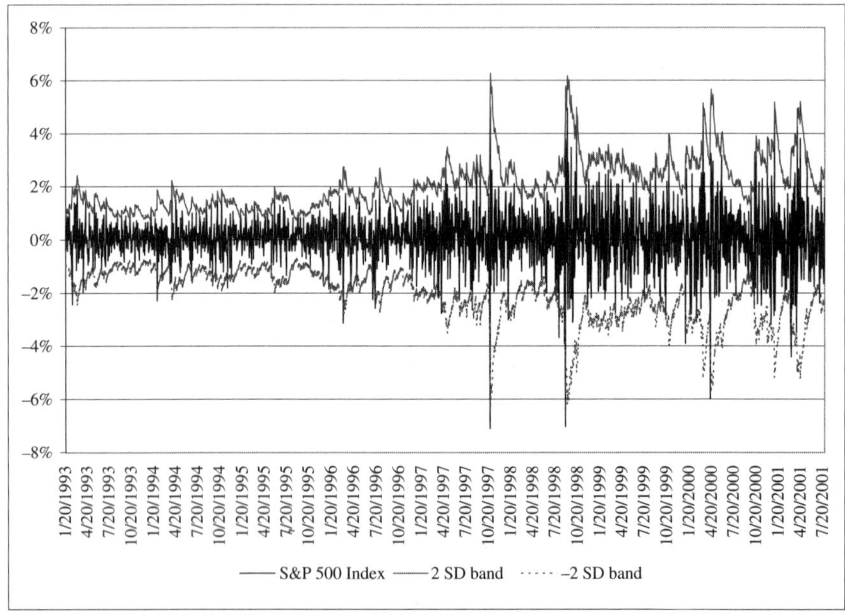

$$R_{t,2} = \ln\left(\frac{P_t}{P_{t-2}}\right) = \ln\left(\frac{P_t}{P_{t-1}}\right) + \ln\left(\frac{P_{t-1}}{P_{t-2}}\right) = R_{t-1} + R_t \qquad (5.63)$$

Thus:

$$r_{t,T} = r_t + r_{t+1} + r_{t+2} + \ldots + r_T \qquad (5.64)$$

If returns are uncorrelated across days, the long-horizon variance as of $t - 1$ is:

$$E_{t-1}[r_{t,T}] = E_{t-1}[r_t^2] + E_{t-1}[r_{t+1}^2] + E_{t-1}[r_{t+2}^2] + \ldots + E_{t-1}[r_T^2] \qquad (5.65)$$

After some transformation, the forecast of variance τ days ahead is:

$$E_{t-1}[r_{t+\tau}^2] = \alpha_0 \frac{1-(\alpha_1+\beta)^\tau}{1-(\alpha_1+\beta)} + (\alpha_1+\beta)^\tau h_t \qquad (5.66)$$

Figure 5-18 displays the effect of different persistence parameters $\alpha_1 + \beta$ on the variance. We start from the long-run value for a given variance, 0.5. Then a shock moves the conditional variance to twice its value,

FIGURE 5-18

Persistence Parameters on the Variance.

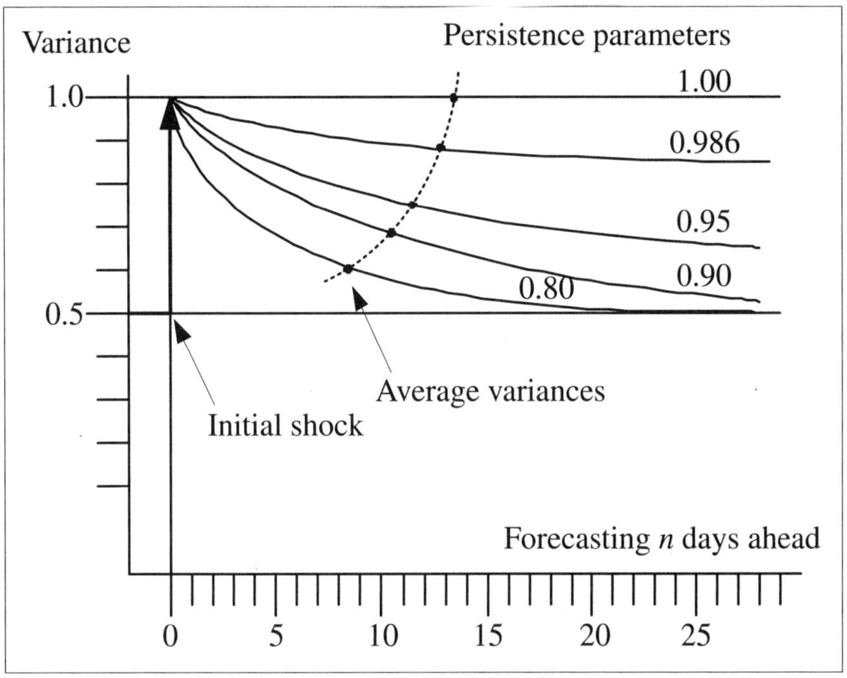

1.0. High persistence means that the shock will decay slowly. For instance, with a persistence of 0.986, the conditional variance is still 0.90 after 20 days. With a persistence of 0.8, the variance drops very close to its long-run value only after 20 days. The dots on each line represent the average daily variance over the following 25 days. High persistence implies that the average variance will remain high.

The parabolic shape of the behaving persistence parameters looks very similar to the cone of forecasted volatilities using the VaR estimates as calculated with the RiskMetrics approach (see Figure 5-19).

5.8.10 The RiskMetrics Approach

RiskMetrics takes a pragmatic approach to modeling risk.[28] Variance forecasts are modeled using an exponential weighting schema. Formally, the forecast for time t is a weighted average of the previous forecast, using weight λ (Equation 5.67), and of the latest squared innovation, using weight $(1 - \lambda)$ (Equation 5.68):

FIGURE 5-19

S&P 500 Returns and VaR Estimates (1.65σ) (*Source: J. P. Morgan,* RiskMetrics Technical Document," 4th ed., *New York: J. P. Morgan, December 1996, chart 5.4. Copyright © 1966 by Morgan Guaranty Trust Company, all rights reserved. Reproduction with permission of RiskMetrics Group, LLC.)*

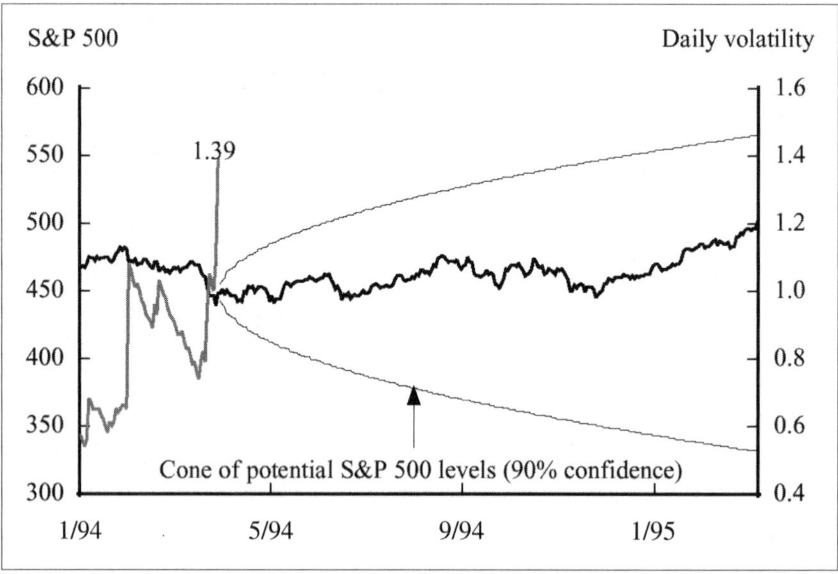

$$\sigma = \sqrt{\frac{1}{T}\sum_{t=1}^{T}(r_t - \bar{r})^2} \tag{5.67}$$

$$\sigma = \sqrt{(1-\lambda)\sum_{t=1}^{T}\lambda^{t-1}(r_t - \bar{r})^2} \tag{5.68}$$

In comparing the two estimators (equal and exponential), the exponentially weighted moving average model depends on the parameter $0 < \lambda < 1$.

The λ parameter is called the *decay factor,* and must be less than unity. It determines the relative weights that are applied to the observations (returns) and the effective amount of data used in estimating volatility. This model can be viewed as a special case of the GARCH process, where α_0 is set to 0 and α_1 and β sum to unity. The model therefore allows for persistence. As shown in Figure 5-20, it appears to produce results that are very close to those achieved with the GARCH model.

FIGURE 5-20

Mean Reversion for the Variance (*Source: J. P. Morgan,* RiskMetrics Technical Document," 4th ed., *New York: J. P. Morgan, December 1996, chart 5.9. Copyright © 1996 by Morgan Guaranty Trust Company, all rights reserved. Reproduction with permission of RiskMetrics Group, LLC.*)

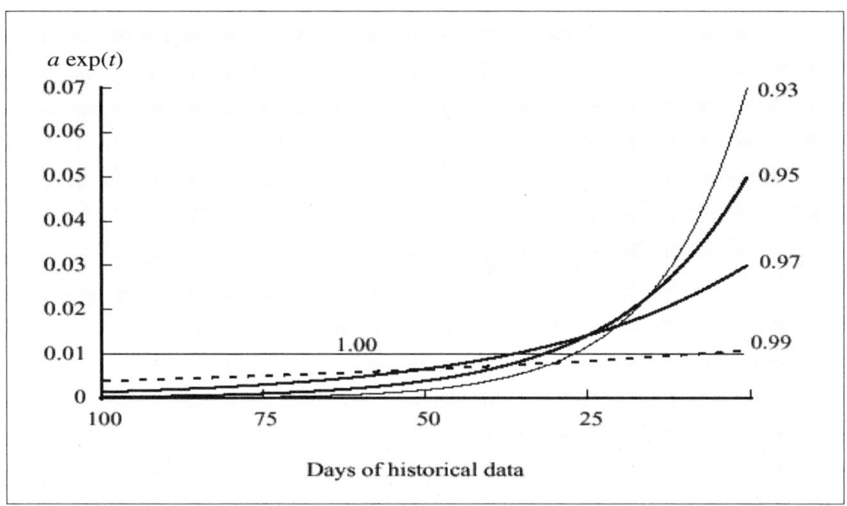

A particularly interesting feature of the exponentially weighted estimator is that it can be written in a recursive form, which, in turn, will be used as a basis for making volatility forecasts. In order to derive the recursive form, it is assumed that an infinite amount of data is available. For example, assuming that the sample mean is zero, we can derive the period $t + 1$ variance forecast, given data available at time t (one day earlier) as:

$$\sigma^2_{1,t+1|t} = \lambda\sigma^2_{1,t-1|t} + (1 - \lambda)\, r^2_{1,t} \tag{5.69}$$

The one-day RiskMetrics volatility forecast is given by:

$$\sigma_{1,t+1|t} = \sqrt{\lambda\sigma^2_{1,t-1|t} + (1 - \lambda)\, r^2_{1,t}} \tag{5.70}$$

The subscript $t + 1 \mid t$ is read "the time $t + 1$ forecast given information up to and including time t." The subscript $t - 1 \mid t$ is read in a similar fashion. This notation underscores the fact that RiskMetrics is treating the variance (volatility) as time dependent. The fact that this period's variance forecast depends on last period's variance is consistent with the observed autocorrelation in squared returns. The volatility is given by:

$$\sigma^2_{1,t+1|t} = (1-\lambda)\sum_{i=0}^{\infty}\lambda^i r^2_{1,t-1}$$

$$= (1-\lambda)(r^2_{1,t} + \lambda r^2_{1,t-1} + \lambda^2 r^2_{1,t-2} + \ldots)$$

$$= (1-\lambda)r^2_{1,t} + \lambda(1-\lambda)(r^2_{1,t-1} + \lambda r^2_{1,t-1} + \lambda^2 r^2_{1,t-2} + \lambda^2 r^2_{1,t-3})$$

$$= \lambda\sigma^2_{1,t-1|t} + (1-\lambda)r^2_{1,t} \quad (5.71)$$

The exponential approach is particularly easy to implement because it relies on one parameter only and thus is more robust than other models to estimation error. In addition, as was the case for the GARCH model, the estimator is recursive; the forecast is based on the previous forecast and the latest innovation. The whole history is summarized by one number, h_{t-1}. This is in contrast to the moving average, for example, where the last n returns must be used to construct the forecast.

The only parameter in this model is the decay factor λ. In theory, this could be found by maximizing the likelihood function, but in practice, this would be a daunting task to perform every day for all the time series in the RiskMetrics database. In the original technical document, the analysis has been performed on a basic set of core data based on 450 time series. An optimization has other shortcomings. The decay factor may vary across series and over time, thus decreasing consistency over different periods. In addition, different values of λ create incompatibilities for the covariance terms and may lead to coefficients of correlation greater than unity, as we will see later. In the original document, RiskMetrics uses only one decay factor for all series, which is set at 0.94 for daily data. However, RiskMetrics currently computes stress testing and VaR based on approximately 500,000 time series from the DataMetrics platform and allows users to define any combination of decay factors, lookback periods, and time horizons, which reflects the underlying data better than the original simplified framework. This document also outlines how risk is computed at different levels of aggregation (from subposition through the entire portfolio) and discusses the various methodologies used (Monte Carlo simulations, historical simulations, etc.).[29]

RiskMetrics also provides risk forecasts over monthly horizons, defined as 25 trading days. In theory, the exponential model should be used to extrapolate volatility over the next day, then the next, and so on until the 25th day, as was done previously for the GARCH model (see Figure 5-21). The persistence parameter for the exponential model is unity. Therefore, it is based on the assumption that there is no mean reversion and the monthly volatility should be the same as the daily volatility. In practice, the estimator is identical to the exponentially weighted estimator at the

FIGURE 5-21

Exponential Volatility Forecast for FTSE Index. (*Data source:* Bloomberg Professional.)

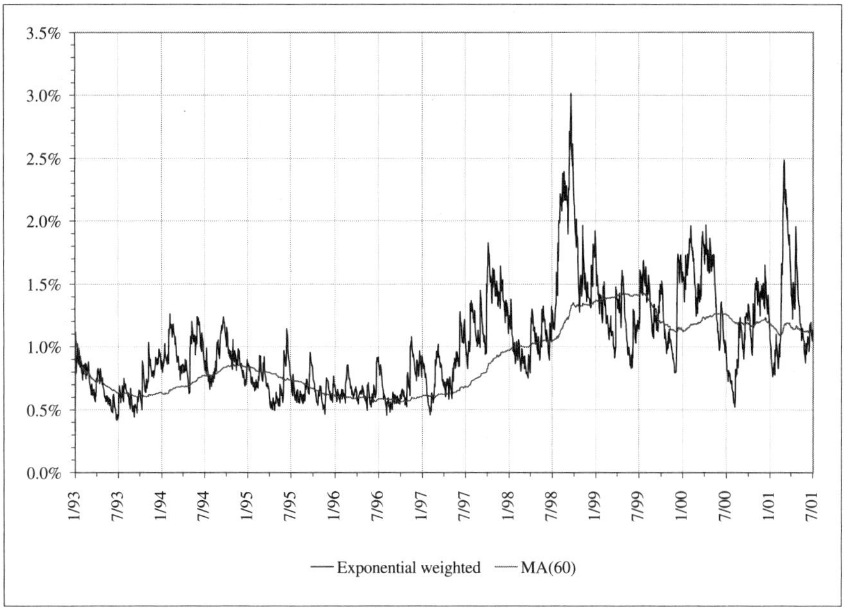

beginning of this section, except that it defines innovations as the 25-day variance. After experimenting with the data, J. P. Morgan chose $\lambda = 0.97$ as the optimal decay factor. Therefore, the daily and monthly specifications are inconsistent with each other. However, they are both easy to use, they approximate the behavior of actual data quite well, and they are robust to misspecifications.

5.8.11 Modeling Correlations

Correlation is of unquestionable importance for portfolio risk—even more so than individual variances. To illustrate the estimation of correlation, we pick two series: the S&P 500 index and the FTSE 100 index.

Over the period from 1996 to 1998, the average daily correlation coefficient [MA(60)] was 0.333. However, we should expect some variation in the correlation coefficient because this time period covers the Asian crisis and the Russian/LTCM crisis. The average correlation was 0.162 in 1995, 0.249 in 1996, 0.305 in 1997, and 0.331 in 1998. As in the case of variance estimation, various methods can be used to capture time variation in correlation: moving average, GARCH, and exponential.

5.8.11.1 Moving Averages

The first method is based on moving averages (MAs), using a fixed window of length *n*. Figure 5-22 presents estimates based on an MA(20) and MA(60). Correlations for the MA(20) start around 0.4 and move between 0.65 and –0.1 until March 1998, when correlation hits a low of –0.45, moving back to 0.7. The correlation falls from 0.76 at the end of January 1999 to –0.34 by April 21, 1999. As can be seen in the figure, the MA(60) follows with some lag and averaging of the swings. These estimates are subject to the same criticisms as before. Moving averages place the same weight on all observations within the moving window and ignore the fact that more recent observations may contain more relevant information than older ones. In addition, dropping observations from the window sometimes has severe effects on the measured correlation.

5.8.11.2 Exponential Averages

In theory, GARCH estimation could be extended to a multivariate framework. The problem is that the number of parameters to estimate increases exponentially with the number of series. With two series, for instance, we need to estimate nine terms, or three α_1, α_0, and β parameters for each of

FIGURE 5-22

Moving Average–Based Correlation Between the S&P 500 Index and the FTSE 100 Index. (*Data source:* Bloomberg Professional.)

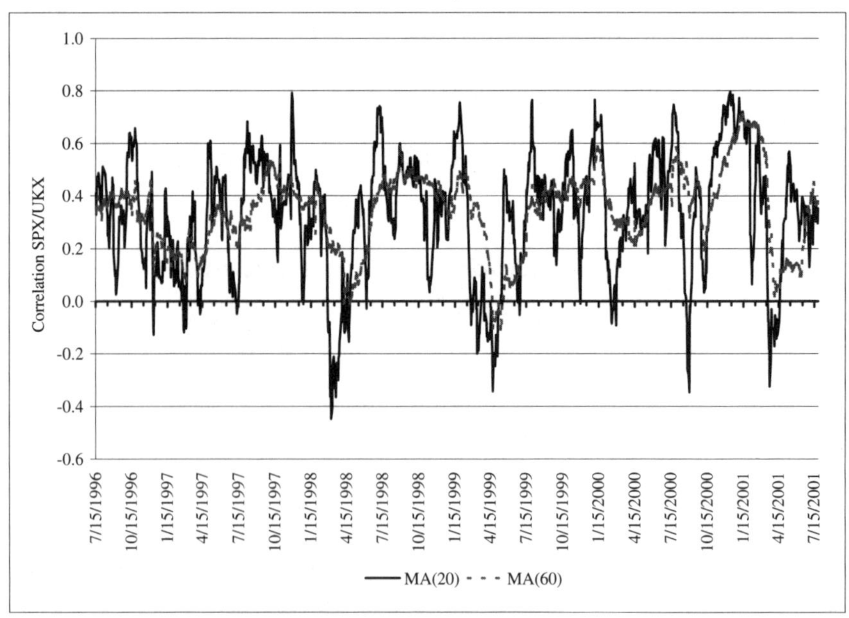

the three covariance terms. For larger samples of securities, this number quickly becomes unmanageable.

The RiskMetrics approach is convincing in its simplicity. Covariances are estimated, much like variances, using an exponential weighting scheme:

$$h_{12,t} = \lambda h_{12,t-1} + (1 - \lambda) r_{1,t-1} r_{2,t-1} \tag{5.72}$$

As before, the decay factor λ is arbitrarily set at 0.94 for daily data and 0.97 for monthly data. The conditional correlation is then:

$$\rho_{12,t} = \frac{h_{12,t}}{\sqrt{h_{1,t} h_{2,t}}} \tag{5.73}$$

Figure 5-23 displays the time variation in the correlation between the S&P 500 index and the FTSE 100 index. The pattern of movements in correlations does not seem too different from the MA model, plotting somewhere between the MA(20) and MA(60).

FIGURE 5-23

Exponential-Weighted Correlation Between the S&P 500 Index and the FTSE 100 Index. (*Data source:* Bloomberg Professional.)

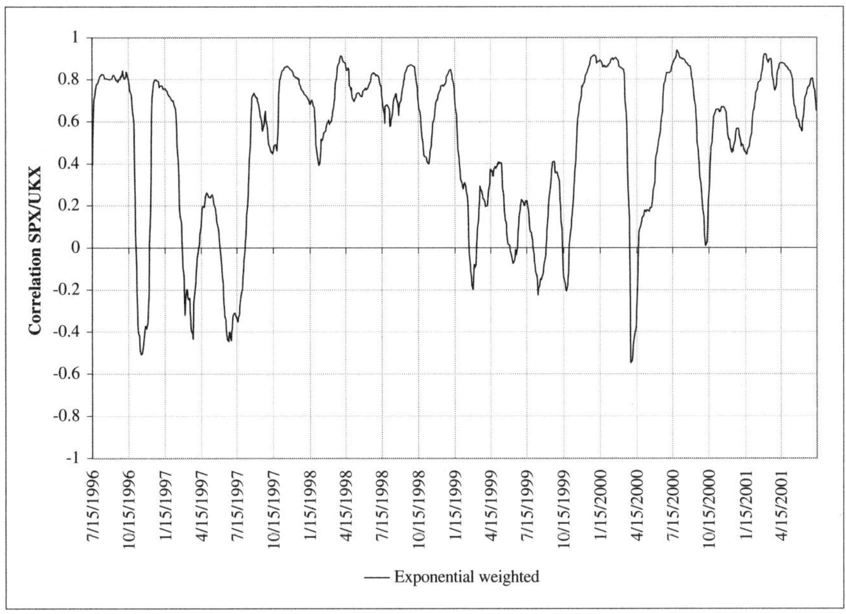

Note that the reason why J. P. Morgan decided to set a common factor λ across all series is to ensure that all estimates of ρ are between -1 and 1. Otherwise, there is no guarantee that this will always be the case.

5.8.11.3 Crashes and Correlations

It is intuitively obvious that low correlations help reduce portfolio risk. It is often argued that correlations increase in periods of global turbulence. Such an observation is particularly worrisome, because increasing correlations occurring at a time of increasing volatility would defeat the diversification properties of portfolios. Measures of VaR based on historical data tend to seriously underestimate the actual risk of failure because both risk and correlation are understated. This double blow could well lead to returns that are far outside the range of forecasts.

Indeed, we expect the structure of the correlation matrix to depend on the type of shocks affecting the economy. Global factors, such as the oil crises and the Gulf War, create increased turbulence and increased correlations. For instance, Longin and Solnik[30] examined the behavior of correlations among national stock markets and found that correlations typically increase by 27 percent (from 0.43 to 0.55) in periods of high turbulence. Assuming a large portfolio (where risk is proportional to $\sqrt{\rho}$), this implies that VaR should be multiplied by a factor of $\sqrt{(0.55/0.43)} = 1.13$. Thus, based solely on the correlation effect, VaR measures could underestimate true risk by 13 percent.

The extent of bias, however, depends on the sign of positions. Higher correlations are harmful to portfolios with only long positions, as is typical of equity portfolios. In contrast, decreasing correlations are dangerous for portfolios with short sales.

Perhaps these discomforting results explain why regulators impose large multiplicative factors on internally computed VaR measures. But these observations also point to the need for stress simulations to assess the robustness of VaR measures to changes in correlations.

Using Option Data

Measures of value at risk are only as good as the quality of forecasts of risk and correlations. Historical data, however, may not provide the best available forecasts of future risks. Situations involving changes in regimes, for instance, are simply not reflected in recent historical data. This is why it is useful to turn to implied forecasts contained in the latest market data.

5.8.11.4 Implied Volatilities

An important function of derivatives markets is arbitrage discovery. Derivatives provide information about market clearing prices, which includes the discovery of volatility. Options are assets whose prices are influenced by a number of factors, all of which are observable save for the volatility of the underlying price. By setting the market price of an option equal to its model value, one can recover an implied volatility.[31] Similarly, implied correlations also can be derived from triplets of options, using, for instance, the Margrabe pricing model.[32]

Correlations are also implicit in so-called quanto options, which also involve two random input variables. For instance, a quantity-adjusted option would be an option struck on a foreign stock index where the foreign currency payoff is translated into dollars at a fixed rate. The valuation formula for such an option also involves the correlation between two sources of risk. Thus, options can potentially reveal a wealth of information about future risks and correlations.

If options markets are efficient, the implied volatility should provide the market's best estimate of future volatility. However, options trading means taking volatility bets. Expressing a view on volatility has become so pervasive in the options markets that prices are often quoted in terms of bid-ask volatility. As options reflect the market consensus about future volatility, there are sound reasons to believe that options-based forecasts should be superior to historical estimates.

The empirical evidence indeed points to the superiority of options data. An intuitive way to demonstrate the usefulness of options data is to analyze the Russian crisis in September to October 1998. Figure 5-24 com-

FIGURE 5-24

Implied Volatility Forecasts for S&P Index Returns. (*Data source:* Bloomberg Professional.)

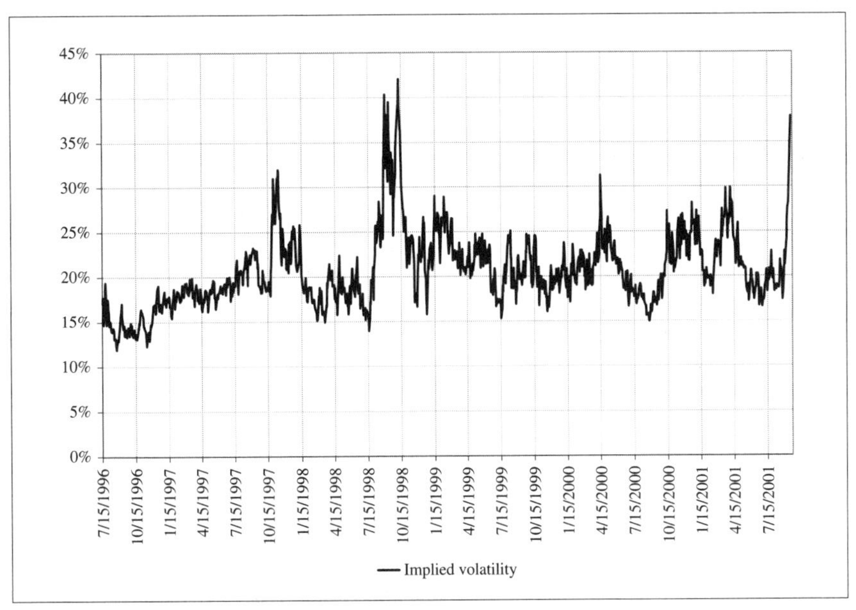

pares volatility forecasts during 1992, including those implied from S&P 500 index options and a moving average with a window of 60 days. It is intuitively obvious that the implied volatility immediately picks up the behavior of the market and reflects the expected volatility to justify current market conditions. As options traders rationally anticipated greater turbulence, the implied volatility was much more useful than time series models.

5.8.11.5 Conclusions

The empirical evidence shows that options contain a wealth of information about price risk that is generally superior to time-series models. This finding is particularly useful in times of stress, when the market has access to current information that is simply not reflected in historical approaches. The drawback of option-implied parameters is that the volume and range of traded options is not sufficiently wide to cover the volatility of all essential financial prices. As more and more options contracts and exchanges are springing up all over the world, traded options data is more readily available. Historical data provides a backward-looking alternative.

The options-based credit model detailed in Section 5.8.11.4 highlights the advantages of an options-based approach:

- Using implied volatilities, the options-based model is forward looking and can be applied in a similar context as the market risk–based options model regarding time horizon.
- The options model does not necessarily require a mean variance normal distribution. Nonlinearity of the underlying asset is captured with an options-based approach for market and credit risk. Operational risk issues can be approached and covered in a similar manner, based on the evaluation of the implied volatility required to calculate the operational risk premium for the historical operational losses as captured through a historical operational risk database.

5.9 LIQUIDITY RISK

The approaches for market risk management under normal conditions traditionally have focused on the distribution of portfolio value changes resulting from moves in the midprice. Under this assumption, market risk is really in a "pure" form: risk in an idealized market with no "friction" in obtaining a fair price. However, many markets possess an additional liquidity component that arises from a trader not realizing the midprice when liquidating a position, but rather the midprice minus the bid-ask spread.

We argue that liquidity risk associated with the uncertainty of the spread, particularly for thinly traded or emerging market securities under adverse market conditions, is an important part of overall risk and therefore an important component and a critical assumption of modeling. The current regulative conceptual approach to measuring market risk does not consider liquidity risk explicitly. Approaches have been developed for modeling liquidity risk that can be easily and seamlessly integrated into standard VaR models.[33] The BIS is inadvertently monitoring liquidity risk, but by not modeling it explicitly and therefore capitalizing against it. Therefore, banks will be experiencing surprisingly many violations of capital requirements, particularly if their portfolios are concentrated in emerging markets. The crash in October 1998 has shown the impact of inadequate liquidity in Russian bonds and the supposed adequacy of quantitative models.

> Portfolios are usually marked to market at the middle of the bid-offer spread, and many hedge funds used models that incorporated this assumption. In late August, there was only one realistic value for the portfolio: the bid price. Amid such massive sell-offs, only the first seller obtains a reasonable price for its security; the rest lose a fortune by having to pay a liquidity premium if they want a sale. . . . Models should be revised to include bid-offer behavior.[34]

The turmoil in the capital markets in October 1998 led experts and laymen alike to cast liquidity risk in the role of the culprit. Inexperienced and sophisticated players alike were caught by surprise when markets dried up. Unsurprisingly, the first to go were the emerging markets in Asia, and, more recently, in Russia. Then the crisis spilled over into the U.S. corporate debt market, which was indeed much more surprising. One of the most famous victims of the 1998 liquidity crisis was Long Term Capital Management (LTCM). Spreads appeared to widen out of the blue; but this could have been predicted. More generally, it is a well-acknowledged fact that the standard VaR concept used for measuring both market and credit risk for tradable securities lacks a rigorous treatment of liquidity risk. At best, the risk for large illiquid positions is adjusted upward in an ad hoc fashion by utilizing a longer time horizon in the calculation of VaR that at best is a subjective estimate of the likely liquidation time of the position. But this holding period adjustment is usually carried out using the square root of time scaling of the variances and covariances rather than a recalculation of variances and covariances for the longer time horizon.[35]

The combination of the recent rapid expansion of emerging market trading activities and the recurring turbulence in those markets has pushed liquidity risk to the forefront of market risk management research. New work in asset pricing has demonstrated how liquidity as a driving factor in risk measurement plays a key role in security valuation and optimal portfolio choice by effectively imposing endogenous borrowing and short-selling constraints, as argued by Longstaff.[36]

Liquidity also plays a major role in transaction costs, as trades of large illiquid positions typically execute at a price away from the midprice.

BARRA's Market Impact Model and other such models quantify the market impact cost, defined as the cost of immediate execution, for establishing and liquidating large positions. Jarrow and Subramanian consider the effect of trade size and execution lag on the liquidation value of the portfolio,[37] proposing a liquidity-adjusted VaR measure that incorporates a liquidity discount, volatility of the liquidity discount, and volatility of the time horizon to liquidation. Although this concept is attractive, there is no available data or procedure to measure the model parameters such as mean and variances for quantity discounts or execution lags for trading large blocks.

Illiquidity can arise from different sources. Conceptually we have to distinguish between risk caused by uncertainty in asset returns and risk due to liquidity constraints. The breakdown of liquidity risk allows a distinction between exogenous liquidity risk, which is not under control of the market participant (market maker or trader), and endogenous liquidity risk, which is the under control of the trader and usually the result of sudden unloading of large positions that the market is unable to absorb efficiently. Conceptually, the current models (which do not distinguish between uncertainty from asset returns or due to liquidity) ignore valuable information contained in the distribution of bid-ask spreads.

Traditional market risk management (under normal conditions) usually deals exclusively with the distribution of portfolio value changes via the distribution of asset/trading returns. These asset/trading returns are based on the midprice, and thus the market risk is really in a "pure" form—risk in an idealized market with no friction in obtaining the fair price. However, many markets possess an additional liquidity component that arises from traders not realizing the midprice when liquidating a position quickly or when the market is moving against them; instead, they realize the midprice minus some spread. Marking to market therefore yields an underestimation of the true risk in such markets, because the realized value on liquidation can deviate significantly from the market midprice. We argue that the deviation of this liquidation price from the midprice, also referred to as the *market impact* or *liquidation cost,* and the volatility of this cost, are important components to model in order to capture the true level of overall risk. We conceptually split uncertainty in market value of an asset, i.e., its overall market risk, into two parts: (1) uncertainty that arises from asset returns, which can be thought of as a pure market risk component, and (2) uncertainty due to liquidity risk.

Conventional VaR approaches, such as J. P. Morgan's RiskMetrics, focus on capturing risk due to uncertainty in asset returns but ignore uncertainty due to liquidity risk. The liquidity risk component is concerned with the uncertainty of liquidation costs. Conceptually, we can express these ideas as a market/liquidity risk plane that considers the joint impact of the two types of risk. Most markets and trading situations fall into regions 1 and 3; we observe that market risk and liquidity risk components are correlated in most cases. For instance, FX derivative products in emerging markets have high market and liquidity risks and therefore fall into region 1. The spot markets for most G-7 currencies, on the other hand, will fall into region 3 due to the relatively low market and liquidity risks involved. Most normal trading activity occurs in these two regions and is subject to exogenous liquidity risk, which refers to liquidity fluctuations driven by factors beyond individual traders' control. We distinguish this from endogenous liquidity risk, which refers to liquidity fluctuations driven by individual actions, such as an attempt to unwind a very large position. A trader holding a very large position in an otherwise stable market, for example, may find him- or herself in region 4. The risk plane (market/liquidity risk) is of course a simplification of a more complex relationship between markets and position sizes, involving both exogenous and endogenous components of liquidity risk. In particular, creating movement along the liquidity axis can be done by moving either across established or emerging markets (i.e., increasing exogenous illiquidity) or within a market by simply increasing one's position size (i.e., increasing endogenous illiquidity).

Exogenous illiquidity is the result of market characteristics; it is common to all market players and unaffected by the actions of any one participant (although it can be affected by the joint action of all or almost all market participants, as happened in several markets in the summer of 1998). The market for liquid securities, such as G-7 currencies, is typically characterized by heavy trading volumes, stable and small bid-ask spreads, and stable and high levels of quote depth. Liquidity costs may be negligible for such positions when marking to market provides a proper liquidation value. In contrast, markets in emerging currencies or thinly traded junk bonds are illiquid and are characterized by high volatilities of spread, quote depth, and trading volume. Endogenous illiquidity, in contrast, is specific to one's position in the market and varies across market participants, and the exposure of any one participant is affected by his or her actions. Endogenous illiquidity is mainly driven by the size of the position: the larger the size, the greater the endogenous illiquidity. A good way to understand the implications of position size is to consider the quote depth, which is the relationship between the liquidation price and the total position size held. Quote depth is defined as the volume of shares available at the market maker's quoted price (bid or ask). Market impact models such as one developed by BARRA quantify this relationship between the transaction price and trade size. If the market order to buy or sell is smaller than the volume available in the market at the quote, then the order transacts at the quote. In this case the market impact cost, defined as the cost of immediate execution, will be half of the bid-ask spread. In our framework, such a position only possesses exogenous liquidity risk and no endogenous risk. If the size of the order exceeds the quote depth, the cost of market impact will be higher than the half-spread. The difference between the total market impact and half-spread is called the *incremental market cost,* and constitutes the endogenous liquidity component in our framework. Endogenous liquidity risk can be particularly important in situations where normally fungible market positions cease to be fungible; a good example would be when the cheapest-to-deliver bond of a futures contract switches. The cheapest-to-deliver bond is a bond that has the same profile as the bonds used in the futures contract. Once the cheapest-to-deliver bond changes in profile, for example because duration is getting shorter because maturity is getting closer, this specific cheapest-to-deliver bond is no longer a fungible position. Later, when the bond is paid back, it disappears from the market. But the futures contract is still in the market. The bonds in the futures contract have to be "switched" from time to time to reflect the correct profile in the contract.

Quantitative methods for modeling endogenous liquidity risk have recently been proposed by Jarrow and Subramanian,[38] Chriss and Almgren,[39] Bertsimas and Lo,[40] and Campbell et al.[41] Jarrow and Subramanian, for example, consider optimal liquidation of an investment portfolio over a fixed horizon. They characterize the costs and benefits of block sale versus slow liquidation and propose a liquidity adjustment to the standard VaR measure. The adjustment, however, requires knowledge of the relationship between the trade size and both the quantity discount and the execution lag. Clearly, there is no readily available data source for quantifying those relationships, which forces one to rely on subjective estimates. In this work we approach the liquidity risk problem from the other side, focusing on methods for quantifying exogenous rather than endogenous liquidity risk. The purpose is to consider two key facts in the liquidity discussion. First, fluctuations in exogenous liquidity risk are often large and important, as is clear from our empirical examples, and they are relevant for all market players, whether large or small. Second, in sharp contrast to the situation for endogenous liquidity risk, the data needed to quantify exogenous liquidity risk is widely available. This is because exogenous liquidity risk is characterized by the volatility of the observed spread with no reference to the relationship of the realized spread to trade size. The upshot is that we can incorporate liquidity risk into VaR calculations in a simple and straightforward way.

Traditional VaR measures are obtained from the distribution of portfolio returns computed at the bid-ask average prices. This implies that the positions can be liquidated at bid-ask prices. This approach conceptually underestimates risk by neglecting the practical fact that liquidation does not occur at the bid-ask average price, but rather at the bid-ask average less half the spread. Thus the spread may fluctuate widely. Use of a simple measure of exogenous liquidity risk, computed using the distribution of observed bid-ask spreads, results in much more appropriate risk result, particularly in emerging market securities. What is the impact for the regulatory capitalization of a trading operation? BIS regulations stipulate monitoring of only the number of VaR violations, not of the way that VaR is computed. Neglecting liquidity risk will lead to underestimation of overall risk, undercapitalization, and too many violations. The BIS regulation, whether intentionally or not, monitors liquidity risk quite appropriately in relation to the qualitative aspects of the regulation. Performance evaluation should also be based on returns adjusted for risk—including liquidity risk. Some financial institutions do this, and due to higher margins many financial institutions have seen growth in their emerging market trading activity. A risk-adjusted view of performance in those markets should account not only for market risk but also for liquidity risk. Otherwise, performance will not be assessed correctly and dealer compensation for liquidity risk will be distorted as it is not under the control of the dealer.

5.10 SUMMARY

The integration of the different risk categories depends on the compatibility of approaches, methodologies, and parameters. Credit risk in the form of specific risks is integrated with market risk in the form of company-specific spread adjustments on top of the generic treasury yield curves, reflecting the company-specific (credit) risk. As discussed in this chapter, the integration of credit and market risk models is more challenging. This is partly due to the fact that the BIS adds values together, ignoring the fact that the underlying valuation models have different roots, assumptions, and parameters. The frequency of the credit events (up- or downgrades) and subsequently the price adjustment follows a different rhythm than market risk valuation, where daily pricing allows a daily frequency. This topic is discussed in Secs. 3.6 to 3.8. For some time, VaR was a favorite measurement approach for everybody and anything. However, more and more, the practical relevance outweighs the fanciness of valuation. The different valuation methodologies, including the advantages and the drawbacks, are discussed to highlight which areas they fit best. Stress testing and limitations of VaR are discussed in detail, emphasizing the important fact that the interpretation of VaR data becomes meaningless unless the relevance of the valuation models, parameters, and assumptions is reexamined on a regular basis. The relevance includes stability of distributions and volatilities including correlations and time-varying risk. Liquidity risk is discussed in detail, as it affects market, credit, and operational risks simultaneously. Market prices react with widening spreads, credit risk reacts with higher specific risks, and operational risk is affected to exposed transaction settlements.

This chapter presents a critical review of many aspects of the previous chapters. It is important to note that technology has helped to integrate market, credit, and operational risk via higher processing capacities, networks and shared information, and the increased rapidity with which companies can close their books and P&L statements. Relevant information for credit risk valuation is disclosed more frequently, which is reflected in more frequent adjustments of credit risk valuations. Systemic risk is becoming more important. Despite the gap between market and credit risk categories, unusual market and credit behavior can trigger systemic risk in a significant way given technology and information networks that spread information in real time. One historical example of systemic risk is the Russian crisis of 1998.

5.11 NOTES

1. Bank for International Settlement (BIS), Basel Committee on Banking Supervision, *The New Basel Capital Accord: Consultative Document, Issued for Comment by 31 May 2001,* Basel, Switzerland: Bank for International Settlement, January 2001.
2. Ibid.
3. The committee will release a complete and fully specified proposal for an additional round of consultation in early 2002 and will finalize the new accord during 2003. The Basel Committee envisions an implementation date of 2005 for the new accord. See Bank for International Settlement (BIS), Basel Committee on Banking Supervision, "Update on the New Basel Capital Accord," press release, Basel, Switzerland: Bank for International Settlement, June 25, 2001.
4. Bank for International Settlement (BIS), Basel Committee on Banking Supervision, *Amendment to the Capital Accord to Incorporate Market Risks,* Basel, Switzerland: Bank for International Settlement, January 1996, modified September 1997.
5. Bank for International Settlement (BIS), Basel Committee on Banking Supervision, *A New Capital Adequacy Framework,* Basel, Switzerland: Bank for International Settlement, June 1999.
6. Bank for International Settlement (BIS), Basel Committee on Banking Supervision, "Progress Towards Completion of the New Basel Capital Accord," press release, Basel, Switzerland: Bank for International Settlement, December 13, 2001.
7. Bank for International Settlement (BIS), Basel Committee on Banking Supervision, "Quantitative Impact Survey of New Basel Capital Accord," press release, Basel, Switzerland: Bank for International Settlement, October 1, 2002.
8. Bank for International Settlement (BIS), Basel Committee on Banking Supervision, "Update on the New Basel Capital Accord," press release, Basel, Switzerland: Bank for International Settlement, June 25, 2001; "Update on the New Basel Capital Accord, Issue 2," press release, Basel, Switzerland: Bank for International Settlement, September 21, 2001; *Results of the Second Quantitative Impact Study,* Basel, Switzerland: Bank for

International Settlement, November 5, 2001; *Potential Modifications to the Committee's Proposals,* Basel, Switzerland: Bank for International Settlement, November 5, 2001; *The Quantitative Impact Study for Operational Risk: Overview of Individual Loss Data and Lessons Learned,* Basel, Switzerland: Bank for International Settlement, January 2002.

9. Bank for International Settlement (BIS), Basel Committee on Banking Supervision, *Results of the Second Quantitative Impact Study,* Basel, Switzerland: Bank for International Settlement, November 5, 2001.

10. Bank for International Settlement (BIS), Basel Committee on Banking Supervision, *The Quantitative Impact Study for Operational Risk: Overview of Individual Loss Data and Lessons Learned,* Basel, Switzerland: Bank for International Settlement, January 2002.

11. Ibid.

12. Bank for International Settlement (BIS), Basel Committee on Banking Supervision, *The New Basel Capital Accord: Consultative Document, Issued for Comment by 31 May 2001,* Basel, Switzerland: Bank for International Settlement, January 2001, para. 19ff.

13. Ibid., para. 586 ff.

14. Ibid., para. 633 ff.

15. The latest approved version, dated May 20, 2001, is officially titled "AIMR-PPS Standards, the U.S. and Canadian Version of GIPS." For details, see www.aimr.org/pdf/gips.pdf and www.aimr.com/standards/pps/pps.html#new.

16. See Anil Bangia, Francis X. Diebold, Til Schuermann, and John D. Stroughair, *Modeling Liquidity Risk, with Implications for Traditional Market Risk Measurement and Management,* University of Pennsylvania, Financial Institutions Center, The Wharton School, June, 1999.

17. See for instance E. I. Altman and D. L. Kao, "Examining and Modeling Corporate Bond Rating Drift," working paper, New York University Salomon Center, New York, 1991. These researchers find that there is positive autocorrelation in S&P downgrades, so a downgrade implies a higher likelihood of a downgrade in the following period. Looking at the S&P rating data, the study finds that an upgrade tends to lead to a "quiet" period. However, this finding applies in particular to the S&P rating methodology. Other credit rating systems are not necessarily subject to this problem in the same way given different assumptions and approaches.

18. Bank for International Settlement (BIS), Basel Committee on Banking Supervision, *Amendment to the Capital Accord to Incorporate Market Risks,* Basel, Switzerland: Bank for International Settlement, January 1996, modified September 1997, para. B4.h.

19. See www.bog.frb.fed.us/BoardDocs/Testimony/1998/19981001.html.

20. For an analysis of this "fallacy," see R. Merton and P. Samuelson, "Fallacy of the Log-Normal Approximation to Portfolio Decision-Making over Many Periods," *Journal of Financial Economics* 1 (1974), 67–94; or W. Harlow, "Asset

Allocation in a Downside Risk Framework," *Financial Analysts Journal* 47 (September 1991), 28–40.

21. Other approaches exist, however. See for instance J. Boudoukh, M. Richardson, and R. Whitelaw, "Expect the Worst," *Risk* (September 1995), 101–105, which describes multivariate density estimation as a nonparametric model that appears to be quite flexible. Also, risk estimators do not necessarily have to rely solely on daily closing prices. Parkinson has shown that using the information in the extreme values (daily high and low) leads to an estimator that is twice as efficient as the usual volatility. For details see M. Parkinson, "The Extreme Value Method for Estimating the Variance of the Rate of Return," *Journal of Business* 53 (1980), 61–65.

22. For details, see R. Engle, "Auto-regressive Conditional Heteroskedasticity with Estimates of the Variance of United Kingdom Inflation," *Econometrica* 50 (1982), 987–1007; and T. Bollerslev, "Generalized Auto-regressive Conditional Heteroskedasticity," *Journal of Econometrics* 31 (1986), 307–327.

23. For an analysis of the theoretical rationale behind the success of GARCH models, see D. Nelson, "ARCH Models as Diffusion Approximations," *Journal of Econometrics* 45 (1990), 7–38.

24. K. French, W. Schwert, and R. Stambaugh, "Expected Stock Returns and Volatility," *Journal of Financial Economics* 19 (1987), 3–29.

25. R. Engle, D. Lilien, and R. Robins, "Estimating Time-Varying Risk Premia in the Term Structure: The ARCH-M Model," *Econometrica* 55 (1987), 391–407.

26. D. Hsieh, "The Statistical Properties of Daily Foreign Exchange Rates: 1974–983," *Journal of International Economics* 24 (1988), 129–145; A. Giovannini and R. Jorion, "The Time-Variation of Risk and Return in the Foreign Exchange and Stock Markets," *Journal of Finance* 44 (1989), 307–325.

27. T. Bollerslev, R. Chou, and K. Kroner, "ARCH Modelling in Finance: A Review of the Theory and Empirical Evidence," *Journal of Econometrics* 52 (1992), 5–59.

28. For more details on the methodology, see J. P. Morgan, *RiskMetrics Technical Document*, 4th ed., New York: J. P. Morgan, December 17, 1996, p. 78.

29. The methods for incorporating this data are fully discussed in Jorge Mina and Jerry Yi Xiao, *Return to RiskMetrics: The Evolution of a Standard*, New York: RiskMetrics Group, 2001.

30. Francis Longin and Bruno Solnik, "Is the Correlation in International Equity Returns Constant: 1960–1990?" *Journal of International Money and Finance* 14 (1995), 3–26.

31. One potential objection to the use of option volatilities is that the Black-Scholes model is, strictly speaking, inconsistent with stochastic volatilities. However, recent research on the effect of stochastic volatilities has shown that the Black-Scholes model performs well for short-term at-the-money options. For further details, see S. Heston, "A Closed-Form Solution for Options with Stochastic Volatility with Applications to Bond and Currency Options," *Review of Financial Studies* 6 (1993), 327–343; J. Duan, "The GARCH Option Pricing Model," *Mathematical Finance* 5 (1995), 13–32; D.

Duffie and D. Lando, "Term Structures of Credit Spreads with Incomplete Accounting Information," working paper, Stanford University Graduate School of Business, 1997; and D. Bates, "Testing Option Pricing Models," Working Paper NBER-5129, Cambridge, MA: National Bureau of Economic Research, 1995.

32. W. Margrabe, "The Value of an Option to Exchange One Asset for Another," *Journal of Finance* 33 (1978), 177–186.

33. Anil Bangia, Francis X. Diebold, Til Schuermann, and John D. Stroughair, *Modeling Liquidity Risk, with Implications for Traditional Market Risk Measurement and Management,* University of Pennsylvania, Financial Institutions Center, The Wharton School, June 1999.

34. Nicholas Dunbar, "Meriwether's Meltdown," *Risk* (October 1998), 32–36.

35. For a discussion on the appropriateness of the time-scaling of variances, see F. X. Diebold, A. Hickman, A. Inoue, and T. Schuermann, "Scale Models," *Risk* 11 (January 1998), 104–107.

36. Francis A. Longstaff, "Optimal Portfolio Choice and Valuation of Illiquid Securities," manuscript, UCLA, Department of Finance, Los Angeles, 1998.

37. R. A. Jarrow and A. Subramanian, "Mopping up Liquidity," *Risk* 10 (December 1997), 170–173.

38. Ibid.

39. N. Chriss and R. Almgren, "Optimal Liquidation," manuscript, University of Chicago, Department of Mathematics, Goldman Sachs & Co., and Courant Institute of Mathematical Sciences, 1998.

40. D. Bertsimas and A. W. Lo, "Optimal Control of Execution Costs," *Journal of Financial Markets* 1 (1998), 1–50.

41. J. Y. Campbell, A. W. Lo, and A. C. MacKinlay, *The Econometrics of Financial Markets,* Princeton, NJ: Princeton University Press, 1997.

CHAPTER 6

Case Studies

6.1 STRUCTURE OF STUDIES

At present, there are standard industry-accepted definitions for market, credit, and systemic risk, but no such definition for operational risk. (The BIS definition of operational risk is not accepted throughout the industry.) For these case studies, therefore, we use the definitions and framework from Chapter 5 and verify case by case the extent to which the structure of this approach can be applied.

The first section of each case study describes the causal events and contributory factors leading to losses at a given financial institution. The following section outlines the effect of the causal events and contributory factors in order to clearly separate the causes, symptoms, and main and side effects. The final section allocates the different findings to the risk areas being affected. This section is key and will highlight to which areas the losses have to be allocated and why management and/or regulatory controls failed.

6.2 OVERVIEW OF CASES

The list of crises, near collapses, and effective collapses involving financial institutions is endless. However, some cases catch the attention of the regulators, and especially the media, and thus drive developments and trigger the implementation of new regulations. This in turn forces the industry to develop new approaches and new processes. Table 6-1 provides an overview of recent incidents in the market. Other cases, such as the losses and consequent shutdown of the London-based Griffin Trading

TABLE 6-1

Overview of Recent Incidents in Financial Institutions

Institution	Date	Cause	Effect
Banco Ambrosiano	1982	Money laundering; fraud; conspiracy leading to multiple murders; complex networking of criminal elements including P2 members, Vatican officials, and high-ranking politicians in many countries.[3]	Loss of $1.4 billion
Bankers Trust	October 27, 1994	Material misrepresentations and omissions to client; lawsuits filed by Procter & Gamble and Gibson Greetings.[4]	$195 million damage; bankruptcy as clients moved business to other banks; takeover in 1999 through Deutsche Bank
Barings	February 23, 1995	Unauthorized trading; failure of controls; lack of understanding of the business, particularly in futures; carelessness in the internal audit department.	Loss of $1.328 billion; bankruptcy (takeover)
BCCI	1991	Weak credit analysis process; missing or incomplete loan documentation; concealment and fraud across the institution; money laundering.[5]	Collapse; $500 billion in estimated damage to taxpayers
Bre-X	November 5, 1997	Deliberate stock manipulation through false claims of gold discovery.[6]	Loss of $120 million
Credit Lyonnais	1994	Inadequate supervision and deregulation supported fraud; loan mismanagement; money laundering; fraud; complex networking of politicians, bankers, and new owners.[7]	Loss of accumulated $24.22 billion; collapse without governmental support
Daiwa	July 1995	Unauthorized trading of U.S. bonds and accumulated losses over 12 years.[8]	Loss of $1.1 billion

Drexel Burnham Lambert	February 9, 1990	Growth and profit were tied to the junk bond market Drexel had created and that crashed. The company was highly leveraged with substantial unsecured short-term borrowing at holding company. Drexel did not and could not obtain committed bank lines of credit to support the unsecured borrowing positions.	$1.3 billion global settlement case; $200 million criminal fine; $400 million civil restitution fund with SEC; bankruptcy
Jardine Fleming	July 1995	Lax controls; fraud; insider trading; selective deal allocations to client account.[9]	Compensation of $19.3 million to client with impacted performance from selective deal allocation; $2.2 million missing from client account
Kidder Peabody	April 1994	Phony profits; superiors did not understand trades; no questions asked because profits were being produced; inadequate supervision; promotion of superstar culture; employment references not checked; payment of bogus bonuses.[10]	Loss of $350 million
LTCM	September 1998	Growth and profit were tied to leverage and large exposures to illiquid emerging market exposures. The company was highly leveraged with substantial unsecured short-term borrowing at holding company. No questions were asked because profits were being produced. Inadequate supervision; promotion of superstar culture (including Nobel Prize winners). LTCM did not and could not sell illiquid positions to support the unsecured borrowing positions as the market went down and investors sold shares of LTCM.	Loss of $3.5 billion; investment of additional $1 million by syndicate of borrowers to avoid crash and systemic crisis; retirement of chairman of UBS

TABLE 6-1

Overview of Recent Incidents in Financial Institutions (*Continued*)

Institution	Date	Cause	Effect
Metallgesellschaft	December 1993	Hedge strategies for oil prices; incorrect economic assumptions. Liquidation of positions failed, strategies led to fraud.	Loss of $1.5 billion
Morgan Grenfell	September 2, 1996	Inadequate supervision; promotion of superstar culture; no questioning of profits and instruments used.[11]	Loss of $260 million
Nasdaq	May 1994	Between 1989 and 1994, several brokers kept spread above unnaturally high levels and generated excessive profits for themselves and their institutions. Article in *Journal of Finance* disclosed excess profits from spread and initiated SEC investigation.[12]	Payment by clients of a spread kept at unnaturally high levels
NatWest	1996	Rogue trading; fraud.[13]	Loss of £90.3 million
Orange County, California	December 1994	Illegal use of state funds; losses from bond trading; false and misleading financial statements; fraud.[14]	Loss of $164 million; bankruptcy
Sumitomo	June 13, 1995	Copper trading errors; failure to segregate duties; no questions asked because profits were produced; inadequate supervision; promotion of superstar culture.	Loss of $2.6 billion

company[1] and of Cendant,[2] or fraud charges against Martin Frankel, are not analyzed. The cases of Metallgesellschaft, Sumitomo, LTCM, and Barings have been selected for detailed analysis.

6.3 METALLGESELLSCHAFT

6.3.1 Background

Starting in 1991, Metallgesellschaft began offering fixed-price contracts with terms of up to 10 years to supply heating oil and gasoline to independent wholesalers and retailers.[15] Firm-fixed contracts supplied the end user with a fixed volume per month for a fixed price over a 5- or 10-year period. The contracts were based on the average price of futures maturing over the next 12 months plus a fixed premium of $3 to $5 per barrel.[16] The same price was offered for the 5- and 10-year contracts, without regard for the time value of credit. Participating firms could also exit the contract if the spot price rose above the contract price. The two parties would then split the difference in the prices. Later, Metallgesellschaft began writing in a mandatory exit if the spot price was higher than the contract price, so that Metallgesellschaft could reduce its exposure to rising oil prices.

In 1993, Metallgesellschaft began offering firm-flexible contracts. These contracts were set at a higher price than the firm-fixed contracts. Under these contracts, a firm could exit and receive the entire difference between the spot price and the contract price multiplied by the remaining barrels in the contract. Metallgesellschaft negotiated most of its contracts in the summer of 1993.[17]

Metallgesellschaft sought to offset the exposure resulting from its delivery commitments by buying a combination of short-dated oil swaps and futures contracts as part of a strategy known as a *stack-and-roll hedge.* A stack-and-roll hedge involves repeatedly buying a bundle, or *stack,* of short-dated futures or forward contracts to hedge a longer-term exposure. Each stack is rolled over just before expiration by selling the existing contracts while buying another stack of contracts for a more distant delivery date; thus the term stack-and-roll. Metallgesellschaft implemented its hedging strategy by maintaining long positions in a wide variety of contract months, which it shifted between contracts for different oil products (crude oil, gasoline, and heating oil) in a manner intended to minimize the costs of rolling over its positions. Metallgesellschaft used short-dated contracts because the futures markets for most commodities have relatively little liquidity beyond the first few contract dates. The gains and losses on each side of the forward and futures transactions should have offset each other.

By September 1993, Metallgesellschaft had committed to sell forward the equivalent of over 150 million barrels of oil for delivery at fixed prices, with most contracts containing 10-year terms. Energy prices were relatively low by recent historical standards during this period and were continuing to fall. As long as oil prices kept falling, or at least did not rise appreciably, Metallgesellschaft stood to make a handsome profit from this marketing arrangement. But a significant increase in energy prices could have exposed the firm to massive losses unless it hedged its exposure.

In December 1993, it was revealed that Refining and Marketing, Inc., a subsidiary of the German conglomerate Metallgesellschaft AG, had experienced losses of approximately $1.5 billion in connection with implementing a hedging strategy in the petroleum futures market.[18] In 1992, the subsidiary had begun a new strategy to sell petroleum to independent retailers, on a monthly basis, at fixed prices above the prevailing market price for periods of up to 5 and even 10 years. To lock in the profits and protect against the risk of rising prices, Metallgesellschaft employed a great many short-term derivative contracts such as swaps and futures on crude oil, heating oil, and gasoline on several exchanges and markets in an attempt to hedge its forward positions with retailers. This led to a timing (maturity) mismatch between the short-term hedges and the long-term liability and also resulted in overhedging (see Table 6-2). While the strategy protected against large price fluctuations, it ignored other risks, including basis risk, dealing risk, liquidity risk, and credit risk. The strategy relied on the prevailing condition of normal backwardation, where the spot price is greater than the futures price. However, due to a sudden large drop in oil prices in the fall of 1993 (due to OPEC's problems sticking to its quotas), the market condition changed into one of contango, where the futures price is greater than the spot price. This had the effect of significantly increasing the costs of Metallgesellschaft's hedging strategy, finally resulting in a loss of $1.5 billion.

Although the petroleum market during that time period was deviating from its historical norm, Metallgesellschaft's problem was with cash flow. Metallgesellschaft entered agreements to supply a defined total volume of heating oil and gasoline to companies over a 5- to 10-year period for a fixed rate. The fixed rate was calculated as a simple 12-month average of the futures prices plus a set premium and did not take into account contract maturity.[19] Metallgesellschaft's customers were obligated to accept monthly delivery of a specified amount of oil or gas for the fixed rate. This arrangement provided customers with an effective means to reduce exposure to oil price volatility risk. In addition, customers were given the option of exiting the contract if the nearest month futures price listed on the New York Mercantile Exchange (NYMEX) was greater than the fixed price defined in the contract. When this option was exercised, Metallgesellschaft made a cash payment to the company for half the difference between the futures price and the fixed price. A company might choose to exercise this option in the event of financial difficulties or if it did not need the product.

TABLE 6-2

Cash Flow Deficit Created by a Maturity-Mismatched Hedge

			Supply Contracts		Futures Stack		Net Position	
Month	Near Month Futures Price, $/Barrel	Next Month Futures Price, $/Barrel	Deliveries, Millions of Barrels	Net Receipts, $ Million	Size of Stack, Millions of Barrels	Monthly Settlement, $ Million	Net Cash Flow, $ Million	Accumulated Net Cash Flow, $ Million
March	20.16	20.30	—	—	154.00	—	—	—
April	20.22	20.42	1.28	1.00	152.70	(12.30)	(11.30)	(11.30)
May	19.51	19.83	1.28	1.90	151.40	(139.00)	(137.10)	(148.40)
June	18.68	18.90	1.28	3.10	150.20	(189.30)	(186.20)	(334.60)
July	17.67	17.92	1.28	4.30	148.90	(184.70)	(180.40)	(515.00)
August	17.86	18.30	1.28	4.00	147.60	(8.90)	(4.90)	(519.90)
September	16.86	17.24	1.28	5.30	146.30	212.50	(207.20)	(727.10)
October	18.27	18.38	1.28	3.50	145.00	150.70	154.20	(572.90)
November	16.76	17.06	1.28	5.40	143.70	234.90	(229.50)	(802.40)
December	14.41	14.80	1.28	8.50	142.50	380.90	(372.40)	(1174.80)

SOURCE: Antonio S. Mello and John E. Parsons, "Maturity Structure of a Hedge Matters: Lessons from the Metallgesellschaft Debacle," *Journal of Applied Finance,* 8/1 (1995), 106–120. Reproduced with permission of The Financial Management Association International.

6.3.2 Cause

In the fall of 1993, Metallgesellschaft went long on approximately 55 million barrels of gasoline and heating oil futures. At that time, the average trading volume for unleaded gas was only between 15,000 and 30,000 barrels. By December of that year, Metallgesellschaft had long positions in energy derivatives equivalent to 185 million barrels of oil. As oil prices fell, Metallgesellschaft was forced to pay the difference, and, by the end of December 1993, losses were just over $1 billion. In addition to the direct losses, rolling over the contracts cost the firm a total of $88 million in October and November alone.

Problems arose because Metallgesellschaft's volume was too high to act as an effective hedge. The company owned so many futures that it had trouble liquidating them. Also, contango caused Metallgesellschaft to perpetually roll into higher futures prices even as the spot prices were falling. In addition, because futures get marked to market each day so that as the price falls, the futures value drops, margin calls were initiated. As these contracts matured, Metallgesellschaft was forced to make large payments to its counterparties, putting further pressure on its cash flows. At the same time, most offsetting gains on its forward delivery commitments were deferred. Had oil prices risen, the accompanying gain in the value of Metallgesellschaft's hedge would have produced positive cash flows that would have offset losses stemming from its commitments to deliver oil at below-market prices. As it happened, however, oil prices fell even further in late 1993 (see Figure 6-1).

6.3.2.1 Hedging Strategy

The hedging strategies used by Metallgesellschaft were very misleading, going from a less appropriate method to final speculative hedging.[20]

- *Short forward.* In 1991, Metallgesellschaft wrote forward contracts of up to 10 years. This strategy was based on Arthur Benson's unproven theory that these contracts were profitable because they guaranteed a price over the cash oil price. There was no certainty that in such a market this situation could continue. Metallgesellschaft's 10-year forward contracts seemed like an action taken by a risk minimizer; however, given 10 years' worth of uncertain market price movement, it would be extremely risky to fix future cash flows for such a long time and ignore the importance of the real value of future cash flows. If Metallgesellschaft expected future cash flows to fund its future operations, the shrinking value of these cash flows would prove insufficient.
- *Forward with option.* Of immediate interest was the sell-back option included in the forward contracts. If we assume the short

FIGURE 6-1

Oil Prices Between January 1993 and December 1994. (*Data source:* Bloomberg Professional.)

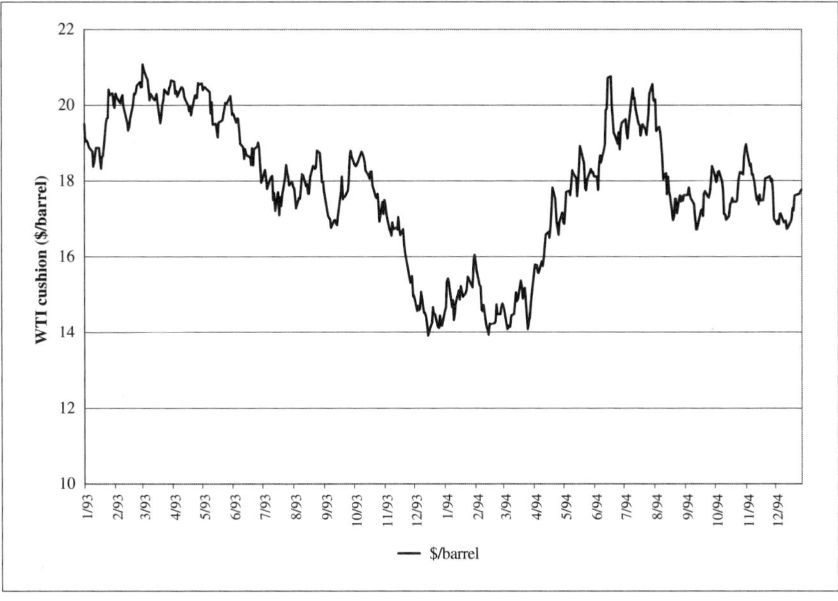

forward strategy to be a risk minimizer, then the sell-back option cast some doubt on it. The sell-back occurred month by month based on the scenario that the front-month NYMEX futures contract price was greater than the fixed price at which Metallgesellschaft was selling its oil products. Metallgesellschaft did not hedge its entire future products price, and, after canceling those forward obligations, it had to pay 50 percent of the difference in cash. There is no benefit from such a cash outflow given that Metallgesellschaft never received cash inflow from the counterparties and that it would never benefit after canceling the forward contracts. In a price swing market, this position could create continuing and enormous cash obligations for Metallgesellschaft. The option items moved Metallgesellschaft from a simple hedger to a market maker, a position that conflicted with its fundamental role.

- *Futures and swaps.* Metallgesellschaft used another strategy to hedge the risk of upward price movements: it entered into huge positions in the futures market for each month, then stacked and rolled over these contracts every month. Thus, contrary to the characteristics of its large forward, Metallgesellschaft entered

> another market, which was marking to market daily, rolling over all 10-year contracts together every month, with constant risk of margin call and cash requirement due to basis risk in a contango market. As Metallgesellschaft built large positions in the futures market, it had to respond to the obligation from the market price swing and short-term cash responsibility and to the 10-year long-term responsibility, while the theoretical gain from the short 10-year forward would not materialize at that time.

The credit risk created thus far led to Metallgesellschaft's final liquidation and loss of $1.5 billion. The notional gain from the short forward did not make up for the loss in futures, and these notional gains could disappear given such a long cycle in the financial market. It is very hard to understand how such a double hedging strategy was allowed.

6.3.2.2 Effect

Moreover, declines in spot and near-term oil futures and forward prices significantly exceeded declines in long-term forward prices. As a result, realized losses from the hedge appeared to exceed any potential offsetting gains accruing to Metallgesellschaft's long-term forward commitments. It was both contango and margin calls that created a major cash crunch for Metallgesellschaft.

German accounting methods made Metallgesellschaft show the futures losses but did not allow the company to show the not yet realized gains from the forward contracts. This caused panic, and Metallgesellschaft's credit rating plummeted. In response to these developments, NYMEX raised its margin requirements for the firm.[21] This action, which was intended to protect the exchange in case of a default, further exacerbated Metallgesellschaft's funding problems. Rumors of the firm's financial difficulties led many of its OTC counterparties to begin terminating their contracts. Others began demanding that it post collateral to secure contract performance. In December 1993, Benson entered into put positions just as the price of crude oil bottomed out.[22]

By the fourth quarter of 1993, Metallgesellschaft's U.S. division needed $1 billion in additional funding and received it even though its credit was faltering. After dismissing the firm's executive chairman, Dr. Heinz Schimmelbusch, Metallgesellschaft's new chairman (turnaround specialist Dr. Kajo Neukirchen) began liquidating the hedge and entering into negotiations to cancel long-term contracts with the company's customers. NYMEX withdrew its hedging exemption once Metallgesellschaft announced the end of its hedging program. The loss of the hedging exemption forced Metallgesellschaft to reduce its positions in energy futures still further. Metallgesellschaft's board of supervisors was forced to negotiate a $1.9 billion rescue package with the firm's 120 creditor banks.

Metallgesellschaft's strategy of paying a floating volatile price in exchange for a fixed price meant the company needed an effective means to manage the price risk. If Metallgesellschaft were to deliver on the contract by purchasing oil on the spot market, the company would be exposed to losses when oil prices increased. Table 6-3 shows that when the spot oil price increased, Metallgesellschaft would incur losses on the delivery of the contract.

To manage the risk of increasing prices, Metallgesellschaft purchased short-term futures contracts for gas and oil on the NYMEX. Normally the markets for oil and gas commodities were in backwardation, which means that the futures prices were less than the current spot prices. By purchasing forward contracts in a backwardation market equal to the amount to be delivered, Metallgesellschaft was able to increase profits when the spot price decreased or to decrease losses when the spot price increased (see Table 6-4).

The historical backwardation term structure of the oil and gas futures markets also presented an opportunity for Metallgesellschaft to earn a profit by hedging. As maturity approaches, the futures and spot prices will normally converge. If the futures price increases as the two prices converge, then the value of the futures contract also increases. A long position established a few months before maturity could then be closed out the month prior to maturity by selling a short position, which generates a net profit. Taking a new long position in a futures contract maturing in a few months, called a *rollover,* extends the hedge. Additional leverage, and thus profit, can be achieved by entering into more contracts.[23]

TABLE 6-3

Three Scenarios for the Amount of Profit Generated per Barrel of Oil on a Six-Month Contract Supplied by Purchasing Oil on the Spot Market

	Stable Spot Price		*Declining Spot Price*		*Increasing Spot Price*	
Date	**Spot**	**Profit**	**Spot**	**Profit**	**Spot**	**Profit**
4/1/01	32.50	0.3331	32.50	0.3331	32.50	0.3331
5/1/01	32.50	0.3331	32.18	0.6581	32.83	0.0081
6/1/01	32.50	0.3331	31.85	0.9799	33.15	–0.3201
7/1/01	32.50	0.3331	31.53	1.2984	33.48	–0.6517
8/1/01	32.50	0.3331	31.22	1.6138	33.82	–0.9865
9/1/01	32.50	0.3331	30.91	1.9260	34.16	–1.3247
Delivery profit per barrel	$2.00		$6.81		$(2.94)	

The assumption is made that prices increase or decrease by 1 percent per month. Formula: Profit = spot price – fixed price.

TABLE 6-4

In a Normal Backwardation Market, Futures Contracts Purchased One Month Before Physical Delivery Increase Profit or Decrease Loss per Barrel.

	Stable Spot Price			*Declining Spot Price*			*Increasing Spot Price*		
Date	**Spot**	**Futures 1 Month Before Delivery**	**Profit**	**Spot**	**Futures 1 Month Before Delivery**	**Profit**	**Spot**	**Futures 1 Month Before Delivery**	**Profit**
4/1/01	32.50	32.18	0.66	32.50	32.18	0.66	32.50	32.18	0.66
5/1/01	32.50	32.18	0.66	32.18	31.85	0.98	32.83	32.50	0.34
6/1/01	32.50	32.18	0.66	31.85	31.93	1.30	33.15	32.82	0.01
7/1/01	32.50	32.18	0.66	31.53	31.22	1.61	33.48	33.15	–0.32
8/1/01	32.50	32.18	0.66	31.22	30.91	1.93	33.82	33.48	–0.65
9/1/01	32.50	32.18	0.66	30.91	30.60	2.24	34.16	33.82	–0.98
Delivery profit per barrel		$3.95			$8.71			$(0.94)	

The assumption is made that the futures contract price with a one-month expiration is 1 percent less than the eventual spot price. Formula: Profit = futures price – fixed price.

The strategy of taking a position in several futures contracts with identical maturities, holding, and then taking an offsetting position before maturity is called a *stack hedge* strategy. A stack hedge is created when a position in futures contracts for a specific maturity is established, but then an offsetting position is taken shortly before maturity. A profit or loss is earned if the futures price increases or decreases.[24]

As long as the spot prices for oil and gas remain relatively stable or increase over the one-month holding period of the stack hedge contracts and the market is in backwardation, then a profit is earned using this strategy. However, if the spot price drops significantly, then losses will be incurred. In the event the spot price drops to less than the futures prices, the market is said to be contango. Entering a long-position stack hedge in a contango market can generate a profit only if spot and futures prices diverge or if spot prices increase while the basis spread does not decrease by an equal amount (i.e., if futures prices increase). Table 6-5 shows the results of holding a long position in futures contracts during a contango and backwardation where the spot price remains stable but the futures price converges. We will assume that if the spot price decreases during backwardation or increases during contango, the futures price remains stable so that the two converge and zero net profit is earned.

The benefits of using a long-position stack hedge when the spot price remains relatively stable or increases can be seen in Table 6-6. As long as the market stays in backwardation, a profit can be earned almost regardless of the direction in which the spot price moves.

TABLE 6-5

Results of Holding a Long Position in Futures Contracts During a Contango and Backwardation

	Date		Rollover	Profit (Loss)
Futures Contract	**Buy**	**Sell**	**Contango**	**Backwardation**
5/01	3/1/01	4/1/01	–0.20	0.20
6/01	4/1/01	5/1/01	–0.20	0.20
7/01	5/1/01	6/1/01	–0.20	0.20
8/01	6/1/01	7/1/01	–0.20	0.20
9/01	7/1/01	8/1/01	–0.20	0.20
Rollover profit per contract			\$(1.00)	\$1.00

The assumption is made that the price of the oil futures contract either increases (backwardation) or decreases (contango) by \$0.20 per barrel during the one-month holding period of the contract. The calculation is based on rollover of only one contract.

TABLE 6-6

Summary of Total Profit Expected Under Each of the Three Scenarios in a Backwardation Market Using 1 and 10 Rollover Contracts

Backwardation Market		Spot Price		
		Stable	Declining	Increasing
1 rollover contract	Delivery profit	$3.95	$8.71	$(0.94)
	Rollover profit	$1.00	—	$1.00
	Total profit	$4.95	$8.71	$0.06
10 rollover contracts	Delivery profit	$3.95	$8.71	$(0.94)
	Rollover profit	$10.00	—	$10.00
	Total profit	$13.95	$8.71	$9.06

The assumption is made that when the spot price decreases, the futures price remains relatively stable.

The term *basis* refers to the difference between the spot price of an item and its futures price. Metallgesellschaft's stack-and-roll hedging strategy exposed it to basis risk—the risk that the price behavior of its stack of short-dated oil contracts might diverge from that of its long-term forward commitments. Because the forward price equals the spot price plus the cost of carry minus the convenience yield, if the convenience yield is high enough to offset the cost of carry, then the forward price is lower than the spot price. This is known as backwardation. A stack-and-roll strategy appeared to offer a means of avoiding carrying costs because short-dated futures markets for oil products have historically tended to exhibit backwardation. In markets that exhibit persistent backwardation, a strategy of rolling over a stack of expiring contracts every month can generate profits. However, a long-dated exposure hedged with a stack of short-dated instruments leaves exposure to curve or contango risk. Buyers of futures and forward contracts should pay a premium for deferred delivery. This premium is known as contango. With contango, the hedge cannot be rolled without a net loss.

In 1993, short-term energy futures exhibited a pattern of contango rather than backwardation for most of the year. Once near-dated energy futures and forward markets began to exhibit contango, Metallgesellschaft was forced to pay a premium to roll over each stack of short-term contracts as they expired. This, however, was only a minor addition to Metallgesellschaft's dilemma.[25]

Metallgesellschaft's financial difficulties were not attributable solely to its use of derivatives; the company had accumulated a heavy debt load in previous years. Metallgesellschaft reported losses of DM 1.8 billion on its operations for the fiscal year ending September 30, 1993, in addition to the DM 1.5 billion loss auditors attributed to its hedging program during the same time frame. The parent firm already had accumulated a cash flow deficit of DM 5.65 billion between 1988 and 1993, which had been financed largely by bank loans. Because of the potential funding risk, Metallgesellschaft should have mitigated the impact by requiring periodic cash settlements from its customers on the forwards. This would have limited the risk of customer default as well as reduced the potential of a cash drain. Also, the firm should have arranged for expanded credit lines to be collateralized by the net value of its forward contracts.[26]

Metallgesellschaft had been using the historical backwardation of the oil market to earn rollover profits, but at the end of 1993 the situation changed to one of contango. The catalyst for this situation was the OPEC cartel, which instituted production quotas that kept spot prices high. Without the production quotas, OPEC countries would have increased oil production, causing spot prices to drop.[27]

Since the contracts Metallgesellschaft had entered into to supply oil were at a fixed rate, the value of these contracts had increased. However, the unexpected move to a contango market caused losses in Metallgesellschaft's long futures. Table 6-7 details three scenarios showing what could have happened to the futures contracts that Metallgesellschaft held to maturity to meet delivery requirements during the contango market. Under the declining spot price scenario, which most closely matches what actually occurred, Metallgesellschaft would earn only $4.91 per barrel in a contango market rather than $8.71 per barrel in a backwardation market (Table 6-6).

Although Metallgesellschaft lost money on each long futures contract purchased in the contango market, the losses on the contracts held to maturity were offset by the increase in the fixed-floating spread. The major problem Metallgesellschaft faced in the contango market resulted from losses on the stacked hedge. Since the stacked hedge was long oil futures, Metallgesellschaft lost money each time a rollover was made. Table 6-8 shows how the rollover losses could have affected the total profit earned by Metallgesellschaft. The losses were exacerbated by the large positions that Metallgesellschaft had in the market, totaling approximately 160 million barrels of oil. In all, Metallgesellschaft lost about $1.5 billion due to the stack hedge and its rollover.

Metallgesellschaft had obviously not anticipated the spot price decrease and the switch to the contango market. It seems that the company's management, led by Arthur Benson, was either speculating that spot prices would not decrease or did not fully understand the company's derivative position. When the spot price fell, it created the need for large amounts of cash to cover the margin calls on the long futures positions. Metallgesellschaft could have easily managed the risk of falling prices by purchasing put options—a move that was not made until December 1993. The spot decrease also had the positive effect of increasing the value of the fixed-rate contracts by an amount equal to the losses in the long futures.

TABLE 6-7

In a Contango Market Using Futures Contracts Purchased One Month in Advance of Physical Asset Delivery, Oil Costs More than If Purchased on the Spot Market

	Stable Spot Price			*Declining Spot Price*			*Increasing Spot Price*		
Date	**Spot**	**Futures 1 Month Before Delivery**	**Profit**	**Spot**	**Futures 1 Month Before Delivery**	**Profit**	**Spot**	**Futures 1 Month Before Delivery**	**Profit**
4/1/01	32.50	32.83	0.01	32.50	32.83	0.01	32.50	32.83	0.01
5/1/01	32.50	32.83	0.01	32.18	32.50	0.34	32.83	33.15	–0.32
6/1/01	32.50	32.83	0.01	31.85	32.17	0.66	33.15	33.48	–0.65
7/1/01	32.50	32.83	0.01	31.53	31.85	0.98	33.48	33.82	–0.99
8/1/01	32.50	32.83	0.01	31.22	31.53	1.30	33.82	34.16	–1.32
9/1/01	32.50	32.83	0.01	30.91	31.22	1.62	34.16	34.50	–1.67
Delivery profit per barrel		$0.05			$4.91			$(4.94)	

The assumption is made that futures contract price one-month expiration is 1 percent greater than the eventual spot price. Formula: Profit = Futures price – Fixed price.

TABLE 6-8

Summary of Total Profit Expected Under Each of the Three Scenarios in a Contango Market Using 1 and 10 Rollover Contracts

Contango Market		Spot Price		
		Stable	Declining	Increasing
1 rollover contract	Delivery profit	$0.05	$4.91	$(4.94)
	Rollover profit	$(1.00)	$(1.00)	—
	Total profit	$(0.95)	$3.91	$(4.94)
10 rollover contracts	Delivery profit	$0.05	$4.91	$(4.94)
	Rollover profit	$(10.00)	$(10.00)	—
	Total profit	$(9.95)	$(5.09)	$(4.94)

The assumption is made that when the spot price increases in a contango market, the futures price remains relatively stable.

However, the daily margin calls required Metallgesellschaft to ask for more than $1.8 billion in loans from its German parent company during the fourth quarter of 1993 to cover the large number of long futures.[28]

Although Metallgesellschaft was having a cash flow crisis due to trying to cover the margin calls, a larger public relations crisis resulted from German accounting requirements. Under the U.S. accounting system for a hedge fund, Metallgesellschaft could have netted out the losses in long futures with the gains in fixed-rate contracts and actually shown a profit.[29] However, using the German rules, Metallgesellschaft could not realize the gains on the fixed-rate forwards. Thus huge losses had to be reported, which caused counterparties to lose confidence.

In conclusion, it seems that management was directly responsible for the financial catastrophe at Metallgesellschaft. If managers had not taken such a large position in long futures, or if they had at least used put options as a hedge for their position, then the magnitude of the cash flow problem could have been reduced. The overall strategy was sound, and, had a little more effort been made by management to analyze worst-case scenarios, the situation could have turned out differently.

6.3.3 Risk Areas Affected

6.3.3.1 Market Risk

The accepted wisdom is that the flaw in Metallgesellschaft's strategy was the mismatch between the short-term hedge and the long-term liability. Merton Miller, a Nobel Prize winner from the University of Chicago, and

Christopher Culp, a consultant, argue that the accepted wisdom is wrong. The so-called stacked hedge used by Metallgesellschaft would have protected the company fully against fluctuations in oil prices. However, regardless of inputs into simulation models and the soundness of the strategy, there were several risks the company's management did not address:

- *Basis risk.* Metallgesellschaft had entered into stacked futures positions in the front-month contracts, which were rolled over at the expiration of each contract (see Table 6-9). The company became exposed to the basis risk because the market moved from the state of normal backwardation to contango. In the contango market, the spot price decreased more than the futures prices. This created rollover losses that were unrecoverable, and, as long as the market stayed in contango, Metallgesellschaft continued to lose on the rollover. This shift in the market to contango mode did not make the hedge bad, it just magnified the cash flow problems.

TABLE 6-9

Valuation of Contracts, Unhedged and Hedged with a Running Stack

Inputs to simulation model	
Duration of contract	10 years
Total delivery obligation	150 million barrels
Monthly delivery	1.25 million barrels
Fixed contract delivery price	\$20/barrel
Cost of delivery	\$2/barrel
Initial spot price of oil	\$17/barrel
Annual interest rate	7%
Annual convenience yield less cost of storage	7%
Cost of external financing	
\$1 million/month	0 basis points
\$10 million/month	0.2 basis points
\$50 million/month	2.2 basis points
Results	
Present value of contract	\$63.6 million
Cost of financing, unhedged	\$4.4 million
Net value of contract, unhedged	\$59.2 million
Cost of financing, rolling stack	\$28.5 million
Net value of contract, rolling stack	\$35.1 million

- *Dealing risk.* Metallgesellschaft had such a huge position in the market that it would have taken 10 days to liquidate. The position was the equivalent of the entire oil output of Kuwait over a period of 85 days. Such a huge position exposed Metallgesellschaft to dealing risk. The company could not get out of its position immediately if things went bad. The trading volume in the heating oil and unleaded gasoline pits usually averaged from 15,000 to 30,000 contracts per day; Metallgesellschaft's reported position was 55,000 contracts. To liquidate this position without influencing the market price would take Metallgesellschaft anywhere from 20 to 55 days. The risk was so large that it became a systemic risk.
- *Liquidity risk.* Metallgesellschaft failed to take into account the huge cash flow problem that would result almost immediately from its strategy. The problem was that the maturity structures of the derivatives were mismatched with the initial forward contracts. Thus, in the event of daily oil price variations, the futures positions would have to be settled due to the mark-to-market feature of this derivative instrument. Meanwhile, the unrealized gains from the forward positions would not translate into cash flow in the near term, as they would only be realized when the contracts expired. Thus, when oil prices decreased because OPEC had problems holding to its quota, Metallgesellschaft was unable to meet margin calls without assistance from its creditors. Even though the cash flows would have balanced out over the life of the hedge, the timing of the cash flows became a very serious problem for Metallgesellschaft. Another complicating issue at the time was the short-term liquidity crisis of the parent company, which had experienced several down years and was forced to sell off assets to meet liquidity needs. Employment had decreased by some 30 percent, to 43,000 employees, and the company was planning on forgoing the next dividend. The subsidiaries were informed that they could not expect to be easily financed by the parent company. Thus Metallgesellschaft chose a particularly poor time to run into funding problems, as its parent could not be of assistance.

6.3.3.2 Credit Risk

The futures and swap positions Metallgesellschaft entered into introduced significant credit risk for the company. The majority of the credit risk was counterparty/settlement risk. If Metallgesellschaft had been subject to banking law, a substantial fraction of capital would have been blocked in regulatory capital. The extraordinary risk concentration might have become obvious and public before the blow-up through banking law auditors and business reports, which require disclosure of the major risks and concentrations.

6.3.3.3 Operational Risk

The company was subject to major operational risk, of which the fraud element is not covered in this analysis: accounting standards contributed substantially to the crisis. Another factor that compounded the problem (and made it possible to "hide" the losses) was the difference between the accounting standards in Germany and the United States. Operating from Germany and processing all accounting transactions and losses according to German accounting standards became a structural operational risk. The German standard required that Metallgesellschaft report its current losses without recognizing the gains on its fixed-rate forwards until they were effectively realized. Thus the company was exposed to a temporary paper loss, which would affect its credit risk, prompting its creditors to require additional margins well above the standard. The banks' panic prevented Metallgesellschaft from rolling over its positions until the long-term delivery contracts expired, which would have left the company with a profit rather than a loss. According to U.S. accounting standards, Metallgesellschaft would have been showing a profit on its strategy, but the lack of foresight to address this issue through a subsidiary or other means left the company vulnerable to a change in market conditions.

6.3.3.4 Systemic Risk

See comments in Section 6.3.3.1 regarding the size of dealing risk leading to systemic risk.

6.3.3.5 Additivity of Risk Management Framework

In this case the BIS framework failed, as Metallgesellschaft is not subject to banking regulation. Internal risk management failed, as positions were reported to management very late in the crisis and hedging activity became more and more speculative. Unless information about rogue trading is known, any regulatory framework will be useless. The management framework failed to recognize the mismatch between the maturity of the original oil contracts and the instruments used to hedge adverse price movements (model risk); to recognize the liquidity impact from the potential cash flows absorbed to cover the margin calls; to recognize the positions in the accounting system; and to supervise employees, given the lack of dual control.

The crisis was triggered by incorrect maturity and cash flow assumptions contained in the investment strategy (model risk) and subsequently not reported as additional operational risk factors contributing to the crisis. It is interesting that market participants knew about the substantial positions and the behavior of Arthur Benson, but top management was not aware of these facts.

Stress testing would have been especially helpful in such a situation, as it would have indicated the substantial potential losses of Metallgesellschaft leading to funding problems.

Had Metallgesellschaft been subject to the BIS and local German banking regulations—apart from management actions—the capital requirements would have been substantially higher. Metallgesellschaft could not have entered the exposures without the capital required by regulations. Stress testing would have indicated that variations in oil prices would break confidence levels and would have shown capital to be inadequate in relation to the risk exposures.

6.4 SUMITOMO

6.4.1 Background

Yasuo Hamanaka was a rogue trader with Sumitomo responsible for the risk management of the company's copper portfolio. Sumitomo, with global assets of $50 billion, maintained a dominant role in copper trading with about 8 percent of the world's supplies of the metal, excluding what is held in the former Eastern Bloc nations and China. The company, which had been in business since the seventeenth century, bought 800,000 tons of copper a year, selling it to affiliates and to the booming market in Southeast Asia. Most of that trading was done by Hamanaka, known as Mr. Five Percent because he and his team controlled at least that share of the world copper market.

Nonetheless, the copper market was relatively small, and this provided Hamanaka with an opportunity to exercise his strategy of capitalizing on copper spot price increases in an effort to corner the market. The strategy failed to minimize its risk against downside risks of falling copper prices. In June 1996, exposure of Hamanaka's illegal transactions sent the price of copper plummeting, resulting in a loss of $2.6 billion. Following the plummeting prices, Sumitomo was able to unwind some of the positions, placing the company in a losing position. Hamanaka was fired and subsequently jailed for his actions in trying to manipulate the price of copper.

6.4.2 Cause

The strategy implemented by Yasuo Hamanaka was quite simple. He worked with brokerage firms such as Merrill Lynch, J. P. Morgan, and Chase to acquire funds to support his transactions. The funds were used to secure a dominant position in copper futures with the purchase of warrants. Hamanaka would buy up physical copper, store it in London Metal Exchange (LME) warehouses, and watch demand drive up the price. His intention was to push up the price of copper and corner the market by acquiring all the deliverable copper in LME warehouses. Since Hamanaka increased his huge long position, it would have been extremely vulnerable to short sales. Peter Hollands, president of Bloomsbury Minerals Economics Ltd. in London, says that was probably the strategy that left Sumitomo so vulnerable and so determined to buy physical copper to boost world copper prices.

Hamanaka was convinced he could drive prices up at will using his huge physical position and sold over-the-counter put options to get cash on the premiums. Put options give their holders the right to sell copper at a predetermined price. Thus, as long as prices were on the upswing, Hamanaka could keep the premiums that the holders paid on the put options. But when copper prices started tumbling, the put holders exercised their puts and Hamanaka had to pay the difference between the strike price and the spot price of copper. His biggest exposure was in a falling spot price.[30]

Given an unusual degree of autonomy within the Sumitomo organization, Hamanaka's intention was to drive up the price of copper to corner the market by acquiring all the deliverable copper in LME warehouses. Implementing the strategy was made easier as he was given the ability to grant power of attorney to brokerage firms to consummate transactions on behalf of Sumitomo without appropriate approval. The lack of oversight apparently allowed Hamanaka to keep two sets of trading books, one reportedly showing big profits for Sumitomo in the buying and selling of copper and copper futures and options and the other a secret account that recorded a dismal tale of billion-dollar losses.

Hamanaka's double-dealing began to unravel in December 1995, when the U.S. Commodity Futures Trading Commission and Britain's Securities and Investments Board, which oversee commodity markets in New York City and London, asked Sumitomo to cooperate in an investigation of suspected price manipulation. Sumitomo later started an in-house investigation of its own. According to CEO Tomiichi Akiyama, in early May 1996 a company auditor uncovered an unauthorized April transaction, the funds for which had passed through an unnamed foreign bank. The trade, which was described as "small in value," led to Hamanaka's office door on the third floor of Sumitomo's headquarters near the Imperial Palace. On May 9, Hamanaka was abruptly reassigned to the post of assistant to the general manager of the Non-Ferrous Metals Division, in what Sumitomo characterized at the time as a promotion. Within days, traders around the world began to realize something was wrong at Sumitomo. In mid-May, a phalanx of commodities firms unloaded their copper holdings in anticipation that Sumitomo would do the same. Prices dropped 15 percent in four days (see Figure 6-2), leaving the international market in an uproar.

6.4.2.1 Intervention by the Commodity Futures Trading Commission

Yasuo Hamanaka's strategy to corner the copper market was most notable not because of his use of derivatives but because his plan included outright fraud and illegal trading practices. Because Sumitomo's positions in the

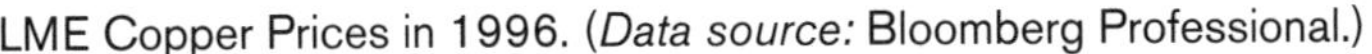

FIGURE 6-2

LME Copper Prices in 1996. (*Data source:* Bloomberg Professional.)

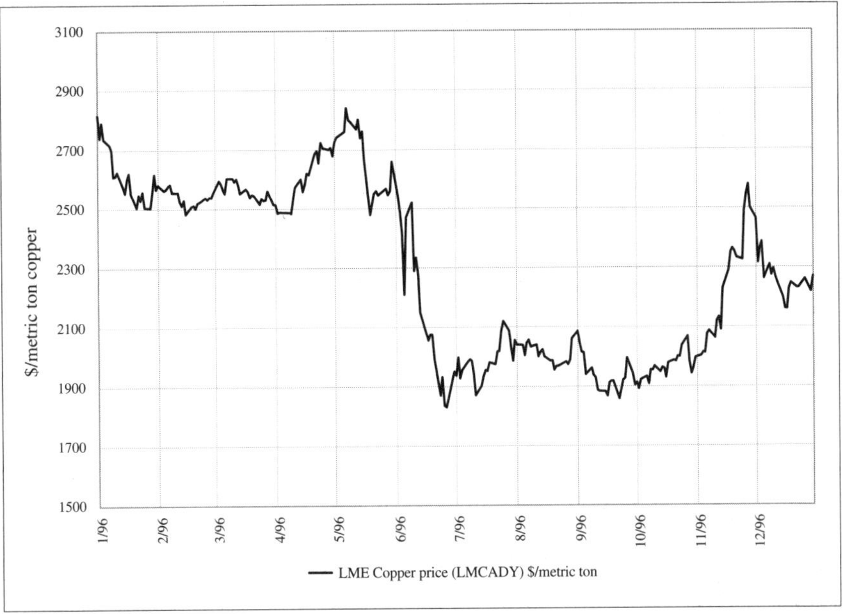

various copper markets artificially manipulated prices and were not related to a "legitimate commercial purpose," Sumitomo was in violation of several sections of the Commodity Exchange Act (CEA).[31] Ultimately, Sumitomo entered into a settlement agreement with the Commodities and Futures Trading Commission (CFTC), agreeing to pay $150 million in fines.[32]

Because the futures market can be manipulated to the detriment of producers or consumers of commodities, Congress expressly prohibits manipulative activity in Sections 6(a), 6(d), and 9(a)(2) of the CEA.[33] While the statutes do not define words like *manipulation, corner,* or *squeeze,* the courts have designed a commonsense approach to interpretation. In Cargill Inc., v. Hardin,[34] the court enumerated the following elements that indicate manipulation: (1) the market participant had the ability to influence market prices; (2) the market participant specifically intended to influence market prices; (3) artificial prices existed; and (4) the market participant created an artificial price.[35] Essentially, when intentional conduct has been engaged in, and that conduct has resulted in a price that does not reflect the basic forces of supply and demand, the courts will presume that manipulation has taken place.[36]

Hamanaka needed a method to generate profits, presumably to offset large losses accumulated as a result of trading in the cash markets.[37] In analyzing the market actions of Sumitomo, the CFTC concluded that as a result of the company's huge physical inventory and its corresponding dominating long futures position, Sumitomo had "expressly [created] artificially high absolute prices and distorted premium of nearby prices over future prices."[38] Furthermore, "Sumitomo deliberately exploited its market dominance [in the futures and physical markets] in order to profit when market prices became artificially high, as Sumitomo had foreseen and planned." Because these positions were not related to Sumitomo's legitimate commercial needs, the resulting price impacts were necessarily artificial and thus in violation of the CEA.[39]

6.4.3 Effect

The effect of the Sumitomo case is typical for disasters triggered by operational risk, with the consequence that the deficiencies in information systems or internal controls will result in unexpected loss. The risk is associated with human error, system failures, and inadequate procedures and controls.

The prevention of an event such as the Sumitomo debacle should include proper internal control measures as well as better portfolio diversification to protect against downside risk. Controls must be in place to prevent such occurrences within an organization. Segregation of duties is vital to proper management of transactions and prevention of fraudulent activities within an organization. Sumitomo should have had a control procedure limiting the ability of copper traders to grant power of attorney to brokerage firms. Such an action on behalf of a company should have appropriate prior approval by senior management. Transactions with a brokerage firm exceeding a certain limit should have multiple approvals by senior management. Senior managers should not allow cash transactions by a trader without appropriate approval from management within the trader's department. Implementing these preventive measures could have prevented some of the transactions that led to huge losses and subsequent civil proceedings.

6.4.4 Risk Areas Affected

6.4.4.1 Market Risk

Put options allow producers the right to sell copper at a set price. As long as the prices were on the upswing, Hamanaka made money and producers lost only the premium on the put options. But when copper prices started tumbling in mid-May and again in June, producers exercised their puts, and Sumitomo swallowed even more losses. This compounded Sumitomo's inability to thwart short sellers due to the company's own desperate sale of long positions, which also drove down prices.

Hamanaka underestimated gamma risk. Gamma measures the parabolic curvature of delta sensitivity. The gamma effect means that position deltas move as the asset price moves, and predictions of revaluation profit and loss based on position deltas are therefore not accurate, except for small moves. Gamma measures the response of an option's delta to changes in rates (gamma = change in delta / change in underlying asset).

6.4.4.2 Credit Risk

Sumitomo dealt with over-the-counter forwards and swaps, where there is a lot of room for subjectivity. Hamanaka was able to sell large quantities of over-the-counter options cheaply, and also financed his positions through large credit lines and prepayment swaps with major banks.

Credit risk in the form of counterparty risk was substantially underestimated, as the concentration in copper trading with a few counterparties was not appropriately recognized and reported to management.

6.4.4.3 Operational Risk

Sumitomo suffered serious control and supervision problems:

- *Lack of management supervision.* Hamanaka was given limitless freedom in handling the copper trade, creating brokerage accounts and bank accounts, executing loan documents, and authorizing cash payments. There was virtually no check on his functional activity. Hamanaka granted power of attorney over Sumitomo trading accounts to brokers. These brokerage firms with power of attorney were doing transactions on margin, which leveraged the position of Sumitomo even higher. It is quite obvious that upper management didn't have the knowledge base to understand these complex transactions.
- *Lack of risk management.* There was no risk management culture at Sumitomo, and even if it had existed, there were a lot of loose ends. Brokerage firms with power of attorney were doing highly leveraged transactions in Sumitomo's name, while Sumitomo thought it was trading cash and futures with the brokerage company.
- *Failure to control the market.* Hamanaka tried to control the market by buying up physical copper, storing it in LME warehouses, and watching demand drive up the price. It's believed that Hamanaka held off huge short sells by purchasing the other side of those short positions.

6.4.4.4 Systemic Risk

Due to fear of facing the market, Hamanaka apparently could not bring himself to accept the fact that even the most successful market manipulator must experience an occasional downward market swing. Rather than sell some of his copper at a loss, he chose to play double or nothing, trying to repeat his initial success by driving prices ever higher, leading to disaster.

6.4.4.5 Additivity of Risk Management Framework

In this case, the BIS framework and internal risk management framework failed, as the positions were unknown to management and undetected by the accounting system until the last minute. Unless information about rogue trading is known, any regulatory framework will be useless. The management framework failed to recognize the substantial concentration risk in trading copper with a few counterparties, especially concentrated in copper instruments; to recognize the positions in the accounting system; and to supervise employees, given the lack of dual control.

Most of the contributing factors are operational risk factors. It is interesting that market participants knew about the substantial positions and the behavior of Yasuo Hamanaka, but Sumitomo's management was not aware of these facts. As a consequence, apart from management actions, the capital requirements would have been substantially higher.

6.5 LTCM

6.5.1 Background

Founded in early 1994, Long Term Capital Management, L.P. (LTCM) is a limited partnership based in Connecticut that operates Long Term Capital Portfolio, L.P., a partnership based in the Cayman Islands. LTCM operates a hedge fund that uses a variety of trading strategies to generate profit, but it initially focused on convergence or relative-value trading. Convergence trading is done by taking offsetting positions in two related securities in hopes of a favorable move in the direction of the price gap. A hedge fund is not defined by statutes, but rather is considered a pooled investment vehicle that is privately organized, administered by professional investment managers, and not widely available to the public. Investors in a hedge fund typically number fewer than 100 institutions and wealthy individuals. Since money is not raised via public offerings, hedge funds avoid the registration and reporting requirements of the federal securities laws. However, hedge funds that trade on organized futures exchanges and that have U.S. investors are required to register with the CFTC as CPOs.[40]

Hedge funds usually focus on one of three general types of investment strategies: (1) taking advantage of global macroeconomic developments; (2) capitalizing on event-driven opportunities including bankruptcies, reorganizations, and mergers; and (3) relative-value trading. LTCM's investment strategy was focused mainly on relative-value trading of fixed-income securities. Here LTCM used sophisticated mathematical models to locate bonds that were closely related to one another but that had a price difference. By taking both a short and a long position in overpriced and underpriced securities, respectively, LTCM would earn a profit as market forces moved to eliminate the arbitrage opportunity. For example, a difference in yields between two U.S. Treasuries with the same maturity and coupon rate but different issuance dates represents an opportunity to profit since market forces should drive the yields to converge.

The relative value strategy worked well for LTCM in 1995 and 1996, with a return on equity of 43 percent and 41 percent, respectively. By 1997, other firms had started copying LTCM's strategy, resulting in fewer opportunities for LTCM to profit from arbitrage in top-quality securities. In an effort to continue generating spectacular returns, LTCM began taking speculative positions in equities and trading extensively in emerging market debt. At one point, Russian debt may have accounted for as much as 8 percent of the total fund value.

At the end of 1998, there were approximately 3000 hedge funds in existence.[41] However, LTCM was unique because of its degree of leverage and scale of activities. Leverage has two different components:

1. *Balance sheet leverage.* Ratio of assets to net worth.
2. *Economic leverage.* Due to its use of repurchase agreements, short sells, and derivative contracts, LTCM saw its capital account mushroom to $7 billion (almost equal to that of Merrill Lynch) by the summer of 1996. The fund struggled throughout 1997, managing to record a gain of only 17 percent.

At the end of 1997, the partners decided to return $2.7 billion to the original investors. The original investors got back $1.82 for every $1 invested in the fund, while still retaining their original $1 investment in the fund.

In the beginning of 1998, the fund had capital of about $4.7 billion and LTCM's leverage reached 28 to 1, or roughly $125 billion. The fund had derivative positions in excess of $1250 billion of notional value. By July, LTCM had mostly uncorrelated (under normal conditions) positions in a wide variety of markets: Danish mortgages, U.S. Treasury bonds, Russian bonds, U.S. stocks, mortgage bonds, Latin American bonds, U.K. bonds, and U.S. swaps.

LTCM wanted the volatility of the fund to be roughly 20 percent on an annualized basis. Before April 1998, the fund's volatility consistently measured 11.5 percent, which was below average. Even after the fund returned its original capital in 1997, its volatility still fell well below 20 percent. With capital of $4.7 billion, a monthly value at risk (VaR) of 5 percent, corresponding to a volatility of 20 percent, is $448 million. In other words, the fund was expected to lose in excess of $448 million in 1 month out of 20 at its target volatility.

On August 17, Russia defaulted on debt and Russian interest rates surged to 200 percent. On August 21, 1998, the Dow fell 280 points by noon and U.S. swap spreads oscillated wildly over a range of 20 points.

(Volatility is around 1 point on a normal day.) They ended 9 points higher, at 76, up from 48 in April. Mortgage spreads and high-yield bonds climbed. LTCM's models considered it a once-in-a-lifetime occurrence and a practical impossibility. On that day, LTCM lost $553 million (15 percent of its capital) when it wasn't supposed to lose more than $35 million on any single day, per the models. This loss was more than 10 times the target daily fund volatility. LTCM had started the year with $4.67 billion; suddenly, it was down to $2.9 billion. LTCM's leverage stood at an untenable 55 times its now shrunken equity (in addition to the massive leverage in derivative bets, such as "equity vol" and swap spreads). Yet the leverage could not be reduced.

One dollar invested in the partnership in March 1994 grew to more than $4 by the end of 1997, but within the first six months of 1998 it dwindled to only 50 cents. More important, the fund was running out of capital. Meeting under the auspices of the Federal Reserve Bank of New York on September 23, the heads of 14 leading banks and investment houses decided to invest $3.65 billion in the fund and obtain a 90 percent stake in LTCM. This was the equivalent of prepackaged bankruptcy.

6.5.2 Cause

The event trigger for the LTCM crisis was model risk. The contributing factors included taking on excessive risks and a general flaw in strategy. The following assumptions and conditions about instruments and models were applied:

- *Risk models relying on portfolio return distribution forecasting.* This is based on the assumption that the past repeats itself in the future. Crisis periods are exceptions where the past is meaningless because volatility increases dramatically and instruments become highly correlated. This is what happened in August 1998.
- *Leverage application.* In theory, market risk does not increase with increase in volume, provided the liquidity of the traded securities is known and the trader does not become the market maker.
- *Relative-value trading.* LTCM spotted arbitrage situations, bet that spreads would narrow and converge (securities that diverged from their historic relationships would eventually converge to the original relationship), and hedged risks. In other words, LTCM would buy huge amounts of six-month-old, 30-year Treasury bonds, and sell equally huge amounts of the just issued but more expensive 30-year Treasury bonds, aiming to profit from the expected convergence in the yields of the two bonds.

The work of Merton and Scholes is grounded in the assumption that there is enough competition in markets that investors can take prices as given and simply react to them. Yet, in 1998, the prices at which LTCM could trade depended on what the market thought LTCM would or could do. Traditional risk measures, which assume that one can trade out of positions without affecting prices, thus become much less useful. LTCM's short-term risk measures took some of these effects into account, but the extent to which prices depended on its positions and actions took the fund's managers by surprise. The problem became critical after the impact of the market events of August 1998:

- LTCM's risk management models relied too heavily on the bell-shaped normal distribution curve, assuming that bad draws occur randomly. A large loss today does not foretell a large loss tomorrow. Unfortunately, in August 1998, risk models indicated that certain events had an infinitesimal probability of happening even though, in reality, they were occurring several times a week.
- LTCM's signature trade, known as equity volatility, comes straight from the Black-Scholes model. It is based on the assumption that the volatility of stocks over time is consistent. Sometimes the market might be more volatile, but it always reverts to form. This theory was guided by the law of large numbers, assuring a normal distribution of quiet trading days and market crashes.

Assuming a swap spread divergence effect, LTCM was betting that the spread between swap rates and liquid treasury bonds would narrow.

For each movement of 5 basis points (BPs), LTCM could make or lose $2.8 million. The expected volatility of the trade over a one-year period involves five such jumps, meaning that, according to its models, LTCM's yearly exposure was no more than $14 million.

The Commodity Futures Trading Commission (CFTC) estimates that 70 percent of all hedge funds have a balance sheet leverage ratio of less than 2 to 1, whereas LTCM, in its year-end 1997 financial statements submitted to the CFTC, showed it had approximately $130 billion in assets on equity capital of $4.8 billion or a ratio of 28 to 1. Approximately 80 percent of LTCM's balance sheet assets were in G-7 nation government bonds. In addition, LTCM had over $1.4 trillion in economic, or off-balance-sheet, leverage, of which $500 billion was in futures exchange contracts and $750 billion was in OTC derivatives.[42]

Although very high compared to the industry average, LTCM's leverage was comparable to the leverage of investment banks at the beginning of 1998. The difference was in LTCM's exposure to certain market risks, which was much greater than for other typical trading portfolios (see Table 6-10), and a global diversification plan that used the same trading strategy in each market.

TABLE 6-10

Leverage Comparison of LTCM Versus Other Large Investment Banks

Institution	Balance Sheet Leverage Ratio	Total Notional Value of OTC and Exchange-Traded Derivatives
LTCM	28 to 1	$1400 billion
Goldman Sachs Group, L.P.	34 to 1	$3410 billion
Lehman Brothers Holdings, Inc.	28 to 1	$2398 billion
Merrill Lynch & Co., Inc.	30 to 1	$3470 billion
Morgan Stanley Dean Witter & Co.	22 to 1	$2860 billion

SOURCE: Commodity Futures Trading Commission (CFTC), "*Hedge Funds, Leverage, and the Lessons of Long-Term Capital Management: Report of the President's Working Group on Financial Markets,* Washington, DC: Commodity Futures Trading Commission, April 1999, www.cftc.gov/tm/hedgefundreport.htm.

In addition to government bonds, LTCM also participated in following markets:

- Mortgage-backed securities, corporate bonds, emerging market bonds, and equity markets
- Futures positions, primarily concentrated in interest rate and equity indexes on major futures exchanges worldwide
- OTC derivatives contracts with over 75 counterparties that included swap, forward, and options contracts

By the end of August 1998, LTCM reportedly had more than 60,000 trades on its books.[43] The circumstances that created the LTCM disaster resulted from the combination of internal and external factors. Government regulatory agencies have known for some time that the unregulated activities of hedge funds could significantly affect financial markets because of their capacity to leverage. However, research by the Federal Reserve Board indicated that banks had adequate procedures in place to manage the credit risk presented by hedge funds. In the case of LTCM, good national economic conditions and the reputation of the management team enticed banks to provide the company with favorable credit arrangements, including no initial margin requirements, that did not adhere to stated policies. This favorable credit treatment allowed LTCM to achieve a high leverage ratio. In addition, LTCM returned $2.7 billion in capital to its investors at the end of 1997 without significantly reducing its positions in the markets, thus pushing the leverage ratio even higher.

In July 1998, LTCM noticed a flaw in its relative-value trading model. Salomon had decided to lower its risk profile by disbanding its bond arbitrage unit. Salomon was selling some of the same positions held by LTCM, which caused a divergence of certain markets that were expected to converge. By the end of the month, LTCM had lost 15 percent of its capital.

International markets were wary because of the turmoil in the economies of Asian countries that had begun in June 1997, causing yields on long-term government bonds in industrial countries to fall. However, most market participants also reasoned that the problems in Asia would lessen worldwide inflationary pressures because of expected weakening in the amount of exports to industrial countries. Thus, the industrial countries largely avoided the negative effects of the Asian crisis. The situation changed in August 1998, when Russia defaulted on government debt obligations and devalued the ruble. This resulted in sizable losses for some investors who had positions that were highly leveraged through collateralized financing. The drop in the value of the ruble in effect caused a global margin call. The Russian default may have also increased investor concern about the risks of investing in other credit-strapped emerging markets. In many emerging markets, both the currency and market value of international debt obligations declined sharply.

Uncertainty about futures prices also broadly affected all financial instruments, causing investors to reduce their tolerance for risk. This created a shift toward the safe and liquid government debt of the major industrial countries, while the yields on both high- and low-quality corporate securities increased sharply. As a result, the spread between rates on corporate and government debt increased substantially around the world.[44]

For LTCM, the dramatic increase in credit spreads meant that its strategy of betting that spreads in all global markets would converge to historical levels was not working, because credit spreads were in fact diverging. Since LTCM had employed the same tactic in markets around the world, there was a lack of diversification that resulted in losing positions in numerous markets. Consequently, LTCM lost 44 percent of its capital in August alone and 52 percent for the year. Because of the high degree of leverage, LTCM would have been unable to make the margin call had it not been for the bail-out package orchestrated by the Federal Reserve Bank of New York.

Problems began for LTCM in July 1998, when Salomon Smith Barney instituted a margin call to liquidate its dollar interest arbitrage opportunities. The interest rate spread arbitrage opportunity on U.S. government bonds and treasuries had blown up on LTCM. The firm had counted on the interest spread closing between the high-liquid and low-liquid treasuries. The crisis in Russia was leading investors to invest in the most liquid U.S. treasuries they could find. This caused the spread to widen instead of close, and convergence turned into divergence. The counterparties of

LTCM began to call for more collateral to cover this divergence. LTCM still believed in its strategy, but required more collateral to cover what it thought were temporary losses.

6.5.3 Effect

LTCM and its investors were impacted most by the following issues:

- The enormous profits LTCM made early on focused the attention of the financial sector on LTCM. This affected LTCM because:

  A large number of imitators appeared in the market. LTCM bought mispriced securities (high yields on a security) while hedging the risk. When imitators did the same, the price of the securities rose, eliminating the profit opportunity LTCM had first identified. This reduced the size of the LTCM trades, decreased the profits on those trades, and destroyed the diversification benefits of the strategy. Rather than acting in isolation, LTCM became the market mover, such that all imitators moved with LTCM. The unfortunate side effect was that seemingly unrelated instruments became linked by common ownership. LTCM partly recognized this in its risk measurement by using correlations that were greater than historical correlations. It also meant that the value of the fund's positions was at the mercy of its imitators pulling out of their positions. In the summer of 1998, Salomon did just that—it closed its bond arbitrage department, resulting in losses for LTCM.

  It put pressure on LTCM to keep pursuing high profits in an environment where this was no longer possible, leading it to create positions in which outsiders would not think it had a competitive advantage.

  It made markets less liquid for LTCM.

- Speculative positions in takeover stocks (e.g., Tellabs, whose share price fell more than 40 percent when it failed to take over Ciena) and investments in emerging markets (e.g., Russia, which represented 8 percent of LTCM's books or $10 billion) caused losses for LTCM.
- There was fallout when spreads widened (as happened during the Russian debt default).
- LTCM was unregulated, which meant it was free to operate in any market without capital charges and with reports required only by the SEC. This enabled LTCM to pursue interest rate swaps with no initial margin (important to its strategy) and implied infinite leverage.

- Financial investors charge a premium to provide liquidity to investors when they want to get out of positions. So, in August 1998, financial intermediaries should have made profits. But federal regulations require banks to use risk management models to set capital. This capital requirement increased with volatility, as banks had to unwind positions themselves and shrink their trading portfolios. As a result, these financial institutions went from being stabilizing to destabilizing forces.
- Adverse price movement caused losses for LTCM.
- Lack of liquidity hampered LTCM's ability to unwind its positions.
- Omitting derivatives, LTCM's leverage was 100 to 1. LTCM routinely borrowed 30 times its equity capital.

6.5.4 Risk Areas Affected

6.5.4.1 Market Risk

Correlation changes or a breakdown of historical relationship is, by definition, a daily VaR that measures maximum loss (confidence level of 99 percent) as that which is exceeded 1 day out of 100 on average. The Russian devaluation and the capital outflows in Brazil started a cycle of losses that developed as positions could not be unwound without creating further losses, which themselves forced further unwinding of positions. This made one-day VaR measures irrelevant, because these measures assume liquidity of positions. As losses forced the unwinding of positions, the crisis spread to unrelated positions, making the returns of unrelated positions highly correlated.[45]

LTCM's trading strategies also made it vulnerable to market shocks. While LTCM traded in a variety of financial markets in a number of different countries, its strategies proved to be poorly diversified. In fact, most of LTCM's trading positions were based on the belief that prices for various risks were high. The company thought that the prices for these risks, such as liquidity, credit, and volatility, were high compared to historical standards. However, these judgments were wrong. In addition, markets proved to be more correlated than LTCM had anticipated, as markets around the world received simultaneous shocks.

LTCM used value-at-risk models, which look backward and assume that as long as markets behave more or less as they have over some past period, a certain amount of losses will likely occur. LTCM studied the relationships between various markets all around the world, bond markets, equity markets, interest rates, and the rate at which those prices changed. When the relationships between these various markets diverged from their historical norms, LTCM would place bets that the norms would reassert themselves.[46]

LTCM's model said the hedge fund was unlikely to lose more than $40 million or so on any given day. But come August 1998, it actually lost more than $500 million in one day, and it lost the same amount in September. Interestingly, even though LTCM lost hundreds of millions of dollars many days during that period, Wall Street has not dropped these models.

LTCM made assumptions based on theoretical model results rather than stress testing. The company assumed that the market would basically behave similarly to how it had in the past, and that the divergence of the spreads it was betting on was limited. It also assumed that market risk would not increase with an increase in volume, provided two things happened: LTCM stuck to liquid instruments and did not get so large that it itself became the market.[47] In sum, the results from stress testing were neglected, or the correlations and volatilities were not stressed enough.

6.5.4.2 Credit Risk

In pursuing the trading strategies mentioned earlier, it appears that LTCM assumed the following:

- That interest rates of liquid and illiquid assets would converge—for example, convergence between liquid treasuries and more complex instruments that command a credit or liquidity premium.
- That it was sufficiently diversified and that its bets were properly hedged. The company also assumed that its models and portfolios used enough stress tests and that risk levels were within manageable limits. In addition, the firm's risk models and risk management procedures may have underestimated the possibility of significant losses.
- That it could be leveraged infinitely on the basis of its reputation.
- Above all, that markets would go up, particularly emerging markets, while credit spreads narrowed.

LTCM was exposed to model risk. LTCM's models indicated that various instruments were mispriced. For example, since 1926, yield spreads between speculative debt-rated Baa bonds and Treasury bonds have ranged from roughly 50 basis points to almost 800 basis points. These large spreads either are due to mispricing (arbitrage profits) or are a market premium that compensates bondholders for the risk they take. It is possible to make large profits based on the mispricing theory, even if it is false. But eventually, if investors are being compensated for taking risks, their bets will result in losses (e.g., they will make profits by selling earthquake insurance only as long as there are no earthquakes). If the bets are highly leveraged, losses can be crippling.

The situation changed dramatically with the Russian default. On August 17, Russia devalued the ruble and declared a moratorium on debt payments. Once again, this sparked a flight to quality as investors shunned risk and sought out liquid assets. As a result, risk spreads widened and many markets around the world became less liquid and more volatile. LTCM was affected, even though the vast majority of its trading risks were related to markets in the major industrialized countries. Thus, LTCM, with 10 percent of its portfolio in Russian securities, found itself losing money on many of its trading positions and nearing insolvency because:

- Some counterparties saw the ongoing crisis as an opportunity to trade against LTCM's known or imagined positions.
- LTCM's counterparties completely ignored the discipline of charging nonbank counterparties initial margin on swap and repo transactions. Collectively, they were responsible for allowing LTCM to build up layer upon layer of swap and repo positions. Their loose practices allowed a nonbank counterparty such as LTCM to write swaps and pledge collateral.
- The results from stress testing were neglected or the credit spreads not stressed enough.

6.5.4.3 Operational Risk

As a registered commodity pool operator (CPO), LTCM filed annual financial statements with the Commodity Futures Trading Commission (CFTC) for the year ending December 31, 1997. The financial statements were audited by Price Waterhouse LLP. LTCM also filed those statements with the National Futures Association (NFA) and provided copies to the fund's investors and lenders. Nothing in the financial statements indicated reason for concern about the fund's financial condition. The fund was well capitalized and very profitable. Its asset-to-capital ratio was similar to that of some other hedge funds as well as many major investment banks and commercial banks.

While the CFTC and the U.S. futures exchanges had detailed daily information about LTCM's reportable exchange-traded futures position through the CFTC's required large trader position reports, no federal regulator received detailed and timely reports from LTCM on its funds' OTC derivatives positions and exposures. Notably, no reporting requirements are imposed on most OTC derivatives market participants.

Furthermore, there are no requirements that a CPO like LTCM provide disclosure documents to its funds' investors or counterparties concerning its derivatives positions, exposures, and investment strategies. It appears that even LTCM's major creditors did not have a complete picture. LTCM's losses in the OTC market make the need for disclosure and transparency obvious.

The Value of Disclosure and Transparency

This is an industrywide issue related to hedge funds. It is important to distinguish between hedging and speculation when using financial derivatives.

Marking to Market

To minimize counterparty risk, LTCM chose derivatives contracts that were marked to market and settled daily, so that no counterparty would be indebted to LTCM for large amounts at any given time. In August 1998, as spreads widened, LTCM was making marked-to-market losses. In other words, long securities were losing value while short securities were gaining value. If LTCM was right about convergence, this was a temporary issue that would be resolved in the long term because the mispricing of the securities would disappear by maturity. Marking to market and the decreased market value of its positions caused LTCM to run out of cash. Although LTCM correctly wanted its investors to commit money for the long term to enable it to take advantage of convergence strategies, it put itself in a position where it could fail before convergence was reached. There was an obvious conflict between hedging strategies and cash requirements.

Transaction Types

The hedge fund was involved in three types of equity trading: "pairs" trading, risk arbitrage (arbitrage positions in merger stocks), and bets on overall market volatility. A major Wall Street firm indicates that LTCM's arbitrage reached $6.5 billion, and positions in individual takeover stocks were 5 to 10 times as large as this Wall Street firm's own arbitrage positions. Some pairs trading positions were even larger. Relative value bets were similar but subtly different. These positions generated profits if LTCM correctly determined that securities were overpriced relative to each other. LTCM differed from the rest of Wall Street in that its investment strategy was backed by detailed and complex computerized analysis of historic patterns of behavior, which allowed it to make confident (but, as it turned out, fallible) predictions about future outcomes.

Liquidity Squeeze

Following the Asian economic crisis, Brazil also devalued its currency. This move created hyperinflation, and interest rates skyrocketed, causing counterparties to lose confidence in themselves and LTCM. As a result of the flight to quality, the spread between liquid and illiquid assets diverged further. With the increased spread, the value of LTCM's collateral assets declined dramatically. LTCM was forced to liquidate assets to meet the margin calls.

Insufficient Risk Management

A significant point that was apparently missed by LTCM and its counterparties and creditors was that while LTCM was diversified across global markets, it did not have a well-diversified strategy. It was betting that, in general, liquidity, credit, and volatility spreads would narrow from historically high levels. When the spreads widened instead in markets across the world, LTCM found itself at the brink of insolvency. In retrospect, it can be seen that LTCM and others underestimated the likelihood that liquidity, credit, and volatility spreads would move in a similar fashion simultaneously in markets across the world.

Essentially, this summarizes the risk of a large loss that LTCM faced owing to its arbitrage strategy. As we have seen, LTCM was highly leveraged. Its on-balance-sheet assets totaled around $125 billion, on a capital base of $4 billion, translating into a leverage of about 30 times. But that leverage was increased 10-fold by LTCM's off-balance-sheet business, where notational principal ran to around $1 trillion. This amount of leverage was reached by using the cash received from borrowing against initial collateral, purchasing securities, and then posting them as collateral for additional borrowing in a continuous cycle. LTCM was leveraged to infinity. Furthermore, as convergence turned to divergence, LTCM sought more borrowed money as capital, convinced that everything would turn out fine. Its leverage was risky due to its magnitude and also to the circumstances for which it relied on a return on investments due to the uncertain global markets. It traded in emerging markets, such as in Russia. The market risk could not be managed or predicted with its models.

The risk that the loss would force liquidation turned into reality as LTCM struggled to raise $500 million in collateral. The more of an asset a company needs to sell, the more capital needs to be available in a very short time period. The number of investors that are ready to buy quickly and at such large amounts is limited.

Another risk was that a forced liquidation would adversely affect market prices. LTCM sold short up to 30 percent of the volatility of the entire underlying French market such that a rapid close-out by LTCM would severely hit the French equity market. The company risked affecting market prices not only due to its own trades, but also as a result of the imitation that occurred in the marketplace. Some of the market players had convergence positions similar or identical to LTCM's, such that if LTCM closed out, there would be a mad panic for everyone to close out.

6.5.4.4 Systemic Risk

Systemic risk is the risk that problems at one financial institution could be transmitted to the entire financial market and possibly to the economy as a whole. Although individual counterparties imposed bilateral trading limits on their own activities with LTCM, none of its investors, creditors, or counterparties provided an effective check on its overall activities. Thus, the only limitations on the LTCM fund's overall scale and leverage were ones provided by its managers and principals. In this setting, the principals, making use of internal risk models, determined the frontier for safe operations of the fund. Moreover, LTCM was unregulated, free to operate in any market without capital charges and with only minimal reporting requirements by the SEC.

What subsequent risks did LTCM face? By mid-September 1998, its capital had shrunk to less than $1 billion, from $4.7 billion at the beginning of the year. LTCM faced severe problems as it tried to unwind some of its positions in illiquid markets. The large size of its positions in many markets contributed to its inability to unwind these positions. As a result, market participants became concerned about the possibility that LTCM could collapse and about the consequences this could have on already turbulent world markets.

With regard to leverage, the LTCM fund's balance sheet on August 31, 1998, included more than $125 billion in assets (see Figure 6-3). Even using the January 1, 1998, equity capital figure of $4.7 billion, this level of assets still implies a balance sheet leverage ratio of more than 25 to 1. The extent of this leverage implies a great deal of risk. Although exact comparisons are difficult, it is likely that the LTCM fund's exposure to certain market risks was several times greater than that of the trading portfolios typically held by major dealer firms. Excessive leverage greatly amplified LTCM's vulnerability to market shocks and increased the possibility of systemic risk. If the LTCM fund had defaulted, the losses, market disruptions, and pronounced lack of liquidity could have

FIGURE 6-3

LTCM's Leverage. (*Source: Commodity Futures Trading Commission* (*CFTC*): Testimony of Brooksley Born, Chairperson, on Behalf of the Commodity Futures Trading Commission before the United States House of Representatives, Subcommittee on Capital Market, Securities and Government Sponsored Enterprises of the Committee on Banking and Financial Services, *Washington, DC: Commodity Futures Trading Commission, March 13, 1999.*)

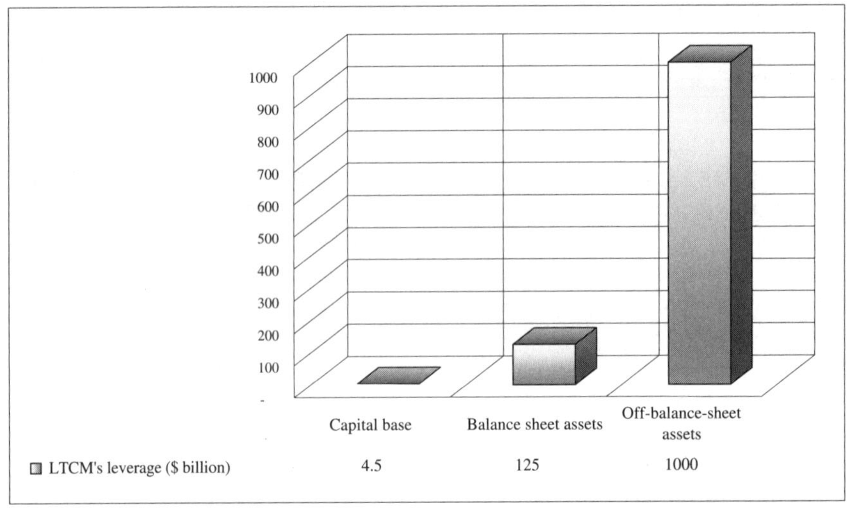

been more severe if not for the use of close-out, netting, and collateral provisions.

6.5.4.5 Additivity of Risk Management Framework

The circumstances leading to the disaster are rooted in the infancy of LTCM. The experience and reputation of its members were renowned throughout the industry. The company was given preferential treatment by investors as well as lending institutions. LTCM was allowed to execute interest rate swaps with no requirement for initial margin, and was also able to use securities purchased with borrowed money to borrow additional money to purchase further securities. In effect, it was able to leverage itself to infinity. This circumstance, coupled with the fact that LTCM kept most of its notational principal off the books, where investors (and the SEC, for that matter) could not monitor it, would prove to be a critical factor in the downfall of the company.[48]

6.6 BARINGS

6.6.1 Background

Barings PLC went bankrupt because it could not meet the trading obligations incurred by Nick Leeson, a British trader at Barings Futures (Singapore). The unauthorized trading positions were made in a fraudulent account from 1992 to 1995. The credit crisis caused by Leeson led to more than $1.39 billion in losses on futures contracts in the Nikkei 225, Japanese Government Bonds (JGB), and euroyen, and options in the Nikkei 225. The value of the venerable 200-year-old Baring Brothers & Co Bank was reduced from roughly $615 million to $1.60, the price it brought from ING, a Dutch financial institution.[49]

Leeson started engaging in unauthorized trading in 1992, and he lost money from day one. In 1994 alone he lost $296 million; however, through creative deception, he showed a gain of $46 million in that year. The primary locus of blame for all the activities that eventually brought down Barings was the lack of an adequate control system to monitor and manage traders' activities. Without such a system in place, unscrupulous traders like Leeson were able to take advantage of the firm and engage in unauthorized activities. Moreover, the environment that allowed the hiding and manipulation of trades, which went virtually undetected, was again directly attributable to Barings' lack of adequate controls. Between 1992 and 1995, the management of Barings had no real concept of Leeson's true profit and loss positions. This is because the details of account 88888 were never transmitted to treasury officials in London. Account 88888 was used by Leeson to cross trades with other Barings accounts and to show false gains on these accounts (while the actual losses were accumulating in the 88888 account). Due to this, Leeson was able to show a flat book exposure while in reality he had huge long and short positions. Leeson probably could have gotten away with his scheme free and clear if it were not for the Kobe earthquake that shattered the Japanese equity markets.

Leeson was authorized to trade Nikkei 225 futures contracts and options contracts on behalf of clients on the Singapore International Monetary Exchange (SIMEX). A Nikkei 225 futures contract is a bundle of stocks that are equal in proportion to the stocks that make up the Tokyo Stock Exchange Nikkei 225 Stock Average. The value of the futures contract is derived from the value of the Nikkei 225 average. A long Nikkei 225 futures position is in the money if the Nikkei 225 average increases, because the futures price will be lower than the actual value of the underlying asset.

Leeson was allowed to take advantage of the arbitrage opportunities that existed between the price of Nikkei 225 futures contracts listed on the Osaka Securities Exchange vs. the Tokyo Stock Exchange and the SIMEX. Barings referred to this arbitrage activity as *switching*. It was imperative to hedge all major proprietary trading positions undertaken on behalf of Barings Securities so that the firm would not be exposed to a large risk. For example, a short futures position is hedged by a long futures position. The gain in the long position will exactly counteract the losses if the short futures position loses value. Leeson was only allowed to make unhedged trades on up to 200 Nikkei 225 futures, 100 Japanese Government Bonds, and 500 euroyen futures contracts. However, Leeson greatly exceeded these allowable limits in unauthorized and unhedged futures trades and exposed Barings to a large amount of risk. His positions were unhedged to maximize the gains if the market moved in a direction favorable to his position. The hedged portion of his position would have to meet margin requirements due to unfavorable market movements. Leeson also engaged in the unauthorized sale of Nikkei 225 put and call options, because doing so meant he could generate premiums without having to meet margin calls. His positions in the options markets were also unhedged in order to maximize his potential gains.

6.6.2 Cause

Leeson was hired as general manager of the newly established Barings Futures (Singapore) office in the spring of 1992. The most notable aspect of his position was that he was in charge of settlement operations and was the Barings Futures floor manager on the SIMEX trading floor. Barings Futures was a subsidiary of Barings Securities. Nick Leeson was the general manager of the Barings Futures (Singapore) office, and he was to report to both the London and Singapore offices. The Singapore office would oversee Leeson's trading activities on the SIMEX, and the London office would oversee his futures and options settlements. However, Barings Securities was a very political company. Individual managers at the field offices, such as Singapore, were fiercely protective of their control over their specific offices. It was difficult for the London headquarters to exercise control over the field offices. Either the managers had excellent past performance, meaning that central control was unnecessary, or they had strong personalities and could successfully thwart attempts from headquarters to increase oversight.

Gordon Bowser, risk manager at Barings Securities (London), was to be responsible for Leeson's futures and options settlements. The senior management of the Singapore office included James Bax, the managing director of the Singapore office and a master of Barings office politics, and Simon Jones, the finance director of the Singapore office and an expert at settling stock trades, but also the possessor of a legendary temper. The pair was known as "Fortress Singapore." Jones took offense at sharing Leeson's oversight responsibilities with Bowser. He felt that if the Singapore office was to oversee Leeson's trading activities on the SIMEX, then it should also oversee his settlements activities.

Bax communicated this disagreement to London, but it was never resolved because the London office did not want to usurp the authority of the Singapore office. The key people in the Singapore office did not fully understand Leeson's role in the organization or were not interested in monitoring his activities. Bax thought Leeson was only running settlements. Jones took little interest in supervising Leeson because he was sharing this responsibility with London.

Mike Killian, head of Global Equity Futures and Options Sales at Barings Investment Bank, on whose behalf Leeson executed trades on the SIMEX, was also responsible for Leeson's activities. However, Killian did not like to take oversight responsibilities and preferred to take credit for a profitable operation. As a result, it was unclear to whom Leeson reported, and his activities were not scrutinized.

On July 3, 1992, Barings Futures (Singapore) established error account 88888 as required by the SIMEX. A few days later, Leeson asked his computer consultant to modify the CONTAC software program so that the trading activity, prices of trades, and positions associated with error account 88888 would not be reported to the London office. A fourth item, margin balances, remained on the report. Leeson knew that trading activity, prices of trades, and positions were processed by the London office and downloaded into First Futures (Barings' internal reporting system) and that margin balances were ignored. Leeson stated that Gordon Bowser had ordered the action because the volume of trades made by Barings Futures (Singapore) on the SIMEX was difficult to settle.

In September 1992, Bowser provided the Barings Futures (Singapore) office with error account 99002, which was to be used as the Barings Futures SIMEX error account. Account 99002 was to be reported to London. However, Leeson kept error account 88888 active to deliberately hide trading losses and unauthorized trades.

Leeson needed funds to meet margin calls and support accumulating losses on his unhedged futures trades. In August 1992, Bowser surprisingly granted Leeson permission to receive funds from London without providing specific information on how these funds would be used. Leeson argued that the difficulty of raising funds from Japanese banks and the peculiarities of SIMEX margin calls required him to have easy access to funds. From 1992 until the collapse, Leeson was able to request and receive funds to meet the margins calls on his unauthorized trades without scrutiny.

Leeson used his position running the back office to further conceal his trading activities. At the end of September 1992, he asked the settlements staff to temporarily debit a Barings receivable account at Citibank Singapore and credit the funds to error account 88888. The transfer was performed in order to hide Leeson's trading losses from Barings Securities (London) monthly reports, which were printed at the end of the month. This first such transaction coincided with the end of Barings Securities' financial year and the start of Deloitte and Touche's 1992 accounting audit. At this time, Leeson also forged a fax from Gordon Bowser stating that error account 88888 had an insignificant balance. The fax kept the accounting firm from discovering his activities.

The specific method Leeson used to cover up his losses and inflate Barings Futures profits was the cross-trade. In a cross-trade, buy and sell orders for the same firm occur on an exchange. Certain rules apply; for example, the transaction must occur at the market price and the bid or offer prices must be declared in the pit at least three times. Leeson would cross-trade between error account 88888 and the following accounts:

- 92000 [Barings Securities (Japan), Nikkei and Japanese Government Bond Arbitrage]
- 98007 [Barings (London), JGB Arbitrage]
- 98008 (Euroyen arbitrage)

This was done to make the trades appear legal per SIMEX rules. Back office staff at Barings Securities (Singapore) would then be ordered to break the trades down into many lots and record them in the Barings accounts at prices differing from the purchase price. In general, the cross-trades were made at prices higher than what Leeson had paid on the SIMEX. In performing cross-trades, Leeson could show a profit for his trading activities on various Barings accounts. However, the gains in accounts 92000, 98007, and 98009 also generated a corresponding loss, which Leeson buried in error account 88888. This activity required the complicity of the Barings Securities (Singapore) clerical staff, which would have been easy to secure by the person in charge of the back office—Nick Leeson.

Leeson was selling straddles on the Nikkei 225. His strategic underlying assumption was that the Nikkei index would be trading in the range of 19,000 to 19,500. In this range he would rake in the money on the premiums of the sold options, while the calls and puts he sold would expire worthless. However, after the Kobe earthquake on January 17, 1995, the Nikkei dropped to 18,950. At that point the straddle strategy was shaky. Leeson started to lose money on the puts, because the (short) value of the put options he sold was starting to overtake the (long) value of the premiums received from selling the puts and calls. Then he made a dangerous gamble; he believed that the market was overreacting and on January 20, three days after the earthquake, he bought 10,814 March 1995 futures contracts. On January 23, the Nikkei dropped 1,000 points to 17,950, and at that point Leeson realized his gamble was a huge mistake. He was facing enormous losses from the long positions that he had just bought, along with unlimited losses on the puts.

In addition to selling straddles, Leeson's reported arbitrage strategy was to go long or short the Nikkei 225 futures on the Osaka exchange, while simultaneously going the other direction on those same Nikkei 225 futures on the SIMEX. This strategy would theoretically take advantage of temporary mispricing differences of the same futures contract on two different exchanges. Since these products were essentially identical (they derived all of their intrinsic value from the same underlying security), any large price differences between the Osaka and SIMEX Nikkei 225 March 1995 futures contracts would be short-lived (or nonexistent) in an efficient market. This trading strategy is what Barings referred to as *switching*. In reality, however, Leeson ignored the switching and was long the March 1995 contract on both exchanges. Therefore, he was doubly exposed to the Nikkei 225 instead of being hedged.

On January 20, the Osaka exchange lost 220 points and the SIMEX lost 195. If Leeson were short on the SIMEX, the net effect would have been (–220 + 195) = –25. However, he was long on both exchanges; therefore, on January 20 he had a loss of (–220 – 195) = –415. During January and February of 1995, Leeson suffered the huge losses that broke Barings.

6.6.2.1 How Leeson Hid the Trades

It is legal for an institution to separate a trade made on an exchange, assuming that the trade is large and that its size might affect the market price of the position. This is done through "block transaction," which effectively splits the transaction into smaller transactions with different counterparts. Leeson traded this way within the Barings accounts (also known as cross-trading). After the transactions, however, when he was splitting the trades into the different accounts, he decided the price at which each trade should be recorded, and did not use the actual price of the trade. This is illegal. Although the sum of the small transaction matches the overall trade, and the books were flat, Leeson was crediting gains to the Barings accounts and was offsetting them by recording losses in the 88888 account. Since he was always losing money, he kept recording losses in this account, and was showing gains in the official books. This way Leeson fooled everybody at Barings and was able to show a profitable net position. Barings' treasury never audited account 88888, which more accurately depicted Leeson's true profits and losses. Account 88888 was a ticking bomb that exploded in February 1995 and broke Barings.[50]

6.6.2.2 Leeson's Assumptions

The facts just discussed show the reasons behind Barings' collapse. When reading them, one openly wonders what made Leeson so aggressive in the derivatives markets, why he thought he could profit from such aggressive tactics, and why he thought he could cover up his activities from his employer. In every case involving huge derivative position losses, one usually sees the "double-down" mentality take effect. In this case, Leeson sealed his fate the first day he decided to eschew the official Barings derivatives trading strategy. He was destined to eventually put himself in a net loss position due to the risky nature of the products he was trading. Once he did this, he had no other option but to keep doubling down in the hope that he could extricate himself from the situation. He could not merely cap his losses and walk away, as that would mean he would have to inform Barings management of his improper trading, and he surely would have been fired by the firm at that point. That is why he did not hedge his positions once he started losing money. To do so might have saved Barings from its eventual collapse, but it would not have been enough to save his job. So, instead, he covered up his illicit trading practices and kept raising the stakes. Leeson had been trading derivative products improperly for some time prior to the disaster in early 1995. Because of his experience, albeit limited, with the Japanese equity markets, he felt confident enough to take some rather large risk positions in early 1995. The Nikkei 225 index had been trading in a very tight range at the beginning of January 1995. Between January 4 and January 11, for example, the Nikkei stayed between 19,500 and 19,700. With his double-long futures position on the SIMEX and OSE and his straddle options, Leeson was betting that the Nikkei 225 index would increase or remain flat. If it stayed flat, he would collect the premiums from his sold put and call options and these options would expire worthless. If the index increased greatly in value, the premium from the sold put options would partially offset the losing call option positions he sold, and he would more than make up for this difference with the windfall profits from the double-long futures positions on the SIMEX and OSE. Aside from his confidence in the volatility and future direction of the Nikkei index, there is another reason Leeson took such a large market gamble. As the case details, Leeson was already £208 million in the hole as of the end of 1994.

6.6.3 Effect

When a terrible earthquake rocked Japan on January 17, 1995, the Nikkei plummeted. Many people explain Leeson's last crazy behavior as evidence that he believed the Nikkei was still undervalued and had overreacted to the disaster, and so continued to add to his futures positions.

Leeson had already built a large quantity of positions. Many people may ask why he did not hedge those positions by building other positions in his account. This is a good question, but Leeson's dilemma was this: he still believed prices would rise and his position would eventually break even or be profitable. However, even if he wanted to hedge those loss positions, he could not do so. If he used the official accounts, which would be reported to Barings, he had to establish huge positions, and he didn't believe the price would crash deeper. Therefore, this strategy seemed too risky. But he could not hedge in his internal 88888 account, either, because in financial trading, a first-in-first-out rule is followed. Leeson's hedging position was to liquidate all his Nikkei long and JGB and euroyen short positions. Thus, the floating loss became realized loss, and Leeson could find no place to recoup these huge losses. What he had to do was to keep them and roll them over with floating loss (a nominal loss not booked yet). In this light, it is very easy to understand the later actions of Leeson. Holding onto the belief that prices would rise, in order to protect his long Nikkei futures, short JGB, and euroyen futures positions and in order to stop the crash of his short put options positions, Leeson executed his final strategy by placing huge amounts of orders to prop up the market.

Barings was on its way to collapse without realizing it due to a continuation of the deceptive practices that Leeson had engaged in since mid-1992. Between January 23 and January 27, 1996, he lost approximately $47,000,000 but was able to present a $55,000,000 profit to London by cross-trading between error account 88888 and Barings account 92000. The London office heard rumors that Barings was not able to meet its margin calls in Asia, but was not concerned because it felt this rumor was based on its long Nikkei futures positions on the Osaka exchange, which were supposedly hedged by corresponding short Nikkei futures position on the SIMEX. After all, Leeson's official trading policy was to short Nikkei 225 futures on SIMEX to hedge Barings' long positions on the Osaka exchange. However, he went long on Nikkei 225 futures, did not hedge these positions, and exposed Barings to significant risk. During January and February 1995, Leeson was still able to receive funds from London to meet margin calls without being questioned. The payments forwarded to Singapore equaled $835 million, whereas Barings only had $615 million in capital. By late February the exposure in the Nikkei futures and options markets that Leeson created was larger than Barings could handle. The enormity of the Nikkei 225 futures margin calls and the losses on the put options bankrupted Barings.

6.6.4 Risk Areas Affected

The collapse of Barings could have been avoided by:

- Making all Barings traders meet London International Financial Futures Exchange (LIFFE) standards
- Managing account settlement and trading functions separately using management information systems
- Exercising rigorous management oversight

6.6.4.1 Market Risk

The risks of Leeson's strategy should be clear. If the market suffered a sharp decline, Leeson would be exposed to tremendous potential losses. The premiums from the call options he sold would have been locked-in profits, since these options would expire worthless in a sinking market. However, the put options he sold were increasing greatly in value as the market declined. With strike prices between 18,500 and 20,000 on the Nikkei 225 index, Leeson faced massive risk on these short put options if they became deep in the money. As the Nikkei plunged down under 18,000 in mid-February 1995, that is exactly what happened. The losses on these short options greatly exceeded the premiums gained on the expired sold call options. Of course, Leeson's double exposure to the March 1995 Nikkei futures contract also left him open to the risks associated with the declining Japanese equity market. When he bought the additional 10,814 contracts on January 20, he further increased this risk. Between January 20 and February 15, the Nikkei dropped an additional 850 points. A declining Nikkei index was a large and obvious market risk that Leeson faced with his derivatives book in early 1995. In addition to market risk, Leeson was also leaving himself exposed to event risk—the risk that something unexpected and not directly related to the market could affect the market. A great example of event risk is the Kobe earthquake of January 17, 1995, which negatively impacted Leeson's prospects for two reasons. First, it helped send the Nikkei index into a tailspin. Second, the earthquake caused increased volatility in these equity markets. Increased volatility adds value to options, both calls and puts. As Leeson was short options at this time, this increase in volatility further helped to destroy him. The short put options exploded in value as they became deeper in the money and as volatility increased.

6.6.4.2 Credit Risk

By late February, Barings' exposure in the Nikkei futures and options markets was larger than the bank could handle. The enormity of the Nikkei 225 futures margin calls and the losses on the put options bankrupted Barings. Leeson created counterparty exposure for other institutions, which finally collapsed the bank.

An appropriate management of counterparty risk and reporting of specific instrument exposures to counterparties would have been an additional signal for management that some exposures were intolerable.

6.6.4.3 Operational Risk

As a result of Barings' derivatives disaster, the market has attempted to head off potential government regulation by improving industry self-regulation. New standards have been developed in accordance with the regulations created by the SEC, FSA, and other national regulators of derivatives sales practices, capital standards, and reporting requirements. Most, if not all, financial firms participating in derivatives have taken a hard second look at their control systems as a result of the Barings collapse. Indeed, some have wondered why a disaster such as this hadn't happened earlier. Valerie Thompson, an experienced trader at Salomon Brothers in London, claims that the deregulation of the British financial sector in the 1980s created a vacuum that was filled by inexperienced traders in the 1990s. Thompson observed that traders were created overnight without the benefit of proper training because firms such as Barings were chasing markets previously dominated by the Americans and Japanese. This inexperience contributed to Leeson's undoing; he didn't have the knowledge or experience to admit his mistakes to upper management.[51]

Perhaps the collapse of Barings was an unfortunate, yet necessary, lesson that the market needed to learn. Graham Newall of BZW Futures notes that upper management now regularly inquires about activity in the omnibus account. Merrill Lynch Futures' Tom Dugan notes that firms are far less tolerant of individual stars these days and that everyone is held accountable for his or her actions. At the Futures Industry Association Exposition in Chicago in October 1996, most industry experts agreed that technology is a key ingredient in preventing scams such as Leeson's in the future. Risk management computer systems have been developed and improved as a result of Barings' demise.[52]

Nick Leeson was obviously a man of questionable character, and this was evident before he was transferred to Barings Securities (Singapore). He was scheduled to appear in court due to the accumulation of unpaid debt and had already been taken to court and ruled against on another unpaid debt charge. Leeson would not have been allowed to trade on the LIFFE due to these problems, and therefore Barings should not have allowed him to trade on the SIMEX. Making one person responsible for managing settlements and the trading floor created a conflict of interest. Leeson was able to use his influence in the back office to hide his actions on the trading floor. Assigning one of these responsibilities to a different manager would have kept Leeson from developing the ability to deceive the London office. Better management information systems were needed to ensure that all account information was available at a central location and that the complete status of all open accounts was known. Finally, Barings management should have monitored Leeson's activities more proactively. Audits should have been performed more frequently and audit recommendations should have been immediately implemented or followed up on. Clearer lines of reporting should have been established, and office politics should not have stood in the way of proper supervision.[53]

After analyzing Leeson's trading and operations activities, the question arises as to what role and responsibility risk management had or could have had. In general, three levels of risk management and valuation processes should be implemented by financial institutions: information and risk reporting, risk control, and risk management.

Information and Risk Reporting

This is a basic process in measuring risk. The senior managers receive the information and reports showing risk created by trades and investments. The reporting side should provide complete, accurate, audited, and precise professionally standard information. Risk reporting is essential in valuing and managing risk.

Leeson violated the principles of risk reporting. He secretly opened account 88888 and sent false information to Barings from the time he arrived in Singapore. He controlled both the front and back offices at Barings Futures (Singapore), which meant he was both chief trader and head of settlements. Taking advantage of his excessive power, he suppressed the information in account 88888, made unauthorized trades, and manipulated profits.

The Barings risk reporting system was flawed. First, there was no one to supervise and assist Leeson in completing the reports and delivering reliable information to his managers. Second, the managers never investigated or doubted the credibility of Leeson's trading activities as detailed in his reports.

If the managers understood the nature of Leeson's job, including arbitrage by taking advantage of the price differences between the SIMEX and the Tokyo Stock Exchange or the Osaka Securities Exchange, they would have been suspicious of the unusual level of profits. Arbitraging the price differences of futures contracts on separate exchanges entails very low risk. The fact that Leeson could make such a huge profit from almost riskless trading is counter to fundamental modern financial theory, which states that low risk equals low return and high risk equals high return. One question should have arisen: if such a low-risk and simple arbitrage could yield such high returns, why did rival banks not execute the same arbitraging strategy? In addition, as the volume of arbitraging trading increases, the price differences tend to decrease, and therefore the potential profit from arbitrage also likely shrinks. Why could Leeson continue arbitraging? Unfortunately no Barings executive recognized the obvious. Even when Leeson's performance accounted for 20 percent of the entire firm's 1993 profits and about half of its 1994 profits, no one tried to determine where the enormous profits were coming from.

Risk Control

Risk control is used to set position limits for traders and business units to prevent individuals from having too much power. It can be used to measure the risk in a variety of risky activities in diverse markets. Leeson continued his unauthorized trading by taking advantage of his positions. He never controlled the risk in his trading in Nikkei, JGB, and euroyen futures as well as straddles in Nikkei options. He took extreme positions without hedging the risk and continued to execute a faulty strategy. The market exposure of his positions exceeded Barings' total capital. In 1994, Barings transferred $354 million to Barings Futures (Singapore) for the margin call from the trading Leeson explained as risk-free arbitrage. It is astonishing that no one even asked Leeson to justify his requests.

Risk Management

Risk management includes the analysis and measurement of positions and strategies. It requires investment experience to supervise the exposures and the persons taking the exposures. Barings had neither the risk controls nor the risk measurement in place to analyze the exposure taken by Nick Leeson, nor the analytical framework to monitor where the huge profits came from and what kinds of risks were being taken to generate the profits.

6.6.4.4 Systemic Risk

The systemic risks in the Barings case were substantial. However, all of the appropriate organizations moved to mitigate the problems created by the debacle. The Singapore stock exchange reacted quickly on the same day Barings was not able to cover the margin calls. The national banks provided additional liquidity to ensure that the markets in London and Singapore did not fall into a liquidity gap. The systemic risk was limited as the loss for counterparty risk was limited to a one-day uncovered margin call, which was settled by Barings and later through ING Groep, which acquired the bankrupt Barings. The systemic risk was further contained by the fact that Leeson's speculation was not supported by an unheated market environment (such as in the months before the October 1987 crash) or the turmoils around the ruble and the Russian bond crisis in August and September 1998.

6.6.4.5 Additivity of Risk Management Framework

The regulatory, supervisory, and corporate governance framework failed completely in the Barings case. The key failures were by weak managers who did not take responsibility for establishing systems and processes that would have prevented the bankruptcy of Barings.

The capital adequacy framework should have required higher capital to support the risk of Leeson's trading strategy, as the strategy did not allow matching and offsetting of the transactions. The internal and external bank auditors should have realized the speculative background and informed the appropriate supervisory authority.

6.7 NOTES

1. BBC News, "Business: The Economy Derivatives Firms Shut Down," London: BBC News, Thursday, December 31, 1998.
2. Denise Lavoie, "Organized Criminal," Associated Press and ABPnews.com, June 22, 1999; "Cendant to Pay $2.8 Billion Fraud Settlement," APBnews.com, December 8, 1999, www.apbnews.com/safetycenter/business/1999/12/08/fraud1208_01.html; SEC press release, "Financial Reporting Case Filed Against Cendant," Washington, DC: SEC, June 14, 2000, www.sec.gov/news/press/2000-80-.txt.
3. "Three Bankers Brought Scandal to the Vatican," *Irish Times* (August 29, 1998); "The Old Man Who Hid Gold Under His Geraniums," *Irish Times* (September 16, 1998).
4. For a discussion of knowledge of the market and the bank's capacity, see David Meerschwarn, *Bankers Trust New York Corporation,* Case Study 9-286-005, Cambridge, MA: Harvard Business School Press, 1985. For the legal case between Procter & Gamble and Bankers Trust, see *Procter & Gamble Co. v. Bankers Trust Co.,* 78 F. 3d 219 (6th Cir. 1996).
5. Senators John Kerry and Hand Brown, *The BCCI Affair: A Report to the Committee on Foreign Relations,* 102d Congress, 2d Session, Senate Print 102-140, Washington, DC: Senate Printing Office, December 1992, www.fas.org/irp/congress/1992/1992_rpt/bcci/index.html; David McKean, *Why the News Media Took So Long to Focus on the Savings and Loan and BCCI Crisis,* Evanston, IL: Northwestern University, Annenberg Washington Program in Communications Policy Studies, 1993.
6. Deloitte & Touche: *BRE-X Corporate Dissemination Services Inc.: The Deloitte & Touche Inc.'s Forensic Investigative Associate Inc. (FIA) Report to BRE-X Minderals,* Deloitte & Touche, 1997.
7. Joseph Fitchett, "The Credit Lyonnais Debacle," *International Herald Tribune* (London; October 3, 1996), p. 13; Ibrahim Warde, "Financiers flamboyants, contribuables brûlés," *Le Monde Diplomatique* (July 1994), 18–19.
8. Alan Greenspan, "Statement to Congress, U.S. Operations of Daiwa Bank, November 27, 1995," *Federal Reserve Bulletin* (January 1996), 31–35; Alan Greenspan, "Statement to Congress: Issues Relating to the U.S. Operations of Daiwa Bank, December 5, 1995," *Federal Reserve Bulletin* (January 1996), 133–138; Eugene A. Ludwig, *Remarks by Eugene A. Ludwig, Comptroller of the Currency, Before the Bank Administration Institute's Asset/Liability and Treasury Management Conference,* Release N6-119, Washington, DC: Office of the

Comptroller of the Currency, October 22, 1996; Mari Yamaguchi, "Convicted Japanese Trader Releases Memoir Accusing Daiwa of Cover-Up," *News Times* (January 7, 1997).

9. Matthew Fletcher, "Whom to Trust? Investors are Spooked by Scandal in Asia's No. 1 Fund Manager," *Asiaweek* (September 27, 1996), www.pathfinder.com/asiaweek/96/0927/bizl.html.

10. Tim Spofford, *Lynch Street,* Kent, OH: Kent State University Press, 1988.

11. IMRO, "IMRO Announces Morgan Grenfell Compensation," Press Release 37/96 (April 16, 1997), London; and IMRO, "IMRO Fines Morgan Grenfell £2,000,000 for Mismanagement of European Funds," Press Release 05/97 (April 16, 1997), London.

13. SFA, "SFA Disciplines NatWest and 2 Individuals," press release, May 18, 2000, www.fsa.gov.uk/sfa/press_releases/2000/sfa8-2000.html; comments in "NatWest Fined for 'Rogue Trader' Loss," *This Is Money,* May 18, 2000, www.thisismoney.com/20000518/nm15300.html; "SFO May Examine NatWest," *Irish Times* (July 31, 2001).

12. "The Big Noise from Columbus: *The Journal of Finance* Breaks the NASDAQ Scandal," *Investment Dealers Digest* (May 22, 1995); Karen Donovan, "Third Circuit Reinstates Nasdaq Suit, Three Brokerage Firms Now Face Securities Class Action," *National Law Journal* (February 16, 1998), B01; *In RE: Nasdaq Market-Makers Antitrust Litigation to: Consolidated Amended Complaint,* M21-68(RWS), Civ. 3996 (RWS), M.D.L. No. 1023.

14. Sarkis Joseph Khoury, "It's the Fundamentals: Stupid! The Orange County Bankruptcy in Perspective," working paper prepared for the Bürgenstock Conference, University of California Riverside, September 1995; Philippe Jorion, *Value-At-Risk: The New Benchmark for Controlling Market Risk,* New York: McGraw-Hill, 1997, p. 32; Philippe Jorion, "Philippe Jorion's Orange County Case: Using Value at Risk to Control Financial Risk," www.gsm.uci.edu.

15. Anatoli Kuprianov, "Derivatives Debacles," *Economic Quarterly* (Federal Reserve Bank of Richmond) 81/4 (Fall 1995), 1.

16. Ibid.

17. Ibid.

18. Reto R. Gallati, *Futures, Options, and Financial Risk Management, Case: Metallgesellschaft,* Reading Package FE829, Boston, MA: Boston University, Fall 2000.

19. Allen B. Frankel and David E. Palmer, "The Management of Financial Risks at German Non-Financial Firms: The Case of Metallgesellschaft," publication no. 560, New York: Board of Governors of the Federal Reserve System; August 1996.

20. *Arthur Benson v. Metallgesellschaft Corp. et al.,* Civ. Act. No. JFM-94-484, U.S. District Court for the District of Maryland, 1994.

21. Anatoli Kuprianov, "Derivatives Debacles," *Economic Quarterly* (Federal Reserve Bank of Richmond) 81/4 (Fall 1995), 1.

22. "Metallgesellschaft: Germany's Corporate Whodunit," *The Economist* (London) 334/7900 (February 4, 1995), 71ff.
23. John Digenan, Dan Felson, Robert Kell, and Ann Wiemert: "Metallgesellschaft: A Case Study," working paper, Illinois Institute of Technology, Stuart School of Business, Financial Markets and Trading Program, undated.
24. Chicago Mercantile Exchange, *Matching CME Quarterly Bankruptcy Index Futures to Different Trading Horizons: A Primer,* Chicago Mercantile Exchange, www.cme.com/qbi/qbiprimer.html.
25. "Metallgesellschaft: Germany's Corporate Whodunit," *The Economist* (London) 334/7900 (February 4, 1995), 71ff.
26. Charles Cathcart, "The Lessons of Metallgesellschaft," *Global Investor* (London) 78 (December 1994–January 1995), 64.
27. Reto R. Gallati, *Futures, Options, and Financial Risk Management, Case: Metallgesellschaft,* Reading Package FE829, Boston, MA: Boston University, Fall 2000.
28. Allen B. Frankel and David E. Palmer, "The Management of Financial Risks at German Non-Financial Firms: The Case of Metallgesellschaft," publication no. 560, New York: Board of Governors of the Federal Reserve System; August 1996.
29. Reto R. Gallati, *Futures, Options, and Financial Risk Management, Case: Metallgesellschaft,* Reading Package FE829, Boston, MA: Boston University, Fall 2000.
30. Jim Kharouf, "The Copper Trader Who Fell from Grace," *Futures* (August 1996).
31. *Commodity Exchange Act,* 7 U.S.C. §§ 6(a), 6(d), 9(a)(2).
32. *Order Instituting Proceedings Pursuant to Sections 6(c) and 6(d) of the Commodity Exchange Act and Findings and Order Imposing Remedial Sanctions,* Docket 98Civ. 4584(MP). Sumitomo was ordered to pay $125 million in civil punitive sanctions and $25 million in restitution to market participants harmed by the scheme.
33. Benjamin E. Kozinn, "The Great Copper Caper: Is Market Manipulation Really a Problem in the Wake of the Sumitomo Debacle?" *Fordham Law Review* (October 2000), 247.
34. *Cargill v. Hardin,* 452 F.2d 1154 (8th Cir., 1971).
35. Ibid., p. 1163.
36. Ibid.
37. Benjamin E. Kozinn, "The Great Copper Caper: Is Market Manipulation Really a Problem in the Wake of the Sumitomo Debacle?" *Fordham Law Review* (October 2000), 247.
38. *Order Instituting Proceedings Pursuant to Sections 6(c) and 6(d) of the Commodity Exchange Act and Findings and Order Imposing Remedial Sanctions,* Docket 98Civ. 4584(MP).

39. Ibid.

40. Commodity Futures Trading Commission, *Testimony of Brooksley Born, Chairperson, on Behalf of the Commodity Futures Trading Commission before the United States House of Representatives, Subcommittee on Capital Market, Securities and Government Sponsored Enterprises of the Committee on Banking and Financial Services,* Washington, DC: Commodity Futures Trading Commission, March 13, 1999.

41. U.S. Government, *Hedge Funds, Leverage, and the Lessons of Long-Term Capital Management: Report of the President's Working Group on Financial Markets,* April, 1999, www.cftc.gov/tm/hedgefundreport.htm.

42. U.S. General Accounting Office, *Long-Term Capital Management, Regulators Need to Focus Greater Attention on Systemic Risk,* October 1999.

43. "Long-Term Capital Management: Technical Note on a Global Hedge Fund," *Thunderbird,* American Graduate School of International Management, 1999.

44. Committee on the Global Financial System, *A Review of Financial Market Events in Autumn 1998,* October 1999.

45. Ibrahim Warde, "LTCM, a Hedge Fund Above Suspicion," *Le Monde Diplomatique* (November 1998), English Internet edition, www.monde-diplomatique.fr/en/1998/11/05warde2.html, accessed August 24, 2000.

46. Philippe Jorion, "Risk Management Lessons from Long-Term Capital Management," Working Paper Series (draft), University of California at Irvine, June 1999.

47. "How LTCM Came to the Edge of the Abyss," *Wall Street Journal* (September 11, 2000), pp. C1, C20.

48. Bank for International Settlement (BIS), Basel Committee on Banking Supervision, *Highly Leveraged Institutions—Sound Practices,* Basel, Switzerland: Bank for International Settlement, January 2000; *Banks' Interaction with Highly Leveraged Institutions,* Basel, Switzerland: Bank for International Settlement, January 1999.

49. Barry Hillenbrand, "The Barings Collapse: Spreading the Blame," *Time* (London) 146/18 (October 30, 1995), www.time.com/time/magazine/archive/1995/951030/banking.box.html; Bank of England, *The Bank of England Report into the Collapse of Barings Bank,* London: HMSO Publications Center, 1995, www.numa.com/ref/barings/bar00.html.

50. Howard G. Chuan-Eoan, "Going For Broke," *Time* 145/10 (March 13, 1995), 18–25.

51. Ibid.

52. Jim Kharouf, Carla Cavaletti, and James T. Holder, "Top 40 Brokers, Technology Key to Stay Alive," *Futures* (December 1996).

53. "Simex Criticizes Barings for Role in Leeson Debacle," *Herald Tribune* (March 16, 1995), p. 1; "Barings Abyss," *Futures* 26/5 (May 1995), 68–74; "BoE Report Details Barings' Guiles, Goofs," *Futures* 26/10 (September 1995), 68–74.

GLOSSARY

ABS See **asset-backed security.**

absolute return Measure of net economic return. Takes into account all costs (for example, cost of funding, balance sheet charges, and administrative expenses).

accrual (Z) bond A long-term, deferred-interest CMO bond that distributes no interest (interest is capitalized) until certain other bonds have been retired.

accumulation plan An investment plan under which an investor may regularly buy specified minimum amounts of investment company shares. Dividends and distributions are usually reinvested automatically. Sometimes referred to as a *systematic plan.* (See **contractual plan.**)

accumulation unit The basic valuation unit of a deferred variable annuity. Such units are valued daily to reflect investment performance and the prorated daily deduction for expenses.

adjustable-rate mortgage (ARM) A mortgage that permits the lender to adjust its interest rate periodically on the basis of movement in a specified index. Also used collectively to refer to ARMs and graduated-payment adjustable-rate mortgages (GPARMs).

ADR See **American Depositary Receipt.**

American Depositary Receipt (ADR) A certificate issued by an American bank as evidence of ownership of foreign shares. The certificate is transferable and can be traded. The original foreign stock certificate is deposited with a foreign branch or correspondent bank of the issuing American bank.

amortization Gradual reduction of mortgage debt through periodic payments scheduled over the mortgage term.

annuity contract A contract issued by an insurance company that provides payments for a specified period, such as for a specified number of years, or for life. (See **variable annuity.**)

arbitrage The simultaneous purchase and sale of the same (or equivalent or related) securities to take advantage of price differences prevailing in separate markets. Pure arbitrage involves trading the same instruments for different prices at the same time.

ARCH See **autoregressive conditional heteroskedascticity.**

ARM See **adjustable-rate mortgage.**

arm's-length transaction A transaction that is conducted as though the parties were unrelated, thus avoiding any semblance of conflict of interest.

ask price A potential seller's lowest declared price for a security.

asset-backed security (ABS) Bonds or debt securities collateralized by the cash flow from a pool of auto loans, credit card receivables, vehicle and equipment leases, consumer loans, and other obligations.

asset liability management Matching the level of debt and amount of assets. Financial institutions carry out asset liability management when they match the maturity of their deposits with the length of their loan commitments to keep from being adversely affected by rapid changes in market prices.

at the money When the strike price of an option is the same as the price of the underlying instrument.

at-the-money forward When the strike price of an option is the same as the forward price of the underlying instrument.

autocorrelation Serial correlation in which observations on the same time series are correlated over time. In mathematical terms, the covariance between data recorded sequentially on the same series is nonzero.

autoregressive conditional heteroskedascticity (ARCH) A time-series process that models volatility as dependent on past returns.

back-office operations Clerical operations at trading institutions that include confirmation and settlement of trades, record keeping, and regulatory compliance.

backtesting A method of testing the validity of VaR models, usually performed by comparing risk forecasts with actual or hypothetical trading results.

balanced fund An investment company that invests in varying proportions from time to time in equity and fixed-income securities for growth and income.

balance-sheet capital The amount of capital reported under generally accepted accounting principles.

Bank for International Settlement (BIS) An agency headquartered in Basel, Switzerland, that serves as an international forum for monetary cooperation and banking regulation.

banker's acceptance A time or sight draft drawn on a commercial bank by a borrower, usually in connection with a commercial transaction.

base currency Currency in which operating gains and losses are measured. Typically this is the reporting currency of a company.

basis The difference between a futures contract price for an item and the current spot price of the same item.

basis risk The potential loss due to small pricing differences between equivalent instruments, such as futures, bonds, and swaps. Hedges are often subject to basis risk.

Basel regulatory market risk capital requirements Minimum requirements for capital that international banks must carry to cushion against adverse market movements.

benchmark A custom or published index of a predetermined set of securities used to compare performance and risk. Asset managers' performance is often gauged against a benchmark of published market indexes.

benchmarking Comparing information about one entity to like information of another entity or composite group for the purpose of determining areas for potential improvement and to identify best practices.

benchmark yield curves Derived yield curves that correspond to a country, industry, or credit rating category; typically generated through a yield-curve-fitting algorithm.

beta (β) A volatility measure relating the rate of return on a security to the return of its market over time. It is defined as the covariance between a security's return and the return on the market portfolio divided by the variance of the return on the market portfolio.

bid price The highest declared price a potential buyer is willing to pay for a security at a particular time.

binomial distribution The distribution of a data set for which there are only two possible outcomes (success and failure).

BIS See **Bank for International Settlement.**

Black-Scholes A model invented by Fischer Black and Myron Scholes for pricing call options based on arbitrage arguments. Key variables are current asset price, exercise price, risk-free rate, time to expiry, and expected standard deviation of the asset.

bond discount The difference between the face amount of a bond and the lower price paid by the buyer.

bond premium The difference between the face amount of a bond and the higher price paid by a buyer.

bonds Debt instruments issued with a maturity greater than one year. The purchase of a bond is comparable to making a loan.

book shares Investment company shares whose ownership is evidenced by records maintained by a transfer agent rather than by physical stock certificates.

break point The volume at which a quantity of securities qualifies for a lower sales charge when purchased. Also, an aggregate amount of investment company assets in excess of which a lower investment advisory fee is rate charged.

broker An agent, often a member of a stock exchange firm or an exchange member, who executes orders to buy or sell securities or commodities and charges a commission. [See Section 2(a)(6) of the Investment Company Act of 1940.]

bunching Grouping transactions in the same security for several investment clients of the same investment advisor to obtain the benefit of lower commission changes or other transaction costs.

calendar spread Options strategy that entails buying two options on the same security with different maturities. If the exercise prices are the same, it is a *horizontal spread.* If the exercise prices are different, it is a *diagonal spread.*

call option A contract that entitles the holder to buy (call), at the holder's option, a specified number of units of a particular security at a specified price at any time until the stated expiration date of the contract. The option generally applies to round lots of securities.

cap An option contract that protects the holder from a rise in interest rates, or some other underlying fundamental, beyond a certain point.

capital asset pricing model (CAPM) A model which relates the expected return on an asset to the expected return on the market portfolio.

CAPM See **capital asset pricing model.**

caps and floors Interest-rate options. *Caps* are an upper limit on interest rates (if you buy a cap, you make money if interest rates move above the cap strike level). *Floors* are a lower limit on interest rates (if you buy a floor, you make money if interest rates move below the floor strike level).

cash-flow map A report that shows net cash flows of foreign-exchange- and interest-rate-related cash flows (typically grouped by maturity, country, or credit rating).

cash flow at risk Estimated potential cash-flow loss (through reduction in revenues or increase in outgoings) due to adverse market movements (for example, unfavorable movements in interest rates, exchange rates, commodity prices, and other markets) within a specific time horizon and subject to a given confidence level.

CBOE See **Chicago Board Options Exchange.**

CD See **certificate of deposit.**

certificate of deposit (CD) Generally, short-term, interest-bearing, negotiable certificates issued by commercial banks or by savings and loan associations against funds deposited with the issuing institution.

change return See **log return.**

Chicago Board Options Exchange (CBOE) A national securities exchange, based in Chicago, that provides a continuous market for trading in derivatives. Various other exchanges, such as the American, Pacific, Philadelphia, and Baltimore and Washington Exchanges, also provide such markets.

churning A process of executing unnecessary portfolio securities transactions to generate commissions.

clearing agency A central location at which members' security transactions are matched to determine the minimum quantities to be received or delivered.

clearing risk The possibility that an institution may not be reimbursed on the same value date for payments made on behalf of customers.

closed-form solution A solution is closed form when an exact solution can be found for a precise mathematical representation of the problem. Otherwise, it is considered an **open-form solution.**

closed-end investment company A mutual fund having a fixed number of shares outstanding, which it does not stand ready to redeem. Its shares are traded similarly to those of other public corporations. [See Section 5(a) of the Investment Company Act of 1940.]

closed-up fund An open-end investment company that no longer offers its shares for sale to the general public but still stands ready to redeem its outstanding shares.

close-out netting An arrangement to settle with one single payment all contracted but not yet due liabilities to and claims on an institution, immediately upon the occurrence of one of a list of defined events, such as the appointment of a liquidator to that institution. (See **netting by novation** and **obligation netting**).

CMO See **collateralized mortgage obligation.**

collar Combination of a cap and a floor that protects the buyer within a band of interest rates.

collateralized mortgage obligation (CMO) Mortgage-backed bond secured by the cash flow of a pool of mortgages.

commercial paper (CP) Short-term, unsecured, promissory notes issued by corporations. Commercial paper is usually sold on a discount basis. [See Section 3(a)(3) of the Securities Act of 1933 and Section 3(a)(10) of the Securities Exchange Act of 1934.]

compliance risk The risk arising from violations or nonconformance with laws, rules, regulations, prescribed practices, or ethical standards.

confidence bands Projected upper and lower boundaries for portfolio returns (e.g., 5 percent band breaks are associated with a 95 percent confidence band).

confidence interval A range of the possible values of a population, usually centered around the mean.

confidence level A specified level of certainty for a statistical prediction (e.g., 95 percent confidence worst-case loss).

confidence level scaling factor A multiplier to scale standard deviation to a specified confidence level, assuming normality (e.g., 1.65 is the confidence level scaling factor to arrive at a 95 percent one-tailed confidence level).

contango An interest factor reflecting the excess of the future price of a commodity contract over the spot price.

contingent lending risk The risk that potential obligations will become actual obligations and will not be repaid on time. Contingent lending risk occurs in products ranging from letters of credit and guarantees to unused loan commitments.

control Defined by Section 2(a)(9) of the Investment Company Act of 1940 as the power to exercise (whether exercised or not) a controlling influence over the management of policies of a company, unless that power results solely from an official position with the company.

conventional mortgage A mortgage that is not insured or guaranteed by the federal government.

convertible bond A bond with an embedded option that allows the holder to convert the bond to common stock.

convertible securities Securities carrying the right (either unqualified or under stated conditions) to exchange the security for other securities of the issuer or of another issuer.

convexity An upward-bowing shape of a security's payoff pattern. In technical parlance, it means that the second derivative of value with respect to some variable is positive.

correlation (ρ) A linear statistical measure of the comovement between two random variables. A correlation ρ (Greek letter rho) ranges from +1.0 to –1.0. Observing clumps of firms defaulting together geographically or by industry is an example of positive correlation of default events.

counterparty The partner in a credit facility or transaction in which each side takes broadly comparable credit risk. When a bank lends a company money, the borrower (not the counterparty) has no meaningful credit risk to the bank. When the same two agree on an at-the-money forward exchange contract or swap, the company is at risk if the bank fails, just as much as the bank is at risk if the counterparty fails (although for the opposite movement in exchange or interest rates). After inception, swap positions often move in or out of the money, and the relative credit risk changes accordingly.

country risk A broad risk category encompassing political risk and transfer risk (also known as *cross-border risk*).

coupon stripping The separation of interest coupons from the corpus of a bearer bond.

covariance (cov) The variability of a portfolio of data sets.

covenants Legal restrictions placed on an organization, often tied to debt issues.

CP See **commercial paper.**

credit (debt) rating A process of ranking obligations (facilities) and, at some banks, obligors (borrowers) according to their relative risk. Moody's and S&P assign both short- and long-term ratings to individual issues of a borrower. Country ratings are also provided.

credit exposure The amount subject to a change in value upon a change in credit quality through either a market-based revaluation in the event of an upgrade or downgrade, or the application of a recovery fraction in the event of default.

credit quality Generally refers to an obligor's relative chance of default, usually expressed in alphabetic terms (e.g., Aaa, Aa, A).

credit-rating methodology Credit ratings are assigned to assess counterparty risk. Credit ratings essentially rank counterparties according to risk of default, risk of loss, or both. There are many forms and many approaches.

credit risk/exposure The risk that a counterparty will not settle a contractual obligation for full value as defined and on time, either when due or at any time thereafter. In exchange-for-value systems, the risk is generally defined to include replacement risk and principal risk.

credit scoring A method of using scorecards to predict an expected default rate. Applicants are ranked according to an expected default rate for each score. Both behavioral scores and application data can be used for new applicants.

credit spreads A spread over government rates to compensate investors for credit risk, typically expressed in basis points (0.01 percent).

cross-currency settlement risk See **foreign-exchange settlement risk.**

currency risk The risk that a change in the value of a foreign currency will affect the value of an asset, liability, or financial instrument that is denominated in the foreign currency.

current exposure For market-driven instruments, the amount it would cost to replace a transaction today should a counterparty default. If there is an enforceable netting agreement with the counterparty, the current exposure would be the net replacement cost; otherwise, it would be the gross amount.

custodian A bank, trust company, or, less frequently, a member of a national securities exchange, responsible for receiving delivery and for the safekeeping of an investment company's cash and securities. [See Section 17(f) of the Investment Company Act of 1940.]

custody arrangements Arrangements under which the trustee's only responsibilities are to ensure the safekeeping of assets and to follow the instructions of approved individuals as set out in the trust agreement.

daily earnings at risk (DEaR) The estimated potential loss of a portfolio's value resulting from an adverse move in market factors over a specific time horizon. Measures the maximum estimated losses on a given position that can be expected to be incurred over a single day, with 95 percent confidence.

daily limits Limits established by exchanges on fluctuations in prices of futures contracts (other than contracts for delivery in the current month) during a trading session.

dealer A person or firm acting as a principal rather than as an agent in buying and selling securities. Mutual fund shares are usually sold through dealers. [See Section 2(a)(11) of the Investment Company Act of 1940.]

DEaR See **daily earnings at risk.**

decay factor (λ) The weight λ (Greek letter lambda) applied in the exponential moving average. It takes a value between 0 and 1. In RiskMetrics, λ is 0.94 in the calculation of volatilities and correlations for a 1-day horizon and 0.97 for a 1-month horizon.

delayed delivery contract A transaction in which delivery and payment are delayed longer than in normal transactions.

delivery versus payment (DVP) A mechanism in an exchange-for-value settlement system that ensures that the final transfer of one asset occurs if and only if the final transfer of other assets occurs. Assets could include monetary assets (such as foreign exchange), securities, or other financial instruments. (See **payment versus payment.**)

delta (δ) The change in a derivative's price in relation to a given and incremental change in the price of the underlying instrument. For example, a delta of –0.5 would imply a –½ percent change in the derivative's price given a 1 percent increase in the underlying asset. (See **volatility.**)

derivative A financial instrument that derives its value from the value and characteristics of another underlying asset, index, or reference rate, called the *underlying instrument.*

diffusion process Process that assumes continuous (as opposed to discrete) price changes of asset prices.

disclosure risk Risk that occurs when acting as an agent for other investors, as an underwriter, or as an advisor on a transaction.

discount The amount of points collected from the mortgagor. The purpose of a discount is to adjust the yield upward above the note rate.

diversification The process of risk reduction achieved by assembling a portfolio of securities with correlations less than 1.

dividends Prorated payments to shareholders from net investment income and realized capital gains.

duration (Macaulay) See **Macaulay duration.**

DVP See **delivery versus payment.**

EaR See **earnings at risk.**

earnings at risk (EaR) The amount of earnings that are at risk over a defined period of time; for example, the earnings that could be claimed by loss over a 10-day time frame by a

2-standard-deviation event. Similar to cash flow at risk, except for necessary adjustments due to accounting treatments of cash flows when determining earnings. Typical adjustments include deferral of cash flows that are subject to deferral accounting treatment, advance treatment of cash flows that are accounted accrually, and inclusion of operating cash flows that are hedged.

economic capital An equity reserve or cushion for unexpected losses. It ensures that a company remains solvent and stays in business even under extreme conditions. It is important to recognize that economic capital is distinct from regulatory capital, which focuses on market and credit risk. Conceptually, economic capital is comprehensive and covers all significant risks.

economic exposures Market exposures that consider how changes in foreign-exchange rates, interest rates, or commodity prices can affect the overall operating environment of a firm (for example, level of demand for products and services). Also called *strategic exposures.*

EDF See **expected default frequency.**

Employee Retirement Income Security Act (ERISA) A federal law enacted in 1974 that set investment guidelines for management of private pension plans and profit sharing plans, including employee vesting and conduct of plan administrators.

enterprise risk The risk of loss associated with the occurrence of firmwide events, such as the loss of key personnel, the loss of important customers, or the risk of litigation. Some of these risks are insurable; some can be actively managed to mitigate their impact.

equity risk Risk that occurs when an institution invests in, holds, or receives equity, equity-like securities, or other junior securities in nonaffiliated entities. These securities include instruments such as common shares, preferred shares, and related derivative instruments.

equity securities Common and preferred stocks and debentures convertible into common stocks.

ERISA See **Employee Retirement Security Act.**

eurodollars U.S. dollars deposited in banks outside the United States.

event risk The risk associated with the occurrence of a single event, such as the default on an individual loan, a failure to process an item accurately, or an act of fraud.

excess returns Returns above the benchmark rate.

excessions Confidence-level band breaks (i.e., observed exceptions or outliers).

ex-dividend A security that no longer carries the right to the most recently declared dividend; or the period of time between the announcement of the dividend and the payment. A security becomes ex-dividend on the ex-dividend date (set by the the NASD), which is usually two business days before the record date (set by the company issuing the dividend). For transactions during the ex-dividend period, the seller, not the buyer, will receive the dividend. Ex-dividend is usually indicated in newspapers with an x next to the stock or mutual fund's name. In general, a stock price drops the day the ex-dividend period starts, since the buyer will not receive the benefit of the dividend payout till the next dividend date. As the stock gets closer to the next dividend date, the price may gradually rise in anticipation of the dividend.

expected default frequency (EDF) The statistically derived likelihood that any given instrument will go into default.

exponential moving average Method of applying weights to a set of data points with the weights declining exponentially over time. In a time series context, this results in weighting recent data more than data from the distant past.

ex-rights Similar to ex-dividends. The buyer of a stock selling ex-rights is not entitled to a rights distribution.

ex-warrants Stocks or bonds trading without attached warrants, entitling holders to subscribe to additional shares within specified periods and at specified prices.

failure to deliver Securities that the selling broker or other financial institution has not delivered to the buyer at the settlement or clearance date.

failure to receive Securities that the buying broker or a financial institution has not received from the seller at the settlement or clearance date.

fair value An estimated value for securities and assets determined in good faith by the board of directors under the Investment Company Act of 1940, and which has no readily available market quotation. [See Section 2(a)(41).]

fat tails See **leptokurtosis.**

fiduciary risk Risk that occurs when an institution is charged with the responsibility of acting as a trustee for third parties. The risk is greatest when placed in this position involuntarily—that is, without having a trust agreement in place that defines the restrictions.

fiduciary services Services involving entrusting assets owned by one party to another party.

final, finality Irrevocable and unconditional.

final settlement Settlement that is irrevocable and unconditional. (See **settlement.**)

fixed income Refers to interest rate instruments (e.g., bonds, zero-coupon bonds, and floating-rate notes). A preferred stock or debt security with a stated percentage or dollar income return.

fixed-rate mortgage A mortgage that provides for only one interest rate for the entire term of the mortgage. If the interest rate changes because of enforcement of the due-on-sale provision, the mortgage is still considered a fixed-rate mortgage.

flat A method of trading in certain types of bonds, usually income bonds that do not pay interest unless it has been earned and declared payable, or bonds on which the issuing corporation has defaulted in paying interest.

floater A debt instrument with a variable coupon, paying a rate indexed to a money market rate.

floor An option contract that protects the holder against a decline in interest rates or some underlying instrument below a certain point.

foreclosure The legal process by which a borrower in default under a mortgage is deprived of the interest in the mortgaged property.

Foreign exchange (FX) risk Risk of loss due to movements in foreign-exchange rates.

foreign-exchange settlement exposure The amount at risk when a foreign-exchange transaction is settled. This equals the full amount of the currency purchased. The exposure lasts from the time that a payment instruction for the currency sold can no longer be cancelled unilaterally until the time the currency purchased is received with finality. (See **credit risk/exposure** and **foreign-exchange settlement risk.**)

foreign-exchange settlement risk The risk that one party to a foreign-exchange transaction will pay the currency it sold but not receive the currency it bought. This is also called *cross-currency settlement risk* or *principal risk.*

forward A contract obligating one party to buy, and the other to sell, a specific asset for a fixed price at a future date.

forward exchange contract An agreement to exchange the currencies of different countries at a specified future date at a specified rate (the *forward rate*). Unlike a securities futures contract, the terms of a forward contract are not standardized.

forward pricing The pricing of mutual fund shares for sale, repurchase, or redemption at a price computed after an order has been received. Mutual fund shares are usually priced once or twice a day.

forward rate agreement (FRA) An agreement to exchange dollar amounts at a specified future date based on the difference between a particular interest-rate index and an agreed fixed rate.

front running Buying or selling securities for an institution in advance of executing a customer's transaction.

fundamental rating models These are typically proprietary models which have been built by individual banks or vendors. They, too, try to predict EDRs; however, they allow changing the firm's balance sheet, stress-testing cash flows, etc. in order to develop an EDR.

futures Contracts covering the sale of financial instruments or physical commodities for future delivery on an exchange. A forward contract that is standardized and traded on an exchange.

futures contract A transferable agreement to deliver or receive during a specific future month a standardized minimum grade or a financial instrument of standardized specification under terms and conditions established by the designated contract market.

FX risk See **foreign-exchange risk.**

gamma (γ) The ratio of an option's change in delta relative to an incremental change in the price of underlying asset. It is a measure of the rate of change of a security's delta.

GPARM Graduated-payment adjustable-rate mortgage. (See **adjustable-rate mortgage.**)

growth fund An investment company investing primarily or entirely in growth-industry securities, emphasizing future capital appreciation over current yield.

growth stock The stock of a company whose earnings are expected to increase, thus raising the market value of the stock. Growth-stock companies generally reinvest a substantial amount of their earnings rather than paying them out in cash dividends.

hedge Transaction that is designed to reduce the risk of a position or a portfolio by taking a corresponding offsetting position. Hedges are good at eliminating market risk, but often result in basis risk.

hedge fund An investment company seeking to minimize market risks by holding securities believed likely to increase in value while simultaneously taking short positions in securities believed likely to decrease in value. The only objective is capital appreciation.

hedging A means of risk protection against extensive loss due to adverse price fluctuations by buying or selling a futures contract or option to offset a present or anticipated position or transaction in the cash market.

historical simulation A nonparametric method of using past data to make inferences about the future. One application of this technique is to take today's portfolio and revalue it using historical price and rate data.

holding period The amount of time that it is assumed that a financial instrument will be retained. The time period over which the risk measurement should apply.

hot spot A measure of contribution to portfolio risk, highlighting significant risk concentration. A trademark of Goldman Sachs.

implied volatility An indication of volatility obtained from observable prices for traded options, and which captures the market's current expectations for the future distribution of market prices.

incentive compensation A fee paid to an investment company's advisor that generally consists of a basic fee plus a bonus (or less a penalty) if the fund's performance exceeds (or fails to match) that of a specified stock index.

incremental VaR A measure of a position's impact on VaR as the position size increases.

independent Implies no correlation or relationship between variables.

individual incentive Objective-based or commission-type incentive, individualized to apply to technicians, professionals, managers, and individual contributors.

information risk Risk arising from lack of sufficient and or timely information, particularly in light of changing economic or market conditions.

International Swap Dealers Association (ISDA) A committee sponsored by this organization was instrumental in drafting an industry standard under which securities dealers would trade swaps. Included in this was a draft of a master agreement by which institutions would outline their rights to net multiple offsetting exposures which they might have to a counterparty at the time of a default.

integrated risk The risk that concentrations and/or interrelationships between risks (i.e., credit and market risk) are not recognized.

interest margin deposit A commodity transaction term for the amount of money or its equivalent, specified by the commodity exchange under which the contract is traded, that is held as a good-faith deposit to ensure that the customer meets the variation margin requirement.

interest method A method of amortizing discount or premium on debt that results in a constant rate of interest on the sum of the face amount of debt and the unamortized premium or discount at the beginning of each period.

interest-rate risk The risk to earnings or capital arising from movements in interest rates. Interest-rate risk arises usually from shift, twist, and butterfly factors; from differences between the timing of rate changes and the timing of cash flows (repricing risk); and from changing rate relationships among different yields.

interest-rate swap A binding agreement between counterparties to exchange periodic interest payments on a predetermined notional principal amount. For example, one party will pay fixed and receive variable interest rate on a $100 million notional principal amount.

internal models approach A proposal by the Basel Committee that permits banks to use approved risk models to calculate market risk capital.

internal rate of return (IRR) The interest rate that, when used as a discount rate, equates the price of a financial instrument to its individual discounted cash flows.

International Organization of Securities Commissions (IOSCO) A committee of supervisory authorities for securities firms in major industrialized countries.

Internet An uncontrolled (not governed, not owned) network of computers linked to one another that provides consistent pathways for communication.

in the money When an option has positive intrinsic value (that is, for a call option, when the price is above the strike, and for a put option, when the price is below the strike).

inverse floater A mortgage-backed bond, usually part of a CMO, bearing an interest rate that declines as an index rate increases, and vice versa.

investment advisor (manager) Under Section 2(a)(20) of the Investment Company Act of 1940, a company providing investment advice, research, and often administrative and similar services for a contractually agreed-on fee, generally based on a percentage of net assets.

Investment Advisory Act of 1940 A law requiring investment advisors and firms providing investment advice to register with the SEC and adhere to SEC regulations.

investment advisory agreement An agreement between an investment company and an investment manager, engaging the investment manager to provide investment advice to the investment company for a fee. [See Sections 15(a), 15(c), and 36(b) of the Investment Company Act of 1940.]

investment company A company, as defined in Section 3(a) of the Investment Company Act of 1940, that primarily invests, reinvests, or trades in securities [Section 3(a)(1)], issues face-amount certificates [Section 3(a)(2)], or is engaged in investing and owning investment securities.

Investment Company Act of 1940 A set of federal laws enforced by the SEC that regulate the registration and activities of investment companies.

investment manager A manager of a portfolio of investments.

IOSCO See **International Organization of Securities Commissions.**

IRR See **internal rate of return.**

ISDA See International Swap Dealers Association.

issuer risk The risk that the market value of a security or other debt instrument may change when the perceived or actual credit standing of the issuer changes.

kurtosis (*K*) Characterization of the relative peakedness or flatness of a distribution when compared to a normal distribution.

lambda (λ) See **decay factor.**

legal and regulatory risk Risk that occurs whenever a bank, a related corporate entity (such as a nonbank subsidiary or affiliate), a transaction, or a customer is subject to a change in exposure resulting from regulatory, civil, or criminal sanctions or litigation. The risk that a country's laws will make certain derivative contracts unenforceable.

leptokurtosis Characterization of the thickness of the tails of a distribution compared to the normal distribution; often called *fat tails.* The situation in which there are more occurrences far from the mean than predicted by a standard normal distribution.

leverage Upside opportunity; amount available to earn as incentive compensation. Also defined as the ratio of equity to loan capital.

LIED See **loss in event of default.**

linear derivative Derivative security whose value changes proportionally with changes in underlying rates. Examples of common linear derivatives are futures, forwards, and swaps.

linear function A payoff pattern that follows a straight line. Any given change in the value of a factor will have the same impact on the price, regardless of the level of the factor.

linear risk For a given portfolio, when the underlying prices or rates change, the incremental change in the payoff of the portfolio remains constant for all values of the underlying prices or rates. When the payoff of the portfolio is not constant, the risk is said to be *nonlinear.*

liquidity At the *enterprise level,* the ability to meet current liabilities as they fall due; often measured as the ratio of current assets to current liabilities. At the *security level,* the ability to trade in volume without directly moving the market price; often measured as bid–ask spread and daily turnover.

liquidity risk The risk that a counterparty (or participant in a settlement system) will not settle an obligation for full value when due. Liquidity risk does not imply that a counterparty or participant is insolvent, because the counterparty or participant may be able to settle the required debit obligations at some later time.

listed security A security listed and traded on a stock exchange.

loan-equivalent risk The risk exposure of a transaction can be converted into one quantity, as if the transaction were a loan of a certain magnitude with specific risks assigned to it.

lognormal distribution Distribution in which the natural logarithms of the data elements are normally distributed.

log return The continuously compounded rate of return is assumed to be normally distributed. If we call this rate r and we call the effective annual rate r_e, then $r_e = e^r - 1$, and because

e^r can never be negative, the smallest possible value for r_e is –1, or –100 percent. Thus this assumption nicely rules out the troublesome possibility of negative prices while still conveying the advantages of working with normal distributions.

long position Denotes ownership or right to possession of securities. Opposite of a *short position,* or a bet that prices will rise. For example, you have a long position when you buy a stock, and will benefit from rising prices.

Long Term Capital Management (LTCM) A famous hedge fund that was rescued by a consortium of banks after extreme market volatility in August 1998 wiped out most of its equity capital.

long-term compensation option gains Gains from the exercise of stock options and/or stock-appreciation rights.

long-term programs Incentives that apply to more than one year; includes both stock and cash plans.

loss in event of default (LIED) The actual loss that will be realized on a position if the counterparty defaults.

LTCM See **Long Term Capital Management.**

Macaulay duration A weighted average term to maturity where the weights are the present value of the cash flows; the weighted average term of a security's cash flow.

macrohedges Portfolio hedges that reduce the risk of a collection of transactions (a large position).

management (investment) company Under Section 4(3) of the Investment Company Act of 1940, any investment company other than a face-amount certificate company [as defined in Section 4(1)] or a unit investment trust [as defined in Section 4(2)].

margin A securities transaction term for the amount of money or its equivalent, specified by the Board of Governors of the Federal Reserve System, that a customer must deposit with a broker in a securities transaction on margin.

marginal statistic A statistic that describes how an asset affects a portfolio. The statistic is obtained by taking the difference between the value of the statistic for the entire portfolio and the value of the statistic for the portfolio without the asset.

marginal VaR Impact of a given position on the total portfolio VaR. (See also **marginal statistic.**)

market exposure For market-driven instruments, there is an amount at risk of default only when the contract is in the money (i.e., when the replacement cost of the contract exceeds the original value). This exposure or uncertainty is captured by calculating the netted mean and standard deviation of exposures.

market liquidity risk The risk that a financial instrument cannot be purchased or liquidated quickly enough or in requisite quantities at a fair price. Also called *product liquidity risk.*

market making A trading style in which dealers publish bids and offer prices at which they are prepared to trade. The long-term goal of market makers is to earn a consistent bid–ask spread on transactions, as opposed to making profits on directional betting. Market making differs from proprietary trading, which takes directional views.

market neutral A trading style that should be uncorrelated to underlying market risks (equity, interest rate, foreign exchange, or commodity), leaving only residual risk. For example, a hedge fund manager can hedge the market risk of a U.S. stock portfolio by shorting S&P 500-Stock Index futures, leaving only firm-specific residual risk.

market price Usually the last reported price at which a security has been sold; or, if the security was not traded or if trading prices are not reported, a price arrived at based on recent bid and ask prices.

market rates Interest rates, equity prices, commodities prices, foreign-exchange rates, credit spreads, futures prices, and other market-related prices or levels.

market risk The risk that changes in market prices and conditions will adversely affect the book or market value of on- or off-balance-sheet positions by movements in equity and interest-rate markets, currency-exchange rates, and commodity prices.

market risk capital requirement The minimum amount of capital needed to support market risk positions, as required by banking regulatory authorities.

market-driven instruments Derivative instruments that are subject to counterparty default (e.g., swaps, forwards, and options). The distinguishing feature of these credit exposures is that their amount is only the net replacement cost—the amount the position is in the money—rather than the full notional amount.

mark to market (MTM) A procedure to adjust the carrying value of a security, option, or futures contract to current value. In the mark-to-market approach, unlike in traditional accrual accounting, positions are valued on a replacement cost basis by marking to the current market price. The position is adjusted to reflect accrued profits and losses.

matrix pricing A statistical technique used to value normal institutional-sized trading units of debt securities without relying exclusively on quoted prices. Factors such as the issue's coupon or stated interest rate, maturity, rating, and quoted prices of similar issues are employed.

MBS See **mortgage-backed security.**

mean (μ) A statistical measure μ (Greek letter mu) of central tendency; sum of the observation values divided by the number of observations. It is the first moment of a distribution.

mean reversion The statistical tendency of a time series to gravitate back toward a long-term historical level. This is manifested on a much longer scale than another similar measure, called *autocorrelation.* Mean reversion and autocorrelation are mathematically independent of one another.

median Central item in a data set after placing the data in increasing order of value.

mode The value that occurs most frequently in a data set.

modified duration An indication of price sensitivity. It is equal to a security's Macaulay duration divided by 1 plus the yield. The approximate percentage change in a bond's price for a 100-basis-point (1 percent) change in interest rates.

moments (of statistical distribution) Statistical distributions show the frequency at which events might occur across a range of values. The most familiar distribution is a normal bell-shaped curve. In general, the shape of any distribution can be described by its infinitely many moments. The first moment is the *mean,* which indicates the central tendency. The second moment is the *variance,* which indicates the width. The third moment is the *skewness,* which indicates any asymmetric leaning either to the left or right. The fourth moment is the *kurtosis,* which indicates the degree of central peakedness or, equivalently, the fatness of the outer tails.

money market fund A mutual fund whose investments are primarily or exclusively in short-term debt securities designed to maximize current income with liquidity and capital preservation, usually maintaining per-share net asset value at a constant amount, such as $1.

Monte Carlo simulation A methodology for solving a problem through the generation of a large number of scenarios and analysis of the collective result, which is generally a probability distribution of possible outcomes.

mortgage Collectively, the security instrument, the note, the title evidence, and all other documents and papers that represent debt-secured real estate.

mortgage-backed security (MBS) Investment-grade securities backed by a pool of mortgages or trust deeds that represent an undivided interest in a pool of mortgages.

MTM See **mark to market.**

mu (μ) See **mean.**

municipal bond fund An investment company whose shares represent holdings solely or largely of securities on which interest is exempt from federal income taxes.

mutual fund The popular name for an open-end management investment company. (See **open-end investment company.**)

NASD See **National Association of Securities Dealers.**

Nasdaq An electronic quotation system for over-the-counter securities sponsored by the NASD, which, in the case of securities traded on the NASD National Market System, reports prices and shares or units of securities trades and other reported market data.

National Association of Securities Dealers (NASD) An association of brokers or dealers, registered as such under Section 15A of the Securities Exchange Act, that supervises and regulates trading by its members in the over-the-counter market.

net asset value per share The value per share of outstanding capital stock of an investment company, computed by dividing net assets by the total number of shares outstanding. [See Rule 2(a)(b)of the Investment Company Act of 1940.] The value per share is usually computed daily by mutual funds.

netting There are at least three types of netting: (1) **Close-out netting.** In the event of counterparty bankruptcy, all transactions or all of a given type are netted at market value. The alternative would allow the liquidator to choose which contracts to enforce, thus creating opportunities to "cherry pick." There are international jurisdictions where the enforceability of netting in bankruptcy has not been legally tested. (2) **netting by novation.** The legal obligation of the parties to make required payments under one or more series of related transactions is canceled and a new obligation to make only the net payment is created. (3) **Settlement or payment netting.** For cash-settled trades, this can be applied either bilaterally or multilaterally and on related or unrelated transactions.

nominee The person, bank, or brokerage in whose name securities are transferred.

nonlinear risk For a given portfolio, when the underlying prices or rates change, the incremental change in the payoff of the portfolio does not remain constant for all values of the underlying prices or rates. When the payoff of the portfolio is constant, the risk is said to be *linear.*

nonparametric analysis When potential market movements are described by assumed scenarios, not by statistical parameters.

nonsystematic risk Diversifiable risk; the portion of the total variability of return that can be eliminated through diversification. To the extent that risk can be reduced through diversification, there is no possible risk premium to compensate management for failing to diversify.

normal distribution A bell-shaped, symmetrical distribution exhibited by some populations of continuous random variables. The normal distribution has a number of very important probability and statistical properties.

notional amount The face amount of a transaction, typically used as the basis for interest payment calculations. For swaps, this amount is not itself a cash flow. Credit exposure arises not against the notional value, but against the present value (market replacement cost) of in-the-money future terminal payments.

obligation netting The legally binding netting of amounts due in the same currency for settlement on the same day for two or more trades. Under an obligation-netting agreement for foreign-exchange transactions, counterparties are required to settle on the due date all of the trades included under the agreement in the form of a single payment in each of the relevant currencies. Depending on the relevant legal system, obligation netting can find a legal basis in constructions such as novation, setoff, or the current account mechanism. (See **close-out netting, netting,** and **netting by novation.**)

odd lot Usually a quantity of securities that is less than an even 100 shares or less than the established trading unit of that security in a particular securities market.

offshore fund An investment company organized outside the United States, whose shares are offered solely to foreign investors.

open contract An unperformed or unsettled contract. May be used in reference to new issues traded when, as, and if issued or in reference to commodity futures trading.

open-end investment company A mutual fund that is ready to redeem its shares at any time and that usually offers its shares for sale to the public continuously. [See Section 5(a)(1) of the Investment Company Act of 1940.]

open-form solution A solution is open form when no exact solution can be found for a precise mathematical representation of the problem. Otherwise, it is considered a **closed-form solution.**

operational risk The risk that controls do not provide adequate protection against fraud, incorrect market valuation, failure to record or settle a deal, settlement with the wrong counterparty, or failure to collect amounts due; the risk of incurring interest charges or other penalties for misdirecting or otherwise failing to make settlement payments on time owing to an error or technical failure.

option A contract between two parties giving one party the right but not the obligation to buy or sell an asset for a specified price; a financial instrument whose payoff is determined by the market value of some underlying instrument.

option-adjusted spread The average spread over the Treasury spot-rate curve, based on potential paths that can be realized in the future for interest rates. The spread is called *option-adjusted* because the potential paths of the cash flows are adjusted to reflect options.

outliers Sudden, unexpectedly large rate or price returns; also called *excessions.*

over-the-counter (OTC) market A market for securities of companies not listed on a stock exchange and traded mainly by electronic communications, such as Nasdaq, or by phone between brokers and dealers who act as principals or brokers for customers and who may or may not be members of a stock exchange.

P&L report See **profit-and-loss report.**

P/E ratio See **price–earnings ratio.**

parametric analysis When a functional form for the distribution of a set of data points is assumed. For example, when the normal distribution is used to characterize a set of returns.

pass-through Principal and interest payments received from borrowers and passed on to investors.

path dependence Inference that an option's value depends not only on the underlying instrument's price at expiration or exercise, but also on the underlying instrument's price history.

payable date The date on which a dividend is payable to holders of record on some previous record date.

payment versus payment (PVP) A mechanism in a foreign-exchange settlement system that ensures that a final transfer of one currency occurs if and only if a final transfer of the other currency or currencies takes place.

peak exposure For market-driven instruments, the maximum (perhaps netted) exposure expected with 95 percent confidence for the remaining life of a transaction.

percent marginal VaR expression in percentage terms of the impact of a given position on the total portfolio VaR.

percentile level A measure of risk describing a worst-case loss at a specified level of confidence; e.g., the probability that the portfolio market falls below the first percentile level (99 percent confidence level) is 1 percent.

performance fee See **incentive compensation.**

portfolio A collection of investments; these can be long (purchased) or short (sold) positions.

portfolio aggregation A methodology for estimating portfolio VaR without using volatilities and correlations; a subset of historical simulation which involves statistical fitting of hypothetical portfolio returns generated from historical market rates.

portfolio risk The risk of loss in a portfolio of assets, loans, and/or other investments. Portfolio risk is not the sum of the individual risks of the positions, as it considers correlations.

portfolio turnover rate A measure of portfolio activity, generally calculated as the amount of transactions for a specific portfolio relative to its average value over one year.

position The buyer of an asset is said to have a *long position,* and the seller of an asset is said to have a *short position.*

prepayment risk The risk of payment of all or part of a mortgage debt before it is due.

presettlement risk The risk that one party of a reciprocal agreement cannot meet its contractual obligation in the settlement of the contract. It is measured in terms of the current economic cost to replace the defaulted contract with another plus the possible price increase in the market.

price–earnings (P/E) ratio The market value of a share of stock divided by its earnings per share.

price makeup sheet A detailed computation of the net asset of a mutual fund.

principal A person, especially a dealer, who buys or sells securities for his or her own account. Also refers to the face amount of a security without accrued interest.

principal risk See **foreign-exchange settlement risk.**

principal underwriter See *distributor* and definition of *underwriter* in Section 2(a)(40) of the Investment Company Act of 1940.

private placement The direct sale of a block of securities of a new or secondary issue to a single investor or group of investors.

product liquidity risk The risk that a financial instrument cannot be purchased or liquidated quickly enough or in requisite quantities at a fair price. Also called *market liquidity risk.*

profit-and-loss (P&L) report A report that shows MTM gains or losses for traders.

prospectus A circular required by the Securities Act of 1933 describing securities being offered for sale to the public. [See Section 2(a)(31) of the Investment Company Act of 1940.]

prudent-man rule Trustees are responsible for ensuring that their actions are consistent with what a reasonably informed person would do with respect to investments.

prudent-person rule Similar to the prudent-man rule, except that the overall portfolio as a whole is the basis for applying the rule, not individual assets.

pure risk A condition in which all possible outcomes and their associated probabilities are known with a high degree of confidence.

pure uncertainty A condition in which neither all possible outcomes nor their associated probabilities are known.

put An option giving the holder the right, but not the obligation, to sell a specific quantity of an asset for a fixed price during a specific period of time.

put option The right, but not the obligation, to sell an asset at a prespecified price on or before a prespecified date in the future.

PVP See **payment versus payment.**

random sample A selection of the data elements drawn from the population in a nonsystematic manner.

RAPM See **risk-adjusted performance measurement.**

RAROC See **risk-adjusted return on capital.**

RAROE See **risk-adjusted return on equity.**

RARORAC Risk-adjusted return on risk-adjusted capital. See **risk-adjusted return on capital.**

registered bond A long-term debt instrument registered on the books of the issuing company in the owner's name; sometimes a debenture, if unsecured, or a note if short or intermediate term.

regulatory capital The minimum amount of capital required under applicable regulations to cover potential losses due to credit or market risks.

relative market risk Risk measured relative to an index or benchmark.

relative return Performance measured relative to a reference or benchmark return.

replacement risk/replacement cost risk The risk that a counterparty to an outstanding transaction for completion at a future date will fail to perform on the settlement date. This failure may leave the solvent party with an unhedged or open market position or deny the solvent party unrealized gains on the position. The resulting exposure is the cost of replacing, at current market prices, the original transaction. (See **credit risk/exposure** and **market risk.**)

repurchase agreement An agreement under which an investment company pays for and receives (purchases) securities from a seller who agrees to repurchase them within a specified time at a specified price.

reputation risk The risk to earnings or capital arising from negative public opinion. This risk is present in such activities as asset management and agency transactions.

residual risk Nonsystemic market-driven risks, including spread risk, basis risk, specific risk, and volatility risk. Residual risk is often defined as *issuer-specific risk.*

restricted security A security that may be sold privately, but that is required to be registered with the SEC or to be exempted from such registration before it may be sold in a public distribution.

return See **yield.**

return on equity (ROE) An amount, expressed as a percentage, earned on a company's common stock investment for a given period.

return on invested capital (ROIC)/return on investment (ROI) An amount, expressed as a percentage, earned on a company's total capital (its common and preferred stock equity plus its long-term funded debt) calculated by dividing total capital into earnings before interest, taxes, and dividends.

return on risk-adjusted capital (RORAC) See **risk-adjusted return on capital.**

reverse repurchase agreement An agreement under which the investment company transfers (sells) securities for cash to another party (purchaser), usually a broker, and agrees to repurchase them within a specified time at a specified price.

reverse split A prorated combination of shares into a smaller number; opposite of **stock split.**

rho (ρ) A measure of the rate of change of an option's value with respect to a change in the risk-free interest rate. (See **correlation.**)

right A privilege offered by a corporation to its shareholders pro rata to subscribe to a certain security at a specified price.

right of accumulation A method permitting the purchase of an aggregation of shares with shares previously acquired and currently owned to qualify for a quantity discount that reduces the sales charge on a single purchase.

risk The variance in outcomes around some central tendency.

risk, pure The condition in which all possible outcomes and their associated probabilities are known with a high degree of confidence.

risk-adjusted performance measurement (RAPM) An umbrella term that refers to RAROC, RORAC, RARORAC, CAPM, etc. The argument over which term to use is meaningless because one concept alone may not give a complete picture.

risk-adjusted return on capital (RAROC) A return on capital that has been adjusted to reflect the riskiness involved in the positions taken to achieve the return. The purpose of capital is to absorb loss. In a RAROC environment, the firm's capital is allocated to each line of business according to the riskiness of that business.

risk-adjusted return on equity (RAROE) A return on equity that has been adjusted to reflect the riskiness involved in the positions taken to achieve the return.

risk-adjusted return on risk-adjusted capital (RARORAC) See **risk-adjusted return on capital.**

risk appetite The level of risk that the board of directors and senior management determine is the appropriate level for their company.

risk-based capital ratio Financial ratio measuring a bank's capital adequacy.

risk capital The firm's own assessment of the amount of capital required to absorb loss and/or to achieve a specific debt rating. Risk that a deterioration in asset quality from losses will impair a bank's capital, requiring the sale of new stock to meet regulatory capital requirements.

risk identification Analysis of the risks that different financial instruments pose to the company, individually and as a group.

risk management process Typically, a sequential, step-by-step process of risk identification, measurement, controls, and monitoring. Risk has to be identified before it can be measured. It has to be measured before a rational control process can be designed.

risk-based limits Limits for market or credit risk that are defined in risk, not notional, terms. Risk-based limits have become a necessity for institutions trading a broad range of financial instruments, among which the same notional exposure can imply very different risks.

RiskMetrics A risk management methodology and database marketed by by J. P. Morgan.

ROE See **return on equity.**

ROI See **return on invested capital/return on investment.**

ROIC See **return on invested capital/return on investment.**

RORAC Return on risk-adjusted capital. See **risk-adjusted return on capital.**

round lot A unit of trading or a multiple of it. On the New York Stock Exchange, the unit of trading is generally 100 shares in stocks and $1000 par value in bonds.

S&P 500 See **Standard & Poor's 500-Stock Index.**

sale against the box Similar to a short sale, except that the seller already owns the stock being sold but keeps possession of it and therefore has to borrow the equivalent stock to deliver to the purchaser.

SEC See **Securities and Exchange Commission.**

secondary marketing A process whereby lenders and investors buy and sell existing mortgages and mortgage-backed securities, thereby providing greater availability of funds for additional mortgage lending by banks, mortgage bankers, and savings institutions.

sector loadings For correlation analysis, a firm or industry group is said to be dependent on underlying economic factors or sectors, such as the market as a whole, interest rates, and oil prices. As two industries "load" (are influenced by) common factors, they become more strongly correlated.

Securities Act of 1933 Act of Congress requiring registration of securities intended for sale to the public in interstate commerce or through the mail. Regulates the contents of prospectuses and similar documents and is intended to ensure that potential investors receive adequate information.

Securities Act of 1934 Act of Congress establishing the SEC, an independent agency, to enforce federal securities laws.

Securities and Exchange Commission (SEC) Independent regulatory agency established by Congress in 1934 to oversee the administration of federal securities laws.

Securities Exchange Act of 1934 Act of Congress regulating securities brokers and dealers, stock exchanges, and the trading of securities in the securities markets.

securitization The process of creating new securities backed or *collateralized* by a package of assets.

seed money An initial amount of capital contributed to a company at its inception. [See Section 14(a) of the Investment Company Act of 1940.]

seller's option A transaction that, by agreement, is to be settled at a date later than is usual for such a transaction.

selling group A group of brokers or dealers that has formed several accounts for the sale of securities, usually for purposes of underwriting.

senior versus subordinated bond A structure typically used for nonconforming loans. It is composed of two types of securities: *senior pass-throughs* (Class A), which are rated securities; and *subordinated securities* (Class B), which supply the credit enhancement for the senior pass-through instrument.

sequential settlement The settlement of payment obligations in different currencies at different times. A sequential settlement system would pay out some currencies to one or more participants before all relevant participants pay in all of the currencies they owe. (See **final settlement, payment versus payment, settlement,** and **simultaneous settlement.**)

serial correlation See **autocorrelation.**

settlement An act that discharges obligations with respect to funds or securities transfers between two or more parties.

settlement date The date on which security transactions are settled by delivering or receiving securities and receiving or paying cash, pursuant to an earlier agreement of purchase and sale called a *trade.* (See **trade date.**)

settlement risk The risk of loss resulting from a counterparty's failure to perform after having received funds or other financial consideration as part of a financial transaction (also known as *Herstatt risk*). During a simultaneous exchange, one party has already paid or delivered its side of the transaction without being able to verify payment by the reciprocal party.

settlement system A system in which settlement takes place.

Sharpe ratio A return-on-risk ratio named after Nobel laureate and Stanford University professor William F. Sharpe. The Sharpe ratio is defined as annual return minus risk-free rate divided by standard deviation of return.

short position Opposite of a long position, or a bet that prices will fall. For example, a short position in a stock will benefit from a falling stock price. If you sell an asset short, you are short the asset. You will benefit if the price falls.

short sale A sale of securities not owned at the time of sale, in anticipation that the price will fall and the securities can then be repurchased at a profit.

SIC See **Standard Industrial Classification.**

sigma (σ) See **standard deviation.**

simultaneous settlement The settlement of payment obligations in different currencies at the same time. A simultaneous settlement system does not pay out any currencies to any participant before all relevant participants pay in all of the currencies they owe. (See **final settlement, payment versus payment, sequential settlement,** and **settlement.**)

skewness Characterization of the degree of asymmetry of a distribution around its mean. Positive skewness indicates a leaning toward positive values (right-hand side); negative skewness indicates a leaning toward negative values (left-hand side).

soft dollars The value of research or services received from broker-dealers in exchange for commissions paid on securities transactions (*hard dollars*).

specific risk Issuer-specific risk; e.g., the risk of holding Yahoo! stock versus an S&P 500 futures contract. According to the capital asset pricing model (CAPM), specific risk is entirely diversifiable.

spot awards Cash and noncash awards recognizing significant individual or team contributions for one-time events.

spot commodity A contract for the delivery of a commodity. The commodity is evidenced by a warehouse receipt.

spread A combination of a put and call option at different prices, one below and the other above the current market price. Also refers to the difference between the bid and ask prices of a security and to the dealer's commission on a security offering.

spread risk The potential loss due to changes in spreads between two instruments. For example, there is a credit spread risk between corporate bonds and government bonds.

square root of time scaling A simple volatility scaling methodology that forecasts long-horizon volatility by multiplying volatility by the square root of time (e.g., 10-day volatility = 1-day volatility × $\sqrt{10}$).

stand-alone standard deviation Standard deviation of value for an asset computed without regard for the other instruments in the portfolio.

Standard & Poor's 500-Stock Index (S&P 500) A market-capitalization-weighted equity index of 500 U.S. stocks.

standard deviation (σ) A statistical measure which indicates the width of a distribution around the mean. A standard deviation σ (Greek letter sigma) is the square root of the second moment (variance) of a distribution.

Standard Industrial Classification (SIC) Four-digit codes used to categorize and uniquely identify business activities.

standby commitment An agreement to accept future delivery of a security at a guaranteed price of fixed yield on the exercise of an option held by the other party to the agreement.

stochastic Involving a random element (variable).

stochastic process A random process whose outcome can be estimated based on a distribution of possible results.

stock dividend A dividend payable in the stock of the issuing corporation.

stock split An increase in the number of outstanding shares of a company's stock to decrease the market price and thus allow for greater distribution of the shares.

stockholder of record A stockholder whose name is registered on the stock transfer books of the issuing corporation.

stop order An order used by a customer to protect a paper profit in a security or to reduce a possible loss in a security. The stop order becomes a market order when the price of the security reaches or sells through the price specified by the customer.

straddle A combination of one put and one option, identical as to the security issue, number of shares, exercise price, and expiration date.

strap A combination of two call options and one put option for the same security issue.

strategic risk The risk to earnings or capital arising from adverse business decisions or improper implementation of those decisions.

street name Securities held in the name of a brokerage concern (a type of nominee) instead of in customers' names. (See **nominee.**)

stress testing The process of determining how much the value of a portfolio can fall under abnormal market conditions. Stress testing consists of generating worst-case stress scenarios (e.g., a stock market crash) and revaluing a portfolio under those stress scenarios.

strike price The stated price for which an underlying asset may be purchased (in the case of a call) or sold (in the case of a put) by the option holder upon exercise of the option contract.

strip A combination of two put options and one call option for the same security issue.

substitute securities Securities that are identical or comparable to assets one is trying to hedge; for example, government bonds, interest-rate swaps, and interest-rate futures may be used as substitute securities for hedging purposes.

swap An agreement by two parties to exchange a series of cash flows in the future; for example, fixed-interest-rate payments for floating-rate payments. Derivative contracts whereby two companies agree to exchange cash flows based on different underlying reference assets. The most common swaps are interest-rate swaps, in which fixed-coupon cash flows are exchanged for floating-rate cash flows. Total return swaps can be structured on just about any underlying reference asset or index; for example S&P 500 Equity Index versus J. P. Morgan EMBI+ Index.

swaptions Options on swaps (e.g., the right, but not the obligation, to buy or sell swaps at a predefined strike rate).

syndicate A group of brokers or dealers who together underwrite and distribute new issues of securities or large blocks of an outstanding issue.

systemic risk The risk that the failure of one participant in a transfer system, or in financial markets generally, to meet its required obligations when due will cause other participants or financial institutions to be unable to meet their obligations when due (including settlement obligations in a transfer system). Such a failure may cause significant liquidity or credit problems and, as a result, might threaten the stability of financial markets.

tail risk Risk of loss due to extreme market movements (e.g., market changes that fall into the tail of the probability distribution).

technical rating models Models that statistically correlate information contained on the obligor's financial statements with SIC codes, bankruptcy data, etc. to calculate debt ratings and probability of default or insolvency.

theta (θ) A measure of the rate of change of an option's value with respect to a change in its time to maturity; refers to time decay of options positions.

thrift A savings and loan association or savings bank whose primary function is to encourage personal savings and home ownership through mortgage lending.

ticker An instrument that prints the price and quantity of a security traded on an exchange within minutes after the trade has been executed.

Tier 1 capital Common stock and qualifying preferred stock.

Tier 2 capital Reserves for loan losses, subordinated debt, and preferred stock.

tracking error The standard deviation of expected portfolio returns versus benchmark returns. The tracking error specifies the active (nonbenchmark) risk in an actively managed portfolio.

trade An agreement of purchase and sale in a securities market, to be settled or performed by payment and delivery on a later settlement date.

trade date The date on which a security transaction that is to be settled on a later settlement date is actually entered into.

trading book A bank's proprietary position in financial instruments which are intentionally held for short-term sale and which are taken on by the institution with the intention of benefiting in the short-term from actual or expected differences between their bid and ask prices.

trading unit The unit by which a security is traded on the exchange, usually 100 shares of stock or $1000 principal amount of bonds. Also called a *round lot.*

transaction risk The risk arising from problems with service or product delivery. It is a function of internal controls, information systems, employee integrity, and operating processes. It is also referred to as *operating* or *operational risk.*

transaction An individual agreement to buy or sell a specific financial instrument.

transfer A change of ownership of a security by delivery of certificates for the security in a sale (against payment of the purchase price in a securities market sale), or by gift, pledge, or other disposition.

transfer agent An agent who maintains records of the names of the company's registered shareholders, their addresses, and the number of shares they own.

transfer risk The risk of loss arising from a particular country imposing restrictions on remittances of capital, dividends, interest, or fees to foreign lenders or investors as part of its economic policy.

trustee Person or entity that is responsible for managing and safekeeping assets in a trust in accordance with the wishes of the trustor.

trustor Person or entity that establishes the trust for the benefit of another individual or entity (the beneficiary).

uncertainty, pure The condition in which neither all possible outcomes nor their associated probabilities are known.

underlying instrument An asset that may be bought or sold.

underwriting The act of distributing a new issue of securities or a large block of issued securities in a secondary offering, commonly including an obligation to purchase the underwritten securities, regardless of whether they can be resold to others.

unit investment trust An investment company, organized under a trust indenture, that issues only redeemable securities that represent an undivided interest in a unit of specified (usually unmanaged) securities. [See Sections 4(3) and 26 of the Investment Company Act of 1940.]

unlisted security A security that is not listed on a securities exchange. (See **over-the-counter market.**)

unregistered securities Securities that are not registered under the Securities Act of 1933.

unwinding positions Reversing positions. That is, if you own a security (are long), sell the security (go short). If you have a short position, buy the security back.

value The market price or fair value of securities. [See **fair value.** See also Rule 2(a)(4) of the Investment Company Act of 1940.]

value at risk (VaR) The predicted worst-case loss at a specific confidence level (e.g., 95 percent) over a certain period of time (e.g., 10 days).

variable annuity A life insurance annuity contract that provides future payments to the holder (the annuitant) usually at retirement, the size of which depends on the performance of the portfolio's securities.

variance A statistical measure which indicates the width of a distribution around the mean. It is the second moment of a distribution. A related measure is *standard deviation,* which is the square root of the variance.

variation margin In commodity operations, last-day point fluctuation—the difference between the settling price of the day before and the last day's settling price—on the net long and short positions.

vega The rate at which the price of an option changes because of a change in the volatility of the underlying instrument.

venture capital An important source of financing for start-up companies or others embarking on new or turnaround ventures that entail some investment risk but offer the potential for above-average future profits.

venture capital limited partnership An investment vehicle organized by a brokerage firm or entrepreneurial company to raise capital for start-up companies or those in the early processes of developing products and services.

volatility (δ) The standard deviation of the natural logarithms of the ratios of data points from one period to the next. The degree of price fluctuation for a given asset, rate, or index. Usually expressed as variance or standard deviation δ (Greek letter delta).

volatility risk Potential loss due to fluctuations in implied option volatilities; often referred to as *vega risk.* Short option positions generally lose money when volatility spikes upward.

warrant The right, but not the obligation, to buy or sell a fixed amount of an underlying asset at a fixed rate in the future; a type of option to purchase additional securities from the issuer. Commonly affixed to certificates for other securities at the time of issuance.

yield The return on investment that an investor receives from dividends or interest, expressed as a percentage of the current market price of the security or, if the investor already owns the security, of the price paid.

yield curves A plot of the market yields of bonds that are alike in every respect except for their remaining terms to maturity.

yield to maturity The rate of return on a debt security held to maturity, used to calculate the stated interest rate, accrual of discount, and amortization of premium.

zero-coupon bond A bond with no periodic coupon payments, redeemed at par value (100 percent of face value) at maturity.

Acharya, V. V., and J. N. Carpenter: "Callable Defaultable Bonds: Valuation, Hedging and Optimal Exercise Boundaries," working paper, New York University, Department of Finance, New York, March 15, 1999.

Aguais, Scott D., and Anthony M. Santomero: "Incorporating New Fixed Income Approaches into Commercial Loan Valuation," *Journal of Lending and Credit Risk Management* 80/6 (February 1998), 58–65, http://fic.wharton.upenn.edu/fic/papers/98.html.

Aguais, S. D., L. Forest, S. Krishnamoorthy, and T. Mueller: "Creating Value from Both Loan Structure and Price," *Commercial Lending Review* (Winter 1997), 1–10.

Alexander, Gordon J., and Jack C. Francis: *Portfolio Analysis,* Englewood Cliffs, New Jersey: Prentice-Hall, 1986, p. 144.

Altman, E. I.: "Financial Ratios, Discriminant Analysis and the Prediction of Corporate Bankruptcy," *Journal of Finance* (September 1968), 589–609.

———: "Measuring Corporate Bond Mortality and Performance," *Journal of Finance* (September 1989), 909–922.

———: "Predicting Financial Distress of Companies: Revisiting the Z-Score and Zeta Models," working paper, New York University Salomon Center, New York, June 1995.

Altman, E. I., T. K. N. Baidya, and L. M. R. Dias: "Assessing Potential Financial Problems for Firms in Brazil," Working Paper 125, New York University Salomon Center, September 1977.

Altman, E. I., and D. L. Kao: "Examining and Modeling Corporate Bond Rating Drift," working paper, New York University Salomon Center, New York, 1991.

———: "The Implications of Corporate Bond Ratings Drift," *Financial Analysts Journal* (May–June 1992), 64–75.

Altman, E. I., and V. M. Kishore: "Defaults and Returns on High-Yield Bonds: Analysis Through 1997," working paper, New York University Salomon Center, January 1998.

Altman, E. I., and P. Narayanan: "An International Survey of Business Failure Classification Models," *Financial Markets, Instruments and Institutions* 6/2 (1997).

Altman, E. I., and A. Saunders: "Credit Risk Measurement: Developments over the Last Twenty Years," *Journal of Banking and Finance* (December 1997), 1721–1742.

Altman, E. I., and H. J. Suggitt: "Default Rates in the Syndicated Loan Market: A Mortality Analysis," Working Paper S-97-39, New York University Salomon Center, New York, December 1997.

Anderson, R., and S. Sunderesan: "A Comparative Study of Structural Models of Corporate Bond Yields," paper presented at the Center for Economic Policy Research (CEPR) Conference, London, September 20, 1998.

Anderson, R., S. Sunderesan, and P. Tychon: "Strategic Analysis of Contingent Claims," *European Economic Review* (1996), 871–881.

Angbazo, L., J-P. Mei, and A. Saunders: "Credit Spreads in the Market for Highly Leveraged Transaction Loans," *Journal of Banking and Finance* (December 1998), 1249–1282.

Anonymous: "Tracking Down Japan's 'Mr. Copper,' " *Reuter's Magazine* (September–October 1996), http://about.reuters.com/magazine/mag96/sepoct96/eqt.htm.

APBnews.com: "Cendant to Pay 2.8 Billion Fraud Settlement," APBnews.com, December 8, 1999, www.apbnew.com/safetycenter/business/1999/12/08/fraud1208_01.html, accessed July 21, 2001.

Arrow, K.: "Le Role des Valeurs Boursieres Pour la Repartition de la Meilleure des Risques," *Econometrie Colloque Internationaux du CNRS* 11 (1953), 41–47.

Arrow, Kenneth J.: *Essays on the Theory of Risk Bearing,* Chicago: Markham, 1971.

Arthur Benson v. Metallgesellschaft Corp. et al., Civ. Act. no. JFM-94-484, U.S. District Court for the District of Maryland, 1994.

Asarnow, E.: "Managing Bank Loan Portfolios for Total Return," paper presented at the Conference on a New Market Equilibrium for the Credit Business, Frankfurt, Germany, March 11, 1999.

Asarnow, E., and J. Marker: "Historical Performance of the U.S. Corporate Loan Market, 1988–1993," *Journal of Commercial Lending* (Spring 1995), 13–22.

Asay, M.: "A Note on the Design of Commodity Option Contracts," *Journal of Finance* 2 (1982), 1–8.

Asiaweek: "Billion-Dollar Man" (December 29, 1995), www.cnn.com/asianow/asiaweek/95/1229/feat5.html, accessed August 20, 2000.

Asquith, P., D. W. Mullins, and E. D. Wolff: "Original Issue High Yield Bonds: Aging Analysis of Defaults, Exchanges and Calls," *Journal of Finance* (September 1989), 923–952.

Aukenthaler, Christoph: *Trust Banking, Theorie und Praxis des Anlagegeschäftes,* PhD thesis, University of Zurich, Bern, Switzerland: Haupt, 1991, p. 244ff.

Auckenthaler, Christoph, and Jürg Gabathuler: *Gedanken zum Konzept eines Total Enterprise Wide Risk Management (TERM),* Zurich: University of Zurich, 1997.

Auckenthaler, Christoph, and Reto R. Gallati: *Eine Zusätzliche Einnahmequelle: Securities Lending,* Zurich: NZZ, April 18, 1996.

Babbel, D. F.: "Insuring Banks Against Systematic Credit Risk," *Journal of Futures Markets* (November 6 1989), 487–506.

Bachelier, Louis: "Theorie de la Speculation," *Annales de l'Ecole Normale Superieure,* 17 (1900), 21–86. English translation by A. J. Boness in Paul H. Cootner (ed.), *The Random Character of Stock Market Prices,* Cambridge, MA: MIT Press, 1967 pp. 17–78.

Bair, S. and S. Milligan: "Voluntary Efforts to Provide Oversight of OTC Derivatives Activities," in R. Klein and J. Lederman (eds.), *Derivatives Risk and Responsibility,* Chicago: Irwin, 1996.

Bangia, Anil, Francis X. Diebold, Til Schuermann, and John D. Stroughair: "Modeling Liquidity Risk, with Implications for Traditional Market Risk Measurement and Management," University of Pennsylvania, Financial Institutions Center, The Wharton School, June 1999.

Bank for International Settlement (BIS), Basel Committee on Banking Supervision: *International Convergence of Capital Measurement and Capital Standards,* Basel, Switzerland: Bank for International Settlement, July 1988.

———: *Delivery Versus Payment in Security Settlement Systems,* Basel, Switzerland: Bank for International Settlement, September 1992.

———: *Measurement of Banks' Exposure to Interest Rate Risk,* Basel, Switzerland: Bank for International Settlement, April 1993.

———: *Amendment to the Capital Accord of July 1988,* Basel, Switzerland: Bank for International Settlement, July 1994.

———: *Basel Capital Accord: The Treatment of the Credit Risk Associated With Certain Off-Balance-Sheet Items,* Basel, Switzerland: Bank for International Settlement, July 1994.

———: *Risk Management Guidelines for Derivatives,* Basel, Switzerland: Bank for International Settlement, July 1994.

———: *Prudential Supervision of Banks' Derivatives Activities,* Basel, Switzerland: Bank for International Settlement, December 1994.

———: *An Internal Model-Based Approach to Market Risk Capital Requirements,* Basel, Switzerland: Bank for International Settlement, April, 1995.

———: *Planned Supplement to the Capital Accord to Incorporate Market Risks,* Basel, Switzerland: Bank for International Settlement, 1995.

———: *Proposal to Issue a Supplement to the Basel Capital Accord to Cover Market Risks,* Basel, Switzerland: Bank for International Settlement, April 1995.

———: *Treatment of Potential Exposure for Off-Balance-Sheet Items,* Basel, Switzerland: Bank for International Settlement, April 1995.

———: *Amendment to the Capital Accord to Incorporate Market Risks,* Basel, Switzerland: Bank for International Settlement, January, 1996; modified September 1997.

———: *Supervisory Framework for the Use of "Backtesting" in Conjunction with the Internal Models Approach to Market Risk Capital Requirements,* Basel, Switzerland: Bank for International Settlement, January 1996.

———: *Settlement Risk in Foreign Exchange Transactions: Report Prepared by the Committee on Payment and Settlement Systems of the Central Banks of the Group of Ten Countries,* Basel, Switzerland: Bank for International Settlement, March 1996.

———: *Interpretation of the Capital Accord for the Multilateral Netting of Forward Value Foreign Exchange Transactions,* Basel, Switzerland: Bank for International Settlement, April 1996.

———: *Survey of Disclosures About Trading and Derivatives Activities of Banks and Securities Firms: Joint Report by the Basel Committee on Banking Supervision and the Technical Committee of the International Organisation of Securities Commissions,* Basel, Switzerland: Bank for International Settlement, November 1996.

———: *Core Principles for Effective Banking Supervision,* Basel, Switzerland: Bank for International Settlement, September 1997.

———: *Principles for the Management of Interest Rate Risk,* Basel, Switzerland: Bank for International Settlement, September 1997.

———: *Framework for the Evaluation of Internal Control Systems,* Basel, Switzerland: Bank for International Settlement, January 1998.

———: *Amendment to the Basel Capital Accord of July 1988,* Basel, Switzerland: Bank for International Settlement, April 1998.

———: *Enhancing Bank Transparency,* Basel, Switzerland: Bank for International Settlement, September 1998.

———: *Framework for Internal Control Systems in Banking Organisations,* Basel, Switzerland: Bank for International Settlement, September 1998.

———: *Operational Risk Management,* Basel, Switzerland: Bank for International Settlement, September 1998.

———: *Supervisory Information Framework for Derivatives and Trading Activities: Joint Report by the Basel Committee on Banking Supervision and the Technical Committee of the International Organisation of Securities Commissions,* Basel, Switzerland: Bank for International Settlement, September 1998.

———: *Banks' Interaction with Highly Leveraged Institutions,* Basel, Switzerland: Bank for International Settlement, January 1999.

———: *Credit Risk Modelling: Current Practices and Applications,* Basel, Switzerland: Bank for International Settlement, April 1999.

———: *A New Capital Adequacy Framework: Consultative Paper by the Basel Committee on Banking Supervision, Issued for Comment by 31 March 2000,* Basel, Switzerland: Bank for International Settlement, June 1999.

———: *Principles for the Management of Credit Risk: Consultative Paper by the Basel Committee on Banking Supervision, Issued for Comment by 30 November 1999,* Basel, Switzerland: Bank for International Settlement, July, 1999.

———: *Sound Practices for Loan Accounting and Disclosure,* Basel, Switzerland: Bank for International Settlement, July 1999.

———: *Risk Concentrations Principles: Joint Report by the Basel Committee on Banking Supervision, the International Organisation of Securities Commissions, and the International Association of Insurance Supervisors,* Basel, Switzerland: Bank for International Settlement, December 1999.

———: *Trading and Derivatives Disclosures of Banks and Securities Firms: Joint Report by the Basel Committee on Banking Supervision and the Technical Committee of the International Organisation of Securities Commissions,* Basel, Switzerland: Bank for International Settlement, December 1999.

———: *Banks' Interactions with Highly Leveraged Institutions: Implementation of the Basel Committee's Sound Practices Paper,* Basel, Switzerland: Bank for International Settlement, January 2000.

———: *Highly Leveraged Institutions—Sound Practices,* Basel, Switzerland: Bank for International Settlement, January 2000.

———: *Industry Views on Credit Risk Mitigation,* Basel, Switzerland: Bank for International Settlement, January 2000.

———: *Range of Practice in Banks' Internal Ratings Systems: Discussion Paper,* Basel, Switzerland: Bank for International Settlement, January 2000.

———: *Best Practices for Credit Risk Disclosure,* Basel, Switzerland: Bank for International Settlement, September 2000.

———: *Asset Securitization, Consultative Document: Supporting Document to the New Basel Capital Accord, Issued for Comment by 31 May 2001,* Basel, Switzerland: Bank for International Settlement, January 2001.

———: *The Internal Ratings-Based Approach, Consultative Document: Supporting Document to the New Basel Capital Accord, Issued for Comment by 31 May 2001,* Basel, Switzerland: Bank for International Settlement, January 2001.

———: *The New Basel Capital Accord: An Explanatory Note,* Basel, Switzerland: Bank for International Settlement, January 2001.

———: *The New Basel Capital Accord: Consultative Document, Issued for Comment by 31 May 2001,* Basel, Switzerland: Bank for International Settlement, January 2001.

———: *Operational Risk, Consultative Document: Supporting Document to the New Basel Capital Accord, Issued for Comment by 31 May 2001,* Basel, Switzerland: Bank for International Settlement, January 2001.

———: *The Standardized Approach to Credit Risk, Consultative Document: Supporting Document to the New Basel Capital Accord, Issued for Comment by 31 May 2001,* Basel, Switzerland: Bank for International Settlement, January 2001.

———: *The Relationship Between Banking Supervisors and Banks' External Auditors: Consultative Document, Issued for Comment by 12 June 2001,* Basel, Switzerland: Bank for International Settlement, February 2001.

———: *Review of Issues Relating to Highly Leveraged Institutions,* Basel, Switzerland: Bank for International Settlement, March 2001.

———: *Conducting a Supervisory Self-Assessment: Practical Application,* Basel, Switzerland: Bank for International Settlement, April 2001.

———: *Essential Elements of a Statement of Cooperation Between Banking Supervisors,* Basel, Switzerland: Bank for International Settlement, May 2001.

———: "Update on the New Basel Capital Accord," press release, Basel, Switzerland: Bank for International Settlement, June 25, 2001.

———: "Update on the New Basel Capital Accord, Issue 2," press release, Basel, Switzerland: Bank for International Settlement, September 21, 2001.

———: *Potential Modifications to the Committee's Proposals,* Basel, Switzerland: Bank for International Settlement, November 5, 2001.

———: *Results of the Second Quantitative Impact Study,* Basel, Switzerland: Bank for International Settlement, November 5, 2001.

———: "Progress Towards Completion of the New Basel Capital Accord," press release, Basel, Switzerland: Bank for International Settlement, December 13, 2001.

———: *The Quantitative Impact Study for Operational Risk: Overview of Individual Loss Data and Lessons Learned,* Basel, Switzerland: Bank for International Settlement, January 2002.

———: "Quantitative Impact Survey of New Basel Capital Accord," press release, Basel, Switzerland: Bank for International Settlement, October 1, 2002.

Bank of England: *The Bank of England Report into the Collapse of Barings Bank,* London: HMSO Publications Center, 1995, www.numa.com/ref/barings/bar00.html, accessed March 31, 1999.

Barone-Adesi, G., and R. Whaley: "Efficient Analytic Approximation of American Option Values," *Journal of Finance* 42 (1987), 301–320.

Bates, D.: "Testing Option Pricing Models," Working Paper NBER-5129, Cambridge, MA: National Bureau of Economic Research, 1995.

———: "Jumps and Stochastic Volatility: Exchange Rate Processes Implicit in PHLX Deutschemark Options," *Review of Financial Studies* 9 (1996), 69–108.

Battley, Nick (ed.), *The European Bond Markets: An Overview and Analysis for Issuers and Investors,* 6th ed., Maidenhead, United Kingdom: McGraw-Hill, 1997.

BBC News: "Business: The Economy Derivatives Firms Shut Down," London: BBC News, December 31, 1998.

Beaver, William H., and George Parker: *Risk Management Problems and Solutions,* Stanford, CA: Stanford University, 1995.

Beckstrom, R., and A. Campbell (eds.): *An Introduction to VAR,* Palo Alto, CA: CATS Software, 1995.

Beder, T.: "VAR: Seductive But Dangerous," *Financial Analysts Journal* 51 (1995), 12–24.

Belkin, B., L. R. Forest, S. D. Aguais, and S. J. Suchower: *Credit Risk Premiums in Commercial Lending* (1), New York: KPMG, August 1998.

———: *Credit Risk Premiums in Commercial Lending* (2), New York: KPMG, August 1998.

Belkin, B., S. J. Suchower, and L. R. Forest: "The Effect of Systematic Credit Risk on Loan Portfolio Value at Risk and Loan Pricing," *CreditMetrics Monitor* (1998), 17–88.

Belkin, B., S. J. Suchower, D. H. Wagner, and L. R. Forest, "Measures of Credit Risk and Loan Value in LAS," *Risk Strategy Practice,* New York: KPMG, 1998.

Bellman, Richard: *Dynamic Programming,* Princeton, NJ: Princeton University Press, 1957.

Berry, Michael, Edwin Burmeister, and Marjorie McElroy: "Sorting Out Risks, Using Known APT-Factors," *Financial Analysts Journal* 3/4 (1988), 29–42.

Bertsimas, D., and A. W. Lo: "Optimal Control of Execution Costs," *Journal of Financial Markets* 1 (1998), 1–50.

Bickel, R., and D. Freedman: "Some Asymptotic Theory for the Bootstrap," *Annals of Statistics* 9 (1981), 1196–1271.

Black, Fischer: "Capital Market Equilibrium with Restricted Borrowing," *Journal of Business* 7 (1972), 444–454.

———: "The Pricing of Commodity Contracts," *Journal of Financial Economics* 3 (1976), 167–179.

Black, Fischer, Michael C. Jensen, and Myron Scholes: "The Capital Asset Pricing Model: Some Empirical Tests," in Michael Jensen, *Studies in the Theory of Capital Markets,* New York: Praeger, 1972.

Black, Fischer, and Myron Scholes: "The Pricing of Options and Corporate Liabilities," *Journal of Political Economy,* 81 (May–June 1973), 637–654.

Blume, M., and D. Keim: "Realized Returns and Defaults on Low-Grade Bonds: The Cohort of 1977 and 1978," *Financial Analysts Journal* 47 (1991), 63–72.

Board of Governors of the Federal Reserve System: "Request for Comment on the Precommitment Approach for Market Risks," Document no. R-0886, Washington, DC, 1995.

Bollerslev, T.: "Generalized Autoregressive Conditional Heteroskedasticity," *Journal of Econometrics* 31 (1986), 307–327.

Bollerslev, T., R. Chou, and K. Kroner: "ARCH Modelling in Finance: A Review of the Theory and Empirical Evidence," *Journal of Econometrics* 52 (1992), 5–59.

Bookstaber, Richard: "Understanding and Monitoring the Liquidity Crisis Cycle," *Financial Analysts Journal* (September–October 2000), 17–22.

Boudoukh, J., M. Richardson, R. Stanton, and R. Whitelaw: "A New Strategy for Dynamically Hedging Mortgage-Backed Securities," *Journal of Derivatives* 2 (Summer 1995), 60–77.

Boudoukh, J., M. Richardson, and R. Whitelaw: "Expect the Worst," *Risk* (September 1995), 101–105.

Boyle, P.: "A Lattice Framework for Option Pricing with Two State Variables," *Journal of Financial and Quantitative Analysis* 23 (1988), 1–12.

———: "Options: A Monte Carlo Approach," *Journal of Financial Economics* 4 (1977), 323–338.

Boyle, P., J. Evnine, and S. Gibbs: "Numerical Evaluation of Multivariate Contingent Claims," *Review of Financial Studies* 2 (1989), 241–250.

Bralver, C., and A. Kuritzkes: "Risk Adjusted Performance Measurement in the Trading Room," *Journal of Applied Corporate Finance* 6 (1993), 104–108.

Brennen, M., and Schwartz, E.: "The Valuation of American Put Options;" *Journal of Finance* 32 (1977), 449–462.

Brenner, M., and Y. H. Eom: "No Arbitrage Option Pricing: New Evidence on the Validity of the Martingale Property," Working Paper 97-10, New York University Salomon Center, New York, 1997.

British Bankers Association: *Operational Risk: The Next Frontier,* London: British Bankers Association, December 1999.

———: *Operational Risk Management Study,* London: British Bankers Association, December 1999.

Brown, S., W. Goetzmann, and S. Ross: "Survival," *Journal of Finance* 50 (1995), 853–873.

Brown, Stephen J., and Mark F. Weinstein: "A New Approach to Testing Asset Pricing Models: The Bilinear Paradigm," *Journal of Finance* 6(1983), 711–743.

Bullinger, Hans-Jörg, Joachim Warschaft, Stefan Bendes, and Alexander Stanke: "Simultaneous Engineering," in Erich Zahn (ed.), *Handbuch Technologiemanagement, Stuttgart:* Schäffer-Pöschel, 1995.

Bullinger, Hans-Jörg: "Customer Focus: Neue Trends für eine zukunftsorientierte Unternehmungsführung," in Hans-Jörg Bullinger (ed.), "Neue Impulse für eine erfolgreiche Unternehmungsführung, 13. IAO-Arbeitstagung," *Forschung und Praxis,* Band 43, Heidelberg u.a., 1994.

Burmeister, Edwin, and Marjorie B. McElroy: "Joint Estimation of Factor Sensitivities and Risk Premia for the Arbitrage Pricing Theory," *Journal of Finance* 7 (1988), 721–735.

Business Week: "LTCM: 'The Fiasco Will Always Be on Their Resumes" (November 1, 2000), www.businessweek.com/print/bwdaily/dnflash/nov2ooo/nf2ooo1101_330.html, accessed December 2, 2000.

Campbell, J. Y., A. W. Lo, and A. C. MacKinlay: *The Econometrics of Financial Markets,* Princeton, NJ: Princeton University Press, 1997.

Caouette, J. B., E. J. Altman, and P. Narayanan: *Managing Credit Risk: The Next Great Financial Challenge,* New York: John Wiley & Sons, 1998.

Carey, M.: "Credit Risk in Private Debt Portfolios," *Journal of Finance* (August 1998), 1363–1387.

Carey, M., M. Post, and S. A. Sharpe: "Does Corporate Lending by Banks and Finance Companies Differ? Evidence on Specialization in Private Debt Contracting," *Journal of Finance* 53 (June 1998), 845–878.

Cargill v. Hardin, 452 F2d 1154 (8th Cir. 1971).

Carty, L. V., and D. Lieberman: *Defaulted Bank Loan Recoveries,* New York: Global Credit Research (Special Report), Moody's Investors Service, 1996.

———: *Corporate Bond Defaults and Default Rates 1938–1995,* New York: Global Credit Research, Moody's Investors Service, January 1996.

Cathcart, Charles: "The Lessons of Metallgesellschaft," *Global Investor* (London) 78 (December 1994–January 1995), 64.

Chen, Nai-Fu: "Some Empirical Tests of the Theory of Arbitrage-Pricing," *Journal of Finance* 12 (1983), 1393–1414.

———: "Financial Investment Opportunities and the Macroeconomy," *Journal of Finance* 6 (1991), 529–554.

Chen, Nai-Fu, Richard Roll, and Stephen A. Ross: "Economic Forces and the Stock Market," *Journal of Business* 3 (1986), 382–403.

Chicago Board Options Exchange: *Market Statistics,* Chicago: 1988.

Chicago Mercantile Exchange: *Matching CME Quarterly Bankruptcy Index Futures to Different Trading Horizons: A Primer,* Chicago Mercantile Exchange, www.cme.com/qbi/qbiprimer.html.

Cho, Chinhyung D.: "On Testing the Arbitrage Pricing Theory: Inter-Battery Factor Analysis," *Journal of Finance* 12 (1984), 1485ff.

Cho, Chinhyung D., Edwin J. Elton, and Martin J. Gruber: "On The Robustness of the Roll and Ross Arbitrage Pricing Theory," *Journal of Financial and Quantitative Analysis* 3 (1984), 1–11.

Choudhury, S. P.: "Choosing the Right Box of Credit Tricks," *Risk* (November 1997), 17–22.

Chriss, N., and R. Almgren: "Optimal Liquidation," manuscript, University of Chicago, Department of Mathematics, Goldman Sachs & Co., and Courant Institute of Mathematical Sciences, Chicago, 1998.

Chuan-Eoan, Howard G.: "Going for Broke," *Time* 145/10 (March 13, 1995), 18–25.

Coates, P. K., and L. F. Fant: "Recognizing Financial Distress Patterns Using a Neural Network Tool," *Financial Management* (Summer 1993), 142–155.

Cohen, K. J., and J. A. Pogue: "An Empirical Evaluation of Alternative Portfolio Selection Models," *Journal of Business* 40 (April 1967), 166–193.

Committee on the Global Financial System: *A Review of Financial Market Events in Autumn 1998,* Basel, Switzerland: Bank for International Settlement, October 1999.

Commodity Exchange Act, 7 U.S.C. §§ 6(a), 6(d), 9(a)(2).

Commodity Futures Trading Commission (CFTC): *Testimony of Brooksley Born, Chairperson, on Behalf of the Commodity Futures Trading Commission before the United States House of Representatives, Subcommittee on Capital Market, Securities and Government Sponsored Enterprises of the Committee on Banking and Financial Services,* Washington, DC: Commodity Futures Trading Commission, March 13, 1999.

———: *Hedge Funds, Leverage, and the Lessons of Long-Term Capital Management: Report of The President's Working Group on Financial Markets,* Washington, DC: Commodity Futures Trading Commission, April 1999, www.cftc.gov/tm/hedgefundreport.html, accessed May 19, 2000.

Coopers & Lybrand: *GARP—Generally Accepted Risk Principles,* London: Coopers & Lybrand, January 1996.

Cox, J., J. Ingersoll, and S. Ross: "A Theory of the Term Structure of Interest Rates," *Econometrica* (1985), 385–407.

Cox, J., and S. Ross: "The Valuation of Options for Alternative Stochastic Processes," *Journal of Financial Economics* 3 (1976), 145–166.

Cox, J., S. Ross, and M. Rubinstein: "Option Pricing: A Simplified Approach," *Journal of Financial Economics* 7 (1979), 229–264.

Credit Suisse First Boston: *CreditRisk+,* technical document, London/New York, October, 1997.

Crosby, Philip B.: *Qualität bringt Gewinn,* Hamburg: McGraw-Hill, 1986.

Crouhy, M., and R. Mark: "A Comparative Analysis of Current Credit Risk Models," paper presented at the Bank of England Conference on Credit Risk Modeling and Regulatory Implications, London, September 21–22, 1998.

Crouhy, M., S. M. Turnbull, and Lee M. Wakeman: "Measuring Risk Adjusted Performance," paper presented at the Center for Economic Policy Research (CEPR) Conference, London, September 20, 1998.

Culp, C., and J. Overdahl: "An Overview of Derivatives: Their Mechanics, Participants, Scope of Activity, and Benefits," in C. Kirsch (ed.), *Financial Services 2000 A.D.: The Dis-*

solving Barriers Among Banks, Mutual Funds and Insurance Companies, Chicago: Irwin, 1996.

Culp, Christopher, and Merton Miller: "Metallgesellschaft and the Economics of Synthetic Storage," *Journal of Applied Corporate Finance* 7 (Winter 1995).

Dantzig, G. B.: *Linear Programming and Extensions,* Princeton, NJ: Princeton University Press, 1963.

Delianedis, G., and R. Geske: "Credit Risk and Risk-Neutral Default Probabilities: Information About Rating Migrations and Defaults," paper presented at the Bank of England Conference on Credit Risk Modeling and Regulatory Implications, London, September 21–22, 1998.

Deloitte & Touche: *BRE-X Corporate Dissemination Services Inc.: The Deloitte & Touche Inc.'s Forensic Investigative Associate Inc. (FIA) Report to BRE-X Minderals,* Deloitte & Touche, 1997.

Derivatives Policy Group: *A Framework for Voluntary Oversight,* New York, 1995.

Derman, E., and I. Kani: "Riding on the Smile," *Risk* (July 1994), 32–39.

Dermine, J.: "Pitfalls in the Application of RAROC in Loan Management," *The Arbitrageur* (Spring 1998), 21–27.

Dhrymes, Phoebus J., Irwin Friend, and Bulent Gultekin: "A Critical Reexamination of the Empirical Evidence on the Arbitrage Pricing Theory," *Journal of Finance* 6 (1984), 323–346.

Dhrymes, Phoebus J., Irwin Friend, Mustafa N. Gultekin, and Bulent N. Gultekin: "New Tests of the APT and Their Implications," *Journal of Finance* 7 (1985), 659–674.

Diebold, F., and R. Mariano: "Comparing Predictive Accuracy," *Journal of Business and Economic Statistics* (May 1995), 253–264.

Diebold, F. X., A. Hickman, A. Inoue, and T. Schuermann: "Scale Models," *Risk* 11 (January 1998), 104–107.

Digenan, John, Dan Felson, Robert Kell, and Ann Wiemert: "Lessons from the Investment Strategy in Energy Futures," class handout, Boston University, undated.

Digenan, John, Dan Felson, Robert Kell, and Ann Wiemert: "Metallgesellschaft: A Case Study," working paper, Illinois Institute of Technology, Stuart School of Business, Financial Markets and Trading Program, undated.

Dimson, E., and R Marsh: "Capital Requirements for Securities Firms," *Journal of Finance* 50 (1995), 821–851.

Donovan, Karen: "Third Circuit Reinstates Nasdaq Suit, Three Brokerage Firms Now Face Securities Class Action," *National Law Journal* (February 16, 1998), B01.

Duan, J.: "The GARCH Option Pricing Model," *Mathematical Finance* 5 (1995), 13–32.

Duffee, G.: "Estimating the Price of Default Risk," *Review of Financial Studies* (Spring 1999), 197–226.

Duffie, D., and M. Huang: "Swap Rates and Credit Quality," *Journal of Finance* (July 1996), 921–950.

Duffie, D., and D. Lando: "Term Structures of Credit Spreads with Incomplete Accounting Information," working paper, Stanford University Graduate School of Business, 1997.

Duffie, D., and K. Singleton: "Simulating Correlated Defaults," paper presented at the Bank of England Conference on Credit Risk Modeling and Regulatory Implications, London, September 21–22, 1998.

Dunbar, Nicholas: "Meriwether's Meltdown," *Risk* (October 1998), 32–36.

Dupire, D.: "Pricing with a Smile," *Risk* (July 1994), 18–20.

The Economist (London): "Metallgesellschaft: Germany's Corporate Whodunit" 334/7900 (February 4, 1995), 71f.

Efron, B.: "Bootstrap Methods: Another Look at the Jackknife," *Annals of Statistics* 7 (1979), 1–26.

Elton, E. J., and M. J. Gruber: "Estimating the Dependence Structure of Share Prices," *Journal of Finance* 28 (December 1973), 1203–1232.

Elton, E. J., and M. J. Gruber: *Modern Portfolio Theory and Investment Analysis,* 5th ed., New York: John Wiley & Sons, 1998.

Engle, R.: "Autoregressive Conditional Heteroskedasticity with Estimates of the Variance of United Kingdom Inflation," *Econometrica* 50 (1982), 987–1007.

Engle, R., D. Lilien, and R. Robins: "Estimating Time-Varying Risk Premia in the Term Structure: The ARCH-M Model," *Econometrica* 55 (1987), 391–407.

Ernst & Young: *Enterprise Risk Management,* New York: Ernst & Young LLP, 2000.

———: *Enterprise Risk Management—Implications for Boards of Directors,* New York: Ernst & Young LLP, 2000.

Estrella, A.: "Formulas or Supervision? Remarks on the Future of Regulatory Capital," paper presented at the Conference on Financial Services at the Crossroads: Capital Regulation in the 21st Century, Federal Reserve Bank of New York, New York, February 26–27, 1998.

Estrella, A., D. Hendricks, J. Karabhu, S. Shin, and S. Walter: "The Price Risk of Options Positions: Measurement and Capital Requirements," *Quarterly Review* (Federal Reserve Bank of New York) 19 (1994), 27–43.

Fadil, M. W.: "Problems with Weighted-Average Risk Ratings: A Portfolio Management View," *Commercial Lending Review* (January 1997), 23–27.

Fama, Eugene: "Efficient Capital Market: A Review of Theory and Empirical Work," *Journal of Finance* 3 (1970), 383–417.

Fama, Eugene: *Foundations of Finance,* New York: Basic Books, 1976.

Fama, Eugene: "Stock Returns, Expected Returns, and Real Activity," *Journal of Finance* 9 (1990), 1089–1109.

Fama, Eugene, and R. Bliss: "The Information in Long-Maturity Forward Rates," *American Economics Review* 77 (1987), 680–692.

Fama, Eugene, and James MacBeth: "Risk, Return and Equilibrium: Empirical Tests," *Journal of Political Economy* 9 (1973), 601–636.

Farrell, J. L.: "The Dividend Discount Model: A Primer," *Financial Analysts Journal* 41 (November–December 1985), 16–19, 22–25.

Fayol, Henri: *General and Industrial Management,* New York: Pitman, 1949. English translation of book originally published in French in 1916.

Federal Reserve System Task Force on Internal Credit Risk Models: *Credit Models at Major U.S. Banking Institutions: Current State of the Art and Implications for Assessments of Capital Adequacy,* Washington, DC: U.S. Government Printing Office, May 1998.

Fehle, F.: "Market Structure and Swap Spreads: International Evidence," working paper, University of Texas at Austin, September 13, 1998.

Financial Times: "Fears over Banks Prompt Surge in Credit Derivatives" (October 7, 1998), 1.

———: "Greenspan Hits Out at Way Banks Treat Risk" (October 12, 1999), 10.

Finger, Christopher: "RMG Volatility Index: Technical Document," New York: RiskMetrics Group, 1998.

Finnerty, J. D.: "Financial Engineering in Corporate Finance: An Overview," *Financial Management* 17 (1988), 14–33.

———: "Credit Derivatives, Infrastructure Finance and Emerging Market Risk," *The Financier* (February 1996), 64–78.

Fisher, L.: "An Algorithm for Finding Exact Rates of Return," *Journal of Business* 39 (1966), 111–118.

Fisher, L., and R. Weil: "Coping with the Risk of Interest-Rate Fluctuations: Returns to Bond Holders from Naive and Optimal Strategies," *Journal of Business* 44 (1971), 408–431.

Fisher, Peter: "PBS Documentary on LTCM," PBS, www.mega.nu:8080/ampp/ltcm.html, accessed October 12, 1998.

Fitchett, Joseph: "The Credit Lyonnais Debacle," *International Herald Tribune* (London; October 3, 1996), 13.

Flannery, M. J., and S. Sorescu: "Evidence of Bank Market Discipline in Subordinated Debenture Yields: 1983–1991," *Journal of Finance* (September 1996), 1347–1377.

Fletcher, Matthew: "Whom to Trust? Investors Are Spooked by Scandal in Asia's No. 1 Fund Manager," *Asiaweek* (September 27, 1996), www.pathfinder.com/asiaweek/96/0927/bizl.html, accessed March 17, 1997.

Forts, J.: "Using Default Rates to Model the Term Structure of Credit Risk," *Financial Analysts Journal* (September–October 1994), 25–32.

Frankel, Allen B., and David E. Palmer: "The Management of Financial Risks at German Non-Financial Firms: The Case of Metallgesellschaft," publication no. 560, New York: Board of Governors of the Federal Reserve System, August 1996.

French, K., W. Schwert, and R. Stambaugh: "Expected Stock Returns and Volatility," *Journal of Financial Economics* 19 (1987), 3–29.

Futures: "Barings Abyss," 26/5 (May 1995), 68–74.

———: "BoE Report Details Barings' Guiles, Goofs," 26/10 (September 1995), 68–74.

Gallagher, Russel B.: "Risk Management: A New Phase of Cost Control," *Harvard Business Review* (September–October 1956).

Gallati, Reto R.: "Multifaktor-Modell für den Schweizer Aktienmarkt, Eine empirische Untersuchung unter besonderer Berücksichtigung der Arbitrage Preis Theorie," PhD thesis, University of Zurich, 1993.

———: *Empirical Application of APT Multifactor-Models to the Swiss Equity Market,* basic report, Zurich: Credit Suisse Investment Research, September 1993.

———: "Anwendung der APT auf dem Schweizer Aktienmarkt," in Christof Kutscher (ed.), *Länderallokation und Titelauswahl für Aktien,* Zurich: Verlag Neue Zürcher Zeitung, 1997, 83–105.

———: "Switzerland, Money Markets," in Nick Battley (ed.), *The European Bond Markets: An Overview and Analysis for Issuers and Investors,* 6th ed., Maidenhead, UK: McGraw-Hill, 1997, p. 1373.

———: "De-Minimis-Regel diskriminiert," *Schweizer Bank* (Zurich) 9 (1998), 41–43.

———: *Methodology for Operational Risk,* Zurich: KPMG, July 1998.

———: *Verzinsliche Wertpapiere, Bewertung und Strategien,* Wiesbaden, Germany: Gabler Verlag, 1999.

———: *Futures, Options, and Financial Risk Management, Case: Metallgesellschaft,* Reading Package FE829, Boston University, Fall 2000.

Gallati, Reto R., and Rudolf Markus: "Asset Allocation: Investment Style and Hedging Style of Internationally Diversified Funds," Working Paper no. 9507, University of St. Gall, 1995.

Garman, M., and S. Kohlhagen: "Foreign Currency Option Values," *Journal of International Money and Finance* 2 (1983), 231–238.

Garvin, David A.: *Managing Quality,* New York: Free Press, 1988.

Geiger, Hans, and Jean-Marc Piaz: "Identifikation und Bewertung von operationellen Risiken," in Henner Schierenbeck (ed.), *Handbuch Bank-Controlling,* 3d ed., Wiesbaden, Germany: Gabler Verlag, 2000.

General Accounting Office: *Financial Derivatives: Actions Needed to Protect the Financial System,* Washington, DC: General Accounting Office, 1994.

———: *Risk-Based Capital: Regulatory and Industry Approaches to Capital and Risk,* Report no. 98-153, Washington, DC: General Accounting Office, 1998.

Geske, R.: "The Valuation of Corporation Liabilities as Compound Options," *Journal of Financial and Quantitative Analysis* (November 1977), 541–552.

———: "A Note on an Analytical Formula for Unprotected American Call Options on Stocks with Known Dividends," *Journal of Financial Economics* 7 (1979), 375–380.

———: "The Valuation of Compound Options," *Journal of Financial Economics* 7 (1979), 63–81.

Geske, R., and H. Johnson: "The American Put Valued Analytically," *Journal of Finance* 39 (1984), 1511–1524.

Ginzberg, A., K. Maloney, and R. Wilner: "Risk Rating Migration and Valuation of Floating Rate Debt," working paper, Citicorp, March, 1994.

Giovannini, A., and R. Jorion: "The Time-Variation of Risk and Return in the Foreign Exchange and Stock Markets," *Journal of Finance* 44 (1989), 307–325.

Gluck, J.: "Measuring and Controlling the Credit Risk of Derivatives," in R. Klein and J. Lederman (eds.), *Derivatives Risk and Responsibility,* Chicago: Irwin, 1996.

Goldman, B., H. Sosin, and M. Gatto: "Path Dependent Options: Buy at the Low, Sell at the High," *Journal of Finance* 34 (1979), 1111–1127.

Gordy, Michael B.: "A Comparative Anatomy of Credit Risk Models," paper presented at the Bank of England Conference on Credit Risk Modeling and Regulatory Implications, London, September 21–22, 1998.

———: *A Comparative Anatomy of Credit Risk Models,* Board of Governors of the Federal Reserve System, Washington, D.C.: U.S. Government Printing Office, December 8, 1998.

Gorton, G., and A. Santomero: "Market Discipline and Bank Subordinated Debt," *Journal of Money, Credit and Banking* (February 1990), 117–128.

Graham, Benjamin, and David L. Dodd: *Security Analysis,* New York: McGraw-Hill, 1934.

Granger, C. W. J., and L. L. Huang: "Evaluation of Panel Data Models: Some Suggestions from Time-Series," Discussion Paper 97-10, University of California, Department of Economics, San Diego, 1997.

Gray, S., and R. Whaley: "Valuing S&P 500 Bear Market Warrants with a Periodic Reset," *Journal of Derivatives* 5 (1997), 99–106.

Green, Christopher J. B.: "The '96 Copper Crisis: Copper Letter," AMM Online—The World Metals Information Network, www.amm.com/ref/hot/green.html, accessed March 31, 1999.

Greenspan, Alan: "Statement to Congress: Issues Relating to the U.S. Operations of Daiwa Bank, December 5, 1995," *Federal Reserve Bulletin* (January 1996), 133–138.

———: "Statement to Congress: U.S. Operations of Daiwa Bank, November 27, 1995," *Federal Reserve Bulletin* (January 1996), 31–35.

———: "Risk Management in the Global Financial System—Before the Annual Financial Markets Conference of the Federal Reserve Bank of Atlanta," Miami Beach, Florida, February 27, 1998.

———: "Measuring Financial Risk in the Twenty-First Century," remarks before a conference sponsored by the Office of the Comptroller of the Currency, Washington, DC, October 14, 1999.

Grinblatt, Mark, and Sheridan Titman: "Approximate Factor Structures: Interpretations and Implications for Empiricial Tests," *Journal of Finance* 12 (1985), 1367–1373.

Group of Thirty Global Derivatives Study Group: *Derivatives: Practices and Principles,* Washington, DC: The Group of Thirty, July 1993.

Gruber, M. J.: *Modern Portfolio Theory and Investment Analysis,* 5th ed., New York: John Wiley & Sons, 1998.

Gupton, Greg M., Christopher C. Finger, and Mickey Bhatia: *CreditMetrics—Technical Document,* New York: Morgan Guaranty Trust Co., April 1997.

Harlow, W.: "Asset Allocation in a Downside Risk Framework," *Financial Analysts Journal* 47 (September 1991), 28–40.

Harrington, Diana R.: *Modern Portfolio Theory, the Capital Asset Pricing Model and Arbitrage Pricing Theory: A User's Guide,* 2d ed., Englewood Cliffs, NJ: Prentice Hall, 1987, p. 35.

Harrison, J. M.: *Brownian Motion and Stochastic Flow Systems,* New York: John Wiley & Sons, 1985.

Harrison, J. M., and D. Kreps: "Martingales and Arbitrage in Multi-Period Security Markets," *Journal of Economic Theory* (1979), 381–408.

Harrison, J. M., and S. R. Pliska: "Martingales and Stochastic Integrals," *Stochastic Processes and Their Applications* (August 1981), 215–260.

Hendricks, D.: "Netting Agreements and the Credit Exposures of OTC Derivatives Portfolios," *Quarterly Review* (Federal Reserve Bank of New York), (Spring 1994), 36–69.

Herald Tribune: "Simex Criticizes Barings for Role in Leeson Debacle" (March 16, 1995), p. 1.

Hertsen, E., and P. Fields (eds.): *Derivative Credit Risk,* London: Risk Publications, 1995.

Heston, S.: "A Closed-Form Solution for Options with Stochastic Volatility with Applications to Bond and Currency Options," *Review of Financial Studies* 6 (1993), 327–343.

Hicks, J. R.: "A Suggestion for Simplifying the Theory of Money," *Economica* (February 1935), 1–19.

———: "Liquidity," *Economic Journal* 72 (December 1962), 787–802.

Hillenbrand, Barry: "The Barings Collapse: Spreading the Blame," *Time* (London) 146/18 (October 30, 1995), www.time.com/time/magazine/archive/1995/951030/banking.box.html, accessed August 20, 2000.

Hotz, Pirmin: *Das Capital Asset Pricing Model und die Markteffizienzhypothese unter besonderer Berücksichtigung der empirisch beobachteten "Anomalien" in den amerikanischen und anderen internationalen Aktienmärkten,* PhD thesis, University of St. Gall, Baar: Victor Hotz AG, 1989, p. 43 ff.

Hsieh, D.: "The Statistical Properties of Daily Foreign Exchange Rates: 1974–1983," *Journal of International Economics* 24 (1988), 129–145.

Hull, J., and A. White: "The Pricing of Options and Asset with Stochastic Volatilities," *Journal of Finance* 42 (1987), 281–300.

IMRO, "IMRO Announces Morgan Grenfell Compensation," Press Release 37/96 (April 16, 1997), London.

———: "IMRO Fines Morgan Grenfell £2,000,000 for Mismanagement of European Funds," Press Release 05/97 (April 16, 1997), London.

Institute of International Finance (IIF): *Recommendations for Revising the Regulatory Capital Rules for Credit Risk: Report of the Working Group on Capital Adequacy,* Washington, DC: Institute of International Finance, 1998.

International Swaps and Derivatives Association (ISDA): *Public Disclosure and Risk Management Activities Including Derivatives,* New York: International Swaps and Derivatives Association, 1995.

———: *Credit Risk and Regulatory Capital,* New York/London: International Swaps and Derivatives Association, March 1998.

Investment Dealers Digest: "The Big Noise from Columbus: *The Journal of Finance* Breaks the NASDAQ Scandal" (May 22, 1995).

Irish Times: "SFO May Examine NatWest" (July 31, 2001).

———: "Three Bankers Brought Scandal to the Vatican" (August 29, 1998).

———: "The Old Man Who Hid Gold Under His Geraniums" (September 16, 1998).

James, C.: *RAROC-Based Capital Budgeting and Performance Evaluation: A Case Study of Bank Capital Allocation,* University of Florida, 1996.

Jarrow, R. A., D. Lando, and S. Turnbull: "A Markov Model for the Term Structure of Credit Spreads," *Review of Financial Studies* (1997), 481–523.

Jarrow, R. A., and A. Subramanian: "Mopping Up Liquidity," *Risk* 10 (December 1997), 170–173.

Jarrow, R. A., and S. M. Turnbull: "The Intersection of Market and Credit Risk," paper presented at the Bank of England Conference on Credit Risk Modeling and Regulatory Implications, London, September 21–22, 1998.

Jarrow, R. A., and D. R. van Deventer: *Practical Usage of Credit Risk Models in Loan Portfolio and Counterparty Exposure Management,* The Kamakura Corporation, March 15, 1999.

Jones, D.: *Emerging Problems with the Accord: Regulatory Capital Arbitrage and Related Issues,* Washington, DC: Federal Reserve Board of Governors, July 1998.

Jones, E. P., S. P. Mason, and E. Rosenfeld: "Contingent Claims Analysis of Corporate Capital Structures: An Empirical Investigation," *Journal of Finance* (July 1984), 611–625.

Jordan, J., and G. Morgan: "Default Risk in Futures Markets: The Customer-Broker Relationship," *Journal of Finance* 45 (1990), 909–933.

Jorion, Philippe: "Asset Allocation with Hedged and Unhedged Foreign Stocks and Bonds," *Journal of Portfolio Management* 15 (Summer 1989), 49–54.

———: *Big Bets Gone Bad: Derivatives and Bankruptcy in Orange County,* San Diego, CA: Academic Press, 1995.

———: "Predicting Volatility in the Foreign Exchange Market," *Journal of Finance* 50 (1995), 507–528.

———: "Risk: Measuring the Risk in Value-At-Risk," *Financial Analysts Journal* (1996).

———: *Value-at-Risk: The New Benchmark for Controlling Market Risk,* New York: McGraw-Hill, 1997, p. 32.

———: "Philippe Jorion's Orange County Case: Using Value at Risk to Control Financial Risk," www.gsm.uci.edu, accessed October 14, 1997.

———: "Risk Management Lessons from Long-Term Capital Management," Working Paper Series (draft), University of California at Irvine, June 1999.

J. P. Morgan: *RiskMetrics Technical Document,* 4th ed., New York: J. P. Morgan, December 17, 1996.

———: *CreditMetrics Technical Document,* New York: J. P. Morgan, April 2, 1997.

Kane, Edward J., and Kimberly Detrask: "Covering Up Trading Losses: Opportunity-Cost Accounting as an Internal Control Mechanism", Boston College/National Bureau of Economic Research (NBER) Working Paper NBER-W6823, Cambridge, MA: National Bureau of Economic Research, December 1998.

Kealhofer, S.: "Managing Default Risk in Derivative Portfolios," in *Derivative Credit Risk: Advances in Measurement and Management,* London: Renaissance Risk Publications, 1995.

Kendall, M.: *Kendall's Advanced Theory of Statistics,* New York: Halsted Press, 1994.

Kerry, John, and Hand Brown: *The BCCI Affair: A Report to the Committee on Foreign Relations,* 102d Congress, 2d Session, Senate Print 102-140, Washington, DC: Senate Printing Office, December 1992, www.fas.org/irp/congress/1992/1992_rpt/bcci/index.html, accessed March 31, 1999.

Kharouf, Jim: "The Copper Trader Who Fell from Grace," *Futures* (August 1996), www.futuresmag.com/library/august96/intrends.html, accessed March 31, 1999.

Kharouf, Jim, Carla Cavaletti, and James T. Holder: "Top 40 Brokers, Technology Key to Stay Alive," *Futures* (December 1996).

Khoury, Sarkis Joseph: "It's the Fundamentals: Stupid! The Orange County Bankruptcy in Perspective," working paper prepared for the Bürgenstock Conference, University of California, Riverside, September 1995.

Klein, R. and Lederman, J. (eds.): *Derivatives Risk and Responsibility,* Chicago: Irwin, 1996.

KMV: *CreditMonitor Overview,* San Francisco: KMV Corporation, 1993.

———: *Portfolio Management of Default Risk,* San Francisco: KMV Corporation, November 15, 1993; revised May 31, 2001.

———: *Global Correlation Factor Structure,* San Francisco: KMV Corporation, August 1996.

———: *KMV and CreditMetrics,* San Francisco: KMV Corporation, 1997.

———: *Portfolio Manager Model,* San Francisco: KMV Corporation, undated.

Kon, Stanley J.: "Models of Stock Returns—A Comparison," *Journal of Finance* 39 (1984), 147–165.

Kooi, Mary: "Analysing Sumitomo," Delivered at SCFOA Meeting, Bürgenstock, November 1996, www.risk.ifci.ch/134800.html, accessed December 12, 1996.

Koyluoglu, H. U., and A. Hickman: *A Generalized Framework for Credit Risk Portfolio Models,* New York: Oliver, Wyman and Co., September 14, 1998.

Kozinn, Benjamin E.: "The Great Copper Caper: Is Market Manipulation Really a Problem in the Wake of the Sumitomo Debacle?" *Fordham Law Review* (October 2000), 247.

KPMG Peat Marwick: *Understanding Risks and Controls: A Practical Guide,* Amsterdam: KPMG International Audit and Accounting Department, March, 1995.

———: "Operational Risk, Control Benchmarking Questionnaire," KPMG, March 1997.
———: *VaR: Understanding and Applying Value-At-Risk,* New York: Risk Publications, 1997.
———: *Loan Analysis System,* New York: KPMG Financial Consulting Services, 1998.

Kreps, D.: "Multiperiod Securities and the Efficient Allocation of Risk: A Comment on the Black-Scholes Option Pricing Model," in J. J. McCall (ed.), *The Economics of Uncertainty and Information,* Chicago: University of Chicago Press, 1982.

Kritzmann, Mark P.: "What Practitioners Need to Know . . . About Uncertainity," *Financial Analysts Journal* (March–April 1991), 17–21.

Kupiec, P.: "Techniques for Verifying the Accuracy of Risk Measurement Models," *Journal of Derivatives* 2 (December 1995), 73–84.

Kupiec, P., and J. O'Brien: "A Pre-Commitment Approach to Capital Requirements for Market Risk," FEDS Working Paper no. 95-34, Washington, DC: Federal Reserve Board of Governors, 1995.

Kuprianov, Anatoli: "Derivatives Debacles," *Economic Quarterly* (Federal Reserve Bank of Richmond) 81/4 (Fall 1995).

Kuritzkes, A.: "Transforming Portfolio Management," *Banking Strategies* (July–August 1998).

Kutscher, Christof (ed.): *Länderallokation und Titelauswahl für Aktien,* Zurich: Verlag Neue Zürcher Zeitung, 1997.

Lavoie, Denise: "Organized Criminal," Associated Press, June 22, 1999.

Leavens, D. H.: "Diversification of Investments," *Trusts and Estates* 80 (May 1945), 469–473.

Lectric Law Library: "11/95 Criminal Complaint & Indictment Against Daiwa Bank," Lectric Law Library, www.lectlaw.com.

Leland, H.: "Corporate Debt Value, Bond Covenants and Optimal Capital Structure," *Journal of Finance* (September 1994), 1213–1252.

———: "Agency Costs, Risk Management and Capital Structure," *Journal of Finance* (July 1998), 1213–1242.

Leland, H., and K. Toft: "Optimal Capital Structure, Endogenous Bankruptcy, and the Term Structure of Credit Spreads," *Journal of Finance* (July 1996), 987–1019.

Levy, H., and H. M. Markowitz: "Approximating Expected Utility by a Function of Mean and Variance," *American Economic Review* 69/3 (June 1979), 308–317.

Lintner, John: "The Valuation of Risk Assets and the Selection of Risky Investments in Stock Portfolios and Capital Budgets," *Review of Economics and Statistics* 47/1 (February 1965), 13–37.

———: "Security Prices, Risk, and Maximal Gains from Diversification," *Journal of Finance* 20 (1965), 587–615.

Litterman, R., and Thomas Iben: "Corporate Bond Valuation and the Term Structure of Credit Spreads," *Journal of Portfolio Management* (Spring 1991), 52–64.

Longin, Francis, and Bruno Solnik: "Is the Correlation in International Equity Returns Constant: 1960–1990?" *Journal of International Money and Finance* 14 (1995), 3–26.

Longstaff, Francis A.: "Optimal Portfolio Choice and Valuation of Illiquid Securities," manuscript, University of California, Los Angeles, Department of Finance, 1998.

Longstaff, Francis A., and E. Schwartz: "Interest Rate Volatility and the Term Structure: A Two-Factor General Equilibrium Model," *Journal of Finance* 47 (1992), 1259–1283.

———: "A Simple Approach to Valuing Risky Fixed and Floating Rate Debt," *Journal of Finance* (July 1995), 789–819.

Lopez, Jose A.: *Regulatory Evaluation of Value-at-Risk Models,* Research and Market Analysis Group, New York: Federal Reserve Bank of New York, 1998.

Lopez, J. A., and M. R. Saidenberg: "Evaluating Credit Risk Models," paper presented at the Bank of England Conference on Credit Risk Modeling and Regulatory Implications, September 21–22, 1998.

Ludwig, Eugene A.: *Remarks by Eugene A. Ludwig, Comptroller of the Currency, Before the Bank Administration Institute's Asset/Liability and Treasury Management Conference,* Release N6-119, Washington, DC: Office of the Comptroller of the Currency, October 22, 1996.

Macaulay, F.: *Some Technical Problems Suggested by the Movements of Interest Rates, Bond Yields and Stock Prices in the United States Since 1856,* New York: National Bureau of Economic Research, 1938.

MacMillan, L.: "Analytic Approximation for the American Put Option," *Advances in Futures and Options Research* 1 (1986), 119–139.

Madan, D. B., and H. Unal: "Pricing the Risks of Default," University of Maryland, College Park, Department of Finance, 1994.

Margrabe, W.: "The Value of an Option to Exchange One Asset for Another," *Journal of Finance* 33 (1978), 177–186.

Markowitz, Harry M.: "Portfolio Selection (1)," *Journal of Finance,* 7 (March 1952), 77–91.

———: "The Optimization of a Quadratic Function Subject to Linear Constraints," *Naval Research Logistics Quarterly* 3 (1956), 111–133.

———: *Portfolio Selection: Efficient Diversification of Investments,* New York: John Wiley & Sons, 1959.

———: *Mean-Variance Analysis in Portfolio Choice and Capital Markets,* Oxford, U.K.: Basil Blackwell, 1987.

———: *Portfolio Selection* (2), 2d ed., Oxford, U.K.: Basil Blackwell, 1992.

Marschak, J.: "Money and the Theory of Assets," *Econometrica* 6 (1938), 311–325.

Martin, Phillip H.: *Speech on Operational Risk Management Presented to the 4th Islamic Banking and Finance Forum, Bahrain, December, 1997,* London: HSBC Holdings PLC., 1999.

McAllister, P. M., and J. J. Mingo: "Commercial Loan Risk Management, Credit Scoring and Pricing: The Need for a New Shared Database," *Journal of Commercial Lending* (May 1994), 6–20.

McCulloch, H.: "Me Tax-Adjusted Yield Curve," *Journal of Finance* 30 (1975), 811–829.

McElroy, Marjorie, Edwin Burmeister, and Wall K. Edwin: "Two Estimators for the APT Model When Factors Are Measured," *Economics Letters* 19 (1985), 271.

McKean, David: *Why the News Media Took So Long to Focus on the Savings and Loan and BCCI Crisis,* Evanston, IL: Northwestern University, Annenberg Washington Program in Communications Policy Studies, 1993.

McKinsey and Company: *CreditPortfolioView,* New York: McKinsey and Company, 1997.

———: *CreditPortfolioView Approach Documentation and User's Documentation,* Zurich: McKinsey and Company, 1998.

McMorris, Frances A.: "Sumitomo's Suit Against J. P. Morgan Seeks $735 Million for Role in Scandal," *Wall Street Journal,* 1999.

McQuown, J. A.: *Market vs. Accounting-Based Measures of Default Risk,* San Francisco: KMV Corporation, 1995.

———: "The Illuminated Guide to Portfolio Management," *Journal of Lending and Credit Risk Management* (August 1997), 29–41.

McQuown, J. A., and S. Kealhofer: *A Comment on the Formation of Bank Stock Prices,* San Francisco: KMV Corporation, April 1997.

Meerschwarn, David: *Bankers Trust New York Corporation,* Case Study 9-286-005, Cambridge, MA: Harvard Business School Press, 1985.

Mella-Barral, P., and W. Perraudin: "Strategic Debt Service," *Journal of Finance* (June 1997), 531–556.

Mello, Antonio S., and John E. Parsons: "Maturity Structure of a Hedge Matters: Lessons from the Metallgesellschaft Debacle," *Journal of Applied Finance* 8/1 (1995), 106–120.

Merrill Lynch: *Credit Default Swaps,* New York: Merrill Lynch, Global Fixed Income Research, October 1998.

Merton, R. C.: "Lifetime Portfolio Selection Under Uncertainty: The Continuous-Time Case," *Review of Economics and Statistics* 51/3 (August 1969), 247–259.

———: "An Analytic Derivation of the Efficient Portfolio Frontier," *Journal of Financial and Quantitative Analysis* 7/4 (September 1972), 1851–1872.

———: "Theory of Rational Option Pricing," *Bell Journal of Economics and Management Science* 4/1 (1973), 141–183.

———: "On the Pricing of Corporate Debt: The Risk Structure of Interest Rates," *Journal of Finance* 29 (June 1974), 449–470.

———: "Option Pricing When Underlying Stock Returns Are Discontinuous." *Journal of Financial Economics* 3 (1976), 125–143.

Merton, R., and Samuelson, P.: "Fallacy of the Log-Normal Approximation to Portfolio Decision-Making over Many Periods," *Journal of Financial Economics* 1 (1974), 67–94.

Miller, M.: "Financial Innovations: The Last Twenty Years and the Next," *Journal of Financial and Quantitative Analysis* 21 (1986), 459–471.

Miller, M. H., and F. Modigilani: "Dividend Policy, Growth and the Valuation of Shares," *Journal of Business* 34 (1961), 411–433.

Miller, R.: "Refining Ratings," *Risk* (August 1998).

Mina, Jorge, and Jerry Yi Xiao: *Return to RiskMetrics: The Evolution of a Standard*, New York: RiskMetrics Group, 2001.

Mingo, J. J.: "Policy Implications of the Federal Reserve Study of Credit Risk Models at Major Banking Institutions," paper presented at the Bank of England Conference on Credit Risk Modeling and Regulatory Implications, London, September 21–22, 1998.

Modigliani, F., and M. H. Miller: "The Cost of Capital, Corporation Finance and the Theory of Investment," *American Economic Review* 48 (1958), 261–297.

Moivre, Abraham de: *Miscellanea Analytica*, London, 1730.

Moore, Nick: "Tracking Down Japan's 'Mr. Copper,' " *Reuter's Magazine* (September–October 1996), http://about.reuters.com/magazine/mag96/sepoct96/cae.html, accessed November 9, 2000.

Moro, B.: "The Full Monte," *Risk* (February 1995), 57–58.

Mortished, Carl: "Merrill Fined Pounds 16m Over Copper Scandal," *Times* (London), 1999.

Mossin, Jan: "Equilibrium in a Capital Asset Market," *Econometrica* 35/4 (October 1966), 768–783.

———: "Optimal Multiperiod Portfolio Policies," *Journal of Business* 41/2 (April 1968), 215–229.

Nasdaq Market-Makers Antitrust Litigation to: Consolidated Amended Complaint, M21-68(RWS), Civ. 3996 (RWS), M.D.L. no. 1023.

Nelson, C., and A. Siegel.: "Parsimonious Modeling of Yield Curves," *Journal of Business* 60 (1987), 473–490.

Nelson, D.: "ARCH Models as Diffusion Approximations," *Journal of Econometrics* 45 (1990), 7–38.

Neumann, Johnann von, and Oskar Morgenstern: *Theory of Games and Economic Behavior*, 3d ed., Princeton, NJ: Princeton University Press, 1967 (1st ed., 1944).

Nickell, P., W. Perraudin, and S. Varotto: "Stability of Rating Transitions," paper presented at the Bank of England Conference on Credit Risk Modeling and Regulatory Implications, London, September 21–22, 1998.

———: "Ratings Versus Equity-Based Credit Risk Modelling: An Empirical Analysis," Working Paper Series (132), London: Bank of England, 2001.

Oda, N., and J. Muranaga: *A New Framework for Measuring the Credit Risk of a Portfolio: The "ExVaR" Model*, Monetary and Economic Studies, Tokyo: Bank of Japan, December 1997.

Office of the Comptroller of the Currency: "Risk Management of Financial Derivatives," Banking Circular BC-277, Washington, DC: Office of the Comptroller of the Currency, 1993.

Overdahl, J., and B. Schachter: "Derivatives Regulation and Financial Management: Lessons from Gibson Greetings," *Financial Management* 24 (1995), 68–78.

Parkinson, M.: "The Extreme Value Method for Estimating the Variance of the Rate of Return," *Journal of Business* 53 (1980), 61–65.

Parseghian, Gregory J.: "Collateralized Mortgage Obligations," in Frank Fabozzi (ed.), *The Handbook of Fixed-Income Securities,* 3d ed., Homewood IL: Irwin, 1991.

Paskov, S., and J. Taub: "Faster Valuation of Financial Derivatives," *Journal of Portfolio Management* 22 (1995), 113–120.

PBS: "Trillion Dollar Bet," *NOVA* no. 2074, broadcast transcript, www.pbs.org/wgbh/nova/transcripts/2704stockmarket.html, accessed March 13, 2000.

Pekarchik, Karin: "LTCM: 'The Fiasco Will Always Be on Their Resumes,' " *BusinessWeek Online* (November 1, 2000), www.businessweek.com:/print/bwdaily/dnflash/nov2ooo/nf2ooo1101_330.html, accessed November 7, 2000.

Perin, Monica: "Feds Charge Broker in $40 Million Euroscheme," *Houston Business Journal* (December 5, 1997).

Perold A., and E. Schulman: "Me Free Lunch in Currency Hedging: Implications for Investment Policy and Performance Standards," *Financial Analysts Journal* 44 (May 1988), 45–50.

Phillips, Susan M.: *Testimony of Governor Susan Phillips,* Federal Reserve Board, September 1996, www.federalreserve.gov/boarddocs/testimony/1996/19960918.html, accessed November 9, 2000.

Powers, M.: "The Day the IMM Launched Financial Futures Trading," *Futures* (May 1992), 52–58.

Procter & Gamble Co. v. Bankers Trust Co., 78 F. 3d 219 (6th Cir. 1996).

Rajan, R.: "Insiders and Outsiders: The Choice Between Informed and Arm's Length Debt," *Journal of Finance* (September, 1992), 1367–1400.

Rawnsley, J.: *Total Risk: Nick Leeson and the Fall of Barings Bank,* New York: Harper, 1995.

Redington, F.: "Review of the Principles of Life-Office Valuations," *Journal of the Institute of Actuaries* 78 (1952), 286–340.

Reinganum, Marc: "Empirical Tests of Multifactor-Pricing Model," *Journal of Finance* 5 (1981), 313–321.

Rendleman, R. Jr., and B. Bartter: "Two-State Option Pricing," *Journal of Finance* 34 (1979), 1093–1110.

RiskMetrics Group: *CreditMetrics Monitor,* New York: RiskMetrics Group, 1998, pp. 17–28.

———: *CorporateMetrics—Technical Document,* New York: RiskMetrics Group, 1999.

———: *Risk Management: A Practical Guide,* New York: RiskMetrics Group, 1999.

Roll, Richard: "An Analytic Valuation Formula for Unprotected American Call Options on Stocks with Known Dividends," *Journal of Financial Economics* 5 (1977), 251–258.

———: "Critique of the Asset Pricing Theory's Tests," *Journal of Financial Economics* 3 (1977), 129–176.

Roll, Richard, and Stephen Ross: "An Empirical Investigation on the Arbitrage Pricing Theory," *Journal of Finance* 12 (1980), 1073–1103.

———: "The Arbitrage Pricing Theory Approach to Strategic Portfolio Planning," *Financial Analysts Journal* 5/6, (1984), 14–26.

———: "A Critical Reexamination of the Empirical Evidence on the Arbitrage Pricing Theory: A Reply," *Journal of Finance* 6 (1984), 347–350.

Ronn, E., and A. Verma: "Pricing Risk-Adjusted Deposit Insurance: An Option-Based Model," *Journal of Finance* (September 1986), 871–896.

Rosenberg, Barr: "Extra-Market Components of Covariance in Security Returns," *Journal of Financial and Quantitative Analysis* 9/2 (March 1974), 263–273.

———: "Choosing a Multiple Factor Model," *Investment Management Review* (Spring 1988), 55–67.

Ross, Stephen A.: "The Arbitrage Theory of Capital Asset Pricing," *Journal of Economic Theory* 13 (1976), 341–360.

———: "Return, Risk and Arbitrage," in Irwin Friend and James Bicksler (eds.), *Risk and Return in Finance,* Cambridge, MA: Ballinger, 1976, pp. 189–218.

Rouvinez, Christoph: "Mastering Delta Gamma," *Risk* (February 1997).

———: *Mastering Delta Gamma,* Zurich: Credit Suisse, 1999.

Roy, A. D.: "Safety First and the Holding of Assets," *Econometrica* 20/3 (July 1952), 431–449.

Rubinstein, M.: "Pay Now, Choose Later," *Risk* (February 1991), 13.

Rubinstein, M., and E. Reiner: "Breaking Down the Barriers," *Risk* (September 1991), 31–35.

———: "Implied Binomial Trees," *Journal of Finance* 49 (1994), 771–818.

Samuelson, P.: "Rational Theory of Warrant Pricing," *Industrial Management Review* 10 (1965), 13–31.

———: "Lifetime Portfolio Selection by Dynamic Stochastic Programming," *Review of Economics and Statistics* 51/3 (August 1969), 239–246.

Sanvicente, A. S., and F. L. C. Bader: "Filing for Financial Reorganization in Brazil: Event Prediction with Accounting and Financial Variables and the Information Content of the Filing Announcement," working paper, São Paulo University, Brazil, March 1996.

Sarig, O., and A. Warga: "The Risk Structure of Interest Rates," *Journal of Finance* 44 (1989), 1351–1360.

Saunders, A.: *Financial Institutions Management: A Modern Perspective,* 2d ed., Burr Ridge, IL: Irwin/McGraw-Hill, 1997.

Saunders, A., A. Srinivasan, and I. Walter: "Price Formation in the OTC Corporate Bond Markets: A Field Study of the Inter-Dealer Market," Working Paper no. 98-89, New York University, Department of Finance, New York, 1998.

Savage, Leonard J.: *The Foundations of Statistics,* New York: John Wiley & Sons, 1954.

Schwartz, E.: "The Valuation of Warrants: Implementing a New Approach," *Journal of Financial Economics* 4 (1977), 79–93.

Schenkel, Roland: "Trial of Weerner K. Rey Opens," Swiss Week, *Neue Zürcher Zeitung* (May 31–June 6, 1999).

Scott, D.: *Multivariate Density Estimation: Theory, Practice and Visualization,* New York: John Wiley & Sons, 1992.

Scott, L.: "Option Pricing When the Variance Changes Randomly: Theory Estimation, and an Application," *Journal of Financial and Quantitative Analysis* 22 (1987), 419–438.

Securities and Exchange Commission: "Financial Reporting Case Filed Against Cendant," press release, June 14, 2000, Washington, DC, www.sec.gov/news/press/2000-80-.txt, accessed July 31, 2001.

Serrill, Michael S.: "Billion-Dollar Loser: A Top Trader at Japan's Sumitomo Created a Disaster. How Did He Hide It for 10 Years?" *Time International* (June 1996).

SFA: "SFA Disciplines NatWest and 2 Individuals," press release, May 18, 2000, www.fsa.gov.uk/sfa/press_releases/2000/sfa8-2000.htm, accessed July 31, 2001.

Shakespeare, William: *The Merchant of Venice,* ca. 1596–1598, Antonio in act 1, scene 1.

Sharpe, William F.: "A Simplified Model for Portfolio Analysis," *Management Science* 9/2 (January 1963), 277–293.

———: "Capital Asset Prices: A Theory of Market Equilibrium Under Conditions of Risk," *Journal of Finance* 19/3 (September 1964), 425–442.

Shea, G.: "Interest Rate Term Structure Estimation with Exponential Splines: A Note," *Journal of Finance* 40 (1985), 319–325.

Shearer, A.: "Pricing for Risk Is the Key in Commercial Lending," *American Banker* (March 21, 1997), 1.

Shepheard-Walwyn, Tim, and Robert Litterman: "Building a Coherent Risk Measurement and Capital Optimization Model for Financial Firms," paper presented at the Conference on Financial Services at the Crossroads: Capital Regulation in the 21st Century, New York, February 26–27, 1998, *FRBNY Economic Policy Review* (October 1998), 173ff.

Shiller, R., and H. McCulloch: "The Term Structure of Interest Rates," Working Paper NBER-2341, Cambridge, MA: National Bureau of Economic Research, 1987.

Shimko, D., N. Tejima, and D. R. van Deventer: "The Pricing of Risky Debt When Interest Rates Are Stochastic," *Journal of Fixed Income* (September 1993), 58–66.

Shukla, Ravi, and Charles Trzcinka: "Sequential Tests of the Arbitrage Pricing Theory: A Comparison of Principal Component Analysis and Maximum Likelihood Factors," *Journal of Finance* 12 (1990), 1541–1564.

Silber, W.: "Innovation, Competition and New Contract Design in Futures Markets," *Journal of Futures Markets* 1 (1981), 123–156.

Smith, Andrew: *Operational Risk Management: Further Analytical Tools,* London: KPMG, January 1997.

Smith, C. W., W. Smithson, and D. S. Wilford: *Managing Financial Risk,* Cambridge, MA: Ballinger, 1990.

Smithson, C., C. W. Smith Jr., and D. S. Wilford: *Managing Financial Risk: A Guide to Derivative Products, Financial Engineering, and Value Maximization,* Chicago, IL: Irwin, 1995.

Society of Actuaries: *1986–1992 Credit Loss Experience Study: Private Placement Bonds,* Schaumburg, IL: Society of Actuaries, 1996.

Solnik, Bruno, and Alrey Freitas: "International Factors of Stock Price Behaviour," in S. Khoury and A. Gosh (eds.), *Recent Developments in International Banking and Finance,* vol. 2, Lexington, MA: Lexington Books, 1988, pp. 259–276.

Spofford, Tim: *Lynch Street,* Kent, OH: Kent State University Press, 1988.

Sprenkle, C.: "Warrant Prices as Indicators of Expectations and Preferences," *Yale Economic Essays* 1 (1961), 172–231.

Stahl, G.: "Confidence Intervals for Different Capital Definitions in a Credit Risk Model," paper presented at Center for Economic Policy Research (CEPR) Conference, London, September 20, 1998.

Standard & Poor's: *Rating Performance 1997: Stability and Transition,* Standard & Poor's Research Report, New York: Standard & Poor's, 1998.

Stiglitz, J., and A. Weiss: "Credit Rationing in Markets with Imperfect Information," *American Economic Review* (June 1981), 393–410.

Studer, Gerold: "Maximum Loss for Measurement of Market Risk," Ph.D. thesis, Swiss Federal Institute of Technology, Zurich, 1997.

Sundaram, R. K.: "Equivalent Martingale Measures and Risk-Neutral Pricing: An Expository Note," *Journal of Derivatives* (Fall 1997), 85–98.

Switzerland Federal Banking Commission: "Guidelines Governing Capital Adequacy Requirements to Support Market Risks," EG-FBC Circular No. 97/1, October 22, 1997.

Taylor, J. D.: "Cross-Industry Differences in Business Failure Rates: Implications for Portfolio Management," *Commercial Lending Review* (January 1998), 36–46.

This Is Money: "NatWest Fined for 'Rogue Trader' Loss" (May 18, 2000), www.thisismoney.com/20000518/nm15300.html, accessed July 31, 2001.

Thunderbird: "Long-Term Capital Management: Technical Note on a Global Hedge Fund," American Graduate School of International Management, 1999.

Tobin, James: "Liquidity Preference as Behavior Towards Risk," *Review of Economic Studies* 26/1 (February 1958), 65–86.

Treacy, W., and M. Carey: "Internal Credit Risk Rating Systems at Large U.S. Banks," *Federal Reserve Bulletin* (November 1998).

Ulmer, Andrew: Unpublished research, in RiskMetrics Group, *Risk Management: A Practical Guide,* New York: RiskMetrics Group, 1999 p. 28.

U.S. Congress: *Safety and Soundness Issues Related to Bank Derivatives Activities,* Washington, DC: U.S. Government Printing Office, 1993.

U.S. General Accounting Office: *Long-Term Capital Management, Regulators Need to Focus Greater Attention on Systemic Risk,* Washington, DC: General Accounting Office, October 1999.

U.S. Government: *Hedge Funds, Leverage, and the Lessons of Long-Term Capital Management: Report of the President's Working Group on Financial Markets,* April 1999, www.cftc.gov/tm/hedgefundreport.htm, accessed June 10, 1999.

Vasicek, O.: *Probability of Loss on a Loan Portfolio,* San Francisco: KMV Corporation, undated.

Vasicek, O., and G. Fong: "Term Structure Modeling Using Exponential Splines," *Journal of Finance* 37 (1982), 339–348.

Vienna, Paul: *An Investors Guide to CMOs,* New York: Salomon Brothers, 1986.

Wall, L., and M. M. Shrikhande: "Credit Derivatives," paper presented at the FMA Conference, Chicago, October 1998.

Wall Street Journal: "How LTCM Came to the Edge of the Abyss" (September 11, 2000), pp. C1, C20.

Warde, Ibrahim: "Financiers flamboyants, contribuables brûlés," *Le Monde Diplomatique* (July 1994), 18–19.

———: "LTCM, a Hedge Fund Above Suspicion" *Le Monde Diplomatique* (November 1998), English Internet edition, www.monde-diplomatique.fr/en/1998/11/05warde2.html, accessed August 24, 2000.

Wasserfallen, Walter, and Heinz Zimmermann: "The Behaviour of Interdaily Exchange Rates," *Journal of Banking and Finance* 9 (1985), 55–72.

Westerfield, Randolph: "An Examination of Foreign Exchange Risk and Fixed and Floating Exchange Rate Regimes," *Journal of International Economics* 7 (1977), 181–200.

Whaley, R.: "On the Valuation of American Call Options on Stocks with Known Dividends," *Journal of Financial Economics* 9 (1981), 207–211.

———: "1993 Derivatives and Market Volatility, Hedging Tools Long Overdue," *Journal of Derivatives* 1 (1993), 71–84.

Wiggins, J.: "Option Values Under Stochastic Volatility: Theory and Empirical Estimates," *Journal of Financial Economics* 19 (1987), 351–372.

Williams, J. B.: *The Theory of Investment Value,* Cambridge, MA: Harvard University Press, 1938.

Wilson, Thomas C.: "Debunking the Myths," *Risk* (April 1994), 67–72.

———: "Credit Portfolio Risk (I)," *Risk* (October 1997).

———: "Credit Portfolio Risk (II)," *Risk* (November 1997).

———: *Credit Risk Modeling: A New Approach,* New York: McKinsey and Company, 1997.

———: "Portfolio Credit Risk (Parts I and II)" *Risk* (September and October 1997).

———: "Portfolio Credit Risk," *FRBNY Economic Policy Review* (October 1998).

Yamaguchi, Mari: "Convicted Japanese Trader Releases Memoir Accusing Daiwa of Cover-up," *News Times* (January 7, 1997).

Zaik, E., J. Walter, and J. G. Kelling: "RAROC at Bank of America: From Theory to Practice," *Journal of Applied Corporate Finance* (Summer 1996), 83–93.

Zhou, C.: "A Jump Diffusion Approach to Modeling Credit Risk and Valuing Defaultable Securities," working paper, Federal Reserve Board of Governors, 1997.

Zimmermann, Heinz: "Zeithorizont, Risiko und Performance, eine Übersicht," *Finanzmarkt und Portfolio Management* 2 (1991), 169.

INDEX